THE ACTS OF THE APOSTLES

PATRI MATRIQVE DILECTISSIMIS

QVI ME VSQVE A PVERO

LITTERARVM SACRARVM STVDIO IMBVERVNT

HVNC LIBRVM

GRATO PIOQVE ANIMO

D. D. D.

FILIVS

THE ACTS OF THE APOSTLES

THE GREEK TEXT WITH INTRODUCTION AND COMMENTARY

BY

F. F. BRUCE, M.A.
Head of the Department of Biblical History and Literature in the University of Sheffield

WM. B. EERDMANS PUBLISHING COMPANY
GRAND RAPIDS, MICHIGAN

ISBN 0-8028-3056-0

First Edition, September 1951

Reprinted, July 1986

Photolithoprinted by Eerdmans Printing Company
Grand Rapids, Michigan, United States of America

CONTENTS

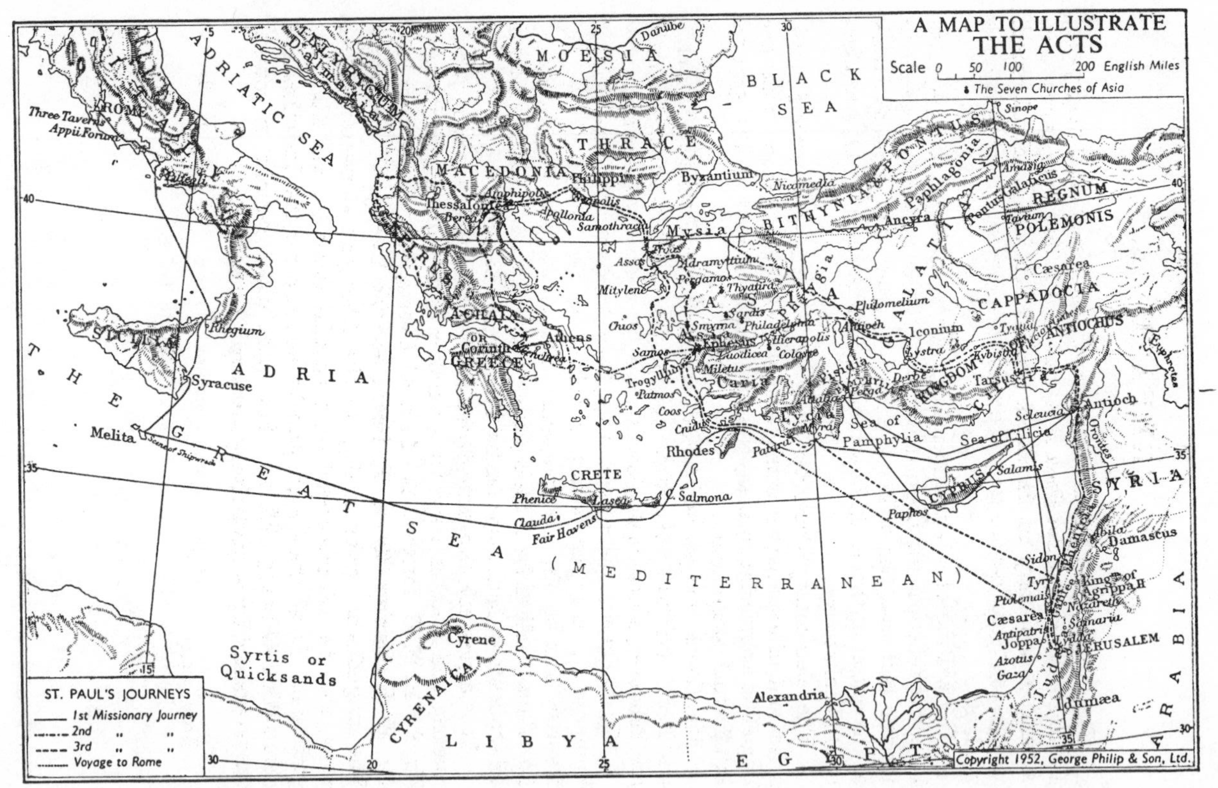
A MAP TO ILLUSTRATE
THE ACTS
Scale 0 50 100 200 English Miles
The Seven Churches of Asia
ST. PAUL'S JOURNEYS
1st Missionary Journey
2nd
3rd
Voyage to Rome
Copyright 1952, George Philip & Son, Ltd.
BLACK SEA
ADRIATIC SEA
ADRIA
THE GREAT SEA
(MEDITERRANEAN)
MOESIA
THRACE
MACEDONIA
ACHAIA OR GREECE
SICILY
Syrtis or Quicksands
CYRENAICA
LIBYA
EGYPT
ARABIA
SYRIA
CAPPADOCIA
GALATIA
BITHYNIA
PONTUS
Paphlagonia
REGNUM POLEMONIS
KINGDOM OF ANTIOCHUS
Mysia
Phrygia
Caria
Lycia
Pamphylia
Sea of Pamphylia
Sea of Cilicia
Danube
Euphrates
Orontes
Rome
Three Taverns
Appii Forum
Puteoli
Rhegium
Syracuse
Melita
Scene of Shipwreck
Thessalonica
Berea
Amphipolis
Neapolis
Apollonia
Philippi
Samothracia
Byzantium
Nicomedia
Ancyra
Amasia
Tavium
Sinope
Caesarea
Troas
Assos
Adramyttium
Mitylene
Pergamos
Thyatira
Sardis
Smyrna
Philadelphia
Hierapolis
Laodicea
Colosse
Ephesus
Chios
Samos
Trogyllium
Miletus
Patmos
Coos
Cnidus
Rhodes
Patara
Myra
Attalia
Perga
Antioch
Philomelium
Iconium
Lystra
Derbe
Tarsus
Seleucia
Antioch
Salamis
Cyprus
Paphos
Athens
Corinth
Cenchrea
CRETE
Phenice
Lasea
C. Salmona
Clauda
Fair Havens
Cyrene
Alexandria
Sidon
Tyre
Ptolemais
Caesarea
Antipatris
Joppa
Lydda
Azotus
Gaza
Damascus
Abila
Nazareth
Samaria
JERUSALEM
Galilee
Judaea
Idumaea
Kingdom of Agrippa II
20
25
30
35
40
15

PREFACE

The present work has been written in the hope that it may prove useful to students of the Book of Acts. It is a long time since a one-volume commentary on the Greek text of Acts has been published, neither too technical nor too popular for the requirements of ordinary students.

The writing of this commentary, which was begun in 1939, and helped to relieve many hours of wartime tedium, is largely responsible for the fact that the writer, who was a teacher of classical Greek at the outset of the work, now finds himself at the end of it a teacher of Biblical studies.

The elementary character of many of the grammatical notes arises out of experience in the lecture-room : it is evident that the linguistic knowledge of many students falls far short of their general intellectual equipment.

The Greek text on which the commentary is based is Westcott and Hort's (without the critical signs) ; reasons for departing from it are, however, occasionally indicated in the notes on the text.

My obligation to others who have laboured in this field is immense ; I am particularly indebted to the works of W. M. Ramsay and to the encyclopædic volumes on *The Beginnings of Christianity* edited by Foakes Jackson and Kirsopp Lake, as indeed all students of Acts must be for many years to come.

It is a pleasure to acknowledge the valuable help given in proof-reading and in other ways by a number of colleagues and friends : Mr. D. E. F.-C. Binyon, the Rev. G. Curtis, Miss A. E. Guilding, Mr. H. H. Huxley, Mr. L. R. Moore and the Rev. J. W. Wenham. The magnificent craftsmanship of the Aberdeen University Press must also be acknowledged—a congenial duty for an Aberdeen graduate. To all these I am greatly indebted for the detection and elimination of many defects. For those which remain, of course, the responsibility is exclusively my own.

F. F. B.

July, 1949.

PREFACE TO THE SECOND EDITION

That a fresh impression of this work should be called for so soon after publication seems to afford gratifying confirmation of the view that there was room for such a one-volume commentary on the Greek text of Acts.

I take this opportunity of expressing my appreciation of the welcome which the commentary has received from scholars whose judgment commands respect. Some reviewers have described it as in some sense a product of the Humanity School of Aberdeen University. This description I esteem a high honour. My debt to the writings of Sir William Ramsay is evident throughout the book, and I am repeatedly amazed by modern writers who deal with areas of New Testament scholarship to which Ramsay made contributions of peculiar value, with hardly so much as a hint that such a person ever lived. My debt to Ramsay's successor, Alexander Souter, is more personal; I owe him much for what I learned from him both in his lecture-room at Aberdeen and in correspondence and conversation in later years.

Attention has been drawn in some quarters to the weakness of this work on the theological side. This is but just; it is not a theological commentary. 'It is, in fact', as one reviewer says, 'a work of the head rather than of the heart: academic and technical rather than contemplative and expository; a manual for the student of the Greek text of the Acts of the Apostles rather than a guide to exegesis for the preacher.' But I hope and believe that the historical and philological material here presented will prove useful as a foundation for the higher exegesis of Acts.

Since the Preface to the first edition was written, a most valuable account of work on Acts during the ten years 1940-50 has appeared from the pen of Dom Jacques Dupont of Louvain: *Les Problèmes du Livre des Actes d'après les Travaux Récents* (Louvain, 1950). The student of Acts will find this an indispensable bibliographical guide, especially for its references to periodical literature which appeared during World War II and was largely inaccessible at the time to scholars in this country, and to some extent remains inaccessible.

The opportunity has been taken of making a number of bibliographical and other additions, and of correcting several defects.

F. F. B.

July, 1952.

ADDENDA

INTRODUCTION

Authorship of Acts (pp. 1 ff.)

For a survey of recent opinions on authorship, destination and date, see Dupont, *op. cit.*, pp. 17 ff.

Early Allusions to Acts (p. 8)

E. J. Goodspeed (*New Chapters in NT Study* [New York, 1937], p. 42) says 'it is clear that Papias knew the Acts' because his account of the death of Judas (quoted by Apollinarius; cf. J. B. Lightfoot, *Apostolic Fathers*, pp. 523 f.) is based on Ac. i. 18 f., and also because his account of Barsabbas Justus (*ap.* Euseb. *HE* iii. 39) is 'a strong contact' with Ac. i. 23. (Papias was contemporary with Polycarp.)

B. P. W. S. Hunt (*Primitive Gospel Sources* [London, 1951], p. 210 n.) suggests that Ac. was not known to the author of the 'Epistle of Barnabas' because, had he known Ac. i. 3, he would not have referred (xv. 9) to 'the eighth day' as the day 'in which Jesus rose from the dead and, having been manifested, ascended into heaven.' This is a precarious inference; see Additional Note on Ac. i. 9 (p. xiv).

P. 9, ll. 22-25

Among the other Apocryphal 'Acts' for which our canonical Ac. served as a model must perhaps be reckoned an Ebionite 'Acts of the Apostles', which H. J. Schoeps (*Theologie und Geschichte des Judenchristentums* [Tübingen, 1949], pp. 381 ff.) discerns as the original source of much of the material in the pseudo-Clementine *Recognitions* and *Homilies*.[1] Hegesippus's account of the martyrdom of James was probably derived, albeit indirectly (*via* the 'Ascents of James'), from some such source. See also Additional Note on Ac. vii. 1 ff. (p. xvi).

Canonicity (p. 10)

It should be emphasized that more is required to establish the canonicity of a document than a demonstration that it was known and quoted by Christians, or even read at meetings of the church, in the earlier part of the second century. Canonicity involves

[1] Cf. also B. H. Streeter, *The Primitive Church* (London, 1929), p. 8; B. W. Bacon, *Studies in Matthew* (London, 1931), pp. 482 ff.

inclusion in a body of writings acknowledged as divinely authoritative, the acknowledged authority of any writing so included being the cause and not the effect of its inclusion.

The importance of including Ac. in the Christian canon would be specially appreciated after Marcion challenged the Catholic Church by the publication of his canon (*c.* A.D. 144). Tertullian's question quoted on p. 34 was particularly applicable to the Marcionites, who emphasized the apostleship of Paul but rejected the one document which put Paul's apostleship on a sound historical basis. In spite of the witness of Ac. to Paul's apostleship, it was unacceptable to the Marcionites because it attested the apostleship of the other apostles as well and represented Paul as living in harmony with them ; but this very fact made it the more valuable now in the eyes of orthodox churchmen. It was from this time, probably, that it came to be called the 'Acts of the Apostles'—a title first given it in the anti-Marcionite Prologue to Lk.—or even, as the Muratorian list calls it with exaggerated anti-Marcionite emphasis, the 'Acts of *all* the Apostles' (cf. p. 1 for both quotations).

The Date of Acts (p. 14)

See T. W. Manson in *BJRL* xxviii (1944), p. 131 n., for the suggestion 'that the date of Mark may be a few years earlier than is usually thought likely. A date before 60 would be quite possible.' But if Mk. cannot be dated so early, one may consider whether the 'former treatise' of Ac. i. 1 may not have been something in the nature of 'Proto-Lk.', written before the appearance of Mk. Cf. C. S. C. Williams in *CQR* cliii (1952), p. 254.

E. J. Goodspeed's arguments (cf. n. 2) are set out at length in his *New Solutions of NT Problems* (Chicago, 1927), chapters vi, vii and viii (pp. 65-109).

The Speeches of Acts (p. 21 n.)

See also W. L. Knox, *Some Hellenistic Elements in Primitive Christianity* (London, 1944), pp. 25 ff. ; M. Dibelius, *Die Reden der Apostelgeschichte* (Heidelberg, 1949) ; J. Dupont, *op. cit.*, pp. 43 ff.

The Sources of Acts (pp. 21 ff.)

See W. L. Knox, *The Acts of the Apostles* (Cambridge, 1948), pp. 16 ff. ; Dupont, *op. cit.*, pp. 35 ff.

The Style and Language of Acts (p. 29 n.)

See also H. F. D Sparks, 'The Semitisms of the Acts', *JTS* N.S. i (1950), pp. 16 ff.

The Purpose and Plan of Acts (pp. 29 ff.)

Schoeps (*Theol. u. Gesch. d. Judenchristentums*) and S. G. F. Brandon (*The Fall of Jerusalem and the Christian Church* [London, 1951], pp. 100 ff., 126 ff., 208 ff.) both represent a partial revival of the Tübingen position. Schoeps believes Ac. to be as tendentious in the one direction as the Ebionite 'Acts of the Apostles', which he considers was written as a counterblast to it, was in the other direction. 'It is impossible that Paul can have spoken in so un-Pauline a fashion and Peter (cf. xv. 10) and James in so Pauline a fashion as the speeches in Ac. wish us to believe' (pp. 445 f.).[1] Brandon (pp. 208 ff.) argues that the Lukan writings reflect a later phase than Mk. does of the new situation which arose after A.D. 70, that Ac. represents a further stage than Mk. does in the process of rehabilitating Paul, and also contains 'a covert polemic' against the Christianity of Alexandria, which he believes had succeeded Jerusalem 'as the citadel of Jewish Christianity and of opposition to Pauline teaching'. The present writer remains convinced that the apologetic of Acts has primary relation to the situation in Rome between A.D. 60 and 64.

Acts and the Pauline Epistles (pp. 38 f.)

The view of the Ac.-Gal. relation here maintained is also given preference by R. Heard, *INT* (London, 1950), p. 183. T. W. Manson, ('The Problem of the Epistle to the Galatians', *BJRL* xxiv [1940], pp. 59 ff.), suggests that the Jerusalem visit of Gal. ii. 1 ff. is not recorded in Ac., but was paid on the eve of Barnabas and Paul's departure for Cyprus and Asia Minor (Ac. xiii. 2 ff.). Cf. J. N. Sanders, *Foundations of the Christian Faith* (London, 1950), pp. 34 ff. A summary of recent views on the matter, and on the more general question of the Council of Jerusalem, is given by Dupont, *op. cit.*, pp. 51 ff.

The Text of Acts (pp. 40 ff.)

Additional studies bearing on the text are presented by M. Dibelius, 'The Text of Acts: An Urgent Critical Task', *Journal of Religion* xxi (1941), pp. 421 ff.; K. W. Clark, *Eight American Praxapostoloi* (Chicago, 1941); W. D. McHardy, 'James of Edessa's Citations from the Philoxenian Text of the Book of Acts', *JTS* xliii (1942), pp. 168 ff., and 'The Philoxenian Text of the Acts in the Cambridge Syriac MS Add. 2053', *JTS* xlv (1944), p. 175; G. D. Kilpatrick, 'Western Text and Original Text in the Gospels and Acts', *JTS* xliv (1943), pp. 24 ff.; R. C. Stone, *The Language of the Latin Text of Codex Bezae* (Univ. of Illinois, 1946); A. F. J. Klijn,

[1] Schoeps refers with approval to the article by W. Mundle, 'Das Apostelbild der Apostelgeschichte', *ZNTW* xxvii (1928), pp. 36 ff.

A Survey of the Researches into the Western Text of the Gospels and Acts (Utrecht, 1949); L. Cerfaux, 'Citations scripturaires et tradition textuelle dans le livre des Actes', *Goguel FS* (Neuchâtel-Paris, 1950), pp. 43 ff.; J. Dupont, *op. cit.*, pp. 25 ff.; M. M. Parvis and A. Wikgren (edd.), *New Testament Manuscript Studies* (Chicago, 1950); P. H. Menoud, 'The Western Text and the Theology of Acts', *Studiorum Noui Testamenti Societas, Bulletin* ii (1951), pp. 19 ff.; C. S. C. Williams, *Alterations to the Text of the Synoptic Gospels and Acts* (Oxford, 1951).

Menoud (*loc. cit.*, p. 28) divides the theological peculiarities of δ into four groups: (*a*) those reflecting anti-Jewish prejudice, (*b*) those indicating a more universalist outlook than β, (*c*) those laying greater weight than β on the action of the Holy Spirit, with reverential amplification of His designation, (*d*) reverential amplification of the name of Christ. (Cf. Williams, *op. cit.*, pp. 54 ff.) According to Menoud, the reverential amplifications of the name of Christ in δ are not so emphatic as those found in the Apostolic Fathers; this, he thinks, may indicate a date for δ earlier than the Apostolic Fathers and not contemporary with them, as Ropes suggested. In any case, the δ revision can be traced back earlier than the β revision, which cannot at present be traced farther back than the third century. Menoud concludes that δ and β 'must be regarded as two different recensions of a lost primitive text. Consequently the question is not so much to make a choice between them, as to work back, if possible, to the primitive text with the aid of both recensions.'

C. C. Torrey's explanation of the Aramaizing character of δ (mentioned on p. 45) has not found support in more recent works on the text. M. Black's explanation (see p. 45 n.) is that in the δ redaction 'more of the primitive "Aramaized" Greek text has been left unrevised than in the redaction . . . represented by the Vatican and Sinaitic Uncials' (*op. cit.*, p. 214). It should be carefully considered how much of the really cogent material in Torrey's case can be accounted for in terms of an Old Syriac influence on the δ recension. The arguments of F. H. Chase in his two books listed on p. 50 n. may require to be reconsidered and restated; according to Williams (*op. cit.*, p. 80) Chase's 'arguments have never been refuted but are commonly ignored, except by some writers in the *Bulletin of the Beza Club*'. Williams goes on to adduce some particularly impressive instances of possible Syriac influence, as well as a few instances of Latin influence (as he points out, even A. C. Clark admitted that D was influenced by d in Ac. xiii. 28 f.; xviii. 21; xix. 29). But Williams concludes this section of his study with a caveat: 'The evidence of "Western" papyri found in Egypt should be enough to warn us, however, against any theory that the whole of the " Western " text of Acts was written either in Syriac or in Latin ' (*op. cit.*, p. 82).

P. 47 : On the bilingual MS. E/e, the account of K. and S. Lake should be noted : ' The Latin has a European text, close to " gigas " . . . and to the quotations of Lucifer, but the Greek is based on a Byzantine text, and its Western readings are translations from the Latin beside it. They cannot, therefore, be used as authority for a Greek Western text, parallel to, or confirming D. It is essentially a Latin MS. with a " conformed " Greek text added to it—Latino-Greek, not Graeco-Latin ' (*The Text of the NT* [London, 1933], p. 20).

P[8], according to Williams (*op. cit.*, pp. 87 f.), ' approximates rather to the " Caesarean " model, oscillating between the B type and the D type of text, though nearer to the former and without supporting the extravagances of the latter.'

BIBLIOGRAPHY

1. *Commentaries*

To those mentioned on pp. 49-51 the following should be added : commentaries by A. Steinmann (in *Die heilige Schrift des NT*, Bonn, 1934) ; by F. W. Grosheide (in *Korte Verklaring der heilige Schrift*, Kampen, 1941-5, and in *Kommentaar op het Nieuwe Testament*, Amsterdam, 1942-9) ; by D. A. Froevig (Oslo, 1944) ; by J. Renié (in *Bible de Letouzey*, Paris, 1949). A second and revised edition of A. Wikenhauser's commentary has appeared (Regensburg, 1951), and forthcoming commentaries are announced by A. Fridrichsen (in the Swedish series *Talkning av Nya Testamentet*, ed. A. Nygren) and by P. H. Menoud (in the French series *Commentaire du Nouveau Testament*, published by Delachaux & Niestlé of Neuchâtel and Paris).

2. *Other Literature*

Add to the list on pp. 51-55 :

J. Bonsirven : *Le Judaïsme palestinien au temps de Jésus-Christ* (Paris, 1934-5).

S. G. F. Brandon : *The Fall of Jerusalem and the Christian Church* (London, 1951).

L. Cerfaux : *La communauté apostolique* (Paris, 1943).

O. Cullmann : *Petrus : Jünger—Apostel—Märtyrer* (Zürich, 1951).

M. Dibelius : *Die Reden der Apostelgeschichte und die Antike Geschichtsschreibung* (Heidelberg, 1949).

M. DIBELIUS and W. G. KÜMMEL : *Paulus* (Sammlung Göschen, Berlin, 1951).[1]

J. DUPONT : *Les Problèmes du livre des Actes d'après les travaux récents* (Louvain, 1950).

L. FINKELSTEIN : *The Pharisees : the Sociological Background of their Faith* (New York, 1938).

—— (ed.) : *The Jews : their History, Culture and Religion* (New York, 1949).

A. GFRÖRER : *Geschichte des Urchristentums,* Bd. i (Stuttgart, 1938).

M. GOGUEL : *Aux Sources de la Tradition Chrétienne : Mélanges offerts à M. Maurice Goguel à l'occasion de son soixante-dixième anniversaire* (Neuchâtel-Paris, 1950).

E. J. GOODSPEED : *Paul* (Philadelphia, 1947).

C. GUIGNEBERT : *Le monde juif vers le Temps de Jésus* (Paris, 1935) ; Eng. tr., *The Jewish World in the Time of Jesus Christ* (London, 1939).

—— *Le Christ* (Paris, 1943).

J. KNOX : *Chapters in a Life of Paul* (Nashville, 1950).

R. MORGENTHALER : *Die lukanische Geschichtsschreibung als Zeugnis* (Zürich, 1948).

R. H. PFEIFFER : *History of New Testament Times with an Introduction to the Apocrypha* (New York, 1949).

H. SAHLIN : *Der Messias und das Gottesvolk : Studien zur protolukanischen Theologie* (Uppsala, 1945).

A. SCHLATTER : *Geschichte der ersten Christenheit* [2] (Stuttgart, 1926).

H. J. SCHOEPS : *Theologie und Geschichte des Judenchristentums* (Tübingen, 1949).

—— *Aus frühchristlicher Zeit* (Tübingen, 1950).

M. SIMON : *Verus Israel* (Paris, 1948).

J. H. WASZINK, W. C. VAN UNNIK, CH. DE BEUS (edd.) : *Het oudste Christendom en die antieke Cultuur,* 2 vols. (Haarlem, Netherlands, 1951).

H. WILL : *Am Urquell : die urchristliche Gemeinde in Jerusalem* (Basel, 1945).

COMMENTARY

i. 9 (p. 71)

ἐπήρθη, καὶ νεφέλη ὑπέλαβεν αὐτὸν κ.τ.λ.] In the primitive apostolic preaching the resurrection and ascension of Christ represent one continuous movement and together constitute His exaltation. The forty days' period of *ver.* 3 is responsible for the arrangement in the Christian calendar which dates Ascension Day on the fortieth day after Easter. But Jesus' exaltation to God's right hand, which is what Ascension Day really commemorates, was not postponed for forty days after His triumph

[1] These works by Dibelius were published posthumously ; he died on Nov. 17, 1947. In his later years he seems to have paid special attention to the historical problems of Ac.

over death. The fortieth day was not the first occasion when He vanished from His companions' sight after His resurrection (cf. Lk. xxiv. 31). Nor are we to suppose that the intervals between His resurrection appearances were spent in some earth-bound state. These appearances, in which He condescended to His disciples' temporal conditions of life, were visitations from that exalted and eternal order to which His 'body of glory' now belonged. What happened on the fortieth day was that this series of frequent though intermittent visitations came to an end, with a scene which brought home to the disciples their Master's heavenly glory.

The reference to the cloud reminds us of the language used of His Parousia (e.g. Mk. xiii. 26 = Lk. xxi. 27; Mk. xiv. 62); cf. also the cloud in the Transfiguration narrative (Mk. ix. 7 = Lk. ix. 34 f.). We may well be intended to think of the cloud of the Shekhinah: 'Jesus is enveloped in the cloud of the divine presence' (A. M. Ramsey, 'What was the Ascension?' *SNTS Bulletin* ii. [1951], pp. 43 ff.). Cf. P. Benoit, 'L'Ascension', *R. Bib.* lvi (1949), pp. 161 ff.

ii. 7 (p. 84)

Γαλιλαῖοι] On the Galilaean dialect cf. also F. Rosenthal, *Die aramaistische Forschung* (Leiden, 1939), p. 108 n. With the following list of nations cf. that of Paulus Alexandrinus (4th cent. A.D.): see F. Cumont, 'La plus ancienne géographie astrologique', *Klio* ix (1909), pp. 263 ff.; S. Weinstock, 'The Geographical Catalogue in Acts ii. 9-11', *JRS* xxxviii (1948), pp. 43 ff.

ii. 13 (p. 87)

γλεύκους] Cf. the words of Elihu in Job xxxii. 18 f., LXX, **ὀλέκει γάρ με τὸ πνεῦμα τῆς γαστρός· ἡ δὲ γαστήρ μου ὥσπερ ἀσκὸς γλεύκους ζέων δεδεμένος.**

ii. 38 (p. 98 n.)

On the baptismal question see H. G. Marsh, *The Origin and Significance of New Testament Baptism* (1941); K. Barth, *The Teaching of the Church regarding Baptism* (1948); W. F. Flemington, *The New Testament Doctrine of Baptism* (1948); O. Cullmann, *Baptism in the New Testament* (1950); G. W. H. Lampe, *The Seal of the Spirit* (1951), pp. 46 ff.

ii. 47 (p. 102)

On the summary which ends with this verse, as on the similar ones in iv. 32-35 and v. 12-16, see P. Benoit, 'Remarques sur les "sommaires" de Actes 2.42 à 5', *Goguel FS*, pp. 1 ff.

iii. 13 (p. 108)

Πελάτου] Cf. also the elder Agrippa's description of Pilate in his account of him to the Emperor Gaius (Philo, *Leg. ad Gai.* 301), ' inflexible, merciless and obstinate '.

iv. 14 (p. 122)

ἀντειπεῖν] *ποιῆσαι ἢ ἀντειπεῖν* D h (representing δ, but d has *contradicere* alone).

v. 1 ff. (p. 131)

P. H. Menoud (' La mort d'Ananias et de Saphira ', *Goguel FS*, pp. 146 ff.) argues that this narrative arose out of the first case of death in the Church.

v. 3 (p. 133)

ἐπλήρωσεν] *ἐπήρωσεν* (' maimed ') ℵ.

v. 37 (p. 148)

ἐν ταῖς ἡμεραῖς τῆς ἀπογραφῆς] Add to bibliography at end of note : F. Spitta in *ZNTW* vii (1906), pp. 281 ff. ; W. Weber in *ZNTW* x (1909), pp. 307 ff. ; M. J. Lagrange, in *R. Bib.*, viii (1911), pp. 60 ff. ; F. Bleckmann in *Klio*, xvii (1921), pp. 104 ff. ; W. Lodder, *Die Schätzung des Quirinius bei Flavius Josephus* (1930) ; E. Groag in Pauly-Wissowa's *Realencyclopädie*, ii. 4 (1931), *s.v.* ' Sulpicius (90) ' ; L. R. Taylor in *A.J.Ph.* liv (1933), pp. 120 ff. ; R. Syme in *Klio*, xxvii (1934), pp. 131 ff. ; A. G. Roos in *Mnemosyne* III. ix (1941), pp. 306 ff. ; F. F. Bruce in *New Schaff-Herzog Relig. Encycl.*, Suppl. Vol. i. (1952), *s.v.* ' Census '.

vi. 1 (p. 151)

Ἑλληνιστῶν] See on this word W. Bauer in his *Gr.-deutsches Wörterbuch zum NT* and H. Windisch in Kittel's *Theol. Wörterbuch zum NT ;* cf. G. Mayeda, *Le langage et l'évangile* (Geneva, 1948), pp. 70 ff.

vii. 1 ff. (p. 160)

On Stephen and his speech see B. W. Bacon, ' Stephen's Speech : its Argument and Doctrinal Relationship ', in *Biblical and Semitic Studies* (Yale Bicentennial Publications, 1901), pp. 213 ff. ; H. J. Schoeps, *Theol. u. Gesch. d. Judenchristentums*, pp. 440 ff. ; M. Simon, ' Saint Stephen and the Jerusalem Temple ', *Journal of Ecclesiastical History*, ii (1951), pp. 127 ff. ; W. Manson, *The Epistle to the Hebrews* (London, 1951), pp. 25 ff. Schoeps, considering the remarkable similarity between Stephen's attitude to the sacrificial cultus and that found later in the pseudo-Clementine literature of the Ebionites, as also between Stephen's rôle in Ac. and that attributed to James the Just in the earliest strata of the Ebionite literature, concludes that Stephen is ' an *ersatz* figure introduced by Luke for tendentious reasons, in order to unload on to him doctrines which he found inconvenient '. Simon, in a critique of Schoeps's argument, concludes that Stephen is the original and the James of the Ebionite literature the tendentious surrogate. W. Manson compares the main emphases of Heb. with those of Stephen's speech, and holds ' that a straight line runs from the teaching and apologia of the proto-martyr to the Epistle to the Hebrews ', and that ' it is to be regarded as a central line in the development of the Christian world-mission '.

vii. 46 (p. 175)

εὑρεῖν σκήνωμα τῷ θεῷ Ἰακώβ] Schoeps (*op. cit.*, p. 238) and F. C. Synge (*Theology*, lv [1952], p. 25) argue for **οἴκῳ** as the true reading; see on the other hand M. Simon (*loc. cit.*, p. 128), who defends **θεῷ**. According to Simon, in the quotation from Ps. cxxxii. 5 the **τόπος** is Jerusalem, the **σκήνωμα** the tent on Zion (cf. 2 Sam. vi. 17; 1 Chr. xv. 1), by contrast with the ' house ' (**οἶκος**) built by Solomon (cf. 2 Sam. vii. 6; 1 Chr. xvii. 5).

vii. 48 (p. 176)

ἐν χειροποιήτοις] For an extended commentary on this idea, see A. Cole, *The New Temple* (London, 1950).

vii. 56 (p. 179)

τὸν υἱὸν τοῦ ἀνθρώπου] See also E. Sjöberg, *Der Menschensohn im äthiopischen Henochbuch* (Lund, 1946); A. Bentzen, *Moses—Messias redivivus—Menschensohn* (Zürich, 1948); T. W. Manson, ' The Son of Man in Daniel, Enoch and the Gospels ', *BJRL* xxxii (1950), pp. 171 ff.; A. E. Guilding, ' The Son of Man and the Ancient of Days ', *EQ* xxiii (1951), pp. 210 ff.; V. Taylor, *Comm. on Mk.* (1952), pp. 119 f., 197 ff., 568 f.

viii. 1 (p. 181)

διωγμὸς μέγας] The persecution appears to have been directed mainly against the Hellenistic believers, who were more closely associated with Stephen; hereafter the Jerusalem Church consists more exclusively of ' Hebrews '.

viii. 9 (p. 184)

Σίμων] See H. J. Schoeps, *op. cit.*, pp. 128 ff., 420 ff., and *Aus frühchristlicher Zeit* (Tübingen, 1950), pp. 239 ff. (' Simon Magus in der Haggada ? '). *μαγεύων*] On the Magi see J. H. Moulton, *Early Zoroastrianism* (London, 1913), pp. 182 ff.

viii. 15 f. (p. 187)

See G. W. H. Lampe, *The Seal of the Spirit*, pp. 64 ff.

viii. 35 (p. 193 n.)

See also H. W. Wolff, *Jesaja* 53 *im Urchristentum* (Berlin, 1950) ; J. Jeremias, ' Zum Problem des leidenden Messias im palästinischen Spätjudentum ', *Goguel FS*, pp. 113 ff. ; E. J. Young, *Isaiah Fifty-Three* (Grand Rapids, 1952) ; H. H. Rowley, *The Servant of the Lord and Other Essays on the OT* (London, 1952), pp. 3 ff. (' The Servant of the Lord in the Light of Three Decades of Criticism '), 61 ff. (' The Suffering Servant and the Davidic Messiah ').

ix. 2 (p. 197)

Further light has been thrown on the ' Covenanters of Damascus ' by the Dead Sea Scrolls discovered in 1947 ; cf. W. H. Brownlee, *The Dead Sea Manual of Discipline* (New Haven, 1951) ; A. Dupont-Sommer, *The Dead Sea Scrolls* (Oxford, 1951) ; B. J. Roberts, ' The Dead Sea Scrolls—Towards a Perspective ', *Transactions of Victoria Institute*, lxxxiv (1952).

ix. 34 (p. 210)

ἰᾶται] Cadbury's *JTS* note (' A Possible Perfect in Acts ix. 34 ') suggests that we should read the perfect *ἴαται* here.

xi. 20 (p. 235)

Ἑλληνιστάς] For *ἑλληνίζω* used of Greeks cf. Plato, *Meno*, 82B (*Ἕλλην μέν ἐστι καὶ ἑλληνίζει*) ; Posidippus, 28 (*οἱ δ' Ἕλληνες ἑλληνίζομεν*). *Ἑλληνισταί* could thus include Greeks, as well as non-Greeks who affected Greek speech and ways.

xi. 26 (p. 238)

Χριστιανούς] Cf. E. J. Bickerman, ' The Name of Christians ', *HTR* xlii (1949), pp. 108 ff.

xii. 17 (p. 248)

Ἰακώβῳ] See H. J. Schoeps, *Aus frühchristlicher Zeit*, pp. 130 ff. (' Jacobus *ὁ δίκαιος καὶ ὠβλίας* ') ; S. G. F. Brandon, *op. cit.*, pp. 46 ff., 95 ff., *et passim.*

xiii. 33 (p. 269)

υἱός μου εἶ σύ κ.τ.λ.] See J. Dupont, 'Filius meus es tu: l'interprétation de Ps. ii. 7 dans le NT', *Recherches de Science Religieuse*, xxxv (1948), pp. 522 ff.; he holds that the primitive Church saw the fulfilment of these words in Christ's resurrection.

xv. 1 ff. (p. 289 n.)

Cf. Tert. *Apol.* 9: '*suffocatis quoque et morticinis abstinemus*'—where, however, there is no explicit reference to Ac. xv.

xv. 20 (p. 300)

καὶ τῆς πορνείας] This is the only place where the text of the decree survives in P^{45}. P. H. Menoud points out that only two basic abstentions (from idol-pollutions and from blood) are common to the four main classes of textual authorities for the decree—P^{45}, β, δ, and Tert. (see on xv. 29). He concludes that the original reading was ***τοῦ ἀπέχεσθαι τῶν ἀλισγημάτων τῶν εἰδώλων καὶ τοῦ αἵματος***, and that our authorities show the tendency to expand the decree to make it cover as many phases of Christian life as possible (*SNTS Bulletin* ii, pp. 22 ff.). Cf. also C. S. C. Williams, *op. cit.*, pp. 72 ff.

xvii. 21 (p. 335 n.)

See also W. Schmid, 'Die Rede des Apostels Paulus vor den Philosophen und Areopagiten in Athen', *Philologus* xcv (1942), pp. 79 ff.; R. Liechtenhan, *Die urchristliche Mission* (1946), pp. 92 ff.

xvii. 23 (p. 335)

ἀγνώστῳ θεῷ] Compare the inscription on an altar on the Palatine, restored 129 B.C. (*CIL* i. 2. 801): '*sei deo sei deiuae sac: C. Sextius C. f. Caluinus de senati sententia restituit*'. But here the vague language is due to the fact that the original dedication could not be recovered.

xviii. 13 (p. 347)

παρὰ τὸν νόμον] Paul was accused of propagating a new religion which was not covered by the protection extended by Roman law to Judaism. Gallio decided that Paul's message was a form of Judaism, and therefore protected by Roman law. On the whole question see S. L. Guterman, *Religious Toleration and Persecution in Ancient Rome* (London, 1951).

xviii. 25 (p. 351)

Ἀπολλῶς] On Apollos and the beginnings of Alexandrian Christianity see S. G. F. Brandon, *op. cit.*, pp. 17 ff., 221 ff.

xix. 13 ff. (pp. 358 ff.)

See B. M. Metzger, 'St. Paul and the Magicians', *Princeton Seminary Bulletin* xxxviii (1944), pp. 27 ff.

xix. 29 (p. 365)

Μακεδόνας] *Μακεδόνα* may quite well have been the original reading, the plural having arisen by dittography of the initial letter of the following word *συνεκδήμους*.

xix. 33 (p. 366)

Ἀλέξανδρον] Presumably a well-known Jew of Ephesus, possibly 'Alexander the coppersmith' of 2 Tim. iv. 14. The Jews probably put him up as their spokesman in order to dissociate themselves publicly from Paul and his colleagues, but the mob was in no mood to draw fine distinctions between people who were united at any rate in refusing to worship Artemis.

xix. 35 (p. 367)

διοπετοῦς] See A. B. Cook, *Zeus* iii (Cambridge, 1940), pp. xii, 881 ff., for the cult of meteorites.

xxiv. 5 (p. 422)

Ναζωραίων] See on this word W. Bauer, *Gr.-deutsches Wörterbuch zum NT*; H. H. Schaeder in Kittel's *Theol. Wörterbuch*; M. Black, *Aramaic Approach to Gospels and Acts*, pp. 143 ff.

xxvii. 17 (p. 460)

χαλάσαντες τὸ σκεῦος] J. Renié (*Recherches de Science Religieuse* xxxv [1948], pp. 272 ff.), following the second suggestion of the three, understands that the ship dropped a floating anchor.

xxvii. 35 (p. 465)

εὐχαρίστησεν] Cf. Bo Reicke, 'Die Mahlzeit mit Paulus auf den Wellen des Mittelmeers', *Theol. Zeitschrift* iv (1948), pp. 401 ff.

xxviii. 31 (p. 481 n.)

See L. P. Pherigo, 'Paul's Life after the close of Acts', *JBL* lxx (1951), pp. 277 ff.

INTRODUCTION

AUTHORSHIP OF ACTS

EXTERNAL EVIDENCE

THE earliest statements about the authorship of Ac. which have survived belong to the last forty years of the second century.

The anti-Marcionite Prologue to Lk. (*c.* 160-180), after giving some account of Luke as the Third Evangelist (see pp. 6 f.), adds *καὶ δὴ μετέπειτα ἔγραψεν ὁ αὐτὸς Λουκᾶς Πράξεις Ἀποστόλων.*

The Muratorian Fragment (*c.* 170-200), which contains an early Roman Canon, gives the following account of Lk. and Ac.:

'Tertium euangelii librum secundum Lucan Lucas iste medicus, post ascensum Christi cum eum Paulus quasi itineris studiosum secum adsumsisset, nomine suo ex ordine conscripsit; dominum tamen nec ipse uidit in carne. Et idem, prout assequi potuit, ita et a natiuitate Iohannis incipit dicere. . . . Acta autem omnium apostolorum sub uno libro scripta sunt. Lucas optimo Theophilo comprehendit, quia sub praesentia eius singula gerebantur, sicuti et semota passione Petri euidenter declarat, sed et profectione Pauli ab urbe ad Spaniam proficiscentis.' [1]

More or less contemporary with these testimonies is the evidence of Irenaeus, who explicitly mentions Luke, '*sectator Pauli*', as the author of the Gospel and Ac. (*Adu. haer.* iii. 1. 1; 14. 1, etc.). Similar testimony is borne by Clement of Alexandria: 'Luke,' he says, 'in the Acts of the Apostles records that Paul said, "Men of Athens, I see that in all things you are very religious"' (*Strom.* v. 12); and again, 'It is acknowledged that Luke wrote with his pen the Acts of the Apostles' (*Adumbr. in* 1 *Pet.*).[2] Tertullian (*Adu. Marc.* iv. 2) and Origen (*ap.* Euseb. *HE* vi. 25) add their witness to the Lukan authorship of the Third Gospel, and hence by implication of Ac. We might go on to add the testimony of Eusebius and Jerome, but it is sufficient to say that from *c.* 170 onwards the consentient opinion of all who write on the subject is that the author of the two works *ad Theophilum* was 'Luke, the beloved physician' of Col. iv. 14.

[1] Emended text as given in Zahn, *Geschichte des NT Kanons*, ii, p. 139.

[2] In this second passage Clement adds that Luke 'translated Paul's Epistle to the Hebrews' (cf. the similar statement in his *Hypotyposes*, *ap.* Euseb. *HE* vi. 14). This epistle's likeness in style to the Lukan writings is 'unquestionably remarkable' (Westcott); but Hebrews is certainly not a translation. The theory mentioned by Clement was an attempt to reconcile the tradition of the Pauline authorship of Heb. current in the East with its obvious dissimilarity in Greek style from the Pauline Epistles.

INTERNAL EVIDENCE

1. The Author was the Third Evangelist

THAT the author of Ac. is identical with the author of the Third Gospel is sufficiently indicated by the opening words of Ac., where the 'first treatise' refers to the Third Gospel.[1] For it can hardly be doubted that the Theophilus addressed in the opening words of Ac. is identical with the Theophilus for whose instruction the Third Gospel was composed, according to the dedication in Lk. i. 1–4. The close similarity in style and language between the two works leads to the same conclusion, as also do the catholic sympathies of both works, the interest in Gentiles, the unusually prominent place given to women in the narrative of both, and the common apologetic tendency. In both works none but Judaean Resurrection-appearances are related, and the end of Lk. dovetails closely into the beginning of Ac. There are other details which strengthen this general impression of unity of authorship; e.g., Lk. is the only Gospel which tells of Christ's appearance before Herod Antipas, and this appearance is alluded to in Ac. iv. 27.

2. The Author was a Companion of Paul

When we examine Ac. itself for indications of authorship, what strikes us most is the presence of sections where the third personal narrative suddenly gives place to one in the first person plural. These 'we' sections are found in xvi. 10-17; xx. 5-xxi. 18; xxvii. 1-xxviii. 16. The most natural explanation of these passages is that in them we have extracts from the personal memoirs of one of Paul's companions. An examination of them indicates that their author joined Paul, Silas and Timothy at Troas during the second missionary journey, and accompanied them to Philippi. Apparently he did not accompany them when they left Philippi, and it is noteworthy that it is at Philippi that we find him next, towards the end of the third missionary tour, when Paul is about to sail for Palestine with the contributions made by the Gentile churches for the relief of poor members of the Jerusalem church (Ac. xx. 4 ff.; cf. Rom. xv. 25 ff.). It does not necessarily follow, of course, that the 'we' author spent the whole of the intervening

[1] The only serious denial of recent times that Ac. was written by the Third Evangelist is A. C. Clark's in *The Acts of the Apostles* (1933), pp. 393 ff., and his arguments are quite unconvincing. They have lately been examined carefully by W. L. Knox in *The Acts of the Apostles* (1948), pp. 2 ff., 100 ff.

time in Philippi. From Philippi he accompanied Paul and his companions to Jerusalem. How he spent the two years of Paul's detention at Caesarea we are not told, but at the end of that period he appears again as Paul's companion on the voyage to Rome, and he describes in vivid and accurate detail the sea-journey with the storm and shipwreck, the safe arrival of the passengers and crew at Malta, and the subsequent journey to Rome.

We have next to decide the relation between these 'we' sections and the rest of Ac. Why are they introduced so unobtrusively? A later writer incorporating into his history the diary of an eyewitness would surely have mentioned the author of so important a contemporary document, in order to enhance its value in the eyes of his readers. *Prima facie* the most reasonable conclusion seems to be that the 'we' of these sections includes the 'I' of i. 1, that the author of the whole narrative was himself present during the periods covered by them, and delicately indicates that at certain points in the course of events he himself joined the company by a simple transition from the third person to the first person plural. Theoretically, of course, it is conceivable that a later writer either incorporated or composed these 'we' sections in such a way as to suggest that he was an eyewitness of the events he narrates. This is in itself unlikely, and if such a device were deliberately adopted to give readers an impression of greater authority than the facts warranted, why did the author omit to give himself a name which would have underlined that authority, and why did he restrict the 'we' narrative for no apparent reason to these short sections?

That the style and language of the 'we' sections cannot be distinguished from those of the rest of the book or of the Third Gospel has been established by more than one investigator—notably by Harnack in *The Acts of the Apostles* and by Hawkins in *Horae Synopticae*. To this linguistic evidence must be added the fact that the 'we' sections form an integral part of the whole work. For example, in ch. viii. we leave Philip the evangelist at Caesarea; we find him there in a 'we' section some twenty years later (xxi. 8), and there he is called 'one of the Seven', which would be unintelligible apart from the narrative of ch. vi. We could, of course, suppose that the author of the whole book so worked over the diary of a companion of Paul as to leave the impress of his own style upon it. But if he worked it over so thoroughly and made it so integral a part of his history, it is very strange that he did not take the obvious step of changing the first into the third person. The most natural conclusion is that the whole book—as well as the Third Gospel—was written by the author of the 'we' sections, and therefore by one who was from time to time a companion of Paul.

3. The Author was Luke the Physician

Which of Paul's many companions was this? We may exclude those other companions mentioned in the 'we' sections as distinct from the author himself. He was, therefore, not Silas, Timothy, Sopater, Aristarchus, Secundus, Gaius, Tychicus or Trophimus. We turn to the Pauline epistles for a clue to his identity. The epistles to the Galatians, Thessalonians, Corinthians and Romans may be put on one side, as none of them seems to have been written during the periods covered by the 'we' sections. If, however, we date the 'Captivity Epistles' during Paul's imprisonment in Rome (Ac. xxviii. 30), we may find him mentioned in these, for we know that he accompanied Paul to Rome. It has, however, been argued by several scholars of late that these letters were written from Ephesus, not from Rome. This is more probable in the case of Philippians than of Ephesians, Colossians and Philemon; to the last three we should continue to attach the traditional Roman dating. All three were written about the same time, and conveyed to Asia from the place where Paul was by Tychicus and Onesimus. Apart from these two, Paul's companions at the time of writing included three Jewish Christians, Aristarchus, Mark and Jesus Justus (Col. iv. 10 f.), and other three, presumably Gentile Christians, Epaphras, Demas and Luke (Col. iv. 12 ff.). Now Luke, as we have seen, is the one to whom Christian antiquity unanimously ascribes the authorship of Ac. and the Third Gospel. He may well have been the 'we' author, so far as the evidence of these epistles goes (cf. also Philm. 24), and he is not mentioned—by name at least—as being in Paul's company in those letters which were written during periods not covered by the 'we' sections.[1] His name plays no prominent part in NT, and therefore there seems no reason why ancient writers should so unanimously ascribe the authorship of Lk. and Ac. to him unless they had good cause to believe that he was the author.

A further argument for the Lukan authorship of both works has often been urged. Luke is called by Paul 'my beloved physician' (ὁ ἰατρὸς ὁ ἀγαπητός, Col. iv. 14), and some investigators have traced characteristic medical diction in Lk. and Ac. The classic work on this aspect of our subject is W. K. Hobart's *The Medical Language of St. Luke* (1882), a thorough but uncritical comparison of the vocabulary and phraseology of Lk.-Ac. with the language of Greek medical writers, particularly Hippocrates, Galen, Dioscorides and Aretaeus. Hobart's argument was reinforced by the more judicious studies of Harnack (*Lukas der Arzt*, 1906 =

[1] There is no good reason for identifying Luke with the Lucius of Rom. xvi. 21, whom Paul includes among his own 'kinsmen'. See *BC* v., pp. 491 f.

Luke the Physician, 1907) and Zahn (*Einleitung in das NT*, 1906 = *Introd. to NT*, 1909). Still more thorough, however, is H. J. Cadbury's *Style and Literary Method of Luke* (1920), where it is argued that the medical element in the language of Lk.-Ac. is not greater than that which we find in the writings of any reasonably educated Greek of that time. We must not fall into the mistake of those who argue from the legal element in Shakespeare's diction that he must have been a lawyer, and therefore Bacon! J. M. Robertson (*The Baconian Heresy*, p. 127) showed that by similar arguments it could be proved that every Elizabethan dramatist was a lawyer. We shall probably be right in concluding that while the presence of medical diction in Lk.-Ac. cannot by itself prove anything about authorship, the more striking instances may properly be used to illustrate, and perhaps even to support, the conclusion reached on other grounds, that the author of the twofold history was Luke the physician.

Thirty-five years ago Rendel Harris argued, on the strength of an Armenian Catena on Ac. with an underlying 'Western' text, that the original 'Western' text of Ac. did contain the writer's name, at xx. 13, which he reconstructed: 'But I Luke, and those who were with me, went on board'.[1] If he was right, then the earliest explicit testimony to Lukan authorship of Ac. must be dated at the latest *c.* A.D. 120, the probable date of the 'Western' recension or 'δ text'. In any case, the words which Rendel Harris wrote in 1913 in connection with this argument are as true now as then:

> 'Thanks to the acuteness of Ramsay's archaeological and historical criticism (and we may add, in spite of its occasional excesses), taken along with the linguistic researches of Hawkins, the studies in medical language of Hobart (again a case often spoiled by the worst extravagances), and finally, the weighty and apparently unanswerable criticisms of Harnack (himself a convert from very different views of the composition of the Lucan writings), we are able to affirm St. Luke's rights over the works commonly attributed to him with an emphasis that has probably not been laid upon them since their first publication' (*The British Friend*, April 1913, quoted in *ET* xxiv. [1912-13], p. 530).

Although in their present form Lk. and Ac. are, strictly speaking, anonymous, they were probably not anonymous originally. What the original title of the twofold work was, we cannot say for certain, but the analogy of similar works suggests that it was *Λουκᾶς πρὸς Θεόφιλον* (*Lucas ad Theophilum*). At first Lk. and Ac. formed a single work in two parts, but after a few decades the first part was

[1] This catena was based mainly on Ephrem and Chrysostom. Rendel Harris's argument was strengthened in 1921, when the Mechitarist Fathers in Vienna published the Armenian translation of Ephrem's commentary on Ac., and these very words were found at xx. 13. F. C. Conybeare renders them: *ego Lucas et qui mecum intrauimus nauem* (*BC* iii., p. 442).

detached and bound up with the other three Gospels, receiving the distinguishing caption *κατὰ Λουκᾶν*. When the two parts were thus separated, the end of the Gospel was apparently modified so as to include a brief reference to the Ascension, and probably at the same time the word *ἀνελήμφθη* was added to Ac. i. 2. As the Ascension accounts in Lk. and Ac. now stand, there seems to be a small discrepancy between them as regards the place and probably the time of that event ; a glance at Lk. xxiv. 51, however, in WH or Nestle's text, shows that the words *καὶ ἀνεφέρετο εἰς τὸν οὐρανόν* are bracketed as a non-Western interpolation.

We infer, then, that the twofold work circulated at first under some such title as 'Luke to Theophilus', and that when the two parts were separated the 'former treatise' had its title changed to 'According to Luke', the author's name being taken over from the original title. The name 'Acts of the Apostles' was probably attached to the second part about the time when its canonicity was recognized (see p. 10).

THE AUTHOR

Nothing certain is known about Luke beyond what we can learn of him from his writings and from Paul's references to him. The information which can be derived from these sources has been summed up above. The only NT passage containing his name which we have not mentioned is 2 Tim. iv. 11, from which we gather that he was in Paul's company shortly before the latter's death.

His name Lucas (*Λουκᾶς*) is familiar as an abbreviation of both Lucanus and Lucius. Several Old Latin MSS of the fifth century give his name as Lucanus. But *Λουκᾶς* appears in inscriptions as a praenomen in Roman names,[1] and must therefore have also been used as an equivalent for Lucius. 'The real argument for Lucius as against Lucanus as the formal name of the Evangelist is the frequency of the former and the rarity of the latter name in the Greek East at this period' (W. M. Calder in *CR* xxxviii. [1924], p. 30). But he cannot with certainty be identified with either of the other Lucii mentioned in NT (Ac. xiii. 1, *q.v.* ; Rom. xvi. 21).

At a fairly early date we meet with a tradition connecting him with Antioch. The anti-Marcionite Prologue to Lk. (*c.* 170) gives the following account of him :

> 'Luke was an Antiochian of Syria, a physician by profession. He was a disciple of the apostles and later accompanied Paul until his martyrdom. He served the Lord without distraction, having neither wife nor children, and at the age of eighty-four he fell asleep in Boeotia, full of the Holy Spirit. While there were already Gospels previously in existence, that according to

[1] W. M. Ramsay, *BRD*, pp. 374 ff. ; M. M. Hardie in *JHS*, xxxii (1912), pp. 130, 145 ff.

Matthew written in Judaea, and that according to Mark in Italy, Luke, moved by the Holy Spirit, composed the whole of this Gospel in the parts about Achaia, showing in the Prologue this very thing, that others had been written before it, and that it was necessary to expound to the Gentile believers the accurate account of the dispensation, so that they should not be distracted by Jewish fables, nor be deceived by heretical and vain imaginations and thus err from the truth. And so right at the beginning we have had handed down to us the Nativity of John, as being most necessary, for John is the beginning of the Gospel, being our Lord's forerunner and companion both in the preparation of the Gospel and in the administration of baptism and the fellowship of the Spirit. This ministry has been mentioned by one of the Twelve Prophets. And afterwards the same Luke wrote the Acts of the Apostles. . . .'

The Antiochian origin of Luke is also mentioned by Eusebius (*Λουκᾶς δὲ τὸ μὲν γένος ὢν τῶν ἀπ' Ἀντιοχείας*, *HE* iii. 4) and by Jerome 'Lucas medicus Antiochensis', *de uir. ill.* 7; 'tertius Lucas medicus, natione Syrus Antiochensis', *Praef. in Comm. in Matt.*). Whether this tradition rests on a stable basis it is difficult to say. It may have arisen from the mention of Lucius at Antioch in Ac. xiii. 1, but this is unlikely, as this Lucius is plainly called a Cyrenean. If we could regard the 'Western' text of Ac. xi. 28 as authentic (*συνεστραμμένων δὲ ἡμῶν*), that would give a starting point for the tradition, but it is more likely that the introduction of 'we' in that verse is due to the tradition, which in that case, however, must have been very early, perhaps 50 years before the anti-Marcionite Prologue. Luke certainly shows an interest in Antioch; e.g., the only member of the Seven whose provenance is stated is 'Nicolas, a proselyte of Antioch' (Ac. vi. 5).[1] Ramsay at one time argued that he was a native of Philippi, from the interest which he shows in that city (cf. especially Ac. xvi. 12). Later, however, Ramsay returned to the Antiochian tradition, suggesting that Luke was a member of the tribe of Makedones, who had settled in Antioch. Thus he was able to retain his view that Luke was the man of Macedonia in xvi. 9. 'His love for Philippi was due to the long and successful evangelization which he carried out there' (*SPT*[14], p. xxxviii.).

If Luke was indeed a native of Antioch, he might well be acquainted with Aramaic, which was spoken in the hinterland of that city, and would thus be able to avail himself of Aramaic sources which have been detected behind both his works. (See R. H. Connolly, 'Syriacisms in St. Luke', *JTS* xxxvii. [1936], p. 383.)

[1] In *The Voyage and Shipwreck of St. Paul*,[4] p. 4, J. Smith notes, by way of illustrating Ac. vi. 5, that out of eight accounts of Napoleon's Russian campaign of 1812—three by Frenchmen, three by Englishmen, and two by Scots—only the two Scots writers mention that the Russian general Barclay de Tolly was of Scots extraction.

Another suggestion of Ramsay is that Titus was Luke's brother —an attractive suggestion, which would help to account for the absence from Luke's narrative of one who appears from the Epistles to have been a very important member of Paul's entourage. Titus was, like Luke, a Gentile (Gal. ii. 3). Luke may then be 'the brother' of 2 Cor. viii. 18 (cf. xii. 18), 'whose praise is in the Gospel' —an identification made by Jerome, following a suggestion of Origen. The identification is supported by the fact that 2 Cor. was written from Macedonia (ii. 13; vii. 5; viii. 1; ix. 2-4), and possibly from Philippi itself, as is stated in the ancient subscriptions of Cod. B and the Peshitta. But these are but speculations, however attractive, and an examination of them does not fall within the scope of this work. Neither does an account of later traditions and legends about Luke. The tradition that he was a painter is late, not being demonstrably earlier than the tenth century.

EARLY ALLUSIONS TO ACTS

1 Clement ii. 1 (A.D. 95), *ἥδιον διδόντες ἢ λαμβάνοντες*. Cf. Ac. xx. 35, though Clement may be quoting this Saying of Jesus from independent knowledge.

Epistle of Barnabas xix. 8 (*c.* A.D. 100), *κοινωνήσεις ἐν πᾶσιν τῷ πλησίον σου, καὶ οὐκ ἐρεῖς ἴδιον εἶναι.* Cf. Ac. iv. 32. Another allusion to the same passage is probably to be found in *Didaché* iv. 8 (*c.* A.D. 100), *συγκοινωνήσεις δὲ πάντα τῷ ἀδελφῷ σου καὶ οὐκ ἐρεῖς ἴδια εἶναι.*

Hermas, *Shepherd:* Vision iv. 2. 4 (*c.* A.D. 100-110), *πιστεύσας ὅτι δι' οὐδένος δύνῃ σωθῆναι εἰ μὴ διὰ τοῦ μεγάλου καὶ ἐνδόξου ὀνόματος.* Cf. Ac. iv. 12.

Ignatius, *Magn.* v. 1 (*c.* A.D 115), *ἕκαστος εἰς τὸν ἴδιον τόπον μέλλει χωρεῖν.* Cf. Ac. i. 25.

Ep. of Polycarp i. 2 (*c.* A.D. 120), *ὃν ἤγειρεν ὁ θεὸς λύσας τὰς ὠδῖνας τοῦ ᾅδου.* Cf. Ac. ii. 24. *Ib.* ii. 1, *ὃς ἔρχεται κριτὴς ζώντων καὶ νεκρῶν.* Cf. Ac. x. 42 (?).

Martyrdom of Polycarp vii. 1 (*c.* A.D. 156), *τὸ θέλημα τοῦ θεοῦ γενέσθω.* Cf. Ac. xxi. 14.

Ep. to Diognetus iii. 4 (*c.* A.D. 150), *ὁ γὰρ ποιήσας τὸν οὐρανὸν καὶ τὴν γῆν καὶ πάντα τὰ ἐν αὐτοῖς, καὶ πᾶσιν ἡμῖν χορηγῶν ὧν προσδεόμεθα, οὐδένος ἂν προσδέοιτο τούτων ὧν τοῖς οἰομένοις διδόναι παρέχει αὐτός.* Cf. Ac. xvii. 24 f.

In some recensions of the *Testaments of the Twelve Patriarchs* there is a panegyric on Paul (*Testament of Benjamin,* xi. 2-5), plainly dependent on Ac., which H. St. J. Thackeray considered to be 'perhaps the earliest evidence for the canonicity of the Acts and the Pauline Epistles' (*The Relation of St. Paul to Contemporary Jewish Thought*, pp. 22 f.). The panegyric, however, is a Christian interpolation of uncertain date, not found in two important authorities for the text, and Thackeray's reasons for dating it earlier than the middle of the second century A.D. are inadequate. (See R. H. Charles, *Apocrypha and Pseudepigrapha of the OT*, ii., pp. 282 ff.; Schürer II. iii. 114 ff.)

In Justin Martyr's first Apology (*c.* A.D. 150), the two following passages contain probable allusions to Ac. With Ac. i. 1 ff. cf. *Apol.* i. 50, *ὕστερον δέ, ἐκ νεκρῶν ἀναστάντος καὶ ὀφθέντος αὐτοῖς καὶ ταῖς προφητείαις ἐντυχεῖν, ἐν αἷς πάντα ταῦτα προείρητο γενησόμενα, διδάξαντος, καὶ εἰς οὐρανὸν ἀνερχόμενον ἰδόντες καὶ πιστεύσαντες καὶ δύναμιν ἐκεῖθεν αὐτοῖς πεμφθεῖσαν παρ' αὐτοῦ λαβόντες καὶ εἰς πᾶν γένος ἀνθρώπων ἐλθόντες, ταῦτα ἐδίδαξαν καὶ ἀπόστολοι προσηγορεύθησαν.*

With Ac. xvii. 25 cf. *Apol.* i. 10, *ἀλλ' οὐ δεῖσθαι τῆς παρὰ ἀνθρώπων ὑλικῆς προσφορᾶς παρειλήφαμεν τὸν θεόν, αὐτὸν παρέχοντα πάντα ὁρῶντες.*

The 'Acts of Paul', composed *c.* A.D. 160 by an orthodox presbyter of the province of Asia, are dependent on the canonical Acts, which served as a model also for the Leucian 'Acts of John' and other apocryphal 'Acts'.

The account by Hegesippus (*c.* A.D. 175) of the stoning of James the Just (Eusebius *HE* ii. 23) contains reminiscences of the account of the stoning of Stephen in Ac. vii. 54 ff. The letter written by the Churches of Vienne and Lyons in A.D. 177 (Euseb. *HE* v. 1 ff.) also refers to Stephen, and seems to imply knowledge of the food-law of Ac. xv. 29 (see footnote on p. 289).

It is sufficiently clear from these allusions, even if some of the passages quoted above are to be otherwise accounted for, that Ac. was generally known in the churches throughout the Empire in the second century. And in view of the close relation between Ac. and the Third Gospel, the evidence for that Gospel is also indirect evidence for Ac. Thus, although Marcion (*c.* A.D. 140) rejected Ac. from his Canon, the fact that his Gospel was a suitably abridged edition of Lk. is an additional piece of evidence, if such were necessary, for the existence of Ac. at that date.[1]

[1] An attempt has recently been made by J. Knox in his *Marcion and the New Testament* (Chicago, 1942) to make our canonical Lk. later than Marcion's Gospel and to date Ac. *c.* A.D. 150, on the ground that Lk.-Ac. was composed under the impulse of Marcion's canon-making and with the object of correcting the Marcionite presentation of Paul and the other Apostles. This theory is both historically improbable and at complete variance with the cogent internal evidence of the first-century authorship of Ac. (see below).

CANONICITY

It is plain that the canonicity of Ac. was firmly established by *c.* A.D. 160-80, and probably it was recognized several decades earlier. Once the canonicity of Lk. was accepted, the same value would inevitably be attached to the companion work written by the same author.

Early in the second century the fourfold Gospel and the Pauline collection were accepted generally as divinely authoritative writings. But these two collections were largely independent of each other. If both collections were to be regarded as parts of one larger collection of authoritative books, there must be some link between them. This link was already in existence; it was Luke's second volume, which is thus the pivotal book of the NT Canon. It provides at one and the same time a sequel to the Gospel story, and an introduction to the Epistles. Against the historical background of Ac. the Pauline letters could be read with greater understanding. And, more important still, Ac. provided independent evidence of the divine authority for Paul's apostolate, and consequently for his letters (see pp. 32 ff.). Thus, without Ac., there might not have been a unified NT Canon as we know it.[1] Its importance in the eyes of Christians at the end of the second century is illustrated by the dictum of Tertullian:

> 'Those who do not accept this book of Scripture can neither belong to the Holy Spirit, seeing that they cannot acknowledge that the Holy Spirit has been sent to the disciples as yet, nor can they claim to be a church, since they are unable to prove at what time and in what swaddling clothes this body was established' (*De praescriptione haereticorum*, xxii).

THE DATE OF ACTS

The allusions to Ac. in the earlier Apostolic Fathers are too indefinite, and the date of these works themselves too uncertain, to enable us to say with confidence that they demand the dating of Ac. much before the end of the first century A.D.

If dependence of Ac. on the *Antiquities* of Josephus could be proved, this would give us A.D. 93 as the *terminus a quo* for dating Ac. But we have indicated elsewhere reasons for rejecting such a dependence (see pp. 24 f.). In that case our only *terminus a quo* is the latest event alluded to in the book itself, the completion of the two years which Paul spent in Rome (xxviii. 30).

[1] The important part played by Ac. in the formation of the NT Canon is specially brought out by Harnack in *The Origin of the New Testament*, pp. 44 ff., 63 ff. E. J. Goodspeed argues that the first collecting of Paul's letters (*c.* A.D. 90) was due to the interest in Paul which was revived and stimulated by the publication of Luke-Acts (*INT* [1937], pp. 210 ff.).

'From this', said Jerome, 'we understand that the book was written in the same city' (*de uir. ill.* 7), probably implying that it was completed at the end of these two years.[1] We can arrive at no certain conclusion about the date of Ac., and still less about the place where it was written, but there are several considerations which tell in favour of its being written in Rome towards the end of Paul's two years of detention there.

(1) Luke betrays surprisingly little acquaintance with the Pauline epistles. At a later date (*c.* A.D. 90), when the *corpus Paulinum* began to be collected, these came to be more generally known among the churches, and could hardly be neglected by a writer drawing up a narrative of the times to which they belong and the activity of their author.

(2) The abrupt manner in which Ac. closes can best be explained thus. Making all allowances for the rhetorical climax of the Good News being proclaimed in the Imperial City 'without let or hindrance' (ἀκωλύτως), we are still left wondering how Paul's appeal fared, and what happened to him afterwards. A few sentences would have sufficed to give us this information.[2] As it is, after the careful and detailed account of the events leading up to the trial, we are left in ignorance of the trial itself. It is almost as if the Third Gospel had come to a sudden end on the eve of our Lord's appearance before Pilate. The suggestion of Ramsay, Zahn and others, that Luke intended to complete his work with a third volume has little to commend it (certainly not the use of πρῶτον in i. 1, *q.v.*). Even if this was his intention, this is a curious place to break off the second volume; the first volume has a more appropriate ending.[3]

(3) There is no certain hint in advance of Paul's death. His words to the Ephesian elders in xx. 25 (38) have been taken as such; but they need not be taken as a foreboding, but simply as a statement of his expectation. His intention at that time was, as we know from Rom. xv. 23 ff., to leave the Aegean area of evangelization for Spain. Therefore, so far as he knew, he would

[1] In the preface to his commentary on Mt., Jerome says that Luke wrote his Gospel 'in the parts of Achaia and Boeotia'; cf. the anti-Marcionite Prologue to Lk., quoted on pp. 6 f. We have no really good external evidence for the place of composition of either volume; it must be deduced, if possible, from internal considerations or from the conclusions we reach about the time of writing.

[2] The comparison with the *Iliad*, which does not go on to complete the life-story of Achilles (as some think it ought to do or once did), is not on all fours. The *Iliad* has as its declared theme the Wrath (μῆνις) of Achilles; it comes to a natural and artistically satisfying end with the purgation of the Wrath. And the death of Achilles is at least foretold in the *Iliad*.

[3] For the view that the abrupt ending of Ac. is to be explained by the author's death, see p. 481 n.

not be in Ephesus again. Whether or not we are to infer from 1 Tim. i. 3; 2 Tim. iv. 12 ff., that he later changed his mind and did re-visit Asia is really irrelevant in this connection, though Harnack, believing that he did re-visit Asia after his first Roman imprisonment, argues that Ac. was written before this second visit, as otherwise Luke would have indicated that Paul's words in xx. 25 were falsified by the event (*Date of Acts*, p. 103). But as diametrically opposite inferences have been drawn from these words the argument from them had better not be pressed either way (see p. 14, n. 2). The fact remains that Luke nowhere indisputably betrays consciousness of Paul's condemnation and execution; had he written after Paul's death, his knowledge of its circumstances would surely have coloured some of his writing, and the note on which Ac. ends would not have been so confident.

(4) The attitude to the Roman power throughout the book makes it difficult to believe that the Neronian persecution of A.D. 64 had begun. The imperial representatives behave with such impartial justice throughout that Paul confidently expects a favourable hearing before the supreme tribunal of the Empire. If Luke were writing at a time when Nero had begun to acquire the everlasting reputation which his attack on the Christians won for him, the atmosphere at the end of Ac., one feels, would have been much less optimistic than it is.

(5) There is no hint throughout the book of the Jewish War of A.D. 66-70, or of the Fall of Jerusalem in which it culminated. If Luke had written after A.D. 70, we might well have expected some indication that the Jewish recalcitrance which he emphasizes had met with this condign punishment, that the 'untoward generation' had met with the judgment from which Peter on the Day of Pentecost urged his hearers to save themselves (ii. 40).

(6) Prominence is given to subjects which were of urgent interest in the Church before the Fall of Jerusalem, but which soon lost their practical importance afterwards, e.g., the terms of Gentile admission to church-fellowship, the relations of Jews and Gentiles in the churches, the food-requirements in the Apostolic Decree of ch. xv., and so on.

(7) To these points we might add that both in conception and in terminology the theology of Ac. gives an impression of primitiveness. This, however, might be due to the sources used, and in any case it is an uncertain criterion; Christian theology remained 'primitive' in some churches longer than in others. Yet the work of a Greek like Luke might have been expected to reflect the more developed Pauline theology. 'Christ' very soon became a proper name in Gentile usage; in Ac. it is still a title. Our Lord is referred to—in reports of speeches—by such 'primitive' titles as

παῖς Θεοῦ (but cf. passages in Didaché and 1 Clement, quoted in note on iv. 27), ὁ υἱὸς τοῦ ἀνθρώπου (vii. 56), ὁ ἴδιος (xx. 28). Christians are still known as disciples (μαθηταί), a name which soon fell out of general use ; it does not appear in the Pauline epistles. The word λαός still refers to the Jewish nation, except in the oxymoron of xv. 14 (ἐξ ἐθνῶν λαόν) and in the Lord's words to Paul in xviii. 10 ; it was speedily transferred, even in NT times, to the Church as the new People of God (cf. Rom. ix. 25 f. ; Tit. ii. 14 ; 1 Pet. ii. 9 f.). Sunday is still 'the first day of the week', as in the Gospels and 1 Cor. xvi. 2 ; it soon became known in the Church as the Lord's Day (κυριακὴ ἡμέρα, *dies dominica*).

The chief difficulty which has been urged against so early a dating arises out of Lk. rather than Ac. itself. Certain references in Lk., it is claimed, demand a date later than A.D. 70 for Lk., and therefore, *a fortiori*, for Ac. Certainly the Jewish War, with the Fall of Jerusalem, is predicted more or less explicitly by our Lord in Lk. xix. 27, 41 ff. ; xxi. 20 ff. ; xxiii. 27 ff. It is, however, absolutely uncritical to assume that every prediction that comes true must be a *vaticinium ex eventu*, quite apart from the consideration that these were the predictions of the Messiah Himself. And the prediction of wars and sieges and sacking of cities is a commonplace of history ; many examples might be collected where the question of divine inspiration does not arise.[1] It is particularly urged, however, that Lk. xxi. 20 is a recasting of Mk. xiii. 14 (= Mt. xxiv. 15) in the light of the actual events of the siege. It is more likely that Luke, writing for a Gentile public, replaced what might be for them an unintelligible apocalyptic allusion by an interpretation ; the surrounding of a city by armies was not so strange an event as to be unpredictable, nor was it unusual for such a manoeuvre to be followed by the desolation of that city. The words may not even be Luke's interpretation, if Blass's suggestion is correct :

'We may suppose that Christ really did speak in both ways, first referring to Daniel's prophecy, and then declaring it Himself ; for it is self-evident that the real speech of Christ must have been much longer than we read it

[1] Blass instances Savonarola's prophecies of the capture of Rome in 1527 which were *printed* 30 years before the event, and which entered into much more remarkable details than any of the predictions recorded in Luke. 'Major utique Christus propheta quam Savonarola ; hujus autem vaticinium longe difficilius fuit quam illius ; nam hostis Romanus praevideri poterat, exercitus Lutheranus non poterat' (Blass, *Ev. sec. Lucam*, p. viii). Prophecies of the impending destruction of London by fire appeared in print for some years before the Great Fire of 1666 (cf. F. Morison, *And Pilate said—*, pp. 261 f.). Metternich in 1851 foretold the circumstances of the rise and fall of the German Empire of 1871-1918, seven distinct predictions which he made being fulfilled (see *The Times Literary Supplement*, 18 April, 1929).

now in any Gospel. Of these two parts, Matthew and Mark give the first, leaving out the second, and Luke gives the second, leaving out the first' (*PG*, p. 46).

C. C. Torrey (*Documents of the Primitive Church*, pp. 20 ff.) believes that the Lukan form is the original (the encompassing of Jerusalem with armies being in perfect accord with the OT prophetic programme as outlined in Zech. xiv. 2, etc.), and that it was replaced by the reference to the abomination of desolation at the time of the crisis in A.D. 40 caused by Caligula's command to set up his image in the Temple.[1]

But the whole question of the date and interrelation of the Synoptic Gospels would have to be discussed in a full consideration of the date of Lk. and Ac. If Ac. was completed *c.* A.D. 62, Lk. must have been a little earlier, and Mk., at least in the form in which Luke knew it, earlier still. There is, indeed, adequate evidence for the view that Luke gathered or set in order much of the material for both parts of his history in Palestine between 57 and 59, that other material was added in Rome, the complete Gospel (= Book I) sent to Theophilus *c.* A.D. 61, and Ac. (= Book II) not very long afterwards.[2]

[1] C. H. Dodd, in *JRS* xxxvii (1947), pp. 47 ff., concludes that the Lukan version of the forecast comes from an independent source and is not coloured by the events of A.D. 66-70.

[2] A convenient summary of the arguments for a later dating of Lk.-Ac. will be found in E. J. Goodspeed's *Introduction to the New Testament* (1937), pp. 191 ff. He enumerates fifteen signs of a later date (*c.* A.D. 90): (1) its literary form; (2) its literary features; (3) its Infancy interest; (4) its Resurrection interest; (5) its doctrine of the Holy Spirit; (6) the interest in punitive miracle; (7) the passing of the Jewish controversy; (8) the interest in Christian psalmody; (9) Church organization; (10) the exaggerated representation of primitive glossolalia; (11) Paul is dead [an inference from Ac. xx. 25, 38, which can, however, be taken as pointing in exactly the opposite direction: cf. Harnack, *Date of Acts*, p. 103]; (12) Paul has risen to hero stature; (13) the emergence of the sects; (14) non-acquaintance with Paul's collected letters [but this gives only a *terminus ante quem*, not a *terminus a quo*]; (15) 'the situation presupposed by the conception of such a work—the wide success achieved by the Greek mission'. Against the cumulative effect of the more telling of these fifteen points must be set the cumulative effect of the points we have already mentioned. Even with regard to the more telling of Goodspeed's points, it is not at all certain that any *one* necessarily demands a later date than A.D. 62. Goodspeed believes, however, that Luke was the author of Lk.-Ac., and allows that his material was gathered earlier. The authorship is a much more important question than the date. But the truth may be that while Lk.-Ac. was *written c.* A.D. 60-62 it did not become generally known to the Church at large until some 20 or 25 years later. Goodspeed argues (*op. cit.*, pp. 210 ff.) that its publication revived interest in Paul and led to the first collecting of the *corpus Paulinum*.

LUKE AS A HISTORIAN

Of all the Evangelists, it is Luke who approaches most nearly the standards of the classical historians. His work, viewed as a historical document, stands in the line of descent from Thucydides. As Thucydides at the outset of his *History of the Peloponnesian War* contrasts his method and purpose with those of his predecessors and contemporaries, so Luke introduces his history with the words, 'Since many have undertaken to draw up a narrative of the events which have taken place among us, . . . I also, having traced the course of everything accurately from the first, have decided to write them to you in order, most excellent Theophilus, so that you may learn the secure basis of the information you have received'.

Then, when Luke has completed the Nativity introduction of his first two chapters, he introduces the main body of his story, the *kerygma* proper, with an elaborate list of synchronisms, designed to fix the time of the ministry of John the Baptist, the preface to Christ's own ministry. In the same way Thucydides, after devoting his first book to introductory matter, commences the history of the Peloponnesian War itself in ii. 2, with just such a synchronism:

> 'The 30 years' truce which was concluded after the conquest of Euboea had lasted 14 years. In the 15th year, in the 48th year of the priestess-ship of Chrysis at Argos, in the ephorate of Aenesias at Sparta, when the archonship of Pythodorus at Athens had but 2 months to run, 6 months after the battle of Potidaea, at the beginning of spring, a Theban force . . . made an armed entry into Plataea.'

Though the most elaborate, the synchronism of Lk. iii. 1 f. is not the only one given by Luke. He relates the story of Christianity to imperial history as no other NT writer does. John the Baptist is born in the reign of Herod (Lk. i. 5), our Lord's Nativity is connected with the enrolment-edict of Augustus (Lk. ii. 1), Quirinius being governor of Syria at the time[1] (Lk. ii. 2). In Ac. the great famine is dated under Claudius (xi. 28), whose edict expelling the Jews from Rome is also mentioned (xviii. 2); and the appearance in the narrative of various Roman officials helps to relate the events recorded to the wider context of Roman history.

The dearth of chronological notes in many parts of his work may simply be due to the lack of such information in his sources. After Luke himself comes on the scene in Ac., such notes are more frequent, not only in the 'we' sections; Paul spends 3 Sabbaths in the Thessalonian synagogue (xvii. 2), 18 months in Corinth (xviii. 11), nearly 3 years in Ephesus (xix. 8 with 10; xx. 31), 3 months in Greece (xx. 3), and then we can trace the course of

[1] A well-known difficulty. See on v. 37.

events almost day by day from Paul's setting sail from Philippi (xx. 6) to his arraignment before Felix (cf. xxiv. 11). Then come the 2 years till Felix's replacement by Festus (xxiv. 27), the accurate notes of time during the voyage to Rome (xxvii. 2 ff.), and the 2 years in Rome (xxviii. 30). The chronology of the latter part of Ac. can thus be determined with a considerable degree of exactness, in contrast to the uncertainty of the earlier chapters.

These earlier chapters contain scenes from the history of the infant Church, admirably selected to give us an impression of its ups and downs, leading up to the increasingly prominent rôle of the Hellenists, the activity and martyrdom of Stephen, the first persecution and dispersal, the conversion of Paul, and the evangelization of Gentiles. They prepare the way for the Pauline mission to which most of the second part of the book is devoted. They give no clear hint of the space of time elapsing between Pentecost and Paul's conversion, so that while some make it 1 year (e.g. W. M. Ramsay), others make it as many as 5 or 6 (e.g. W. L. Knox). The true figure is probably somewhere between these extremes; if the Crucifixion took place in A.D. 30, we may date Paul's conversion about A.D. 33.

Both in the Third Gospel and in Ac., Luke restricts himself to the limits of a single papyrus roll. He makes full use of the space at his disposal; Lk. is the longest and Ac. the second longest book of the NT. We need not quarrel with Luke because his choice of what to include and what to omit does not coincide with what ours would be. It need not be considered *de rigueur* in an academic study of a book of Scripture to ignore the factor of divine inspiration; and we may well believe that Luke's selection was an 'inspired' selection, and one that admirably served his purpose. But in view of the restricted space, his repetitions are the more striking. Paul's conversion is narrated 3 times (ix. 1 ff.; xxii. 3 ff.; xxvi. 2 ff.), the story of Cornelius is told twice, and parts of it more frequently (x. 1 ff.; xi. 4 ff.; xv. 7 ff.), the Apostolic Decree of Jerusalem is quoted thrice (xv. 20, 29; xxi. 25). Thus we recognize the importance attached by Luke to the conversion of Paul, the evangelization of Gentiles, and their title to equal rights in the Church with Jews, on the ground of faith in Christ alone.

Luke departs from the Thucydidean tradition in his attitude to the supernatural. Yet he is not an uncritical and credulous swallower of the miraculous. It is not simply that 'miracles of healing, and indeed miracles of any kind, have a strong attraction for him'.[1] As in the Gospels and elsewhere in the NT, the 'wonders' (τέρατα) which are narrated in Ac. are 'signs' (σημεῖα)—signs,

[1] P. Gardner in *Cambridge Biblical Essays*, p. 386.

that is to say, of the invasion of this age by the Messianic Age; they are 'mighty works' (δυνάμεις), 'the powers of the Age to come', manifestations of the Power of God, and an essential part of the proclamation of the Good News.[1] To reject the supernatural out of hand just because it is supernatural, without considering the circumstances or the evidence, is as unscientific as to accept it uncritically. The reader's estimate of the necessary theological approach will of course depend on his theological outlook, on his attitude to the Person of Christ; but Christians who accept the crowning wonders of the Incarnation and Resurrection cannot logically deny the *possibility* of their being accompanied by lesser 'signs', especially if these are supported by strong evidence.

As in the Prologue to the twofold work, so in other places Luke insists on accuracy (ἀκρίβεια) in the recording of important events.[2] When we test him by his own standard, he emerges from the test with remarkable credit. His reliability in matters of history, and especially of geography, has been abundantly demonstrated by the long and brilliant research of the late Sir William Ramsay. Ramsay started in early life with the conviction that Ac. belonged to the middle of the second century A.D., but he was compelled by his archaeological discoveries in Asia Minor and by his wide and accurate acquaintance with the life of the Roman Empire to conclude 'that it must have been written in the first century and with admirable knowledge'.[3] One of the most impressive examples of Luke's accuracy is in the titles of the various officials in the Empire mentioned throughout his pages, details of which will be found *passim* in the Commentary.[4] This accuracy is the more striking because titles of provincial governors changed suddenly at times if the status of provinces was changed. Luke's accuracy betokens not only contemporary knowledge but a natural accuracy of mind, and if his trustworthiness is vindicated in points where he can be checked, we should not assume that he is less trustworthy where we cannot test his accuracy.

The accuracy of the voyage-narrative of ch. xxvii. was vindicated 100 years ago by James Smith of Jordanhill in *The Voyage and Shipwreck of St. Paul* (1848; 4th ed., 1880), a work which remains indispensable on the subject, and which certainly ought to be reprinted.

Where Luke has been accused of inaccuracy, it has usually been on the ground of real or fancied disagreement with Josephus (see on v. 36 f.; xxi. 38). On this we may remark that Josephus

[1] See A. Richardson, *The Miracle-Stories of the Gospels* (1940).

[2] Cf. Ac. xviii. 26; xxiii. 15.

[3] *Pauline and Other Studies*, p. 199.

[4] See, e.g., on xiii. 7; xvi. 19 f., 35; xvii. 6, 19; xviii. 12; xix. 31, 35, 38; xxviii. 7, 16.

is certainly not *more* distinguished for accuracy, and where we have simply the one author's word against the other's, Luke is at least as likely to be right as Josephus.[1] (See further pp. 24 f.)

THE SPEECHES OF ACTS

It is well known that the speeches which classical historians put into the mouths of their characters were admittedly not intended to be a *verbatim* account of what was actually said. The fashion in this respect was set by Thucydides, who gives this account of his procedure :

> 'As for the speeches made by various persons either on the eve of the war or during its actual course, it was difficult for me to remember exactly the words which I myself heard, as also for those who reported other speeches to me. But I have recorded them in accordance with my opinion of what the various speakers would have had to say in view of the circumstances at the time, keeping as closely as possible to the general gist of what was really said' (Thuc. i. 22).

The speeches of Thucydides are thus not merely rhetorical exercises, but may be regarded as giving a general impression of the sort of thing said on certain occasions. Later historians, however, tended to concentrate more on the rhetorical exercise, paying less attention to historical fact or even probability. Their speeches were deliberately composed as the most polished examples of their style.

Luke's speeches, however, can hardly have been intended to exhibit the Lukan style in its most polished form. He could compose when necessary in very elegant Greek, but the style of many of the speeches in Ac. is inferior to that of the narrative. This is markedly so in the earlier chapters ; and the most natural conclusion is that the style of those early speeches represents the language of men whose Greek was none of the purest, or else that the writer is translating with considerable literalness from an Aramaic source.

The speeches in Ac. must not be considered in isolation from those in Lk., where we have the other Synoptists for comparison. It is agreed by Synoptic students that Luke reports with great faithfulness the sayings and speeches which he found in his Gospel sources. In *BC* ii., pp. 106 ff., F. C. Burkitt examines the eschatological discourse in Lk. xxi. in relation to the earlier form in Mk.

[1] Cf. Ed. Meyer's remark on the story of the death of Herod Agrippa I as related by Luke (Ac. xii. 21 ff.) and Josephus (*Ant.* xix. 8. 2) : 'In outline, in date, and in the general conception, both accounts are in full agreement. By its very interesting details, which are by no means to be explained as due to a "tendency" or a popular tradition, Luke's account affords a guarantee that it is at least just as reliable as that of Josephus' (*Ursprung und Anfänge des Christentums*, iii, pp. 167 f.).

xiii., and shows that in spite of changes and differences, it is substantially the same speech: 'what concerns us here is not that Luke has changed so much, but that he has invented so little' (p. 115). If this is the verdict on Luke in places where his fidelity to his source can be controlled, we should not without good reason suppose that he was not equally faithful where his sources are no longer available for comparison.

The large part which OT quotations play in the earlier speeches of Ac. is not surprising in a Jewish setting; this is not beyond the wit of a clever writer to invent. But there is evidence that many of these quotations, with their interdependent exegesis (cf. ii. 25 ff. with xiii. 33 ff.), are derived from a very early collection of *testimonia* or proof-texts, the use of which can be traced back to the earliest days of Christian history. The scholar to whose researches we are chiefly indebted for our knowledge of the early use of these *testimonia*, the late Dr. Rendel Harris, expressed the following opinion on the distribution of *testimonia* in Ac.:

> 'It will be observed that these instances which we have been studying are taken from speeches, of Paul and the other Apostles, and that there is nothing of the kind in Luke's ordinary narration. He, at all events, does not turn aside to tell us that "Then was fulfilled that which was spoken of by the prophet". If Luke does not use the method of *Testimonies* on his own account, he is quite clear that it was the Apostolic method. It was either what they actually said or what they ought to have said. But if we concede that the *Testimony Book* was behind Luke, the historian of the Acts, it seems absurd to deny that it was behind the speakers with whom he had intercourse and whom he professed to report. The natural consequence is that we have a report of speeches which cannot be very far from their actual utterance' (*Testimonies*, ii, p. 80).

Most of the speeches in the first half of Ac. are reports of the proclaiming of the good news to Jewish audiences, and most of these are put into the mouth of Peter. When we consider that from these speeches we can reconstruct an outline of the Gospel story starting from the baptism of John, when we consider that this corresponds to the scope of Mk., which itself is constructed on the framework of just such an outline,[1] and which is traditionally considered to rest on the authority of Peter, we have good reason for confidence that here we are face to face with the Christian *kerygma* in its primitive form. This confidence is supported by the primitive Christology of these speeches and by other marks of early date, such as the hope expressed that 'all the house of Israel', to whom the proclamation is first made, may repent as a nation, that the Messianic Age may be inaugurated at once (cf. ii. 36; iii. 19 ff.).

[1] See C. H. Dodd in *ET* xliii (1931-2), pp. 396 ff.

It is beside the point to object, as so many have done, that Peter's speeches in Ac. are too Pauline, or that Paul's speech in the synagogue at Pisidian Antioch (xiii. 16 ff.) is too Petrine. We have Paul's own word for it that he preached the same Gospel as the other apostles (1 Cor. xv. 11); the similarities of subject-matter, style, and even of OT quotation, running through all these reports of the early *kerygma*, whether Peter's or Paul's, are only what we should expect in the light of the lessons we have learned from the comparatively new discipline of Form Criticism. It is significant, however, that it is in Paul's preaching that the idea of justification is first introduced (see on xiii. 38 f.). Of the *kerygma* as exhibited in the first half of Ac., Prof. Dodd writes:

> 'But a comparison with the *data* of the Pauline epistles makes it certain that at least the substance of this *kerygma*, with its historical core, is as early as the time of Paul, and that it represents the gospel which he declared to be common to him and the original apostles, the tradition which he received and handed on. When we further observe that most of the forms of the *kerygma* in Acts show in their language a strong Aramaic colouring, we may recognize the high probability that in these passages we are in fairly direct touch with the primitive tradition of the Jesus of history' (*History and the Gospel*, p. 73).

We should observe, however, that primitive though the Christology of these early speeches may be, it is none the less a real Christology; just as every classification and cross-section of the Gospels presents us with a theological portrayal of Jesus as Messiah, Son of God and Saviour, so do these summaries of the original *kerygma* in the early speeches of Ac. In them, Jesus is the divinely appointed Saviour, put to death in accordance with the determinate counsel and foreknowledge of God, raised from the dead by the power of God and exalted as Lord and Christ.

The examples of Gospel preaching to pagans have also been illuminated by Form Criticism. These examples are the brief summary of the address of Paul and Barnabas at Lystra (xiv. 15-17) and Paul's *Areopagitica* at Athens (xvii. 22 ff.). The 'form' of these speeches has been shown, especially by Ed. Norden in *Agnostos Theos* (1913), to conform to the 'form' in which all religious propaganda at that time was cast. What made the difference, of course, was not the 'form' or mould, but what was put into it. The appeal to natural revelation in these speeches is in agreement with Paul's argument in Rom. i. 19 ff.

The most important speeches in Ac., apart from the evangelistic ones, are apologetic in character. The first of these is Stephen's defence in ch. vii., in which we find adumbrated ideas later developed by Paul and the writer to the Hebrews. Paul's chief apologetic speeches are those of chs. xxii. and xxvi., which are subtly adapted to two very different audiences. His speech to the Ephesian elders in xx. 18 ff., which is partly hortatory and partly apologetic, is the only address to Christians ascribed to him in Ac.; it is significant therefore to find this speech full of parallels to his epistles, such as are lacking in his other speeches in Ac.

Even the minor speeches in Ac., e.g. those of Gamaliel (v. 35 ff.), the Ephesian town-clerk (xix. 35 ff.), and Tertullus (xxiv. 2 ff.), are very much in character, and in keeping with their circumstances. Further notes on the respective speeches will be found at appropriate places throughout the Commentary. We fully endorse the conclusion of F. J. Foakes Jackson:

> 'Whatever these speeches may be, it cannot be disputed that they are wonderfully varied as to their character, and as a rule admirably suited to the occasion on which they were delivered. Luke seems to have been able to give us an extraordinarily accurate picture of the undeveloped theology of the earliest Christians, and to enable us to determine the character of the most primitive presentation of the gospel. However produced, the speeches in Acts are masterpieces, and deserve the most careful attention' (*The Acts of the Apostles*, p. xvi.).

These considerations, with others which we have looked at, give us good ground for believing that the speeches in Ac. are not Luke's invention, but summaries giving at least the gist of what was really said on the various occasions, and therefore valuable and independent sources for the life and thought of the primitive Church.[1]

THE SOURCES OF ACTS

> 'We should constantly remember that source-criticism in the New Testament is largely guess-work' (F. J. Foakes Jackson, *The Acts of the Apostles*, p. xv.).

Once it is established that the author of Ac. was Luke, the companion of Paul, it follows that for a great part of his second volume he had the advantage of personal knowledge, which he did not have in writing the Gospel. The 'we' sections at least, and possibly some other parts of the second half of Ac., give the story of things that took place in his actual presence, while so close a companion of Paul had the best possible source of information about the Apostle's life and travels. For a considerable part of Ac., therefore, the only sources required by Luke were his own experiences in Paul's company, probably recorded in his diary, and the information which he had every opportunity of receiving from Paul himself.

[1] I have discussed this subject in greater detail in my Tyndale Lecture, *The Speeches in the Acts* (London, 1944).

For the events of chs. i.-viii; ix. 32- xi. 24; xii. 1-24, Luke had neither his own experience, so far as we know,[1] nor that of Paul, to guide him. But we are not without hints as to the persons on whom he depended for the history of those early days. Much, probably most, of his information was acquired orally, but we cannot exclude the possibility that at a fairly early date the experiences of the infant Church were recorded in written documents.

Those to whom Luke refers in his Prologue as having 'undertaken to draw up a narrative of the events which have taken place among us' may, in addition to telling the story of Jesus, have gone on to relate the events which followed His ascension.

We may regard it as morally certain that one of the writers to whom Luke was indebted was Mark. Mark first appears in Ac. xii. 12, where a certain distinction invests the house of Mary his mother. Owing to the apparent mutilation of the end of Mk., it is impossible to say at what point the Second Gospel ended; but it is conceivable that Mark's account of the Passion and Resurrection was followed by an account of the birth of the Jerusalem Church,[2] which Luke used as a source for Ac., just as he used Mark's earlier narrative as a source for Lk. But there were many in Jerusalem who could give Luke details of the early days when he visited the city in A.D. 57 (e.g. Mnason: see on xxi. 16), and the use of a written source as distinct from oral information must remain not proven. C. C. Torrey, in *The Composition and Date of Acts* (1916), argues from Semitisms in the first half of Ac. that everything from i. 1*b* to xv. 35 is simply the translation of one Aramaic document. As in his work on the Gospels, Torrey has accumulated much interesting information on the Aramaic sources behind our Greek text, but has probably overstated his case. His work on Ac. is carefully examined by J. de Zwaan in *BC* ii., pp. 44 ff., where it is shown that the strongest case for an Aramaic source can be made out for i. 1-v. 16; ix. 31-xi. 18, and perhaps part of chs. xii. and xv. It is in these sections that Torrey's most illuminating elucidations of textual difficulties occur (see on iii. 16; iv. 25; x. 36 ff.), and we may postulate an underlying Aramaic document there with more confidence than anywhere else in Ac.

These sections which betray Aramaic origin deal with the first days of the Jerusalem Church and the early ministry and adventures

[1] Unless for the founding of the Church at Antioch: cf. xi. 27 D.

[2] F. C. Burkitt thought it possible that Mk. 'may have lost about a third of its original contents, and that the work once dealt with the period covered by Acts i-xii' (*Christian Beginnings*, p. 83). Cf. W. K. Lowther Clarke's suggestion in *Theology*, xxix (1934), pp. 106 f., that Mark's Gospel ended originally at xvi. 8, and was followed by a lost δεύτερος λόγος which began with the Resurrection appearances. Similar suggestions were made earlier by B. Weiss and F. Blass; see on xii. 12.

of Peter. We may therefore ascribe them to a Jerusalem source, without necessarily supposing that all the information they contain was derived from one source only. It is precarious to use the criterion of duplicate narratives to divide the early chapters between a 'Jerusalem A Source' and a 'Jerusalem B Source', as did Harnack (*Acts of the Apostles*, pp. 162 ff.). True, we have in the first five chapters two sermons by Peter (ii. 14 ff.; iii. 12 ff.), two arrests of the apostles (iv. 3; v. 18), two defences before the Sanhedrin (iv. 8 ff.; v. 29 ff.), two estimates of the number of converts (ii. 41; iv. 4), and two accounts of the primitive community of goods (ii. 44 f.; iv. 32 ff.). But these pairs are not simply doublets, and the narrative of chs. i.-v. reads smoothly and continuously enough without having recourse to source-analysis. The sermon of ch. iii. arises out of the miracle at the Beautiful Gate, recorded as an example of the 'wonders and signs' of ii. 43; the arrest and examination of v. 18 ff. follow naturally on the earlier dismissal with a caution in iv. 21; the 5000 of iv. 4 represents an increase on the 3000 of ii. 41 not unnatural in a mass-movement of the kind; the miracle in the Temple added its impression to that made by the gift of tongues a short time previously. The account of the community of goods is inserted a second time to introduce the contrasted stories of Barnabas and Ananias.

The section vi. 1-viii. 3 forms a single unit, for much of which Luke may have been indebted to Paul as probably as to anyone else. Paul, a Cilician Jew, must have heard Stephen's synagogue disputations, and he was probably a hearer of his defence as he was certainly a witness of his death. For the same section another possible witness was Philip, in whose house at Caesarea Luke spent several days on the way to Jerusalem (xxi. 8 ff.). Harnack (*LP*, pp. 153 ff.) argued that much of the material peculiar to the Third Gospel was derived from the household of Philip (see on xxi. 9). Philip, too, could tell Luke of the dispersion which followed the death of Stephen (viii. 1*b*), and of the evangelization of Samaria and the conversion of the Ethiopian.

In xi. 19-30 we have the beginning of an Antiochene narrative, which is resumed in xii. 25-xiii. 3, and introduces the account of Barnabas, and Paul's first missionary journey. If Luke was indeed a native of Antioch, whether we follow the δ text of xi. 28 or not, then this Antiochene narrative may depend on Luke's personal knowledge of the events. If, on the other hand, he was not present at the events described in this narrative, he had many other opportunities of information; Paul must have known of the situation which led to his being invited to Antioch by Barnabas; there may even have been an Antiochene document recording the origins of the church at Antioch and including the story of the first missionary journey, a report of which was given to the Antiochene church by Barnabas and Paul on their return (xiv. 27). Paul himself, of course, was a first-hand witness for this journey, as also for the Council of Jerusalem and the events leading up to it. Antioch and Jerusalem would both have some sort of record of the Council.[1]

In ch. xvi. the first 'we' section commences, and Paul himself may have been an authority for the events of xvii. 1-xx. 4. Luke had also opportunities of learning facts from Paul's companions; Aristarchus, for example, may have been his authority for the vividly told narrative of the riot at Ephesus (cf. xix. 29). From the beginning of the second 'we' section in xx. 5 to the end of Ac., the story is told in considerable detail, and we have the impression that even in the parts of those final chapters not included in the 'we' narrative, Luke was not very far from the centre of events.

It is clear that the Pauline epistles were not used by Luke as sources of information; this suggests a date for Ac. before the *corpus Paulinum* began to circulate.

As regards non-Christian sources, many writers have maintained that Luke must have known the *Antiquities* of Josephus, published *c.* A.D. 93. The case for Luke's dependence on Josephus is given most elaborately by M. Krenkel in *Josephus und Lucas* (1894). (Cf. also P. W. Schmiedel's arts. on 'Lysanias' and 'Theudas' in *Enc. Bib.*) The evidence for such a dependence, however, will not bear examination. Since there are so many instances where Luke and Josephus tell of the same persons and events, it is surprising that the only parts of Josephus which Luke is alleged to have used amount to two or three columns—which he did not read properly. As far as Ac. is concerned, the case for Luke's dependence on Josephus rests on two passages, the reference to Theudas and Judas in v. 36 f., and to the Egyptian in xxi. 38. The difficulty about Theudas is discussed in the Commentary *ad loc.* It is strange that a discrepancy should be taken to prove dependence, but it is pointed out that in *Ant.* xx. 5. 1 f. Josephus describes the insurrection of Theudas in the procuratorship of Fadus, and then tells how the sons of Judas, the leader of the revolt of A.D. 6, were executed by the successor of Fadus. This is supposed to account for Luke's order, Theudas-Judas. But only a very cursory and careless glance at the passage in Josephus could lead a reader to suppose that Theudas preceded Judas. Similarly the reference in xxi. 38 to 'the Egyptian who . . . led out into the desert 4000 men of the Sicarii' is explained as due to the fact that in *BJ* ii. 13. 3 ff. Josephus describes (1) the Sicarii, (2) the false prophets who led men into the wilderness, (3) the Egyptian who led 30,000 men

[1] For the theory that Luke has here mistaken two separate accounts of the same series of events for two separate series of events, see p. 38.

out of the desert. There is nothing here to suggest literary dependence; as for discrepancies, Luke is as likely to be right as Josephus. On the whole comparison, there is no ground for believing that either Luke or Josephus was acquainted with the other's work.[1] One of the most important points of contact between the two writers is the narrative of the death of Herod Agrippa I (see pp. 18 n., 249 ff.) and it is perfectly plain that each account is independent of the other. The evidence may best be summed up in E. Schürer's words: 'Either Luke had not read Josephus, or he had forgotten all about what he had read' (*Zeitschrift für wissenschaftliche Theologie*, xix [1876], p. 582).

The linguistic arguments for Luke's dependence on Josephus are equally unconvincing. Krenkel argued that Lk.-Ac. has 178 peculiar words in common with Josephus, which are not in LXX, as against 87 in common with LXX, which are not in Josephus. De Zwaan (*BC* ii, pp. 81 f.) shows that reference to Hatch and Redpath's Concordance to the LXX, which is later than Krenkel's work, reduces the former figure to about 100, and when allowance is made among these for nautical terms and terms belonging to the political vocabulary of the Roman Empire, which two writers of the first century A.D. would naturally have in common, this part of Krenkel's argument appears almost as weak as the other.

There is a little scope for Form Criticism in Ac., in the sermons (see pp. 18 ff.), and in the healing-miracles, the escapes from prison, and the story of the voyage and shipwreck. We may compare the healing-miracles with those in the Gospels, where the main elements in the stories are (1) the intractable nature of the disease, (2) the cure, (3) the effect produced. These are, of course, the natural points to emphasize in a healing narrative; and all we can deduce from the similarity between such narratives is that there was a recognized vocabulary and form for such narratives, which was generally followed. R. Reitzenstein (*Die hellenistischen Wundererzählungen*, pp. 120 ff.) traces in various literatures a similar common framework for stories of escape from prison. Of these there are three in Ac. (v. 19; xii. 6 ff.; xvi. 25 ff.), similarities between which are pointed out in the Commentary. The resemblance between the 'form' used by Luke and that found, e.g. in the

[1] Luke's reference to 'Lysanias, tetrarch of Abilene' in Lk. iii. 1, has been thought due to his misreading of *Ant.* xix. 5. 1, where Claudius bestows on Agrippa I in A.D. 41 'Abila, that had belonged to Lysanias', or of *Ant.* xx. 7. 1, where Agrippa II receives in A.D. 53 'Abila, which had been the tetrarchy of Lysanias'. The only Lysanias mentioned by Josephus was killed in 36 B.C. (*Ant.* xv. 4. 1). But there is good evidence for a younger Lysanias, tetrarch at the time indicated by Luke: cf. Schürer, I, ii. 335 ff.; Ramsay, *BRD*, pp. 297 ff.; E. Meyer, *Ursprung und Anfänge des Christentums*, i, pp. 47 ff.; A. H. M. Jones, *The Herods of Judaea*, pp. 69, 208.

Bacchae of Euripides and in the 'Acts of Thomas' is striking, but proves only that Luke inherited a literary tradition, and cast these stories in recognized literary moulds. The use of such moulds in no way affects the historicity of the narratives themselves. As for the narrative in ch. xxvii., it contains Homeric reminiscences (see on *vv.* 29, 41). The *Odyssey* gives us the oldest surviving descriptions of Mediterranean seafaring. For Greek and Roman literature, Homer set the fashion in which such stories should be told, and Luke follows this fashion. Here again, the historicity of the narrative is not affected; all that is proved is that Luke was heir to a Greek literary tradition.

THE STYLE AND LANGUAGE OF ACTS

Whatever truth there may be in the late tradition that Luke was a painter, he certainly was an artist in words. Many will endorse the verdict of Renan, that his Gospel 'is the most beautiful book there is'.[1] How immensely poorer we should be without his description of the herald angels with their *Gloria in excelsis*, the Parables of the Good Samaritan and the Prodigal Son, the story of the Emmaus road! It is the same artist who in his second book depicts for us in vivid and unforgettable words the scene where Peter stands and knocks at Mary's door, the earthquake at Philippi, the uproar in the Ephesian theatre, the riot in Jerusalem when Paul was arrested, the appearance of Paul before Agrippa, the storm and shipwreck on the voyage to Rome, the fire of sticks and the viper at Malta.

Renan also said of Lk. that it was 'the most literary of the Gospels'.[2] We may extend this judgment to Ac. and call the combined work the most literary part of the NT. Of Luke, Jerome says: 'qui inter omnes euangelistas eruditissimus fuit, quippe ut medicus'. We find more really classical Greek in Luke's writings than anywhere else in the NT, or in the Greek Bible, for that matter, although even in Luke's writings there is also a great deal of Greek that is not classical. The Prologue to the twofold work, Lk. i. 1-4, is composed in idiomatic Greek, which contrasts strikingly with the markedly Hebraic idiom of the Nativity narratives which immediately follow. We are probably right in concluding that where Luke's Greek is idiomatic he is composing freely, and that where his Greek is Semitizing, he is either imitating the style of the LXX or following one of his sources with considerable fidelity.

In Ac. we have good literary Greek in the Areopagitica of xvii. 22 ff. (*ver.* 21 is described by Ed. Norden as the most Attic thing in

[1] *The Gospels* (Eng. tr.), p. 148. [2] *Ib.*, p. 147.

the NT), in the exordium of the address to Felix (xxiv. 10 ff.), and in the Apologia before Agrippa in ch. xxvi.[1] In general, we may describe Luke's style as good Hellenistic Greek, somewhat more literary than the Greek of most NT writers. The most important literary form which he retains is the use of the optative, which was very rare in the Koiné vernacular and in NT. There are 67 examples of the opt. in NT, 38 of which are volitive.[2] Of the 67, Luke has 28, 11 in Lk. and 17 in Ac. The only examples of the potential opt. in NT occur in Lk.-Ac. Once it occurs in an affirmative sentence, in the polite assertion *εὐξαίμην ἄν* (xxvi. 29); twice in a direct question (viii. 31; xvii. 18); the remaining examples are in indirect questions (v. 24; x. 17; Lk. i. 62; vi. 11; ix. 46; xv. 26). For other uses of the opt. in Ac. see viii. 20; xvii. 11, 27; xxi. 33; xxv. 16, 20; xxvii. 12, 39.

Other literary forms retained by Luke are the fut. inf. (see on xi. 28; xxiii. 30; xxiv. 15; xxvi. 7; xxvii. 10), and the fut. ptc. expressing purpose (see viii. 27; xx. 22; xxii. 5; xxiv. 11, 17).

He makes an accurate distinction between tenses (see on vii. 26; xv. 37; xxvi. 11), especially in the imperative (contrast x. 15; xviii. 9; xx. 10, with vii. 60; ix. 38; xvi. 28; xxiii. 21). There is a significant distinction between the subjunctive and indicative in v. 38 f. and between the opt. and indic. in xxi. 33. Although *μή* is the usual negative with participles, he sometimes uses *οὐ* with participles to express direct negation (vii. 5; xxvi. 22; xxviii. 17-19).

Also characteristic of the style of Ac. are the use of litotes (e.g. *οὐκ ἀσήμου*, xxi. 39; *οὐχ ὁ τυχών*, xix. 11; xxviii. 2; and especially *οὐκ ὀλίγος*, xii. 18, etc.), double prepositions (e.g. *ἕως ἐπί*, xvii. 14), *δὲ καί* in an adversative sense (e.g. xxii. 28), the use of *τοῦ* with infin. to express purpose (e.g. iii. 2, 12; vii. 19; x. 25; xiv. 9; xv. 20; xx. 3; xxi. 12; xxvi. 18), Attic attraction (e.g. i. 1 f.; vii. 45; ix. 36), and the indefinite use of *τις* (e.g. iii. 2; v. 1 f.; very characteristic of Lk.-Ac.).

Luke has a much ampler vocabulary than the other NT writers According to the data in Hawkins' *Horae Synopticae*, he uses 732 words which do not appear elsewhere in NT: 261 in Lk. only, 413 in Ac. only, and 58 common to Lk. and Ac. Of these 732, about

[1] See on *vv.* 2, 4, 5, 13, 26, 29. But even in this speech we have awkward constructions: see on *vv.* 3, 20. The curious construction in *vv.* 22 f. seems due to the fact that, instead of quoting the arguments used by Paul, Luke simply indicated their nature by quoting the headings to groups of OT *testimonia* in an early collection of these.

[2] Of these 38, 15 are accounted for by the phrase *μὴ γένοιτο*, used 14 times by Paul and once by Luke (Lk. xx. 16). Of the remaining 23 volitive opts., Paul has 15, Jude has 2, Mk., Lk., Ac., Heb., 1 Pet., 2 Pet. have one each. Paul has 31 or 32 optatives altogether.

475 are found in LXX. Luke's characteristic words and phrases are so evenly distributed between all parts of Lk.-Ac., including the 'we' sections, as to give the strongest support to belief in unity of authorship throughout. As the argument depends on an accumulation of details too numerous to be given here, reference should be made to Hawkins (*op. cit.*) and to Harnack (*The Acts of the Apostles*).

The language of Ac. contains several anacolutha (e.g. iv. 5 f.) and involved constructions, especially in the speeches (e.g. x. 36 ff.; xxvi. 3). Specially curious phenomena are a mixture of the gen. abs. with the acc. and infin. (xxiii. 30) and ὅτι followed by the acc. and infin. (xxvii. 10), notes on which will be found in the Commentary.

A few Latinisms occur; e.g. ἱκανὸν λαβεῖν, xvii. 9 (*satis capere*), ἀγοραῖοι ἄγονται, xix. 38 (*conuentus aguntur*), ὄψεσθε αὐτοί, xviii. 15 (*uideritis ipsi*), possibly τιθέναι γόνατα, vii. 60; ix. 40 (*genua ponere*), and, according to Blass, οὐ μετὰ πολλὰς ταύτας ἡμέρας, i. 5 (*non post multos hos dies*, vg), though Burney and Torrey, possibly with greater justification, take this as an Aramaism.

When we speak of Semitisms in NT Greek, we must distinguish Hebraisms from Aramaisms, for the syntax of Hebrew is in many ways quite different from that of Aramaic. Hebraisms are most likely to be due to LXX influence, Aramaisms to Aramaic sources, whether oral or written.

Most of the NT writers were very familiar with the LXX. Its language influenced their style much as the language of the AV has influenced the style of many English writers. Luke can use this 'Biblical Greek' as readily as any other NT writer. But he shows a sense of fitness in his use of it, for it is found most abundantly in those parts of his work where he has a Palestinian or Jewish setting. This style is therefore more characteristic of the first half of Ac. than of the second. The most common Hebraism in Luke's style is his use of ἐγένετο δέ ('and it came to pass'), which in Ac. is regularly followed by the acc. and infin. Another common Hebraism is the use of ἐν τῷ with infin., as in Ac. ii. 1. In Ac. xii. 3 προσέθετο συλλαβεῖν is another Hebraism. It is remarkable that Luke affects this particular Hebraism twice in the Parable of the Vineyard (Lk. xx. 11 f.) where the parallel passages in the other Synoptists (Mt. xxi. 36; Mk. xii. 4 f.) have ordinary Greek idioms. Yet another of these Septuagintalisms is probably to be seen in ἀποκριθεὶς . . . εἶπεν, viii. 24, etc. (plural, ἀποκριθέντες εἶπον, iv. 19), 'he (they) answered and said'.

Apart from this LXX influence on Luke's style, we have to reckon with Aramaisms. As we have seen in the section on the sources of Ac., these are found chiefly in i. 1-v. 16; ix. 31-xi. 18, and in parts of chs. xii. and xv. The fullest treatment of the Aramaic substratum in Ac. is C. C. Torrey's *Composition and Date of Acts*, where he argues that most of the first fifteen chapters are translated from an Aramaic document.[1] Some difficult expressions in the Greek of the early chapters are apparently simplified by being turned literally into idiomatic Aramaic, but it is unlikely that the first twelve or fifteen chapters are translated from Aramaic as a whole. The most convincing points made by Torrey are noticed in the Commentary.

The argument from the medical language of Luke has already been noticed (pp. 4 f.). While this argument can no longer be used to prove that the author was a physician, yet if we have been led to conclude on other grounds that the author was a physician (as we have), the medical element in the language of Lk.-Ac. has illustrative value.[2]

THE PURPOSE AND PLAN OF ACTS

For Luke's own account of the purpose of his history, we turn to the Prologue to the Third Gospel, which applies to the whole of his twofold work *Ad Theophilum:*

> 'Since many have undertaken to draw up a narrative of the events which have taken place among us, as they have been handed down to us by those who were from the beginning eye-witnesses and ministers of the Word, I also, having traced the whole course of events accurately from the very first, have decided to write them for you in order, most excellent Theophilus, so that you may know the secure basis of the information you have received.'

Then, after the introductory Nativity and Childhood narratives, he gives a brief summary of the activity of John the Baptist, leading up to the real subject of his Gospel—the public ministry, Passion and Resurrection of Jesus. In the opening sentence of Ac., he characterizes the 'former treatise' as an account 'of all that Jesus began both to do and teach'. The word 'began' should not be regarded here as a redundant auxiliary after the Aramaic idiom; rather it is emphatic, implying that Luke is now about to

[1] G. F. Moore believes that the first part of Ac. 'has used, directly or indirectly, Aramaic sources' (*Judaism* i., pp. 187, 189); B. W. Bacon says that the whole history from Lk. i. 4 to Ac. xii. 25, 'with slight exceptions, is Petrine in point of view and Aramaic in sources and language-coloration' (*Studies in Matthew* [1930], p. 34).

[2] In addition to works mentioned in this section, valuable information on the language and style of Luke will be found in Plummer's commentary on Lk. in *ICC*, pp. xli. ff.; Moulton-Howard's *Gr. of NT Gk.*, i. and ii., *passim*; H. J. Cadbury's *Style and Literary Method of Luke*, and two chapters in *BC* ii.: 'The Use of the Greek Language in Acts' by J. de Zwaan (pp. 30 ff.), and 'The Use of the Septuagint in Acts' by W. K. L. Clarke (pp. 66 ff.).

tell us what Jesus *continued* to do after his Ascension. The second treatise might then be fittingly called 'The Acts of the Risen Christ', or, since the Risen Christ acts through His Spirit in the Church, 'The Acts of the Holy Spirit'.

The Holy Spirit, promised by the Lord (i. 8), comes upon the disciples on the Day of Pentecost (ch. ii.), enabling them to speak with tongues, to proclaim the Good News with convicting effect and to perform 'signs and wonders' in the Name of Christ, and, above all, uniting them into one Body, the Church. Throughout Ac. the Spirit is in the foreground. The supernatural is emphasized because it bears witness to His operation. He speaks through prophets, foretelling the dearth (xi. 28), so that the church at Antioch may take timely steps to provide for their brethren at Jerusalem; His is the supreme authority behind the Apostolic Decree (xv. 28); He directs the course of missionary activity, selecting Barnabas and Saul for the work (xiii. 2), and prescribing the route to be taken (xvi. 6 ff.). The whole progress of Paul to Rome is Spirit-guided; in all the book there is nothing which is unrelated to the Holy Spirit.

Equally clear is the writer's intention to defend Christianity and Paul against the accusations of various opponents. In the Third Gospel neither Pontius Pilate nor Herod Antipas finds any substance in the charges brought against Jesus, and the centurion at the Cross pronounces Him a righteous man (Lk. xxiii. 14 f., 47). The innocence of Christianity before the Law is emphasized. In Ac., wherever Paul goes in the Roman world, he usually establishes good relations with the Gentile authorities. At Ephesus he is on friendly terms with the Asiarchs and the town-clerk declares his innocence. In Philippi the magistrates have to eat humble pie for beating and imprisoning him. Though his Jewish opponents try to prejudice the minds of the authorities against him, they are usually unsuccessful: at Corinth, Gallio refuses to listen to them; in Palestine Felix and Festus find no basis for their accusations, and Herod Agrippa II is convinced of his innocence; the closing verses of ch. xxvi. show complete agreement on that point between Festus, Agrippa, Bernice and their assessors. So marked is this apologetic tendency that some have inferred that Ac. or even Lk.-Ac. was written to supply the information required for Paul's defence before the imperial tribunal in Rome.[1] This can hardly have been the main purpose of the book, however, though it may have been a subordinate consideration; there is much in Ac., as for example the theological interest we have mentioned above, which would

[1] E.g. M. Aberle in *Theologische Quartalschrift*, 1855, pp. 173 ff. and 1863, pp. 84 ff.; D. Plooij in *Exp.* VIII. viii (1914), pp. 511 ff. and VIII. xiii (1917), pp. 108 ff.; G. S. Duncan, *SPEM*, p. 97.

be irrelevant for the purpose. The object of the apologetic was probably wider. There was an intelligent reading public, or rather listening public, at Rome, and Luke may have availed himself of this opportunity to rebut in the Imperial City itself the popular charges brought against Christianity by insisting on its complete and acknowledged innocence before the law of the Empire.

Rome is the goal towards which the whole of Ac. tends. The Gospel spread out from Palestine in every direction, but the direction in which Luke is interested is the road that leads to Rome. Hence he emphasizes the rise of Gentile evangelization, the Holy Spirit's choice of Paul and Barnabas for this work, the spread of the Gospel through Asia Minor to Europe, and at last the chain of events by which Paul achieves his long-conceived desire to see Rome. As Rome draws near, the interest quickens, and the climax is reached when Paul is established at the heart of the Empire, 'proclaiming the kingdom of God and teaching the story of the Lord Jesus Christ, with all boldness, without let or hindrance' —the triumphant peroration ἀκωλύτως expressing Luke's exultation over the situation with which he concludes his work. Here is the final apologetic: not only do the provincial governors place no obstacle in the way of the Gospel, but in Rome itself the chief exponent of the Gospel is allowed to proclaim it unhindered. It seems unlikely that this joyful note could have been struck in quite this way after the Neronian persecution and martyrdom of Paul.

It could not be denied, however, that the Christian preachers had met with opposition everywhere. The readers might well ask how this came about, if the movement was so innocent as Luke maintained. On a few occasions, Luke points out, trouble arose when financial interests were threatened by the Gospel (cf. Ac. xvi. 19; xix. 24 ff.). But throughout the book the chief cause of the tumults which attended the preaching of the Gospel in so many cities is Jewish opposition. In the 'former treatise' it was the insistence of the Jewish multitude, egged on by their rulers, that caused Pilate to hand Jesus over for crucifixion, against his better judgment; and although the disciples enjoyed the favour of the people in the early days of the Church, they incurred very quickly the anger of the rulers. It was the discounting of the cherished Jewish prerogatives, however, that aroused their bitterest wrath; we get a foretaste of it in the prosecution of Stephen, and it knew no bounds when Paul carried through the Empire the offer of salvation to Gentiles without requiring submission to Jewish rites and ceremonies. Luke emphasizes their envy; they refused the Christ themselves, although in Jerusalem itself and from synagogue to synagogue throughout the Empire they regularly received the first opportunity of accepting Him, and their anger was roused because the Gentiles accepted what they refused.[1] It is striking that the initiative in the opposition to Paul came more from Jews of the Dispersion than from those of Palestine. It was Jews from the province of Asia who stirred up the trouble which led to Paul's arrest in Jerusalem. It was in order to be safe from the plots of his own countrymen that Paul appealed to Caesar. All the way through Ac., along with the expansion of the Gospel among the Gentiles, goes its rejection by the Jewish nation as a whole, until at last in Rome Paul has to say in words such as he had already used elsewhere: 'This salvation of God has been sent to the Gentiles; they indeed will hear it' (Ac. xxviii. 28).

From Jerusalem to Rome, however, many individual Jews did believe, although the nation as a whole did not. The Church was at first composed entirely of Jews. But the circle widened. From the beginning it included Jews of the Dispersion as well as Jerusalem Jews. Before long the Hellenists in the Church began to claim their rights as against the 'Hebrews', and had seven representatives of their own appointed. Stephen, the most outstanding of these, showed an exceptionally farsighted comprehension of the breach with Judaism which was involved in the principles of the Gospel. Philip, another of the Seven, then appears preaching the Gospel in Samaria, which was only half-Jewish, and both he and Peter evangelize Western Palestine, which was half-Gentile. In ch. viii. an Ethiopian believes and is baptized; in ch. x. a Roman centurion and his household accept the Gospel, and the descent of the Spirit upon them shows that faith in Christ alone, apart from any ritual, suffices for acceptance before God. In ch. xi. Gentiles are evangelized on a larger scale at Antioch, and from Antioch goes forth the mission to Cyprus and Asia Minor of chs. xiii. and xiv., in the course of which Gentile converts are united in Church fellowship without having to be circumcised or to submit to the Jewish law. All this alarms the more orthodox Jewish members of the Jerusalem church, but when their Apostles and elders meet to discuss the question with delegates from Antioch, it is decided that the evidence leaves no room for doubt that circumcision and the other ceremonies are not required from Gentile believers. Their right to full Church privileges through faith in Christ alone is vindicated. This was all of high importance in the eyes of Luke, who was himself a Gentile; it is natural, therefore, that this should be one of the prominent themes in Ac.

It is plain that Paul is Luke's hero, and the main object of some passages of Ac. seems to be to show how Paul stands head and shoulders above other men. This is so, for example, in the voyage and shipwreck story of ch. xxvii., where at the most critical juncture

[1] Cf. xiii. 45 ff.; xiv. 19; xvii. 5 ff., 13; xviii. 12 ff.; xx. 19.

Paul stands out as master of the situation. But Ac. not only reveals the greatness of Paul's character; it also establishes the validity of his apostleship. This tendency of Ac. is the more important when we consider how Paul's apostleship was compared disadvantageously with that of the Twelve in several quarters, as the Galatian and Corinthian correspondence testifies. Incidents therefore seem to be selected by Luke in order to show how Paul's apostleship was confirmed by the same signs as was Peter's. Does Peter heal a lame man (iii. 2 ff.)? So does Paul (xiv. 8 ff.). Has Peter's shadow healing power (v. 15)? So have Paul's kerchiefs (xix. 12). Does Peter exorcize (v. 16)? So does Paul (xvi. 18). Has Peter a victorious encounter with a sorcerer (viii. 18 ff.)? So has Paul (xiii. 6 ff.). Does Peter raise the dead (ix. 36 ff.)? So does Paul (xx. 9 ff.).[1] It was apparently objected to Paul's apostolic claim that it was founded on visions, whereas the Twelve had been personal companions of Jesus 'in the days of His flesh'. This objection is explicit later in the Ebionite *Clementine Homilies*, where Paul is presented under the guise of Simon Magus (cf. *Clem. Hom.* xvii. 13), but we can perhaps see it reflected in some passages in the Epistles where Paul vindicates his apostleship (cf. 2 Cor. xii. 1). But Luke shows that while Paul was commissioned in a vision to go as Apostle to the Gentiles (Ac. xxii. 17-21), Peter was the first to evangelize Gentiles, and that as the result of a vision (Ac. x. 9 ff.).

This parallelism between the 'Acts of Peter' and the 'Acts of Paul' has long been noted, and recognized as being due to the author's intention to defend Paul's apostolic dignity.[2] But it does not follow, as F. C. Baur and his followers maintained, that the parallel incidents were *invented* by the author in order to minimize the difference between Peter and Paul; the truth is that the author *selected* from the record of actual events accessible to him those which best subserved the aim he had in view in composing his work.

The measure of Luke's success in his vindication of Paul's apostolic claims was early recognized—for example, by Tertullian, who points out to those heretics who rejected Ac. while accepting the Pauline epistles that in rejecting the former they reject the only independent evidence for the apostolic authority of the latter:

[1] It might be added that both Peter (v. 19; xii. 7 ff.) and Paul (xvi. 25 ff.) have miraculous escapes from prison, though this is scarcely a sign of apostolicity.

[2] E.g. by F. C. Baur, *Über den Ursprung des Episcopats* (Tübingen, 1838); A. Schneckenburger, *Über den Zweck der Apostelgeschichte* (Berne, 1841). Baur rejected while Schneckenburger maintained the historicity of Ac. See Baur's critique of Schneckenburger in *Paul: his Life and Works*, pp. 5 ff

'I may here say to those who reject the *Acts of the Apostles*: "It is first necessary that you show us who this Paul was, both what he was before he was an apostle, and how he became an apostle"—so very great is the use which they make of him in respect of other questions also' (*De praescriptione haereticorum* xxiii).

ACTS AND THE PAULINE EPISTLES

The agreement depicted in Ac. between Paul on the one hand and Peter and James on the other on the basic principles of the Gospel was regarded by the Tübingen school of critics of last century[1] as a sure mark of the late and unhistorical character of the book. Reading the four Pauline epistles whose genuineness they admitted (Gal., Rom., 1 and 2 Cor.) in the light of the Hegelian dialectic interpretation of history, with its pattern of thesis, antithesis and synthesis, they recognized in Ac. the synthesis, the latest stage, belonging to the latter half of the second century. The thesis and antithesis were represented by Peter and Paul, who violently opposed one another, Paul advocating complete liberty from the Jewish law, Peter insisting on its continued observance by Gentile believers as well as Jews. Obviously, if this interpretation of history were true, Ac. must be unhistorical, but in truth the picture of events in these four Pauline epistles must be equally unhistorical. While in Gal. Paul insists that he received the Gospel and his commission to preach it direct from God, and through no human mediation, in 1 Cor. xv. 11 he equally insists that the Gospel he preached was essentially the same as that preached by the original Apostles. This is implied even in Gal., the epistle which seemed to those critics to lend most colour to their theory; when Peter, John and James gave Paul and Barnabas the right hand of fellowship (Gal. ii. 9), there was no hint of any difference in the substance of the preaching, the only difference in question relating to the respective mission-fields which each group was to serve. Paul pronounces a solemn and repeated anathema on any who should preach a different Gospel from that which he preached (Gal. i. 8 f.), but he says nothing to imply that the Jerusalem Apostles were liable to his anathema.

The picture of Peter in Gal. accords well with the one we find in Ac., and both differ from the fictitious Peter of Tübingen imagination. According to Gal. ii. 11 ff., Peter's personal conviction, like Paul's, was that no distinction should be made, even socially, between Jewish and Gentile believers. In Antioch, 'before certain people came from James, he ate with the Gentiles; but when they came, he withdrew and separated himself'—not because he had changed his convictions, but 'fearing those of the circumcision'. But what had happene d reviously to convince Peter, orthodox

[1] E.g. F. C. Baur, A. Schwegler, E. Zeller.

Jew, that there was nothing wrong in eating with Gentiles? We find the explanation in Ac. x., where we read how he had learned not to call common what God had cleansed. Peter's action at Antioch was a lapse, and it is evident that Paul's rebuke had its effect, for we find him maintaining true Christian liberty in Ac. xv.

Besides maintaining that the writer of Ac. made Peter too Pauline, the Tübingen critics also insisted that he made Paul too Petrine, in his attempt to reconcile the irreconcilable. The Paul who in Ac. accepts the decisions of the Apostolic Council, circumcises Timothy, and undertakes to perform a rite in the Temple to calm those who were alarmed at rumours of his rejection of all ritual obligations—this Paul was, to them, far removed from the uncompromising controversialist of Gal. Is the Paul of Ac. really the Paul of the Epistles? In Gal. we must remember that Paul was dealing in white-hot urgency with a situation which threatened the very foundations of the Gospel. For the Paul of the Epistles, outward acts in themselves were neither good nor bad, except as the intention made them so. The truly emancipated man is not in bondage to his liberty. If he wishes for certain proper purposes to perform a ritual act not sinful in itself he will do so, not as under an obligation, but freely. If meat offered to idols is set before him, and there is no risk of causing offence to others by eating it, he will eat it and give God thanks; to him an idol is nothing in the world. If expediency demands that a half-Jew be circumcised for his greater usefulness in the Gospel, Paul will circumcise him; in such a case circumcision is simply a minor surgical operation performed for a practical purpose. But the more narrow type of mind will never grasp the difference between doing such things freely and doing them as religious obligations with a view to securing divine favour. To them Paul's behaviour appears as rank inconsistency. So it appeared to his Judaizing and other opponents in his own day; so it has appeared to many Biblical critics in more recent times, and they have therefore dubbed Ac. unhistorical. An apostle must not be inconsistent! But the consistency which some expect from Paul is that 'foolish consistency' which Emerson called 'the hobgoblin of little minds, adored by little statesmen and philosophers and divines';[1] for such a consistency little

[1] 'Essay on Self-Reliance', *Works* (Bohn), i, 24. Cf. the remarks of Foakes Jackson: 'This charge of lack of consistency is a delight to men of limited intelligence, who desire some one whom they can understand, and will always say exactly what they expect of him. As they cannot find such a man in Paul, his utterances often appear to them to be illogical. But this is not because he is really inconsistent, for no one held to great principles more consistently, but because of his exceptional breadth of view, and his power of seeing that there is more than one side to every question' (*Life of St. Paul*, p. 15).

minds will search the life of Paul in vain, for his was pre-eminently a great mind. On the great basic principles of Christianity he was uncompromising; where these were not affected he was the most adaptable of men. He circumcised Timothy, but solemnly warned the Galatian Christians against the practice. Why? Because *they* were being taught to regard it as necessary to complete their salvation, and such an attitude would bring them into bondage to rites and ceremonies, away from the liberty with which Christ had made them free.[1] Similarly, one who ate meat offered to idols with consciousness of the idol might violate his conscience in so doing; let him therefore refrain. But one to whom the meat was just a piece of meat like any other and to whom the idol meant nothing at all might eat freely; though the grace of Christ would lead him to refrain if another's conscience might be injured by his eating. Paul himself endeavoured to be in Jerusalem for various festivals, and associated himself with purificatory rites; yet he challenges the Galatians: 'You observe days and months and seasons and years' (Gal. iv. 10). The difference lay in the intention; they were acting in such a way as to lose the very liberty of which Paul availed himself. Paul's real attitude to such matters is given in Rom. xiv. 5 f.:

> 'One man regards one day above another; another judges every day alike. Let every man be fully persuaded in his own mind. He who regards the day, regards it unto the Lord; and he who eats, eats unto the Lord, for he thanks God; and he who does not eat, unto the Lord he does not eat, and thanks God.'

In his attitude to the Jews, the Paul of Ac. is also the Paul of the Epistles. It is the Paul who repeats in Rom., 'To the Jew, first, and also to the Greek', who in Ac. visits the synagogues first in city after city, and who in Pisidian Antioch declares to the envious Jews: 'It was necessary that the word of God should be spoken to you first'. It is the Paul who suffers so much from Jewish hostility in Ac. who can speak of the Jews in 1 Th. ii. 15 f. as those 'who killed both the Lord Jesus and the prophets, and have persecuted us, and do not please God, and are contrary to all men, forbidding us to speak to the Gentiles, that they should be saved'. It is also the Paul who in Ac. refuses to stop offering the Gospel to his brethren according to the flesh in spite of all his bitter experiences at their hands, who in Rom. ix. 2 f. tells of his great sorrow and unceasing anguish of heart at their refusal to receive

[1] But even in Gal., he insists that circumcision in itself is immaterial (v. 6); only when performed as a religious act does it carry with it the obligation to do the whole law. Cf. 1 Cor. vii. 18 f., μὴ ἐπισπάσθω, which evidently means that converted Jews, like Paul himself, need not cease to observe ancestral customs (cf. Ac. xxi. 21, 24).

the Gospel, and is willing himself to be accursed, if only his heart's desire and prayer to God for their salvation be accomplished.

The Paul who in Ac. labours with his hands in Corinth and Ephesus, and bids the Ephesian elders learn a lesson from him in this respect, is the Paul who in the Epistles shows the same example and teaches the same lesson to the Thessalonians and Corinthians.[1]

The Paul who in Ac. can adapt himself so readily to Jew and Gentile, learned and unlearned, Areopagus and Sanhedrin, synagogue audience and city mob, Roman governor and King Agrippa, is the Paul who speaks in 1 Cor. ix. 19 ff.:

> 'For though I am free from all, I have made myself the slave of all, that I might win the more. To the Jews I was as a Jew, that I might win the Jews; to those under the law, as under the law (not being myself under the law), that I might win those under law; to those without law, as without law (not being without law towards God, but under the law of Christ), that I might win those without law; to the weak I was weak, that I might win the weak; I have become all things to all men, that by all means I might save some.'

The Paul who in Ac. is God's 'chosen vessel' to bear His Name before the Gentiles claims in the Epistles to have been divinely set apart, even from birth, for this very purpose (Ac. ix. 15; Gal. i. 15 f.; Rom. i. 1 ff.).

It is plain that the narrative of Ac. is in no way dependent on what can be gleaned from the Epistles about the course of events during the 30 years it covers. Luke may have seen Paul's letters, but if he did, he has successfully concealed all knowledge of them. An author writing in later years, when the Epistles were in more general circulation among the churches, would almost certainly have availed himself of such first class evidence.

Yet Ac. and the Epistles throw considerable light on each other. We can read several of the Epistles with greater understanding because Ac. gives us some account of the founding and progress of the churches to which they were written. We understand the references to Apollos in 1 Cor. the better for our introduction to him in Ac. We are better informed about the Gentile collection for the Jerusalem believers by combining the information of Ac. and the Epistles than we should be if we had only one or the other of these sources of information; as it is, the references in the one throw light upon those in the other.

When comparing the historical information which we can gather from the Epistles with the narrative of Ac. we meet several difficulties—not, however, insuperable. If we compare the account of Paul's conversion and its sequel in Ac. ix. with Paul's own

[1] Cf. Ac. xx. 33-35, with notes *ad loc.* For the agreement between the Pauline epistles and the Pauline speeches in Ac. see further pp. **20 f.** and the Commentary *passim.*

narrative in Gal. i., we find that Luke gives in greater detail what Paul passes over briefly (the actual conversion), whereas the events of the following three years and the first Jerusalem visit are given with much more explicitness by Paul. Luke mentions no visit to Arabia, nor does he explain that the only apostles whom Paul saw in Jerusalem were Peter and James the Lord's brother. These details were important for Paul's argument in Gal.; Luke passes over them in general terms—*ἡμέρας τινάς* (Ac. ix. 19), *ἡμέραι ἱκαναι* (ix. 23), *τοῖς μαθηταῖς* (ix. 26), *τοὺς ἀποστόλους* (ix. 27). The escape in the basket is related by Paul in 2 Cor. xi. 32 f., where he represents the danger as coming from the ethnarch of Aretas; Luke says it came from the Jews. Judging from later experiences, we need not be surprised if Paul's Jewish opponents enlisted the co-operation of non-Jews against him.

The correspondence of the Jerusalem visits of Ac. and Gal. is a vexed question. The view taken in this Commentary is that the visit of Gal. ii. 1 ff. is the visit of Ac. xi. 30. The purpose of the visit—famine-relief—is hinted at in Gal. ii.10; Paul's statement (Gal. ii. 2) that he went up by revelation is explained by the prophecy of Agabus in Ac. xi. 28. The third visit (Ac. xv.) is not mentioned in Gal., and this can best be explained if this visit had not been paid at the time when Gal. was written. Otherwise, it is amazing that Paul should make no mention of the Apostolic Decree, which would have afforded the most convincing support to his argument. It follows that Gal. must have been addressed to South Galatian churches, and is the earliest of Paul's extant epistles. This view is that adopted by Ramsay,[1] F. C. Burkitt,[2] C. W. Emmet,[3] G. S. Duncan,[4] A. W. F. Blunt,[5] and at one time by K. Lake.[6] Prof. Lake, however, in his later works,[7] has adopted the view first expounded by J. Wellhausen [8] and E. Schwartz,[9] that the visits of Ac. xi. and xv. are really one and the same. Schwartz argued further that the missionary journeys following each of these visits were also one and the same, Luke having found in different sources two variant traditions of the same series of events and failed to realize that they referred to the same events. This view is unnecessarily complicated, to say nothing of its unflattering implications for Luke's intelligence.[10] Apart from this

[1] *SPT*[14], pp. xxii, xxxi, 54 ff.; *The Teaching of Paul*, pp. 372 ff.

[2] *Christian Beginnings*, pp. 116 ff.

[3] Commentary on Gal. in Reader's Commentary series; *BC* ii, pp. 265 ff.

[4] Commentary on Gal. in Moffatt Commentary series.

[5] Commentaries on Ac. and Gal. in Clarendon Bible series.

[6] *EEP*, pp. 297 ff.

[7] *BC*; *Introduction to the New Testament*.

[8] *Nachrichten d. kgl. Gesellschaft d. Wissenschaften zu Göttingen*, 1907 pp. 1 ff.

[9] *Ib.* pp. 263 ff.

[10] R. Eisler combines acceptance of the Wellhausen-Schwartz reconstrnction

consideration, we prefer the correspondence mentioned above, and accept the Apostolic Council as historical.[1] The situation in which it met is outlined on pages 287 ff.

For the movements of Paul and his companions during the second missionary journey, we have some first-hand information from 1 Th. iii. 1-6. This agrees substantially with what we find in Ac. xvii. 14-xviii. 5; such differences as there are arise from the omission and addition of different details by the two authors. For the sequence of events, which we can reconstruct from a comparison of both sources, see on xvii. 14.

From the Corinthian epistles we can derive much information (though not so much as we should like) about the period xviii. 18-xx. 3, which is passed over rapidly by Luke. It is clear from these epistles that Paul's relations with the church at Corinth during his stay at Ephesus were marred by trouble of various kinds, of which Ac. gives no hint. Timothy's visit to Macedonia in Ac. xix. 22 is possibly referred to in 1 Cor. iv. 17; xvi. 10, but belongs more probably to a somewhat later period. Paul expresses his intention of following him in 1 Cor. xvi. 5 f. His intention of wintering in Corinth may have been fulfilled in his three months' stay there (Ac. xx. 3). But we gather from 2 Cor. xii. 14; xiii. 1 f., that the visit of Ac. xx. 2 f. was at least Paul's third visit to Corinth. He must therefore have paid a second visit some time previously in the course of his Ephesian ministry, probably after the writing of 1 Cor., the sorrowful visit implied in 2 Cor. ii. 1.[2]

There are various indications in the Corinthian epistles that Paul's life was in peculiar danger at times during his residence in Ephesus (cf. 1 Cor. xv. 30-32; 2 Cor. i. 8 ff.). The only hint of danger given by Luke is the story of the riot in the theatre (Ac. xix. 23 ff.), but Paul's words seem to imply greater peril than was apparently involved in the riot. Some scholars whose names carry weight [3] have argued for an Ephesian imprisonment (or more than

with vindication of Luke's accuracy by supposing a subsequent dislocation of the text of Ac. The original order he supposes to have been: xi. 25 f.; xiii. 1-xv. 2; xi. 27-30; xv. 3-33; xv. 34; xii. 25; xii. 1-24; xv. 35-41 (*Enigma of the Fourth Gospel* [1938], p. 80). This re-arrangement will probably meet with as much approval as most of Dr. Eisler's theories.

[1] See also W. L. Knox, *The Acts of the Apostles* (1948), pp. 40 ff., where much the same conclusion is reached.

[2] For this period see W. Sanday's art. on 'Corinthians' in *Enc. Bib.*; J. H. Kennedy, *The Second and Third Epistles to the Corinthians*; K. Lake, *EEP*, pp. 117 ff.; G. S. Duncan, *SPEM*, pp. 165 ff.; T. W. Manson, 'St. Paul in Ephesus', in *BJRL*, xxiii (1939), pp. 182 ff.; xxiv (1940), pp. 59 ff., xxvi (1941-2), pp. 101 ff., 327 ff.

[3] Especially A. Deissmann in *Anatolian Studies presented to Sir W. M. Ramsay* (1923), pp. 121 ff.; W. Michaelis, *Die Gefangenschaft des Paulus in Ephesus* (1925); G. S. Duncan, *SPEM*.

one), during which the 'Captivity Epistles' may have been written. It is not unlikely that Phil. was written at this time;[1] in that case Phil. ii. 19 must be linked with Ac. xix. 22; Phil. ii. 24 with Ac. xx. 1. As for Col., Phm. and Eph., they are more probably to be assigned to the Roman captivity. Luke's scanty account of the Ephesian ministry seems to indicate that he was not with Paul during those years; we know, however, that he went to Rome with Paul, and was with him when Col. and Phm. were written.

Paul's statement in Ac. xxiv. 17 that he came to bring alms and offerings to his nation is illuminated by the references to the Gentile collection for the Jerusalem believers (1 Cor. xvi. 1 ff.; 2 Cor. viii. 1-ix. 15; Rom. xv. 25 ff.). These references also explain why so many representatives of Gentile churches accompanied Paul on his last visit to Jerusalem; we may reasonably infer that they went as delegates bearing the contributions of their respective churches. In this as in several other respects the Epistles and Ac. supplement and explain each other.[2]

In short, after a comparison of this nature our verdict on Ac. may be pronounced in the words of F. C. Burkitt:

> 'But when we come to test it by the Letters of Paul we find it to be historical, not fabulous: it is a real guide to us, even for the earliest period' (*Christian Beginnings*, p. 144).

THE TEXT OF ACTS

The original text of NT must be recovered as far as possible by a comparison of the various types of text current in the early Christian centuries, as these have been preserved in manuscripts, ancient versions, and in Biblical quotations in early Christian writers.

Early in the fourth century there came into being a recension of the NT text which combined many distinctive features of the chief existing texts. This recension was possibly made under the supervision of Lucian of Syrian Antioch (d. 312), whence it has been called the Syrian or Antiochian text;[3] but as it soon found its way to Byzantium (Constantinople) and was diffused from that centre, it is perhaps most convenient to refer to it as the Byzantine text. During the following centuries this text increasingly superseded other and earlier forms of text; the great mass of later MSS.

[1] See J. H. Michael's commentary on Phil. in the Moffatt Commentary series.

[2] On the subject of 'undesigned coincidences' between Ac. and the Epistles, W. Paley's *Horae Paulinae*, first published in 1790, may still be consulted with profit.

[3] This text is the NT part of that revision of the whole Greek Bible, the OT part of which is known as the 'Lucianic' text. See *BC* iii, pp. cclxxxi ff.

and versions from the fifth century onwards is Byzantine in character. This was, by and large, the text of the first printed editions of the Greek NT, the text which came to be known as the *Textus Receptus*, the text underlying the great English versions of the sixteenth and seventeenth centuries, including, of course, that of 1611.

But the circumstances under which this text seems to have originated, the fact that it is not represented in quotations in writers of the first three centuries A.D., and the secondary relation which it plainly bears to other early forms of text, make it quite clear that wherever it differs from these earlier texts, the earlier are almost always to be preferred. Several references to Byzantine readings are given in the commentary, and though they may very occasionally represent the original text better than the rival readings (see, e.g., on iv. 17 ; xvi. 13), the secondary nature of the peculiarly Byzantine readings is generally apparent. The Byzantine text of Ac. is represented in the uncials H L P S and in the majority of minuscules, but it has usually been found sufficient for our purpose to indicate their readings by the abbreviation 'byz.', without specifying the individual MSS.

The text of Westcott and Hort, which is the text printed in this work, represents what they called by the question-begging name of 'Neutral Text', because, in their view, it contains none of the aberrations characteristic of the other text families. It is, however, better to call it the Alexandrian text, after the place in which it was current, or, as in this commentary, the β text, after the usual symbol for its most important representative, Codex B (Vaticanus). Codices B and ℵ (Sinaiticus) preserve this text in a very pure form, and so also, for Ac., do Codex A (Alexandrinus) and the minuscules 81 and 1175.

The main criticism of WH as a reproduction of the β text is that it follows B even where the weight of other β authorities is against it. (See for example on iv. 1 ; xxvii. 37, 39.) In several places the β text is probably better represented by Nestle's resultant text. Still, WH is as near to the basic β text as makes little difference. But when we have said this, we have not yet discovered whether it is as near to the text of the original NT autographs. Westcott and Hort themselves believed that it was ; in their view the β text was an excellent representative of the original, as is probably reflected in their term, the 'Neutral' text. There is, however, another candidate for the honour of representing more accurately the original text, and it is none too easy to decide between the rival claims.

This other candidate is usually known as the 'Western' text, because it is represented mainly by the bilingual Codex Bezae (a Graeco-Latin MS. of the Gospels and Ac., written probably in the fifth century in some part of Western Europe, possibly Sicily), the African Latin version (represented in Ac. by the sixth century Codex Floriacensis), and quotations in Tertullian, Cyprian, the Latin translation of Irenaeus, and Augustine. A similar text, however, is found in the East, represented in the Gospels principally by the Old Syriac version, and in Ac. by quotations in Ephrem's commentary on that book and in the Armenian catena mentioned on page 5,[1] and by notes on variant readings in the Harclean Syriac. The Harclean Syriac is a revision made in 616 by Thomas of Harkel (Heraclea) of the Philoxenian version of 508.[2] Thomas's revision consisted mainly in bringing the Philoxenian into line with the prevalent Byzantine text, but in Ac. he also gives a large number of 'Western' readings, for the most part in marginal notes, but also in some 95 asterisked additions in the body of his text, with the result that, next to Codex D (Bezae), the Harclean Syriac is our most important authority for the 'Western' text of Ac. He carried out his revision in the library of the Enaton near Alexandria, using as his standards 'accurate and approved' Greek MSS., presumably of a Byzantine character, but the sources of his variant readings are not easily determined. Some of them he may have taken from earlier Syriac versions, but others he probably found in a Greek MS. of a 'Western' type. The latter is made all the more likely because most of his variant readings are cast in the same slavishly literal translation-Syriac as he used for his text. The 'Western' MS. which he probably used seems to have been similar in character to a papyrus fragment, No. 1571 in the Michigan collection (P^{38}), containing Ac. xviii. 27-xix. 6, 12-16, first published by H. A. Sanders in *HTR* xx. (1927), pp. 1-19.[3] This fragment belongs to the fourth century, if not, as Sanders thinks, to the third, and its text is decidedly 'Western'. Two other papyrus fragments

[1] Ephrem's commentary on Ac. extant in an Armenian translation (see p. 5 n.) and the Armenian catena are printed in translation on opposite pages in *BC* iii, pp. 373 ff. The text on which they are based is probably the otherwise lost Old Syriac version of Ac. The Old Syriac Gospels are extant in the Curetonian and Sinaitic MSS. Burkitt argued that the 'Western' element in the Old Syriac Gospels was due to the influence of Tatian's *Diatessaron*, which was made in Rome about A.D. 170 from Gk. MSS. of a 'Western' type. Whether this is so or not, the influence of the *Diatessaron* obviously could not account for the 'Western' character of the Old Syriac Ac., used by Ephrem, which resembles the African Latin Ac. much more than the Sinaitic Syriac resembles the African Latin Gospels.

[2] Reference should be made to G. Zuntz, *The Ancestry of the Harklean New Testament* (Oxford 1945), and to reviews in *JTS* xlviii (1947), pp. 92 ff.

[3] Also published in A. C. Clark's *Acts of the Apostles*, pp. 220 ff., in *BC* v, pp. 262 ff., and in *Michigan Papyri* iii (1936), pp. 14 ff. See also A. C. Clark's article in *JTS* xxix (1928), pp. 18 ff.

of Ac. may be mentioned because of their 'Western' character: P^{48} (Società Italiana 1165), containing Ac. xxiii. 11-16, 24-29, belonging apparently to the third century, published by G. Vitelli in *Papiri greci e latini*, x. (1932), pp. 112 ff., and by A. C. Clark in *The Acts of the Apostles* (1933), pp. 409 ff.; and P^{29} (Oxyrhynchus 1597), containing part of Ac. xxvi. 7 f., 20, belonging to the third or fourth century, published in *Oxyrhynchus Papyri*, xiii. (1919), pp. 10 ff., and in *BC* iii., pp. 235, 237. The presence of the 'Western' text in Egypt in the third and fourth centuries, before the date of the great uncials, is very important.

As we have called the Alexandrian text the β text after Cod. B, so we may call the 'Western' text the δ text, after its principal representative, Cod. D. The δ text has marked peculiarities in the Gospels (especially Lk.) and in Ac. In the main, it is distinguished from the β text by additions, some of which can be accounted for as scribal or editorial amplifications, while others are not so easily explained, and seem to have some primitive authority behind them.[1]

The claims of the δ text to be regarded as the best representative of the original cannot be dismissed lightly. It has very ancient attestation, and can be traced in versions as independent of each other as the Old Latin and the Old Syriac, both of which go back to the second half of the second century. It appears in patristic citations earlier than the β text does. Internally, however, the evidence for regarding it as superior to the β text is less convincing. A longer text should not invariably be regarded as later than a shorter text, but many of the readings in δ which are longer than the corresponding readings of β are definitely secondary in character. The many amplifications of our Lord's name (cf. i. 21; ii. 38; vii. 55; xiii. 33) are plainly later and pious expansions; so also are phrases like 'in the name of the Lord Jesus Christ' when these are absent from the β text (cf. vi. 8; xiv. 10; xviii. 8) and references to the Spirit over and above those found in β (cf. xv. 7, 29, 32; xix. 1; xx. 3). Similar too, is the frequent harmonization of OT quotations to the LXX form. Some of the longer δ readings are of the nature of glosses, e.g. the addition of 'Jesus' in xvii. 31 and of 'Christ' in xix. 5. Other modifications have the effect of making difficult passages in the β text read more smoothly; e.g. the construction in iii. 16; iv. 25; the chronology in xiii. 20;

[1] Beside these additions, the δ text sometimes omits passages contained in the β text (cf. Lk. xxiv. 36, 40, 51 f.). There is good ground for regarding some of these as β text additions or interpolations. WH, however, unwilling to detract from the β text's reputation for purity, called them not 'Neutral interpolations' but 'Western non-interpolations'. For this curious and clumsy locution we may use the slightly altered and more intelligible 'Non-Western interpolations'.

the removal by omission of the difficulty about ἑπτά and ἀμφοτέρων in the β text of xix. 14 ff. In the latter place, had the β editor been abridging the δ text, he would not have gone out of his way to insert an apparently inconsistent detail which he did not find in the longer text. In the δ text of the Apostolic Decree in xv. 20, 29, an ethical precept is added, the Negative Golden Rule, which is generally admitted to be an interpolation even by those who defend the priority of the δ text; but even if it be removed, the Decree in the δ text remains purely ethical, while in the β text it is mainly concerned with food regulations. Here we have neither expansion nor abridgement, but alteration, and if we ask in which direction the alteration was likely to take place, we must remember that after A.D. 70 the relation between Jews and Gentiles in the Church was no longer the burning question that it had previously been, and the tendency would be to replace by purely ethical precepts those primitive food-regulations which had been laid down to facilitate social intercourse between Jewish and Gentile Christians.

Some of the δ additions are attractive, and might be accepted with greater confidence if they did not keep such questionable company. Such are Simon the sorcerer's copious tears in viii. 24; Cornelius's dispatch of a servant to meet Peter in x. 25; Peter's missionary activity on the way back from Caesarea to Jerusalem, xi. 2 (to be taken along with the δ version of Paul's journey from Caesarea to Jerusalem in xxi. 17); the seven steps of xii. 10; the jailor's securing the other prisoners before attending to Paul and Silas, xvi. 30; Paul's inserting the name of Jesus in the Scripture lessons in the Corinthian synagogue, xviii. 4; his haste to keep the feast (Passover) at Jerusalem, xviii. 21; the hours during which he lectured at Ephesus, xix. 9; the Ephesian populace running into the square, xix. 28; the handing over of Paul to the stratopedarch, xxviii. 16. Some of these added details give the impression of local knowledge, though others may have been deduced from the narrative, or even invented by the expander (though it is often difficult to see why). In xx. 4 a strong case can be made out for preferring *Δουβήριος* of δ to *Δερβαῖος* of β. But the general impression is that the δ text is secondary, though its priority has been ably championed, notably by A. C. Clark in *The Acts of the Apostles*. The best and, I think, convincing work in favour of the superiority of the β text to δ is *The Text of Acts*, by J. H. Ropes (= *BC* iii.). A good summary of the evidence is given by Sir F. Kenyon in a 32-page brochure, *The Western Text in the Gospels and Acts* (1939). He gives his verdict against the priority of δ, while admitting that several of its readings contain 'instances of local knowledge which give the impression of authenticity' (p. 26), and concludes that in Ac., 'the editor of the δ text (if we do not accept it as original) must have had access to material of good quality, such as an alternative draft by Luke, or a copy made by one of Paul's companions who felt himself at liberty to amplify the narrative from his own knowledge' (p. 31). This would explain the presence in δ of apparently authentic details, while leaving us free to regard as secondary the majority of the expansions in which it abounds.

The phenomenon presented by δ, of a secondary Gk. text which is more Aramaizing than the superior β text, has led C. C. Torrey to formulate the very plausible theory that the Gospels and Ac. were translated from the Gk. into an Aramaic 'Targum' towards the end of the first century, and that this 'Targum', being mistaken for the original Semitic text of these books, was very soon afterwards retranslated into Gk. with constant reference to the existing Gk. text.[1] This retranslation, he believes, was the basis of the δ text of the Gospels and Ac., its speedy though short-lived popularity being due to the idea that it was a closer representative of the original Semitic documents than was the β text. If this hypothesis were accepted (and it seems to satisfy many of the *linguistic* phenomena better than any other), it would follow that unsupported δ readings, however inherently attractive, have little independent value for the criticism of the standard Gk. text.

Another account of the origin of the δ text is that offered with some diffidence by Ropes, that it represents a revised recension made very early in the second century, perhaps in connection with an early stage in the formation of the NT Canon: 'The reviser's aim was to improve the text, not to restore it, and he lived not far from the time when the New Testament canon in its nucleus was first definitely assembled. It is tempting to suggest that the "Western" text was made when Christian books valued for their antiquity and worth were gathered and disseminated in a collection which afterwards became the New Testament, and that the two processes were parts of the same great event, perhaps at Antioch —in other words, that the "Western" text was the original "canonical" text (if the anachronism can be pardoned) which was later supplanted by a "pre-canonical" text of superior age and merit' (*BC* iii., p. ccxlv.). This suggestion and Torrey's need not be entirely exclusive of each other.

[1] *Documents of the Primitive Church*, pp. 112 ff. Torrey maintains that the practice of 'targuming' was very popular about this time. With the process of translation and retranslation envisaged by Torrey we may compare the Aramaic 'Gospel of the Nazarenes' (probably a 'Targum' of Mt.) which Jerome claims to have translated into Gk. and Lat. under the impression that it was the Aram. original of Mt. (see his *De Viris Illustribus* 2, etc.). A different explanation of the Aramaisms in the δ text is given by M. Black, *An Aramaic Approach to the Gospels and Acts* (1946), pp. 212 ff.

The view expressed by F. Blass and supported by Th. Zahn, that Luke made two editions of Ac., the δ text being the first and β the second, breaks down under close examination.

It appears, then, that β is superior to δ, but this need not mean that β is equivalent to the original text. The Chester Beatty papyrus of the Gospels and Ac. (P^{45}) has shown that a century before our best witnesses for the β text there existed in Egypt a text of the Gospels—or at least of Mk.—similar to that which we had previously learned to call the Caesarean text,[1] a short text, generally resembling β, but with some affinities to δ. We must take account of the possibility that there was a 'Caesarean' text of Ac. as well, and that it may represent the original text even better than β. In a study of 'The Nature of the Text of the Chester-Beatty Papyrus in the Acts' in *JTS* xxxviii (1937), pp. 383 ff., R. V. G. Tasker finds 'that the text of P^{45}, the oldest Egyptian fragments of Acts preserved, is a distinctive "non-Western" text, probably older than the texts of the Great Uncials and of D, and presenting the same kind of characteristics as that known as the Caesarean text of the Gospels, and that possibly it is the text used by Origen'. Further work must be done on this question before any pronouncement can be made with confidence, and we may hope that more documents may come to light to serve as material for the research. In the commentary most of the noteworthy readings of P^{45} are mentioned. In any case, β is sufficiently close to the Caesarean text to give us confidence that whichever be the better of the two, either will represent with substantial faithfulness the original text of Ac.

In the textual notes in this Commentary, special attention is paid to the readings of the δ text (especially of Cod. D[2]) and of

[1] So called first by B. H. Streeter (*The Four Gospels*, pp. 77 ff., 598 f.), because it appeared that while Origen used MSS. of a β type for Mk. at Alexandria his works written after his removal to Caesarea in 231 show the use of MSS. akin to Codd. Θ, W, 1 and its related minn. (118, 131, 209, 1582), 13 and related minn. (69, 124, 230, 346, 543, 788, 826, 828, 983, 1689, 1709), 28, 565, 700, and the Old Georgian version. It was shown by K. Lake, however, in *HTR* xxi (1928), pp. 207 ff., that Origen possibly used a 'Caesarean' text of Mk. even before leaving Egypt, and certainly used a β text for a short time after coming to Caesarea (but thereafter a 'Caesarean' text exclusively). The discovery and study of P^{45} shows that a 'Caesarean' text of Mk. was current in Egypt about that time. As the 'Caesarean' text was soon adopted in Caesarea, however, and radiated from there, the name may conveniently be retained (on the same principle as we call the later text Byzantine, although it probably originated in Antioch). Kenyon suggests the term 'α text' for the Byzantine (after Cod. A, which is Byzantine in the Gospels), and 'γ text' for the Caesarean.

[2] Ac. viii. 29-x. 14; xxi. 2-10, 15-18; xxii. 10-20; xxii. 29-xxviii. 31, are wanting from D; viii. 20-x. 4; xx. 31-xxi. 2; xxi. 7-10; xxii. 2-10; xxii. 20-xxviii. 31 are wanting from d (the Latin part of the same MS).

the Byzantine text, and of some recently found papyri, especially P^{45}. The following are the symbols most frequently occurring in the textual notes:[1]

UNCIALS

e p a c r ℵ (Sinaiticus) saec. iv, β text.
e a c p r A (Alexandrinus) saec. v, β in Ac., byz. in Gospels.
e a c p r B (Vaticanus), saec. iv, β.
e a c p r C (Ephraemi), saec. v, β in Ac., mixed in Gospels.
e a D (Bezae), saec. v-vi, bilingual, δ.
a E (Laudianus), saec. vi-vii, bilingual, byz.
a H (Mutinensis), saec. ix, byz.
a c p L (Angelicus), saec. ix, byz.
a c p r P (Porphyrianus), saec. ix, byz.
a c p S (Laurensis ii), saec. ix-x, byz.
e W (Washington), the Freer Gospels, saec. iv-v, Caesarean.
e Θ (Koridethianus), saec. ix, Caesarean.
e a c p Ψ (Laurensis), saec. viii, β.
a 0175 (Società Italiana 125), saec. v, Ac. vi. 7-15.
a 066 (Leningrad), saec. v, Ac. xxviii. 8-17.

N.B.—ℵ*A*B*C*D*, etc. First hand in ℵ ABCD etc.
$ℵ^{a}ℵ^{b}ℵ^{ca}ℵ^{cb}ℵ^{cc}ℵ^{d}$. Correctors of ℵ.
A^{vid}. Apparent reading of A.
A^{corr}. Corrector of A.
B^2 B^3. Second and third hands in B.

PAPYRI

a P^{8} (Berlin 8683), saec. iv, Ac. iv. 31-37; v. 2-9; vi. 1-6, 8-15, β.
a P^{29} (Oxyrhynchus 1597), saec. iii-iv, Ac. xxvi. 7 f., 20, δ.
a P^{33} (Wessely 190), saec. vi-vii, Ac. xv. 22-24, 27-32, β.
a P^{38} (Michigan 1571), saec. iii-iv, Ac. xviii. 27-xix. 6, 12-16, δ.
a P^{41} (Wessely 237), saec. xii-xiii, Gk. and Sah., parts of Ac. xvii. 28–xxii. 17, β.
e a P^{45} (Chester Beatty), saec. iii, parts of Ac. iv. 27-xvii. 17, β or Caesarean.
a P^{48} (Società Italiana 1165), saec. iii, Ac. xxiii. 11-16, 24-29, δ.

MINUSCULES (Minn.)

The great majority of minn. exhibit a Byzantine text. A β text is found in the following (among others):—

e a c p 33 (Paris), saec. x or earlier (influenced by byz.).
a 81 (Brit. Mus.), saec. xi, agreeing closely with B.
a c p 1175 (Patmos), saec. x, akin to 81, with some δ readings.

[1] The letters *e a c p r* printed before the symbols of the MSS. indicate that the MS. in question contains in whole or in part the Gospels (*e*), Acts (*a*), the Catholic Epistles (*c*), the Pauline Epistles and Hebrews (*p*), the Revelation (*r*).

A δ text is found in the following (among others) :—

a 36 (Oxford), saec. xii.
p a c r 69 (Leicester), saec. xv. (' Caesarean ' in Mk.).
a c p r 88 (Naples), saec. xii.
a c p r 181 (Rome), saec. xi.
a p c 429 (Wolfenbüttel), saec. xiv-xv.
e a p c 431 (Strasbourg), saec. xii.
a p c 614 (Milan), saec. xiii.
a c p 915 (Escurial), saec. xiii.
e a c p 1149 (Chalcis), saec. xiii.
a c p 1518 (Constantinople), saec. xv.
a c p r 1611 (Athens), saec. xii.
a p c 1739 (Athos), saec. x.
a c p 1898 (Athens), saec. x.
e a c p 2147 (Leningrad), saec. xii.
a c p 2298 (Paris), saec. xi-xii.

VERSIONS

Latin

vet. lat. Old Latin, saec. ii-iv.
e a d Latin part of D.
a e Latin part of E.
e a c p r g Cod. Gigas Holmiensis, saec. xiii, only Ac. and Rev. pre-vg.
a c r h Cod. Floriacensis, African Latin, δ, saec. vi.
m Speculum ps.-Augustini, saec. ix.
e a c p r p Cod. Perpinianus, saec. xiii (Old Latin only in Ac. 1^{1}-13^{5}; 28^{16-31}; the rest of the book is mainly vg).
r Lectionary (Schlettstadt), saec. vii-viii.
a s Cod. Bobiensis, saec. v-vi.
t Liber comicus (Paris, orig. Toledo), lectionary, saec. xi.
vg Vulgate (A.D. 384-386).

Syriac

e syr. sin. and syr. cur. Sinaitic and Curetonian MSS. of the Old Syriac Gospels, saec. ii.
pesh. Peshitta (*c.* A.D. 411).
hcl. Harclean text (*c.* 616).
hcl.* Asterisked additions in Harclean text.
hcl. mg. δ readings in Syriac in the margin of the Harclean version.
hcl. mg. gr. Harclean marginal readings in Greek.

Egyptian (Coptic)

sah Sahidic version (Upper Egyptian, formerly called Thebaic), saec. iii.
boh Bohairic version (Lower Egyptian, formerly called Memphitic), saec. vii.

Other Versions

arm. Armenian, saec. v, revision of older ' Caesarean ' text.
eth. Ethiopic, saec. iv-vii.
vet. bohaem. Old Bohemian, saec. xiv (from vet. lat.).
cod. tepl(ensis). A copy of the German NT (translated from vet lat.), saec. xiv.

PATRISTIC CITATIONS

Amb.	Ambrose of Milan (Lat.), saec. iv.
Ambst.	' Ambrosiaster ' (Lat.), saec. iv.
Ath. lat.	Latin version of Athanasius of Alexandria (Gk.), saec. iv.
Aug.	Augustine of Hippo (Lat.), saec. iv-v.
Chrys.	Chrysostom of Byzantium (Gk.), saec. iv-v.
Clem. Alex.	Clement of Alexandria (Gk.), saec. ii-iii.
Cypr.	Cyprian of Carthage (Lat.), saec. iii.
Did.	Didymus of Alexandria (Gk.), saec. iv.
Eph.	Ephrem Syrus (Syriac), saec. iv.
Epiph.	Epiphanius of Cyprian Salamis (Gk.), saec. iv-v.
Fulg.	Fulgentius of Ruspe (Lat.), saec. v-vi.
Greg. Illib.	Gregory of Elvira (Lat.), saec. iv.
Hier.	Jerome (Lat.), saec. iv-v.
Hil.	Hilary of Poitiers (Lat.), saec. iv.
Iren.	Irenaeus of Lyons (Gk.), saec. ii.
Iren. lat.	Latin version of Irenaeus, saec. iv.
Lucif.	Lucifer of Cagliari (Lat.), saec. iv.
Orig.	Origen of Alexandria and Caesarea (Gk.), saec. iii.
Tert.	Tertullian of Carthage (Lat.), saec. ii-iii.

SELECT BIBLIOGRAPHY

1. COMMENTARIES, CRITICAL EDITIONS, WORKS ON THE TEXT

In *BC* ii. (1922), pp. 429, Dr. J. W. Hunkin mentions as ' the three best commentaries in English upon the Acts ' those of R. B. Rackham (Westminster Commentaries, 1902), R. J. Knowling (EGT, 1900), and T. E. Page (Macmillan, 1886, etc.). Other English commentaries worth mentioning before 1922 are those by J. R. Lumby (Camb. Bib., 1882 ; CGT, 1894) ; C. Wordsworth[4] (London, 1887) ; F. Rendall (London, 1897) ; J. V. Bartlet (Cent. Bib., 1902) ; H. T. Andrews (Westminster NT, 1908) ; W. M. Furneaux (Oxford, 1912) ; W. Kelly[2] (London, 1914) ; W. F. Burnside (CGT, 1916). Since 1922 we have had the commentaries of A. W. F. Blunt (Clarendon Bib., 1923), L. E. Browne (Indian Church Commentaries, 1925), F. J. Foakes Jackson (Moffatt NT Commentaries, 1931), and J. A. Findlay (SCM Press, 1934). But towering far above all other works on Ac. in English is the encyclopædic work edited by Foakes Jackson and Kirsopp Lake, *The Beginnings of Christianity*, Part I, vols. i.-v. (Macmillan, 1920-33). The first two volumes contain Prolegomena and Criticism by various scholars ; vol. iii. by J. H. Ropes, *The Text of Acts* (1926), is devoted to the peculiar textual problems of Ac., which it tackles with a thoroughness and scholarship which are beyond praise, making this volume one of superlative value for the student of NT textual criticism. Vol. iv. (1933), by K. Lake and H. J. Cadbury, contains the Commentary proper, along with a new

English translation of Ac., while vol. v. is in the nature of an Appendix to the Commentary, containing Additional Notes by various writers. These volumes will for long be an indispensable aid to the study of Ac.

Besides the volume by Ropes, another important treatment of the text of Ac. is *The Acts of the Apostles*, by A. C. Clark (Oxford, 1933), containing a new critical edition with textual apparatus, and the most elaborate statement in English of the case for accepting the ' Western ' or δ text as the original.[1] With the volumes of Ropes and Clark, the student has at his disposal nearly all the arguments in favour of the originality of the β and δ texts respectively, both sides being presented with high scholarship and ample citation of the relevant material. The reviews of Ropes's work by F. C. Burkitt in *JTS* xxviii. (1927), pp. 194 ff., and of Clark's work by B. H. Streeter in *JTS* xxxiv. (1933), pp. 232 ff., may also be consulted with advantage. A judicious appraisal of the question will be found in Sir F. G. Kenyon's *The Western Text of the Gospels and Acts* (London, 1939).

Of German editions and commentaries we may mention B. Weiss's critical edition in *TU* ix. 3, 4, *Die Apostelgeschichte; textkritische Untersuchungen und Textherstellung* (Leipzig, 1893); F. Blass's *Acta Apostolorum sive Lucas ad Theophilum liber alter; editio philologica* (Göttingen, 1895), followed by *Acta Apostolorum secundum formam quae videtur Romanam* (Leipzig, 1896), in which he propounded his theory of Luke's two-fold recension of his history, the ' Roman ' recension (represented by the δ text) being the later in Lk. and the earlier in Ac.; A. Hilgenfeld's *Actus Apostolorum graece et latine secundum antiquissimos testes* (Berlin, 1899); the commentaries of A. Schlatter (Calw and Stuttgart, 1902), R. Knopf (in *SNT*, 2nd ed., Göttingen, 1907), H. H. Wendt (in the Meyer series, 9th ed., Göttingen, 1913), and G. Hoennicke (Leipzig, 1913). To Hans Lietzmann's *Handbuch zum NT* a volume on Ac. was contributed by E. Preuschen (Tübingen, 1912), but a new one by H. W. Beyer is announced. Beyer is also the author of *Die Apostelgeschichte übersetzt und erklärt* (Göttingen, 1938), a part of the German NT edited by P. Althaus and J. Behm. Th. Zahn's *Die Urausgabe der Apostelgeschichte des Lucas* (Leipzig, 1916), the ninth part of his *Forschungen zur Geschichte des neutestamentlichen*

[1] This work of Clark superseded his earlier and shorter study, *The Primitive Text of the Gospels and Acts* (Oxford, 1914). See also J. R. Harris, *A Study of Codex Bezae* (Cambridge, 1891) and *Four Lectures on the Western Text of the New Testament* (Cambridge, 1894); F. H. Chase, *The Old Syriac Element in the Text of Codex Bezae* (London, 1893) and *The Syro-Latin Text of the Gospels* (London, 1894); J. M. Wilson, *The Acts of the Apostles translated from the Codex Bezae, with an Introduction on its Lucan Origin and Importance* (London, 1923).

Kanons, restated the Blass theory of a double recension of Ac. by Luke himself, the *Urausgabe* being represented by the δ text. This was followed by Zahn's commentary on Ac. in his *Kommentar zum NT* (Leipzig, 1919, 1921). Nor must we omit the section on Ac. in the *Kommentar zum NT aus Talmud und Midrasch*, by H. L. Strack and P. Billerbeck: vol. ii. (Munich, 1924), pp. 588-773. A recent German commentary from the Roman Catholic side is A. Wikenhauser's *Die Apostelgeschichte* (Regensburg, 1938). O. Bauernfeind has contributed the volume on Ac. to the *Theologischer Handkommentar zum NT* (Leipzig, 1939).

In French the most important commentaries are those by A. Loisy (Paris, 1920), from the Modernist side, and by E. Jacquier (Paris, 1926), from the Roman Catholic side.

Also worthy of mention are J. de Zwaan's *Die Handelingen der Apostelen* (Groningen, 1920), and the *Commentarius in Actus Apostolorum*[7] by A. Camerlynck and A. van der Heeren (Bruges, 1923).

2. OTHER LITERATURE

B. W. BACON: *The Story of St. Paul* (London, 1905).

—— *Jesus and Paul* (New York, 1921).

S. BARING-GOULD: *A Study of St. Paul* (London, 1897).

J. V. BARTLET: *The Apostolic Age* (Edinburgh, 1902).

—— *Church-Life and Church-Order during the first four centuries* (Oxford, 1943).

G. A. BARTON: *The Apostolic Age and the New Testament* (Philadelphia and London, 1936).

F. C. BAUR: *Das Christentum und die christliche Kirche der drei ersten Jahrhunderte* [3] (Tübingen, 1863); Eng. tr., *The Church History of the first three Centuries* (London, 1878-9).

—— *Paulus, der Apostel Jesu Christi: sein Leben und Wirken* [2] (Leipzig, 1866); Eng. tr., *Paul, his Life and Works* (London, 1873-5).

T. D. BERNARD: *The Progress of Doctrine in the New Testament* [5] (London, 1900).

C. BIGG: *The Origins of Christianity* (Oxford, 1909).

M. BLACK: *An Aramaic Approach to the Gospels and Acts* (*Oxford*, 1946)

F. BLASS: *Philology of the Gospels* (London, 1898).

W. BOUSSET: *Die Religion des Judentums im späthellenistischen Zeitalter*,[3] hrsg. H. Gressmann (Tübingen, 1926).

A. BREUSING: *Die Nautik der Alten* (Bremen, 1886).

F. C. BURKITT: *Christian Beginnings* (London, 1924).

H. J. CADBURY: *Style and Literary Method of Luke* (Cambridge, Mass., 1920).

—— *The Making of Luke-Acts* (New York, 1927).

S. J. CASE: *The Evolution of Early Christianity* (Chicago, 1914).

M. P. CHARLESWORTH: *Trade-Routes and Commerce of the Roman Empire* [2] (Cambridge, 1926).

F. H. CHASE: *The Credibility of the Acts of the Apostles* (London, 1902).

C. CLEMEN: *Die Apostelgeschichte im Lichte der neueren text-, quellen-, und historisch-kritischen Forschungen* (Giessen, 1905).

J. R. COHU: *St. Paul and Modern Research* (London, 1911).

W. J. CONYBEARE and J. S. HOWSON: *The Life and Epistles of St. Paul* (London, 1852, etc.).

C. T. CRAIG: *The Beginning of Christianity* (New York, 1943).

G. H. DALMAN: *Die Worte Jesu* [2] (Leipzig, 1930); Eng. tr., *The Words of Jesus* (Edinburgh, 1902).

—— *Jesus-Jeschua* (Leipzig, 1929); Eng. tr., *Jesus-Jeshua* (London, 1929).

W. D. DAVIES: *Paul and Rabbinic Judaism* (London, 1948).

G. A. DEISSMANN: *Bibelstudien* (Marburg, 1895) and *Neue Bibelstudien* (Marburg, 1897); combined Eng. tr., *Bible Studies* [2] (Edinburgh, 1909).

—— *Licht vom Osten* [4] (Tübingen, 1923); Eng. tr., *Light from the Ancient East* (London, 1927).

—— *Paulus* [2] (Tübingen, 1925); Eng. tr., *Paul* [2] (London, 1926).

M. DIBELIUS: *Paulus auf dem Areopag* (Heidelberg, 1939).

E. DOBSCHÜTZ: *Die urchristlichen Gemeinden, sittengeschichtliche Bilder* (Leipzig, 1902); Eng. tr., *Christian Life in the Primitive Church* (London, 1904).

—— *Probleme des apostolischen Zeitalters* (Leipzig, 1904).

—— *Das apostolische Zeitalter* (Halle, 1904); Eng. tr., *The Apostolic Age* (London, 1909).

C. H. DODD: *The Meaning of Paul for To-day* (London, 1920).

—— *The Mind of Paul* (Manchester, 1934).

—— *The Apostolic Preaching and its Developments* (London, 1936).

—— *History and the Gospel* (London, 1938).

G. S. DUNCAN: *St. Paul's Ephesian Ministry* (London, 1929).

—— *The Epistle of Paul to the Galatians* (London, 1934).

B. S. EASTON: *The Purpose of Acts* (London, 1936).

M. S. ENSLIN: *Christian Beginnings* (New York, 1938).

F. W. FARRAR: *The Life and Work of St. Paul* (London, 1879, etc.).

—— *The Early Days of Christianity* (London, 1882, etc.).

F. FIELD: *Notes on the Translation of the New Testament* (Cambridge, 1899), pp. 110 ff.

F. J. FOAKES JACKSON: *Studies in the Life of the Early Church* (New York, 1924).

—— *The Rise of Gentile Christianity* (London, 1927).

—— *The Life of St. Paul* (London, 1927).

—— *Peter, Prince of Apostles* (London, 1927).

—— *Josephus and the Jews* (London, 1930).

P. GARDNER: *The Speeches of St. Paul in Acts*, in *Cambridge Biblical Essays*, ed. H. B. Swete (Cambridge, 1909), pp. 379 ff.

—— *The Religious Experience of St. Paul* (London, 1911).

T. R. GLOVER: *Paul of Tarsus* (London, 1925).

—— *The World of the New Testament* (Cambridge, 1931).

M. GOGUEL: *Le livre des Actes* (Paris, 1922).

—— *La Naissance du Christianisme* (Paris, 1946).

—— *L'Église Primitive* (Paris, 1947).

A. HARNACK: *Chronologie der altchristlichen Litteratur* (Leipzig, 1897).

—— *Mission und Ausbreitung des Christentums* [4] (Leipzig, 1923); Eng. tr., *Mission and Expansion of Christianity* [2] (London, 1908).

—— *Lukas der Arzt* (Leipzig, 1906); Eng. tr., *Luke the Physician* (London, 1907).

—— *Die Apostelgeschichte* (Leipzig, 1908); Eng. tr., *The Acts of the Apostles* (London, 1909).

A. Harnack: *Entstehung und Entwicklung der Kirchenfassung und des Kirchenrechts in den zwei ersten Jahrhunderten* (Leipzig, 1910); Eng. tr., *The Constitution and Law of the Church in the first two Centuries* (London, 1910).

—— *Neue Untersuchungen zur Apostelgeschichte und zur Abfassungszeit der synoptischen Evangelien* (Leipzig, 1911); Eng. tr., *Date of the Acts and of the Synoptic Gospels* (London, 1911).

—— *Ist die Rede des Paulus in Athen ein ursprünglicher Bestandteil der Apostelgeschichte?* (Leipzig, 1913).

—— *Die Entstehung des Neuen Testaments* (Leipzig, 1914); Eng. tr., *The Origin of the New Testament* (London, 1925).

J. R. Harris: *Testimonies*, i. (Cambridge, 1916); ii. (Cambridge, 1920).

E. Hatch: *The Organization of the Early Christian Churches* [3] (London, 1888).

J. C. Hawkins: *Horae Synopticae* [2] (Oxford, 1909), pp. 174 ff.

W. K. Hobart: *The Medical Language of St. Luke* (Dublin, 1882).

F. J. A. Hort: *Judaistic Christianity* (London, 1894).

—— *The Christian Ecclesia* (London, 1897).

A. M. Hunter: *Paul and his Predecessors* (London, 1940).

G. Johnston: *The Doctrine of the Church in the New Testament* (Cambridge, 1943).

A. H. M. Jones: *The Herods of Judaea* (Oxford, 1938).

J. Klausner: *Min Yeshua' wĕ-'ad Paulos* [in Hebrew] (Tel Aviv, 1939-40); Eng. tr., *From Jesus to Paul* (London, 1943).

A. Klostermann: *Probleme im Aposteltexte* (Gotha, 1883).

W. L. Knox: *St. Paul and the Church of Jerusalem* (Cambridge, 1925).

—— *St. Paul and the Church of the Gentiles* (Cambridge, 1939).

—— *Some Hellenistic Elements in Primitive Christianity* (London, 1944).

—— *The Acts of the Apostles* (Cambridge, 1948).

M. Krenkel: *Beiträge zur Aufhellung der Geschichte und der Briefe des Apostels Paulus* (Braunschweig, 1890).

K. Lake: *The Earlier Epistles of St. Paul* (London, 1911).

—— *Landmarks in the History of Early Christianity* (London, 1920).

—— *Paul: His Heritage and Legacy* (London, 1934).

E. Lekebusch: *Die Composition und Entstehung der Apostelgeschichte* (Gotha, 1854).

R. Liechtenhan: *Die urchristliche Mission* (Zürich, 1946).

H. Lietzmann: *Geschichte der alten Kirche:* (i) *Die Anfänge* [2] (Berlin, 1936); Eng. tr., *Beginnings of the Christian Church* (London, 1937).

J. B. Lightfoot: *Dissertations on the Apostolic Age* (London, 1892).

—— *Biblical Essays* (London, 1893).

A. C. McGiffert: *History of Christianity in the Apostolic Age* (Edinburgh, 1897).

A. H. M'Neile: *St. Paul: His Life, Letters, and Christian Doctrine* (Cambridge, 1920).

J. G. Machen: *The Origin of Paul's Religion* (New York, 1921).

T. W. Manson: *Sadducee and Pharisee* (Manchester, 1938).

—— *St. Paul in Ephesus* (Manchester, 1939-42).

—— *The Work of St Luke* (Manchester, 1944.).

A. Meyer: *Die Moderne Forschung über die Geschichte des Urchristentums* (Tübingen, 1897).

Ed. Meyer: *Ursprung und Anfänge des Christentums* (Stuttgart & Berlin, 1921-3).

G. F. Moore: *Judaism* (Cambridge, Mass., 1927-30).

A. D. Nock: *St. Paul* (London, 1938).

C. F. NOLLOTH: *The Rise of the Christian Religion: a Study in Origins* (London, 1917).
ED. NORDEN: *Die antike Kunstprosa* (Leipzig, 1909).
—— *Agnostos Theos* (Leipzig, 1912).
A. OMODEO: *Prolegomeni alla Storia dell' Età Apostolica* (Messina, 1920).
F. OVERBECK: Introduction to W. M. L. de Wette's *Kurze Erklärung der Apostelgeschichte, 4te Auflage, bearbeitet und stark erweitert von Frz. Overbeck* (Leipzig, 1870); Eng. tr. of the Introduction appears as preface to E. Zeller's *The Contents and Origin of the Acts of the Apostles* (London, 1875).
W. PALEY: *Horae Paulinae* (London, 1790, etc.).
A. PALLIS: *Notes on St. Luke and the Acts* (Oxford, 1928).
O. PFLEIDERER: *Urchristentum* [2] (Berlin, 1902); Eng. tr. *Primitive Christianity* (London, 1906-11).
A. T. PIERSON: *The Acts of the Holy Spirit* [2] (London, 1913).
G. T. PURVES: *Christianity in the Apostolic Age* (New York, 1900).
W. M. RAMSAY: *Historical Geography of Asia Minor* (London, 1890).
—— *The Church in the Roman Empire* [4] (London, 1895).
—— *Historical Commentary on the Epistle to the Galatians* (London, 1899).
—— *Pauline and Other Studies* (London, 1906).
—— *The Cities of St. Paul* (London, 1907).
—— *Luke the Physician* (London, 1908).
—— *The First Christian Century* (London, 1911).
—— *The Teaching of Paul in Terms of the Present Day* [2] (London, 1914).
—— *The Bearing of Recent Discovery on the Trustworthiness of the New Testament* (London, 1914).
—— *St. Paul the Traveller and Roman Citizen* [14] (London, 1920).
R. REITZENSTEIN: *Die hellenistischen Wundererzählungen* (Leipzig, 1906).
E. RENAN: *Les Apôtres* (Paris, 1866); Eng. tr., *The Apostles* (London, 1869).
—— *St. Paul* (Paris, 1869); Eng. tr., *St. Paul* (London, 1887).
A. T. ROBERTSON: *Luke the Historian in the Light of Research* (Edinburgh, 1920).
J. H. ROPES: *The Apostolic Age in the Light of Modern Criticism* (London, 1906).
W. SANDAY: *The Apostolic Decree* (Leipzig, 1908).
TH. SCHERMANN: *Propheten- und Apostellegenden* (Leipzig, 1907).
M. SCHNECKENBURGER: *Über den Zweck der Apostelgeschichte* (Berne, 1841).
E. SCHÜRER: *Geschichte des jüdischen Volkes im Zeitalter Jesu Christi* [4] (Leipzig, 1909); Eng. tr., *History of the Jewish People in the Time of Jesus Christ* (Edinburgh, 1892-1901).
E. SCHWARTZ: *Über den Tod der Söhne Zebedaei* (Berlin, 1904).
A. SCHWEGLER: *Geschichte des nachapostolischen Zeitalters* (Tübingen, 1846).
E. F. SCOTT: *The Nature of the Early Church* (New York, 1941).
D. SMITH: *Life and Letters of St. Paul* (London, 1919).
J. SMITH: *The Voyage and Shipwreck of St. Paul* [4] (London, 1880).
F. SPITTA: *Die Apostelgeschichte: ihre Quellen und deren geschichtlicher Wert* (Halle, 1891).
—— *Zur Geschichte und Litteratur des Urchristentums* (Göttingen, 1893-1907).
J. I. STILL: *St. Paul on Trial* (London, 1923).
B. H. STREETER: *The Four Gospels* (London, 1924, etc.), pp. 529 ff.
—— *The Primitive Church* (London, 1929).
H. B. SWETE (ed.): *Essays on the Early History of the Church and the Ministry* (London, 1918).
H. ST. J. THACKERAY: *The Relation of St. Paul to Contemporary Jewish Thought* (London, 1900).
—— *Josephus. the Man and the Historian* (New York, 1929).

C. C. Torrey : *The Composition and Date of Acts* (Cambridge, Mass., 1916).
—— *Documents of the Primitive Church* (New York, 1941).
H. Weinel : *Paulus : der Mensch und sein Werk* (Tübingen, 1904) ; Eng. tr., *St. Paul : the Man and His Work* (London, 1906).
J. Weiss : *Über die Absicht und den literarischen Charakter der Apostelgeschichte* (Göttingen, 1897).
—— *Paulus and Jesus* (Tübingen, 1909) ; Eng. tr., *Paul and Jesus* (London, 1909).
—— *Das Urchristentum* (Göttingen, 1914-17) ; Eng. tr., *History of Primitive Christianity* (London, 1937).
C. Weizsäcker : *Das apostolische Zeitalter der christlichen Kirche*[3] (Tübingen, 1902) ; Eng. tr., *The Apostolic Age of the Christian Church* (Edinburgh, 1894-5).
J. Wellhausen : *Noten zur Apostelgeschichte* (Berlin, 1907).
—— *Kritische Analyse der Apostelgeschichte* (Berlin, 1914).
P. Wernle : *Die Anfänge unserer Religion* (Tübingen, 1901) ; Eng. tr., *The Beginnings of Christianity* (London, 1903).
A. Wikenhauser : *Die Apostelgeschichte und ihr Geschichtswert* (Münster, 1921).
J. M. Wilson : *The Origin and Aim of the Acts of the Apostles* (London, 1912).
Th. Zahn : *Skizzen aus dem Leben der alten Kirche* (Leipzig, 1908).
—— *Grundriss der Geschichte des apostolischen Zeitalters* (Leipzig, 1929).
E. Zeller : *Die Apostelgeschichte nach ihrem Inhalt und Ursprung kritisch untersucht* (Stuttgart, 1854) ; Eng. tr., *The Contents and Origin of the Acts of the Apostles* (London, 1875-6).

CHRONOLOGICAL TABLE

	A.D.
Ministry of John the Baptist	Autumn 27-Autumn 28
Baptism of Jesus	Spring 28
Early Judaean Ministry of Jesus	Summer 28
Galilaean Ministry of Jesus	Autumn 28-Autumn 29
Jesus in Judaea and Peraea	Autumn 29-Spring 30
Crucifixion, Resurrection, Ascension, Pentecost	April-May 30
Conversion of Saul of Tarsus	*c.* 33
His first post-conversion visit to Jerusalem	*c.* 35
Death of James son of Zebedee ; imprisonment and escape of Peter ; death of Herod Agrippa I	Spring 44
Famine in Judaea ; Barnabas and Paul sent with relief from Antioch to Jerusalem	*c.* 46
First Missionary Journey ; Barnabas and Paul visit Cyprus and Asia Minor	47-48
Epistle to the Galatians	*c.* 48
Apostolic Council at Jerusalem	*c.* 49
Second Missionary Journey ; Lystra, Derbe, Troas, Philippi, Thessalonica, Beroea, Athens, to Corinth	*c.* 49-50
Epistles to the Thessalonians	late 50
Paul in Corinth	Autumn 50-Spring 52
Gallio becomes proconsul of Achaia	July 51
Paul's hasty visit to Palestine	Spring-Summer 52
Paul at Ephesus	Autumn 52-Summer 55
First Epistle to the Corinthians	Spring 54
Paul's sorrowful visit to Corinth	Summer or Autumn 54

Murder of Silanus, proconsul of Asia	late 54
EPISTLE TO THE PHILIPPIANS	? late 54 or early 55
Paul sends Titus to Corinth and Timothy and Erastus to Macedonia	early 55
Paul in Troas	Autumn 55
Paul in Macedonia and Illyricum	Winter 55-Autumn 56
SECOND EPISTLE TO THE CORINTHIANS	56
Paul in Corinth	Winter 56-57
EPISTLE TO THE ROMANS	early 57
Paul's arrival and arrest in Jerusalem	May 57
Paul detained at Caesarea	57-59
Paul sails for Rome	September-October 59
Paul in Malta	Winter 59-60
Paul arrives in Rome	February 60
EPISTLES TO COLOSSIANS, PHILEMON, EPHESIANS	*c.* 60-61
Death of James the Just in Jerusalem	61
End of Paul's Roman detention	late 61 or early 62
Great Fire of Rome; persecution of Christians	64
Death of Paul	? 65
Outbreak of Jewish War	66
Destruction of Jerusalem	70

In the absence of exact chronological indications, many of these dates are only approximate, and a margin of two or three years must be allowed for some of them. See C. H. Turner in *HDB* i, pp. 403 ff.; K. Lake in *BC* v, pp. 445 ff.

ROMAN EMPERORS IN NEW TESTAMENT TIMES

Augustus (Lk. ii, 1)	27 B.C.-A.D. 14
Tiberius (Lk. iii. 1; xx. 22 ff.; xxiii. 2; Jn. xix. 12, 15)	A.D. 14-37
Gaius (Caligula)	37-41
Claudius (Ac. xi. 28; xviii. 2)	41-54
Nero (Ac. xxv. 11 f., 21, etc.)	54-68
Galba	68-69
Otho	69
Vitellius	69
Vespasian	69-79
Titus	79-81
Domitian	81-96
Nerva	96-98
Trajan	98-117

RULERS OF JUDAEA IN NEW TESTAMENT TIMES

Herod the Great, king (Mt. ii. 1 ff.; Lk. i. 5)	37-4 B.C.
Archelaus, ethnarch (Mt. ii. 22)	4 B.C.-A.D. 6
PROCURATORS:	
Coponius (Jos. *Ant.* xviii. 1. 1)	*c.* A.D. 6-9
Marcus Ambivius (Jos. *Ant.* xviii. 2. 2)	*c.* A.D. 9-12
Annius Rufus (Jos. *Ant.* xviii. 2. 2)	*c.* 12-15
Valerius Gratus (Jos. *Ant.* xviii. 2. 2)	15-26
Pontius Pilatus (Lk. iii. 1, etc.; Jos. *Ant.* xviii. 2. 2, etc.)	26-36
Marcellus (Jos. *Ant.* xviii. 4. 2)	*c.* 36-37
Marullus (Jos. *Ant.* xviii. 6. 10)	*c.* 37-41

King:	
Herod Agrippa I (Ac. xii. 1 ff.; Jos. *Ant.* xviii. 6. 10, etc.)	41-44
Procurators:	
Cuspius Fadus (Jos. *Ant.* xix. 9. 2)	*c.* 44-46
Tiberius Julius Alexander (Jos. *Ant.* xx. 5. 2)	*c.* 46-48
Cumanus (Jos. *Ant.* xx. 5. 2)	48-52
Antonius Felix (Ac. xxiii. 24, etc.; Jos. *Ant.* xx. 7. 1, etc.)	*c.* 52-59
Porcius Festus (Ac. xxiv. 27, etc.; Jos. *Ant.* xx. 8.9 ff.)	*c.* 59-61
Albinus (Jos. *Ant.* xx. 9. 1)	61-65
Gessius Florus (Jos. *Ant.* xx. 11. 1)	65-66

JEWISH HIGH PRIESTS IN NEW TESTAMENT TIMES

Appointed by Herod the Great (37-4 B.C.):	
Hananel	37-36 B.C.
Aristobulus, last of the Hasmoneans	? Spring-Autumn 36 B.C.
Hananel (restored)	*c.* 36-30 B.C.
Jesus son of Phabes	*c.* 30-23 B.C.
Simon son of Boethus	*c.* 23-5 B.C.
Matthew son of Theophilus	*c.* 5 B.C.
Joseph son of Ellem	*c.* 5-4 B.C.
Joazar son of Boethus	*c.* 4 B.C.
Appointed by Archelaus, ethnarch of Judaea (4 B.C.-A.D. 6):	
Eleazar son of Boethus	*c.* 4-3 B.C.
Jesus son of See	*c.* 3 B.C.-A.D. 6
Joazar son of Boethus (second time)	A.D. 6
Appointed by Quirinius, Legate of Syria (A.D. 6-9):	
Annas son of Seth	A.D. 6-15
Appointed by Valerius Gratus, Procurator of Judaea (15-26):	
Ishmael son of Phabi	A.D. 15-16
Eleazar son of Annas	A.D. 16-17
Simon son of Kami	A.D. 17-18
Joseph Caiaphas, son-in-law of Annas	A.D. 18-36
Appointed by Vitellius, Legate of Syria (35-39):	
Jonathan son of Annas	A.D. 36-37
Theophilus son of Annas	A.D. 37-41
Appointed by Herod Agrippa I, King of Judaea (41-44):	
Simon Cantheras, son of Boethus	A.D. 41-42
Matthias son of Annas	A.D. 42-43
Elioenai son of Cantheras	A.D. 43-44
Appointed by Herod of Chalcis (44-48):	
Joseph son of Kami	*c.* A.D. 44-47
Ananias son of Nebedaeus	*c.* A.D. 47-58
Appointed by Herod Agrippa II (50-100):	
Ishmael son of Phabi	*c.* A.D. 58-60
Joseph Kabi son of Simon	A.D. 60-61
Ananus son of Annas	A.D. 61
Jesus son of Damnaeus	*c.* A.D. 61-63
Jesus son of Gamaliel	*c.* A.D. 63-65
Matthias son of Theophilus son of Annas	*c.* A.D. 65-68
Appointed by the People during the War:	
Phinehas son of Samuel	A.D. 68-70

HEROD THE GREAT AND HIS DESCENDANTS[1]

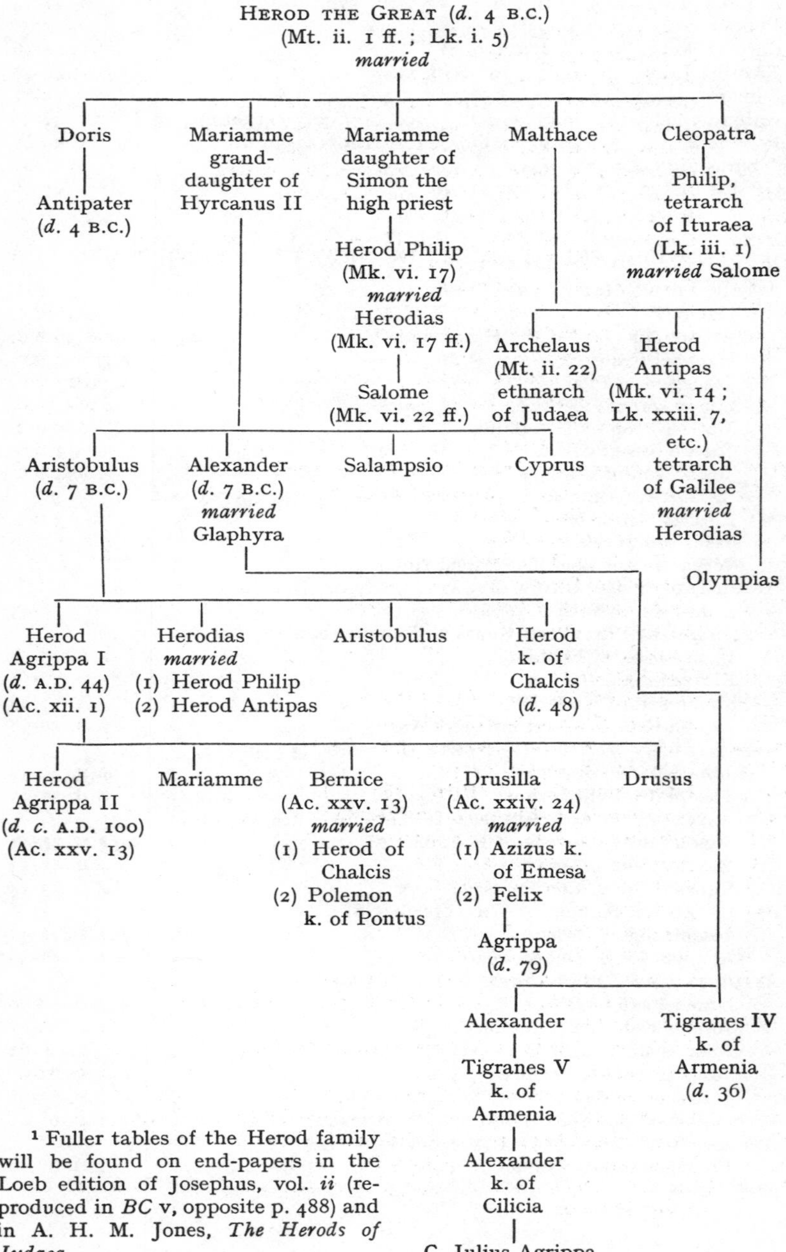

[1] Fuller tables of the Herod family will be found on end-papers in the Loeb edition of Josephus, vol. *ii* (reproduced in *BC* v, opposite p. 488) and in A. H. M. Jones, *The Herods of Judaea.*

LIST OF ABBREVIATIONS

AJT — *American Journal of Theology.*
Ant. — *Antiquities* (of Josephus).
AV — Authorized Version.
BC — *Beginnings of Christianity* (ed. Jackson and Lake).
BGU — *Griechische Urkunden* from Berlin *Ägyptische Urkunden.*
BJ — *Bellum Judaicum* (*Jewish War,* by Josephus).
BJRL — *Bulletin of the John Rylands Library,* Manchester.
BRD — *Bearing of Recent Discovery,* etc. (Ramsay).
BS — *Bible Studies* (Deissmann).
CDA — *Composition and Date of Acts* (Torrey).
CE — *The Christian Ecclesia* (Hort).
CGT — *Cambridge Greek Testament.*
CIG — *Corpus Inscriptionum Graecarum.*
CIL — *Corpus Inscriptionum Latinarum.*
CR — *Classical Review.*
CRE — *Church in the Roman Empire* (Ramsay).
DAC — *Dictionary of the Apostolic Church* (Hastings).
DB — *Dictionary of the Bible.*
DCG — *Dictionary of Christ and the Gospels* (Hastings).
DPC — *Documents of the Primitive Church* (Torrey).
EEP — *Earliest Epistles of St. Paul* (Lake).
EGT — *Expositor's Greek Testament.*
Enc. Bib. — *Encyclopaedia Biblica.*
Ep. Barn. — Epistle of Barnabas.
EQ — *Evangelical Quarterly.*
ERE — *Encyclopaedia of Religion and Ethics.*
ET — *Expository Times.*
EV — English Version(s).
Exp. — *The Expositor.*
HDB — Hastings' *Dictionary of the Bible.*
HE — *Historia Ecclesiastica* (Eusebius).
Hobart — Hobart's *Medical Language of St. Luke.*
HTR — *Harvard Theological Review.*
IG — *Inscriptiones Graecae* (Berlin, 1873-).
ILS — *Inscriptiones Latinae Selectae* (Dessau).
INT — *Introduction to the New Testament.*
JBL — *Journal of Biblical Literature.*
JHS — *Journal of Hellenic Studies.*
Jos. — Josephus.
JRS — *Journal of Roman Studies.*
JTS — *Journal of Theological Studies.*
LAE — *Light from the Ancient East* (Deissmann).
LC — Lake and Cadbury's Commentary (= *BC* iv.).
LP — *Luke the Physician* (Harnack).
LS[9] — Liddell and Scott's *Greek-English Lexicon* (9th ed.).
LXX — Septuagint.
MG — Moulton and Geden's *Concordance to the Greek Testament.*
MH — Moulton and Howard's *Grammar of New Testament Greek.*
MM — Moulton and Milligan's *Vocabulary of the Greek Testament.*
MT — Massoretic Text of the Hebrew Old Testament.
Nachr. Gött. Ges. — *Nachrichten der königlichen Gesellschaft der Wissenschaften zu Göttingen.*

NT New Testament.
OGIS *Orientis Graeci Inscriptiones Selectae* (W. Dittenberger).
OT Old Testament.
P Papyrus, Papyri ; *P. Flor.:* Florentine ; *P. Oxy.:* Oxyrhynchus.
PG *Philology of the Gospels* (Blass).
PL *Patrologia Latina* (Migne).
Proleg. Moulton's *Prolegomena* (= MH i.).
Ps. Sol. Psalms of Solomon.
RV Revised Version.
Schürer Schürer's *History of the Jewish People* (Eng. tr.).
Sib. Or. Sibylline Oracles.
Sir. The Wisdom of Jesus ben Sira (Ecclesiasticus).
SNT *Die Schriften des Neuen Testaments* (ed. J. Weiss).
SPEM *St. Paul's Ephesian Ministry* (Duncan).
SPT *St. Paul the Traveller*, etc. (Ramsay).
Syll. *Sylloge Inscriptionum Graecarum* (W. Dittenberger), ed. 3.
TB Babylonian Talmud.
TJ Jerusalem (Palestinian) Talmud.
TR ' Textus Receptus '.
TU *Texte und Untersuchungen.*
WH Westcott and Hort.
ZNTW *Zeitschrift für neutestamentliche Wissenschaft.*

For abbreviations used in notes on the text, see pp. 47 ff.

SYNOPSIS OF ACTS

I. THE BIRTH OF THE CHURCH, i. 1-v. 42.

1. Introduction.
   (*a*) Prologue, i. 1-5.
   (*b*) The Ascension, i. 6-12.
   (*c*) In the Upper Room, i. 13-14.
   (*d*) Matthias succeeds Judas Iscariot, i. 15-26.

2. The Day of Pentecost.
   (*a*) The Descent of the Spirit, ii. 1-4.
   (*b*) The Crowd's Amazement, ii. 5-13.
   (*c*) Peter's Sermon, ii. 14-36.
   (*d*) Call to Repentance, ii. 37-40.
   (*e*) The First Christian Church, ii. 41-47.

3. A Miracle and its Consequences.
   (*a*) Healing of the Lame Man, iii. 1-10.
   (*b*) Peter's Address in Solomon's Colonnade, iii. 11-26.
   (*c*) Arrest of Peter and John ; Increase of the Church, iv. 1-4.
   (*d*) Peter and John before the Sanhedrin, iv. 5-12.
   (*e*) The Sanhedrin dismiss Peter and John, iv. 13-22.
   (*f*) Peter and John return ; the Disciples pray, iv. 23-31.

4. All Things in Common.
   (*a*) Progress of the Church ; Community of Goods, iv. 32-35
   (*b*) Generosity of Barnabas, iv. 36-37.
   (*c*) Deceit and Death of Ananias, v. 1-6.
   (*d*) Death of Sapphira, v. 7-11.

5. The Apostles before the Sanhedrin again.

(*a*) Signs and Wonders, v. 12-16.
(*b*) Second Imprisonment and Examination of the Apostles, v. 17-32.
(*c*) Gamaliel's Counsel ; the Apostles again dismissed, v. 33-42.

II. PERSECUTION LEADS TO EXPANSION, vi. 1-ix. 31.

1. Stephen.

(*a*) The Appointing of the Seven, vi. 1-6.
(*b*) Fresh Progress, vi. 7.
(*c*) Stephen's Activity arouses Opposition, vi. 8-vii. 1.
(*d*) Stephen's Defence, vii. 2-53.
(*e*) Martyrdom of Stephen, vii. 54-viii. 1*a*.

2. Philip.

(*a*) Persecution and Dispersion, viii. 1*b*-3.
(*b*) Philip in Samaria, viii. 4-8.
(*c*) Simon Magus believes and is baptized, viii. 9-13.
(*d*) Peter and John visit Samaria, viii. 14-24.
(*e*) The Preachers return to Jerusalem, viii. 25.
(*f*) Philip and the Ethiopian, viii. 26-40.

3. Conversion of Saul of Tarsus.

(*a*) Saul's Expedition to Damascus, ix. 1-2.
(*b*) The Voice from Heaven, ix. 3-9.
(*c*) Ananias sent to Saul, ix. 10-19*a*.
(*d*) Saul preaches in Damascus, ix. 19*b*-22.
(*e*) Saul escapes from Damascus, ix. 23-25.
(*f*) Saul in Jerusalem ; he is sent to Tarsus, ix. 26-30.
(*g*) The Church enjoys Peace and Prosperity, ix. 31.

III. ACTS OF PETER : THE GENTILES BROUGHT IN, ix. 32-xii. 24.

1. Peter in Western Palestine.

(*a*) Peter at Lydda ; the Healing of Aeneas, ix. 32-35.
(*b*) Peter at Joppa ; the Raising of Tabitha, ix. 36-43.

2. The Story of Cornelius.

(*a*) Cornelius the Centurion's Vision, x. 1-8.
(*b*) Peter's Vision, x. 9-16.
(*c*) The Messengers of Cornelius arrive at Joppa, x. 17-23*a*.
(*d*) Peter enters the House of Cornelius, x. 23*b*-33.
(*e*) The Good News first preached to Gentiles, x. 34-43.
(*f*) The Gentiles, receiving the Holy Spirit, are baptized, x. 44-48.

3. Peter Defends his Action.

(*a*) Peter accused of Intercourse with Gentiles, xi. 1-3.
(*b*) Peter's Defence, xi. 4-17.
(*c*) Peter's Defence accepted—for the Present at least, xi. 18.

4. Antioch.

(*a*) The First Gentile Church, xi. 19-26.
(*b*) Famine-Relief Expedition to Judaea, xi. 27-30.

5. Herod Agrippa I and the Church.

(*a*) Martyrdom of James ; Imprisonment and Escape of Peter, xii. 1-19.
(*b*) Death of Herod Agrippa I, xii. 20-23.
(*c*) The Gospel continues to progress, xii. 24.

IV. PAUL'S FIRST MISSIONARY JOURNEY AND THE APOSTOLIC DECREE, xii. 25-xvi. 5.

1. Barnabas and Saul.
   - (*a*) Return of the Famine-Relief Delegation, xii. 25.
   - (*b*) Barnabas and Saul sent from Antioch to evangelize, xiii. 1-3.

2. Cyprus.
   - (*a*) The Missionaries arrive in Cyprus, xiii. 4-5.
   - (*b*) The Incident at Paphos, xiii. 6-12.

3. Pisidian Antioch.
   - (*a*) Arrival at Pisidian Antioch, xiii. 13-15.
   - (*b*) Paul's Sermon in Pisidian Antioch, xiii. 16-41.
   - (*c*) Paul's Sermon arouses Interest, xiii. 42-43.
   - (*d*) Gentile Interest arouses Jewish Envy, xiii. 44-52.

4. Iconium, Lystra, Derbe.
   - (*a*) Adventures in Iconium, xiv. 1-7.
   - (*b*) The Miracle at Lystra, xiv. 8-18.
   - (*c*) Persecution at Lystra; they visit Derbe and return to Syrian Antioch, xiv. 19-28.

5. The Council at Jerusalem.
   - (*a*) Judaizers visit Antioch, xv. 1-2.
   - (*b*) Paul and Barnabas go up to Jerusalem, xv. 3-5.
   - (*c*) The Council meets; Peter's Speech, xv. 6-11.
   - (*d*) The Missionaries address the Council, xv. 12.
   - (*e*) The Speech of James, xv. 13-21.
   - (*f*) The Letter to the Gentile Churches, xv. 22-29.

6. The Letter received in Antioch and the Anatolian Churches.
   - (*a*) The Church at Antioch receives the Letter, xv. 30-35.
   - (*b*) Paul's second Missionary Journey commences, xv. 36-41.
   - (*c*) In the Province of Galatia; Timothy joins them, xvi. 1-4.
   - (*d*) The Churches grow in Faith and Numbers, xvi. 5.

V. EVANGELIZATION ON THE SHORES OF THE AEGEAN, xvi. 6-xix. 20.

1. Philippi.
   - (*a*) The Missionaries are called to Macedonia, xvi. 6-10.
   - (*b*) Troas to Philippi, xvi. 11-12*a*.
   - (*c*) The Conversion of Lydia, xvi. 12*b*-15.
   - (*d*) The Pythoness, xvi. 16-18.
   - (*e*) Imprisonment of Paul and Silas, xvi. 19-24.
   - (*f*) Deliverance from Prison; Conversion of the Jailer, xvi. 25-34.
   - (*g*) Paul and Silas asked to leave Philippi, xvi. 35-40.

2. Thessalonica to Athens.
   - (*a*) Thessalonica, xvii. 1-4.
   - (*b*) Trouble in Thessalonica, xvii. 5-9.
   - (*c*) Beroea, xvii. 10-15.
   - (*d*) Paul waits for his Companions in Athens, xvii. 16-21.
   - (*e*) Paul before the Areopagus, xvii. 22-34.

3. Corinth.
   - (*a*) Paul arrives at Corinth, xviii. 1-4.
   - (*b*) He spends Eighteen Months in Corinth, xviii. 5-11.
   - (*c*) Paul before Gallio, xviii. 12-17.

4. Ephesus.

(a) Hasty Visit to Palestine, xviii. 18-23.
(b) Apollos, xviii. 24-28.
(c) Paul and the Twelve Disciples at Ephesus, xix. 1-7.
(d) Paul leaves the Synagogue for the School of Tyrannus, xix. 8-10.
(e) Signs and Wonders at Ephesus, xix. 11-19.
(f) Progress reported, xix. 20.

VI. PAUL PLANS TO VISIT ROME VIA JERUSALEM AND ACHIEVES HIS AIM IN AN UNEXPECTED WAY, xix. 21-xxviii. 31.

1. He Leaves Ephesus for Macedonia and Greece.

(a) Paul makes Plans for the Future, xix. 21-22.
(b) The Riot at Ephesus, xix. 23-41.
(c) Paul's Visit to Macedonia and Greece, xx. 1-6.

2. The Journey to Jerusalem.

(a) Paul at Troas ; Fall and Recovery of Eutychus, xx. 7-12.
(b) From Troas to Miletus, xx. 13-16.
(c) Paul's Address to the Elders of Ephesus, xx. 17-38.
(d) Arrival at Tyre, xxi. 1-6.
(e) Arrival at Caesarea, xxi. 7-9.
(f) Agabus reappears, xxi. 10-14.
(g) Arrival at Jerusalem, xxi. 15-16.

3. Paul at Jerusalem.

(a) Meeting with James and the Elders, xxi. 17-26.
(b) Riot in the Temple ; Paul rescued by the Romans, xxi. 27-36.
(c) Paul obtains Leave to address the Crowd, xxi. 37-40.
(d) Paul addresses the Crowd ; he relates his Conversion, xxii. 1-16.
(e) Paul relates his Vision in the Temple, xxii. 17-21.
(f) The Tumult renewed ; Paul reveals his Roman Citizenship, xxii, 22-29.
(g) Paul before the Sanhedrin, xxii. 30-xxiii. 10.
(h) The Lord appears to Paul by Night, xxiii. 11.
(i) The Plot against Paul, xxiii. 12-15.
(j) Paul's Nephew reveals the Plot to the Tribune, xxiii. 16-22.
(k) Lysias prepares to send Paul away, xxiii. 23-25.
(l) Letter from Lysias to Felix, xxiii. 26-30.

4. Paul at Caesarea ; He appears before Felix and Festus.

(a) Paul taken to Caesarea, xxiii. 31-35.
(b) Paul accused before Felix, xxiv. 1-9.
(c) Paul's Defence before Felix, xxiv. 10-21.
(d) Felix adjourns the Proceedings, xxiv. 22-23.
(e) Paul's Interviews with Felix, xxiv. 24-26.
(f) Festus succeeds Felix ; Paul left in Custody, xxiv. 27.
(g) Festus visits Jerusalem, xxv. 1-5.
(h) Paul appeals to Caesar, xxv. 6-12.

5. Paul and Agrippa.

(a) Agrippa II and Bernice visit Festus, xxv. 13-22.
(b) Paul brought before Agrippa, xxv. 23-27.
(c) Paul's ' Apologia Pro Vita Sua ', xxvi. 1-23.
(d) Interchange between Festus, Paul and Agrippa, xxvi. 24-29
(e) Agreement on Paul's Innocence, xxvi. 30-32.

6. The Voyage and Shipwreck of Paul.

(*a*) The Voyage to Myra, xxvii. 1-5.
(*b*) They trans-ship at Myra and sail to Crete, xxvii. 6-8.
(*c*) Paul's Advice neglected, xxvii. 9-12.
(*d*) They are caught by the Wind Euraquilo, xxvii. 13-20.
(*e*) Paul's Encouragement, xxvii. 21-26.
(*f*) They approach Land, xxvii. 27-29.
(*g*) The Sailors' Attempt to escape frustrated, xxvii. 30-32.
(*h*) Paul again encourages the Ship's Company, xxvii. 33-38.
(*i*) The Shipwreck, xxvii. 39-41.
(*j*) They all get safe to Land, xxvii. 42-44.

7. In Malta.

(*a*) Welcome at Malta ; Paul and the Viper, xxviii. 1-6.
(*b*) Deeds of Healing in Malta, xxviii. 7-10.

8. Rome !

(*a*) The Last Lap : ' And so we came to Rome ', xxviii. 11-15.
(*b*) Paul handed over to be kept under Guard, xxviii. 16.
(*c*) Paul's first Interview with the Roman Jews, xxviii. 17-22.
(*d*) Paul's second Interview with the Roman Jews, xxviii. 23-29.
(*e*) The Gospel advances unhindered in Rome, xxviii. 30-31.

TEXT AND COMMENTARY

I. THE BIRTH OF THE CHURCH, i. 1-v. 42

1. INTRODUCTION i. 1–26

(a) Prologue, i. 1-5

Τὸν μὲν πρῶτον λόγον ἐποιησάμην περὶ πάντων, ὦ Θεόφιλε, ὧν 1
ἤρξατο Ἰησοῦς ποιεῖν τε καὶ διδάσκειν ἄχρι ἧς ἡμέρας ἐντειλάμενος 2
τοῖς ἀποστόλοις διὰ πνεύματος ἁγίου οὓς ἐξελέξατο ἀνελήμφθη· οἷς 3
καὶ παρέστησεν ἑαυτὸν ζῶντα μετὰ τὸ παθεῖν αὐτὸν ἐν πολλοῖς
τεκμηρίοις, δι' ἡμερῶν τεσσεράκοντα ὀπτανόμενος αὐτοῖς καὶ λέγων
τὰ περὶ τῆς βασιλείας τοῦ θεοῦ. καὶ συναλιζόμενος παρήγγειλεν 4
αὐτοῖς ἀπὸ Ἱεροσολύμων μὴ χωρίζεσθαι, ἀλλὰ περιμένειν τὴν ἐπαγγελίαν τοῦ πατρὸς ἣν ἠκούσατέ μου· ὅτι Ἰωάνης μὲν ἐβάπτισεν ὕδατι, 5
ὑμεῖς δὲ ἐν πνεύματι βαπτισθήσεσθε ἁγίῳ οὐ μετὰ πολλὰς ταύτας
ἡμέρας.

i. 1

These verses provide a connection between the two parts of Luke's history, and partly summarize the closing scenes of the Gospel. The Prologue to the Gospel (Lk. i. 1-4) is really the Prologue to the twofold work Lk.-Ac.

Τὸν μὲν πρῶτον λόγον ἐποιησάμην] i.e., the Third Gospel. *μέν* is anacoluthic ; the following *δέ* is not expressed. We should not infer from the use of *πρῶτος* rather than *πρότερος* that Luke intended his Gospel to be the first of three treatises. Just as we loosely use 'first' for 'former' even when only two things are in question, so in Hellenistic Gk. *πρότερος* was largely superseded by *πρῶτος*. Cf. *πρῶτός μου ἦν*, Jn. i. 15 ; *ἐμὲ πρῶτον ὑμῶν μεμίσηκεν*, Jn. xv. 18. Luke never uses *πρότερος*, and it is very rare in the papyri. *λόγος* is used for a division of a work which covered more than one papyrus roll. Ac. is thus the second division of the work *Lucas ad Theophilum*. Lk. and Ac. covered one papyrus roll each, and as they are the two longest books in NT (Lk. is longer than Ac.), it is clear that Luke made the fullest possible use of his space.

ὦ Θεόφιλε] Theophilus is addressed as *κράτιστε Θεόφιλε* in Lk. i. 3. The title *κράτιστος* properly belongs to the equestrian rank (Lat. *egregius*), but is also used in a more general sense (Lat. *optimus*). Elsewhere in Ac. it indicates an official position : cf. xxiii. 26 ; xxiv. 3 ; xxvi. 25.

It is unnecessary to suppose, as several writers from Origen onwards have done, that Theophilus ('dear to God') is a symbolical name, either of the individual addressed [1] or of the class of readers in view. It occurs as a proper name from the third century B.C. onwards (see MM); and the custom of dedicating books to distinguished persons was common at this time.

An interesting parallel to the twofold address to Theophilus in Lk. i. 3 and Ac. i. 1 is the twofold address by Josephus to his patron Epaphroditus [2] at the beginning of both parts of his work *Against Apion*. In particular, *κράτιστε ἀνδρῶν Ἐπαφρόδιτε* in *Ap*. i. 1 should be compared with *κράτιστε Θεόφιλε* in Lk. i. 3, and *διὰ μὲν οὖν τοῦ προτέρου βιβλίου, τιμιώτατέ μοι Ἐπαφρόδιτε, κ.τ.λ.* in *Ap*. ii. 1 should be compared with *τὸν μὲν πρῶτον λόγον ἐποιησάμην . . . ὦ Θεόφιλε* in Ac. i. 1. This affords an additional indication, if such were needed, that in Lk. and Ac. we are dealing, not with two works, but with two parts of one work.

ἤρξατο] As the Gospel tells us what Jesus *began* to do and teach, so Ac. tells us what He *continued* to do and teach, by His Spirit in the apostles, after His Ascension. Cf. Heb. ii. 3 (*ἀρχὴν λαβοῦσα λαλεῖσθαι διὰ τοῦ κυρίου*); also Mk. i. 1, where the history from the preaching of John to the Resurrection is called *ἀρχὴ τοῦ εὐαγγελίου Ἰησοῦ Χριστοῦ*. *ἤρξατο* is emphatic here, and should not be regarded merely as a Semitizing auxiliary (see on ii. 4).

ποιεῖν τε καὶ διδάσκειν] All our canonical Gospels comprise narrative and discourse, the Good News *about* Jesus and the Good News proclaimed *by* Jesus.

i. 2

ἄχρι ἧς ἡμέρας] Cf. Mt. xxiv. 38. Attic attraction for *ἄχρι τῆς ἡμέρας ᾗ*. Cf. *ver*. 22.

ἄχρι ἧς ἡμέρας ἐντειλάμενος τοῖς ἀποστόλοις διὰ πνεύματος ἁγίου οὓς ἐξελέξατο ἀνελήμφθη] D has *ἄχρι ἧς ἡμέρας ἀνελήμφθη ἐντειλάμενος τοῖς ἀποστόλοις διὰ πνεύματος ἁγίου οὓς ἐξελέξατο καὶ ἐκέλευσε κηρύσσειν τὸ εὐαγγέλιον*. This text is evidently conflate; the original δ text is probably represented by Augustine, *c. Fel*. i. 4 and *c. ep. Fund*. 9: *in die quo apostolos elegit per spiritum sanctum et praecepit praedicare euangelium*. This would represent *ἐν ᾗ ἡμέρᾳ τοὺς ἀποστόλους ἐξελέξατο διὰ πνεύματος ἁγίου καὶ ἐκέλευσεν κηρύσσειν τὸ εὐαγγέλιον*, which A. C. Clark prints as the original text. The omission of *ἀνελήμφθη* is noteworthy, because the δ text of Lk. xxiv. 51 omits *καὶ ἀνεφέρετο εἰς τὸν οὐρανόν*, a clause which WH bracket as a non-Western interpolation. Perhaps these words were added to Lk. xxiv. 51 and *ἀνελήμφθη* to Ac. i. 2 after the two parts of *Lucas ad Theophilum* were separated and began to circulate

[1] E.g. B. H. Streeter supposes Theophilus may have been T. Flavius Clemens, the cousin of the Emperor Domitian (*The Four Gospels*, pp. 534 ff.).

[2] To whom the *Antiquities* were also dedicated (*Vita*, 76; *Ant*. praef. 2).

independently. The β text here is awkward, chiefly because of the unnatural separation of οὓς ἐξελέξατο from τοῖς ἀποστόλοις, but otherwise it gives good sense: 'until the day on which He was taken up, having given commandment by the Holy Spirit to the Apostles whom He had chosen'. For the commandment cf. Lk. xxiv. 49. With ἀνελήμφθη cf. ἀνάλημψις, Lk. ix. 51.

i. 3

παρέστησεν ἑαυτὸν ζῶντα] From the Gospels and 1 Cor. xv. 5-7 we can collect nine or ten such appearances, some in Judaea and some in Galilee.

παθεῖν] Used thus absolutely of our Lord's Passion in xvii. 3; xxvi. 23.

τεκμηρίοις] Aristotle defines τεκμήριον as ἀναγκαῖον σημεῖον, 'a compelling sign' (*Rhet.* i. 2. 16).

διὰ τεσσεράκοντα ἡμερῶν] Not continuously (in which case the accusative without a preposition would have been used), but at intervals. This is the only place in NT where the lapse of time between the Resurrection and Ascension is stated.

ὀπτανόμενος] The only NT occurrence of this verb, a new present formation on the model of the aor. pass. ὤφθην in its intransitive sense 'appear'. It is found in LXX (Num. xiv. 14[1]; 3 K. viii. 8; Tob. xii. 19), Poimandres, and the papyri from second century B.C. onwards.

λέγων τὰ περὶ τῆς βασιλείας τοῦ θεοῦ] Developing the teaching He had given them before the Crucifixion. We should understand βασιλεία not in a territorial sense but in the sense of kingship, royal rule, sovereignty. From the earliest times in Israel, *melekh* ('king') was a title of God (cf. Ex. xv. 18). His sovereignty is universal (Ps. ciii. 19), but on earth was specially manifested in the nation of Israel. With the fall of Israel's independence, there arose a new conception of the Kingdom of God as something to be manifested fully at a future date, and it is in the light of this later conception (especially as revealed in Dan. ii. 44; vii. 13 f., etc.) that we are to understand the NT references to the Kingdom. In NT the Kingdom of God is represented as having 'drawn nigh' in the coming of the Christ (Mk. i. 15, etc.). So in Ac. viii. 12; xxviii. 23, 31 we find the Kingdom of God closely associated with 'the story of Jesus' (τὰ περὶ τοῦ Ἰησοῦ). In narrating the events of His life, death, resurrection and exaltation the apostles proclaimed 'the good news of the Kingdom'—the same good news as had been announced earlier by Jesus Himself, but now amplified and illuminated by these great salvation-bringing events. We may reasonably infer that the teaching which our Lord gave about the

[1] As a variant reading to ὀπτάζω.

Kingdom of God during these forty days was intended to make clear to the disciples the bearing of His crucifixion and resurrection on the message of the Kingdom. 'The kingdom of God is conceived as coming in the events of the life, death, and resurrection of Jesus, and to proclaim these facts, in their proper setting, is to preach the Gospel of the Kingdom of God' (C. H. Dodd, *The Apostolic Preaching and its Developments*, pp. 46 f.).

The similar phrase ἡ βασιλεία τῶν οὐρανῶν, peculiar to Mt., reflects the reverential Aramaic use of *shĕmayyā* ('the heavens') as a substitute for *'Ĕlāhā* ('God'); cf. Dan. iv. 26, 'the heavens do rule', with iv. 25, 'the Most High ruleth'. There is no difference in meaning between 'the kingdom of God' and 'the kingdom of heaven'. By the drawing nigh of the Kingdom, the Age to come has invaded the present age, and those who now receive the Kingdom by faith belong spiritually to the coming Age and share its life even while temporally they still belong to this age.

i. 4

συναλιζόμενος] If this is from συναλίζω in its regular sense, the meaning will be 'being gathered together with (them)', but the singular is awkward, and we should expect the perfect tense, not the present. Other suggestions are (1) that it is derived from ἅλς and means lit. 'eating salt with' (so hcl. *mithmallaḥ*), and then more generally 'eating with' (so vg. *conuescens*, pesh. *'ekhal 'amhūn laḥmā*); (2) that it is a spelling variant of συναυλιζόμενος ('dwelling with'), which is the reading of many minn. (inc. 614) and patristic citations. So Augustine, in common with some vet. lat. and vg. codd., translates it by the verb *conuersari* (similarly *conuiuens* d); Ephrem Syrus also understood it thus.

ἀπὸ Ἱεροσολύμων μὴ χωρίζεσθαι] Cf. Lk. xxiv. 49. As elsewhere in NT, we find in Ac. both Ἰερουσαλήμ (the transliteration of the Heb. word) and Ἱεροσόλυμα (the Hellenized neut. plur. form). It is difficult to draw any certain conclusion from the distribution of the two forms, but the former seems normally to suggest a Jewish, the latter a Gentile atmosphere (not, however, in this verse.)[1] The Hellenized form represents an attempt to give the word a Gk. etymology, from ἱερός ('sacred') and Σόλυμοι, the Solymi, a nation of Asia Minor, with whom the fancy of some Gentile historians connected the Jews (cf. Jos. *Ap.* i. 22; Tac. *Hist.* v. 2; Juv. *Sat.* vi. 544). As Ἱεροσόλυμα is a conscious formation from ἱερός, it

[1] See J. V. Bartlet, 'The Twofold use of "Jerusalem" in the Lucan Writings', in *ET* xiii. (1901-2), pp. 157f. According to MG, Ἱεροσόλυμα occurs 7 times in Ac. i-xv (Torrey's I Acts) and 18 times in Ac. xvi-xxviii (Torrey's II Acts); Ἰερουσαλήμ occurs 27 times in i-xv and 12 times in xvi-xxviii.

should have a rough breathing, *pace* WH (cf. Lat. *Hierosolyma*): the smooth breathing is, on the other hand, appropriate for Ἰερουσαλήμ (cf. *ver.* 8), transliterated from Heb. *Yĕrūshālēm* (or, as the Massoretes pointed it, *Yĕrūshālaim*).

τὴν ἐπαγγελίαν] i.e., the Holy Spirit: cf. Lk. xxiv. 49; also Eph. i. 13 (τῷ πνεύματι τῆς ἐπαγγελίας τῷ ἁγίῳ); Jn. xiv. 16 f., 26; xv. 26; xvi. 7-13.

τοῦ πατρός] Subjective genitive; it is the Father who promises; in ii. 33, τὴν . . . ἐπαγγελίαν τοῦ πνεύματος τοῦ ἁγίου, the genitive is objective; it is the Spirit who is promised.

ἣν ἠκούσατέ μου] Reversion from indirect to direct speech. Cf. Lk. v. 14. For the opposite construction, a transition from direct to indirect speech, cf. Ac. xxiii. 23 f.

i. 5

ὅτι Ἰωάνης μὲν ἐβάπτισεν ὕδατι, ὑμεῖς δὲ ἐν πνεύματι βαπτισθήσεσθε ἁγίῳ] Cf. the words of John himself, Mt. iii. 11; Mk. i. 8; Lk. iii. 16; καὶ πυρί is omitted here, as in Mk. i. 8. The words of Christ here are quoted in Ac. xi. 16; cf. also xix. 4.[1]

ἐν πνεύματι] ἐν instrumental, representing Aram. *bĕ*, which in this sense is also represented by the simple dative, as in ὕδατι. Cf. ἐν ὕδατι . . . ἐν πνεύματι, Mt. iii. 11; ὕδατι . . . πνεύματι, Mk. i. 8.

οὐ μετὰ πολλὰς ταύτας ἡμέρας] About ten days, as events proved. The construction is not a native Gk. one; Burney and Torrey explain it as an Aramaism; Blass, with less probability, takes it to be a Latinism.

(b) The Ascension, i. 6-12

Οἱ μὲν οὖν συνελθόντες ἠρώτων αὐτὸν λέγοντες Κύριε, εἰ ἐν τῷ 6
χρόνῳ τούτῳ ἀποκαθιστάνεις τὴν βασιλείαν τῷ Ἰσραήλ; εἶπεν πρὸς 7
αὐτούς Οὐχ ὑμῶν ἐστὶν γνῶναι χρόνους ἢ καιροὺς οὓς ὁ πατὴρ ἔθετο
ἐν τῇ ἰδίᾳ ἐξουσίᾳ, ἀλλὰ λήμψεσθε δύναμιν ἐπελθόντος τοῦ ἁγίου 8
πνεύματος ἐφ' ὑμᾶς, καὶ ἔσεσθέ μου μάρτυρες ἔν τε Ἰερουσαλὴμ καὶ
ἐν πάσῃ τῇ Ἰουδαίᾳ καὶ Σαμαρίᾳ καὶ ἕως ἐσχάτου τῆς γῆς. καὶ 9
ταῦτα εἰπὼν βλεπόντων αὐτῶν ἐπήρθη, καὶ νεφέλη ὑπέλαβεν αὐτὸν
ἀπὸ τῶν ὀφθαλμῶν αὐτῶν. καὶ ὡς ἀτενίζοντες ἦσαν εἰς τὸν οὐρανὸν 10
πορευομένου αὐτοῦ, καὶ ἰδοὺ ἄνδρες δύο παριστήκεισαν αὐτοῖς ἐν
ἐσθήσεσι λευκαῖς, οἳ καὶ εἶπαν Ἄνδρες Γαλιλαῖοι, τί ἑστήκατε 11
βλέποντες εἰς τὸν οὐρανόν; οὗτος ὁ Ἰησοῦς ὁ ἀναλημφθεὶς ἀφ' ὑμῶν εἰς
τὸν οὐρανὸν οὕτως ἐλεύσεται ὃν τρόπον ἐθεάσασθε αὐτὸν πορευόμενον

[1] According to Aug. *Ep.* 265, 3, some Latin codices had *baptizabitis* or *incipietis baptizare;* Ropes thinks it likely 'that the active voice was an attempt of purely Latin origin to find here the commission to baptize which both Luke and Acts lack' (*BC* iii., p. 4).

εἰς τὸν οὐρανόν. Τότε ὑπέστρεψαν εἰς Ἰερουσαλὴμ ἀπὸ ὄρους τοῦ 12
καλουμένου Ἐλαιῶνος, ὅ ἐστιν ἐγγὺς Ἰερουσαλὴμ σαββάτου ἔχον
ὁδόν.

i. 6

With *ver.* 6 the δεύτερος λόγος properly begins. This paragraph describes the disciples' last meeting with their Master on Olivet, where they saw Him ascend to heaven. In the δ text this is Luke's only account of the Ascension. It is possible that it was so originally: see on *ver.* 2.

Οἱ μὲν οὖν] A favourite formula in Ac. for opening a new section of the narrative, connecting it with the preceding section. Cf. i. 18; ii. 41; v. 41; viii. 4, 25; ix. 31; xi. 19; xii. 5; xiii. 4; xv. 3, 30; xvi. 5. Translate μὲν οὖν by 'so, then'.

ἠρώτων αὐτὸν λέγοντες] The participle is pleonastic; this use is a characteristic Semitism.

Κύριε] A common form of address to our Lord from the earliest days of His ministry. As a title of respect or courtesy it may be rendered 'Sir' (cf. x. 4; xvi. 30). As applied to Jesus, however, the word early acquired the much fuller sense in which it is employed in LXX as a divine title, whether as the equivalent of the Ineffable Name Jehovah (Heb. *Yahweh*) or of *'Ādōn, 'Adōnay*. See on ii. 21, 36; x. 36.

εἰ] Introducing a direct question, as in vii. 1; xix. 2; xxi. 37; xxii. 25.

ἀποκαθιστάνεις τὴν βασιλείαν τῷ Ἰσραήλ] This interest in the hope of an earthly and national kingdom (cf. Mk. x. 35 ff.) gave place after Pentecost to the proclamation of the spiritual kingdom of God, into which men might enter through repentance and faith in Christ. See on *ver.* 3; viii. 12; xx. 25; xxviii. 23. For ἀποκαθιστάνεις see on iii. 21, ἀποκατάστασις.

i. 7

οὐχ ὑμῶν ἐστὶν γνῶναι] 'It does not belong to you to know', i.e. 'it is not your concern'. Cf. Mt. xxiv. 36; Mk. xiii. 32; 1 Th. v. 1 ff. The δ text was probably οὐδεὶς δύναται γνῶναι, 'no one can know' (cf. Zahn, *Urausgabe*).

χρόνους ἢ καιροὺς] χρόνους refers to the time that must elapse before the final establishment of the Kingdom; καιρούς to the critical events accompanying its establishment. Cf. 1 Th. v. 1 (with Lightfoot's and G. Milligan's notes *ad loc.*); Tit. i. 2 f.; also Trench *Syn.* lvii.

οὓς ὁ πατὴρ ἔθετο ἐν τῇ ἰδίᾳ ἐξουσίᾳ] 'which the Father has placed in His own jurisdiction', or 'which the Father has fixed by (instrumental ἐν) His own authority'. The latter rendering is perhaps to be preferred in the light of xvii. 26.

i. 8

λήμψεσθε δύναμιν] Cf. Lk. xxiv. 49, *ἕως οὗ ἐνδύσησθε ἐξ ὕψους δύναμιν*. The *δύναμις* is that supernatural power by which miracles (*δυνάμεις*, cf. ii. 22) were wrought and the preaching made effective.

ἔσεσθέ μου μάρτυρες] Cf. Isa. xliii. 10; xliv. 8, and Lk. xxiv. 48 (*ὑμεῖς μάρτυρες τούτων*). The idea of witness is prominent in the preaching throughout Ac., cf. ii. 32; iii. 15; v. 32; x. 39; xiii. 31; xxii. 15, etc.

ἕως ἐσχάτου τῆς γῆς] In Ps. Sol. viii. 16 *ἀπ' ἐσχάτου τῆς γῆς* means 'from Rome'; this sense may be in the writer's mind here, since the book ends with Paul's arrival in Rome, but the expression in a wider sense is common in LXX: cf. xiii. 47, a citation from Isa. xlix. 6. The whole verse, including the promise of the Spirit, the gift of power, and the geographical instructions, forms a summary of the narrative of Ac.; chs. i-vii are placed in Jerusalem, viii-ix in Judaea and Samaria, and x-xxviii take us step by step from Caesarea to Rome.

i. 9

βλεπόντων αὐτῶν] ℵ A C 81 byz; *αὐτῶν βλεπόντων* B; om δ.

i. 10

ἀτενίζοντες ἦσαν] The periphrastic use of *εἰμί* with the ptc. is very common in Lk.-Ac. Of 86 NT examples given in MH ii, pp. 451 f., 28 are from Lk. and 24 from Ac. The construction [1] occurs in classical Gk. (e.g. Thuc. iv. 54; Aristoph. *Acharn.* 484, etc.), so there is no need to explain it as due to the influence of the similar Aram. idiom, though this influence may account for some occurrences, e.g. xxii. 19 f. *'Ατενίζω*, a favourite word of Luke, who is responsible for 12 out of its 14 NT occurrences, 'is used by the medical writers to denote a peculiar fixed look' (Hobart, p. 76).

καὶ ἰδού] Cf. xvi. 1; xxvii. 24; Lk. vii. 12; xxiv. 4. The pleonastic *καί* may indicate the simultaneity of the two events: 'then, behold'. The expression, however, is a Semitism found in LXX, where it represents Heb. *wĕ-hinnēh*, usually introducing an apodosis (cf. Aram. *wĕ-hā*).

παριστήκεισαν] Classical *παρειστήκεσαν*. For the itacism see on iii. 19; ix. 7.

[1] See Gudmund Björck, *ΗΝ ΔΙΔΑΣΚΩΝ*: *Die periphrastischen Konstruktionen im Griechischen* (Uppsala, 1940).

ἐσθήσεσι] Dat. pl. of the rare word *ἔσθησις*, for which MM quote a papyrus of A.D. 159-60. It is also found in Lk. xxiv. 4, except in ℵ B D, which have *ἐσθῆτι*, which is the reading of δ here.

λευκαῖς] For white as the colour of angels' garb, cf. Mt. xxviii. 3 ; Jn. xx. 12, etc. Lk. xxiv. 4 has *ἐν ἐσθῆτι ἀστραπτούσῃ*.

i. 11

οἳ καὶ] *καί* emphasizes the relative.

οὕτως . . . ὃν τρόπον] He was taken up in a cloud (*ver.* 9) and in glory (1 Tim. iii. 16) ; the Son of man is pictured as coming in the clouds (Dan. vii. 13 ; Mk. xiii. 26 ; xiv. 62 ; Rev. i. 7, etc.) and in great glory (Mk. xiii. 26 ; Mt. xxv. 31, etc.).

i. 12

ἀπὸ ὄρους τοῦ καλουμένου Ἐλαιῶνος] The common noun *ἐλαιών*, ' oliveyard ' (Lat. *oliuetum*, whence ' Olivet ') occurs at least 30 times in papyri between the first and third centuries A.D. Cf. Jos. *Ant.* vii. 9. 2, *διὰ τοῦ Ἐλαιῶνος ὄρους*. The nominative is possibly to be read in Lk. xix. 29 ; xxi. 37 (and in Mk. xi. 1 if *τῶν* be omitted), rather than the gen. pl. of *ἐλαία*, as WH print it (*ἐλαιῶν*). It is otherwise referred to as *τὸ ὄρος τῶν ἐλαιῶν* ' the hill of the olives ', e.g., Lk. xix. 37 ; xxii. 39. The suffix *-ών* denotes a place where persons or things are to be found : so *ἀμπελών* (' vineyard '), the place of *ἄμπελοι* (' vines '), *νυμφών* (' bride-chamber '), the place of the *νύμφιος* (' bridegroom ') and *νύμφη* (' bride '). Olivet lay to the east of Jerusalem.

σαββάτου ἔχον ὁδόν] lit. ' having a sabbath day's journey ', i.e. between itself and the city. A sabbath day's journey was 2000 cubits or 6 furlongs (*στάδια*). This calculation was based on Ex. xvi. 29 interpreted by Num. xxxv. 5. The Heb. term is *tĕḥūm ha-shabbāth* (' the limit of the sabbath ') ; the relevant laws are dealt with in the Mishna tractates *Shabbāth* and *'Erūbīn*. According to Jos. *BJ* v. 2. 3 the distance from Jerusalem to Olivet is 6 stadia ; according to *Ant.* xx. 8. 6 it is 5 stadia. Bethany (Lk. xxiv. 50) lies on the eastern slopes of Olivet, about 15 stadia from the city (Jn. xi. 18).

(c) In the Upper Room, i. 13-14

Καὶ ὅτε εἰσῆλθον, εἰς τὸ ὑπερῷον ἀνέβησαν οὗ ἦσαν καταμένοντες, 13
ὅ τε Πέτρος καὶ Ἰωάνης καὶ Ἰάκωβος καὶ Ἀνδρέας, Φίλιππος καὶ
Θωμᾶς, Βαρθολομαῖος καὶ Μαθθαῖος, Ἰάκωβος Ἁλφαίου καὶ Σίμων
ὁ ζηλωτὴς καὶ Ἰούδας Ἰακώβου. οὗτοι πάντες ἦσαν προσκαρτεροῦντες 14
ὁμοθυμαδὸν τῇ προσευχῇ σὺν γυναιξὶν καὶ Μαριὰμ τῇ μητρὶ τοῦ
Ἰησοῦ καὶ σὺν τοῖς ἀδελφοῖς αὐτοῦ.

i. 13.

ὑπερῷον] Zahn and others suggest, with some show of probability, that this was the room where the Last Supper was held. The upper room of large dwelling-houses was generally used as a dining-room, or sublet to poorer people. The house where the Supper was held has also been supposed to be the house of Mary the mother of Mark (cf. xii. 12).

ἦσαν καταμένοντες] For the construction see on *ver.* 10.

ὅ τε Πέτρος κ.τ.λ.] Cf. the lists in Mt. x. 2 ff.; Mk. iii. 16 ff.; Lk. vi. 14 ff. The first nine names occur in all four lists, in somewhat varying order (but Peter, Philip, and James the son of Alphaeus are always first, fifth and ninth respectively). Simon Zelotes, who comes tenth in Lk. and Ac., is the same as Simon the Cananaean, who comes eleventh in Mt. and Mk. It seems, then, that we should identify *Ἰουδας Ἰακώβου* of Lk. and Ac. ('Judas not Iscariot' of Jn. xiv. 22) with Thaddaeus of Mt. and Mk.

Ἰάκωβος Ἀλφαίου] *Ἀλφαῖος* is Aram. *Ḥalphai*. There is no good ground for identifying this name with the *Κλωπᾶς* of Jn. xix. 25,[1] or for supposing that this James was in any way related to Jesus (see on *ver.* 14).

Σίμων ὁ ζηλωτής] The Zealots were a fanatical party, who championed the cause of Jewish political independence, which they thought should be won by force. G. F. Moore suggested that their name was associated with the statement about Phinehas in Num. xxv. 13, *ἐζήλωσεν τῷ θεῷ αὐτοῦ* (cf. *BC* i, p. 423 *n.*). See also on xxi. 20. They are commonly identified with the 'fourth philosophic party' which Josephus (*Ant.* xviii. 1. 1, 6) says was founded by Judas, who revolted against the Romans in A.D. 6 (see on v. 37). They preserved the spirit of his revolt, and nursed the flames of rebellion which burst out in A.D. 66. (But see *BC* i., pp. 421 ff.) The Aram. equivalent is *qan'anā* or *qannāyā*, which appears in the Hellenized form *Καναναῖος* in Mt. x. 4; Mk. iii. 19. Cf. Jos. *BJ* iv. 3. 9; 5. 1; 6. 3; vii. 8. 1.

Ἰούδας Ἰακώβου] 'Judas the son of James', the 'Judas not Iscariot' of Jn. xiv. 22 (where syr. cur. has 'Judas Thomas', i.e. 'Judas the Twin'). We cannot identify his father with any other James in NT. Thaddaeus, according to Dalman (*Jesus-Jeshua*, p. 5), is Gk. in origin, representing an Aramaized form *Thaddai* which goes back through *Θευδᾶς* (cf. v. 36) to *Θεόδοτος* or a similar Gk. name. Others regard it as derived from Aram. *taddā*, 'breast', and this seems more likely. But there is a further possibility that in Mt. x. 3 and Mk. iii. 18 Thaddaeus may represent a corruption of *Yaddai*, a hypocoristic form of Judas.

[1] According to Hegesippus (*ap.* Euseb. *HE* iii. 11), Clopas was the brother of Joseph, our Lord's foster-father.

i. 14

ὁμοθυμαδὸν] A favourite adverb of Luke, who uses it 10 times (all in Ac.). The one other NT occurrence is in Rom. xv. 6.

τῇ προσευχῇ] The article probably indicates the appointed service of prayer: cf. ii. 42; vi. 4.

σὺν γυναιξὶν] Including no doubt those who accompanied Jesus from Galilee (Lk. viii. 2) and those who were present at the Cross and at the grave (Mt. xxvii. 55 f.; Mk. xv. 40; xvi. 1; Lk. xxiv. 10; Jn. xix. 25). δ has *σὺν ταῖς γυναιξὶν καὶ τέκνοις*, 'with their wives and children'.

καὶ] 'including', 'and in particular'.

Μαριὰμ τῇ μητρὶ τοῦ Ἰησοῦ] This is the last recorded appearance of the Mother of our Lord. It is significant that she is found in prayer with His disciples. *Μαριάμ* is the OT name Miriam; it also appears in the Hellenized forms *Μαρία* (cf. xii. 12) and (in Josephus) *Μαριάμη*, *Μαριάμμη*, or *Μαριάμνη*.

τοῖς ἀδελφοῖς αὐτοῦ] Cf. 1 Cor. ix. 5. What actual relation the brethren of the Lord bore to Him has for long been a vexed question, but the *onus probandi* lies on those who wish to understand *ἀδελφοί* in another than its usual sense. In Mt. xiii. 55; Mk. vi. 3 these brethren are named as James, Joses (or Joseph), Simon, and Judas. They did not believe in the Lord before His death (Jn. vii. 5), but were convinced by His resurrection; James had a special post-resurrection interview with Him (1 Cor. xv. 7). For James cf. xii. 17; xv. 13; xxi. 18. Judas was presumably the writer of the Epistle of Jude (cf. Jude 1).

In the fourth century Epiphanius argued that these brethren were sons of Joseph by a (hypothetical) former wife. This view had been held by many before his time, but others, such as Tertullian, had insisted on taking the word in its natural sense of blood-relationship, and understanding the brethren to be children of Joseph and Mary. A Roman Christian, Helvidius, now came forward as a champion of the latter interpretation, in order to attack the prevalent view that virginity was superior to matrimony, and Jerome wrote a treatise in reply (*adu. Heluidium de perpetua uirginitate b. Mariae*), in which he propounded a new view, that the brethren were the Lord's cousins, the sons of Alphaeus by 'Mary of Clopas' whom he (probably wrongly) inferred from Jn. xix. 25 to be the Virgin's sister. Of the sons of this other Mary we know two by name, 'James the little' and Joses (Mk. xv. 40). But James the little, far from being James the Lord's brother, was possibly called 'the little' in contrast to the latter's prominence.[1]

[1] See J. B. Lightfoot, 'The Brethren of the Lord' in his *Galatians*, pp. 252 ff.; J. B. Mayor, *The Epistle of St. James*, pp. v. ff.; Th. Zahn, 'Brüder und Vettern Jesu' in *Forschungen zur Geschichte des NT Kanons*, vi. (1900), pp. 225 ff.; J. Chapman in *JTS* vii. (1906), pp. 424 ff.

(d) Matthias succeeds Judas Iscariot, i. 15-26

Καὶ ἐν ταῖς ἡμέραις ταύταις ἀναστὰς Πέτρος ἐν μέσῳ τῶν ἀδελφῶν 15
εἶπεν (ἦν τε ὄχλος ὀνομάτων ἐπὶ τὸ αὐτὸ ὡς ἑκατὸν εἴκοσι) Ἄνδρες 16
ἀδελφοί, ἔδει πληρωθῆναι τὴν γραφὴν ἣν προεῖπε τὸ πνεῦμα τὸ ἅγιον
διὰ στόματος Δαυεὶδ περὶ Ἰούδα τοῦ γενομένου ὁδηγοῦ τοῖς συλλαβοῦσιν
Ἰησοῦν, ὅτι κατηριθμημένος ἦν ἐν ἡμῖν καὶ ἔλαχεν τὸν κλῆρον τῆς 17
διακονίας ταύτης.—Οὗτος μὲν οὖν ἐκτήσατο χωρίον ἐκ μισθοῦ τῆς 18
ἀδικίας, καὶ πρηνὴς γενόμενος ἐλάκησεν μέσος, καὶ ἐξεχύθη πάντα
τὰ σπλάγχνα αὐτοῦ. καὶ γνωστὸν ἐγένετο πᾶσι τοῖς κατοικοῦσιν 19
Ἰερουσαλήμ, ὥστε κληθῆναι τὸ χωρίον ἐκεῖνο τῇ διαλέκτῳ αὐτῶν
Ἀκελδαμάχ, τοῦτ' ἔστιν Χωρίον Αἵματος.—Γέγραπται γὰρ ἐν Βίβλῳ 20
Ψαλμῶν

> *Γενηθήτω ἡ ἔπαυλις αὐτοῦ ἔρημος*
> *καὶ μὴ ἔστω ὁ κατοικῶν ἐν αὐτῇ,*

καὶ

> *Τὴν ἐπισκοπὴν αὐτοῦ λαβέτω ἕτερος.*

δεῖ οὖν τῶν συνελθόντων ἡμῖν ἀνδρῶν ἐν παντὶ χρόνῳ ᾧ εἰσῆλθεν καὶ 21
ἐξῆλθεν ἐφ' ἡμᾶς ὁ κύριος Ἰησοῦς, ἀρξάμενος ἀπὸ τοῦ βαπτίσματος 22
Ἰωάνου ἕως τῆς ἡμέρας ἧς ἀνελήμφθη ἀφ' ἡμῶν, μάρτυρα τῆς ἀνα-
στάσεως αὐτοῦ σὺν ἡμῖν γενέσθαι ἕνα τούτων. καὶ ἔστησαν δύο, Ἰωσὴφ 23
τὸν καλούμενον Βαρσαββᾶν, ὃς ἐπεκλήθη Ἰοῦστος, καὶ Μαθθίαν.
καὶ προσευξάμενοι εἶπαν Σὺ κύριε καρδιογνῶστα πάντων, ἀνάδειξον 24
ὃν ἐξελέξω, ἐκ τούτων τῶν δύο ἕνα, λαβεῖν τὸν τόπον τῆς διακονίας 25
ταύτης καὶ ἀποστολῆς, ἀφ' ἧς παρέβη Ἰούδας πορευθῆναι εἰς τὸν
τόπον τὸν ἴδιον. καὶ ἔδωκαν κλήρους αὐτοῖς, καὶ ἔπεσεν ὁ κλῆρος 26
ἐπὶ Μαθθίαν, καὶ συνκατεψηφίσθη μετὰ τῶν ἕνδεκα ἀποστόλων.

i. 15

Καὶ ἐν ταῖς ἡμέραις ταύταις] This or a similar phrase marks the beginning of a new division of the story in the first half of Ac. (cf. vi. 1; xi. 27). It indicates a more definite break than *μὲν οὖν* does (see on *ver.* 6).

τῶν ἀδελφῶν] There are both Jewish and Gentile parallels to this use of *ἀδελφοί* to denote members of the same religious community—Jewish in OT, and cf. ii. 29; vii. 2; xiii. 15; xxii. 1; xxviii. 17; and Gentile in papyri from the second century B.C. onward. δ has *μαθητῶν* here, probably to avoid confusion with the *ἀδελφοί* of *ver.* 14.

ὀνομάτων] 'persons', as in Rev. iii. 4; xi. 13; Num. i. 18, 20; xxvi. 53, 55.

ἐπὶ τὸ αὐτὸ] 'altogether'; the phrase seems to have acquired a quasi-technical sense not unlike *ἐν ἐκκλησίᾳ* ('in church fellowship') in NT (cf. ii. 1, 47; 1 Cor. xi. 18, 20; xiv. 23) and the Apostolic Fathers. Cf. MH ii., p. 473.

ὡς] Luke habitually modifies numbers by *ὡς* or *ὡσεί*. Cf. ii. 41; iv. 4; v. 7, 36; x. 3; xiii. 18, 20; xix. 7, 34; Lk. iii. 23, etc.

ἑκατὸν εἴκοσι] There were by this time over 500 believers (1 Cor. xv. 6), of whom the majority probably remained in Galilee. It is unnecessary to see any significance in 120 being 10 times the full number of apostles, or the sum of all whole numbers from 1 to 15 inclusive (see on xxvii. 37).

i. 16

Ἄνδρες ἀδελφοί] This use of *ἄνδρες* (cf. *ἄνδρες Γαλιλαῖοι, ver.* 11) is a classical Gk. idiom, and represents nothing in the Aramaic spoken by Peter (cf. Dalman, *Jesus-Jeshua*, p. 22). The word is otiose, and does not necessarily exclude women. Translate, 'Brethren'. The expression seems to have belonged to synagogue phraseology (cf. xiii. 15). Chase (*Credibility*, p. 123) refers to 4 Macc. viii. 19 as the only example of *ἄνδρες ἀδελφοί* he could find outside Ac., where it is frequent.

ἔδει πληρωθῆναι τὴν γραφήν] 'The Scripture had to be fulfilled', the implication being that it was fulfilled in the fate of Judas. δ has δεῖ, as if it still had to be fulfilled (by the election of Matthias). That certain things had to happen because the Scriptures foretelling them had to be fulfilled is taught in all four Gospels, especially in connection with the Passion of Christ. See, e.g., Mk. xiv. 49; Lk. xxiv. 26.

ἣν προεῖπε τὸ πνεῦμα τὸ ἅγιον διὰ στόματος Δαυεὶδ] Cf. iv. 25; Mk. xii. 36, etc., for the work of the Holy Spirit in the inspiration of OT. The Psalmist is His mouthpiece. We are not surprised therefore to find the words of the Psalms and other OT passages applied to circumstances not envisaged by the writers.

περὶ Ἰούδα κ.τ.λ.] It was his apostasy, not his death, that necessitated the filling of the vacancy; there is no suggestion of filling the vacancy left by the martyrdom of James the son of Zebedee (xii. 2).

i. 17

ἔλαχεν τὸν κλῆρον] Both *λαχεῖν* and *κλῆρος* originally imply apportioning and receiving by lot, but this sense has disappeared; tr. 'he received his portion'.

i. 18

WH mark off this verse and the next by dashes as a parenthesis, rightly. It is not part of Peter's speech, but an explanatory insertion by Luke. The impression given in the parenthesis is of events which took place several years previously, not a bare seven weeks before. If the story was known to all the dwellers in

Jerusalem, there was no need for Peter to rehearse it to his audience, but we can understand why Luke should insert it for the benefit of Theophilus. The expression τῇ διαλέκτῳ αὐτῶν suits Luke better than Peter. There are well-known differences in this account of Judas's death from that in Mt. xxvii. 3 ff. The main problems are: (1) Who bought the field? (2) How did Judas die? (3) Why was the place called 'The Field of Blood'?

Οὗτος μὲν οὖν ἐκτήσατο χωρίον] In Mt. xxvii. 7, it was the priests who bought the Potter's Field with the thirty pieces of silver. A common explanation (favoured, e.g., by Jacquier) is that, considering the money as legally belonging to Judas, they bought the field in his name.

ἐκ μισθοῦ τῆς ἀδικίας] The genitive is either objective ('the reward he received for his unrighteousness') or a Semitic adjectival genitive ('his unrighteous reward'). For the former cf. ἡ κόλασις τῆς ἀδικίας αὐτοῦ, Ezek. xiv. 4; εἰς κόλασιν ἀδικίας, Ezek. xliv. 12; 2 Pet. ii. 13, 15; with the latter cf. Lk. xvi. 8 f.; xviii. 6. The reference is to the 30 shekels (tetradrachms) paid him for betraying Jesus (Mt. xxvi. 15).

πρηνὴς γενόμενος] lit. 'having become prone', i.e. falling flat. In vet. lat. the phrase is variously rendered: *pronus factus* d e p; *in faciem prostratus* g Ambr. These are replaced in vg by *suspensus*, a harmonization with Mt. xxvii. 5. Augustine (*c. Fel.* i. 4) combines the hanging and the falling: *collum sibi alligauit et deiectus in faciem diruptus est medius*, the most obvious way of reconciling the two accounts.

There is evidence, however, that πρηνής may be taken here in the sense 'swelling up', as if connected with πρήθω or πίμπρημι (cf. xxviii. 6). So apparently it was taken in vet. syr., if we can judge from its witnesses, the secondary Armenian and Georgian versions, and from a comment of Ephrem (see *BC* iii, p. 391). In Wisd. iv. 19 (ῥήξει αὐτοὺς ἀφώνους πρηνεῖς), πρηνεῖς is rendered *inflatos* in vg. A tradition that Judas did actually swell up was current in early times, and Papias was quoted as an authority for it (cf. Lightfoot, *Apostolic Fathers*, pp. 523 f., 534 f.). This tradition was apparently due to a desire to accommodate the fate of Judas to that generally thought appropriate for traitors (like the nephew of Aḥiqar [1]), heretics (like Arius), and tyrants (like Antiochus IV). Cf. the discussion by F. H. Chase in *JTS* xiii. (1912), 278 ff., 415.

ἐλάκησεν] From λάσκω, to crack or burst; an accompanying noise is implied, cf. *crepuit* vg.

ἐξεχύθη πάντα τὰ σπλάγχνα αὐτοῦ] Cf. Amasa in 2 Sam. (LXX 2 K.) xx. 10, ἐξεχύθη ἡ κοιλία αὐτοῦ εἰς τὴν γῆν.

[1] See R. H. Charles, *Apocrypha and Pseudepigrapha*, ii. pp. 715 ff.

i. 19

τῇ διαλέκτῳ αὐτῶν] Aramaic, which by this time had replaced Heb. as the vernacular of the Jews in Palestine and farther east.

Ἁκελδαμάχ] Aram. *ḥăqal dĕmā.* The rough breathing in WH represents the initial guttural, as in *Ἁλφαίου, ver.* 13. The final -*χ* represents nothing in the Aram. pronunciation, but was an orthographical device to transliterate the final א (*'aleph*). Cf. *Σειράχ* as a transliteration of Sira, in the name of the author of Ecclesiasticus. Dalman (*Gr. des jüd.-pal. Aram.*, p. 202) calls -*χ* the sign of an indeclinable. A. Klostermann suggested that the original name was *ḥăqal dĕmakh,* 'field of sleep', i.e. a cemetery (Gk. *κοιμητήριον,* from *κοιμάω*). Cf. Mt. xxvii. 7, according to which it was used to bury strangers in. In Mt. the explanation of the name *Ἀγρὸς αἵματος* seems to be that it was purchased with blood-money. Probably both explanations were current.

i. 20

Γέγραπται γὰρ] It is not suggested that the primary reference of these two passages is to Judas. In so far, however, as the character of Judas corresponded to the descriptions in Pss. lxix and cix, these passages could be applied to him. The titles of both these Pss. ascribe them to David. As the things said of David were interpreted in a Messianic sense, so David's enemies could be regarded as foreshadowing the enemies of Christ. Probably at an early date collections were made for ready reference of 'Testimonies', or OT passages fulfilled in the Gospel narrative:[1] cf. J. R. Harris, *Testimonies* Part I (1916), Part II (1920). See on xxvi. 23.

Γενηθήτω . . . ἐν αὐτῇ] From Ps. lxix. 25 (LXX lxviii. 26). The LXX[2] wording is slightly different:

> *γενηθήτω ἡ ἔπαυλις αὐτῶν ἠρημωμένη,*
> *καὶ ἐν τοῖς σκηνώμασιν αὐτῶν μὴ ἔστω ὁ κατοικῶν.*

ἔπαυλις] In the papyri this word usually means a homestead.

τὴν ἐπισκοπὴν αὐτοῦ λαβέτω ἕτερος] From Ps. cix. 8 (LXX cviii.), with *λαβέτω* (imperative) for LXX *λάβοι* (optative).

[1] It is reasonable to regard the instruction given by Jesus Himself to His disciples on the fulfilment of OT prophecy (cf. Lk. xxiv. 25 ff., 44 ff.) as forming the nucleus of these collections of 'Testimonies'.

[2] LXX quotations in the commentary are taken, of course, from those forms in which the pre-Christian Greek OT has come down to us. In the 1st century A.D. the Pentateuch was the only part of this translation which existed in a 'standard' version; no doubt, for the rest of the OT in particular, there were many more variant forms of the Greek translation than have survived to our day. See P. E. Kahle, *The Cairo Geniza* (1947), pp. 132 ff.

ἐπισκοπήν] lit. 'overseership', not in a technical sense; the meaning here is the same as that of *διακονία* in *vv.* 17, 25, and of *ἀποστολή* in *ver.* 25.

For other traces of a collection of 'Testimonies' about Judas cf. Mt. xxvii. 9 f.; Jn. xiii. 18, and xvii. 12 (*ἵνα ἡ γραφὴ πληρωθῇ*).

i. 21

ἐν παντὶ χρόνῳ ᾧ] *ἐν* is omitted before *ᾧ*, being understood from its earlier occurrence before the antecedent.

εἰσῆλθεν καὶ ἐξῆλθεν ἐφ' ἡμᾶς] Telescoped construction for *εἰσῆλθεν ἐφ' ἡμᾶς καὶ ἐξῆλθεν παρ' ἡμῶν*. For the idiom cf. ix. 28; it is a Semitism common in OT (e.g. Dt. xxxi. 2; 2 Sam. iii. 25; Ps. cxxi. 8 [LXX cxx.], etc.). *ἐφ' ἡμᾶς*, 'over us' (RV mg.), may further suggest our Lord's relation to His disciples.

κύριος Ἰησοῦς] δ characteristically adds *χριστός*: such amplifications of our Lord's name are evidence of the secondary nature of this text. Cf. iii. 13; iv. 33; viii. 16; xi. 20; xv. 11; xvi. 31; xix. 5; xxi. 13, and see further on ii. 38; vii. 55; xiii. 33.

i. 22

ἀρξάμενος] Though formally agreeing with *Ἰησοῦς*, this use of the ptc. is really adverbial. Cf. x. 37; xi. 4; Mt. xx. 8; Lk. xxiii. 5; xxiv. 27, 47; Jn. viii. 9. Torrey (*CDA*, pp. 25-7) regards *ἀρξάμενος ἀπὸ . . . ἕως* as an Aram. idiom, representing *mĕshārē min . . . 'ad*, 'from . . . to'.

ἧς] Attic attraction, for *ἐν ᾗ*. Cf. *ver.* 2.

μάρτυρα τῆς ἀναστάσεως] Note the emphasis on personal witness as an essential apostolic qualification, especially with regard to the Resurrection (cf. 1 Cor. ix. 1; xv. 8 f.). The experience here required corresponds to the scope of Mk. and of the primitive Kerygma (see on x. 36).

i. 23

ἔστησαν] δ has *ἔστησεν*, as if Peter nominated them.

Ἰωσὴφ κ.τ.λ.] To be distinguished from Judas Barsabbas (xv. 22) and from Jesus called Justus (Col. iv. 11). According to Eusebius (*HE* iii. 39) and Philip of Side (*Hist. Christ.*), Papias told on the authority of Philip's daughters (see on xxi. 9) how this man, when challenged by unbelievers, drank serpent's poison in the Lord's name, with no harmful consequences (cf. Mk. xvi. 18).

Βαρσαββᾶν] A patronymic: Aram. *Bar-Shabbā* ('son of the Sabbath', i.e. born on the Sabbath) or, less probably, *Bar-Sābā* ('son of the elder'). δ (D d g p t vg.codd.) has *Βαρνάβαν*, confusing him with the Joseph surnamed Barnabas in iv. 36.

Ἰοῦστος] It was a common practice for Jews to assume a Gentile name, frequently bearing some resemblance to their Jewish name: see on xvii. 5. See *ET* x (1898-9), p. 527, for a Rabbinic parallel quoted by Eb. Nestle.

Μαθθίαν] A contracted form of Mattithiah (' gift of Jah ').

i. 24

προσευξάμενοι εἶπαν] The aor. ptc. is simultaneous: cf. the reverse construction *προσηύξατο . . . εἰπών* in Mk. xiv. 39.

κύριε] The prayer is perhaps addressed to Jesus: see below on *ἐξελέξω*.

καρδιογνῶστα] Cf. xv. 8, *ὁ καρδιογνώστης θεός*. The word occurs chiefly in Christian liturgical literature.

ἐξελέξω] The same verb is used in *ver.* 2 of the choosing of the apostles; it is appropriate, therefore, that Jesus should be the subject here as there.

i. 25

παρέβη] ' transgressed '.

εἰς τὸν τόπον τὸν ἴδιον] The phrase is euphemistic; *ἴδιον* is emphatic. Cf. *ἕκαστος εἰς τὸν ἴδιον τόπον μέλλει χωρεῖν*, Ignat. *Magn.* v. 1; *εἰς τὸν ὀφειλόμενον αὐτοῖς τόπον*, Polycarp, *Ep.* ix. 2; *εἰς τὸν ὀφειλόμενον τόπον τῆς δόξης*, 1 Clem. v. 4, the first referring to both bliss and woe, the second and third to bliss.

i. 26

ἔδωκαν κλήρους αὐτοῖς] ' they cast lots for them '. We should have expected *ἔβαλον* rather than *ἔδωκαν*, but ' to give a lot ' is the Heb. idiom. The procedure of casting lots after nomination (*κλήρωσις ἐκ προκρίτων*) is similar to that introduced by Solon for electing Athenian magistrates (Aristotle, *Ath. Pol.* 8). In OT the casting of lots was a recognized way of ascertaining the divine will (cf. Prov. xvi. 33). For the employment of Urim and Thummim for this purpose cf. 1 Sam. xiv. 41, LXX. There is no record of the disciples' resorting to this procedure after Pentecost.

ἕνδεκα] δ has *δώδεκα*. Augustine has the conflate text *deputatus est cum undecim apostolis duodecimus*.

2. The Day of Pentecost, ii. 1–47.

(a) The Descent of the Spirit, ii. 1-4

Καὶ ἐν τῷ συνπληροῦσθαι τὴν ἡμέραν τῆς πεντηκοστῆς ἦσαν πάντες 1
ὁμοῦ ἐπὶ τὸ αὐτό, καὶ ἐγένετο ἄφνω ἐκ τοῦ οὐρανοῦ ἦχος ὥσπερ φερο- 2
μένης πνοῆς βιαίας καὶ ἐπλήρωσεν ὅλον τὸν οἶκον οὗ ἦσαν καθήμενοι,

καὶ ὤφθησαν αὐτοῖς διαμεριζόμεναι γλῶσσαι ὡσεὶ πυρός, καὶ ἐκάθισεν 3
ἐφ' ἕνα ἕκαστον αὐτῶν, καὶ ἐπλήσθησαν πάντες πνεύματος ἁγίου, καὶ 4
ἤρξαντο λαλεῖν ἑτέραις γλώσσαις καθὼς τὸ πνεῦμα ἐδίδου ἀποφθέγγεσθαι αὐτοῖς.

ii. 1

Καὶ ἐν τῷ συνπληροῦσθαι] ἐν τῷ with the infinitive is a favourite Lukan construction, especially to discharge the function of a time-clause: cf. iii. 26; iv. 30; viii. 6; ix. 3; xi. 15; xix. 1. It occurs 32 times in Lk., as against 3 in Mt. and 2 in Mk. Such phrases, according to F. Krapp (*Der substantivierte Infinitiv*, Heidelberg, 1892), are characteristic of historical writers from second century B.C. to first century A.D. For ἐν τῷ συνπληροῦσθαι cf. Lk. ix. 51. δ has here καὶ ἐγένετο ἐν ταῖς ἡμέραις ἐκείναις τοῦ συνπληροῦσθαι κ.τ.λ.

τὴν ἡμέραν τῆς πεντηκοστῆς] The construction is compressed; συνπληροῦσθαι is used in LXX and NT to express the completion of a *period*. Actually, it was the 7 weeks since Passover that had been fulfilled. But the Heb. name of the festival, *shābū'ōth* ('weeks'), includes the 7 weeks. Vg pesh have the plural, as if rendering τὰς ἡμέρας. For the festival cf. Ex. xxiii. 16*a*; xxxiv. 22*a*, Lev. xxiii. 15 ff.; Num. xxviii. 26 ff.; Dt. xvi. 9 ff. It was originally the festival of firstfruits of the wheat-harvest.

ἐπὶ τὸ αὐτό] See on i. 15. We are not told where they were. It may have been in the Temple precincts, where they would have had the best opportunity of addressing a large audience; according to Lk. xxiv. 53 they were continually there.

ii. 2

πνοῆς] For the wind as an emblem of the Spirit of God cf. Ezek. xxxvii. 9; Jn. iii. 8.

ἐπλήρωσεν] Ephrem Syrus says the house was filled with fragrance. Cf. Isa. vi. 4.

οἶκον] This can refer to the Temple as well as to a private house: cf. vii. 47; Isa. vi. 4 and freq. in LXX.

ii. 3

ὤφθησαν] Intrans., 'appeared'.

διαμεριζόμεναι] 'distributed among them', rather than 'cloven'.

γλῶσσαι ὡσεὶ πυρός] F. H. Chase (*Credibility*, pp. 34 f.) and others suggest that this appearance was caused by the rays of the rising sun suddenly shining through the Temple colonnade upon them. The metaphor γλῶσσαι may be suggested by the γλῶσσαι of *ver.* 4. But a mystical experience is probably indicated. For the association of the Holy Spirit with fire cf. Mt. iii. 11; Lk. iii. 16.

ἐκάθισεν] The subject is probably γλῶσσα (understood from γλῶσσαι) or possibly πῦρ. As the tongues of fire were distributed among them, one sat on each of them. So, when the Spirit descended from heaven upon our Lord in the form of a dove, ἔμεινεν ἐπ' αὐτόν (Jn. i. 32).

ii. 4

ἐπλήσθησαν πάντες πνεύματος ἁγίου] For such an instantaneous filling of the Spirit resulting in inspired utterance, cf. iv. 8, 31; xiii. 9; Lk. i. 41, 67.

ἤρξαντο] Possibly an example of the redundant auxiliary, representing Aram. *shārē* used to form a periphrastic variant of the simple verb: see on xi. 4, 15; xviii. 26; xxiv. 2; xxvii. 35.

λαλεῖν ἑτέραις γλώσσαις] The phenomenon of glossolalia has appeared in many forms.[1] The context here implies that the disciples' words made good sense to those who understood the various languages or dialects, but were unintelligible to others. Their hearers probably all spoke either Gk. or Aram. as their native tongue. The disciples, suddenly delivered from the peculiarities of their Galilaean speech, praised God and rehearsed His mighty works in such a way that each hearer recognized with surprise his own native language or dialect. No such surprise is expressed when Peter addresses the multitude (*vv.* 14 ff.), though we may infer that in this address he continued to speak without those Galilaean peculiarities which might otherwise have hindered people from other parts from understanding him. The Corinthian glossolalia does not seem to have been quite the same as this, to judge from Paul's deprecating description of it (1 Cor. xiv. 23). The effect of the Pentecostal glossolalia was better understanding on the part of the hearers; this does not appear to have been so at Corinth, nor is it so in many circles where the gift of tongues is cultivated nowadays. The test as to whether this or any other form of utterance represents the Holy Spirit's activity is this: Does it edify the hearer? Does it help him to become a Christian, or to be a better Christian than he already is?

ἀποφθέγγεσθαι] Of weighty or oracular utterance; e.g., in LXX it is used of prophesying in 1 Chr. xxv. 1, of soothsaying in Mic. v. 12.

(b) The Crowd's Amazement, ii. 5-13

Ἦσαν δὲ ἐν Ἰερουσαλὴμ κατοικοῦντες Ἰουδαῖοι, ἄνδρες εὐλαβεῖς 5
ἀπὸ παντὸς ἔθνους τῶν ὑπὸ τὸν οὐρανόν· γενομένης δὲ τῆς φωνῆς ταύτης 6
συνῆλθε τὸ πλῆθος καὶ συνεχύθη, ὅτι ἤκουσεν εἷς ἕκαστος τῇ ἰδίᾳ

[1] See K. Lake, *EEP*, pp. 241 ff.; A. L. Drummond, *Edward Irving and his Circle* (1937), pp. 236 ff., 278 ff., *et passim*, and his bibliography on p. 300.

διαλέκτῳ λαλούντων αὐτῶν· ἐξίσταντο δὲ καὶ ἐθαύμαζον λέγοντες 7
Οὐχὶ ἰδοὺ πάντες οὗτοί εἰσιν οἱ λαλοῦντες Γαλιλαῖοι; καὶ πῶς ἡμεῖς 8
ἀκούομεν ἕκαστος τῇ ἰδίᾳ διαλέκτῳ ἡμῶν ἐν ᾗ ἐγεννήθημεν; Πάρθοι 9
καὶ Μῆδοι καὶ Ἐλαμεῖται, καὶ οἱ κατοικοῦντες τὴν Μεσοποταμίαν,
Ἰουδαίαν τε καὶ Καππαδοκίαν, Πόντον καὶ τὴν Ἀσίαν, Φρυγίαν τε καὶ 10
Παμφυλίαν, Αἴγυπτον καὶ τὰ μέρη τῆς Λιβύης τῆς κατὰ Κυρήνην, καὶ
οἱ ἐπιδημοῦντες Ῥωμαῖοι, Ἰουδαῖοί τε καὶ προσήλυτοι, Κρῆτες καὶ 11
Ἄραβες, ἀκούομεν λαλούντων αὐτῶν ταῖς ἡμετέραις γλώσσαις τὰ
μεγαλεῖα τοῦ θεοῦ. ἐξίσταντο δὲ πάντες καὶ διηποροῦντο, ἄλλος πρὸς 12
ἄλλον λέγοντες Τί θέλει τοῦτο εἶναι; ἕτεροι δὲ διαχλευάζοντες 13
ἔλεγον ὅτι Γλεύκους μεμεστωμένοι εἰσίν.

ii. 5

ἦσαν . . . κατοικοῦντες] For the construction see on i. 10.

ἐν Ἰερουσαλήμ] ℵ^c B D byz.; *εἰς Ἰερουσαλήμ* ℵ* A. Cf. ix. 21.

Ἰουδαῖοι] om. ℵ. Blass, Ropes and Lake support the omission, but even so it is unlikely that Gentiles are in view here.

εὐλαβεῖς] om. Aug. In NT *εὐλαβής* is used only of Jews: e.g. in viii. 2 of those who buried Stephen, in xxii. 12 of Ananias, in Lk. ii. 25 of Simeon.

ἀπὸ παντὸς ἔθνους τῶν ὑπὸ τὸν οὐρανόν] i.e., from every land where there were Jews. We may compare the Jewish tradition that at the giving of the Law the voice of God was heard in every nation under heaven.[1] The Rabbis reckoned the languages of the world to be 70 in all, according to the number of nations in Gen. x.

ii. 6

φωνῆς] The *ἦχος* of *ver.* 2 or the inspired utterance of *ver.* 4? The latter seems more likely, but we need not exclude the former. For *φωνή* with *γίνομαι* cf. vii. 31; x. 13; xix. 34; Lk. i. 44; iii. 22; ix. 35 f.

τὸ πλῆθος] Here in a non-technical sense, 'the populace'; for a different sense cf. iv. 32.

τῇ ἰδίᾳ διαλέκτῳ] While *διάλεκτος* does not exactly correspond to the modern sense of 'dialect', having the wider meaning 'manner of speech', yet 'dialect' is pretty much what is meant here: cf. the variant expression *ταῖς ἡμετέραις γλώσσαις* in *ver.* 11.

ii. 7

Οὐχὶ ἰδού] B; *οὐκ ἰδού* A C; *οὐχ ἰδού* ℵ D 81 WH mg. For aspiration before *ἰδεῖν* cf. *ἀφίδω*, Phil. ii. 23. The occasional aspiration of this verb and its compounds is found in the best MSS.

[1] Cf. Midrash *Tanḥuma* 26c. Cf. also the tradition preserved in TB *Pesaḥim* 68 b: 'the Feast of Weeks . . . is the day on which the Torah was given.'

This expression is used in LXX in rhetorical questions, and 'in time became the recognised equivalent for the classical ἆρ' οὐ;' (Thackeray, *Gr. of OT in Gk.*, i. 125 f.). Torrey thinks that here it represents Aram. *lā hā* (found in pesh Mt. xxiv. 2).

Γαλιλαῖοι] For the peculiarities of Galilaean speech cf. Mt. xxvi. 73; Mk. xiv. 70; Lk. xxii. 59.

'The Galilean dialect is specially mentioned as having an indistinct pronunciation of the gutturals (which was, and still is, characteristic of the Samaritans), and also as a dialect in which syllables were often swallowed in such a way that the meaning of words and phrases often became doubtful to a southern Jew. The Talmud has many amusing anecdotes about this dialect' (A. Neubauer, 'The Dialects of Palestine in the Time of Christ', in *Studia Biblica*, i [1885], p. 51).

ii. 8

τῇ ἰδίᾳ διαλέκτῳ ἡμῶν] 'our very own dialect'. For the collocation of *ἴδιος* and the genitive of the personal pronoun cf. Tit. i. 12; 2 Pet. iii. 16. In the papyri it occurs as early as the Ptolemaic period.

ii. 9

Πάρθοι καὶ Μῆδοι καὶ Ἐλαμεῖται, καὶ οἱ κατοικοῦντες τὴν Μεσοποταμίαν] In these countries lived descendants of the 10 tribes (commonly miscalled the 'lost' tribes), and of members of the 2 tribes who did not return from exile. Artaxerxes III planted Jewish captives in Hyrcania on the Caspian (*c.* 350 B.C.). These settlements were augmented by voluntary immigration, so that there were millions of Jews in those parts. Their vernacular was Aramaic. Cf. Jos. *Ant.* xi. 5. 2; xv. 2. 2; xviii. 9. 1 ff., and the preface to *BJ* which tells how that work was first composed in Aram. for the benefit of the Jews in Babylonia and neighbouring regions. 'Parthians and Medes' are linked in 1 Enoch lvi. 5 as the chief nations in the league against Israel. (See Schürer, II. ii. 223.)

Ἰουδαίαν] Perhaps in the wider prophetic sense, 'the land of the Jews', from the Egyptian border to the Euphrates, which would explain the omission from this list of Syria, which according to Philo and Josephus was full of Jews. So Jerome on Isa. xi. 6 ff. substitutes Syria for Judaea in quoting this verse. A difficulty has been felt in the absence of the article before *Ἰουδαίαν*, as the word is properly an adjective. 'The anarthrous *Ἰουδαίαν* . . . is certainly corrupt', says Blass (*Gr.* 153, *n.* 1). Aug. *unit.* and pesh read 'Jews' (so Zahn); Aug. *c. ep. Fund.* and Tert. *adu. Iud.* 7 have *Armeniam:* Bentley suggested *Ἰνδίαν*, Burkitt *Γορδυαίαν* (Kurdistan), W. L. Knox *Ἰωνίαν*. We may keep the text, in spite of the difficulty; the analogy of the accompanying place-names is sufficient to explain the anarthrous Ἰουδαίαν.

Καππαδοκίαν, Πόντον τε καὶ τὴν Ἀσίαν, Φρυγίαν τε καὶ Παμφυλίαν] All these were districts of Asia Minor, which was full of Jews, as may be seen from the second half of Ac. Ἰουδαῖοι καθ' ἑκάστην πόλιν εἰσὶ παμπληθεῖς Ἀσίας τε καὶ Συρίας, says Philo (*Leg. ad Gai.* 245). Cf. xv. 21, where Asia Minor is chiefly in question. From Pontus they crossed the Black Sea; Jewish inscriptions have been found even in the Crimea.

ii. 10

Αἴγυπτον] Jews had lived continuously in Egypt from the time of Psammetichus II (*c.* 590 B.C.), receiving fresh accessions from time to time. Philo and Josephus *passim* bear witness to their numbers and influence there. The former estimated in A.D. 38 that the Jewish population of Egypt was about a million; 2 out of the 5 wards of Alexandria were Jewish (*In Flaccum*, 6, 8).

Κυρήνην] For the Jews of Cyrenaica cf. vi. 9; xi. 20; xiii. 1, and Simon of Cyrene in the Passion story. Cf. also 1 Macc. xv. 23; 2 Macc. ii. 23; Jos. *Ap.* ii. 4; *BJ* vii. 11; *Ant.* xiv. 7. 2; xvi. 6. 1, 5; *Vita* 76. Ptolemy I (323-283 B.C.) settled a number of Jews in Cyrenaica, to ensure its loyalty.

οἱ ἐπιδημοῦντες Ῥωμαῖοι] 'the visitors from Rome'. Some of these may have returned and formed the nucleus of the Roman church, of the origin of which we have no historical record. 'Rome was the seat of a Jewish community numbered by thousands' (Schürer, II, ii. 232).

προσήλυτοι] In LXX προσήλυτος represents Heb. *gēr*, used of a sojourner in the land of Israel, a stranger within the gates: cf. Attic μέτοικος, a resident alien, to whom certain rights and privileges were accorded by law. Both *gēr* and προσήλυτος were subsequently employed to denote those Gentiles who undertook the complete observance of the Jewish law and were admitted into full fellowship with Israel. For proselytization three things were necessary, (1) circumcision (in the case of males), (2) baptism (for ritual purification),[1] (3) the offering of sacrifice. The real test was naturally circumcision, which partly explains why proselytization was more common among women. Many men were content with that looser attachment to the synagogue usually implied in the term 'God-fearers' (cf. x. 2; xiii. 16; xvii. 17, etc.).[2]

[1] See 'Jewish Proselyte Baptism and the Baptism of John', by H. H. Rowley, in *Hebrew Union College Annual*, xv. (1940), pp. 313 ff.

[2] The distinction sometimes made between 'proselytes of righteousness' and 'proselytes of the gate', as full proselytes and 'God-fearers' respectively,

ii. 11

Κρῆτες] For Jews in Crete cf. Tit. i. 10 ff.; Jos. *BJ* ii. 7. 1; *Ant.* xvii. 12. 1; *Vita* 76. The wife of Josephus was a Cretan Jewess.

Ἄραβες] Arabia in Graeco-Roman usage generally meant the kingdom of the Nabataean Arabs, then at the height of its power under Aretas IV (9 B.C.-A.D. 40). It lay between the Red Sea and the Euphrates, Petra being the capital. At one time it had included Damascus, which, however, belonged to the Roman province of Syria from 64 B.C. onward. See on ix. 23 ff.

λαλούντων . . . τὰ μεγαλεῖα τοῦ θεοῦ] = *μεγαλυνόντων τὸν θεόν*, 'magnifying God', as in x. 46. The Jewish authorities in Palestine seem to have sanctioned the use of any language in reciting the *Shĕma'* ('Hear, O Israel', etc.), the *Shĕmōneh 'Esrēh*[1] (the 'Eighteen Benedictions'), and the Grace at meals. So the praise of God in various tongues and dialects was a frequent sound in Jerusalem during the great festivals, when so many pilgrims of the Dispersions were present. Now, to their surprise, these pilgrims hear those words of praise uttered in their own languages, by Galilaeans of all people! The reversal of the curse of Babel is surely in the writer's mind.

ii. 12

ἐξίσταντο] As in *ver.* 7: cf. *ἐξέστησαν*, x. 45, in a similar context.

διηπoροῦντο] Luke is the only NT writer to use this word: cf. v. 24; x. 17; Lk. ix. 7. In these three places the active is used.

Τί θέλει τοῦτο εἶναι;] 'What does this mean?' Cf. xvii. 20, *τίνα θέλει ταῦτα εἶναι.*

ii. 13

διαχλευάζοντες] The only NT occurrence of this word. Cf. the only NT occurrence of the simple verb *χλευάζω* in xvii. 32.

is a fiction. The former were religious proselytes, the latter 'strangers within the gates' in the OT sense of foreigners living in the land of Israel.

That even a full proselyte was not in every respect on a par with a native Israelite seems indicated by Mishna, *Bikkurim*, i. 4: 'These may bring the first-fruits but they may not make the Avowal [Dt. xxvi. 3]: the proselyte may bring them but he may not make the Avowal since he cannot say, "Which the Lord sware unto our fathers to give us". But if his mother was an Israelite he may bring them and make the Avowal. And when he prays in private he should say, "O God of the fathers of Israel"; and when he is in the synagogue he should say, "O God of your fathers". But if his mother was an Israelite he may say, "O God of our fathers".'

[1] For the text of this, the chief Jewish prayer, cf. Schürer, II. ii. 85 ff.; Westcott, *Hebrews*, pp. 208 ff.; Singer, *Authorised Daily Prayer Book*, pp. 44 ff.

ἔλεγον] Imperfect tense, here indicating the repeated remarks of a number of people.

ὅτι] ὅτι *recitantis*, introducing direct speech.

Γλεύκους] The only NT occurrence of γλεῦκος, which is found first in Aristotle: 'sweet wine', i.e., wine still fermenting. The vintage of the current year had not yet come, but there were means of keeping wine sweet all the year round. Cato (*De Re Rustica* 120) gives one such recipe for keeping new wine from becoming sour: '*mustum si uoles totum annum habere, in amphoram mustum indito, et corticem oppicato, demittito in piscinam, post xxx diem eximito; totum annum mustum erit*'.

In 1 Cor. xiv. 23 Paul points out that glossolalia may be mistaken for madness.

(c) Peter's Sermon, ii. 14-36

Σταθεὶς δὲ ὁ Πέτρος σὺν τοῖς ἕνδεκα ἐπῆρεν τὴν φωνὴν αὐτοῦ καὶ 14
ἀπεφθέγξατο αὐτοῖς Ἄνδρες Ἰουδαῖοι καὶ οἱ κατοικοῦντες Ἰερουσαλὴμ πάντες, τοῦτο ὑμῖν γνωστὸν ἔστω καὶ ἐνωτίσασθε τὰ ῥήματά
μου. οὐ γὰρ ὡς ὑμεῖς ὑπολαμβάνετε οὗτοι μεθύουσιν, ἔστιν γὰρ ὥρα 15
τρίτη τῆς ἡμέρας, ἀλλὰ τοῦτό ἐστιν τὸ εἰρημένον διὰ τοῦ προφήτου 16
Ἰωήλ

Καὶ ἔσται ἐν ταῖς ἐσχάταις ἡμέραις, λέγει ὁ θεός, 17
ἐκχεῶ ἀπὸ τοῦ πνεύματός μου ἐπὶ πᾶσαν σάρκα,
καὶ προφητεύσουσιν οἱ υἱοὶ ὑμῶν καὶ αἱ θυγατέρες ὑμῶν,
καὶ οἱ νεανίσκοι ὑμῶν ὁράσεις ὄψονται,
καὶ οἱ πρεσβύτεροι ὑμῶν ἐνυπνίοις ἐνυπνιασθήσονται·
καί γε ἐπὶ τοὺς δούλους μου καὶ ἐπὶ τὰς δούλας μου 18
ἐν ταῖς ἡμέραις ἐκείναις ἐκχεῶ ἀπὸ τοῦ πνεύματός μου,
καὶ προφητεύσουσιν.
Καὶ δώσω τέρατα ἐν τῷ οὐρανῷ ἄνω 19
καὶ σημεῖα ἐπὶ τῆς γῆς κάτω,
αἷμα καὶ πῦρ καὶ ἀτμίδα καπνοῦ· 20
ὁ ἥλιος μεταστραφήσεται εἰς σκότος
καὶ ἡ σελήνη εἰς αἷμα
πρὶν ἐλθεῖν ἡμέραν Κυρίου τὴν μεγάλην καὶ ἐπιφανῆ.
Καὶ ἔσται πᾶς ὃς ἐὰν ἐπικαλέσηται τὸ ὄνομα Κυρίου σωθήσεται. 21

Ἄνδρες Ἰσραηλεῖται, ἀκούσατε τοὺς λόγους τούτους. Ἰησοῦν τὸν 22
Ναζωραῖον, ἄνδρα ἀποδεδειγμένον ἀπὸ τοῦ θεοῦ εἰς ὑμᾶς δυνάμεσι
καὶ τέρασι καὶ σημείοις οἷς ἐποίησεν δι' αὐτοῦ ὁ θεὸς ἐν μέσῳ ὑμῶν,
καθὼς αὐτοὶ οἴδατε, τοῦτον τῇ ὡρισμένῃ βουλῇ καὶ προγνώσει τοῦ 23
θεοῦ ἔκδοτον διὰ χειρὸς ἀνόμων προσπήξαντες ἀνείλατε, ὃν ὁ θεὸς 24
ἀνέστησεν λύσας τὰς ὠδῖνας τοῦ θανάτου, καθότι οὐκ ἦν δυνατὸν
κρατεῖσθαι αὐτὸν ὑπ' αὐτοῦ· Δαυεὶδ γὰρ λέγει εἰς αὐτόν 25

Προορώμην τὸν κύριον ἐνώπιόν μου διὰ παντός,
ὅτι ἐκ δεξιῶν μού ἐστιν ἵνα μὴ σαλευθῶ.
διὰ τοῦτο ηὐφράνθη μου ἡ καρδία καὶ ἠγαλλιάσατο ἡ γλῶσσά μου, 26
ἔτι δὲ καὶ ἡ σάρξ μου κατασκηνώσει ἐπ' ἐλπίδι·
ὅτι οὐκ ἐνκαταλείψεις τὴν ψυχήν μου εἰς ᾅδην, 27
οὐδὲ δώσεις τὸν ὅσιόν σου ἰδεῖν διαφθοράν.
ἐγνώρισάς μοι ὁδοὺς ζωῆς, 28
πληρώσεις με εὐφροσύνης μετὰ τοῦ προσώπου σου.

Ἄνδρες ἀδελφοί, ἐξὸν εἰπεῖν μετὰ παρρησίας πρὸς ὑμᾶς περὶ τοῦ πατρι- 29
άρχου Δαυείδ, ὅτι καὶ ἐτελεύτησεν καὶ ἐτάφη καὶ τὸ μνῆμα αὐτοῦ
ἔστιν ἐν ἡμῖν ἄχρι τῆς ἡμέρας ταύτης· προφήτης οὖν ὑπάρχων, καὶ 30
εἰδὼς ὅτι ὅρκῳ ὤμοσεν αὐτῷ ὁ θεὸς ἐκ καρποῦ τῆς ὀσφύος αὐτοῦ
καθίσαι ἐπὶ τὸν θρόνον αὐτοῦ, προιδὼν ἐλάλησεν περὶ τῆς ἀναστάσεως 31
τοῦ χριστοῦ ὅτι οὔτε ἐνκατελείφθη εἰς ᾅδην οὔτε ἡ σὰρξ αὐτοῦ εἶδεν
διαφθοράν. τοῦτον τὸν Ἰησοῦν ἀνέστησεν ὁ θεός, οὗ πάντες ἡμεῖς 32
ἐσμὲν μάρτυρες. τῇ δεξιᾷ οὖν τοῦ θεοῦ ὑψωθεὶς τήν τε ἐπαγγελίαν 33
τοῦ πνεύματος τοῦ ἁγίου λαβὼν παρὰ τοῦ πατρὸς ἐξέχεεν τοῦτο ὃ
ὑμεῖς καὶ βλέπετε καὶ ἀκούετε. οὐ γὰρ Δαυεὶδ ἀνέβη εἰς τοὺς 34
οὐρανούς, λέγει δε αὐτός

Εἶπεν Κύριος τῷ κυρίῳ μου Κάθου ἐκ δεξιῶν μου
ἕως ἂν θῶ τοὺς ἐχθρούς σου ὑποπόδιον τῶν ποδῶν σου. 35

ἀσφαλῶς οὖν γινωσκέτω πᾶς οἶκος Ἰσραὴλ ὅτι καὶ κύριον αὐτὸν καὶ 36
χριστὸν ἐποίησεν ὁ θεός, τοῦτον τὸν Ἰησοῦν ὃν ὑμεῖς ἐσταυρώσατε.

On the authenticity of this and other speeches in Ac., cf. Introduction, pp. 18 ff. This speech suits exactly the time and circumstances of its delivery. It consists of (1) introduction (*vv.* 14-21), (2) account of the death, resurrection and exaltation of Jesus (*vv.* 22-36), interspersed with (3) Scriptural proofs (*vv.* 25-8, 34 f.), followed, after a brief interruption, by (4) exhortation to repentance. The same fourfold pattern can be traced in the sermons in chs. iii., x., xiii.

ii. 14

σὺν τοῖς ἕνδεκα] While all the believers received the gift of the Spirit (*πάντες*, *vv.* 1, 4), the Twelve (including Matthias) presented themselves to the populace as the leaders.

ἐπῆρεν τὴν φωνὴν αὐτοῦ καὶ ἀπεφθέγξατο αὐτοῖς] A common LXX phrase, reflecting Heb. idiom. While *ἐπῆρεν τὴν φωνήν* can be paralleled from classical Gk. (e.g. Demosthenes *De Corona* 291, *ἐπάρας τὴν φωνήν*), as it stands here it is a characteristic Semitizing pleonasm.

ἀπεφθέγξατο] Cf. *ἀποφθέγγεσθαι* in *ver.* 4; probably here, as there, the word implies inspired utterance. Cf. Winer *ap.* Grimm-Thayer, p. 69.

Ἄνδρες Ἰουδαῖοι] 'Fellow-Jews': cf. *ἄνδρες Ἰσραηλεῖται, ver.* 22; *ἄνδρες ἀδελφοί, ver.* 29. See on i. 16.

ἐνωτίσασθε] The only NT occurrence of this word, which is derived from *οὖς* ('ear') and is frequent in LXX in the sense 'give ear' (like Heb. *he'ezīn*, from *'ōzen*, 'ear').

ii. 15

ὥρα τρίτη] i.e. reckoning from sunrise, and therefore about 9 a.m. The Jews did not eat until the fourth hour (on the Sabbath, they dined at the sixth hour: Jos. *Vita* 54).

ii. 16

διὰ] 'through', the preposition regularly used in this connection: the Holy Spirit was the real speaker, the prophet but His mouthpiece.

Ἰωήλ] om D Iren.lat Hil Aug Greg.Illib. It may be a non-Western interpolation. For the anonymity with which other quotations from the Book of the Twelve Prophets are introduced, cf. vii. 42; xiii. 40; xv. 15.

ii. 17

The quotation is from Joel ii. 28-32 (iii. 1-5 Heb.), with variations to be noted. It may be observed that the context in Joel contains a call to repentance, which would be followed by forgiveness (cf. *ver.* 38 below), and by the coming of the Day of the Lord, the commencement of the Messianic Age (see on iii. 19 ff. below).

καὶ ἔσται . . . ἐκχεῶ] A Hebraism (cf. *ver.* 21), usually rendered in EV, 'And it shall come to pass (that). . . .' See on iv. 5 for Luke's own treatment of this idiom.

ἐν ταῖς ἐσχάταις ἡμέραις, λεγει ὁ θεός] These words replace LXX *μετὰ ταῦτα, καὶ*. Cf. Isa. ii. 2, *ὅτι ἔσται ἐν ταῖς ἐσχάταις ἡμέραις κ.τ.λ.*

ἀπὸ τοῦ πνεύματός μου] Partitive use of *ἀπό*, as in *ver.* 18. This use is common in Mod. Gk. Cf. *ἐκ* in *ver.* 30.

καὶ οἱ νεανίσκοι . . . καὶ οἱ πρεσβύτεροι] These two classes are in reverse order in MT and LXX. The quotation was probably made from memory.

ἐνυπνίοις ἐνυπνιασθήσονται] For this use of the verb with the dat. of the corresponding noun cf. *ver.* 30; iv. 17; v. 28; xxiii. 14. Here the LXX texts vary; some have the acc. *ἐνύπνια*, which more accurately represents the Heb.

ii. 18

καὶ προφητεύσουσιν] Not in LXX, and omitted by δ, probably to harmonize with LXX.

ii. 19

ἄνω . . . σημεῖα . . . κάτω] These three words are not in LXX.

αἷμα καὶ πῦρ καὶ ἀτμίδα καπνοῦ] Omitted by δ, perhaps as not being applicable to the circumstances of Pentecost. But Peter's hearers may have associated the phenomena described in *vv.* 19 f. with those which attended the preternatural darkness on Good Friday.

ii. 20

ὁ ἥλιος μεταστραφήσεται εἰς σκότος καὶ ἡ σελήνη εἰς αἷμα] Cf. Rev. vi. 12, *ὁ ἥλιος ἐγένετο μέλας ὡς σάκκος τρίχινος, καὶ ἡ σελήνη ὅλη ἐγένετο ὡς αἷμα*, signifying the advent of the *Dies Irae*, in terms suggested by Joel's prophecy.

ἐπιφανῆ] 'splendid', 'glorious'. The MT has *nōrā* ('terrible'), for which the LXX translators read *nir'eh* ('conspicuous').

ii. 21

καὶ ἔσται . . . σωθήσεται] See on *ver.* 17.

Κυρίου] i.e. Jehovah (Heb. *Yahweh*), as in *ver.* 20. But the practical application here, as in Rom. x. 13, is to Jesus (see on *ver.* 36). This is one of several places where words referring to Jehovah in OT are in NT applied to Jesus: cf. Isa. xlv. 23 in Rom. xiv. 11 and Phil. ii. 10 f.; Ps. xxxiv. 8 in 1 Pet. ii. 3; Isa. viii. 13 in 1 Pet. iii. 15.

ii. 22

ἄνδρες Ἰσραηλεῖται] See on *ver.* 14.

Ἰησοῦν τὸν Ναζωραῖον] This title is found in vi. 14; xxii. 8; xxvi. 9; Mt. xxvi. 71; Lk. xviii. 37; Jn. xviii. 5, 7; xix. 19; and cf. *Ἰησοῦ Χριστοῦ τοῦ Ναζωραίου*, iii. 6; iv. 10. In spite of other suggestions, it seems fairly certain that *Ναζωραῖος* means 'of Nazareth' (= Heb. *Noṣrī*, with metathesized vowel), synonymous with *Ναζαρηνός*, Mk. i. 24; x. 47; xiv. 67 (where it corresponds to *Ναζωραῖος* of Mt. xxvi. 71); xvi. 6; Lk. iv. 34; xxiv. 19. Thus *Ἰησοῦν τὸν Ναζωραῖον* here = *Ἰησοῦν τὸν Ναζαρηνόν* (Mk. xvi. 6) = *Ἰησοῦν τὸν ἀπὸ Ναζαρέθ* (Ac. x. 38). Mt. ii. 23, *ὅπως πληρωθῇ τὸ ῥηθὲν διὰ τῶν προφητῶν ὅτι Ναζωραῖος κληθήσεται*, suggests a word-play on Heb. *nēṣer* ('Branch', Isa. xi. 1) [less probably on Heb. *nāṣar* ('guard') or even, despite the difference in the second radical, on *nāzīr* ('separated', 'Nazirite': cf. Judg. xiii. 5, 7)]. See G. F. Moore in *BC* i., pp. 426 ff.; W. O. E. Oesterley in *ET* lii. (1940-1), pp. 410 ff.; W. F. Albright in *JBL* lxv. (1946), pp. 397 ff. See further on xxiv. 5, where the Christians are called *Ναζωραῖοι*.

ἀποδεδειγμένον] 'appointed', 'designated': cf. *προκεχειρισμένον*, iii. 20; *ὡρισμένος*, x. 42; *ἐν ἀνδρὶ ᾧ ὥρισεν*, xvii. 31. δ has *δεδοκιμασμένον*, whence Iren.lat and vg *adprobatum*, but Tert *destinatum* reflects *ἀποδεδειγμένον*.

ἀπὸ] Denoting the agent (classical *ὑπό*): cf. iv. 36; xv. 4, 33; xx. 9.

ὑμᾶς] *ἡμᾶς* D.

δυνάμεσι καὶ τέρασι καὶ σημείοις] Our Lord's miracles were signs of the Messianic Age, 'the powers of the age to come' of Heb. vi. 5, showing that in Him the divine kingdom had broken into the world and was in operation (Lk. xi. 20). They are called 'mighty works' (*δυνάμεις*) because they were manifestations of the divine power which resided in Him. For *τέρατα* and *σημεῖα* cf. *vv.* 19, 43. Here and in the briefer allusion in x. 38 we have the only explicit NT allusions outside the Gospels to our Lord's miracles. For the witness of the miracles cf. Jn. iii. 2; vii. 31; xiv. 10; xv. 24. That the Messiah was expected to do miracles is implied by Jos. *Ant.* xx. 8. 6.

ii. 23

τοῦτον] Resumes and emphasizes by its position the preceding accusative: cf. iv. 10; vii. 35.

τῇ ὡρισμένῃ βουλῇ] Cf. iii. 18; iv. 28; xvii. 3; xxvi. 23; Lk. xxii. 22; xxiv. 26, 46, etc., for the predestined character of the death of Christ.

προγνώσει] Cf. *προεγνωσμένου*, 1 Pet. i. 20, in the same connection.

ἔκδοτον] = *παράδοτον*, as in Jos. *Ant.* vi. 13. 9; xiv. 13. 8; xviii. 9. 7.

διὰ χειρὸς] Reflecting Aram. *bĕ-yad* (lit. 'in the hand'), if an Aram. source lies behind this report. Torrey points out that the Aram. behind *ἔκδοτον διὰ χειρὸς ἀνόμων* would be the same as behind *παραδίδοται εἰς τὰς χεῖρας τῶν ἁμαρτωλῶν* in Mk. xiv. 41. Cf. xvii. 25; xix. 11; xxi. 11; xxiv. 7; xxviii. 17 for prepositional phrases with *χείρ*.

ἀνόμων] Perhaps referring to the Romans; they are frequently called *rĕshā'īm* ('wicked men') by Jewish writers; *malkūth hā-rĕshā'īm* (lit. 'kingdom of the wicked') means the Roman Empire. Cf. Mk. xiv. 41. If this interpretation is right, it is a mark of the genuineness of the speech; Luke would never have designated the Romans thus.

προσπήξαντες] 'having nailed up'; *σταυρόω* soon became the stereotyped word.

ἀνείλατε] Cf. iii. 13; iv. 10; v. 30; vii. 52, etc., for the insistence that the immediate moral responsibility for the death of Christ rested with His own countrymen. His humiliation, here emphasized as a result of divine predestination, was used by the Jews as an argument against His Messiahship (one of the names by which they called Him was *ha-tālūy*, 'the hanged one').

ii. 24

ὃν ὁ θεὸς ἀνέστησεν] Cf. iii. 15; iv. 10; v. 30; x. 40; xiii. 30; 1 Pet. i. 21, etc. To the predestined suffering and death of Christ Peter now adds His resurrection and exaltation. Cf. 1 Pet. i. 11, *τὰ εἰς Χριστὸν παθήματα καὶ τὰς μετὰ ταῦτα δόξας*, as the burden of OT prophecy.

λύσας τὰς ὠδῖνας τοῦ θανάτου] For *λύσας τὰς ὠδῖνας* cf. Job xxxix. 2 (*ὠδῖνας δὲ αὐτῶν ἔλυσας*). For *τὰς ὠδῖνας τοῦ θανάτου* cf. *ὠδῖνες θανάτου*, Ps. xviii. 4 (LXX xvii. 5) and cxvi. 3 (LXX cxiv. 3); *ὠδῖνες ᾅδου*, Ps. xviii. 5 (LXX xvii. 6). Polycarp *Ep.* i. 2 (*λύσας τὰς ὠδῖνας τοῦ ᾅδου*) echoes the present passage. Torrey sees behind *ὠδῖνας* here Aram. *ḥabalayyā*, which means 'bonds' as well as 'pangs', the former sense being more suitable with *λύσας*. Similarly LXX sometimes translates Heb. *ḥebel*, 'cord', 'bond', by *ὠδίς*, as if it were *ḥēbel*, 'pang', e.g. in the three passages from Pss. quoted above.

ii. 25

εἰς αὐτόν] 'with regard to Him'. For this sense of *εἰς* cf. *εἰς τὰ ἕτοιμα*, 2 Cor. x. 16; *εἰς ἑαυτὸν . . . εἰς τὸν ἕτερον*, Gal. vi. 4; *εἰς Χριστὸν καὶ [εἰς] τὴν ἐκκλησίαν*, Eph. v. 32; *τὰ εἰς Χριστὸν παθήματα*, 1 Pet. i. 11; and the similar sense of *πρός* in Heb. i. 7, *πρὸς . . . τοὺς ἀγγέλους*, 'concerning the angels'.

προορώμην κ.τ.λ.] The quotation is from Ps. xvi. 8-11 (LXX xv.). The argument is that the words of the Psalm cannot refer to David, since his soul did go to Sheol and his body did see corruption; they must therefore refer to the Messianic King, of whom David was a figure, and in whose name he spoke these words. These words were fulfilled in Jesus of Nazareth, and in no other; therefore Jesus must be the Messiah. Cf. Paul's argument from this Psalm in xiii. 34-37, and the similar treatment of Ps. cx. in *vv.* 34 ff. below.

προορώμην] With loss of temporal augment, as in LXX. In Hellenistic Gk., *προορῶμαι* (middle voice) is used without the idea of *fore*seeing ; so RV 'I beheld'. LXX uses it here to render Heb. *shiwwīthī*, 'I have set'. Contrast the active προιδών in *ver.* 31 with the full sense of foreseeing.

ii. 26

μου ἡ καρδία] ℵ B ; ἡ καρδία μου ℵ^c A C D 81 byz (following LXX.)

ἠγαλλιάσατο ἡ γλῶσσά μου] LXX substitutes ἡ γλῶσσά μου for MT *kĕbōdī*, 'my glory'. To 'my glory rejoices' the Midrash on this Psalm adds 'over King Messiah'. (The original sense may have been *kĕbēdī*, 'my liver', in parallelism with 'my heart'.)

ἐπ' ἐλπίδι] So LXX for Heb. *lā-beṭaḥ*, 'in safety' (RV), or 'in confidence', as in Prov. i. 33.

ii. 27

ὅτι οὐκ ἐνκαταλείψεις τὴν ψυχήν μου εἰς ᾅδην] 'because Thou wilt not abandon my soul (*or* life) to Hades' (εἰς ᾅδην represents Heb. *li-Shĕ'ōl*, '*to* Sheol', though the Gk. by itself might equally well mean '*in* Hades'). Hades, as in classical Gk., is the abode of the souls of all the dead. Originally it meant not the nether world itself, but the god of that region ; hence the classical use of the genitive Ἅιδου after εἰς and ἐν, instead of the acc. and dat. respectively, which we find in Hellenistic Gk. : cf. Lk. xvi. 23, ἐν τῷ ᾅδῃ.

οὐδὲ δώσεις τὸν ὅσιόν σου ἰδεῖν διαφθοράν] This clause, the second half of Ps. xvi. 10, is quoted again in xiii. 35 in the course of a similar argument. For δίδωμι with the infinitive, cf. x. 40 ; xiv. 3.

τὸν ὅσιόν σου] In LXX ἅγιος and ὅσιος are usually employed to render Heb. *qādōsh* and *ḥāsīd* respectively ; whereas *qādōsh* primarily means 'set apart', *ḥāsīd* primarily means one who has experienced the *ḥesed* ('plighted love', 'lovingkindness') of God, one who enjoys a covenant-relation with Him (cf. Ps. l. 5, where 'my saints' is *ḥasīday*). God Himself is bound by this covenant-relation and is therefore Himself *ḥāsīd* (translated 'gracious' in Ps. cxlv. 17 RV). Apart from LXX quotations, however, it is difficult to draw a distinction in NT between ἅγιος and ὅσιος. See also on xiii. 34 f.

ii. 29

Ἄνδρες ἀδελφοί] See on i. 16.

ἐξὸν] = ἐξόν ἐστιν or ἔξεστιν. It is not the classical accusative absolute, a usage which had by now been replaced by the genitive. Cf. ἃ οὐκ ἐξὸν ἀνθρώπῳ λαλῆσαι, 2 Cor. xii. 4 ; also ἐξὸν ἦν, Mt. xii. 4 ; ἦν ἐξόν, Esth. iv. 2.

πατριάρχου] 'head of a family'. This word seems to have been coined for LXX, on the analogy of such Hebrew terms as *rōsh hā-'ābōth* (lit., ' head of the fathers '). The title in NT is usually restricted to Abraham, Isaac, Jacob and Jacob's twelve sons: cf. vii. 8 f.; Heb. vii. 4.

τὸ μνῆμα αὐτοῦ] Cf. Neh. iii. 16; Jos. *BJ* i. 2. 5; *Ant.* vii. 15. 3; xiii. 8. 4; xvi. 7. 1. It lay to the south of the city, not far from Siloam.

ii. 30

ὅρκῳ ὤμοσεν κ.τ.λ.] An allusion to Ps. cxxxii. 11 (LXX cxxxi.),

ὤμοσεν Κύριος τῷ Δαυεὶδ ἀλήθειαν, καὶ οὐ μὴ ἀθετήσει αὐτήν·
Ἐκ καρποῦ τῆς κοιλίας σου θήσομαι ἐπὶ τὸν θρόνον σου.

ὅρκῳ ὤμοσεν] For the construction see on *ver.* 17 and iv. 17. The LXX, following the Heb., emphasizes ὤμοσεν by adding ἀλήθειαν, but here it is emphasized by the addition of ὅρκῳ.

ἐκ καρποῦ] Partitive use of ἐκ (cf. similar use of ἀπό, *ver.* 17). The phrase ἐκ καρποῦ is treated as a noun and made the object of καθίσαι, ' God had sworn to him with an oath to set *of the fruit of his loins* (i.e. one of his descendants) upon his throne'. The unusual construction gave rise to various expansions, e.g. D has ἐκ καρποῦ τῆς καρδίας αὐτοῦ κατὰ σάρκα ἀναστῆσαι τὸν χριστὸν καὶ καθίσαι κ.τ.λ. A similar expansion in byz is represented by AV. καρδίας in D may be a corruption of an original δ reading κοιλίας, an assimilation to LXX. But C. C. Torrey supposes that ὀσφύος was targumed as *beṭen*, which was then re-translated as καρδίας. For κατὰ σάρκα cf. Rom. i. 3; ix. 5, with reference to Christ.

καθίσαι] Should be taken as transitive, ' to set ', with ἐκ καρποῦ as the object. It is grammatically possible to take it as intransitive, ' to sit ', with ἐκ καρποῦ as subject, but the transitive use agrees better with θήσομαι of LXX.

ii. 31

προιδὼν] See on προορώμην, *ver.* 25.

ii. 32

τοῦτον τὸν Ἰησοῦν] Note the emphatic position, as in *vv.* 22 f., 36; iv. 10, etc.

ἀνέστησεν ὁ θεός] Cf. *ver.* 24, and references there. As in *ver.* 24, ἀνέστησεν is to be taken here of the Resurrection. For another sense, see on iii. 22, 26; xiii. 33.

οὗ] Neuter, ' of which fact ', rather than masculine, ' whose '. The former suits the emphasis of the sentence better; and cf. i. 22, μάρτυρα τῆς ἀναστάσεως αὐτοῦ. Cf. iii. 15.

ii. 33

τῇ δεξιᾷ] 'by the right hand': instrumental dative: cf. Ps. cxviii. 16 (LXX cxvii), *δεξιὰ Κυρίου ὕψωσέν με*. The expression is not unconnected, however, verbally at least, with *ἐκ δεξιῶν μου*, quoted in *ver.* 34. Cf. *ἐν δεξιᾷ*, Heb. xii. 2.

τήν τε ἐπαγγελίαν τοῦ πνεύματος τοῦ ἁγίου λαβὼν παρὰ τοῦ πατρὸς] Cf. i. 4. For Christ's mediation in the giving of the Spirit to men by the Father, cf. Jn. xiv. 16, 26; xvi. 7. For the sense cf. Ps. lxviii. 18 (LXX lxvii. 19), *ἀναβὰς εἰς ὕψος . . . ἔλαβες δόματα*.

τοῦτο] Some forms of δ (Iren.lat hcl) have *τοῦτο τὸ δῶρον*, which gives the proper sense of *τοῦτο*. Torrey would render, 'hath poured it out, as you have both seen and heard', taking *ὅ* to represent Aram. *dī*, which might also mean 'as'.

The story of the humiliation needed no proof, as everyone knew of the trial and crucifixion; the resurrection and exaltation are here proved from Scripture, as they are later to be proved by the enduring activity of Jesus (iii. 6; iv. 10, etc.), by the witnessing of His followers (iv. 20, etc.), and by the testimony of the Holy Spirit (v. 32).

ii. 34

οὐ γὰρ Δαυεὶδ ἀνέβη] 'For it was not David that ascended'; the words of Ps. cx. 1, therefore, cannot refer to him. While the emphasis of this clause is not such as explicitly to deny that the soul of David was in heaven at the time of speaking, the wording would have been different had Peter believed that David and the other saints of pre-Christian times were transferred from Hades to heaven at the time of Christ's resurrection or ascension, as some have taught. Cf. Calvin, *Institutio* ii. 16. 8-12; Pearson *On the Creed*, Article V. Eph. iv. 8 (quotation from Ps. lxviii. 19) has no bearing on such a transference.

εἶπεν Κύριος τῷ κυρίῳ μου κ.τ.λ.] Ps. cx. 1 (LXX cix.). The first *Κύριος* represents Heb. *Yahweh*, the second *'ādōn*. Notice that when anarthrous *Κύριος* represents *Yahweh*, WH print it with a capital, otherwise *κύριος* has a small initial. Our Lord's use of this Psalm (Mt. xxii. 42 ff. = Mk. xii. 35 ff. = Lk. xx. 41 ff.) shows that in His time the Messianic reference of the Psalm was generally accepted, as it was also by some later Rabbis. Cf. its use in 1 Cor. xv. 25; Heb. i. 13, and especially the application of its fourth verse in Heb. v. 6 ff. The argument is similar to that based on Ps. xvi. above; as the words cannot apply to David, they must apply to the Messiah; Jesus did in fact ascend to heaven, and so satisfies the terms of the Scripture. And when once He has been proved to be Messiah (as in *vv.* 25 ff.), then all Messianic prophecies can be applied to Him.

ii. 36

πᾶς οἶκος Ἰσραήλ] The only NT occurrence of this expression (cf. Ezek. xxxvii. 11), which is common in Jewish prayers, e.g. in the *Qaddīsh* [1] (*bĕ-ḥayyē dī kol bēth Yisrā'ēl*, 'during the life of all the house of Israel').

καὶ κύριον αὐτὸν καὶ χριστὸν ἐποίησεν ὁ θεός, κ.τ.λ.] The foundation truth on which the Church was built. The first Christian sermon culminates in the first Christian 'creed': cf. *κύριος Ἰησοῦς* (Rom. x. 9; 1 Cor. xii. 3); *κύριος Ἰησοῦς Χριστός* (Phil. ii. 11). Cf. *χριστὸς κύριος* in Lk. ii. 11, and *βασιλεὺς αὐτῶν χριστὸς κύριος*, of the Messianic Age, in Ps. Sol. xvii. 36. The Scriptures quoted prove Jesus to be the Messiah; Ps. cx. vindicates His right to the title Lord in the sense of *'ādōn*, but *κύριος* as henceforth used of Him has a higher dignity even than this; it represents the Ineffable Name of God (cf. *ver.* 21). This title as given to Jesus depends for its fullest significance on the Resurrection: cf. Rom. x. 9 (note the parallelism of the two conditional clauses); xiv. 9; Phil. ii. 9 (where the *ὄνομα τὸ ὑπὲρ πᾶν ὄνομα* is probably *κύριος*). The Aram. equivalent of *κύριος* was *mar* (cf. *māranā*, 'our Lord', in 1 Cor. xvi. 22); the Aram. equivalent of *χριστός* ('anointed') was *Mĕshīḥā*, Hellenized as *Μεσσίας*. The Messiahship of Jesus was made public in a sense at His baptism (cf. x. 38, *ἔχρισεν*), but confirmed by the Resurrection.

In this and other sermons in the earlier part of Ac. we should observe the absence of the Pauline emphasis on the pre-existence of Jesus, on His unique relation to the Father, on His sin-bearing, on justification (contrast Paul's own words in xiii. 39), on the moral and spiritual power of the Resurrection, on the sanctifying influence of the Holy Spirit. What we do find is Christian preaching of an obviously primitive character, against the background of Jewish Messianic expectation. That this should be so in a report written by a Gentile, and by one who came so much under Paul's influence as Luke did, is a compelling token of the genuineness of these speeches.

τοῦτον τὸν Ἰησοῦν ὃν ὑμεῖς ἐσταυρώσατε] Note the emphasis on *τοῦτον τὸν Ἰησοῦν*, as in *ver.* 32, and the contrast between God's treatment of Him and theirs; *ὃν ὑμεῖς ἐσταυρώσατε*, forming the peroration of the address, was well calculated to increase their sense of guilt and provoke their repentant outcry. Cf. iv. 10.

[1] A brief Aram. prayer which recurs in the synagogue service: cf. Singer, *Authorised Daily Prayer Book*, p. 37. It probably arose out of the ascription at the end of the sermon.

(d) Call to Repentance, ii. 37-40

'Ακούσαντες δὲ κατενύγησαν τὴν καρδίαν, εἶπάν τε πρὸς τὸν 37
Πέτρον καὶ τοὺς λοιποὺς ἀποστόλους Τί ποιήσωμεν, ἄνδρες ἀδελφοί;
Πέτρος δὲ πρὸς αὐτούς Μετανοήσατε, καὶ βαπτισθήτω ἕκαστος 38
ὑμῶν ἐν τῷ ὀνόματι 'Ιησοῦ Χριστοῦ εἰς ἄφεσιν τῶν ἁμαρτιῶν ὑμῶν,
καὶ λήμψεσθε τὴν δωρεὰν τοῦ ἁγίου πνεύματος· ὑμῖν γάρ ἐστιν ἡ ἐπαγ- 39
γελία καὶ τοῖς τέκνοις ὑμῶν καὶ πᾶσι τοῖς εἰς μακρὰν ὅσους ἂν προσ-
καλέσηται Κύριος ὁ θεὸς ἡμῶν. ἑτέροις τε λόγοις πλείοσιν διεμαρτύ- 40
ρατο, καὶ παρεκάλει αὐτοὺς λέγων Σώθητε ἀπὸ τῆς γενεᾶς τῆς σκολιᾶς
ταύτης.

ii. 37

κατενύγησαν τὴν καρδίαν] Cf. Ps. cix. 16 (LXX cviii), *κατανενυγμένον τῇ καρδίᾳ*. The phrase is used here of that conviction of guilt which leads to repentance. Contrast *διεπρίοντο* in v. 33; vii. 54.

εἶπάν τε] According to Blass, *τε* denotes a closer affinity between the connected clauses than *καί* or *δέ*: 'and so they said'.

λοιπούς] om. D.

Τί ποιήσωμεν] Deliberative subjunctive: 'what are we to do?' D has *Τί οὖν ποιήσομεν*, and after *ἄνδρες ἀδελφοί* D hcl.mg (representing δ) add *ὑποδείξατε ἡμῖν*.

ii. 38

Πέτρος δὲ πρὸς αὐτούς] B has no verb of saying, understanding *εἶπεν* from *εἶπαν* in *ver*. 37. ℵ A C D 81 have *φησιν* after *μετανοήσατε*, while byz has *ἔφη*.

Μετανοήσατε] The call to repentance had been previously sounded by John the Baptist (Mt. iii. 2) and by our Lord (Mt. iv. 17, etc.). It was an essential element in the announcing of the Good News: cf. iii. 19; viii. 22; xvii. 30; xx. 21; xxvi. 20. Repentance (*μετάνοια*, 'change of mind') involves a turning with contrition from sin to God; the repentant sinner is in the proper condition to accept the divine forgiveness. In LXX *μετανοέω* almost always represents Heb. *nāḥam* in the Niphal form, lit. 'to comfort oneself'. See further on iii. 19.

βαπτισθήτω] Baptism as an outward sign of repentance and remission of sins was no new thing in Judaism, and the command would occasion no undue surprise. John the Baptist came *κηρύσσων βάπτισμα μετανοίας εἰς ἄφεσιν ἁμαρτιῶν* (Mk. i. 4). The main difference between John's baptism (for which cf. xviii. 25; xix. 3 f.) and that on the day of Pentecost was that the latter was associated with the name of Jesus and the gift of the Spirit. For the fuller significance of Christian baptism cf. Rom. vi. 3 ff. (with Sanday and Headlam's notes *ad loc.*). Here we have a more primitive conception, a further testimony to the truth of the narrative.[1]

ἐν τῷ ὀνόματι Ἰησοῦ Χριστοῦ] So x. 48. The phrase is probably to be distinguished from *εἰς τὸ ὄνομα τοῦ κυρίου Ἰησοῦ* in viii. 16; xix. 5 (*q.v.*). Here *ἐν* is to be understood instrumentally; the name of Jesus Christ is an 'accompanying circumstance' of the baptism. According to xxii. 16 the person baptized called at his baptism on the name of Jesus (cf. *ver.* 21 above), probably by way of confessing faith in Him. Cf. J. A. Robinson's note on Eph. v. 26, *ἐν ῥήματι*. The baptism, indeed, was doubly associated 'with the name of Jesus Christ', as the baptizer also named it over the person baptized (cf. xv. 17; Jas. ii. 7). For *ἐν*, א A 81 byz have *ἐπί*. *ἐπὶ τῷ ὀνόματί τινος* means 'on the authority of someone' (cf. Lk. xxiv. 47).

Ἰησοῦ Χριστοῦ] δ prefixes *κυρίου*, as in v. 42; x. 48; for similar amplification see on i. 21; vii. 55; xiii. 33. *Χριστοῦ* must be regarded not as a personal name, but as a title, as regularly in Ac.; perhaps we should translate 'Jesus the Messiah' or 'Jesus as Messiah', to bring this out.

εἰς ἄφεσιν τῶν ἁμαρτιῶν ὑμῶν] To be taken with *μετανοήσατε* as well as with *βαπτισθήτω*. Cf. iii. 19; v. 31; Lk. xxiv. 47.

δωρεὰν] 'free gift': used of the Holy Spirit in viii. 20; x. 45; xi. 17; cf. Jn. iv. 10, where the *ὕδωρ ζῶν*, the 'living water', is an emblem of the Spirit (as in Jn. vii. 37 ff.).

ii. 39

ὑμῖν . . . ὑμῶν] *ἡμῖν . . . ἡμῶν* D.

καὶ τοῖς τέκνοις ὑμῶν] The promise of the 'covenant of grace' is not only to the present generation but also to those yet to come: cf. the promises to Noah (Gen. ix. 9), to Abraham (Gen. xiii. 15; xvii. 7 ff.; Gal. iii. 16), and to David (Ps. xviii. 50; lxxxix. 34 ff.; cxxxii. 11 f.).

καὶ πᾶσι τοῖς εἰς μακρὰν κ.τ.λ.] The promise is not only to those distant in time but to those in distant places as well, even—as it

[1] *Note on Baptism in Ac.* Baptism in water (such as John's) is distinguished from baptism with the Holy Spirit (i. 5, etc.). Those who receive the latter, however, may also be baptized in water (cf. xi. 16 with x. 47); and there is one example of people who had previously received John's baptism receiving Christian baptism as a preliminary to receiving the Spirit (xix. 3 ff.). John's was a baptism of repentance (xiii. 24; xix. 4), as was also Christian baptism (ii. 38), but as John's pointed forward to Jesus (xix. 4), it became obsolete when He came. Christian baptism followed faith in the Lord Jesus (xvi. 31 ff.); it was associated with His name (ii. 38; viii. 16, etc.), which was invoked by the person baptized (xxii. 16); it signified the remission (ii. 38) or washing away of sins (xxii. 16); sometimes it preceded (ii. 38; viii. 15 ff.; xix. 5), sometimes followed (x. 47 f.) the receiving of the Spirit.

soon appeared—to Gentiles. Two OT passages are here alluded to: Isa. lvii. 19 (*εἰρήνην ἐπ' εἰρήνην τοῖς μακρὰν καὶ τοῖς ἐγγὺς οὖσιν*), and Joel ii. 32, following the words quoted in *vv.* 17 ff. (*καὶ εὐαγγελιζόμενοι, οὓς Κύριος προσκέκληται*). Note the conjunction of men's calling on the Lord with His calling them.

ii. 40

διεμαρτύρατο] 'testified by argument': cf. viii. 25; x. 42; xviii. 5; xx. 21, 23, 24; xxiii. 11; xxviii. 23; Lk. xvi. 28. The Lukan writings account for 10 out of its 15 NT occurrences. Cf. Demosthenes, *Callicles* iv., *διεμαρτύρατο*, 'formally protested'.

Σωθῆτε ἀπὸ τῆς γενεᾶς τῆς σκολιᾶς ταύτης] Cf. Dt. xxxii. 5; Ps. lxxviii. 8 (LXX lxxvii.); Phil. ii. 15 for the epithet. For other epithets applied to that generation cf. Mt. xvi. 4 (*γενεὰ πονηρὰ καὶ μοιχαλίς*); xvii. 17 (*γενεὰ ἄπιστος καὶ διεστραμμένη*), etc. By its rejection of the Messiah (cf. Lk. xvii. 25), it had incurred inevitable judgment (cf. Mt. xxiii. 36; Lk. xi. 50 f.); the only way to escape the coming judgment was to accept the Good News. With *σωθῆτε* cf. *σωθήσεται*, quoted from Joel in *ver.* 21. In both places the word applies to a 'remnant' (cf. Joel ii. 32) which would be delivered from the judgment destined to overtake the mass of the people. Early Christian preaching, like much of the teaching of our Lord, is characterized by a prominent eschatological element (cf. iii. 19 ff.).

(e) The First Christian Church, ii. 41-47

Οἱ μὲν οὖν ἀποδεξάμενοι τὸν λόγον αὐτοῦ ἐβαπτίσθησαν, καὶ προσ- 41
ετέθησαν ἐν τῇ ἡμέρᾳ ἐκείνῃ ψυχαὶ ὡσεὶ τρισχίλιαι. ἦσαν δὲ προσ- 42
καρτεροῦντες τῇ διδαχῇ τῶν ἀποστόλων καὶ τῇ κοινωνίᾳ, τῇ κλάσει
τοῦ ἄρτου καὶ ταῖς προσευχαῖς. Ἐγίνετο δὲ πάσῃ ψυχῇ φόβος, πολλὰ 43
δὲ τέρατα καὶ σημεῖα διὰ τῶν ἀποστόλων ἐγίνετο. πάντες δὲ οἱ 44
πιστεύσαντες ἐπὶ τὸ αὐτὸ εἶχον ἅπαντα κοινά, καὶ τὰ κτήματα καὶ τὰς 45
ὑπάρξεις ἐπίπρασκον καὶ διεμέριζον αὐτὰ πᾶσιν καθότι ἄν τις χρείαν
εἶχεν· καθ' ἡμέραν τε προσκαρτεροῦντες ὁμοθυμαδὸν ἐν τῷ ἱερῷ, 46
κλῶντές τε κατ' οἶκον ἄρτον, μετελάμβανον τροφῆς ἐν ἀγαλλιάσει καὶ
ἀφελότητι καρδίας, αἰνοῦντες τὸν θεὸν καὶ ἔχοντες χάριν πρὸς ὅλον 47
τὸν λαόν. ὁ δὲ κύριος προσετίθει τοὺς σωζομένους καθ' ἡμέραν ἐπὶ
τὸ αὐτό.

ii. 41

Οἱ μὲν οὖν] Commencing a new paragraph: 'So then, those (who welcomed his word were baptized)'. See on i. 6.

ψυχαὶ] 'persons', as freq. in LXX, rendering Heb. *nephesh*. Cf. *ver.* 43; iii. 23; vii. 14; xxvii. 37.

ii. 42

ἦσαν δὲ προσκαρτεροῦντες] For the construction see on i. 10; cf. *ἦσαν προσκαρτεροῦντες*, i. 14.

τῇ διδαχῇ τῶν ἀποστόλων] δ adds *ἐν Ἰερουσαλήμ*. For NT testimony to the authority of apostolic teaching cf. 1 Cor. xii. 28; xiv. 37; Eph. ii. 20; iii. 5. The apostles' teaching was authoritative because it was delivered as the teaching of the Lord *through* the apostles; cf. the title of the *Didaché*.

τῇ κοινωνίᾳ] For the practical force of the word *κοινωνία* cf. its use in Rom. xv. 26; Heb. xiii. 16. Here it may refer to the practice of *vv.* 44 f. below, but not exclusively so, as 'the breaking of the bread and the prayers' are also to be understood as expressions of this 'fellowship'.

τῇ κλάσει τοῦ ἄρτου] The phrase is found elsewhere only in Lk. xxiv. 35; but cf. *ver.* 46; xx. 7. 11; xxvii. 35; Mt. xxvi. 26; Mk. xiv. 22; Lk. xxii. 19; xxiv. 30; 1 Cor. x. 16; xi. 24 for *κλάω ἄρτον*. Heb. *pāras* and Aram. *pĕras* ('to break') were used absolutely in the special sense of breaking bread and saying grace (cf. Jastrow's Dictionary *s.v.*). Is the reference here to the Eucharist, to an Agape, or to an ordinary meal? Perhaps to all three, if we are to gather from *ver.* 46 that they took the principal meal of the day in each other's houses, observing the Lord's Supper each time they did so. R. Otto (*The Kingdom of God and the Son of Man*, pp. 312 ff.) argues rightly that the Lord's Supper is referred to; while a meal usually followed, the emphasis on the act of breaking the bread shows this 'circumstance wholly trivial in itself' to be 'the significant element of the celebration. . . . But it could only be significant when it was a signum, viz. of Christ's being broken in death'.

ταῖς προσευχαῖς] 'in the prayers' (another expression of the fellowship). Prayers in their own meetings are primarily meant, but the public Jewish prayers are not excluded (cf. iii. 1).

ii. 43

ἐγίνετο δὲ πάσῃ ψυχῇ φόβος] Cf. v. 5, 11. The imperfect denotes that the fear which fell on all who heard the words of Peter was no momentary panic, but continued to be a feature of the days that followed.

τέρατα καὶ σημεῖα] See on *ver.* 22. The collocation of the two words is common in LXX and NT (cf. also *ver.* 19; iv. 30; v. 12; vi. 8; vii. 36; xiv. 3; xv. 12), and is found also in pagan writers. A sample of these 'wonders and signs' is given in ch. iii. The apostles' miracles, like those of their Lord, were 'signs' of the advent of the Messianic Age.

διὰ τῶν ἀποστόλων ἐγίνετο] ℵ A C minn vg boh add *ἐν Ἰερουσαλήμ· φόβος τε ἦν μέγας ἐπὶ πάντας*. Pesh adds *ἐν Ἰερουσαλήμ* only. The shorter text is found in BD 81 byz e g p.

ii. 44

ἐπὶ τὸ αὐτό] See on i. 15 for the special sense of this phrase: 'together in Christian fellowship'. They may have been recognized as a separate synagogue (Aram. *kĕnishtā*, Heb. *kĕnēseth*) within the Jewish community, the 'Synagogue of the Nazarenes' (see on v. 11; vi. 9; xxiv. 5).

εἶχον ἅπαντα κοινά] Further details of this communal life are given in iv. 32 ff.

ii. 45

καὶ τὰ κτήματα καὶ τὰς ὑπάρξεις] D imports the construction of iv. 34, *καὶ ὅσοι κτήματα εἶχον ἢ ὑπάρξεις*. If a distinction is to be made between *κτήματα* and *ὑπάρξεις*, they probably refer to real and personal property respectively. See on v. 1.

ἐπίπρασκον καὶ διεμέριζον αὐτά] Imperfect, indicating a regular practice: cf. iv. 34 f. δ adds *καθ' ἡμέραν*, from *ver.* 46: cf. also vi. 1, *ἐν τῇ διακονίᾳ τῇ καθημερινῇ*.

καθότι ἄν τις χρείαν εἶχεν] Iterative *ἄν* with imperfect, as in iv. 35 (same phrase) and 1 Cor. xii. 2 (*ὡς ἂν ἤγεσθε*).

ii. 46

καθ' ἡμέραν] These words apply to the whole sentence as far as *πρὸς ὅλον τὸν λαόν* (*ver.* 47).

ἐν τῷ ἱερῷ] Cf. Lk. xxiv. 53. Their favourite meeting-place in the Temple was Solomon's colonnade (v. 12).

κλῶντές τε κατ' οἶκον ἄρτον] This could not conveniently be done in the Temple precincts, so it took place 'by households' (a rendering supported in the papyri). AV 'from house to house', though not a literal translation, may give the sense fairly well. For this 'breaking bread' see on *ver.* 42. It was a daily occurrence. Cf. also 1 Cor. x. 16 ff.; xi. 20 ff.

ἀφελότητι καρδίας] Probably means 'generosity'; this is the only NT occurrence of *ἀφελότης*, which occurs in Vettius Valens[1] 240. 15, *ὑπ' ἀφελότητος καὶ ἀδιοικήσεως προδεδομένος* ('betrayed by simplicity and lack of practical capacity'). Cf. Eph. vi. 5; Col. iii. 22; 1 Chr. xxix. 17; Wisd. i. 1 for *ἁπλότης καρδίας* in this sense.

[1] For a supplement to the references to Vettius Valens given *passim* in MM, recourse should be had to a valuable article, 'Vettius Valens and the New Testament', in *EQ* ii. (1930), pp. 389 ff., by E. K. Simpson, to which I have been indebted in the course of this work.

ii. 47

ἔχοντες χάριν πρὸς ὅλον τὸν λαόν] 'enjoying all the people's favour'; cf. v. 13. The stricter Jewish Christians of Jerusalem were held in general respect for long (generally speaking, until the rising of A.D. 132); cf. the account by Hegesippus of James the Just, quoted in Euseb. *HE* ii. 23. As regularly in LXX and NT, *λαός* is used of the people of Israel. D has *τὸν κόσμον*, which Nestle thought was due to a confusion between Aram. *'ālmā*, 'the world', and *'ammā*, 'the people'; but Torrey (*DPC*, p. 145) points out that in popular Aram. *kūlē 'ālmā*, 'all the world', is used like Fr. *tout le monde* in the sense of 'everybody'.

ὁ δὲ κύριος προσετίθει κ.τ.λ.] The Lord Himself reserves the prerogative of adding new members to His community; the duty of believers is to receive those whom Christ has received (Rom. xv. 7).

τοὺς σωζομένους] The force of the pres. ptc. here is probably iterative, i.e. they were added to the community as they were saved. But we might almost translate *τοὺς σωζομένους* by 'the remnant', in view of the force of the verb in *vv.* 21, 40 (see on *ver.* 40). The 'remnant' of the old Israel also formed the nucleus of the new Israel.

ἐπὶ τὸ αὐτό] D adds *ἐν τῇ ἐκκλησίᾳ*, probably a gloss explaining *ἐπὶ τὸ αὐτό* (see on *ver.* 44 and i. 15). Torrey (*CDA*, pp. 10 ff.) points out that *laḥdā*, the regular Aram. equivalent of *ἐπὶ τὸ αὐτό* meant also 'exceedingly' (*σφόδρα*) in Judaean Aram., and suggests that the latter is the sense intended here. But *ἐπὶ τὸ αὐτό* in the sense already mentioned ('in church fellowship') makes good sense here.

3. A Miracle and its Consequences, iii. 1–iv. 31.

(a) Healing of the Lame Man, iii. 1-10

Πέτρος δὲ καὶ Ἰωάνης ἀνέβαινον εἰς τὸ ἱερὸν ἐπὶ τὴν ὥραν τῆς 1
προσευχῆς τὴν ἐνάτην, καί τις ἀνὴρ χωλὸς ἐκ κοιλίας μητρὸς αὐτοῦ 2
ὑπάρχων ἐβαστάζετο, ὃν ἐτίθουν καθ' ἡμέραν πρὸς τὴν θύραν τοῦ ἱεροῦ
τὴν λεγομένην Ὡραίαν τοῦ αἰτεῖν ἐλεημοσύνην παρὰ τῶν εἰσπορευομένων
εἰς τὸ ἱερόν, ὃς ἰδὼν Πέτρον καὶ Ἰωάνην μέλλοντας εἰσιέναι εἰς τὸ 3
ἱερὸν ἠρώτα ἐλεημοσύνην λαβεῖν. ἀτενίσας δὲ Πέτρος εἰς αὐτὸν 4
σὺν τῷ Ἰωάνῃ εἶπεν Βλέψον εἰς ἡμᾶς. ὁ δὲ ἐπεῖχεν αὐτοῖς προσ- 5
δοκῶν τι παρ' αὐτῶν λαβεῖν. εἶπεν δὲ Πέτρος Ἀργύριον καὶ χρυσίον 6
οὐχ ὑπάρχει μοι, ὃ δὲ ἔχω τοῦτό σοι δίδωμι· ἐν τῷ ὀνόματι Ἰησοῦ
Χριστοῦ τοῦ Ναζωραίου περιπάτει. καὶ πιάσας αὐτὸν τῆς δεξιᾶς 7
χειρὸς ἤγειρεν αὐτόν· παραχρῆμα δὲ ἐστερεώθησαν αἱ βάσεις αὐτοῦ
καὶ τὰ σφυδρά, καὶ ἐξαλλόμενος ἔστη καὶ περιεπάτει, καὶ εἰσῆλθεν 8

σὺν αὐτοῖς εἰς τὸ ἱερὸν περιπατῶν καὶ ἁλλόμενος καὶ αἰνῶν τὸν θεόν. 9
καὶ εἶδεν πᾶς ὁ λαὸς αὐτὸν περιπατοῦντα καὶ αἰνοῦντα τὸν θεόν, ἐπε- 10
γίνωσκον δὲ αὐτὸν ὅτι οὗτος ἦν ὁ πρὸς τὴν ἐλεημοσύνην καθήμενος
ἐπὶ τῇ ῾Ωραίᾳ Πύλῃ τοῦ ἱεροῦ, καὶ ἐπλήσθησαν θάμβους καὶ ἐκστάσεως
ἐπὶ τῷ συμβεβηκότι αὐτῷ.

We are now given a sample of the 'many wonders and signs' of ii. 43.

iii. 1

Πέτρος δὲ καὶ 'Ιωάνης] The leaders of the Twelve. This John is certainly John the son of Zebedee. These two, along with James the brother of John, had formed an inner circle admitted to special intimacy with the Lord, e.g. on the Mount of Transfiguration (Mk. ix. 2) and in Gethsemane (Mk. xiv. 33). Peter and John are again found together in viii. 14 (cf. also Lk. xxii. 8; Gal. ii. 9).

ἀνέβαινον] MM quote papyrus parallels for *ἀναβαίνω* of going up to a temple: cf. Lk. xviii. 10; Jn. vii. 14. The word would be appropriate in any case because of the situation of the Temple in Jerusalem. The imperfect implies that they 'were going up' when the incident occurred.

εἰς τὸ ἱερὸν] *ἱερόν* is used of the entire edifice; *ναός* of the actual sanctuary ('the Holy Place'), to which the priests alone had access. On the more exact sense of *εἰς τὸ ἱερόν* see on *ver.* 2.

ἐπὶ τὴν ὥραν τῆς προσευχῆς τὴν ἐνάτην] The stated times for prayer were (1) early morning, the time of the morning sacrifice; (2) the ninth hour (about 3 p.m.), the time of the evening oblation; (3) at sunset (cf. Schürer, II. i. 290 f.). Josephus (*Ant.* xiv. 4. 3) says that the sacrifices were offered *δὶς τῆς ἡμέρας, πρωΐ τε καὶ περὶ τὴν ἐνάτην ὥραν*. D adds *τὸ δειλινόν* before *ἐπὶ τὴν ὥραν*, indicating that it was the hour of the evening oblation. Cf. Ex. xxix. 39 ff.; Lev. vi. 20 ff., etc.

iii. 2

χωλὸς ἐκ κοιλίας μητρὸς αὐτοῦ] Cf. *ἀπὸ κοιλίας μητρός μου*, Judg. xvi. 17; *ἐκ κοιλίας μητρός μου*, Ps. xxii. 10 (xxi. 11 LXX), and similar OT phrases. In Luke's writings *κοιλία* always means 'womb', as also in Mt. xix. 12; Jn. iii. 4; Gal. i. 15. Elsewhere in NT it is used of the digestive organs. The note of the duration of the malady is characteristic of Luke (cf. ix. 33; xiv. 8; Lk. xiii. 11), but does not of itself indicate medical authorship; similar notes are given in Mk. v. 25; ix. 21; Jn. v. 5; ix. 1.

ὑπάρχων] If we press the full meaning of this verb, it means that he was already lame when this incident took place; as this is obvious in any case, we should regard *ὑπάρχων* as the equivalent of *ὤν*.

ἐτίθουν] Classical *ἐτίθεσαν*. The ending *-ουν* is borrowed from the verbs in *-έω*. Cf. iv. 35. The 3 plur. act. is here used impersonally for the 3 sing. pass., a usage common in Heb. and Aram., but unusual in Gk. apart from *λέγουσι*, *φασί*, 'they say'.

πρὸς τὴν θύραν τοῦ ἱεροῦ τὴν λεγομένην Ὡραίαν] The proper identification of this gate is a matter of some dispute, but the weight of available evidence is in favour of identifying it with the Nicanor Gate (as it is called in the Mishna, *Middoth* ii. 3), leading from the Court of the Gentiles into the Women's Court, and with the gate of Corinthian bronze described by Josephus (*BJ* v. 5. 3) as 'far exceeding in value those plated with silver and set in gold'.

τοῦ αἰτεῖν] This use of *τοῦ* with infin. to express purpose is classical enough, but it is more frequent in NT than in classical writers, especially in the writings of Luke and Paul: see on *τοῦ περιπατεῖν*, *ver.* 12.

παρὰ τῶν εἰσπορευομένων εἰς τὸ ἱερόν] The outer court had been enclosed by Herod, and was not equal in sacredness to the rest of the Temple buildings. Gentiles might enter it, but they were strictly debarred from penetrating beyond it (see on xxi. 28). Hence this outer area, called in the Mishna 'the mountain of the house', came to be known as the Court of the Gentiles. Thus Jewish worshippers might well regard themselves as not entering the *ἱερόν* proper until they had passed from this court to the inner courts, through the Nicanor Gate or any other of the nine 'gates of the sanctuary'.

iii. 3

ἠρώτα ἐλεημοσύνην λαβεῖν] The imperfect *ἠρώτα* suggests the reiterated appeal of beggars. For the infin. *λαβεῖν* after *ἠρώτα* cf. *ᾐτήσατο εὑρεῖν*, vii. 46; also *αἰτῶν λαβεῖν*, Aristophanes, *Plutus* 240.

iii. 4

ἀτενίσας] See on i. 10. D has *ἐμβλέψας*, but adds *ἀτενίσας τοῖς ὀφθαλμοῖς αὐτοῦ* in *ver.* 3, has *ἀτένισον* for *βλέψον* in *ver.* 4, and continues (*ver.* 5), *ὁ δὲ ἀτενίσας αὐτοῖς προσδοκῶν τι λαβεῖν παρ' αὐτῶν*—obviously a corrupt text, followed as it is by *εἶπεν δὲ ὁ Πέτρος* at the beginning of *ver.* 6.

iii. 5

ἐπεῖχεν] Sc. *τὸν νοῦν* or *τοὺς ὀφθαλμούς*. Cf. 1 Tim. iv. 16; Job xxx. 26; Sir. xxxiv. 2; 2 Macc. ix. 25.

iii. 6

οὐχ ὑπάρχει μοι] We can take *ὑπάρχω* in its full sense here, of what one has in store : ' I do not possess '.

ἐν τῷ ὀνόματι] i.e. ' by the authority ', ' with the power '.

περιπάτει] Cf. Mk. ii. 9. The power by which Jesus had healed the paralytic was shown to be still operative in the healing of this lame man.

iii. 7

ἐστερεώθησαν] praef *ἐστάθη καὶ* D h (repr. δ). *στερεόω* ' was, in medical language, applied to the bones in particular ' (Hobart, p. 35 ; he quotes Hippocrates and Galen in confirmation).

βάσεις] Hobart (pp. 34 f.) quotes examples of this word from Hippocrates and Galen, and says, ' The words employed to describe the seat of the lameness tend to show that the writer was acquainted with medical phraseology, and had investigated the nature of the disease under which the man suffered '. The associations of *βάσις*, however, are literary rather than professional ; it seems to have been poetic in origin. Cf. Wisd. xiii. 18 (*τὸ μηδὲ βάσει χρῆσθαι δυνάμενον*) ; Plato, *Timaeus* 92*a* (*θεοῦ βάσεις ὑποτιθέντος πλείους τοῖς μᾶλλον ἄφροσιν*).

σφυδρά] Classical *σφυρά*. The form here can be paralleled only from Hesychius and *P Flor* 391. 53, 56. The word is used properly of the projecting ankle-bones, then of the ankles themselves. Hobart quotes Galen for its use. It is not a distinctively medical word, though its collocation with *βάσεις* may suggest medical finesse. On this verse and the following Harnack says, ' That which the physician observes during the months of the ordinary *gradual* cure of a lame man is here compressed into a moment ' (*LP* p. 191).

iii. 8

περιεπάτει] add *χαιρόμενος* D ; *g[audens] et exultans* h. δ probably had *χαίρ<ων καὶ ἀγαλλι>ώμενος*.

ἁλλόμενος] Cf. Isa. xxxv. 6, *τότε ἁλεῖται ὡς ἔλαφος χωλός*.

iii. 10

ἐπεγίνωσκον] *ἐπιγινώσκω* implies taking cognizance of a specific fact ; the force of *ἐπί* is ' directive ', not intensive (cf. J. A. Robinson on Eph., pp. 248 ff.) ; see also on iv. 13.

ὁ πρὸς τὴν ἐλεημοσύνην καθήμενος] ' he who used to sit for alms ' : the pres. ptc. has imperfect force.

ἐπὶ τῷ συμβεβηκότι] *ἐπὶ τῷ γεγενημένῳ* D.

(b) Peter's Address in Solomon's Colonnade, iii. 11-26

Κρατοῦντος δὲ αὐτοῦ τὸν Πέτρον καὶ τὸν Ἰωάνην συνέδραμεν 11
πᾶς ὁ λαὸς πρὸς αὐτοὺς ἐπὶ τῇ στοᾷ τῇ καλουμένῃ Σολομῶντος
ἔκθαμβοι. ἰδὼν δὲ ὁ Πέτρος ἀπεκρίνατο πρὸς τὸν λαόν Ἄνδρες 12
Ἰσραηλεῖται, τί θαυμάζετε ἐπὶ τούτῳ, ἢ ἡμῖν τί ἀτενίζετε ὡς ἰδίᾳ
δυνάμει ἢ εὐσεβείᾳ πεποιηκόσιν τοῦ περιπατεῖν αὐτόν; ὁ θεὸς Ἀβραὰμ 13
καὶ Ἰσαὰκ καὶ Ἰακώβ, ὁ θεὸς τῶν πατέρων ἡμῶν, ἐδόξασεν τὸν παῖδα
αὐτοῦ Ἰησοῦν, ὃν ὑμεῖς μὲν παρεδώκατε καὶ ἠρνήσασθε κατὰ πρόσωπον
Πειλάτου, κρίναντος ἐκείνου ἀπολύειν· ὑμεῖς δὲ τὸν ἅγιον καὶ δίκαιον 14
ἠρνήσασθε, καὶ ᾐτήσασθε ἄνδρα φονέα χαρισθῆναι ὑμῖν, τὸν δὲ ἀρχηγὸν 15
τῆς ζωῆς ἀπεκτείνατε, ὃν ὁ θεὸς ἤγειρεν ἐκ νεκρῶν, οὗ ἡμεῖς μάρτυρές
ἐσμεν. καὶ τῇ πίστει τοῦ ὀνόματος αὐτοῦ τοῦτον ὃν θεωρεῖτε καὶ 16
οἴδατε ἐστερέωσεν τὸ ὄνομα αὐτοῦ, καὶ ἡ πίστις ἡ δι' αὐτοῦ ἔδωκεν
αὐτῷ τὴν ὁλοκληρίαν ταύτην ἀπέναντι πάντων ὑμῶν. καὶ νῦν, ἀδελφοί, 17
οἶδα ὅτι κατὰ ἄγνοιαν ἐπράξατε, ὥσπερ καὶ οἱ ἄρχοντες ὑμῶν· ὁ δὲ 18
θεὸς ἃ προκατήγγειλεν διὰ στόματος πάντων τῶν προφητῶν παθεῖν
τὸν χριστὸν αὐτοῦ ἐπλήρωσεν οὕτως. μετανοήσατε οὖν καὶ ἐπι- 19
στρέψατε πρὸς τὸ ἐξαλιφθῆναι ὑμῶν τὰς ἁμαρτίας, ὅπως ἂν ἔλθωσιν
καιροὶ ἀναψύξεως ἀπὸ προσώπου τοῦ κυρίου καὶ ἀποστείλῃ τὸν 20
προκεχειρισμένον ὑμῖν χριστὸν Ἰησοῦν, ὃν δεῖ οὐρανὸν μὲν δέξασθαι 21
ἄχρι χρόνων ἀποκαταστάσεως πάντων ὧν ἐλάλησεν ὁ θεὸς διὰ στόματος
τῶν ἁγίων ἀπ' αἰῶνος αὐτοῦ προφητῶν. Μωυσῆς μὲν εἶπεν ὅτι 22
Προφήτην ὑμῖν ἀναστήσει Κύριος ὁ θεὸς ἐκ τῶν ἀδελφῶν ὑμῶν ὡς
ἐμέ· αὐτοῦ ἀκούσεσθε κατὰ πάντα ὅσα ἂν λαλήσῃ πρὸς ὑμᾶς. ἔσται 23
δὲ πᾶσα ψυχὴ ἥτις ἂν μὴ ἀκούσῃ τοῦ προφήτου ἐκείνου ἐξολεθρευ-
θήσεται ἐκ τοῦ λαοῦ. καὶ πάντες δὲ οἱ προφῆται ἀπὸ Σαμουὴλ καὶ 24
τῶν καθεξῆς ὅσοι ἐλάλησαν καὶ κατήγγειλαν τὰς ἡμέρας ταύτας.
ὑμεῖς ἐστὲ οἱ υἱοὶ τῶν προφητῶν καὶ τῆς διαθήκης ἧς ὁ θεὸς διέθετο 25
πρὸς τοὺς πατέρας ὑμῶν, λέγων πρὸς Ἀβραάμ Καὶ ἐν τῷ σπέρματί
σου εὐλογηθήσονται πᾶσαι αἱ πατριαὶ τῆς γῆς. ὑμῖν πρῶτον ἀναστήσας 26
ὁ θεὸς τὸν παῖδα αὐτοῦ ἀπέστειλεν αὐτὸν εὐλογοῦντα ὑμᾶς ἐν τῷ
ἀποστρέφειν ἕκαστον ἀπὸ τῶν πονηριῶν ὑμῶν.

iii. 11

Κρατοῦντος δὲ αὐτοῦ τὸν Πέτρον καὶ τὸν Ἰωάνην συνέδραμεν πᾶς ὁ λαὸς πρὸς αὐτοὺς ἐπὶ τῇ στοᾷ τῇ καλουμένῃ Σολομῶντος] D has *ἐκπορευομένου δὲ τοῦ Πέτρου καὶ Ἰωάνου συνεξεπορεύετο κρατῶν αὐτούς· οἱ δὲ θαμβηθέντες ἔστησαν ἐν τῇ στοᾷ ἡ καλουμένη Σολομῶνος.* Without regarding this as the original text, we may take it as a true account of what actually happened. δ frequently makes explicit what is implicit in β, as if the readers could not be trusted to draw the correct inference for themselves. The apostles and the healed man, after worshipping in the Temple, emerged (probably through the Beautiful Gate) into the Outer Court, and made their way to its eastern side, the man still shouting his praise. The populace gathered to watch them as they approached Solomon's colonnade, which ran the whole length of the east side of the Outer Court. Solomon's colonnade, in which Jesus walked at the Feast of the Dedication, perhaps less than a year previously (Jn. x. 23), became the regular meeting-place of the Jerusalem Christians (v. 12). The breach of concord in D, *τῇ στοᾷ ἡ καλουμένη*, is similar to what we find regularly in the Apocalypse (e.g. *τῆς καινῆς Ἰερουσαλήμ, ἡ καταβαίνουσα*, Rev. iii. 12).[1]

iii. 12

Ἄνδρες Ἰσραηλεῖται] So ii. 22; cf. ii. 14 and see on i. 11.

ἀτενίζετε] See on i. 10.

εὐσεβείᾳ] For this, the reading of the Gk. MSS, *ἐξουσίᾳ* is the reading of h p[2] vg.codd pesh arm Chrys al. Iren.lat. omits *ἢ εὐσεβείᾳ*.

ὡς . . . πεποιηκόσιν] For *ὡς* with ptc. meaning 'as though', cf. xxiii. 15, 20; xxvii. 30.

τοῦ περιπατεῖν αὐτόν] Cf. *τοῦ αἰτεῖν*, *ver.* 2. The final use of *τοῦ* with infin. is characteristic of Lk.-Ac. Cf. ix. 15; x. 25; xiv. 18; xv. 20; xx. 3, 27; xxvii. 1; Lk. xvii. 1; xxi. 22. Paul is the only other NT writer who makes any marked use of this construction.

iii. 13

ὁ θεὸς Ἀβραὰμ καὶ Ἰσαὰκ καὶ Ἰακώβ, ὁ θεὸς τῶν πατέρων ἡμῶν] This formula, going back to Ex. iii. 6 (*ἐγώ εἰμι ὁ θεὸς τοῦ πατρός σου, θεὸς Ἀβραὰμ καὶ θεὸς Ἰσαὰκ καὶ θεὸς Ἰακώβ*), occurs frequently in various forms: cf. vii. 32; Mt. xxii. 32 = Mk. xii. 26 = Lk. xx. 37. Here and in vii. 32 δ repeats *θεός* before *Ἰσαάκ* and *Ἰακώβ*, in conformity with LXX. In this fuller form the phrase occurs in the opening formula of the 'Eighteen Benedictions'.

ἐδόξασεν τὸν παῖδα αὐτοῦ] An allusion to Isa. lii. 13, *ἰδοὺ συνήσει ὁ παῖς μου καὶ ὑψωθήσεται καὶ δοξασθήσεται σφόδρα*. Cf. also Wisd. ii. 13, where it is said of the righteous man *παῖδα Κυρίου ἑαυτὸν ὀνομάζει*, and 2 Baruch lxx. 9 ('my servant Messiah').[2] The Targum of Jonathan ben Uzziel adds 'Messiah' as epexegetic of 'my servant' in Isa. xlii. 1; lii. 13. *παῖς* is here to be rendered 'Servant', as in *ver.* 26; iv. 27, 30, the reference being to the

[1] If C. C. Torrey's theories of the origin of the δ text and of the original language of Rev. are right, this breach of concord ('nominative in apposition') both in D and in Rev. may reflect an Aramaic construction. See *DPC*, p. 176.

[2] I.e. the Syriac Apocalypse of Baruch: Charles's *Apocrypha and Pseudepigrapha*, ii. pp. 470 ff.

Isaianic ideal *'Ebed Yahweh.* The Voice from heaven at our Lord's baptism identified Him with the Isaianic Servant ; ὁ ἀγαπητός, ἐν σοὶ εὐδόκησα (Mk. i. 11 ; Lk. iii. 22) echoes Isa. xlii. 1, ὁ ἐκλεκτός μου, ὃν εὐδόκησεν ἡ ψυχή μου, as does also the word ἐκλελεγμένος in the Lukan version of the Voice at the Transfiguration (Lk. ix. 35). (For Ps. ii. 7, which is connected with Isa. xlii. 1 by the Voice on both occasions, see on xiii. 33.) Our Lord himself explicitly interpreted His Messiahship in terms of the Isaianic Servant (in Lk. xxii. 37 He directly applies to Himself the words καὶ μετὰ ἀνόμων ἐλογίσθη from Isa. liii. 12, and 'many' in Mk. x. 45 ; xiv. 24 echoes 'many' in Isa. liii. 11 f.), and so do the NT writers generally (cf. Mt. viii. 17 ; xii. 18 ff. ; Jn. xii. 38 ; Rom. iv. 25 ; x. 16 ; Heb. ix. 28 ; 1 Pet. ii. 22-25 ; Rev. v. 6). See further on viii. 35. But παῖς did not gain general currency as a title of Jesus (see on iv. 27). δ characteristically adds Χριστόν after Ἰησοῦν : see on i. 21.

ὑμεῖς] On the question of Jewish moral responsibility for the crucifixion cf. ii. 23 ; iv. 10 ; v. 30 ; vii. 52 ; xiii. 28 ; 1 Th. ii. 15.

κατὰ πρόσωπον] This prepositional phrase is probably a Semitism here, though it is not unknown in classical Gk. (cf. Xen. *Cyr.* vi. 3. 35, τὴν κατὰ πρόσωπον τῆς ἀντίας φάλαγγος τάξιν, 'the post in front of the opposing phalanx').

Πειλάτου] Pontius Pilate, procurator of Judaea, A.D. 26-36. The fullest account of his career in Judaea is given by Josephus in *Ant.* xviii. 3. 1-4.2. Whether intentionally or not, he consistently offended Jewish public opinion, and his rule was marked by several savage acts of bloodshed (cf. Lk. xiii. 1). He was recalled to Rome to justify himself, but before his arrival Tiberius died (March, A.D. 37), and Pilate was not reappointed. According to Eusebius (*HE* ii. 7) he committed suicide. He is remembered almost exclusively for his part in the condemnation of our Lord ; even the sole reference to him by a pagan Roman historian is in this connection ; Tacitus, in reference to the Christians, says, 'They took their name from Christ, who had been executed by the procurator Pontius Pilate when Tiberius was Emperor' (*Ann.* xv. 44).[1]

κρίναντος ἐκείνου ἀπολύειν] Cf. Lk. xxiii. 16, 22, ἀπολύσω. This phrase forms the antithesis to ὑμεῖς μὲν παρεδώκατε καὶ ἠρνήσασθε, instead of a principal clause with δέ. D, taking κρίναντος ('having decided') to mean 'having judged', alters the text to τοῦ κρίναντος, ἐκείνου ἀπολύειν αὐτὸν θέλοντος.

iii. 14

ὑμεῖς δὲ . . . ἠρνήσασθε] Adversative to κρίναντος ἐκείνου ἀπολύειν: this δέ is not the correlative to μέν in *ver.* 13.

[1] *auctor nominis eius Christus Tiberio imperitante per procuratorem Pontium Pilatum supplicio adfectus erat.*

τὸν ἅγιον καὶ δίκαιον] Both ὁ ἅγιος and ὁ δίκαιος are Messianic titles. For the former cf. Mk. i. 24 = Lk. iv. 34 ; 1 Jn. ii. 20 ; also Ac. iv. 27, 30 (cf. further ὅσιος in ii. 27 [*q.v.*] ; xiii. 35). For the latter, cf. vii. 52 ; xxii. 14 ; Jas. v. 6 ; 1 Jn. ii. 1 ; also Mt. xxvii. 19, 24 ; Lk. xxiii. 47. The emphasis on Messiah's righteousness has its roots in OT : cf. e.g., 2 Sam. xxiii. 3 ; Isa. xxxii. 1 ; liii. 11 ; Zech. ix. 9. In 1 Enoch xxxviii. 2 'the Righteous One' is used as a title of Messiah ; in xlvi. 3, 'this is the Son of man who has righteousness, with whom righteousness dwells' ; in liii. 6, 'the righteous and elect one' ; cf. Ps. Sol. xvii. 35, καὶ αὐτὸς βασιλεὺς δίκαιος. In 1 Enoch the plural form, 'righteous and holy ones', is used of the Messianic people (xxxviii. 5 ; xlviii. 1, 7 ; li. 2), suggesting the close relation between Messiah and His people. So the Isaianic title *'Ebed Yahweh* is used of both, and regularly in OT the same adjectives are applied to Israel and Israel's God.

ἠρνήσασθε] D substitutes the non-Lukan ἐβαρύνατε ('ye oppressed'), thus avoiding the repetition of ἠρνήσασθε in two consecutive verses. C. C. Torrey (*DPC*, p. 145) suggests that ἐβαρύνατε is a rendering of Aram. *kabbēdtūn*, a misreading of *kaddēbtūn*, the natural equivalent of ἠρνήσασθε of β.[1] But it is by no means certain that *kabbēdtūn* could mean ἐβαρύνατε. One might think rather of the Aphel *'akhbēdtūn*.

ἄνδρα φονέα] For this appositional use of ἀνήρ, cf. Lk. v. 8 ; xxiv. 19 ; for its use in the voc. plur., see on i. 11. The murderer was Barabbas (cf. Lk. xxiii. 19).

χαρισθῆναι] 'to be given over', whether for life, as here and xxvii. 24, or for death, as xxv. 11, 16.

iii. 15

τὸν . . . ἀρχηγὸν τῆς ζωῆς] 'the Author of life' : in Aram this would be the same as τὸν ἀρχηγὸν τῆς σωτηρίας in Heb. ii. 10, as Aram. *ḥayyē* is the equivalent of both ζωή and σωτηρία. ἀρχηγός also occurs in v. 31 (ἀρχηγὸν καὶ σωτῆρα) and Heb. xii. 2 (τὸν τῆς πίστεως ἀρχηγόν). It is quite classical, and combines the ideas of originator and leader. In LXX it is used, e.g., of the heads of the tribes of Israel, Num. xiii. 2 f. Here and in Heb. ii. 10 it denotes Christ as the *Source* of life and salvation ; in v. 31 (*q.v.*) the meaning 'Prince' or 'Leader' is uppermost ; in Heb. xii. 2, the meaning 'Leader', 'Exemplar'.

ὃν ὁ θεὸς ἤγειρεν ἐκ νεκρῶν] in strong contrast to ὑμεῖς . . . ἠρνήσασθε κ.τ.λ. Cf. the similar contrast in ii. 23 f. ; iv. 10.

[1] Other explanations of ἐβαρύνατε from Hebrew or Aramaic were offered by Nestle, Chase and others (see Blass *PG*, pp. 194 ff.). For another explanation, tracing ἐβαρύνατε through Lat. *aggrauastis* (so Iren.lat.) to ἡττήσατε, a misreading for ᾐτήσατε, see J. Rendel Harris, *A Study of Codex Bezae*, pp. 162 ff.

οὗ ἡμεῖς μάρτυρές ἐσμεν] 'of which fact we are witnesses': cf. ii. 32. The emphasis on personal witness of the Resurrection is maintained (see on i. 22).

iii. 16

καὶ τῇ πίστει τοῦ ὀνόματος αὐτοῦ τοῦτον ὃν θεωρεῖτε καὶ οἴδατε ἐστερέωσεν τὸ ὄνομα αὐτοῦ] Several attempts have been made to get rid of the awkwardness of this sentence as it stands. F. C. Burkitt (*JTS* xx. [1919], pp. 324 f.) suggested that a colon be placed before *τοῦτον*, and the preceding words be joined to *ver.* 15, thus: 'whereof we are witnesses, even to faith in His name: this man, whom ye see and know, His name hath made strong'. Thus 'ugly repetition is turned into characteristically Lucan rhetoric'. But it is awkward to have the genitive *οὗ* and dative *τῇ πίστει* together dependent on *μάρτυρές ἐσμεν*. LC suggest that *τὸ ὄνομα αὐτοῦ* is a marginal gloss to explain δι' *αὐτοῦ*. According to C. C. Torrey (*CDA*, pp. 14 ff.), *ἐστερέωσεν τὸ ὄνομα αὐτοῦ* represents Aram. *taqqēph shĕmēh*, which should be pointed *taqqīph sāmēh*, *ὑγιῆ ἐποίησεν αὐτόν*, the meaning of the passage then being, 'and by faith in His name He has made whole this man whom you see and know'. This seems the most attractive solution of the difficulty.

ἐστερέωσεν] Cf. *ἐστερεώθησαν*, *ver.* 7.

ἡ πίστις ἡ δι' αὐτοῦ] Cf. 1 Pet. i. 21, *τοὺς δι' αὐτοῦ πιστοὺς εἰς θεόν*. Was the faith theirs or his? Probably both. It is uncertain whether *δι' αὐτοῦ* means 'through Him' or 'through it' (i.e. His name: cf. x. 43), but in either case the essential meaning is the same.

ὁλοκληρίαν] The only NT occurrence. 'The noun *ὁλοκληρία* does not seem to be used in the medical writers; the adjective *ὁλόκληρος*, however, is frequently, both in its more general meaning of "complete", "entire", and also in the same sense as by St. Luke, of "complete soundness of body"' (Hobart, p. 193). The noun is found in Plutarch and the papyri.

ἀπέναντι] lit. 'opposite'; here a substitute for *πρό*, like *κατὰ πρόσωπον* in *ver.* 13. Cf. xvii. 7, where it means 'against'.

iii. 17

καὶ νῦν, ἀδελφοί, οἶδα ὅτι κατὰ ἄγνοιαν ἐπράξατε] δ has *καὶ νῦν, ἄνδρες ἀδελφοί, ἐπιστάμεθα ὅτι ὑμεῖς μὲν κατὰ ἄγνοιαν ἐπράξατε τὸ πονηρόν*—harmonizing *ἀδελφοί* to the more usual *ἄνδρες ἀδελφοί*, and adding *τὸ πονηρόν* to point the moral.

κατὰ ἄγνοιαν] Cf. 1 Tim. i. 13, *ἀγνοῶν ἐποίησα*, where Paul refers to himself; 1 Cor. ii. 8, *εἰ γὰρ ἔγνωσαν, οὐκ ἂν τὸν κύριον τῆς δόξης ἐσταύρωσαν*. Peter's words here may be reminiscent of the Word from the Cross in Lk. xxiii. 34 (*πάτερ, ἄφες αὐτοῖς, οὐ γὰρ οἴδασιν* τί ποιοῦσιν), which is certainly genuine, despite its omission by ℵ[a] B D* W Θ a b syr.sin sah boh eth al (see B. H. Streeter, *The Four Gospels*, pp. 138 f.).

iii. 18

ἃ προκατήγγειλεν . . . παθεῖν τὸν χριστὸν αὐτοῦ] The Messiah as such is not represented as suffering in OT. The Isaianic Servant is so represented, and the apostles followed Jesus Himself in interpreting His Messiahship in terms of the Servant prophecies. See on *ver.* 13 ; viii. 35. For the belief that the sufferings of Messiah were predicted cf. ii. 23 and references *ad loc.* For τὸν χριστὸν αὐτοῦ cf. Ps. ii. 2, quoted in iv. 26.

iii. 19

μετανοήσατε οὖν καὶ ἐπιστρέψατε] For μετανοήσατε see on ii. 38. In LXX ἐπιστρέφω is the word most often used to render Heb. *shūb*, 'return'. Sometimes both words are found together in LXX as here, e.g. Joel ii. 14, τίς οἶδεν εἰ ἐπιστρέψει καὶ μετανοήσει ; (Heb. *mī yōdēa' yāshūb wĕ-niḥām*).

πρὸς τὸ ἐξαλιφθῆναι] For πρὸς τό with infin., cf. Lk. xviii. 1, πρὸς τὸ δεῖν πάντοτε προσεύχεσθαι. The construction is not found elsewhere in the Lukan writings. ἐξαλιφθῆναι is the classical ἐξαλειφθῆναι. By NT times the pronunciation of ι, ει, η, υ had become identical, like *ee* in Eng. *see*. Hence we have frequent variations of spelling, e.g. -ια and -εια are used interchangeably in many nouns. This process is called itacism (*ita* being the later pronunciation of *eta*, which in earlier Gk. represented a long open *e*).

iii. 20

ὅπως ἂν ἔλθωσιν] ὅπως ἄν with subjunctive is literary ; in NT it occurs only here and xv. 17 (from LXX) ; Lk. ii. 35 ; Rom. iii. 4 (from LXX).

καιροὶ ἀναψύξεως] In LXX ἀνάψυξις occurs only in Ex. viii. 15, in the sense 'respite' (Heb. *rĕwāḥāh*). In Hellenistic Gk. it had the meaning 'rest', 'respite'. The reference here is probably to the return of Messiah. (Cf. ἀποκατάστασις, *ver.* 21.) From this promise of Peter it has been inferred that if the Jewish nation had accepted the Gospel then, the Kingdom of God would speedily have been established on earth. Cf. Paul's argument in Rom. xi. 12, 15. This at least is clear, that here as in ii. 36 (γινωσκέτω πᾶς οἶκος Ἰσραήλ) Peter urged that the Jews as a nation should repent of the rejection of Jesus and receive Him as Messiah. The nation as a whole declined this offer, and while Ac. records the progressive acceptance of the Gospel by Gentiles in one place after another, it records at the same time its rejection by Jewish communities in nearly every one of these places.

ἀπὸ προσώπου] Semitism for *ἀπό*. Cf. v. 41; vii. 45; also *κατὰ πρόσωπον* in *ver.* 13, *πρὸ προσώπου* in xiii. 24; *ἐπὶ προσώπου* in xvii. 26.

προκεχειρισμένον] 'appointed'. Cf. xxii. 14; xxvi. 16, of Paul. It is probable that *προ-* means 'forth' rather than 'before' in the temporal sense; for the meaning cf. *ἀποδεδειγμένον* in ii. 22 and *ὡρισμένος*, x. 42; *ὥρισεν*, xvii. 31. Translate: 'and that He may send Jesus, who has been appointed Messiah for you'.

iii. 21

ἄχρι χρόνων ἀποκαταστάσεως πάντων] These words imply the Lord's absence for a certain period, until the fulfilment of prophetic scriptures. With *ἀποκατάστασις* we may compare *ἀποκαθιστάνεις* in i. 6, but the sense here cannot be restricted to the restoration of the kingdom to Israel. Cf. also in Mt. xvii. 11 and Mk. ix. 12 the expectation that Elijah should come (cf. Mal. iv. 5) to restore (*ἀποκαθιστάνειν*) all things. This restoration is called the 'regeneration' (*παλινγενεσία*) in Mt. xix. 28, 'when the Son of man shall sit on the throne of His glory'. *ἀποκατάστασις* may here be rendered 'establishment', 'fulfilment', referring to the fulfilment of all OT prophecy, culminating in the establishment of God's kingdom on earth. This rendering finds support in papyri and inscriptions, and also in LXX (cf. Ps. xvi. 5;[1] Job viii. 6; 2 Macc. xii. 39; xv. 20). So Torrey, who gives an Aramaic retroversion, *'ad 'iddānē hăqāmūth kōllā dī mallel 'Elāhā* (*CDA*, p. 29; cf. Dalman, *Words of Jesus*, p. 178), and cf. pesh *'admā lĕ-mūlāyā dĕ-zabne dĕ-kulheyn 'ayleyn dĕ-malel 'Alāhā* ('until the fulness of the times of all that God has spoken'). The sense of 'restoration' should perhaps not be entirely excluded; for the renovation of all nature at the inauguration of the Messianic reign cf. Rom. viii. 18-23; 4 Ezra vii. 75; xiii. 26-29; 1 Enoch xlv. 5; li. 4, etc. This meaning is also well attested in papyri; cf. MM.

ἀπ' αἰῶνος] 'from eternity': a phrase used in LXX for Heb. *mē-'ōlām*. δ (D h Tert Iren.lat.) omits it here, but cf. Lk. i. 70, *καθὼς ἐλάλησεν διὰ στόματος τῶν ἁγίων ἀπ' αἰῶνος προφητῶν αὐτοῦ.*

iii. 22

Μωυσῆς] This spelling, derived from LXX, reflects the attempt to derive the name from Coptic *mōu* ('water') and *esēs* ('saved'), i.e., 'saved from the water' (cf. Jos. *Ant.* ii. 9. 6; *Ap.* i. 31; Philo, *Vit. Moys.* i. 17).

εἶπεν] δ adds *πρὸς τοὺς πατέρας ἡμῶν.*

[1] LXX. Ps. xv. 5.

iii. 22f.

Προφήτην κ.τ.λ.] The quotation is from Dt. xviii. 15 ff., *προφήτην ἐκ τῶν ἀδελφῶν σου ὡς ἐμὲ ἀναστήσει σοι Κύριος ὁ θεός σου, αὐτοῦ ἀκούσεσθε κατὰ πάντα ὅσα ᾐτήσω παρὰ Κυρίου τοῦ θεοῦ σου . . . καὶ λαλήσει αὐτοῖς καθότι ἂν ἐντείλωμαι αὐτῷ· καὶ ὁ ἄνθρωπος, ὃς ἐὰν μὴ ἀκούσῃ ὅσα ἐὰν λαλήσῃ ὁ προφήτης ἐπὶ τῷ ὀνόματί μου, ἐγὼ ἐκδικήσω ἐξ αὐτοῦ.* The concluding part of the present citation, however, bears a greater resemblance to Lev. xxiii. 29, *πᾶσα ψυχή, ἥτις μὴ ταπεινωθήσεται ἐν αὐτῇ τῇ ἡμέρᾳ ταύτῃ, ἐξολεθρευθήσεται ἐκ τοῦ λαοῦ αὐτῆς.* Dt. xviii. 15 ff. was a favourite proof-text in the early Church: cf. vii. 37 and the allusions in Jn. i. 21; vi. 14; vii. 40. The primary meaning of the passage in Dt. is that the children of Israel should not have recourse to magic arts, in imitation of their heathen neighbours, when they wished to ascertain the divine will; if God had any communication to make to them He would raise up a prophet as He had raised up Moses, and they should listen to him. It is clear, however, that in later times the passage was interpreted among the Jews as referring to one particular Prophet who was to come (cf. Jn. i. 21; vi. 14; vii. 40), and by Christians this Prophet was naturally identified with our Lord, who Himself perfectly embodied the revelation of God and fulfilled all the law and the prophets. This passage was no doubt one of the 'Testimonies' which seem to have been collected in early Christian times for apologetic purposes: see on i. 20; xxvi. 23. Obviously the quotation here, in its conflate form, was not taken direct from OT, and the fact that this form reappears *verbatim* in *Clementine Recognitions* i. 36 may be regarded as showing that in both cases it was taken from a collection of 'Testimonies'. Conflation of this kind, however, is natural in a spoken address (cf. ii. 17; vii. 7, etc.), and the author of the *Recognitions* may have taken the quotation direct from Ac. In some respects the quotation here is closer to the Heb. than is LXX; e.g. *ἔσται δέ* at the beginning of *ver.* 23 represents Heb. *wĕ-hāyāh* (Dt. xviii. 19), which is not translated in LXX. For the construction of *ἔσται δέ* cf. *καὶ ἔσται*, ii. 17, 21.

iii. 24

καὶ . . . δὲ] 'Yes, and' or 'And also'.

καὶ πάντες δὲ οἱ προφῆται ἀπὸ Σαμουὴλ καὶ τῶν καθεξῆς ὅσοι ἐλάλησαν καὶ κατήγγειλαν τὰς ἡμέρας ταύτας] The construction of this sentence is not clear. As it stands, it may be rendered, 'Yes, and all the prophets from Samuel and his successors who spoke and announced these days'—which is not a proper sentence. We might join it to the preceding sentence, and translate: 'Moses said . . . and so also did all the prophets from Samuel and his successors who spoke and announced these days'—but Samuel and the prophets after him did not say what Moses said, though the meaning may simply be that they foretold the Coming One. The best sense is given if we translate *καί* before *κατήγγειλαν* as 'also': the meaning will then be, 'Yes, and all the prophets who spoke, from Samuel and his successors, also announced these days'. But our first rendering may be right, even if it is ungrammatical; anacoluthon is not unknown in the speeches of Ac., and the Gk. of this speech is obscure and awkward as it stands in other places as well: see on *ver.* 16. Torrey gives an Aram. retroversion, *wĕ-khol nĕbiyayyā min Shmū'ēl wĕ-dī bāthrēh dī mallēlū wĕ-hakhrīzū yōmayyā hā'illēn*, 'and all the prophets who spoke from Samuel onwards through his successors, announced these days' (*CDA*, pp. 29 f.).

iii. 25

οἱ υἱοὶ . . . τῆς διαθήκης] Cf. *τῶν υἱῶν τῆς διαθήκης μου*, Ezek. xxx. 5; *υἱοὶ τῆς διαθήκης*, Ps. Sol. xvii. 17. Such a Jewish idiom as this (Heb. *bĕnē bĕrīth*), like the solemn formula with which the speech begins, is a mark of genuineness, reflecting a time when the breach between the church and the synagogue was not so wide as it later became.

Καὶ ἐν τῷ σπέρματί σου εὐλογηθήσονται πᾶσαι αἱ πατριαὶ τῆς γῆς] Free quotation from Gen. xii. 3 (*καὶ ἐνευλογηθήσονται ἐν σοὶ πᾶσαι αἱ φυλαὶ τῆς γῆς*); xviii. 18 (*ἐνευλογηθήσονται ἐν αὐτῷ πάντα τὰ ἔθνη τῆς γῆς*); xxii. 18 (*καὶ ἐνευλογηθήσονται ἐν τῷ σπέρματί σου πάντα τὰ ἔθνη*). Note the use of *πατριαί* ('families'), instead of *φυλαί* ('tribes'). The Heb. of Gen. xii. 3 has *mishpāḥāh* ('family'), so that the Gk. of this quotation is more accurate than LXX (cf. *ver.* 23). In the present passage the 'seed' of Abraham is interpreted of Christ, through whom blessing was being offered, as in the similar quotation in Gal. iii. 8.

iii. 26

ὑμῖν πρῶτον] i.e., to you first of all the families of the earth. This order is maintained throughout the book: Jews receive the offer first (cf. Rom. i. 16; ii. 10), and as they were first in privilege, so they were first in responsibility if they repudiated the offer (Rom. ii. 9).

ἀναστήσας] 'having raised up': here perhaps not of the Resurrection, but in the sense of *ἀναστήσει*, *ver.* 22, of His incarnation or the beginning of His public ministry; see also on xiii. 33, and the similar sense of *ἐγείρω* in v. 30.

ἐν τῷ ἀποστρέφειν] For ἐν τῷ with infin., see on ii. 1. The construction here is not temporal but instrumental ('by turning'). Cf. iv. 30. ἀποστρέφειν is probably transitive, with ἕκαστον as its object.

(c) Arrest of Peter and John: Increase of the Church, iv. 1-4

Λαλούντων δὲ αὐτῶν πρὸς τὸν λαὸν ἐπέστησαν αὐτοῖς οἱ ἀρχιερεῖς 1
καὶ ὁ στρατηγὸς τοῦ ἱεροῦ καὶ οἱ Σαδδουκαῖοι, διαπονούμενοι διὰ τὸ 2
διδάσκειν αὐτοὺς τὸν λαὸν καὶ καταγγέλλειν ἐν τῷ Ἰησοῦ τὴν ἀνάστασιν
τὴν ἐκ νεκρῶν, καὶ ἐπέβαλον αὐτοῖς τὰς χεῖρας καὶ ἔθεντο εἰς τήρησιν 3
εἰς τὴν αὔριον, ἦν γὰρ ἑσπέρα ἤδη. πολλοὶ δὲ τῶν ἀκουσάντων τὸν 4
λόγον ἐπίστευσαν, καὶ ἐγενήθη ἀριθμὸς τῶν ἀνδρῶν ὡς χιλιάδες πέντε.

iv. 1

λαὸν] δ adds τὰ ῥήματα ταῦτα.

ἀρχιερεῖς] B C 4 arm eth; ἱερεῖς א A δ byz lat sah boh pesh hcl Chrys Lucif. ἱερεῖς should probably be preferred, as in RV. These priests may have formed part of the Temple guard.

ὁ στρατηγὸς τοῦ ἱεροῦ] Cf. v. 24, 26; Lk. xxii. 4, 52; Jos. *BJ* ii. 17. 2; vi. 5. 3; *Ant.* xx. 6. 2; 9. 3. This officer is to be identified with the *sāgān* who came next in rank to the High Priest, and superintended arrangements for the preservation of order in and around the Temple. See Schürer, II. i. 257 ff. (The plur. *sĕgānīm* occurs in OT in the sense 'rulers', 'governors', and is usually rendered στρατηγοί in LXX.)

Σαδδουκαῖοι] Cf. v. 17; xxiii. 6 ff.; Mt. xxii. 23 = Mk. xii. 18 = Lk. xx. 27; Jos. *BJ* ii. 8. 14; *Ant.* xiii. 5. 9; xviii. 1. 4. The origin of the name is obscure.[1] It may be that the party grew out of a movement founded by an unknown Zadok, or, more probably, that the name is intended to indicate their loyalty to the tradition of the priestly family of Zadok, commended by Ezekiel (xliv. 15 f.; xlviii. 11) for the purity of their worship. They claimed to represent the ancient standpoint in religion and morals, and emphasized the priestly point of view. The priestly families belonged for the most part to this party, and as the continued enjoyment of the priestly prerogatives and, indeed, the peace of the land and political existence of the people depended on Roman goodwill, they tried to co-operate as far as possible with the Roman authorities, and set their face sternly against religious or nationalist aspirations which might incur the wrath of the ruling power. They rejected as innovations belief in the world

[1] T. W. Manson in *BJRL* xxii. (1938), pp. 144 ff., suggests that it represents a Semitized form of σύνδικοι, 'fiscal controllers'.

of spirit-beings (angels and demons), which appears so regularly in Jewish post-exilic literature, and in individual immortality or at least resurrection. It is natural, then, to find them in opposition to a movement based upon belief in the Resurrection. See further on xxiii. 8.

iv. 2

διαπονούμενοι] 'annoyed': here and at xvi. 18 are the only NT occurrences.[1] For this sense MM quote *ἐγὼ ὅλος διαπονοῦμαι* from a papyrus of 2 B.C.

καταγγέλλειν ἐν τῷ Ἰησοῦ τὴν ἀνάστασιν τὴν ἐκ νεκρῶν] The meaning seems to be that they proved from the fact of Jesus' resurrection (*ἐν τῷ Ἰησοῦ*, 'in the case of Jesus') the general principle of resurrection, which the Sadducees denied. Cf. Paul's argument in 1 Cor. xv. 12 ff.; also Ac. xxiii. 6 ff.; xxiv. 15; xxvi. 6 ff. D has *ἀναγγέλλειν τὸν Ἰησοῦν ἐν τῇ ἀναστάσει τῶν νεκρῶν*.

iv. 3

ἐπέβαλον αὐτοῖς τὰς χεῖρας καὶ ἔθεντο εἰς τήρησιν] For the Sanhedrin's power of arrest cf. v. 17 f.; Mk. xiv. 43. It could deal on its own authority with offences against Jewish law, but could not carry out the death penalty without the procurator's ratification. For one particular offence, trespassing by Gentiles beyond the Temple barriers into the Inner Court (see on iii. 2; xxi. 28 f.), the Jewish court had the right to sentence even Roman citizens to death—an extraordinary concession, which shows how far Rome was willing to go in deference to Jewish religious sentiment. Cf. Jos. *BJ* vi. 2. 4, where Titus asks, *οὐχ ἡμεῖς δὲ τοὺς ὑπερβάντας ὑμῖν ἐπετρέψαμεν, κἂν Ῥωμαίων τις ᾖ;* The stoning of Stephen (vii. 58 f.) was an excess of jurisdiction, as was the killing of James the Just (Jos. *Ant.* xx. 9. 1; Euseb. *HE* ii. 23). For the composition of the Sanhedrin see on *ver.* 5 and *ver.* 15.

iv. 4

ἐγενήθη] 'had become'. This is the only example[2] in Ac. of this form (passive, for middle *ἐγένετο*), but D has it in vii. 13; xx. 3, 16. It is frequent in the Epistles.

ὡς χιλιάδες πέντε] An increase on the 3000 of ii. 41. In Biblical Gk. the forms compounded of a numeral adverb and *χίλιοι* (like *τρισχίλιαι*, ii. 41) are regularly replaced after 5000 by the cardinal number followed by *χιλιάδες*. Here the latter form is used for 5000

[1] Also Mk. xiv. 4, D W Θ 565.

[2] The imperative *γενηθήτω* occurs in the LXX quotation at i. 20.

itself. A curious exception is ἑπτακισχιλίους in Rom. xi. 4 for LXX ἑπτὰ χιλιάδας. In Mod. Gk. χιλιάδες has driven out χίλιοι except when χίλιοι stands alone meaning '*one* thousand'.

(d) Peter and John before the Sanhedrin, iv. 5-12

Ἐγένετο δὲ ἐπὶ τὴν αὔριον συναχθῆναι αὐτῶν τοὺς ἄρχοντας καὶ 5
τοὺς πρεσβυτέρους καὶ τοὺς γραμματεῖς ἐν Ἰερουσαλὴμ (καὶ Ἅννας 6
ὁ ἀρχιερεὺς καὶ Καιάφας καὶ Ἰωάννης καὶ Ἀλέξανδρος καὶ ὅσοι
ἦσαν ἐκ γένους ἀρχιερατικοῦ), καὶ στήσαντες αὐτοὺς ἐν τῷ μέσῳ 7
ἐπυνθάνοντο Ἐν ποίᾳ δυνάμει ἢ ἐν ποίῳ ὀνόματι ἐποιήσατε τοῦτο
ὑμεῖς; τότε Πέτρος πλησθεὶς πνεύματος ἁγίου εἶπεν πρὸς αὐτούς 8
Ἄρχοντες τοῦ λαοῦ καὶ πρεσβύτεροι, εἰ ἡμεῖς σήμερον ἀνακρινόμεθα 9
ἐπὶ εὐεργεσίᾳ ἀνθρώπου ἀσθενοῦς, ἐν τίνι οὗτος σέσωσται, γνωστὸν 10
ἔστω πᾶσιν ὑμῖν καὶ παντὶ τῷ λαῷ Ἰσραὴλ ὅτι ἐν τῷ ὀνόματι Ἰησοῦ
Χριστοῦ τοῦ Ναζωραίου, ὃν ὑμεῖς ἐσταυρώσατε, ὃν ὁ θεὸς ἤγειρεν
ἐκ νεκρῶν, ἐν τούτῳ οὗτος παρέστηκεν ἐνώπιον ὑμῶν ὑγιής. οὗτός 11
ἐστιν ὁ λίθος ὁ ἐξουθενηθεὶς ὑφ' ὑμῶν τῶν οἰκοδόμων, ὁ γενόμενος εἰς
κεφαλὴν γωνίας. καὶ οὐκ ἔστιν ἐν ἄλλῳ οὐδενὶ ἡ σωτηρία, οὐδὲ γὰρ 12
ὄνομά ἐστιν ἕτερον ὑπὸ τὸν οὐρανὸν τὸ δεδομένον ἐν ἀνθρώποις ἐν ᾧ
δεῖ σωθῆναι ἡμᾶς.

iv. 5

ἐγένετο δὲ] This, followed by the accusative and infinitive, is the regular form taken in Ac. by the Hebraism 'and it came to pass (Heb. *wayyĕhī*) that . . .'. Two other forms occurring in NT are ἐγένετο followed without an intervening conjunction by the indicative, or followed by καί and the indicative. They represent LXX influence on NT language (cf. ii. 17, 21; iii. 23). This construction is Luke's favourite Septuagintalism. Cf. J. H. Moulton, *Proleg.*, p. 16.

συναχθῆναι τοὺς ἄρχοντας κ.τ.λ.] D has συνήχθησαν οἱ ἄρχοντες κ.τ.λ. The alteration was intended to avoid the anacoluthon caused by the change in *ver.* 6 from the accusative to the nominative. The three categories here mentioned made up the Sanhedrin (see on *ver.* 15). The Sanhedrin is sometimes referred to by all or some of its constituent parts: e.g. οἱ ἀρχιερεῖς καὶ οἱ πρεσβύτεροι καὶ οἱ γραμματεῖς (Mk. xiv. 53, etc.), οἱ ἀρχιερεῖς καὶ οἱ γραμματεῖς (Lk. xxii. 2, etc.), οἱ ἀρχιερεῖς καὶ οἱ πρεσβύτεροι (*ver.* 23; xxiii. 14; xxv. 15, etc.), οἱ ἀρχιερεῖς καὶ πᾶν τὸ συνέδριον (xxii. 30, etc.). As a rule the ἀρχιερεῖς come first, as the leading members of the Sanhedrin. Besides the actual High Priest, the ἀρχιερεῖς included ex-High Priests and members of the high-priestly families. Here, then, as in *ver.* 8, ἄρχοντες may be regarded as an alternative for ἀρχιερεῖς (cf. xxiii. 5). Josephus never has both words together; he uses ἄρχοντες for ἀρχιερεῖς in *BJ* ii. 16. 1; 17. 1 *bis*; 21. 7. (In Lk. xxiii. 13 and xxiv. 20, where ἄρχοντες are mentioned in addition to ἀρχιερεῖς, the former word must refer to the members of the Sanhedrin generally.)

πρεσβυτέρους] The most general word for members of the Sanhedrin, whence the body was called the πρεσβυτέριον (cf. xxii. 5; Lk. xxii. 66). From early times the 'elders of Israel' (cf. Ex. iii. 16; xxiv. 1; Num. xi. 16, etc.) occupied an influential and representative position, forming the centre of the people's life. See further on *ver.* 15. The name came to be applied to the leaders in the Jerusalem church (cf. xi. 30) and in the Gentile churches (cf. xiv. 23).

γραμματεῖς] The 'scribes' were the professional students and teachers of the Scriptures (their function is more accurately expressed by the German *Schriftgelehrte*), and they belonged mostly to the Pharisaic party (see on v. 34). They were prominent figures in synagogue life, and some of them had teaching-pitches in the Temple courts (cf. Lk. ii. 46).

iv. 6

καὶ Ἅννας ὁ ἀρχιερεὺς] καὶ may be rendered 'including in particular'; some of the prominent members present are singled out for special mention, and this may in part mitigate the awkwardness of the anacoluthon caused by the sudden change of case. Note the rough breathing in Ἅννας in WH; this represents more accurately Heb. *Ḥānān* (Hellenized Ἀνάνος, of which Ἅννας is a shorter form). In Josephus he is called Ἀνάνος, and is said to have been the son of Seth. Appointed High Priest by Quirinius when the latter became legate of Syria in A.D. 6 (see on v. 37), he held office until A.D. 15, when he made way for Ishmael ben Phabi, who received his appointment from Valerius Gratus, procurator of Judaea (15-26). Cf. Jos. *BJ* v. 12. 2; *Ant.* xviii. 2. 1 f.; xx. 9. 1. Even after his deposition Annas enjoyed great prestige, and by the time we are now dealing with he was the senior ex-High Priest. Several members of his family became High Priests: his sons Eleazar (16-17), Jonathan (36-37), Theophilus (37-41), Matthias (*c.* 42) and Ananus (61), his grandson Matthias, son of Theophilus (65-66 or later), and his son-in-law Caiaphas (18-36). His prestige is reflected in NT by his being coupled with Caiaphas in Lk. iii. 2 as High Priest (ἐπὶ ἀρχιερέως Ἅννα καὶ Καιάφα), and by our Lord's appearance before him for a private examination before He was led before the Sanhedrin in the palace of Caiaphas.

Καιάφας] His personal name was Joseph. According to Jn. xviii. 13 he was son-in-law to Annas. He was appointed to the High Priesthood by the procurator Valerius Gratus in A.D. 18, and held it for eighteen years, a longer period than any other High Priest in NT times. The fact that Pilate left him in office during his ten years' procuratorship suggests that the two had an understanding. As High Priest he would be President of the Sanhedrin, though he may have deferred to the seniority of Annas when the latter was present.[1] When Vitellius, legate of Syria, visited Judaea in 36 after Pilate's departure (see on iii. 13), he deposed Caiaphas, and appointed Jonathan the son of Annas in his place. Caiaphas is chiefly remembered for the leading part he played in the arrest, trial and execution of Jesus, which he regarded as dictated by the highest considerations of national safety (cf. Jn. xi. 49 ff.); and in the eyes of Jesus Himself he bore the heaviest responsibility (Jn. xix. 11). Cf. Jos. *Ant.* xviii. 2, 2; 4, 3.

'Ιωάννης] He cannot be identified with certainty. R. Eisler may be right in identifying him with Theophilus, son of Annas, High Priest 37-41 (*The Enigma of the Fourth Gospel*, pp. 44 f.).[2] A more likely identification is suggested by the reading of δ, *'Ιωνάθας*, instead of *'Ιωάννης* of *β*. The δ text may be right, and if so, probably refers to Jonathan, son of Annas, who succeeded Caiaphas in 36, and was himself succeeded a year later by his brother Theophilus. Herod Agrippa I offered to reinstate him, but he declined, asking that the office be conferred on his other brother Matthias. He was assassinated by the Sicarii (see on xxi. 38) during the procuratorship of Felix. Cf. Jos. *Ant.* xviii. 4. 3; 5. 3; xix. 6. 4; xx. 8. 5.

'Αλέξανδρος] Otherwise unknown. F. W. Farrar (*Life of St. Paul*, i. 107), following Bishop Pearson, says he was perhaps Alexander the Alabarch, the brother of Philo, mentioned in Jos. *Ant.* xviii. 8. 1; this is as impossible as his other suggestion (following John Lightfoot) that John here was Yohanan ben Zakkai; this John and Alexander were both plainly of the high-priestly family.

[1] A. Edersheim, *Life and Times of Jesus the Messiah*, i, p. 264, concludes that 'although Annas was deprived of the Pontificate, he still continued to preside over the Sanhedrin'—a conclusion with which Schürer disagrees, maintaining that 'as regards the time of Christ it may be held as certain . . . that the office of president was always occupied by *the high priest for the time being*, and that too in virtue of his being such' (II. i. 180 ff.). See on xxiii. 5.

[2] We may dismiss Eisler's further theory, that he was John the Evangelist, the disciple who was known to the High Priest (Jn. xviii. 15), and the John who, according to Polycrates (*ap.* Euseb. *HE* v. 24), 'being a priest wore the *petalon*' (the gold plate in front of the sacerdotal turban).

καὶ ὅσοι ἦσαν ἐκ γένους ἀρχιερατικοῦ] 'and all who were of high-priestly family'. After Herod deprived the Hasmonean dynasty of the high priesthood, the High Priests were chosen from a few families, among which the families of Boethus and Annas were pre-eminent. The adj. ἀρχιερατικός, which does not occur elsewhere in NT, occurs in Jos. *Ant.* iv. 4. 7; vi. 6. 3; xv. 3. 1 (ἀρχιερατικοῦ γένους), and in inscriptions.

iv. 7

Ἐν ποίᾳ δυνάμει ἢ ἐν ποίῳ ὀνόματι] Instrumental ἐν (cf. iii. 6).

ὑμεῖς] Scornfully emphatic, the more so by its position at the end of the sentence: 'people like you'.

iv. 8

πλησθεὶς πνεύματος ἁγίου] Implying inspiration. The permanent indwelling of the Holy Spirit in a believer must be contrasted with special moments of inspiration, such as the present, which was a fulfilment of our Lord's promise in Mk. xiii. 11 and parallel passages. With the aor. ptc. contrast the adj. πλήρης in vi. 5, where Stephen's abiding character is in view.

Ἄρχοντες τοῦ λαοῦ] See on *ver.* 5.

iv. 9

ἀνακρινόμεθα] In Attic Gk., this verb is used of a preliminary inquiry; in later Gk., of any legal questioning (cf. xii. 19; xxiv. 8; xxv. 26; xxviii. 18).

ἐν τίνι] 'by what means': instrumental ἐν, as in *vv.* 7, 12.

σέσωσται] σῴζω is used both of physical and spiritual health; here of physical; in *ver.* 12 there is a transition to the spiritual sense.

iv. 10

ὃν ὑμεῖς ἐσταυρώσατε] Again the Jewish rulers' responsibility for the crucifixion is pressed home. Cf. the same phrase in ii. 36, where also their treatment of Jesus is contrasted with God's, as here (ὃν ὁ θεὸς ἤγειρεν ἐκ νεκρῶν).

ὑγιής] Some forms of δ (E e h Cypr hcl.mg) add καὶ ἐν ἄλλῳ οὐδένι, probably introduced from *ver.* 12, where καὶ οὐκ ἔστιν ἐν ἄλλῳ οὐδένι ἡ σωτηρία is lacking in h Cypr Iren.lat Aug. *pecc. merit.* i. 52.

iv. 11

ὁ λίθος κ.τ.λ.] From Ps. cxviii. 22 (LXX cxvii),

> λίθον ὃν ἀπεδοκίμασαν οἱ οἰκοδομοῦντες,
> οὗτος ἐγενήθη εἰς κεφαλὴν γωνίας.

Cf. Mk. xii. 10 and parallels; 1 Pet. ii. 7; Ep. Barn. vi. 4, where these words are quoted direct from LXX and applied to Christ. For ἐξουθενέω cf. Lk. xviii. 9; xxiii. 11. It is used in LXX in 1 Sam. (LXX 1 K.) viii. 7 (once, and possibly twice); x. 19, to render *mā'as*, the same Heb. word as is rendered ἀπεδοκίμασαν in Ps. cxviii. 22. The related verb ἐξουδενέω is found in the best MSS. in Mk. ix. 12.

iv. 12

σωτηρία] Including, of course, the healing of the lame man, but embracing, and indeed emphasizing, spiritual healing and deliverance from judgment (as in ii. 21, 40, 47); so σωθῆναι at the end of this verse.

ἕτερον] 'implies a difference of kind, which is not involved in ἄλλο' (J. B. Lightfoot on Gal. i. 6).

τὸ δεδομένον] The art. with the ptc., although there is none with the noun, suggests that the emphasis is on the one name which *is* given rather than on any other in which there is no salvation.

(e) The Sanhedrin dismiss Peter and John, iv. 13-22

Θεωροῦντες δὲ τὴν τοῦ Πέτρου παρρησίαν καὶ Ἰωάνου, καὶ κατα- 13
λαβόμενοι ὅτι ἄνθρωποι ἀγράμματοί εἰσιν καὶ ἰδιῶται, ἐθαύμαζον,
ἐπεγίνωσκόν τε αὐτοὺς ὅτι σὺν τῷ Ἰησοῦ ἦσαν, τόν τε ἄνθρωπον 14
βλέποντες σὺν αὐτοῖς ἑστῶτα τὸν τεθεραπευμένον οὐδὲν εἶχον ἀντειπεῖν.
κελεύσαντες δὲ αὐτοὺς ἔξω τοῦ συνεδρίου ἀπελθεῖν συνέβαλλον πρὸς 15
ἀλλήλους λέγοντες Τί ποιήσωμεν τοῖς ἀνθρώποις τούτοις; ὅτι μὲν 16
γὰρ γνωστὸν σημεῖον γέγονεν δι' αὐτῶν πᾶσιν τοῖς κατοικοῦσιν Ἰερουσαλὴμ φανερόν, καὶ οὐ δυνάμεθα ἀρνεῖσθαι· ἀλλ' ἵνα μὴ ἐπὶ πλεῖον 17
διανεμηθῇ εἰς τὸν λαόν, ἀπειλησώμεθα αὐτοῖς μηκέτι λαλεῖν ἐπὶ τῷ
ὀνόματι τούτῳ μηδενὶ ἀνθρώπων. καὶ καλέσαντες αὐτοὺς παρήγ- 18
γειλαν καθόλου μὴ φθέγγεσθαι μηδὲ διδάσκειν ἐπὶ τῷ ὀνόματι τοῦ
Ἰησοῦ. ὁ δὲ Πέτρος καὶ Ἰωάνης ἀποκριθέντες εἶπαν πρὸς αὐτούς 19
Εἰ δίκαιόν ἐστιν ἐνώπιον τοῦ θεοῦ ὑμῶν ἀκούειν μᾶλλον ἢ τοῦ θεοῦ
κρίνατε, οὐ δυνάμεθα γὰρ ἡμεῖς ἃ εἴδαμεν καὶ ἠκούσαμεν μὴ λαλεῖν. 20
οἱ δὲ προσαπειλησάμενοι ἀπέλυσαν αὐτούς, μηδὲν εὑρίσκοντες τὸ 21
πῶς κολάσωνται αὐτούς, διὰ τὸν λαόν, ὅτι πάντες ἐδόξαζον τὸν θεὸν
ἐπὶ τῷ γεγονότι· ἐτῶν γὰρ ἦν πλειόνων τεσσεράκοντα ὁ ἄνθρωπος 22
ἐφ' ὃν γεγόνει τὸ σημεῖον τοῦτο τῆς ἰάσεως.

iv. 13

παρρησίαν] In classical Gk., 'freedom of speech', as a democratic right; here of the confidence and forthrightness with which the apostles spoke under the prompting of the Holy Spirit (see on *ver.* 8); so in *vv.* 29, 31.

καταλαβόμενοι] For the middle, of grasping with the mind, cf. x. 34; xxv. 25; Eph. iii. 18.

ἀγράμματοι] 'unversed in the learning of the Jewish schools' (Grimm). The sense 'illiterate', quoted by MM from the papyri, is probably not intended here. Cf. Jn. vii. 15, where the words *πῶς οὗτος γράμματα οἶδεν μὴ μεμαθηκώς;* express surprise, not that Jesus could write, but that He could teach and discuss subjects which normally were beyond the scope of those who had not received a Rabbinical education. For the same reason the Sanhedrin was surprised at Peter and John, who though untrained *'ammē hā-'āreṣ* ('people of the land'), could sustain a theological disputation with the supreme court of the nation.

ἰδιῶται] lit., 'private persons', 'laymen'. The word appears as a loan-word in later Hebrew and Aramaic, in the form *hedyōṭ*, 'unskilled', 'commoner' (e.g., Targ. 1 Sam. xviii. 23; Job xxx. 8; Mishna *Mō'ēd Qāṭān* i. 8; *Sanh.* x. 2). Cf. 2 Cor. xi. 6. Suidas (*s.v. ἰδιώτης*) regards the word as synonymous with *ἀγράμματος*.

ἐπεγίνωσκόν τε αὐτοὺς ὅτι σὺν τῷ Ἰησοῦ ἦσαν] 'and they took cognizance of the fact that they had been with Jesus'. They knew this before (we need not find such an 'almost insuperable' discrepancy with *ver.* 2 as LC suppose), but now they directed special attention to it as an important piece of relevant evidence. (This is the force of *ἐπιγινώσκω*: see on iii. 10.) They may have remembered how Jesus, despite His lack of Rabbinical training, 'knew letters' (Jn. vii. 15) and 'taught as one having authority' (Mk. i. 22). And now these men, claiming the authority of His name, had wrought a cure so plain as to be beyond gainsaying. Unable or unwilling to draw the proper conclusion, they kept silence.

iv. 15

συνεδρίου] 'court of law', 'council'. It is this word (composed of *σύν* and *ἕδρα*) which appears in Heb. and Aram. in the transliterated form *sanhedrīn*. (The *h* indicates that the rough breathing did not always disappear in Gk. pronunciation, though it was not represented in spelling, when a prefix preceded it in composition. The spelling with *-im* instead of *-in* is due to the notion that this is a plural ending, whereas here it represents Gk. *-ιον*.) The supreme court is regularly called *συνέδριον* in NT: cf. Jos. *Ant.* xiv. 9. 3-5; xv. 6. 2; xx. 9. 1; *Vita* 12 (*τὸ συνέδριον τῶν Ἱεροσολυμειτῶν*). It is also called the *πρεσβυτέριον* (xxii. 5; Lk. xxii. 66), the *γερουσία*, 'senate' (v. 21; *Ant.* xii. 3. 3; xiii. 5. 8), and the *βουλή*, 'council' (*BJ* ii. 15. 6; 16. 2; v. 13. 1; *Ant.* xx. 1. 2). In the Mishna its other names, apart from *sanhedrīn*, are *bēth dīn ha-gādōl* ('the great law-court'), *sanhedrīn gĕdōlāh*

(' great court '), *sanhedrīn shel shib'īm wā'eḥād* (' court of the seventy-one ').

This body, the supreme court of the Jewish people, was identified by rabbinical exegesis with the council of 70 elders of Num. xi. 16, but the Sanhedrin of NT times cannot certainly be traced earlier than the Greek period. It is first mentioned as the γερουσία (' senate ') in Jos. *Ant.* xii. 3. 3, in the report of a letter written by Antiochus III after the battle of Panion (198 B.C.). The Hellenistic kings granted the Jews considerable local autonomy, and the High Priest at the head of the Jewish commonwealth presided over the senate and regulated the internal affairs of the nation. (Cf. 1 Macc. vii. 33; xi. 23; xii. 6, 35; xiii. 36; xiv. 20, 28; 2 Macc. i. 10; iv. 44; xi. 27; Judith iv. 8; xi. 14; xv. 8.) In *Ant.* xiii. 16. 5 the court appears in the reign of Salome Alexandra (76-67 B.C.) as τῶν Ἰουδαίων οἱ πρεσβύτεροι. After the Roman conquest (63 B.C.) the High Priest retained the προστασία τοῦ ἔθνους (*Ant.* xx. 10). Gabinius, when governor of Syria (57-55 B.C.), disturbed the supremacy of the court, but this was later restored: cf. *Ant.* xiv. 9. 3-5, where it appears exercising jurisdiction in Galilee as well as in Judaea (under Antipater, *c.* 47 B.C.), and where for the first time it is called συνέδριον. See on *ver.* 5, and cf. Schürer, II. i. 163 ff.

After the Fall of Jerusalem in A.D. 70, a new Sanhedrin, religious and not political in character, was established at Jabneh by R. Yohanan ben Zakkai; its President (*nāsī* or *rōsh bēth dīn*) was usually an eminent scholar. The Mishna and later Jewish tradition project the constitution of this later Sanhedrin back into the time of the Second Temple, making notable Rabbis like Hillel and Gamaliel Presidents of the Sanhedrin (see on xxiii. 5).

Some Jewish scholars, notably Adolf Büchler in *Das Synhedrion in Jerusalem* (Vienna, 1902), have maintained that a religious Sanhedrin existed in the time of the Second Temple alongside the political one, and that while the High Priest presided *ex officio* over the latter, scholars presided over the former, as tradition asserts. This view has recently been put forward anew by Solomon Zeitlin, in *Who Crucified Jesus?* (1942), where he argues that the pro-Roman political Sanhedrin was the only section of the Jewish nation responsible for the Crucifixion. (See critique by N. B. Stonehouse in the *Westminster Theological Journal*, v, May 1943, pp. 137-165.)

See the articles ' Sanhedrin ' by J. Z. Lauterbach in the *Jewish Encyclopaedia*, by W. Bacher in *HDB*, by I. Abrahams in *ERE*; the first supports the theory of two Sanhedrins, the second opposes it, the third gives the arguments for both views without taking sides.

ἀπελθεῖν] δ has ἀπαχθῆναι, ' to be led off ' (see on xii. 19).

iv. 16

φανερόν] D has φανερότερον (for φανερώτερον)—an elative comparative (' very clear ', ' all too clear '): cf. x. 28 D (βέλτιον ἐφίστασθε); xxv. 10 (κάλλιον ἐπιγινώσκεις), and perhaps xxiv. 22, ἀκριβέστερον εἰδώς.

iv. 17

ἀλλ'] Correlative to μέν in *ver.* 16.

διανεμηθῇ] δ (E e g h hcl.mg Lucif—not D) adds τὰ ῥήματα ταῦτα.

ἀπειλησώμεθα] byz prefixes ἀπειλῇ, ' with a threat ', whence

AV 'let us straitly threaten them' (RV omits 'straitly'). This reading reflects the Heb. device of emphasizing a finite verb by prefixing the absolute infinitive (e.g. Ex. iii. 7, *rā'ōh rā'īthī*, 'I have certainly seen': LXX *ἰδὼν εἶδον*, quoted in vii. 34). This 'characteristic' reading here 'one is strongly tempted to accept', say MM, for it 'clearly reflects the literal rendering of a Semitic original reported to Luke from an eye-witness—was it Paul? Homoeoteleuton and unfamiliarity to Greek ears would account for the loss of the noun in ℵ A B D Pesh., etc. (so Blass).' Cf. ii. 17, 30; v. 28; xxiii. 14; also *ἐπιθυμίᾳ ἐπεθύμησα*, Lk. xxii. 15; *χαρᾷ χαίρει*, Jn. iii. 29; *προσευχῇ προσηύξατο*, Jas. v. 17, etc.

iv. 18

καὶ καλέσαντες αὐτοὺς] δ has *συγκατατιθεμένων δὲ αὐτῶν τῇ γνώμῃ φωνήσαντες αὐτούς*, 'and when they agreed to the decision, having called them'.

μὴ φθέγγεσθαι μηδὲ διδάσκειν] Note the pres. infin.: they were to stop doing something which they had already begun to do, 'give up speaking and teaching': so *μηκέτι λαλεῖν* in *ver.* 17. This prohibition was probably regarded as giving a legal excuse for the prosecution in v. 17 ff.; cf. v. 28.

ἐπὶ τῷ ὀνόματι τοῦ Ἰησοῦ] It is difficult to distinguish here *ἐπὶ τῷ ὀνόματι* (see on ii. 38) from *ἐν τῷ ὀνόματι* (cf. iii. 6); the former implies authority, but so also may the latter, if the context requires it. See further on ii. 38; viii. 16 for the distinction between *ἐν τῷ ὀνόματι* and *εἰς τὸ ὄνομα*. Notice that in this verse we have indirect speech; in the direct speech of *ver.* 17 the personal name of Jesus is avoided, as frequently in later Jewish references to Him (e.g., He is sometimes referred to as *Pĕlōnī*, 'So and so').

iv. 19

ἀποκριθέντες εἶπαν] A good example of the redundant Hebraizing use of the verb 'answer': cf. v. 29; viii. 24, 34; xxv. 9, and freq. in the Synoptic Gospels. Jn. prefers *ἀπεκρίθη καὶ εἶπεν* (plur. *ἀπεκρίθησαν καὶ εἶπαν*), a more literal rendering of the common OT phrase *wayya'an wayyōmer* (plur. *wayya'ănū wayyōmĕrū*). Note also the 'simultaneous' use of the aor. ptc. *ἀποκριθέντες* (cf. v. 29; x. 33; xxii. 24).

ὑμῶν ἀκούειν μᾶλλον ἢ τοῦ θεοῦ] Cf. v. 29, and the words of Socrates in Plato, *Apology* 29D, *πείσομαι δὲ μᾶλλον τῷ θεῷ ἢ ὑμῖν.*

iv. 20

οὐ δυνάμεθα . . . μὴ λαλεῖν] 'we cannot give up speaking' for the pres. infin. see on *ver.* 18.

iv. 21

προσαπειλησάμενοι] 'having threatened further' (*πρός*, 'in addition'); this is the only NT occurrence of the word.

μηδὲν εὑρίσκοντες τὸ πῶς κολάσωνται αὐτούς] The ptc. is used in a causal sense. The art. precedes the indirect question *πῶς κολάσωνται αὐτούς* as if it were a noun. This clause explains the positive element in *μηδέν*: this was what they could not find. *κολάσωνται* is deliberative subjunctive, like *ποιήσωμεν* in *ver.* 16.

iv. 22

ἐτῶν γὰρ ἦν πλειόνων τεσσεράκοντα] 'an age at which such cures no longer occur' (Harnack, *LP*, p. 191). For this note of the patient's age cf. Mk. v. 42; Lk. viii. 42; and see on iii. 2 for notes of the duration of disease. These notes cannot be pressed as evidence of medical interest, as some of them occur in non-Lukan parts of NT.

γεγόνει] Unaugmented form for *ἐγεγόνει*. Such a dropping of the augment is not infrequent in the pluperfect; cf. xiv. 23; Mt. vii. 25; Mk. xiv. 44; xv. 7, 10; xvi. 9; Lk. xix. 15; Jn. xi. 30, 57; 1 Jn. ii. 19. Here ℵ A E P al have the augmented form: cf. also xxvi. 32; Lk. xi. 22; xvi. 20; Jn. ix. 22; xi. 44. Cf. MH ii, p. 190.

(f) Peter and John return; the Disciples pray, iv. 23-31

Ἀπολυθέντες δὲ ἦλθον πρὸς τοὺς ἰδίους καὶ ἀπήγγειλαν ὅσα 23
πρὸς αὐτοὺς οἱ ἀρχιερεῖς καὶ οἱ πρεσβύτεροι εἶπαν. οἱ δὲ ἀκούσαντες 24
ὁμοθυμαδὸν ἦραν φωνὴν πρὸς τὸν θεὸν καὶ εἶπαν Δέσποτα, σὺ ὁ ποιήσας
τὸν οὐρανὸν καὶ τὴν γῆν καὶ τὴν θάλασσαν καὶ πάντα τὰ ἐν αὐτοῖς, ὁ 25
τοῦ πατρὸς ἡμῶν διὰ πνεύματος ἁγίου στόματος Δαυεὶδ παιδός σου
εἰπών

Ἵνα τί ἐφρύαξαν ἔθνη
καὶ λαοὶ ἐμελέτησαν κενά;
παρέστησαν οἱ βασιλεῖς τῆς γῆς 26
καὶ οἱ ἄρχοντες συνήχθησαν ἐπὶ τὸ αὐτὸ
κατὰ τοῦ κυρίου καὶ κατὰ τοῦ χριστοῦ αὐτοῦ.

συνήχθησαν γὰρ ἐπ' ἀληθείας ἐν τῇ πόλει ταύτῃ ἐπὶ τὸν ἅγιον παῖδά 27
σου Ἰησοῦν, ὃν ἔχρισας, Ἡρῴδης τε καὶ Πόντιος Πειλᾶτος σὺν ἔθνεσιν
καὶ λαοῖς Ἰσραήλ, ποιῆσαι ὅσα ἡ χείρ σου καὶ ἡ βουλὴ προώρισεν 28
γενέσθαι. καὶ τὰ νῦν, κύριε, ἔπιδε ἐπὶ τὰς ἀπειλὰς αὐτῶν, καὶ δὸς 29
τοῖς δούλοις σου μετὰ παρρησίας πάσης λαλεῖν τὸν λόγον σου, ἐν 30
τῷ τὴν χεῖρα ἐκτείνειν σε εἰς ἴασιν καὶ σημεῖα καὶ τέρατα γίνεσθαι
διὰ τοῦ ὀνόματος τοῦ ἁγίου παιδός σου Ἰησοῦ. καὶ δεηθέντων αὐτῶν 31

ἐσαλεύθη ὁ τόπος ἐν ᾧ ἦσαν συνηγμένοι, καὶ ἐπλήσθησαν ἅπαντες τοῦ ἁγίου πνεύματος, καὶ ἐλάλουν τὸν λόγον τοῦ θεοῦ μετὰ παρρησίας.

iv. 23

πρὸς τοὺς ἰδίους] 'to their own (people)': cf. xxiv. 23; Jn. i. 11; xiii. 1. See further on xx. 28, for the similar sense of the sing. *τοῦ ἰδίου*.

οἱ ἀρχιερεῖς καὶ οἱ πρεσβύτεροι] See on *vv.* 5, 15. They are the general members of the Sanhedrin. They are also called *βουλευταί* ('councillors'), Mk. xv. 43 = Lk. xxiii. 50; *BJ* ii. 17. 1.

iv. 24

ὁμοθυμαδόν] See on i. 14. Before this word D has *ἐπιγνόντες τὴν τοῦ θεοῦ ἐνέργειαν.*

Δέσποτα] 'Sovereign Lord': cf. Lk. ii. 29; Rev. vi. 10 for this form of address to God. Cf. also 3 Macc. ii. 2, *δέσποτα πάσης τῆς κτίσεως*. In 2 Tim. ii. 21; 2 Pet. ii. 1; Jude 4 *δεσπότης* is used of Christ. The correlative word is *δοῦλος*, as in *ver.* 29; Lk. ii. 29. That this prayer is addressed to the Father is clear from the repeated phrase, 'Thy holy Servant Jesus' (*vv.* 27, 30).

ὁ ποιήσας τὸν οὐρανὸν κ.τ.λ.] Cf. xiv. 15; xvii. 24. The words reflect such OT passages as Ex. xx. 11; Neh. ix. 6 (LXX 2 Esdr. xix. 6); Ps. cxlvi. 6 (LXX cxlv); Isa. xlii. 5; Wisd. xiii. 3, 4, 9. The invocation of God as Creator here and elsewhere has been considered liturgical, from the stereotyped character of the wording.

iv. 25

ὁ τοῦ πατρὸς ἡμῶν διὰ πνεύματος ἁγίου στόματος Δαυεὶδ παιδός σου εἰπών] A well-known crux. It is curious how often the Gk. becomes obscure when the apostles are speaking. The only way to translate the Gk. as it stands is to regard David himself as the 'mouth' (i.e. mouthpiece[1]) of the Holy Spirit: 'who didst say through Thy servant David our father, the mouthpiece of the Holy Spirit'; but apart from the questionable sense, this involves a straining of the order of the words. δ attempts to mend matters by omitting *τοῦ πατρὸς ἡμῶν* and inserting *διὰ τοῦ* before *στόματος* thus: *ὃς διὰ πνεύματος ἁγίου διὰ τοῦ στόματος ἐλάλησας Δαυεὶδ παιδός σου*, 'who through the Holy Spirit didst speak through the mouth of David Thy servant'. Hort suggests that *τοῦ πατρός* is a corruption of *τοῖς πατράσιν*. H. W. Moule (*ET* li. [1939-40], p. 396) ingeniously suggests that the writer put down a first draft of the sentence and then made corrections, and that a copyist,

[1] For *στόμα* in this sense cf. Theocritus vii. 37, *καὶ γὰρ ἐγὼν Μοισᾶν καπυρὸν στόμα*, 'for indeed I am a clear-sounding mouth (i.e. mouthpiece) of the Muses'.

misunderstanding the signs for deletion or addition, combined words which are really alternative. C. C. Torrey (*CDA* 16 ff.), assuming an Aram. original, explains the obscurity as due to the common confusion between Aram. masc. pronoun *hū* and the corresponding fem. or neut. form *hī*. The Gk. text represents Aram. *hū dī 'abūnā lĕ-phūm rūḥā dī qūdshā Dāwīd 'abdākh 'āmar;* but if we read neut. *hī* for masc. *hū*, *Dāwīd* becomes the subject, and the meaning is: 'that which our father David, Thy servant, said by the mouth of the Holy Spirit'. This is a very attractive solution of 'the extreme difficulty of text, which doubtless contains a primitive error' (WH).

iv. 25f.

ἵνα τί ἐφρύαξαν ἔθνη κ.τ.λ.] An exact quotation from Ps. ii. 1f., LXX. The expression *ἵνα τί* (cf. vii. 26; Mt. ix. 4; xxvii. 46; Lk. xiii. 7; 1 Cor. x. 29) is elliptical, for *ἵνα τί γένηται;* It is not uncommon in the later classical writers (e.g. Plato, *Apol.* 26 D, *ἵνα τί ταῦτα λέγεις;*). The active *φρυάσσω* is found only here and in Ps. ii. 1, LXX; the middle is found in late Greek writers. It is primarily used of the neighing of high-fed, spirited horses. Ps. ii. is one of the principal sources for the concept of the Messiah and His divine Sonship. Our first record of its Messianic interpretation is Ps. Sol. xvii. 26, where the Messianic king (the *χριστὸς κύριος* of *ver.* 36), will 'dash in pieces the pride of the sinner like a potter's vessels, break all their substance with a rod of iron'. For the Messianic interpretation of this Psalm see further on xiii. 33, and cf. Heb. i. 5; v. 5; Rev. ii. 27; xii. 5; xix. 15.

iv. 27

παῖδα] See on iii. 13. In the present context *παῖς* may be intended to bear the meaning 'Son' as well as 'Servant' (cf. Ps. ii. 7, *υἱός μου εἶ σύ*). Cf. *ver.* 30; also the formula *διὰ Ἰησοῦ τοῦ παιδός σου* in the *Didaché* ix. 2 f., x. 2; *διὰ τοῦ ἠγαπημένου παιδὸς αὐτοῦ Ἰησοῦ Χριστοῦ*, 1 Clem. lix. 2; *διὰ Ἰησοῦ Χριστοῦ τοῦ ἠγαπημένου παιδός σου*, *ib.* lix. 3; *Ἰησοῦς Χριστὸς ὁ παῖς σου*, *ib.* lix. 4.

ὃν ἔχρισας] Referring to *χριστοῦ*, *ver.* 26. Cf. x. 38. The reference is probably to His baptism, when He was publicly manifested to Israel and addressed as the Son of God.

Ἡρῴδης] i.e., Herod Antipas. Luke alone tells the story of Christ's appearance before Herod (Lk. xxiii. 7 ff.). Other NT references to this Herod are Mt. xiv. 1-11=Mk. vi. 14-28; Mk. viii. 15; Lk. iii. 1, 19 f.; viii. 3; ix. 7–9; xiii. 31, 32 (where Jesus calls him 'that fox'); Ac. xiii. 1. He is chiefly remembered for the sorry part he played in the imprisonment and death of John the Baptist.

He was the son of Herod the Great by his Samaritan wife Malthace, and the younger full brother of Archelaus (Mt. ii. 22). In the division of their father's kingdom (4 B.C.) Antipas received Galilee and Peraea, over which he ruled with the title tetrarch until A.D. 39. He was the ablest son of his father, and like him was a great builder: the construction of Tiberias on the Lake of Galilee was his work (A.D. 22). On his way to Rome about A.D. 23 he lodged with his half-brother Herod Philip (not the Philip of Lk. iii. 1), and became infatuated with the latter's wife Herodias, who was herself the daughter of another of their half-brothers, Aristobulus. In order to marry her he divorced his wife, the daughter of Aretas, the Nabataean king (see on ii. 11; ix. 23), who seized an opportunity later to declare war on Antipas and inflict a crushing defeat on him. When in A.D. 37 Herod Agrippa, the brother of Herodias, received from the new Emperor Gaius (Caligula) the title of 'king' (see on xii. 1), Antipas set out for Rome, at the instigation of Herodias, to ask that the royal title be conferred on himself as well. (He is called 'king' in Mt. xiv. 9; Mk. vi. 14 ff., but this was probably a mere courtesy title given him by his Galilaean subjects.) Agrippa now satisfied an old grudge against Antipas by denouncing him to the Emperor as a plotter of insurrection; as a result, Antipas was deposed from his tetrarchy and sent into banishment. Herodias, who remained a free agent, showed a redeeming feature by voluntarily sharing his exile. Cf. Jos. *BJ* i. 28. 1, 4; 32. 7; 33. 7; ii. 2. 3; 9. 6; *Ant.* xvii. 1. 3; 8. 1; 9. 4; 11. 4; xviii. 5. 1-4; 6. 2; 7. 1 f. Cf. also A. H. M. Jones, *The Herods of Judaea*; A. W. Verrall, 'Christ before Herod' in *The Bacchants of Euripides and other Essays*, pp. 335-390; W. M. Christie, *Palestine Calling*, pp. 45 ff.

Πόντιος Πειλᾶτος] See on iii. 13.

σὺν ἔθνεσιν καὶ λαοῖς 'Ισραήλ] Thus they interpreted Ps. ii. i f.; the *ἔθνη* are the Gentiles, the *λαοί* the Jews; the *βασιλεῖς* are represented by Herod, the *ἄρχοντες* by Pilate.[1]

iv. 28

προώρισεν] For the fore-ordained character of the death of Christ see on ii. 23; iii. 18.

iv. 29

ἔπιδε] In NT only here and at Lk. i. 25, there too of God. This concurs with the classical usage: cf. Homer, *Odyssey*, xvii. 487, *θεοὶ . . . ἀνθρώπων ὕβριν τε καὶ εὐνομίην ἐφορῶντες*.

[1] See for a slightly different interpretation Tert. *de resurr. carn.* 20: 'In the person of Pilate the heathen raged, and in the person of Israel the people imagined vain things; the kings of the earth in Herod and the rulers in Annas and Caiaphas, were gathered together', etc.

iv. 30

ἐν τῷ τὴν χεῖρα ἐκτείνειν σε] Instrumental use of ἐν τῷ with infin., as in iii. 26. The phrase 'with a stretched out arm' is common in OT, though its LXX rendering is different from what we have here (see on xiii. 17).

iv. 31

ἐσαλεύθη] 'shook as with an earthquake'; a sign of divine assent: cf. ii. 2 f.; Ex. xix. 18; Isa. vi. 4; 4 Ezra vi. 15, 29.

μετὰ παρρησίας] See on *ver.* 13. At the end of this verse δ adds παντὶ τῷ θέλοντι πιστεύειν.

4. ALL THINGS IN COMMON, iv. 32–v. 11.

(a) Progress of the Church; Community of Goods, iv. 32-35

Τοῦ δὲ πλήθους τῶν πιστευσάντων ἦν καρδία καὶ ψυχὴ μία, καὶ 32
οὐδὲ εἷς τι τῶν ὑπαρχόντων αὐτῷ ἔλεγεν ἴδιον εἶναι, ἀλλ' ἦν αὐτοῖς
πάντα κοινά. καὶ δυνάμει μεγάλῃ ἀπεδίδουν τὸ μαρτύριον οἱ ἀπόστολοι 33
τοῦ κυρίου Ἰησοῦ τῆς ἀναστάσεως, χάρις τε μεγάλη ἦν ἐπὶ πάντας
αὐτούς. οὐδὲ γὰρ ἐνδεής τις ἦν ἐν αὐτοῖς· ὅσοι γὰρ κτήτορες χωρίων 34
ἢ οἰκιῶν ὑπῆρχον, πωλοῦντες ἔφερον τὰς τιμὰς τῶν πιπρασκομένων
καὶ ἐτίθουν παρὰ τοὺς πόδας τῶν ἀποστόλων· διεδίδετο δὲ ἑκάστῳ 35
καθότι ἄν τις χρείαν εἶχεν.

With this summary cf. the earlier one in ii. 41-47. Both end with a description of the community of goods. This repetition is not sufficient warrant for concluding that ii. 1-40 and iii. 1-iv. 31 are duplicate narratives. The present section is designed to introduce the incidents of Barnabas and Ananias.

iv. 32

πλήθους] 'congregation'; in LXX the word usually means 'multitude', but twice (Ex. xii. 6; 2 Chr. xxxi. 18) it represents Heb. *qāhāl*, normally rendered ἐκκλησία (see on v. 11). In Attic Gk. πλῆθος is used of the civic community. Cf. the cognate Lat. *plebs*, which also came to be used in an ecclesiastical sense ('laity', 'parishioners'), e.g., by Cyprian, Victorinus Afer, Jerome and Rufinus (cf. Welsh *plwyf*, 'parish'). For πλῆθος of a Christian company, cf. vi. 2, 5; xv. 12, 30; of a Jewish company, ii. 6; xix. 9; xxiii. 7; xxv. 24; in the general sense of 'multitude', xiv. 1; xvii. 4; cf. xxi. 22 δ.

ψυχὴ μία] δ adds καὶ οὐκ ἦν διάκρισις ἐν αὐτοῖς οὐδεμία, which adds nothing to the sense.

iv. 33

δυνάμει] i.e., the power of God manifested in mighty works (*δυνάμεις*) : see on ii. 22.

ἀπεδίδουν τὸ μαρτύριον οἱ ἀπόστολοι τοῦ κυρίου Ἰησοῦ τῆς ἀναστάσεως] 'the apostles bore their (*τό*) witness to the resurrection of the Lord Jesus'. The order of the genitives in B is a little confusing; Soden and Ropes prefer the order of δ, *τῆς ἀναστάσεως τοῦ κυρίου Ἰησοῦ* (so also P^8 and perhaps P^{45}). D adds *Χριστοῦ* after *Ἰησοῦ*, ℵ A have *τῆς ἀναστάσεως Ἰησοῦ χριστοῦ τοῦ κυρίου*.

N.B.—*ἀπεδίδουν* for classical *ἀπεδίδοσαν*, with ending from verbs in *-όω* or *-έω*.

iv. 34

ἐνδεής] Cf. Dt. xv. 4, *ὅτι οὐκ ἔσται ἐν σοὶ ἐνδεής*.

κτήτορες] Frequent in papyri for owners of real estate.

iv. 35

ἐτίθουν] For the ending see on iii. 2, and cf. *ἀπεδίδουν*, *ver.* 33.

διεδίδετο] Note *-ετο* for *-οτο*, under the influence of the thematic conjugation: cf. *ἀπεδίδουν*, *ver.* 33; *παρεδίδετο*, 1 Cor. xi. 23.

καθότι ἄν τις χρείαν εἶχεν] Iterative *ἄν* with imperf.: cf. ii. 45 for the same clause.

(b) Generosity of Barnabas, iv. 36-37

Ἰωσὴφ δὲ ὁ ἐπικληθεὶς Βαρνάβας ἀπὸ τῶν ἀποστόλων, ὅ ἐστιν 36
μεθερμηνευόμενον Υἱὸς Παρακλήσεως, Λευείτης, Κύπριος τῷ γένει,
ὑπάρχοντος αὐτῷ ἀγροῦ πωλήσας ἤνεγκεν τὸ χρῆμα καὶ ἔθηκεν παρὰ 37
τοὺς πόδας τῶν ἀποστόλων.

The description of the community of goods is now followed by two examples of the way it worked out in practice, in the one, happily; in the other, disastrously.

iv. 36

ἐπικληθεὶς] Cf. *ἐπεκλήθη*, i. 23, where another Joseph has a distinctive surname.

Βαρνάβας . . . Υἱὸς Παρακλήσεως] *παράκλησις* may mean either 'consolation' or 'exhortation'. If the former, *Βαρνάβας* probably represents Aram. *Bar-nawḥā* or *Bar-nĕwāḥā*, 'son of refreshment' (in NT times, as now, Gk. *β* was pronounced *v*). If 'son of exhortation' is the meaning, the word may be *Bar-nĕbiyyā*, 'son of the prophet', or rather the cognate Palmyrene *Bar-Nebō* (cf. Deissmann

BS, p. 188; Torrey, *CDA*, p. 30). Cf. παρεκάλει, of Barnabas, xi. 23. The idiom υἱὸς παρακλήσεως is characteristically Semitic; 'son of exhortation' means 'one who exhorts': cf. Lk. v. 34; x. 6; xvi. 8; xx. 34, 36.

ἀπὸ] Of the agent: see on ii. 22. δ has ὑπό.

Λευείτης] Despite the provisions of Num. xviii. 20 and Dt. x. 9 priests and Levites do not seem in practice to have been debarred from owning landed estates; cf. Jer. xxxii. 7 ff., Jos. *Vita*, 76 (both Jeremiah and Josephus were members of priestly families). Levites performed Temple functions inferior to those carried out by the priests.

Κύπριος] For other references to Cyprus and Cypriote Jews cf. xi. 19f.; xiii. 4; xv. 39; xxi. 3, 16; xxvii. 4. See on xiii. 4 for the position of Cyprus in the Roman Empire. Jews first settled in the island under the Ptolemys. They were expelled from it in A.D. 117 after having revolted. As the cousin of Mark, Barnabas had Jerusalem as well as Cypriote connections. He next appears at ix. 27.

τῷ γένει] Dative of reference, 'by family': cf. xviii. 2, 24.

iv. 37

ὑπάρχοντος αὐτῷ ἀγροῦ] ὑπάρχω, of what one has in possession. This is the only example in Ac. of ἀγρός: elsewhere χωρίον is used in this sense (cf. *ver.* 34; i. 18 f.; v. 3, 8; xxviii. 7).

(c) Deceit and Death of Ananias, v. 1-6.

Ἀνὴρ δέ τις Ἁνανίας ὀνόματι σὺν Σαπφείρῃ τῇ γυναικὶ αὐτοῦ 1
ἐπώλησεν κτῆμα καὶ ἐνοσφίσατο ἀπὸ τῆς τιμῆς, συνειδυίης καὶ τῆς 2
γυναικός, καὶ ἐνέγκας μέρος τι παρὰ τοὺς πόδας τῶν ἀποστόλων ἔθηκεν.
εἶπεν δὲ ὁ Πέτρος Ἁνανία, διὰ τί ἐπλήρωσεν ὁ Σατανᾶς τὴν καρδίαν 3
σου ψεύσασθαί σε τὸ πνεῦμα τὸ ἅγιον καὶ νοσφίσασθαι ἀπὸ τῆς τιμῆς
τοῦ χωρίου; οὐχὶ μένον σοὶ ἔμενεν καὶ πραθὲν ἐν τῇ σῇ ἐξουσίᾳ ὑπῆρχεν; 4
τί ὅτι ἔθου ἐν τῇ καρδίᾳ σου τὸ πρᾶγμα τοῦτο; οὐκ ἐψεύσω ἀνθρώποις
ἀλλὰ τῷ θεῷ. ἀκούων δὲ ὁ Ἁνανίας τοὺς λόγους τούτους πεσὼν 5
ἐξέψυξεν· καὶ ἐγένετο φόβος μέγας ἐπὶ πάντας τοὺς ἀκούοντας.
ἀναστάντες δὲ οἱ νεώτεροι συνέστειλαν αὐτὸν καὶ ἐξενέγκαντες ἔθαψαν. 6

While the historian takes pleasure in reporting the progress of the movement, the increase of the church, and the generosity of Barnabas, he does not omit a discreditable story of the kind that follows, as he might well have done. This is an early example of Luke's honesty as a narrator: cf. also xv. 39.

v. 1

δὲ] Adversative, in contrast to Barnabas.

Ἁνανίας] Note the rough breathing in WH. The name is the OT Hananiah (Heb. *Ḥănan-Yāh*, ' Jah is gracious ') : cf. Ἅννας, iv. 6.

ὀνόματι] Dat. of reference, like γένει in iv. 36.

Σαπφείρῃ] Aram. *shappīrā*, ' beautiful '. J. Klausner (*From Jesus to Paul*, pp. 289 f.) suggests the identification of this Sapphira with the person named on an ossuary found in Jerusalem in 1923, in both Hebrew (or Aramaic) and Greek : שפירא and *CAΦEIPA*.

κτῆμα] i.e., landed property, as is clear from *ver.* 3, χωρίου (cf. Prov. xxiii. 10 LXX, where κτῆμα represents Heb. *sādeh*, ' field '). See on ii. 45.

v. 2

ἐνοσφίσατο ἀπὸ τῆς τιμῆς] Cf. Josh. vii. 1, of Achan's action, ἐνοσφίσατο ἀπὸ τοῦ ἀναθέματος. A study of the conscious or unconscious parallels between Josh. and Ac. would be rewarding.[1] *Ver.* 4 makes it clear that the fault of Ananias did not lie in wrongfully appropriating what did not belong to him (his continued right to dispose as he wished of his own property is emphasized), but in pretending to give all when he gave only part. νοσφίζομαι is originally a poetic word, its primary meaning being to ' turn one's back on ' (so in Homer) ; it first appears in prose, with the sense ' peculate ', ' purloin ', in Xen. *Cyr.* iv. 2. 42, and thereafter freq. in Hellenistic writers and in papyri. Cf. Tit. ii. 10.

v. 3

Σατανᾶς] Heb. *sāṭān*, originally a common noun, meaning ' adversary ' (e.g., 1 K. xi. 14 ; Ps. cix. 6),[2] appears as a personal name for the angel who in Job i. 6 ff. and Zech. iii. 1 ff. accuses men before God (cf. Rev. xii. 10) and who in 1 Chr. xxi. 1 tempts them to evil (as here). The Greek form in *-ᾶς* is derived from the Aram. *status emphaticus* in *-ā*. In the inter-canonical literature the conception of Satan is developed and shows marked signs of Iranian influence. In NT he is identified with Baʿal-Zĕbūl (lit. ' lord of the high place '), ' prince of the demons ' (Mt. xii. 24 ff.), and is referred to as ' the evil one ' (cf. Mk. iv. 15 with Mt. xiii. 19).

[1] Cf. *BC* ii., pp. 68 f.

[2] H. Torczyner in *ET* xlviii. (1936-7), pp. 563 ff., argues that the Heb. form was originally *shāṭān*, from *shūṭ*, ' to rove ', ' go to and fro ' (as in Job i. 7 ; ii. 2), and compares the similar activity of the eyes of God in 2 Chr. xvi. 9 ; Zech. iv. 10. The primary idea of the name would then be ' one who roves ' through the earth to take note of the doings of men and report them to God.

He has his kingdom, angels, and children in opposition to the kingdom, angels, and children of God (Mt. xii. 26; xxv. 41; 1 Jn. iii. 10). He is the 'prince of this world' (Jn. xvi. 11), the 'god of this age', who blinds the minds of the unbelieving (2 Cor. iv. 4), the 'prince of the power of the air, the spirit that now works in the sons of disobedience' (Eph. ii. 2). He is identified with the serpent which seduced Eve, and true to his pristine character, is still 'the deceiver of the whole world' (cf. Rom. xvi. 20; 2 Cor. xi. 2 f.; Rev. xii. 9; xx. 2). The Gk. equivalent of his name is διάβολος, 'calumniator': see x. 38; xiii. 10.

ἐπλήρωσεν] vg. *temtauit*, reflecting ἐπείρασεν (attested also in Ath.lat Did Epiph Fulg), a corruption due to the omission of λ. For Satan's action on the heart cf. Lk. xxii. 3; Jn. xiii. 2, 27.

τὸ πνεῦμα τὸ ἅγιον] The Holy Spirit is here clearly regarded as personal: cf. *ver.* 4, ἐψεύσω . . . τῷ θεῷ.

v. 4

οὐχὶ μένον σοὶ ἔμενεν καὶ πραθὲν ἐν τῇ σῇ ἐξουσίᾳ ὑπῆρχεν;] The communism was plainly voluntary. The negative οὐχί controls the whole sentence, and is to be taken with ὑπῆρχεν as well as with ἔμενεν. Otherwise we might put the question mark after ἔμενεν and take the following words as a statement ('and having been sold it was still in your authority'), but this is less natural.

τί ὅτι] Cf. *ver.* 9. Elliptical; sc. ἐστιν between τί and ὅτι, 'Why (is it) that . . . ?'

ἔθου ἐν τῇ καρδίᾳ] Cf. xix. 21; also ἔθετο Δανιὴλ ἐπὶ τὴν καρδίαν αὐτοῦ, Dan. i. 8 (Theod.); θέσθε ἐν ταῖς καρδίαις ὑμῶν, Hagg. ii. 18.

τὸ πρᾶγμα τοῦτο] δ has <τὸ> πονηρὸν τοῦτο (cf. iii. 17).

οὐκ ἐψεύσω ἀνθρώποις ἀλλὰ τῷ θεῷ] It was to God that the lie was told, because it was to Him that the gift was offered. Cf. ψεύδομαι followed by dat. here, 'to tell lies to', with its construction with acc. in *ver.* 3, 'to deceive'. The parallelism of τὸ πνεῦμα τὸ ἅγιον in *ver.* 3 with τῷ θεῷ here indicates that the Holy Spirit is God.

v. 5

πεσὼν] D prefixes παραχρῆμα from *ver.* 10, to heighten the dramatic effect.

ἐξέψυξεν] 'breathed out his soul (*or* life)'; in NT only here, *ver.* 10, and xii. 23 (Mod. Gk. ξεψυχῶ). In Ezek. xxi. 7 it means 'to faint'. Cf. ἐκπνέω, Mk. xv. 37, 39; Lk. xxiii. 46. 'The very rare word ἐκψύχειν seems to be almost altogether confined to the medical writers, and very seldom used by them' (Hobart, p. 37; he quotes Hippocrates, Galen, Aretaeus). To Hobart's examples MM add Herondas iv. 29, ἢν μὴ λάβῃ τὸ μῆλον, ἐκ τάχα ψύξει (N.B. the tmesis). That Christians may be visited with premature death for grievous sin is taught elsewhere in NT: cf. 1 Cor. xi. 30; Jas. v. 20; 1 Jn. v. 16 f., and perhaps 1 Cor. v. 5; 1 Tim. i. 20. Some commentators, while admitting that Ananias may have died of shock, find it difficult to believe that Sapphira died from the same cause the same afternoon: 'the addition of Sapphira adds such improbability as lies in a coincidence' (A. W. F. Blunt). But given the likelihood of the man's death from this cause (according to Dr. Blunt, 'the death of Ananias by itself is not difficult to credit, if we remember the excitement of the time. The sudden detection of his guilt may well have produced a mortal convulsion of feeling in him'), there is little improbability in the death of Sapphira, who in addition to the surprise of detection and the conviction of guilt, suffered the shock of her husband's sudden death.

v. 6

ἀναστάντες] This and the corresponding ptc. of *ἐγείρω*, followed by a verb of motion, are cited in MH (ii, p. 453) as examples of an idiom common in Heb. and Aram., and classified among the Semitizing redundant uses of the ptc. See on iv. 19, and cf. viii. 27; ix. 39; x. 20, 23; xxii. 10.

οἱ νεώτεροι] Cf. *ver.* 10, *οἱ νεανίσκοι.* Probably the younger men of the community, and not professional buriers.

συνέστειλαν] 'wrapped up': LC render 'gathered up', citing vg *amouerunt*, Lucif. *sustulerunt*, and referring to this meaning of *συστέλλω* in Plutarch, *Aratus* 22. 1037 A, *συστείλαντες ἑαυτούς*. In its only other NT occurrence, 1 Cor. vii. 29, it means 'to shorten'. 'In medical language the word is very frequent and its use varied: one use was almost identical with that here, viz. "to bandage a limb", "to compress by bandaging"' (Hobart, p. 38: he quotes Hippocrates, Galen, Dioscorides).

ἐξενέγκαντες] *ἐκφέρω* is used technically in the sense 'to carry out for burial'; cf. *vv.* 9 f. For its ordinary sense cf. *ver.* 15.

(d) Death of Sapphira, v. 7-11

Ἐγένετο δὲ ὡς ὡρῶν τριῶν διάστημα καὶ ἡ γυνὴ αὐτοῦ μὴ εἰδυῖα 7
τὸ γεγονὸς εἰσῆλθεν. ἀπεκρίθη δὲ πρὸς αὐτὴν Πέτρος Εἰπέ μοι, εἰ 8
τοσούτου τὸ χωρίον ἀπέδοσθε; ἡ δὲ εἶπεν Ναί, τοσούτου. ὁ δὲ Πέ- 9
τρος πρὸς αὐτήν Τί ὅτι συνεφωνήθη ὑμῖν πειράσαι τὸ πνεῦμα Κυρίου;
ἰδοὺ οἱ πόδες τῶν θαψάντων τὸν ἄνδρα σου ἐπὶ τῇ θύρᾳ καὶ ἐξοίσουσίν

σε. ἔπεσεν δὲ παραχρῆμα πρὸς τοὺς πόδας αὐτοῦ καὶ ἐξέψυξεν· 10
εἰσελθόντες δὲ οἱ νεανίσκοι εὗρον αὐτὴν νεκράν, καὶ ἐξενέγκαντες
ἔθαψαν πρὸς τὸν ἄνδρα αὐτῆς. Καὶ ἐγένετο φόβος μέγας ἐφ᾽ ὅλην 11
τὴν ἐκκλησίαν καὶ ἐπὶ πάντας τοὺς ἀκούοντας ταῦτα.

v. 7

Ἐγένετο δὲ ὡς ὡρῶν τριῶν διάστημα καὶ ἡ γυνὴ αὐτοῦ . . . εἰσῆλθεν] 'And there elapsed (lit., took place, *ἐγένετο*) an interval of about three hours, and his wife came in.' It is possible, on the other hand, that we have here an *ἐγένετο* construction of the Semitizing kind (see on iv. 5), but this would be the form where *ἐγένετο* is followed by *καί* and the indic., which is not the form used in Ac., and *ὡς ὡρῶν τριῶν διάστημα* would have to be taken as an adverbial phrase. The former rendering is more likely. Note the characteristic Lukan *ὡς* before *τριῶν* (see on i. 15).

v. 8

ἀπεκρίθη] She had not spoken ; here, as in some other places in NT and LXX, *ἀποκρίνομαι* means simply 'to address' : cf. iii. 12, *ἀπεκρίνατο*.

τοσούτου] Genitive of price.

v. 9

Τί ὅτι] See on *ver*. 4.

συνεφωνήθη ὑμῖν] i.e., *conuenit inter uos*, 'there was an agreement between you'. The verb is used with *μετά* in Mt. xx. 2, but elsewhere it takes the dat., as here (so Mt. xx. 13 ; MM give papyrus parallels). Cf. Demaratus, *Arcadica*, *ap*. Stob. *Flor*. 39. 32, *συνεφώνησε τοῖς δήμοις*.

πειράσαι τὸ πνεῦμα Κυρίου] Cf. *τί πειράζετε Κύριον;* Ex. xvii. 2 ; *οὐκ ἐκπειράσεις Κύριον τὸν θεόν σου*, Dt. vi. 16, quoted by our Lord in His temptation. The idea in this tempting is 'seeing how far you can go' (LC).

v. 10

ἐξέψυξεν] See on *ver*. 5.

ἐξενέγκαντες] D pesh have *συστείλαντες ἐξήνεγκαν καί* (cf. *ver*. 6).

v. 11

Καὶ ἐγένετο φόβος μέγας] As in *ver*. 5 : cf. ii. 43.

ἐφ᾽ ὅλην τὴν ἐκκλησίαν] The first occurrence in Ac. (but cf. ii. 47 D) of *ἐκκλησία*, which became the regular word for the

Christian community, both in its local (or visible) and universal (or invisible) sense. At what point the Christians began to adopt it as the name for their community is uncertain, though it was no doubt very early. It was one of the possible Gk. equivalents for Aram. *kĕnishtā*, and the primitive Jerusalem church was perhaps known as the *kĕnishtā* ('synagogue') of the Nazarenes. (Another Gk. equivalent of *kĕnishtā* was *συναγωγή*, which was normally reserved, however, for a local Jewish community or meeting-place, though it is also used occasionally of Christian meetings: see on vi. 9.)

The word *ἐκκλησία* has both a Gentile and a Jewish background. In Attic Gk. it was the name of the citizen body in its legislative capacity; this usage obtained in many other Greek cities (e.g. Ephesus: cf. xix. 32, 39, 41). But it is against the Jewish background only that we can understand the early Christian usage. In LXX it is used for the 'congregation' of Israel, the nation in its theocratic aspect, organized as a religious community (cf. Dt. ix. 10; xviii. 16; xxiii. 1 f.; xxxi. 30; Josh. viii. 35, where *ἐκκλησία* represents Heb. *qāhāl*, frequently also rendered by *συναγωγή*:[1] see further on vii. 38). Philo and Josephus also use *ἐκκλησία* thus, apparently in preference to *συναγωγή*.

The Christian Ecclesia was both new and old—new, because of its relation and witness to Jesus as the Messiah and to the epochal events of the Cross and Resurrection and outpouring of the Spirit; old, in that it was the continuation and successor of the original 'Congregation of the Lord', which had previously been restricted to one nation, but now was thrown open to all believers everywhere. For the NT usage of *ἐκκλησία* see F. J. A. Hort, *The Christian Ecclesia*; G. Johnston, *The Doctrine of the Church in the NT*; K. L. Schmidt *s.v.* *ἐκκλησία* in Kittel's *Theol. Wörterbuch zum NT*.

[1] In Dt. and the following OT books, except Jer. and Ezk., *qāhāl* is regularly rendered by *ἐκκλησία* in LXX; in Gen.-Num., Jer. and Ezk., it is regularly rendered by *συναγωγή* which is also used throughout LXX as the equivalent of Heb. *'ēdāh*. See on vi. 9; xx. 28. The Aram. equivalent of *'ēdāh*, and occasionally of *qāhāl*, was *kĕnishtā*, which may not only have been the term by which the Christian community was first known in Jerusalem, but also, probably, the Aram. word represented by *ἐκκλησία* in the sayings of Jesus in Mt. xvi. 18; xviii. 17. In the latter passage the Sinaitic Syriac has *kĕnūshtā* (its rendering of the former passage is not available, as Mt. xvi. 16-xvii. 13 is missing from the MS.; the Curetonian and Peshitta have *'edtā* in both passages). See K. L. Schmidt in G. Kittel's *Theologisches Wörterbuch zum NT*, iii. 528 f. The view here expressed is contested by J. Y. Campbell in *JTS* xlix. (1948), pp. 130 ff.; he argues that in Christian usage *ἐκκλησία* first meant a 'meeting', then a 'congregation', and only later acquired its catholic sense.

5. The Apostles before the Sanhedrin again, v. 12-42

(a) Signs and Wonders, v. 12-16

Διὰ δὲ τῶν χειρῶν τῶν ἀποστόλων ἐγίνετο σημεῖα καὶ τέρατα πολλὰ 12
ἐν τῷ λαῷ· καὶ ἦσαν ὁμοθυμαδὸν πάντες ἐν τῇ Στοᾷ Σολομῶντος· τῶν 13
δὲ λοιπῶν οὐδεὶς ἐτόλμα κολλᾶσθαι αὐτοῖς, ἀλλ' ἐμεγάλυνεν αὐτοὺς
ὁ λαός, μᾶλλον δὲ προσετίθεντο πιστεύοντες τῷ κυρίῳ πλήθη ἀνδρῶν 14
τε καὶ γυναικῶν· ὥστε καὶ εἰς τὰς πλατείας ἐκφέρειν τοὺς ἀσθενεῖς 15
καὶ τιθέναι ἐπὶ κλιναρίων καὶ κραβάττων, ἵνα ἐρχομένου Πέτρου κἂν
ἡ σκιὰ ἐπισκιάσει τινὶ αὐτῶν. συνήρχετο δὲ καὶ τὸ πλῆθος τῶν πέριξ 16
πόλεων Ἰερουσαλήμ, φέροντες ἀσθενεῖς καὶ ὀχλουμένους ὑπὸ πνευ-
μάτων ἀκαθάρτων, οἵτινες ἐθεραπεύοντο ἅπαντες.

This paragraph is a summary or interlude between the preceding and following incidents.

v. 12

Διὰ δὲ τῶν χειρῶν κ.τ.λ.] Cf. *διὰ χειρὸς ἀνόμων* ii. 23.

ἐγίνετο σημεῖα καὶ τέρατα πολλὰ] Cf. ii. 43.

καὶ ἦσαν ὁμοθυμαδὸν πάντες ἐν τῇ Στοᾷ Σολομῶντος] Cf. ii. 44, 46. For Solomon's colonnade see on iii. 11. This seems to have been their public meeting place. Certainly no ordinary building would have sufficed for their increasing numbers. Probably this is the part of the Temple meant in ii. 46, as it may have been the place where Peter addressed the crowds at Pentecost. The breaking of bread took place privately, at home (see on ii. 46).

v. 13

τῶν δὲ λοιπῶν οὐδεὶς ἐτόλμα κολλᾶσθαι αὐτοῖς] If we take the text as it stands, 'the rest' will be the Jews who did not believe, and their reason for not daring to join the company which enjoyed such popularity will be the warning of Ananias and Sapphira's fate. F. C. Burkitt (*JTS* xx [1919], p. 326) says: 'Luke uses *κολλᾶσθαι* of attaching oneself to somebody without a regular introduction, which may sometimes be successful (Acts viii. 29) but not always (ix. 26)'; no one dared join the believers on his own authority, that is; each had to be received and baptized. But this, as LC rightly say, 'scarcely seems to fit well with the following verse'. Blass suggested for *κολλᾶσθαι* the meaning 'meddle', which according to LC gives 'far the best sense' and 'has the additional advantage of giving a natural meaning to *μᾶλλον*', but 'is open to the fatal objection that there seems to be no clear evidence for κολλᾶσθαι in this sense'.[1] A. Pallis emends κολλᾶσθαι αὐτοῖς to κωλῦσαι αὐτούς, and follows A. Hilgenfeld in emending λοιπῶν to Λευειτῶν, rendering 'And of the Levites none dared to prevent them' (i.e. from holding meetings in the Temple precincts).

ἀλλ ἐμεγάλυνεν αὐτοὺς ὁ λαός] om P^{45}. Cf. ii. 47.

v. 14

προσετίθεντο] Cf. the same verb in ii. 41, 47; xi. 24. According to H. St. J. Thackeray in *JTS* xxx (1929), p. 363, προστίθεσθαι came in certain passages of Josephus to be used as a synonym for πιστεύειν.

τῷ κυρίῳ] Dat. after προσετίθεντο or πιστεύοντες? For the former cf. xi. 24; for the latter cf. xviii. 8. Formally, it is probably to be taken with πιστεύοντες, but in sense it may go with either or both. With the dat., πιστεύω means 'to believe or trust (somebody or something)', as distinct from πιστεύω εἰς, 'believe in', and πιστεύω ἐπί, 'believe on'. In Lk.-Ac. πιστεύω occurs with dat. nine times, with εἰς three times, with ἐπί five times (followed once by dat., four times by acc.). Cf. *Proleg.*, pp. 67 f.

v. 15

ὥστε καὶ] 'so that they actually'.

πλατείας] sc. ὁδούς, 'broadways', 'main streets', 'squares' (cf. Ital. *piazza*, Fr. *place*, Ger. *Platz*).

ἐκφέρειν] In *vv.* 6, 9 f., used in a technical sense; here in the ordinary sense, 'carry out'.

ἐπὶ κλιναρίων καὶ κραβάττων] Luke has four words for a sick bed: κλίνη, κλινίδιον, and these two. He is the only NT writer to use κλινίδιον and κλινάριον. In Lk. v. 19, 24 he has κλινίδιον for κράβαττος of Mk. ii. 4 ff.: κράβαττος, apparently of Macedonian origin, means strictly a camp-bed. Later MSS. have κράββατος, probably a dialect variant, which (in its diminutive form κραββάτιον) is represented by Mod. Gk. κρεββάτι. Cf. MH ii. 102.

ἐρχομένου Πέτρου] Either gen. abs., 'as Peter came', or gen. after σκιά, '(the shadow) of Peter coming'.

ἡ σκιὰ] Cf. the effect of Paul's handkerchiefs and aprons, xix. 12.

[1] The objection would not be so fatal if we could follow Torrey in supposing that κολλᾶσθαι αὐτοῖς represents Aram. *lĕ-hithlaḥāmāh 'amhōn*, which could equally well mean 'to contend with them' (*CDA*, pp. 31 f.). But he later abandoned this suggestion in favour of the view that Aram. *sēbūthā*, 'the elders', was misread as *shērīthā*, 'the rest', the original meaning having been: 'of *the elders* no one dared join himself to them; nevertheless *the common people* magnified them, . . . multitudes both of men and women' (*DPC*, p. 96; cf. *ET* xlvi. [1934-5], pp. 428 f.).

ἐπισκιάσει] Note the future after *ἵνα* and *κἄν* (*καὶ ἄν*). D has *ἐπισκιάσῃ*. As there was no distinction in pronunciation between *ει* and *η* in Hellenistic Gk., 'the passage is wholly useless for any argument as to the use of *ἵνα* with a future' (*Proleg.*, p. 35). Cf. xxi. 24.

αὐτῶν] δ adds by way of explanation, *ἀπηλλάσσοντο γὰρ ἀπὸ πάσης ἀσθενείας ὡς εἶχεν ἕκαστος αὐτῶν*, 'for they were set free from every sickness which each of them had' (so, with variations, DE d e g p vg.codd. Lucif).

v. 16

πέριξ] Only here in NT.

ἀσθενεῖς καὶ ὀχλουμένους ὑπὸ πνευμάτων ἀκαθάρτων] He distinguishes between sickness and demon possession. Cf. xix. 12; Lk. iv. 40 f.; vi. 17 f.; vii. 21; xiii. 32. For *ὀχλεῖσθαι* cf. Lk. vi. 18, T.R. The 'quasi-medical use' of this word, says E. K Simpson, 'is amply sustained by the practice of [Vettius] Valens, who employs the verb with specifications of disease, and makes *σωματικαὶ ὀχλήσεις* his stock-term for "bodily maladies"' (e.g. 163. 22).

(b) Second Imprisonment and Examination of the Apostles v. 17-32

Ἀναστὰς δὲ ὁ ἀρχιερεὺς καὶ πάντες οἱ σὺν αὐτῷ, ἡ οὖσα αἵρεσις 17
τῶν Σαδδουκαίων, ἐπλήσθησαν ζήλου καὶ ἐπέβαλον τὰς χεῖρας ἐπὶ 18
τοὺς ἀποστόλους καὶ ἔθεντο αὐτοὺς ἐν τηρήσει δημοσίᾳ. Ἄγγελος 19
δὲ Κυρίου διὰ νυκτὸς ἤνοιξε τὰς θύρας τῆς φυλακῆς ἐξαγαγών τε
αὐτοὺς εἶπεν Πορεύεσθε καὶ σταθέντες λαλεῖτε ἐν τῷ ἱερῷ τῷ λαῷ 20
πάντα τὰ ῥήματα τῆς ζωῆς ταύτης. ἀκούσαντες δὲ εἰσῆλθον ὑπὸ 21
τὸν ὄρθρον εἰς τὸ ἱερὸν καὶ ἐδίδασκον. Παραγενόμενος δὲ ὁ ἀρχιερεὺς καὶ οἱ σὺν αὐτῷ συνεκάλεσαν τὸ συνέδριον καὶ πᾶσαν τὴν γερουσίαν
τῶν υἱῶν Ἰσραήλ, καὶ ἀπέστειλαν εἰς τὸ δεσμωτήριον ἀχθῆναι αὐτούς.
οἱ δὲ παραγενόμενοι ὑπηρέται οὐχ εὗρον αὐτοὺς ἐν τῇ φυλακῇ, ἀνα- 22
στρέψαντες δὲ ἀπήγγειλαν λέγοντες ὅτι Τὸ δεσμωτήριον εὕρομεν 23
κεκλεισμένον ἐν πάσῃ ἀσφαλείᾳ καὶ τοὺς φύλακας ἑστῶτας ἐπὶ τῶν
θυρῶν, ἀνοίξαντες δὲ ἔσω οὐδένα εὕρομεν. ὡς δὲ ἤκουσαν τοὺς 24
λόγους τούτους ὅ τε στρατηγὸς τοῦ ἱεροῦ καὶ οἱ ἀρχιερεῖς, διηπόρουν
περὶ αὐτῶν τί ἂν γένοιτο τοῦτο. Παραγενόμενος δέ τις ἀπήγγειλεν 25
αὐτοῖς ὅτι Ἰδοὺ οἱ ἄνδρες οὓς ἔθεσθε ἐν τῇ φυλακῇ εἰσὶν ἐν τῷ ἱερῷ
ἑστῶτες καὶ διδάσκοντες τὸν λαόν. τότε ἀπελθὼν ὁ στρατηγὸς σὺν 26
τοῖς ὑπηρέταις ἦγεν αὐτούς, οὐ μετὰ βίας, ἐφοβοῦντο γὰρ τὸν λαόν,
μὴ λιθασθῶσιν· ἀγαγόντες δὲ αὐτοὺς ἔστησαν ἐν τῷ συνεδρίῳ. καὶ 27
ἐπηρώτησεν αὐτοὺς ὁ ἀρχιερεὺς λέγων Παραγγελίᾳ παρηγγείλαμεν 28
ὑμῖν μὴ διδάσκειν ἐπὶ τῷ ὀνόματι τούτῳ, καὶ ἰδοὺ πεπληρώκατε τὴν

*'Ιερουσαλὴμ τῆς διδαχῆς ὑμῶν, καὶ βούλεσθε ἐπαγαγεῖν ἐφ' ἡμᾶς τὸ
αἷμα τοῦ ἀνθρώπου τούτου. ἀποκριθεὶς δὲ Πέτρος καὶ οἱ ἀπόστολοι* 29
εἶπαν Πειθαρχεῖν δεῖ θεῷ μᾶλλον ἢ ἀνθρώποις. ὁ θεὸς τῶν πατέρων 30
ἡμῶν ἤγειρεν 'Ιησοῦν, ὃν ὑμεῖς διεχειρίσασθε κρεμάσαντες ἐπὶ ξύλου· 31
*τοῦτον ὁ θεὸς ἀρχηγὸν καὶ σωτῆρα ὕψωσεν τῇ δεξιᾷ αὐτοῦ, τοῦ δοῦναι
μετάνοιαν τῷ 'Ισραὴλ καὶ ἄφεσιν ἁμαρτιῶν· καὶ ἡμεῖς ἐσμὲν μάρτυρες* 32
τῶν ῥημάτων τούτων, καὶ τὸ πνεῦμα τὸ ἅγιον ὃ ἔδωκεν ὁ θεὸς τοῖς 32
πειθαρχοῦσιν αὐτῷ.

v. 17

'Αναστὰς] Semitizing use of the ptc., as in LXX (see on *ver.* 6); it means little more than 'thereupon'. The ptc. here agrees with the nearest nominative, *ἀρχιερεύς*. The reading of p indicates an early corruption of *ἀναστὰς* to *Ἄννας* (*Annas autem . . .*).

ὁ ἀρχιερεὺς καὶ πάντες οἱ σὺν αὐτῷ] Another way of referring to the Sanhedrin: see on iv. 5.

ἡ οὖσα αἵρεσις τῶν Σαδδουκαίων] Although Sadducees are explicitly mentioned here, Pharisees were also present (cf. *ver.* 34). The high-priestly group were mostly Sadducees. Since they formed a considerable proportion of the court, and the High Priest seems to have been *ex officio* President of the Sanhedrin in those days, the influence of the Sadducees in its counsels was great, hence their special mention here. But see on *ver.* 34 for the counter-influence of the Pharisees. *αἵρεσις* ('party') is used of the Pharisees in xv. 5; xxvi. 5; of the Nazarenes in xxiv. 5; so also xxiv. 14; xxviii. 22; it is used in 1 Cor. xi. 19 and Gal. v. 20 of divisions in the churches, and in 2 Pet. ii. 1 of heresies. In a Greek context it means a philosophic school: cf. Jos. *Ant.* xviii. 1, where the Pharisees, Sadducees, Essenes, and even the Zealots (!) are misleadingly called 'philosophies' (*φιλοσοφίαι*).

For *ἡ οὖσα αἵρεσις*, 'the local party', cf. xi. 22; xiii. 1; xiv. 13; xxviii. 17. This use of the ptc. of *εἰμί* 'introduces some technical phrase . . . and is almost equivalent to *τοῦ ὀνομαζομένου*' (Ramsay, *CRE*, p. 52, on *τοῦ ὄντος Διός*, xiv. 13 D). Perhaps the best rendering is 'local': cf. the English use of 'existing' in the sense of 'present' (e.g., 'the existing government'). J. de Zwaan (*BC* ii, pp. 56 ff.) thinks this usage is developed from the use of *ὤν* with an adverbial extension, as in xvi. 3; xix. 35; xxii. 5.

ζήλου] 'envy', because of the apostles' popularity. *B** has *ζήλους*: for the neuter cf. 2 Cor. ix. 2 א B 33; Phil. iii. 6 א* A B D* F G. The classical masc. (cf. xiii. 45) is rare in LXX. The word is neuter in Mod. Gk., which has regularized the prevalent tendency in Hellenistic Gk.

v. 18

ἐπέβαλον τὰς χεῖρας ἐπὶ τοὺς ἀποστόλους] Cf. iv. 3, ἐπέβαλον αὐτοῖς τὰς χεῖρας, and note the different construction.

ἐν τηρήσει δημοσίᾳ] 'in public ward': cf. iv. 3. D adds, from Jn. vii. 53, καὶ ἐπορεύθη εἷς ἕκαστος εἰς τὰ ἴδια.

v. 19

Ἄγγελος δὲ Κυρίου] The doubly anarthrous ἄγγελος Κυρίου is the LXX phrase for Heb. *mal'akh Yahweh*, the special angel who represented God: see on vii. 30, 38. For ἄγγελος Κυρίου cf. viii. 26; xii. 7, 23; Mt. i. 20, 24; ii. 13, 19; xxviii. 2; Lk. i. 11; ii. 9. According to Dalman, 'one must not seek to find in this "*the* angel of the Lord" of the Old Testament. ἄγγελος is defined by κυρίου as a messenger of God' (*Words of Jesus*, p. 183). But the difficulty of distinguishing the 'angel of the Lord' from the 'Spirit of the Lord' in viii. 26 ff. suggests that in NT, as in OT, the ἄγγελος Κυρίου denotes the presence or agency of God Himself.

ἤνοιξε τὰς θύρας τῆς φυλακῆς κ.τ.λ.] For the release see on xii. 7 ff. (especially for the angelic agency); xvi. 25 ff.

v. 20

σταθέντες] Not redundant here; it suggests steadfastness.

τῆς ζωῆς ταύτης] See on iii. 15. In Aram. *ḥayyē* means both 'life' and 'salvation' and there would be no difference between τῆς ζωῆς ταύτης here and τῆς σωτηρίας ταύτης in xiii. 26; pesh renders both phrases by *dĕ-ḥaye*.

v. 21

ὑπὸ τὸν ὄρθρον] 'at daybreak'; quite classical.

παραγενόμενος] παραγενόμενοι B*.

ὁ ἀρχιερεὺς καὶ οἱ σὺν αὐτῷ] See on *ver*. 17.

συνεκάλεσαν] ἐγερθέντες τὸ πρωῒ καὶ συγκαλεσάμενοι D.

τὸ συνέδριον καὶ πᾶσαν τὴν γερουσίαν τῶν υἱῶν Ἰσραήλ] Cf. Ex. xii. 21, πᾶσαν γερουσίαν υἱῶν Ἰσραήλ. καί is probably epexegetic, 'seeing that there can be no question as to the identity of the two conceptions συνέδριον and γερουσία' (Schürer, II. i. 172). See on iv. 5, 15.

v. 22

οἱ δὲ παραγενόμενοι ὑπηρέται] D has οἱ δὲ ὑπηρέται παραγενόμενοι καὶ ἀνοίξαντες τὴν φυλακήν, inserting clumsily, as in *ver*. 21, participles and details which add nothing to our real knowledge.[1] The ὑπηρέται were probably Levites of the Temple watch, under the command of the captain (cf. *ver*. 26, and see on iv. 1).

[1] p vg hcl* also add 'opened the prison', which thus appears to be a δ reading.

v. 23

ὅτι] *ὅτι recitantis*: see on ii. 13.

τοὺς φύλακας ἑστῶτας ἐπὶ τῶν θυρῶν] Cf. xii. 6, *φύλακές τε πρὸ τῆς θύρας ἐτήρουν τὴν φυλακήν.*

v. 24

τί ἂν γένοιτο τοῦτο] The direct form would presumably be *τί γενήσεται τοῦτο*, but in the indirect greater indefiniteness is suggested by the construction with *ἄν*. Cf. Lk. vi. 11, where *τί ἂν ποιήσαιεν* is 'the hesitating substitute for the direct *τί ποιήσομεν;*' (*Proleg.*, p. 198). The potential optative with *ἄν* was a purely literary construction in NT times, and Luke is the only NT author who uses it: cf. viii. 31; x. 17; xvii. 18; xxi. 33; xxvi. 29; Lk. i. 62; ix. 46; xv. 26; xviii. 36 D.

v. 25

εἰσὶν . . . ἑστῶτες καὶ διδάσκοντες] See on i. 10 for the periphrasis.

v. 26

ἦγεν] Imperfect, because the manner of the act is vividly portrayed. In *ver.* 27 (*ἀγαγόντες δέ*) the conclusion of the act is what is contemplated.

οὐ μετὰ βίας] Emphatic. D accidentally omits *οὐ*.

v. 27

ἀρχιερεὺς] *ἱερεύς* D; *pontefix*[1] d; *praetor* h. The reading of h probably represents *στρατηγός* (for which d has *praetor* in *ver.* 26 and h in iv. 1).

v. 28

Παραγγελίᾳ παρηγγείλαμεν] For the Semitism see on iv. 17. LC quote from *P Oxy* 1411 (A.D. 260) *παραγγέλματι παραγγελῆναι.* The word (whether verb or noun) is used in papyri of official notification to follow or refrain from some course.

ἐπαγαγεῖν ἐφ' ἡμᾶς τὸ αἷμα τοῦ ἀνθρώπου τούτου] Cf. Mt. xxvii. 25, *τὸ αἷμα αὐτοῦ ἐφ' ἡμᾶς.*

τοῦ ἀνθρώπου τούτου] Note again the avoidance of the name of Jesus: cf. iv. 17. D has *ἐκείνου* for *τούτου.*

v. 29

ἀποκριθεὶς δὲ Πέτρος καὶ οἱ ἀπόστολοι εἶπαν] See on iv. 19 both for the grammar and for the sentiment of their reply. Note that

[1] *Sic* (for *pontifex*).

ἀποκριθεὶς agrees with *Πέτρος*, *εἶπαν* with *Πέτρος καὶ οἱ ἀπόστολοι.* The text of D has been corrupted ; the true δ text is represented by h : *respondens autem Petrus dixit ad il[lum] : cui obaudire oportet, deo an hominibus ? ille aut[em ait : deo].* (30) *et dixit Petrus ad eum : deus patrum,* etc.

v. 30

ἤγειρεν] Probably not of the resurrection, but of the inauguration of His ministry : see on iii. 26, *ἀναστήσας*. Cf. Judg. iii. 9, etc., *ἤγειρεν Κύριος σωτῆρα τῷ Ἰσραὴλ καὶ ἔσωσεν αὐτούς.*

ὑμεῖς] Emphatic ; the Sanhedrin, led by the priestly party, took the initiative in having Him crucified.

διεχειρίσασθε] Cf. xxvi. 21, of violent handling (' did away with ').

κρεμάσαντες ἐπὶ ξύλου] The reference is to Dt. xxi. 22 f., *καὶ κρεμάσητε αὐτὸν ἐπὶ ξύλου . . . ὅτι κεκατηραμένος ὑπὸ θεοῦ πᾶς κρεμάμενος ἐπὶ ξύλου* (cf. Jos. *Ant.* iv. 8. 6 for the Jewish law of blasphemy based on this). Cf. also x. 39 and Gal. iii. 13, and for *ξύλον* meaning ' tree ' in this sense, cf. xiii. 29 ; 1 Pet. ii. 24. This use of *ξύλον* for a gibbet goes back through LXX to Heb. *'ēṣ*, which denotes both a tree and the stake or pole on which bodies of executed criminals were hung. Cf. also Lat. *arbor infelix* for a cross. For another sense of *ξύλον* (' stocks ') cf. xvi. 24. The proper meaning of the word is ' wood '. With the language of *vv.* 30 ff. cf. that of iii. 13 ff.

v. 31

τοῦτον] Emphatic : cf. ii. 23.

ἀρχηγὸν καὶ σωτῆρα] For *ἀρχηγός* see on iii. 15 ; for *σωτήρ* cf. the quotation from Judg. iii. 9 in the note on *ἤγειρεν* in *ver.* 30 ; *ἀρχηγός* is used in Judg. xi. 6, 11 of Jephthah as the military leader (*qāṣīn*) of Israel. The allusions to Judg. are significant in the light of other Jewish references ; e.g., in the eleventh of the Eighteen Benedictions, ' Restore our judges as at the first ' (cf. Isa. i. 26). Cf. Ps. Sol. xvii. 23 ff. ; Sib. Or. iii. 652 ff., where Messiah is depicted as a royal captain triumphing over the ungodly nations. As for *σωτήρ*, the ideas of ' healing ' and ' salvation ' are also frequent in Jewish thought : cf. Ps. Sol. x. 9 (*τοῦ κυρίου ἡ σωτηρία*), the eighth of the Eighteen Benedictions (' Heal us, O Lord, and we shall be healed ; save us, and we shall be saved ' [from Jer. xvii. 14]), etc. This, of course, goes back to OT language (cf. Judg. iii. 9 above ; Ps. cvi. 47 ; cxviii. 25 ; Isa. lxiii. 8 f., etc.).

ὕψωσεν] Cf. *ὑψωθείς*, ii. 33 ; *ὑπερύψωσεν*, Phil. ii. 9.

τοῦ δοῦναι μετάνοιαν κ.τ.λ.] *τοῦ* (א B) is omitted by A D byz. T. E. Page compares Lk. xxiv. 47 f., where Jesus ' orders that there be proclaimed as by heralds (*κηρυχθῆναι*) " repentance "—the condition He imposes as a Prince, and " remission of sins "—the reward He offers as a Saviour '. Note that the nation of Israel as a whole is still offered the privilege, first of accepting the Gospel, and then of being evangelists to the Gentile world, in fulfilment of Isa. xlii. 6; xlix. 6 (quoted in xiii. 47 below). Cf. ii. 36; iii. 19-26.

v. 32

καὶ ἡμεῖς ἐσμὲν μάρτυρες] Cf. i. 8; ii. 32 f.; iii. 15; the emphasis on personal witness is maintained. Page, continuing the comparison quoted in the notes on *ver.* 31, compares Lk. xxiv. 48.

ῥημάτων] Probably ' things ' rather than ' words ': cf. x. 37; Lk. ii. 15, 17, 19.

(c) Gamaliel's Counsel: the Apostles again dismissed, v. 33-42

οἱ δὲ ἀκούσαντες διεπρίοντο καὶ ἐβούλοντο ἀνελεῖν αὐτούς. 33
'Αναστὰς δέ τις ἐν τῷ συνεδρίῳ Φαρισαῖος ὀνόματι Γαμαλιήλ, νομοδιδά- 34
σκαλος τίμιος παντὶ τῷ λαῷ, ἐκέλευσεν ἔξω βραχὺ τοὺς ἀνθρώπους
ποιῆσαι, εἶπέν τε πρὸς αὐτούς Ἄνδρες 'Ισραηλεῖται, προσέχετε 35
ἑαυτοῖς ἐπὶ τοῖς ἀνθρώποις τούτοις τί μέλλετε πράσσειν. πρὸ γὰρ 36
τούτων τῶν ἡμερῶν ἀνέστη Θευδᾶς, λέγων εἶναί τινα ἑαυτόν, ᾧ προσ-
εκλίθη ἀνδρῶν ἀριθμὸς ὡς τετρακοσίων· ὃς ἀνῃρέθη, καὶ πάντες ὅσοι
ἐπείθοντο αὐτῷ διελύθησαν καὶ ἐγένοντο εἰς οὐδέν. μετὰ τοῦτον 37
ἀνέστη 'Ιούδας ὁ Γαλιλαῖος ἐν ταῖς ἡμέραις τῆς ἀπογραφῆς καὶ ἀπέ-
στησε λαὸν ὀπίσω αὐτοῦ· κἀκεῖνος ἀπώλετο, καὶ πάντες ὅσοι ἐπείθοντο
αὐτῷ διεσκορπίσθησαν. καὶ τὰ νῦν λέγω ὑμῖν, ἀπόστητε ἀπὸ τῶν 38
ἀνθρώπων τούτων καὶ ἄφετε αὐτούς· (ὅτι ἐὰν ᾖ ἐξ ἀνθρώπων ἡ βουλὴ
αὕτη ἢ τὸ ἔργον τοῦτο, καταλυθήσεται· εἰ δὲ ἐκ θεοῦ ἐστίν, οὐ 39
δυνήσεσθε καταλῦσαι αὐτούς·) μή ποτε καὶ θεομάχοι εὑρεθῆτε.
ἐπείσθησαν δὲ αὐτῷ, καὶ προσκαλεσάμενοι τοὺς ἀποστόλους δείραντες 40
παρήγγειλαν μὴ λαλεῖν ἐπὶ τῷ ὀνόματι τοῦ 'Ιησοῦ καὶ ἀπέλυσαν.
Οἱ μὲν οὖν ἐπορεύοντο χαίροντες ἀπὸ προσώπου τοῦ συνεδρίου ὅτι 41
κατηξιώθησαν ὑπὲρ τοῦ ὀνόματος ἀτιμασθῆναι· πᾶσάν τε ἡμέραν ἐν 42
τῷ ἱερῷ καὶ κατ' οἶκον οὐκ ἐπαύοντο διδάσκοντες καὶ εὐαγγελιζόμενοι
τὸν χριστὸν 'Ιησοῦν.

v. 33

ἀκούσαντες] *ἀκούοντες* P P^{45} al.

διεπρίοντο] Cf. vii. 54, literally of sawing asunder, hence of being rent with vexation. Contrast *κατενύγησαν*, of conviction of sin, ii. 37.

v. 34

Φαρισαῖος] Evidence for the representation of Pharisees in the Sanhedrin. Cf. xxiii. 6 ff.; Jos. *BJ* ii. 8. 14; 17. 3; *Ant.* xviii. 1. 3; *Vita* 38 f. The word is derived from Aram. *pĕrash*, 'to separate'; the passive participle *pĕrīsh* in its plural emphatic form is *pĕrīshayyā*, 'the separated ones', whence Gk. plur. *Φαρισαῖοι*, sing. *Φαρισαῖος*.[1] In Hellenistic times the pious members of the community, the *ḥăsīdīm*, who spent their time in studying the Law (oral as well as written) and expounding its application to the circumstances of the day, opposed the popular Hellenizing tendencies. In the conflict precipitated by Antiochus Epiphanes (175-163 B.C.), they lent their support to the Maccabees in the struggle for religious freedom, but once this was gained they held aloof from the fight for political independence, strongly disapproving of the self-seeking policies of the later Hasmoneans and their assumption of the High Priesthood. This is the most probable explanation of their nickname, 'the separated ones'. Till the nation came under Roman overlordship, which they regarded as a national punishment, they were regularly in opposition to the ruling party, except under Queen Salome Alexandra (76-67 B.C.). Under Herod (37-4 B.C.) their power increased, but in NT times they were in a minority on the Sanhedrin, though their popular support was such that their opponents could not disregard them. Cf. Jos. *Ant.* xviii. 1. 4, according to which the Sadducean magistrates professed Pharisaic principles in order to win popular goodwill (*ὁπότε γὰρ ἐπ' ἀρχὰς παρέλθοιεν, ἀκουσίως μὲν καὶ κατ' ἀνάγκας, προχωροῦσι δ' οὖν οἷς ὁ Φαρισαῖος λέγει, διὰ τὸ μὴ ἂν ἄλλως ἀνεκτοὺς γενέσθαι τοῖς πλήθεσιν*). The expression *ἀρχιερεῖς καὶ Φαρισαῖοι* combines both elements in the Sanhedrin: cf. Mt. xxi. 45; xxvii. 62; Jn. vii. 32, 45; xi. 47, 57; xviii. 3. The influence of the Pharisees was enhanced by the fact that the scribes (see on iv. 5) belonged chiefly to their party: cf. the common collocation 'scribes and Pharisees' in the Gospels. They were accepted by the people as religious patriots and spiritual leaders. They consistently

[1] Cf. Dalman, *Jesus-Jeshua*, p. 13. This derivation accords best with the passive sense of *pĕrīsh*. W. O. E. Oesterley (*The Jews and Judaism during the Greek Period*, pp. 245 ff.) connects another sense of *pĕrash*, 'to interpret', with the Pharisees' expounding of the law, and suggests that those who prefer the meaning 'separated' may regard it as a nickname given them by the Sadducees for forming themselves into a body of teachers in opposition to the priestly teachers. The Pharisees probably acquiesced the more readily in the name *pĕrīshayyā* (Heb. *pĕrūshīm*) because it could also mean 'separated' in the sense of 'holy'; indeed in the Midrashim we find *pārūsh* in place of *qādōsh* (cf. G. F. Moore, *Judaism*, i, pp. 60 f.). T. W. Manson (*BJRL* xxii [1938], 153 ff.) thinks the original sense was 'Persianizers', because of their eschatology and angelology.

refused to countenance aspirations to political independence, and after the fall of Jerusalem in A.D. 70 it was they who preserved some measure of national continuity in Palestine, by reconstituting the Sanhedrin for certain limited purposes and by continuing the study of the Law at Jabneh. Unlike the Sadducees, they believed in the resurrection of the dead and in the existence of a spirit world; they also believed that the divine decrees and human freewill were so combined that man could act virtuously or viciously as he chose (Jos. *Ant.* xviii. 1. 3: cf. R. Aqiba in *Pirqe Aboth* iii. 19, 'Everything is foreseen, yet freedom of choice is given'). See on xxiii. 6 ff.

Γαμαλιήλ] Gamaliel I, *Rabbān Gamli'ēl ha-zāqēn* (the elder), the teacher of Saul of Tarsus (xxii. 3), belonged to the liberal school of Hillel. He modified the Sabbath law and forbade divorce proceedings to be annulled without the wife's knowledge. Jewish tradition glorifies him as a most celebrated teacher, but frequently confuses him with his illustrious grandson, Gamaliel II. 'Since Rabban Gamaliel the elder died there has been no more reverence for the Law; and purity and abstinence (*pĕrīshūth*, lit., 'separation') died out at the same time' (Mishna, *Soṭa* ix. 15).

νομοδιδάσκαλος] Cf. Lk. v. 17; 1 Tim. i. 7. It is not found outside NT except in ecclesiastical writers who derive it thence; but cf. Plutarch, *Cato Maior* xx. 4, *νομοδιδάκτης*.

τίμιος] Applied in the superlative to a favourite pupil by Vettius Valens, 157. 32.

v. 35

εἶπέν τε πρὸς αὐτούς κ.τ.λ.] Luke's knowledge of what happened when the apostles were put out could have been derived from Paul, who, if he was not present himself (see on viii. 1), may have heard it from Gamaliel (see on iv. 17). 'The doctrine preached by Gamaliel is sound Pharisaic teaching; God is over all, and needs no help from men for the fulfilment of His purposes; all men must do is to obey, and leave the issue to Him' (J. A. Findlay).[1]

αὐτούς] *τοὺς ἄρχοντας καὶ τοὺς συνέδρους* D (*σύνεδροι* is unexampled in NT, but is found in classical Gk.).

προσέχετε ἑαυτοῖς] A Lukan phrase: cf. xx. 28; Lk. xvii. 3; xxi. 34. See on xv. 29.

[1] Cf. the dictum of Aqiba's pupil R. Yohanan the sandal-maker: 'Every assembly which is in the name of heaven will finally be established, but that which is not in the name of heaven will not finally be established' (*Pirqe Aboth* iv. 14).

v. 36

πρὸ . . . τούτων τῶν ἡμερῶν] ‘ some time ago ’ : cf. xxi. 38.

Θευδᾶς] According to Josephus (*Ant.* xx. 5. 1), a magician called Theudas led a large company to the Jordan, promising that at a word of command he would divide the river, that they might cross it dryshod. Cuspius Fadus, who was procurator at the time (*c.* 44-46), sent a body of cavalry against them, who routed the multitude, and brought the head of Theudas to Jerusalem. Luke has been suspected of inaccuracy, because this Theudas rose about 40 years after Judas (who, according to *ver.* 37, rose after Theudas). A. C. Clark thought the discrepancy might be due to an accidental transposition of lines in the archetype of all our MSS. ; the original order would then have been Judas-Theudas. But this does not explain how Gamaliel, speaking not later than 36, could have referred to the Theudas of Josephus. Luke's error, if error it is, is twofold. Some (following Krenkel) have tried to account for it on the ground that Josephus, in the section following his account of Theudas, mentions the sons of Judas. But only a very careless and cursory glance at Josephus could give a reader the impression that Judas himself came after Theudas. And it is not at all likely that Ac. is so late as the *Antiquities* (*c.* 93). If the discrepancy were insoluble, we might well prefer the testimony of an accurate writer like Luke to that of an author so liable to blunders as Josephus. But it is not insoluble ; it is quite likely that Gamaliel is referring to another Theudas, who flourished before A.D. 6. It is, of course, unsafe in general to get over a difficulty of this kind by assuming that the person in question is someone else of the same name, but the assumption is permissible here (1) because of Luke's proved high standard of accuracy, (2) because Theudas is a common name (it is a contraction of Theodorus, Theodotus, Theodosius, etc.), occurring also in inscriptions (e.g., *CIG* 2684, 3563, 3920, 5698), (3) because there were many such risings under similar leaders (cf. xxi. 38) : according to Jos. *Ant.* xvii. 10. 4 there were innumerable tumults and disorders in Judaea after the death of Herod the Great (4 B.C.), and this may well have been one of those. So Origen says Θευδᾶς πρὸ τῆς γενέσεως Ἰησοῦ γέγονέ τις παρὰ Ἰουδαίοις (*c. Cels.* i. 57) ; cf. J. B. Lightfoot in Smith's *DB*, i, p. 40.

λέγων εἶναί τινα ἑαυτόν] Just possibly this may mean ‘ claiming to be Messiah ’, but it is best to take it literally, as in the corresponding Eng. idiom, ‘ claiming to be somebody ’. See on viii. 9, whence probably the δ reading here is borrowed, τινα μέγαν.

ἀνῃρέθη] κατελύθη αὐτὸς δι᾽ αὐτοῦ D (not d or h).

ἐγένοντο εἰς οὐδέν] Cf. for γίνεσθαι εἰς Mt. xxi. 42 (from LXX) ; Lk. xiii. 19 ; Jn. xvi. 20 ; Rev. viii. 11 ; xvi. 19 ; cf. also εἶναι εἰς, viii. 20, etc. This may be a Hebraism, εἰς with acc. representing the Heb. use of *lĕ* (' to ') with a noun to express the complement (see on vii. 21; xiii. 22, 47). If this is the construction here, the meaning is ' became nothing '. It is perfectly likely, however, that it is a straightforward Gk. construction, ' came to nothing ' (cf. τὸ μηδὲν εἰς οὐδὲν ῥέπει, Euripides, *frag*. 536).

v. 37

Ἰούδας ὁ Γαλιλαῖος] According to Josephus (*BJ* ii. 8. 1; vii. 8. 1; *Ant*. xviii. 1. 1; xx. 5. 2) Judas of Gamala in Gaulanitis (he also calls him Judas the Galilean) opposed the census carried out by Quirinius in A.D. 6 (see next note). Along with one Sadduk, a Pharisee, he proclaimed a religious revolution, contending that since God alone was Israel's king, to Him alone should tribute be paid. The movement was unsuccessful, but it led to the formation of the party of the Zealots (see on i. 13), so that Gamaliel was unduly optimistic if he thought it had come to naught. This Judas is possibly the same as Judas the son of Hezekiah, who in the year of Herod's death gained possession of weapons stored at Sepphoris in Galilee and distributed them among his followers; he then attacked the government and is even said by Josephus to have aimed at the royal crown (cf. *BJ* ii. 4. 1; *Ant*. xvii. 10. 5). It must be remembered that Josephus, for reasons of his own, consistently describes patriotic risings as brigand activities.

ἐν ταῖς ἡμέραις τῆς ἀπογραφῆς] When Archelaus was deposed by Augustus in A.D. 6, Judaea was added to the imperial province of Syria, the legate of which, Quirinius, proceeded to hold a census in the whole province. Judas and Sadduk regarded this census as the prelude to enslavement, and struck for liberty. The census of Lk. ii. 1 was earlier, ' in the days of Herod ' (Lk. i. 5; Mt. ii. 1), i.e., not after 4 B.C. The reference to Quirinius in Lk. ii. 2 implies, not that he held this earlier census, but that it was made while he was governor of Syria. There is some evidence that he had the status of an imperial legate in Syro-Cilicia between 10 and 7 B.C. Cf. W. M. Ramsay, *Was Christ Born at Bethlehem?* pp. 109 ff., 227 ff.; *BRD* pp. 255 ff.; *JRS* vii (1917), pp. 273 ff.; W. M. Calder in *Discovery* i (1920), pp. 100 ff.; *CR* xli (1927), p. 151; T. Corbishley in *JRS* xxiv (1934), pp. 43 ff.; *Klio* xxix (1936), pp. 81 ff.; *Scripture* i (1946), pp. 77 ff.; MM s.v. ἀπογραφή.[1]

[1] Th. Zahn identifies the rising of *Ant*. xviii. 1. 1 (under Judas of Gamala) with that of *Ant*. xvii. 10. 5 (under Judas, son of Hezekiah), placing the one rising in the year of Herod's death. ' The insurrection of Judas, the rise of the party of the Zealots (Luke vi. 15; Acts i. 13; v. 37), the deposition of the high priest Joazar, who had been installed in office a few months before, and the taxing under the direction of Quirinius, took place in the first year

λαόν] 'a host'.

ἀπώλετο] Possibly means not merely 'was undone' but 'was killed'. Cf. the fifth century *Acts of Pilate*, v. 1, concerning Jannes and Jambres: 'and whereas the signs which they did were not of God, they perished and those also that believed on them'.

πάντες ὅσοι] om πάντες D P^{45}.

v. 38

τὰ νῦν] Emphatic, 'in the present case': cf. iv. 29. B* omits τὰ.

ἄφετε αὐτούς] ἐάσατε αὐτοὺς μὴ μιάναντες τὰς χεῖρας D.

Cf. from *Acts of Pilate* (*loc. cit.*): 'let him alone and contrive not any evil against him: if the signs which he doeth are of God, they will stand, but if they be of men, they will come to nought' (Nicodemus begging Pilate to acquit Jesus).

ἐάν] With the pres. subjunctive ᾖ, a rare construction for an open condition referring to the *present*, but the force may be, 'If it turn out to be'. In the next verse, we have εἰ with the pres. indic., indicating that Luke approves the second alternative, and therefore expresses it by means of a less remote construction. We cannot argue that *Gamaliel* regarded the second alternative as the more probable; the interplay of conditional constructions belongs to Luke's Gk., not to Gamaliel's Aram.

ἐξ ἀνθρώπων . . . ἐκ θεοῦ] Cf. Lk. xx. 4, τὸ βάπτισμα Ἰωάνου ἐξ οὐρανοῦ ἦν ἢ ἐξ ἀνθρώπων;

βουλὴ . . . ἔργον] Cf. Lk. xxiii. 51, τῇ βουλῇ καὶ τῇ πράξει.

v. 39

καταλῦσαι αὐτούς] δ adds οὔτε ὑμεῖς οὔτε βασιλεῖς οὔτε τύραννοι· ἀπέχεσθε οὖν ἀπὸ τῶν ἀνθρώπων τούτων.

μή ποτε καὶ θεόμαχοι εὑρεθῆτε] 'The warning of Ac. v. 39 might . . . start from either "Perhaps you will be found", or "Do not be found": the former suits the ποτε better' (*Proleg.*, p. 193). Cf. Homer, *Iliad* vi. 129, οὐκ ἂν ἔγωγε θεοῖσιν ἐπουρανίοισι μαχοίμην.

v. 40

ἐπὶ τῷ ὀνόματι τοῦ Ἰησοῦ] Indirect speech: what they said may have been ἐπὶ τῷ ὀνόματι τούτῳ, as in *ver.* 28; iv. 17.

after Herod's death (March 4-3 B.C.). Josephus, who places these events in the year A.D. 6-7, although he reproduces them in part in the year 4-3 B.C., has made a mistake of a decade, and, in other respects as well, displays a serious lack of critical judgment' (Zahn, *INT* iii, p. 98). The problem of the mention of Quirinius in Lk. ii. 2 is solved more summarily by B. S. Easton (*Comm. on Lk.* [1926], *ad loc.*) and J. W. Jack (*ET* xl [1928-9], pp. 496 f.), who suppose that the original reading there was not Quirinius but Saturninus (legate of Syria, 8-6 B.C.).

v. 41

ἐπορεύοντο] Imperfect; the manner of their going (*χαίροντες*) is emphasized.

ἀπὸ προσώπου] See on iii. 20.

κατηξιώθησαν ὑπὲρ τοῦ ὀνόματος ἀτιμασθῆναι] Note the oxymoron of *κατηξιώθησαν . . . ἀτιμασθῆναι*. For *ὑπὲρ τοῦ ὀνόματος* cf. 3 Jn. 7. This absolute use of *τὸ ὄνομα* is common in the Apostolic Fathers. For the general sense cf. also xxi. 13; 1 Pet. iv. 16. *καταξιόω* occurs also in Lk. xx. 35; 2 Th. i. 5; it appears in Vettius Valens (e.g. 38. 33; 39. 4; 85. 12; 222. 24) with a suggestion of promotion or preferment.

v. 42

κατ' οἶκον] Cf. ii. 46.

τὸν χριστὸν Ἰησοῦν] Either 'the Messiah Jesus' or 'that the Messiah was Jesus'. Cf. xviii. 5. The position of the article is to be noted.

II. PERSECUTION LEADS TO EXPANSION, vi. 1-ix. 31

1. STEPHEN, vi. 1-viii. 1*a*

(a) The Appointing of the Seven, vi. 1-6

Ἐν δὲ ταῖς ἡμέραις ταύταις πληθυνόντων τῶν μαθητῶν ἐγένετο 1
γογγυσμὸς τῶν Ἑλληνιστῶν πρὸς τοὺς Ἐβραίους ὅτι παρεθεωροῦντο
ἐν τῇ διακονίᾳ τῇ καθημερινῇ αἱ χῆραι αὐτῶν. προσκαλεσάμενοι δὲ 2
οἱ δώδεκα τὸ πλῆθος τῶν μαθητῶν εἶπαν Οὐκ ἀρεστόν ἐστιν ἡμᾶς
καταλείψαντας τὸν λόγον τοῦ θεοῦ διακονεῖν τραπέζαις· ἐπισκέψασθε 3
δέ, ἀδελφοί, ἄνδρας ἐξ ὑμῶν μαρτυρουμένους ἑπτὰ πλήρεις πνεύματος καὶ σοφίας, οὓς καταστήσομεν ἐπὶ τῆς χρείας ταύτης· ἡμεῖς 4
δὲ τῇ προσευχῇ καὶ τῇ διακονίᾳ τοῦ λόγου προσκαρτερήσομεν. καὶ 5
ἤρεσεν ὁ λόγος ἐνώπιον παντὸς τοῦ πλήθους, καὶ ἐξελέξαντο Στέφανον,
ἄνδρα πλήρη πίστεως καὶ πνεύματος ἁγίου, καὶ Φίλιππον καὶ Πρό-
χορον καὶ Νικάνορα καὶ Τίμωνα καὶ Παρμενᾶν καὶ Νικόλαον προσήλυτον
Ἀντιοχέα, οὓς ἔστησαν ἐνώπιον τῶν ἀποστόλων, καὶ προσευξάμενοι 6
ἐπέθηκαν αὐτοῖς τὰς χεῖρας.

vi. 1

Ἐν δὲ ταῖς ἡμέραις ταύταις] Marking the beginning of a new division in the book: see on i. 15; cf. xi. 27.

πληθυνόντων τῶν μαθητῶν] 'as the disciples were multiplying'. The word μαθηταί, earlier used of the personal followers of Jesus before His ascension, is used in Ac. as a name for Christians in general. See on xi. 26 for other names for Christians.

Ἑλληνιστῶν] The first occurrence of this word in Greek literature. Its meaning, therefore, has to be deduced from the contexts in which it is found. Here it is contrasted with Ἑβραίους. The usual explanation (Chrysostom's) is that Ἑλληνισταί were Greek-speaking Jews—here, of course, such Greek-speaking Jews as were members of the church. The strict Jerusalem Jews boycotted the use of Gk., cultivating the vernacular Aram., if not Mishnaic Hebrew (which the Rabbis used much as mediaeval scholars used Latin), and so there was a linguistic cleavage. Other suggestions are that they were Jewish proselytes who had joined the church, such as Nicolas in *ver.* 5 (E. C. Blackman, *ET* xlviii [1936-7], 524 f.); that they were Greek-speaking Gentiles who had been converted at Pentecost (H. J. Cadbury, *BC* v, 59 ff.); that Ἑλληνιστής was a party-name which had a short vogue in the early church, the correlative of Ἰουδαϊστής (G. P. Wetter, A. D. Nock). Perhaps we should not regard it as a technical term, but simply as meaning 'Greek speakers'. The context will then determine more exactly what kind of Greek speakers they were: here, Greek-speaking Jewish Christians; in ix. 29, probably Greek-speaking Jews in the synagogues; in xi. 20, probably Gentiles. Cadbury (*BC* v, pp. 59 ff.) points out that Ἑλληνιστής is used in the Semitic part of Ac., but Ἕλλην in the Hellenistic part.

Ἑβραίους] Observe that WH print this word with a smooth breathing, representing Heb. ע (*'ayin*). The word here stands in opposition to Ἑλληνιστῶν, and apparently means Hebrew or Aramaic-speaking Jews, whether of Palestine or, like Paul (Phil. iii. 5, Ἑβραῖος ἐξ Ἑβραίων), of the Dispersion. Elsewhere Ἑβραῖος is not so restricted.

ἐν τῇ διακονίᾳ τῇ καθημερινῇ] We gather that a daily distribution was made out of the common funds, provided by the voluntary pooling of resources (ii. 44 f.; iv. 34 f.). The extreme poverty of many in the Jerusalem church later 'acted as a bond to unite the scattered congregations in active ministration . . . and at the beginning it stimulated the primitive Church to originate a better organisation' (Ramsay, *SPT*, p. 373). Note that καθημερινός, though a compound adj., has three terminations, 'like its classical predecessor καθημέριος' (MH ii, p. 158). Its only other occurrence in the Gk. Bible is Judith xii. 15, τὴν καθημερινὴν δίαιταν.

αἱ χῆραι αὐτῶν] Widows were naturally among the neediest members. Cf. Jas. i. 27; 1 Tim. v. 9 ff. D adds ἐν τῇ διακονίᾳ τῶν Ἑβραίων (cf. h, *a ministris Hebraicorum*).

vi. 2

οἱ δώδεκα] Common in Mk. and Lk.; cf. 1 Cor. xv. 5. Only here in Ac., but cf. *οἱ ἕνδεκα*, i. 26; ii. 14.

τὸ πλῆθος] See on iv. 32.

Οὐκ ἀρεστόν ἐστιν] = *non placet*, so *ἤρεσεν* in *ver.* 5 = *placuit*. *ἀρεστός* is the verbal adjective of *ἀρέσκω* ('to please'), and is hence used in the sense 'fitting', 'satisfactory'.

διακονεῖν τραπέζαις] Perhaps *τράπεζα* is used here in the financial sense: cf. Mt. xxi. 12 = Mk. xi. 15; Jn. ii. 15. Note the verb *διακονεῖν*, and the corresponding noun *διακονία* in *vv.* 1, 4. These words are not here used in any restricted or technical sense. Nor are the Seven called *διάκονοι*, though of course they were *διάκονοι* in the ordinary sense of 'servants'. It is an anachronism to apply to NT persons and conditions names which have acquired a stereotyped ecclesiastical sense. The NT has, generally speaking, no *technical* vocabulary for functions in the churches and for those who discharge them but uses ordinary Gk. words, which had best be rendered by ordinary Eng. words.

vi. 3

ἐπισκέψασθε δέ, ἀδελφοί, ἄνδρας ἐξ ὑμῶν] δ has *τί οὖν ἐστιν, ἀδελφοί; ἐπισκέψασθε ἐξ ὑμῶν αὐτῶν ἄνδρας.* For *τί οὖν ἐστιν;* cf. xxi. 22. B has *ἐπισκεψώμεθα* for *ἐπισκέψασθε*, probably from a desire not to exclude the Twelve from a share in the selection of the Seven; but this reading is at variance not only with all other authorities, but also with *ver.* 6.

μαρτυρουμένους] 'to whom witness is borne', i.e., good witness: cf. x. 22; xvi. 2; xxii. 12.

ἑπτὰ] *septem viri mensis ordinandis*, as Ramsay calls them (*SPT*, p. 375). In xxi. 8 they are simply called 'the Seven'.

πλήρεις] *πλήρης* A E H P al. There was no difference in pronunciation between the two forms, and this may be the cause of the confusion. But *πλήρης* may be right: see on *πλήρη*, *ver.* 5.

πνεύματος] Here without *ἁγίου*, but *πνεύματος ἁγίου* in *ver.* 5 indicates that the Holy Spirit is meant.

καταστήσομεν] The Twelve were to give their approval to the congregation's selection of the Seven.

ἐπὶ τῆς χρείας ταύτης] They were not, however, restricted to this service: Stephen and Philip, for example, shone as public speakers. The NT force of *χρεία* is usually 'need', but in Hellenistic Gk. it generally means 'office', as here.

vi. 4

τῇ προσευχῇ] As in i. 14: cf. ii. 42, *ταῖς προσευχαῖς*. The regular worship of the church is what is meant.

τῇ διακονίᾳ τοῦ λόγου] i.e., preaching. Cf. Lk. i. 2, ὑπηρέται . . . τοῦ λόγου.

vi. 5

ἤρεσεν ὁ λόγος ἐνώπιον κ.τ.λ.] A Semitism: cf. Mt. xviii. 14, οὐκ ἔστιν θέλημα ἔμπροσθεν τοῦ πατρός μου.

καὶ ἐξελέξαντο κ.τ.λ.] All seven have Greek names. As they were elected in the interest of the Hellenists, it was only natural that they themselves should be Hellenists, and one of them (Nicolas) was not even a Jew by birth, but a proselyte. They were probably regarded as the leaders of the Hellenists in the church. Their appointment, therefore, was a step forward towards the equality of Jew and Gentile in the church, although there was as yet no question of admitting Gentiles who were not already proselytes.

πλήρη] B C^{corr}; πλήρης ℵ A C D byz al. By all canons of probability, πλήρης must be the true reading, as the tendency would be to change πλήρης to πλήρη. We must conclude that πλήρης was used indeclinably: cf. *ver.* 3; xix. 28 (A E L 33); Mk. iv. 28 (C*); viii. 19 (A F G M al); Jn. i. 14 (where πλήρης, if indecl., may refer to δόξαν rather than to λόγος); 2 Jn. 8 (L). 'In almost every NT occurrence of an oblique case of this word we meet with the indeclinable form in good uncials' (*Proleg.*, p. 50). Cf. Job. xxi. 24 LXX (ℵ A B C); Vettius Valens 298. 26. Papyrus parallels commence in the second century B.C., and are abundant after the first century A.D. Latin readers who read in their versions *plenum fidei* may have been struck by the resemblance to the fine old Roman character of Flamininus, described by Ennius: *ille uir haud magna cum re, sed plenus fidei.*

Φίλιππον] See on viii. 5 ff.; xxi. 8 f. Nothing more is heard in NT about the other five.

Νικόλαον προσήλυτον 'Αντιοχέα] The inclusion of a proselyte (see on ii. 10) is significant. So also is the fact that Nicolas is the only one of the Seven whose place of origin is mentioned. This reflects Luke's interest in Antioch (cf. Introduction, pp. 6 f., and xi. 19 ff.; xiii. 1). That Jews were very numerous in Antioch we learn from Jos. *BJ* vii. 3. 3. From the time of Irenaeus (*adu. haer.* i. 26. 3; cf. iii. 11. 1) attempts were made to connect the Nicolaitans of Rev. ii. 6, 15 with this Nicolas. That they were called after *some* Nicolas seems plain from the formation of the name, but there seems no good reason for identifying him with this Nicolas.

vi. 6

ἐπέθηκαν αὐτοῖς τὰς χεῖρας] For the sequence ἐπισκέψασθε . . . ἐπέθηκαν αὐτοῖς τὰς χεῖρας, cf. Num. xxvii. 16 ff., ἐπισκεψάσθω . . . ἄνθρωπον ὃς ἔχει πνεῦμα ἐν ἑαυτῷ καὶ ἐπιθήσεις τὰς χεῖράς σου ἐπ' *αὐτόν*. The Heb. word there used for 'laying on' is *sāmakh;* hence the ceremony was called *sĕmīkhāh*, and according to the Mishna members of the Sanhedrin were so admitted (*Sanh.* iv. 4). The ceremony in this case indicated the conferring of authority by the Twelve on the Seven whom the people had chosen. See further on viii. 17; ix. 17; xiii. 3; xix. 6 for various circumstances in which a similar ceremony took place. The root idea seems to have been the transference of something already possessed by the person performing the ceremony; so in Lev. iii. 2; xvi. 21, *sāmakh* is used in connection with the sin-offering, for the symbolical transference of sin. (Cf. also xxviii. 8; Mk. v. 23, etc., for the imposition of hands in healing; 1 Tim. iv. 14 for the conferment by this means of a spiritual gift.)

(b) Fresh Progress, vi. 7

Καὶ ὁ λόγος τοῦ θεοῦ ηὔξανεν, καὶ ἐπληθύνετο ὁ ἀριθμὸς τῶν 7
μαθητῶν ἐν Ἰερουσαλὴμ σφόδρα, πολύς τε ὄχλος τῶν ἱερέων
ὑπήκουον τῇ πίστει.

vi. 7

This verse is one of several reports of progress which serve to punctuate the sections of the narrative of Ac.: cf. ix. 31; xii. 24; xvi. 5; xix. 20; xxviii. 31.

πολύς τε ὄχλος τῶν ἱερέων ὑπήκουον] An interesting fact. For *ἱερέων* ℵ minn.aliquot pesh have *Ἰουδαίων*, h has *in templo*, representing *ἐν τῷ ἱερῷ*.

ὑπήκουον τῇ πίστει] Here *πίστις* is almost equal to *εὐαγγέλιον* (cf. *ὑπακούουσιν τῷ εὐαγγελίῳ*, 2 Th. i. 8), the *fides quae creditur* rather than the *fides quâ creditur:* for this sense cf. 1 Tim. i. 19; iv. 6; vi. 10.

(c) Stephen's Activity arouses Opposition, vi. 8-vii. 1

Στέφανος δὲ πλήρης χάριτος καὶ δυνάμεως ἐποίει τέρατα καὶ 8
σημεῖα μεγάλα ἐν τῷ λαῷ. Ἀνέστησαν δέ τινες τῶν ἐκ τῆς συνα- 9
γωγῆς τῆς λεγομένης Λιβερτίνων καὶ Κυρηναίων καὶ Ἀλεξανδρέων
καὶ τῶν ἀπὸ Κιλικίας καὶ Ἀσίας συνζητοῦντες τῷ Στεφάνῳ, καὶ οὐκ 10
ἴσχυον ἀντιστῆναι τῇ σοφίᾳ καὶ τῷ πνεύματι ᾧ ἐλάλει. τότε ὑπέβαλον 11
ἄνδρας λέγοντας ὅτι Ἀκηκόαμεν αὐτοῦ λαλοῦντος ῥήματα βλάσφημα
εἰς Μωυσῆν καὶ τὸν θεόν· συνεκίνησάν τε τὸν λαὸν καὶ τοὺς πρεσβυτέρους 12
καὶ τοὺς γραμματεῖς, καὶ ἐπιστάντες συνήρπασαν αὐτὸν καὶ ἤγαγον 13
εἰς τὸ συνέδριον, ἔστησάν τε μάρτυρας ψευδεῖς λέγοντας Ὁ ἄνθρωπος

οὗτος οὐ παύεται λαλῶν ῥήματα κατὰ τοῦ τόπου τοῦ ἁγίου τούτου
καὶ τοῦ νόμου, ἀκηκόαμεν γὰρ αὐτοῦ λέγοντος ὅτι Ἰησοῦς ὁ Ναζωραῖος 14
οὗτος καταλύσει τὸν τόπον τοῦτον καὶ ἀλλάξει τὰ ἔθη ἃ παρέδωκεν
ἡμῖν Μωυσῆς. καὶ ἀτενίσαντες εἰς αὐτὸν πάντες οἱ καθεζόμενοι ἐν 15
τῷ συνεδρίῳ εἶδαν τὸ πρόσωπον αὐτοῦ ὡσεὶ πρόσωπον ἀγγέλου.
Εἶπεν δὲ ὁ ἀρχιερεύς Εἰ ταῦτα οὕτως ἔχει; 16

vi. 8

πλήρης χάριτος καὶ δυνάμεως] We have already been told that he was full of faith and the Holy Spirit. It is possible that *χάρις* has here its earlier sense of 'charm', i.e. spiritual charm: cf. iv. 33; Lk. iv. 22. The *δύναμις* is that divine power which is manifested in 'mighty works' (see on ii. 22; iv. 33) or, as is said here, in 'wonders and great signs'.

τέρατα καὶ σημεῖα μεγάλα] Cf. ii. 22, 43; iv. 30; v. 12; vii. 36; viii. 13; xiv. 3.

ἐν τῷ λαῷ] The *λαός* is the Jewish people, as regularly. D adds *διὰ τοῦ ὀνόματος κυρίου Ἰησοῦ Χριστοῦ*, a conflation of 'by the name of the Lord' (hcl*) and *in nomine Iesu Christi* (h).

vi. 9

ἐκ τῆς συναγωγῆς] The origin of the synagogue is quite obscure; its rise and development are probably to be dated in Persian times. It is believed by many that synagogues are intended by the *mō'ădē 'Ēl* of Ps. lxxiv. 8 (? *c.* 350 B.C.). If so, it is the only OT reference to synagogues. But W. O. E. Oesterley (*The Psalms*, p. 68) denies that this can be the meaning of the expression. Their primary purpose was for the reading and exposition of the Law. The synagogue, especially in the Dispersion, was the centre round which the life of the Jewish community revolved. For the synagogue service see on xiii. 14 ff. The Heb. name of the synagogue was *bēth ha-kĕnēseth*, 'the house of gathering' (Aram. *kĕnishtā*); *συναγωγή* is thus a fairly literal rendering. Other names in Gk. were *συναγώγιον* (Philo, *Leg. ad Gai.* 311; *De somniis* ii. 127; *CIG* 9908); *προσευκτήριον* (Philo, *Vit. Moys.* ii. 216); *σαββατεῖον* (Jos. *Ant.* xvi. 6. 2), but the most common name, next to *συναγωγή* itself (which appears in *BJ* ii. 14. 4 f.; vii. 3.3; *Ant.* xix. 6. 3; Philo, *Quod omnis probus liber* 81 [of Essene meeting-places], etc.), is *προσευχή* (see on xvi. 13; cf. also Jos. *Vita* 54; Philo, *Flacc.* 41, 45, 122; *Leg. ad Gai.* 134, 155, 346, 371; 3 Macc. vii. 20; Juvenal, *Sat.* iii. 296; inscriptions, etc.). In Jas. ii. 2; Hermas, *Mand.* xi. 9, 13 f.; Justin, *Dial.* 63; Ignatius, *ad Polyc.* iv. 2; Dion.

Alex. *ap.* Euseb. *HE* vii. 9, 11, a Christian meeting is called a συναγωγή (and cf. ἐπισυναγωγή, Heb. x. 25).[1]

τῆς λεγομένης Λιβερτίνων καὶ Κυρηναίων καὶ Ἀλεξανδρέων καὶ τῶν ἀπὸ Κιλικίας καὶ Ἀσίας] Opinions differ as to the number of synagogues indicated here. Schürer (II. ii. 57) says there are certainly five, viz., those of the (1) Libertini, (2) Cyreneans, (3) Alexandrians, (4) Cilicians, (5) Asians. A plurality of synagogues is not surprising; there were several in the larger towns: Philo, *Leg. ad Gai.* 137 f., 156 f., speaks of several in Alexandria and Rome. A synagogue of Alexandrians at Jerusalem is mentioned in the Tosefta, *Megillah* iii. 6; TJ *Megillah* iii. 1. 73d.

If we take 'those from Cilicia and Asia' closely together, as sharing one synagogue, the sum will be four. If, similarly, we also take 'Cyreneans and Alexandrians' closely together, the sum will be three (so T. E. Page). This can be reduced to two, if we regard καὶ Κυρηναίων καὶ Ἀλεξανδρέων as epexegetic of Λιβερτίνων (so LC, who render, 'the synagogue which is called that of the Libertini, both Cyrenians and Alexandrians, and of those from Cilicia and Asia'). Or we could take τῶν ἀπὸ Κιλικίας καὶ Ἀσίας as also epexegetic of Λιβερτίνων, in which case one synagogue only is in question. Much depends on the meaning of Λιβερτίνων. According to Schürer, they were Roman freedmen, descended from Jews sent by Pompey as prisoners to Rome, and soon liberated (cf. Philo, *Leg. ad Gai.* 155). These may have been included, but the word need not refer exclusively to them. A *libertinus* (the Lat. word here transliterated into Gk.) was either a *libertus* ('freedman') or the son of a *libertus* (cf. Suetonius, *Claudius* xxiv. 1). Deissmann (*LAE*, p. 441) thinks they were freedmen of the Imperial household. Jewish freedmen, according to Tacitus (*Ann.* ii. 85), seem to have been regarded as a state problem. I am inclined to think that one synagogue is meant, attended by Jewish freedmen or descendants of freedmen from the various places mentioned. The characteristic Lukan λεγομένης may be intended to apologize for the foreign word.

A tempting emendation is suggested by the reading 'Libyans' for 'Libertines' in the Armenian versions and Syriac commentaries. The form Λιβύων given by Tischendorf is improbable, but Beza's conjecture Λιβυστίνων is attractive. If this reading be adopted, we have the Jews of Libya, Cyrene, and Alexandria named in their geographical order. (Cf. Blass, *PG*, pp. 69 f.) But there is no sufficient reason to reject Λιβερτίνων.

[1] In LXX, συναγωγή appears in Gen.-Num., Jer. and Ezk. as the regular equivalent of *qāhāl* (elsewhere in LXX rendered by ἐκκλησία), and throughout LXX it is the almost invariable equivalent of *'ēdāh* (which is never rendered by ἐκκλησία). See on v. 11; vii. 38; xx. 28.

ἀπὸ Κιλικίας] The synagogue, no doubt, which Paul attended. He may have been a *libertinus*, if his father or remoter ancestor gained his citizenship by manumission (see on xxii. 28).

καὶ Ἀσίας] om A D.

vi. 10

τῇ σοφίᾳ καὶ τῷ πνεύματι ᾧ ἐλάλει] D has *τῇ σοφίᾳ τῇ οὔσῃ ἐν αὐτῷ καὶ τῷ πνεύματι τῷ ἁγίῳ ᾧ ἐλάλει διὰ τὸ ἐλέγχεσθαι αὐτοὺς ἐπ' αὐτοῦ μετὰ πάσης παρρησίας. μὴ δυνάμενοι οὖν ἀντοφθαλμεῖν τῇ ἀληθείᾳ κ.τ.λ.* This δ text is found also in h vg.codd hcl.mg tepl vet. bohaem. Note *ἀντοφθαλμεῖν* ('withstand'), which in the ordinary NT text occurs only in xxvii. 15 (*q.v.*). For the sense cf. Lk. xxi. 15, *ἐγὼ . . . δώσω ὑμῖν στόμα καὶ σοφίαν ᾗ οὐ δυνήσονται ἀντιστῆναι.*

vi. 11

ὑπέβαλον] 'put up', 'suborned'; of introducing in an underhand manner with fraudulent intent. Cf. Appian, *Bell. ciu.* i. 74, *ὑπεβλήθησαν κατήγοροι.* The Lat. versions have *summiserunt*.

ῥήματα βλάσφημα] Cf. Mk. xiv. 64. The Mosaic law on blasphemy (Num. xv. 30) was at this time more widely interpreted than in the later Rabbinic law (*Sanh.* vii. 5), according to which blasphemy involved the use of the Ineffable Name. Cf. Dalman, *Words of Jesus*, p. 314.

vi. 12

εἰς τὸ συνέδριον] See on iv. 15.

vi. 13

κατὰ τοῦ τόπου τοῦ ἁγίου τούτου καὶ τοῦ νόμου] *τούτου* B C; om א A D al. With the terms of Stephen's accusation we may compare the charges brought against Christ (Mk. xiv. 56 ff., 64) and against Paul (Ac. xxi. 28). As in our Lord's accusation, so in Stephen's, the charges were perversions of what had actually been said. What Stephen had said may be judged from the tenor of his reply. His declaration (vii. 48) that the Most High does not dwell in temples made with hands might easily be interpreted as blasphemy 'against this holy place'. It is clear that Stephen advanced beyond the apostles' earlier position in relation to official Judaism, and saw more clearly the inevitability of a break. In more ways than one he was the forerunner of Paul and of the writer to the Hebrews.

vi. 14

ὁ Ναζωραῖος οὗτος] See on ii. 22; *οὗτος* is here perhaps contemptuous.

καταλύσει τὸν τόπον τοῦτον] Exactly what they had said about Jesus Himself (Mk. xiv. 58); the charge rose out of His saying 'Destroy this temple' (Jn. ii. 19) and possibly His prediction of the destruction of the temple (Mk. xiii. 2).

ἀλλάξει τὰ ἔθη ἃ παρέδωκεν ἡμῖν Μωυσῆς] He may have spoken of the transitory character of the Mosaic ceremonial; out of the mouths of his accusers we have here a tribute to Stephen's far-sighted comprehension of what was involved in the Gospel. No wonder his teaching was anathema to orthodox Jews! For the language, Page compares Juvenal, *Sat.* xiv. 102, '*tradidit arcano quodcumque uolumine Moyses*'.

vi. 15

ὡσεὶ πρόσωπον ἀγγέλου] For *ὡσεί* cf. ii. 3; Lk. iii. 23; xxii. 44. Cf. also for the shining face Moses on Sinai (Ex. xxxiv. 29 ff.) and Christ at His transfiguration (Mt. xvii. 2). Cf. Esth. xv. 13 LXX, *εἶδόν σε, κύριε, ὡς ἄγγελον θεοῦ.* δ adds *ἑστῶτος ἐν μέσῳ αὐτῶν.*

vii. 1

Εἶπεν δὲ ὁ ἀρχιερεύς Εἰ ταῦτα οὕτως ἔχει;] *εἶπεν δὲ ὁ ἀρχιερεὺς τῷ Στεφάνῳ Εἰ ἄρα τοῦτο οὕτως ἔχει;* D. For *εἰ* introducing a direct question, cf. i. 6; xix. 2; xxi. 37; xxii. 25.

(d) Stephen's Defence, vii. 2-53

ὁ δὲ ἔφη Ἄνδρες ἀδελφοὶ καὶ πατέρες, ἀκούσατε. Ὁ θεὸς τῆς 2
δόξης ὤφθη τῷ πατρὶ ἡμῶν Ἀβραὰμ ὄντι ἐν τῇ Μεσοποταμίᾳ πρὶν ἢ
κατοικῆσαι αὐτὸν ἐν Χαρράν, καὶ εἶπεν πρὸς αὐτόν Ἔξελθε ἐκ τῆς γῆς 3
σου καὶ τῆς συγγενείας σου, καὶ δεῦρο εἰς τὴν γῆν ἣν ἄν σοι δείξω·
τότε ἐξελθὼν ἐκ γῆς Χαλδαίων κατῴκησεν ἐν Χαρράν. κἀκεῖθεν μετὰ 4
τὸ ἀποθανεῖν τὸν πατέρα αὐτοῦ μετῴκισεν αὐτὸν εἰς τὴν γῆν ταύτην εἰς
ἣν ὑμεῖς νῦν κατοικεῖτε, καὶ οὐκ ἔδωκεν αὐτῷ κληρονομίαν ἐν αὐτῇ 5
οὐδὲ βῆμα ποδός, καὶ ἐπηγγείλατο δοῦναι αὐτῷ εἰς κατάσχεσιν αὐτὴν
καὶ τῷ σπέρματι αὐτοῦ μετ' αὐτόν, οὐκ ὄντος αὐτῷ τέκνου. ἐλάλησεν 6
δὲ οὕτως ὁ θεὸς ὅτι ἔσται τὸ σπέρμα αὐτοῦ πάροικον ἐν γῇ ἀλλοτρίᾳ,
καὶ δουλώσουσιν αὐτὸ καὶ κακώσουσιν ἔτη τετρακόσια· καὶ τὸ ἔθνος 7
ᾧ ἂν δουλεύσουσιν κρινῶ ἐγώ, ὁ θεὸς εἶπεν, καὶ μετὰ ταῦτα ἐξελεύ-
σονται καὶ λατρεύσουσίν μοι ἐν τῷ τόπῳ τούτῳ. καὶ ἔδωκεν αὐτῷ 8
διαθήκην περιτομῆς· καὶ οὕτως ἐγέννησεν τὸν Ἰσαὰκ καὶ περιέτεμεν
αὐτὸν τῇ ἡμέρᾳ τῇ ὀγδόῃ, καὶ Ἰσαὰκ τὸν Ἰακώβ, καὶ Ἰακὼβ τοὺς
δώδεκα πατριάρχας. Καὶ οἱ πατριάρχαι ζηλώσαντες τὸν Ἰωσὴφ 9

ἀπέδοντο εἰς Αἴγυπτον· καὶ ἦν ὁ θεὸς μετ' αὐτοῦ, καὶ ἐξείλατο αὐτὸν 10
ἐκ πασῶν τῶν θλίψεων αὐτοῦ, καὶ ἔδωκεν αὐτῷ χάριν καὶ σοφίαν ἐναντίον Φαραὼ βασιλέως Αἰγύπτου, καὶ κατέστησεν αὐτὸν ἡγούμενον
ἐπ' Αἴγυπτον καὶ ὅλον τὸν οἶκον αὐτοῦ. ἦλθεν δὲ λιμὸς ἐφ' ὅλην 11
τὴν Αἴγυπτον καὶ Χαναὰν καὶ θλίψις μεγάλη, καὶ οὐχ ηὕρισκον
χορτάσματα οἱ πατέρες ἡμῶν· ἀκούσας δὲ Ἰακὼβ ὄντα σιτία εἰς 12
Αἴγυπτον ἐξαπέστειλεν τοὺς πατέρας ἡμῶν πρῶτον· καὶ ἐν τῷ δευτέρῳ 13
ἐγνωρίσθη Ἰωσὴφ τοῖς ἀδελφοῖς αὐτοῦ, καὶ φανερὸν ἐγένετο τῷ
Φαραὼ τὸ γένος Ἰωσήφ. ἀποστείλας δὲ Ἰωσὴφ μετεκαλέσατο Ἰακὼβ 14
τὸν πατέρα αὐτοῦ καὶ πᾶσαν τὴν συγγένειαν ἐν ψυχαῖς ἑβδομήκοντα
πέντε, κατέβη δὲ Ἰακὼβ εἰς Αἴγυπτον. καὶ ἐτελεύτησεν αὐτὸς 15
καὶ οἱ πατέρες ἡμῶν, καὶ μετετέθησαν εἰς Συχὲμ καὶ ἐτέθησαν ἐν τῷ 16
μνήματι ᾧ ὠνήσατο Ἀβραὰμ τιμῆς ἀργυρίου παρὰ τῶν υἱῶν Ἑμμὼρ
ἐν Συχέμ. Καθὼς δὲ ἤγγιζεν ὁ χρόνος τῆς ἐπαγγελίας ἧς ὡμολόγησεν 17
ὁ θεὸς τῷ Ἀβραάμ, ηὔξησεν ὁ λαὸς καὶ ἐπληθύνθη ἐν Αἰγύπτῳ, ἄχρι 18
οὗ ἀνέστη βασιλεὺς ἕτερος ἐπ' Αἴγυπτον, ὃς οὐκ ᾔδει τὸν Ἰωσήφ.
οὗτος κατασοφισάμενος τὸ γένος ἡμῶν ἐκάκωσεν τοὺς πατέρας τοῦ 19
ποιεῖν τὰ βρέφη ἔκθετα αὐτῶν εἰς τὸ μὴ ζωογονεῖσθαι. ἐν ᾧ καιρῷ 20
ἐγεννήθη Μωυσῆς, καὶ ἦν ἀστεῖος τῷ θεῷ· ὃς ἀνετράφη μῆνας τρεῖς
ἐν τῷ οἴκῳ τοῦ πατρός· ἐκτεθέντος δὲ αὐτοῦ ἀνείλατο αὐτὸν ἡ θυγά- 21
τηρ Φαραὼ καὶ ἀνεθρέψατο αὐτὸν ἑαυτῇ εἰς υἱόν. καὶ ἐπαιδεύθη 22
Μωυσῆς πάσῃ σοφίᾳ Αἰγυπτίων, ἦν δὲ δυνατὸς ἐν λόγοις καὶ ἔργοις
αὐτοῦ. Ὡς δὲ ἐπληροῦτο αὐτῷ τεσσερακονταετὴς χρόνος, ἀνέβη 23
ἐπὶ τὴν καρδίαν αὐτοῦ ἐπισκέψασθαι τοὺς ἀδελφοὺς αὐτοῦ τοὺς υἱοὺς
Ἰσραήλ. καὶ ἰδών τινα ἀδικούμενον ἠμύνατο καὶ ἐποίησεν ἐκδίκησιν 24
τῷ καταπονουμένῳ πατάξας τὸν Αἰγύπτιον. ἐνόμιζεν δὲ συνιέναι 25
τοὺς ἀδελφοὺς ὅτι ὁ θεὸς διὰ χειρὸς αὐτοῦ δίδωσιν σωτηρίαν αὐτοῖς,
οἱ δὲ οὐ συνῆκαν. τῇ τε ἐπιούσῃ ἡμέρᾳ ὤφθη αὐτοῖς μαχομένοις 26
καὶ συνήλλασσεν αὐτοὺς εἰς εἰρήνην εἰπών Ἄνδρες, ἀδελφοί ἐστε· ἵνα
τί ἀδικεῖτε ἀλλήλους; ὁ δὲ ἀδικῶν τὸν πλησίον ἀπώσατο αὐτὸν εἰπών 27
Τίς σὲ κατέστησεν ἄρχοντα καὶ δικαστὴν ἐπ' ἡμῶν; μὴ ἀνελεῖν με 28
σὺ θέλεις ὃν τρόπον ἀνεῖλες ἐχθὲς τὸν Αἰγύπτιον; ἔφυγεν δὲ Μωυσῆς 29
ἐν τῷ λόγῳ τούτῳ, καὶ ἐγένετο πάροικος ἐν γῇ Μαδιάμ, οὗ ἐγέννησεν
υἱοὺς δύο. Καὶ πληρωθέντων ἐτῶν τεσσεράκοντα ὤφθη αὐτῷ ἐν τῇ 30
ἐρήμῳ τοῦ ὄρους Σινὰ ἄγγελος ἐν φλογὶ πυρὸς βάτου· ὁ δὲ Μωυσῆς 31
ἰδὼν ἐθαύμασεν τὸ ὅραμα· προσερχομένου δὲ αὐτοῦ κατανοῆσαι ἐγένετο
φωνὴ Κυρίου Ἐγὼ ὁ θεὸς τῶν πατέρων σου, ὁ θεὸς Ἀβραὰμ καὶ Ἰσαὰκ 32
καὶ Ἰακώβ. ἔντρομος δὲ γενόμενος Μωυσῆς οὐκ ἐτόλμα κατανοῆσαι.
εἶπεν δὲ αὐτῷ ὁ κύριος Λῦσον τὸ ὑπόδημα τῶν ποδῶν σου, ὁ γὰρ τόπος 33
ἐφ' ᾧ ἕστηκας γῆ ἁγία ἐστίν. ἰδὼν εἶδον τὴν κάκωσιν τοῦ λαοῦ μου 34
τοῦ ἐν Αἰγύπτῳ, καὶ τοῦ στεναγμοῦ αὐτοῦ ἤκουσα, καὶ κατέβην
ἐξελέσθαι αὐτούς· καὶ νῦν δεῦρο ἀποστείλω σε εἰς Αἴγυπτον. Τοῦτον 35
τὸν Μωυσῆν, ὃν ἠρνήσαντο εἰπόντες Τίς σὲ κατέστησεν ἄρχοντα καὶ
δικαστήν, τοῦτον ὁ θεὸς καὶ ἄρχοντα καὶ λυτρωτὴν ἀπέσταλκεν σὺν
χειρὶ ἀγγέλου τοῦ ὀφθέντος αὐτῷ ἐν τῇ βάτῳ. οὗτος ἐξήγαγεν αὐτοὺς

*ποιήσας τέρατα καὶ σημεῖα ἐν τῇ Αἰγύπτῳ καὶ ἐν Ἐρυθρᾷ Θαλάσσῃ
καὶ ἐν τῇ ἐρήμῳ ἔτη τεσσεράκοντα. οὗτός ἐστιν ὁ Μωυσῆς ὁ εἴπας* 37
*τοῖς υἱοῖς Ἰσραήλ Προφήτην ὑμῖν ἀναστήσει ὁ θεὸς ἐκ τῶν ἀδελφῶν
ὑμῶν ὡς ἐμέ. οὗτός ἐστιν ὁ γενόμενος ἐν τῇ ἐκκλησίᾳ ἐν τῇ ἐρήμῳ* 38
*μετὰ τοῦ ἀγγέλου τοῦ λαλοῦντος αὐτῷ ἐν τῷ ὄρει Σινὰ καὶ τῶν πατέρων
ἡμῶν, ὃς ἐδέξατο λόγια ζῶντα δοῦναι ὑμῖν, ᾧ οὐκ ἠθέλησαν ὑπήκοοι* 39
*γενέσθαι οἱ πατέρες ἡμῶν ἀλλὰ ἀπώσαντο καὶ ἐστράφησαν ἐν ταῖς
καρδίαις αὐτῶν εἰς Αἴγυπτον, εἰπόντες τῷ Ἀαρών Ποίησον ἡμῖν* 40
*θεοὺς οἳ προπορεύσονται ἡμῶν· ὁ γὰρ Μωυσῆς οὗτος, ὃς ἐξήγαγεν
ἡμᾶς ἐκ γῆς Αἰγύπτου, οὐκ οἴδαμεν τί ἐγένετο αὐτῷ. καὶ ἐμοσχο-* 41
*ποίησαν ἐν ταῖς ἡμέραις ἐκείναις καὶ ἀνήγαγον θυσίαν τῷ εἰδώλῳ, καὶ
εὐφραίνοντο ἐν τοῖς ἔργοις τῶν χειρῶν αὐτῶν. ἔστρεψεν δὲ ὁ θεὸς καὶ* 42
*παρέδωκεν αὐτοὺς λατρεύειν τῇ στρατιᾷ τοῦ οὐρανοῦ, καθὼς γέγραπται
ἐν Βίβλῳ τῶν προφητῶν*

*Μὴ σφάγια καὶ θυσίας προσηνέγκατέ μοι
ἔτη τεσσεράκοντα ἐν τῇ ἐρήμῳ, οἶκος Ἰσραήλ;
καὶ ἀνελάβετε τὴν σκηνὴν τοῦ Μολόχ* 43
*καὶ τὸ ἄστρον τοῦ θεοῦ Ῥομφά,
τοὺς τύπους οὓς ἐποιήσατε προσκυνεῖν αὐτοῖς.
καὶ μετοικιῶ ὑμᾶς ἐπέκεινα Βαβυλῶνος.*

Ἡ σκηνὴ τοῦ μαρτυρίου ἦν τοῖς πατράσιν ἡμῶν ἐν τῇ ἐρήμῳ, καθὼς 44
*διετάξατο ὁ λαλῶν τῷ Μωυσῇ ποιῆσαι αὐτὴν κατὰ τὸν τύπον ὃν ἑωράκει,
ἣν καὶ εἰσήγαγον διαδεξάμενοι οἱ πατέρες ἡμῶν μετὰ Ἰησοῦ ἐν τῇ κατα-* 45
*σχέσει τῶν ἐθνῶν ὧν ἐξῶσεν ὁ θεὸς ἀπὸ προσώπου τῶν πατέρων ἡμῶν
ἕως τῶν ἡμερῶν Δαυείδ· ὃς εὗρεν χάριν ἐνώπιον τοῦ θεοῦ καὶ ᾐτήσατο* 46
εὑρεῖν σκήνωμα τῷ θεῷ Ἰακώβ. Σολομῶν δὲ οἰκοδόμησεν αὐτῷ 47
οἶκον. ἀλλ᾽ οὐχ ὁ ὕψιστος ἐν χειροποιήτοις κατοικεῖ· καθὼς ὁ 48
προφήτης λέγει

Ὁ οὐρανός μοι θρόνος, 49
*καὶ ἡ γῆ ὑποπόδιον τῶν ποδῶν μου·
ποῖον οἶκον οἰκοδομήσετέ μοι, λέγει Κύριος,
ἢ τίς τόπος τῆς καταπαύσεώς μου;
οὐχὶ ἡ χείρ μου ἐποίησεν ταῦτα πάντα;* 50

Σκληροτράχηλοι καὶ ἀπερίτμητοι καρδίαις καὶ τοῖς ὠσίν, ὑμεῖς ἀεὶ 51
*τῷ πνεύματι τῷ ἁγίῳ ἀντιπίπτετε, ὡς οἱ πατέρες ὑμῶν καὶ ὑμεῖς.
τίνα τῶν προφητῶν οὐκ ἐδίωξαν οἱ πατέρες ὑμῶν; καὶ ἀπέκτειναν τοὺς* 52
*προκαταγγείλαντας περὶ τῆς ἐλεύσεως τοῦ δικαίου οὗ νῦν ὑμεῖς προ-
δόται καὶ φονεῖς ἐγένεσθε, οἵτινες ἐλάβετε τὸν νόμον εἰς διαταγὰς* 53
ἀγγέλων, καὶ οὐκ ἐφυλάξατε.

'Stephen's apology' is not so much a forensic defence as a statement of the teaching which had caused such irritation. This teaching marks a great advance on the more conservative Jerusalem Christianity of chs. i-v, and in several ways foreshadows the teaching of Paul and of the Epistle to the Hebrews. The main arguments are: (1) God is not locally restricted and does not inhabit material buildings; His people similarly should not be tied to any particular spot; (2) the Jewish nation has always been rebellious; as previous generations opposed the prophets from Moses onwards, so this generation has killed 'the Righteous One'. Some parallels with Hellenistic Jewish thought, noticed below, help to show the appropriateness and support the authenticity of the speech.

vii. 2

ὁ θεὸς τῆς δόξης] a title found in Ps. xxix. 3 (LXX xxviii).

ὄντι ἐν τῇ Μεσοποταμίᾳ] The full name is *Συρία Μεσοποταμία*, a rendering of Aram-Naharaim ('Aram of the two rivers'), that part of North Syria lying between the Orontes and the Euphrates (the Egyptian Naharin). The ancient Mesopotamia was not coterminous with the modern Iraq, and did not include the well-known city of Ur near the mouth of the Euphrates, which is commonly identified with the 'Ur of the Chaldees' (Heb. *Ūr Kasdīm*) where Abraham lived 'before he dwelt in Haran'. Probably therefore the Biblical Ur of the Chaldees should be placed farther north, which would accord better with Jewish tradition. The name may originally have been connected with Urartu,[1] or (more probably) with Arpachshad on the Tigris.[2]

πρὶν ἢ κατοικῆσαι αὐτὸν ἐν Χαρράν] According to Gen. xi. 31-xii. 5, the words quoted in *ver.* 3 below were spoken after Abraham's arrival in Haran (RV gives correct sense). But Gen. xv. 7 and Neh. ix. 7 state that God brought Abraham from Ur, implying a divine communication there as well, which is also indicated by Philo, *de Abrahamo* 71; Jos. *Ant.* i. 7.

Χαρράν] The OT Haran, mod. Harran, known also in ancient times as Carrhae, in N.W. Mesopotamia. It was a flourishing city in the nineteenth and eighteenth centuries B.C. In the same district place-names have been discovered corresponding to the names of some members of Abraham's family: e.g. Nahor, Serug and Terah (see W. F. Albright, *From the Stone Age to Christianity* [1940], pp. 179 f.).[3]

[1] So LC: 'it must be remembered that the district of Van was known to the Assyrians as Urartu and that they described the inhabitants of that district as Chaldees' (i.e. *Ḫaldi*, not to be confused with *Kaldu*, the Chaldaeans who lived in lower Babylonia). Greek writers know of Chaldaeans (*Χαλδαῖοι*) in the districts of Armenia and Pontus (e.g. Xenophon, *Anab.* iv. 3. 4; v. 5. 17; *Cyrop.* iii. 1. 34; Strabo, xii. 3. 18 ff., 28 f.; Plutarch, *Lucullus* 14; Stephanus the Byzantine *s.v.* *Χαλδαῖοι* calls them *ἔθνος πλησίον τῆς Κολχίδος*).

[2] Cf. W. J. Phythian-Adams, *The Fulness of Israel* (1938), pp. 51 ff.; J. & J. B. E. Garstang, *The Story of Jericho* (1940), pp. 15 f.

[3] Mention should be made of the view held by some that Aram-Naharaim or Paddan-Aram is Syria of Damascus, the two rivers being in that case Abana

vii. 3

καὶ εἶπεν κ.τ.λ.] From Gen. xii. 1, *καὶ εἶπεν Κύριος τῷ Ἀβράμ, Ἔξελθε ἐκ τῆς γῆς σου καὶ ἐκ τῆς συγγενείας σου καὶ ἐκ τοῦ οἴκου τοῦ πατρός σου, εἰς τὴν γῆν ἣν ἄν σοι δείξω.*

καὶ δεῦρο] Only in the Lucianic recension of LXX. The adv. *δεῦρο* was used quite early as a verb: cf. *ver.* 34, and the plural formation *δεῦτε*, Mt. xi. 28, etc.

vii. 4

τότε ἐξελθὼν ἐκ γῆς Χαλδαίων κατῴκησεν ἐν Χαρράν] In Gen. xi. 27–xii. 5 Terah is represented as the leader of the expedition from Ur to Haran. Terah would be the recognized leader while he lived, even though Abraham was the moving spirit.

γῆς Χαλδαίων] In LXX *ἡ χώρα τῶν Χαλδαίων* is the regular translation of *'Ūr Kasdīm*. This 'land of the Chaldaeans' Josephus places in Mesopotamia.

μετὰ τὸ ἀποθανεῖν τὸν πατέρα αὐτοῦ] Cf. Philo, *de migratione Abrahami* 177, *ὅτι πρότερον μὲν ἐκ τῆς Χαλδαϊκῆς ἀναστὰς γῆς Ἀβραὰμ ᾤκησεν εἰς Χαρράν, τελευτήσαντος δὲ αὐτῷ τοῦ πατρὸς ἐκεῖθι κἀκ ταύτης μετανίσταται.* A comparison of the chronological data of Gen. xi. 26, 32; xii. 4 would suggest that Terah's death at the age of 205 took place 60 years after Abraham's departure from Haran. The older Bible chronologers dealt with this difficulty by taking Gen. xi. 25 to mean that Terah was 70 when his oldest son Haran was born, while Abraham may have been born 60 years later.[1]

μετῴκισεν] Understand *ὁ θεός* as subject.

εἰς ἣν ὑμεῖς νῦν κατοικεῖτε] A clear example of the Hellenistic encroachment of *εἰς* upon *ἐν*. D adds *καὶ οἱ πατέρες ἡμῶν οἱ πρὸ ἡμῶν*, hcl* 'and your fathers before you'.

vii. 5

καὶ οὐκ ἔδωκεν αὐτῷ κληρονομίαν ἐν αὐτῇ οὐδὲ βῆμα ποδός] The wording reflects Dt. ii. 5 (*οὐ γὰρ μὴ δῶ ὑμῖν ἀπὸ τῆς γῆς αὐτῶν οὐδὲ βῆμα ποδός*), where the reference is to Mount Seir.

δοῦναι αὐτῷ εἰς κατάσχεσιν αὐτὴν καὶ τῷ σπέρματι αὐτοῦ μετ' αὐτόν] A quotation from Gen. xvii. 8 (*καὶ δώσω σοι καὶ τῷ σπέρματί*

and Pharpar, and Haran being Haran el-Awamid, 15 miles east of Damascus. See, e.g., H. M. Wiener, *The Origin of the Pentateuch* (1912), pp. 99 ff.; W. M. Christie, *Palestine Calling* (1939), pp. 92 ff.; and cf. the name of Abraham's servant, Dammeseq Eliezer (Gen. xv. 2), with the statement of Nicolaus of Damascus that 'Abraham reigned at Damascus' (*ap.* Jos. *Ant.* i. 7. 2).

[1] The Samaritan Pentateuch gives Terah's age at death as 145, and a similar LXX reading may lie behind the present passage and Philo, *loc. cit.* There are other passages in Stephen's speech which presume readings no longer extant in our LXX texts but preserved in the Samaritan Pentateuch. See P. E. Kahle, *The Cairo Geniza* (1947), pp. 143 ff.

σου μετὰ σὲ τὴν γῆν ἣν παροικεῖς, πᾶσαν τὴν γῆν Χαναάν, εἰς κατάσχεσιν αἰώνιον). Cf. similar promises to Jacob (Gen. xlviii. 4) and Moses (Dt. xxxii. 49).

εἰς κατάσχεσιν] Cf. *ver.* 45, where *κατάσχεσις* means not so much 'having in possession' as 'taking in possession'.

οὐκ ὄντος κ.τ.λ.] The ordinary rule is that the negative with a ptc. is *μή*, but *οὐ* is not unnaturally found where an explicit negative fact is stated (cf. xxvi. 22; xxviii. 17, 19; and Moulton, *Proleg.*, pp. 231 f.).

vii. 6f.

ὅτι ἔσται . . . ἐξελεύσονται] From Gen. xv. 13 f., *ὅτι πάροικον ἔσται τὸ σπέρμα σου ἐν γῇ οὐκ ἰδίᾳ, καὶ δουλώσουσιν αὐτοὺς καὶ κακώσουσιν αὐτοὺς καὶ ταπεινώσουσιν αὐτοὺς τετρακόσια ἔτη. τὸ δὲ ἔθνος, ᾧ ἐὰν δουλεύσωσιν, κρινῶ ἐγώ· μετὰ δὲ ταῦτα ἐξελεύσονται ὧδε μετὰ ἀποσκευῆς πολλῆς.*

πάροικον] A theme throughout the speech (cf. Heb. xi. 8-16). The people of God should sit loose to any earthly country. The only land that Abraham possessed was what he bought for a burying-place (see on *ver.* 16). Cf. *vv.* 29, 44, 47.

ἐν γῇ ἀλλοτρίᾳ] Gen. xv. 13 LXX has *ἐν γῇ οὐκ ἰδίᾳ*, but cf. Ex. ii. 22, *πάροικός εἰμι ἐν γῇ ἀλλοτρίᾳ.*

τετρακόσια ἔτη] According to Ex. xii. 40 MT, the sojourning in Egypt lasted 430 years, for which 400 might be taken as a round number. But Rabbinical exegesis reckoned 400 years from the birth of Isaac to the Exodus: cf. Gal. iii. 17 (following Ex. xii. 40 LXX), where the 430 years stretch from the promise made to Abraham to the Exodus. See on xiii. 20.

ᾧ ἐὰν δουλεύσουσιν] The use of *ἄν* with fut. indic. is post-classical, being a mixture of two constructions, (1) the simple future, and (2) *ἄν* with the aorist subjunctive, the classical indefinite construction, which B has here, following LXX. Cf. Mk. viii. 35; Lk. xii. 8; xvii. 33.

καὶ λατρεύσουσίν μοι ἐν τῷ τόπῳ τούτῳ] From the words addressed to Moses in Ex. iii. 12 (*ἐν τῷ ἐξαγαγεῖν σε τὸν λαόν μου ἐξ Αἰγύπτου καὶ λατρεύσετε τῷ θεῷ ἐν τῷ ὄρει τούτῳ*), where the place referred to is Sinai. Here it is Palestine. With the telescoping of distinct quotations cf. the telescoping of distinct events in *ver.* 16 below. Cf. also, particularly for the inclusion of *λατρεύω* in the promise to Abraham, the words of the Magnificat, Lk. i. 73-75.

vii. 8

διαθήκην περιτομῆς] Cf. Gen. xvii. 10, *καὶ αὕτη ἡ διαθήκη . . . περιτμηθήσεται ὑμῶν πᾶν ἀρσενικόν.*

οὕτως] LC suggest the emphatic meaning, 'thus, while there was still no holy place, all the essential conditions for the religion of Israel were fulfilled'.

περιέτεμεν αὐτὸν τῇ ἡμέρᾳ τῇ ὀγδόῃ] Cf. Gen. xxi. 4, *περιέτεμεν δὲ Ἀβραὰμ τὸν Ἰσαὰκ τῇ ὀγδόῃ ἡμέρᾳ.*

πατριάρχας] See on ii. 29. The word is used for the sons of Jacob in 4 Macc. xvi. 25 (along with Abraham, Isaac and Jacob, who are so called also in vii. 19), and in the title of the Greek version of *Testaments of the Twelve Patriarchs.*

vii. 9

ζηλώσαντες τὸν Ἰωσὴφ ἀπέδοντο εἰς Αἴγυπτον] Cf. Gen. xxxvii. 11 (*ἐζήλωσαν δὲ αὐτὸν οἱ ἀδελφοὶ αὐτοῦ*); xlv. 4 (*ἐγώ εἰμι Ἰωσὴφ ὁ ἀδελφὸς ὑμῶν, ὃν ἀπέδοσθε εἰς Αἴγυπτον*).

vii. 10

καὶ ἦν ὁ θεὸς μετ' αὐτοῦ] Cf. Gen. xxxix. 2, 3, 21.

καὶ ἔδωκεν αὐτῷ χάριν] The exact words occur in Gen. xxxix. 21, followed by *ἐναντίον τοῦ ἀρχιδεσμοφύλακος.*

σοφίαν] A reference no doubt to his interpretation of dreams and his advice to store the corn against the years of famine: cf. Gen. xli. 38 f.

ἐναντίον Φαραὼ βασιλέως Αἰγύπτου] These words occur in Gen. xli. 46, preceded by *ἔστη.*

κατέστησεν αὐτὸν κ.τ.λ.] Cf. Ps. cv. 21 (LXX civ),

κατέστησεν αὐτὸν κύριον τοῦ οἴκου αὐτοῦ
καὶ ἄρχοντα πάσης τῆς κτίσεως αὐτοῦ.

Cf. also Gen. xli. 40 f., 43, and xlv. 8 (*καὶ ἐποίησέν με . . . κύριον παντὸς τοῦ οἴκου αὐτοῦ καὶ ἄρχοντα πάσης γῆς Αἰγύπτου*).

vii. 11

ἦλθεν δὲ λιμὸς ἐφ' ὅλην τὴν Αἴγυπτον καὶ Χαναάν] Cf. Gen. xli. 54 ff. (*καὶ ἐγένετο λιμὸς ἐν πάσῃ τῇ γῇ . . . καὶ ἐπείνασεν πᾶσα ἡ γῆ Αἰγύπτου*); xlii. 5 (*ἦν γὰρ ὁ λιμὸς ἐν γῇ Χαναάν*).

θλίψις μεγάλη] For the words cf. Mt. xxiv. 21; Rev. ii. 22; vii. 14, where much more than famine is meant.

οὐχ ηὕρισκον] Note the imperfect, 'could not find'.

χορτάσματα] Originally of animals' feeding-stuffs, 'provender'; later used in wider sense of men's food as well.

vii. 12

ἀκούσας δὲ Ἰακὼβ ὄντα σίτια εἰς Αἴγυπτον] Cf. Gen. xlii. 1 f., *ἰδὼν δὲ Ἰακὼβ ὅτι ἐστὶν πρᾶσις ἐν Αἰγύπτῳ εἶπεν . . . ἰδοὺ ἀκήκοα ὅτι ἐστὶν σῖτος ἐν Αἰγύπτῳ.*

εἰς Αἴγυπτον] Note again the encroachment of εἰς on ἐν. D, following LXX, has ἐν: cf. viii. 23 (but in xi. 25 D has εἰς for ἐν).

πρῶτον] 'a first time'. Ramsay (*BRD* 254*n.*) argues that the meaning must be first of three, the third occasion being when the whole family of Israel went down. But πρῶτον here is intended to balance ἐν τῷ δευτέρῳ in *ver.* 13. See on i. 1.

vii. 13

ἐν τῷ δευτέρῳ] ἐπὶ τῷ δευτέρῳ D. As Joseph appeared to his brethren twice, so did Moses twice 'visit his brethren' (*vv.* 23 ff.). Some have seen a reference here to Christ's second coming (cf. iii. 20 f.), when *His* brethren κατὰ σάρκα will recognize *Him* (cf. Zech. xii. 10).

ἐγνωρίσθη Ἰωσὴφ τοῖς ἀδελφοῖς αὐτοῦ] D has ἀνεγνωρίσθη for ἐγνωρίσθη, following LXX ἀνεγνωρίζετο (Gen. xlv. 1).

vii. 14

ἐν] 'consisting of', 'amounting to', 'in all'. Cf. Mk. iv. 8 *bis.* The construction here is taken from Dt. x. 22, ἐν ἑβδομήκοντα (A F add πέντε) ψυχαῖς κατέβησαν οἱ πατέρες σου εἰς Αἴγυπτον, where ἐν represents Heb. *bĕ.*

ἐν ψυχαῖς ἑβδομήκοντα πέντε] The MT of Gen. xlvi. 27; Ex. i. 5; Dt. x. 22 says seventy persons (including Jacob, and Joseph and his two sons); the LXX of Gen. xlvi. 27 and Ex. i. 5 says seventy-five persons, omitting Jacob and Joseph, but giving Joseph *nine* sons, instead of the two of MT (Gen. xlvi. 27). Philo, *de migratione Abrahami* 199 ff., reconciles the discrepant accounts by saying that in the smaller figure the number five, which symbolizes the senses, has been omitted, signifying the transition from the recalcitrant Jacob to Israel, the man with the vision of God (as though from Heb. *'īsh rō'eh 'Ēl,* 'man seeing God')—a typical example of Philo's allegorizing method. Josephus (*Ant.* ii. 7. 4: vi. 5. 6) follows the Hebrew number.

vii. 15

εἰς Αἴγυπτον] ℵ A C D byz; om B.

αὐτὸς] Jacob; his death is recorded in Gen. xlix. 33, and the deaths of his sons in Ex. i. 6.

vii. 16

καὶ μετετέθησαν εἰς Συχὲμ κ.τ.λ.] Jacob was buried at Hebron, in the cave of Machpelah, which Abraham had bought for 400 silver shekels from Ephron the Hittite (Gen. xxiii. 16; xlix. 29 ff.; l. 13). Joseph was buried at Shechem, in the piece of ground which

Jacob had bought for 100 pieces of silver from the sons of Hamor (Josh. xxiv. 32). Josephus (*Ant.* ii. 8. 2) says that Jacob's other sons were buried at Hebron. The telescoping of two transactions in this verse may be compared with other examples of compression in this speech, e.g. the apparent telescoping of two calls of Abraham in *ver.* 2, and of two quotations in *ver.* 7.

εἰς Συχὲμ] Shechem, between Mounts Ebal and Gerizim. Its name in NT times was Mabartha (Jos. *BJ* iv. 8. 1); it was refounded by Vespasian *c.* A.D. 72 as Flavia Neapolis, whence its modern name Nablus. The mention of a place now belonging to the schismatic Samaritans (cf. Jn. iv. 5 f., 12) was little calculated to conciliate the audience.

ἐν Συχέμ] ℵ B C; *τοῦ Συχέμ* δ byz (whence AV '*the father* of Shechem': cf. Josh. xxiv. 32 MT, EV); *τοῦ ἐν Συχέμ* ℵ[c] A al.

vii. 17

ηὔξησεν ὁ λαὸς καὶ ἐπληθύνθη] Cf. Ex. i. 7, *οἱ δὲ υἱοὶ Ἰσραὴλ ηὐξήθησαν καὶ ἐπληθύνθησαν.*

ὡμολόγησεν] *ἐπηγγείλατο* P^{45} δ; *ὤμοσεν* 81 byz. For *ὤμοσεν* cf. Lk. i. 73 from Gen. xxii. 16, and for *ὡμολόγησεν* and *ὤμοσεν* as variants cf. Mt. xiv. 7 with Mk. vi. 23.

vii. 18

ἀνέστη βασιλεὺς ἕτερος ἐπ' Αἴγυπτον, ὃς οὐκ ᾔδει τὸν Ἰωσήφ] From Ex. i. 8, the reference being to the Eighteenth Dynasty, founded by Aahmes (1567 B.C.), who expelled the Asiatic Hyksos rulers, or else to the Nineteenth Dynasty which followed it (1319 B.C.). It is usually thought that Joseph's patron was a Hyksos king (so, e.g., W. F. Albright); A. S. Yahuda, however, thinks he was a native Egyptian king of pre-Hyksos times (*The Accuracy of the Bible* [1934], pp. 41 ff.), while H. H. Rowley argues that he was Ikhnaton, *c.* 1377-1360 (*From Joseph to Joshua* [1950], pp. 116 ff.).

οὐκ ᾔδει τὸν Ἰωσήφ] The δ text has *οὐκ ἐμνήσθη τοῦ Ἰωσήφ* (D E g p).

vii. 19

κατασοφισάμενος] Cf. Ex. i. 10, *δεῦτε οὖν κατασοφισώμεθα αὐτούς.* The word naturally had a somewhat different connotation in Pharaoh's mouth and in Stephen's; what was 'wise dealing' to the former was 'crafty business' to the latter. LC render it here 'exploited'. Elsewhere in the Greek Bible *κατασοφίζομαι* occurs only in Judith v. 11 (of Pharaoh, as here); x. 19 (*δυνήσονται κατασοφίσασθαι πᾶσαν τὴν γῆν*).

ἐκάκωσεν] The word occurs in Ex. i. 11, in connection with the tasks imposed on them.

τοῦ ποιεῖν τὰ βρέφη ἔκθετα αὐτῶν] 'to expose their infants'. An explanatory phrase, involving some idea of purpose, loosely appended to the principal clause. Cf. Lk. i. 74; xxiv. 25.

εἰς τὸ μὴ ζωογονεῖσθαι] Final construction. ζωογονέω occurs in Ex. i. 18, in Pharaoh's expostulation with the midwives. Cf. Lk. xvii. 33. The literal sense is 'to generate life'; but the force of -γονέω is weakened, so that both in LXX and in NT the word means 'to preserve life'.

vii. 20

ἀστεῖος τῷ θεῷ] Cf. Ex. ii. 2, ἰδόντες δὲ αὐτὸ ἀστεῖον ἐσκέπασαν αὐτὸ μῆνας τρεῖς, whence Heb. xi. 23, διότι εἶδον ἀστεῖον τὸ παιδίον. So Jos. *Ant.* ii. 9. 7 (παῖδα μορφῇ τε θεῖον); Philo, *Vit. Moys.* i. 9 (γεννηθεὶς οὖν ὁ παῖς εὐθὺς ὄψιν ἐνέφαινεν ἀστειοτέραν ἢ κατ' ἰδιώτην). τῷ θεῷ may be taken in its full sense, 'in the sight of God' (cf. xxiii. 1; 2 Cor. x. 4; also similar phrases in Lk. i. 6, 15; ii. 52; xxiv. 19). Such phrases, however, were frequently used with elative force (so EV, 'exceeding fair'): cf. Jonah iii. 3 (πόλις μεγάλη τῷ θεῷ) and similar phrases in Gen. x. 9; 1 Sam. xvi. 12; Ps. lxxx. 10 (LXX lxxix. 11). As the LXX examples indicate, this is a Semitic idiom, but cf. in Mod. Gk. the use of θεο- as a prefix to indicate 'very' (A. Thumb, *Handbook of the Modern Greek Vernacular*, p. 74, quotes θεότρελλος, 'quite crazy').

vii. 21

ἐκτεθέντος δὲ αὐτοῦ] The gen. abs. is used although the person referred to is indicated twice by the acc. αὐτόν. Cf. xxii. 17, μοι . . . μου . . . με.

ἀνείλατο] Used in the Koiné of acknowledging or adopting as one's child. In Ex. ii. 5, however, it is used non-technically, of taking up the basket in which Moses was. The way in which Stephen shows his acquaintance with the LXX text by using its vocabulary without actual quotation is noteworthy; it suggests an extemporaneous speech rather than a conscious literary composition. (See on *ver.* 43, Βαβυλῶνος.)

ἡ θυγατὴρ Φαραώ] The identification of this princess with Hatshepsut, daughter of Thothmes I and recognized by him as his legitimate successor, who ruled Egypt jointly with her nephew Thothmes III from 1490 to 1468 B.C., would be chronologically not improbable, if with A. S. Yahuda, J. Garstang, J. W. Jack and others we could date the Exodus under Moses *c.* 1450-1440 B.C. But the Exodus belongs almost certainly to the 13th century B.C.

ἀνεθρέψατο αὐτὸν ἑαυτῇ εἰς υἱόν] The reflexive idea is expressed twice, both by the use of the middle and by *ἑαυτῇ* (cf. LXX quotation in Jn. xix. 24). For the predicative use of *εἰς* in *εἰς υἱόν* cf. v. 36; xiii. 22, 47; xix. 27. Here, at any rate, it is a Hebraism, from Ex. ii. 10, *ἐγενήθη αὐτῇ εἰς υἱόν* (Heb. *lĕ-bēn*).

vii. 22

καὶ ἐπαιδεύθη Μωυσῆς πάσῃ σοφίᾳ Αἰγυπτίων] Josephus (*Ant.* ii. 9. 6) describes the unique wisdom of Moses; Philo (*Vit. Moys.* i. 20 ff.) credits him with proficiency in arithmetic, geometry, poetry, music, philosophy, astrology, and all branches of education. 'The Hellenists, in works designed for heathen readers, represent him as the father of all science and culture. He was, according to Eupolemus, the inventor of alphabetical writing. . . . Artabanus tells us the Egyptians owed to him their whole civilisation' (Schürer II, i. 343). Stephen expresses himself with greater moderation.

δυνατὸς ἐν λόγοις καὶ ἔργοις αὐτοῦ] Cf. Lk. xxiv. 19, *δυνατὸς ἐν ἔργῳ καὶ λόγῳ*. That Moses was *δυνατὸς ἐν λόγοις* may seem to contradict Ex. iv. 10, but the reference may be to written words. For his prowess *ἐν ἔργοις* cf. the story in Jos. *Ant.* ii. 10 of his leading the expedition against the Ethiopians.

vii. 23

ὡς δὲ ἐπληροῦτο αὐτῷ τεσσερακονταετὴς χρόνος] His age at this time is not given in Exodus, but this statement is paralleled in Rabbinical writings which divide his life of 120 years into three equal parts. Cf. Ex. vii. 7; Dt. xxxiv. 7. In Ex. ii. 11 (quoted Heb. xi. 24) we read simply *μέγας γενόμενος*. For the sense of *ἐπληροῦτο* cf. ii. 1, *συνπληροῦσθαι*.

ἀνέβη ἐπὶ τὴν καρδίαν αὐτοῦ] A Semitism: cf. Isa. lxv. 16; Jer. iii. 16 (*οὐκ ἀναβήσεται ἐπὶ καρδίαν*); xliv. 21; li. 50; Ezek. xxxviii. 10; 1 Cor. ii. 9, and freq. in the *Shepherd* of Hermas.

τοὺς ἀδελφοὺς αὐτοῦ τοὺς υἱοὺς Ἰσραήλ] Verbatim from Ex. ii. 11.

vii. 24

ἀδικούμενον] The δ text adds *ἐκ τοῦ γένους*.

ἠμύνατο] 'assisted', 'defended'. 'The word may have almost fallen out of the colloquial language, to judge from its rarity in LXX and NT, and the absence of occurrences in papyri' (MM).

ἐποίησεν ἐκδίκησιν] lit., 'wrought an avenging', a periphrasis for the simple verb *ἐξεδίκησεν* (cf. Lk. xviii. 3 ff., 7 ff.). Such a periphrasis in Attic Gk. would be formed with the middle *ποιοῦμαι*.

πατάξας τὸν Αἰγύπτιον] Verbatim from Ex. ii. 12; D completes the quotation by adding *καὶ ἔκρυψεν αὐτὸν ἐν τῇ ἄμμῳ*.

vii. 25

ἐνόμιζεν δὲ συνιέναι τοὺς ἀδελφούς] Note the parallel; Moses appeared as a messenger of peace, and was rejected; the same happened to Christ. The idea of this verse is not found in OT. Philo (*Vit. Moys.* i. 40 ff.) describes Moses' championship of the Israelites at this period of his life as a settled policy. Though rejected by his brethren the first time, he was accepted by them as their deliverer when he visited them the second time. In this he resembled Christ (see on *ver.* 13).

vii. 26

συνήλλασσεν] Imperfect: 'tried to reconcile'. AV has 'curiously blundered into the right meaning by mistranslating a wrong text' (*Proleg.*, p. 129). *συνήλασεν* byz., from *συνελαύνω*, would mean that he '"drove" them to shake hands'.

Ἄνδρες, ἀδελφοί ἐστε] D has the more formal *τί ποιεῖτε, ἄνδρες ἀδελφοί;*

ἵνα τί] See on iv. 25. The question in LXX is *διὰ τί σὺ τύπτεις τὸν πλησίον*; (Ex. ii. 13).

vii. 27

ἀπώσατο] Not in LXX: cf. *ver.* 39 below.

vii. 28

τίς σὲ κατέστησεν . . . τὸν Αἰγύπτιον;] Quotation from Ex. ii. 14.

vii. 29

ἐν τῷ λόγῳ τούτῳ] For causal *ἐν*, 'on account of', cf. xxiv. 16. It is paralleled elsewhere in Bib. Gk. and papyri.

ἐγένετο πάροικος] Cf. Ex. ii. 22, *πάροικός εἰμι ἐν γῇ ἀλλοτρίᾳ.* See on *vv.* 6, 44, 47 for Stephen's stress on the 'pilgrim' theme.

ἐν γῇ Μαδιάμ] Probably in the region of Aqaba.

υἱοὺς δύο] Gershom and Eliezer (Ex. ii. 22; xviii. 3 f.).

vii. 30

ὤφθη αὐτῷ ἐν τῇ ἐρήμῳ τοῦ ὄρους Σινὰ ἄγγελος ἐν φλογὶ πυρὸς βάτου] Cf. Ex. iii. 1*b*-2*a*, *καὶ ἤγαγεν τὰ πρόβατα ὑπὸ τὴν ἔρημον καὶ ἦλθεν εἰς τὸ ὄρος Χωρήβ. ὤφθη δὲ αὐτῷ ἄγγελος Κυρίου ἐν φλογὶ πυρὸς ἐκ τοῦ βάτου.*

Σινά] The mountain is called Horeb in Ex. iii. 1; its identity with Sinai is implied by Ex. iii. 12; Dt. i. 6, etc., alongside Ex. xix. 11 ff.

ἄγγελος] The *ἄγγελος Κυρίου* (see on v. 19), the special representative of God in His dealings with men, called in Heb. *mal'akh Yahweh* (or *mal'akh pānāw*, 'the angel of His face [presence]', e.g., Isa. lxiii. 9): cf. *vv.* 35, 38, 53 below. In Ex. iii. the Person who speaks to Moses is called *ἄγγελος Κυρίου, ὁ κύριος*, and *ὁ θεός*; so here the angel speaks with the voice of the Lord (*ver.* 31), claims to be God (*ver.* 32), and is called *ὁ κύριος* (*ver.* 33).

vii. 31

κατανοῆσαι] 'to master the mystery' (*Proleg.*, p. 117); the aorist marks the completion of a mental process.

ἐγένετο φωνὴ Κυρίου] D has *ὁ κύριος εἶπεν αὐτῷ λέγων*.

vii. 32

Ἐγὼ ὁ θεὸς τῶν πατέρων σου, ὁ θεὸς Ἀβραὰμ καὶ Ἰσαὰκ καὶ Ἰακώβ] From Ex. iii. 6 (*ἐγώ εἰμι ὁ θεὸς τοῦ πατρός σου, θεὸς Ἀβραὰμ καὶ θεὸς Ἰσαὰκ καὶ θεὸς Ἰακώβ*), where the words follow the command to remove his shoes. δ follows LXX in repeating *θεός* before *Ἰσαάκ* and *Ἰακώβ*, as at iii. 13 (*q.v.*).

ἔντρομος δὲ γενόμενος] Cf. xvi. 29; Heb. xii. 21. The adj. is post-classical; it is found in LXX, Plutarch, and the Palatine Anthology.

vii. 33

εἶπεν δὲ αὐτῷ κ.τ.λ.] From Ex. iii. 5 (*ὁ δὲ εἶπεν . . . λῦσαι τὸ ὑπόδημα ἐκ τῶν ποδῶν σου, ὁ γὰρ τόπος ἐν ᾧ σὺ ἕστηκας γῆ ἁγία ἐστίν*). The removal of the shoes was a mark of respect to the divine presence, as it was a mark of respect to one's host when visiting him.

vii. 34

ἰδὼν εἶδον . . . αὐτούς] From Ex. iii. 7 f. (*ἰδὼν εἶδον τὴν κάκωσιν τοῦ λαοῦ μου τοῦ ἐν Αἰγύπτῳ καὶ τῆς κραυγῆς αὐτῶν ἀκήκοα . . . καὶ κατέβην ἐξελέσθαι αὐτούς*): cf. Ex. ii. 24 (*καὶ εἰσήκουσεν ὁ θεὸς τὸν στεναγμὸν αὐτῶν*).

ἰδὼν εἶδον] A Semitism, representing the Heb. construction of the absolute infin. with the finite verb to express emphasis, 'I have certainly seen' (see on iv. 17; v. 28; cf. Mt. xiii. 14; Mk. iv. 12; Eph. v. 5; Heb. vi. 14).

καὶ νῦν δεῦρο ἀποστείλω σε εἰς Αἴγυπτον] From Ex. iii. 10, substituting *εἰς Αἴγυπτον* for *πρὸς Φαραὼ βασιλέα Αιγύπτου*. P^{45} omits *νῦν*.

ἀποστείλω] Futuristic use of subjunctive, a survival of the primary force of this mood. Cf. perhaps δεῦρο δείξω σοι in Rev. xvii. 1; xxi. 9; also ἄφες ἐκβάλω τὸ κάρφος, Mt. vii. 4. For a classical parallel to its use with δεῦρο, cf. Euripides, *Bacchae* 341, δεῦρό σου στέψω κάρα.

vii. 35

τοῦτον κ.τ.λ.] Note the emphatic use of οὗτος (as in ii. 23, etc.) five times in *vv.* 35-38. Both Moses and Jesus, though rejected by their brethren, were chosen by God to deliver them.

τοῦτον ὁ θεὸς καὶ ἄρχοντα καὶ λυτρωτὴν ἀπέσταλκεν] Cf. what is said of Jesus in v. 31.

ἀπέσταλκεν] This perfect, 'with the forest of aorists all round, is more plausibly conformed to them, and it happens that this word is alleged to have aoristic force elsewhere. But, after all, the abiding results of Moses' mission formed a thought never absent from a Jew's mind' (*Proleg.*, p. 144).

δικαστήν] ℵ A C 81 δ add ἐφ' ἡμῶν, as in *ver.* 27; Ex. ii. 14.

σὺν χειρὶ] A B C D 81; ἐν χειρί ℵ byz.

σὺν χειρὶ ἀγγέλου τοῦ ὀφθέντος αὐτῷ] 'by the hand of an angel, (namely) the one who appeared to him'. For the construction see on iv. 12.

ἐν τῇ βάτῳ] βάτος, though usually fem. in Hellenistic Gk., is masc. in LXX.

vii. 36

ἐξήγαγεν αὐτοὺς ποιήσας κ.τ.λ.] The relation of the aor. ptc. ποιήσας to ἐξήγαγεν is debatable. We could take it as simultaneous, making ἐξήγαγεν refer to the 40 years' leadership of Moses from the Exodus onwards; but it is better to take it with the ordinary force of an aorist participle, and suppose that the words after ἐν γῇ Αἰγύπτῳ were added without strict regard to the grammar of the preceding words.

τέρατα καὶ σημεῖα ἐν τῇ Αἰγύπτῳ] Cf. Ex. vii. 3 (καὶ πληθυνῶ τὰ σημεῖά μου καὶ τὰ τέρατα ἐν γῇ Αἰγύπτῳ); also Ps. cv. 27 (LXX civ), ἔθετο αὐτοῖς τοὺς λόγους τῶν σημείων αὐτοῦ καὶ τῶν τεράτων ἐν γῇ Χάμ. The doing of 'wonders and signs' is another point of resemblance between Moses and Jesus (see on ii. 22).

ἐν τῇ ἐρήμῳ ἔτη τεσσεράκοντα] Verbatim from Num. xiv. 33. Cf. also *Assumption of Moses*, iii. 11, '*Moyses . . . qui multa passus est in Aegypto et in mari rubro et in eremo annis quadraginta*' (probably a partial reminiscence of this verse).

vii. 37

προφήτην κ.τ.λ.] From Dt. xviii. 15: see on iii. 22. Its introduction here is to point further the parallel between Moses and Christ.

ὡς ἐμέ] δ adds *αὐτοῦ ἀκούσεσθε*, to harmonize with OT.

vii. 38

ἐν τῇ ἐκκλησίᾳ] In Dt. xviii. 16, immediately following the words quoted in the previous verse, *ἐκκλησία* represents Heb. *qāhāl* ('congregation') referring to the meeting of the people to receive the Law. As Moses was with the old Ecclesia, so Christ is with the new, and it is still a pilgrim Church, 'the Church in the desert'. Cf. Heb. ii. 12, where the words *ἐν μέσῳ ἐκκλησίας ὑμνήσω σε*, applied to Christ, are quoted from Ps. xxii (xxi LXX). 22, *ἐκκλησία* being the equivalent of *qāhāl*. See on v. 11.

μετὰ τοῦ ἀγγέλου] According to Jubilees i. 27; ii. 1, an angel talked with Moses on Sinai (see also on *vv.* 35, 53); cf. Ex. xxxiii. 14, 'My presence (*pānay*, lit., "My face") shall go' (LXX renders *pānay* by *αὐτός*, 'I myself'); so Isa. lxiii. 9, 'the angel of His presence saved them' (LXX quite differently, *οὐ πρέσβυς οὐδ' ἄγγελος, ἀλλ' αὐτὸς ἔσωσεν αὐτούς*, 'not a messenger nor an angel but Himself saved them'). On the other hand, LXX introduces angels where they are absent from MT in Dt. xxxiii. 2, *Κύριος ἐκ Σινὰ ἥκει . . . ἐκ δεξιῶν αὐτοῦ ἄγγελοι μετ' αὐτοῦ*.

μετὰ τοῦ ἀγγέλου . . . καὶ τῶν πατέρων ἡμῶν] LC suggest that this reflects Heb. *bēn . . . ū-bēn*, 'between . . . and', representing Moses as mediator between God and Israel: cf. Gal. iii. 19.

ἐδέξατο] *ἐξελέξατο* B, certainly corrupt.

λόγια ζῶντα] Cf. Rom. iii. 2 for *λόγια* used of the Law; for the epithet cf. Heb. iv. 12 (*ζῶν γὰρ ὁ λόγος τοῦ θεοῦ*); 1 Pet. i. 23 (*διὰ λόγου ζῶντος θεοῦ καὶ μένοντος*).

vii. 39

ἀπώσαντο] Cf. *ver.* 27.

ἐστράφησαν ἐν ταῖς καρδίαις αὐτῶν εἰς Αἴγυπτον] Cf. Num. xiv. 3 f., *νῦν οὖν βέλτιον ἡμῖν ἐστιν ἀποστραφῆναι εἰς Αἴγυπτον . . . ἀποστρέψωμεν εἰς Αἴγυπτον*.

vii. 40

εἰπόντες τῷ Ἀαρών κ.τ.λ.] From Ex. xxxii. 1, *συνέστη ὁ λαὸς ἐπὶ Ἀαρὼν καὶ λέγουσιν αὐτῷ Ἀνάστηθι καὶ ποίησον ἡμῖν θεούς, οἳ προπορεύσονται ἡμῶν· ὁ γὰρ Μωυσῆς οὗτος, ὁ ἄνθρωπος ὃς ἐξήγαγεν ἡμᾶς ἐξ Αἰγύπτου, οὐκ οἴδαμεν τί γέγονεν αὐτῷ*.

ὁ γὰρ Μωυσῆς οὗτος] *Nominativus pendens*, followed by resumptive *αὐτῷ*. Cf. Lk. xii. 10 ; xiii. 4 ; xxiii. 50-52, etc. ; the construction can be freq. paralleled from classical, Hellenistic and Mod. Gk.

vii. 41

ἐμοσχοποίησαν] Not found elsewhere. Great as was the classical Gk. facility for composition, it was even greater in later Gk. Cf. other compounds in -*ποιέω* as *ὀχλοποιέω* (xvii. 5) and *εἰρηνοποιέω* (Col. i. 20). The corresponding LXX passage has *καὶ ἐποίησαν αὐτὰ μόσχον χωνευτόν* (Ex. xxxii. 4). The noun *μοσχοποιία* occurs in Justin, *Dial. c. Tryph.* 19, 73, 102, 132.

ἀνήγαγον θυσίαν] MM quote an inscription of 127 B.C. to illustrate the sacrificial sense of *ἀνάγω*.

ἐν τοῖς ἔργοις τῶν χειρῶν αὐτῶν] Cf. *τὰ εἴδωλα τῶν ἐθνῶν ἀργύριον καὶ χρυσίον, ἔργα χειρῶν ἀνθρώπων*, Ps. cxv. 4 (LXX cxiii. 12) ; cxxxv. 15 (LXX cxxxiv).

vii. 42

ἔστρεψεν] Intransitive, as so often also in compounds of *στρέφω* : cf. *ἐπιστρέφω* in iii. 19.

παρέδωκεν αὐτοὺς] Cf. Rom. i. 24, 26, 28 ; Ps. cvi. 41 (LXX cv). For the principle that men are left to the consequences of their settled choice cf. Hos. iv. 17 ; Mt. xv. 14.

τῇ στρατιᾷ τοῦ οὐρανοῦ] The heavenly bodies : cf. Dt. iv. 19 ; xvii. 3 ; 2 Chr. xxxiii. 3, 5 ; Jer. vii. 18 (LXX, for MT ' queen of heaven ') ; viii. 2 ; xix. 13 ; Zeph. i. 5.

vii. 42f.

ἐν βίβλῳ τῶν προφητῶν] i.e., in the Book of the Twelve (' Minor ') Prophets, whose prophecies form one book in the Heb. Bible. This quotation is from Amos v. 25-27. The difference between the MT and LXX is considerable. In MT, Amos, writing on the eve of the Assyrian invasions which brought an end to the northern kingdom of Israel, warns Israel that the Assyrian king will deport them ' beyond Damascus ', and that they will carry thither the very instruments of that idolatry for which God brings this calamity upon them (cf. RV mg.). The LXX form, quoted here with variations, places this idolatry as far back as the wilderness period.

Μὴ σφάγια καὶ θυσίας προσηνέγκατέ μοι] They offered sacrifices indeed, but as their hearts were rebellious against God, He could not regard them as offered to Him : a constant burden of OT prophecy. Cf. Isa. i. 10 ff. ; Jer. vii. 22 ff. ; Hos. vi. 6 ; Mic. vi. 6 ff. ; Ps. l. 8 ff. ; li. 16 f., etc.

ἐν τῇ ἐρήμῳ] om B.

vii. 43

τὴν σκηνὴν τοῦ Μολόχ] As opposed to the *σκηνή* of *ver.* 44. MT has *Sikkūth malkĕkhem*, 'Siccuth your king'. *Sikkūth* seems to be Akkadian *Sakkut* (a name of Ninib, god of the planet Saturn) with the vowels of *shiqqūṣ*, 'abomination' (so Moloch,[1] better Molech, a title of various Canaanite deities, is simply *melekh*, 'king', with the vowels of *bōsheth*, 'shame'). LXX *σκηνήν* is due to the similarity between *Sikkūth* and *sukkāh*, 'tent'.

τὸ ἄστρον τοῦ θεοῦ 'Ρομφά, τοὺς τύπους οὓς ἐποιήσατε] MT has *Kiyyūn ṣalmēkhem kōkhab 'elōhēkhem 'asher 'asīthem lākhem*, 'Kiyyun your images, the star of your gods that you made for yourselves'. *Kiyyun* is Assyrian *Kaiwanu*, another name of Ninib, spelt (like *Sikkuth*) with the vowels of *shiqqūs*. *'Ρομφά*, the reading of B, is one of many corruptions (cf. *'Ρομφάν* ℵ, *'Ρεμφάμ* D) of *'Ρεφάν* (C) or *'Ραιφάν* (ℵ^c A), the LXX form. This resembles *Repa*, a name of Seb, the Egyptian god of the planet Saturn, possibly substituted by the Alexandrian translators of OT for the less intelligible *Kiyyun* (cf. Hort in WH App. *ad loc.*).

προσκυνεῖν αὐτοῖς] Replacing LXX *ἑαυτοῖς*.

ἐπέκεινα Βαβυλῶνος] For LXX *ἐπέκεινα Δαμάσκου*. Amos was foretelling the Assyrian captivity, a suitable punishment for those who practised Assyrian star-worship; Stephen has the Babylonian captivity in his mind, as was not unnatural in one speaking in Jerusalem. This is perhaps the most striking example of quotation from memory in an impassioned speech; we should not expect it in a literary composition. δ in its harmonizing zeal replaces *ἐπέκεινα Βαβυλῶνος* by the paraphrase *ἐπὶ τὰ μέρη Βαβυλῶνος*, which no doubt were 'beyond Damascus'. That a Hellenist like Stephen should quote LXX or indeed deliver his whole speech in Gk. is not surprising.

vii. 44

ἡ σκηνὴ τοῦ μαρτυρίου] By contrast with 'the tabernacle of Moloch' (*ver.* 43). The *μαρτύριον* consisted of the tables of the Law, which also gave the name *κιβωτὸς μαρτυρίου* to the Ark in which they were kept. In LXX *ἡ σκηνὴ τοῦ μαρτυρίου* renders not only *'ōhel 'ēdūth* (correctly), but also *'ōhel mō'ēd*, 'tent of meeting'.

ὁ λαλῶν τῷ Μωυσῇ] Reminiscent of the words so frequent in the Pentateuch, *καὶ ἐλάλησεν Κύριος πρὸς Μωυσῆν* (Ex. xxv. 1, etc.).

[1] Mention should be made of O. Eissfeldt's argument that Molech was no deity, but that the name represents Phoenician *molk*, a term for human sacrifice attested in Carthaginian inscriptions (*Molk als Opferbegriff im Punischen und Hebräischen und das Ende des Gottes Moloch*, 1935).

ποιῆσαι αὐτὴν κατὰ τὸν τύπον ὃν ἑωράκει] Cf. Ex. xxv. 40, *ὅρα ποιήσεις κατὰ τὸν τύπον τὸν δεδειγμένον σοι ἐν τῷ ὄρει.* This *τύπος* may be contrasted with the idolatrous *τύποι* of *ver.* 43. The conception of the earthly tent as the copy of a heavenly pattern, which bears a resemblance to Platonic doctrine, is developed in Heb. ix. 1 ff. A movable tent was more suitable for a pilgrim people than a house such as Solomon's. The fact that God Himself could not be restricted to any one building or place should be reflected in a similar avoidance of such restriction by His people. For *τύπον* D here has *παράτυπον* (cf. *παράδειγμα* in Ex. xxv. 9).

vii. 45

διαδεξάμενοι] 'having received it in turn'.

Ἰησοῦ] i.e., Joshua: cf. Heb. iv. 8. It was felt to be appropriately significant that the leader into the earthly Canaan should have borne the same name as the Leader into the heavenly rest. See Justin, *Dial. c. Tryph.* 113 ff.

ἐν τῇ κατασχέσει] 'while they were taking possession'. In LXX *κατάσχεσις* means 'having possession'. Cf. *ver.* 5.

ἀπὸ προσώπου] For the Semitism cf. iii. 20; v. 41.

ἕως τῶν ἡμερῶν Δαυείδ] May refer both to *διαδεξάμενοι* and to *ἐξῶσεν*, but principally to the former. Successive generations received the tent until David's time (cf. 2 Sam. vii. 6), after which it was replaced by Solomon's temple; also it was not until David's time that the land was thoroughly conquered by Israel.

vii. 46

ᾐτήσατο εὑρεῖν] See on iii. 3.

εὑρεῖν σκήνωμα τῷ θεῷ Ἰακώβ] Cf. Ps. cxxxii. 5 (LXX cxxxi), *ἕως ἂν εὕρω τόπον τῷ κυρίῳ, σκήνωμα τῷ θεῷ Ἰακώβ.* For *θεῷ*, ℵ B D H S 429 sah have *οἴκῳ*. Perhaps *θεῷ* was an early emendation for *οἴκῳ*, itself a still earlier corruption of the original, which Hort, followed by Ropes, suggested might be *κυρίῳ* (written $\overline{κω}$), which occurs in the LXX context. The Heb. word here rendered *θεῷ* in LXX is *'ābīr*, 'Mighty One' (rendered *δυνάστης* in Gen. xlix. 24, etc.). LC, preferring *οἴκῳ*, understand, 'David wished to build a habitation (of God) for the house of Jacob'; this, however, gives awkward connection with the next verse.

vii. 47

Σολομῶν δὲ οἰκοδόμησεν αὐτῷ οἶκον] Cf. 1 K. (LXX 3 K.) vi. 2, *ὁ οἶκος ὃν ᾠκοδόμησεν ὁ βασιλεὺς Σαλωμὼν τῷ κυρίῳ.* A house with foundations was less appropriate for a pilgrim people. It is significant that in Heb. ix. 1 ff. it is the wilderness tent, not the

Jerusalem temple, that is taken as a type of God's spiritual dwelling among His people.

οἰκοδόμησεν] Unaugmented: WH give this form as an alternative to the augmented *ᾠκ-* everywhere except Mt. xxi. 33; Lk. iv. 29. (But the *ᾠκ-* form in Lk. iv. 29 may be regarded as 'reduplication.')

vii. 48

ἀλλ' οὐχ ὁ ὕψιστος] Note the emphasis. Other deities might be conceived of as so dwelling, but not the Most High. D weakens the emphasis with *ὁ δὲ ὕψιστος οὐ κατοικεῖ.* The title *ὕψιστος* had both a Jewish and a Gentile background, and thus served as a bridge between Jew and Gentile in talking of God. It is the translation of Heb. *'Elyōn* (cf. Gen. xiv. 18; Dt. xxxii. 8), Aram. *'Illāyā* (cf. Dan. iii. 26, etc.). For its use as a title of deity among Gentiles see on xvi. 17.

ἐν χειροποιήτοις] Cf. xvii. 24, *οὐκ ἐν χειροποιήτοις ναοῖς κατοικεῖ.* (Cf. also xix. 26, *θεοὶ οἱ διὰ χειρῶν γινόμενοι.*)

That God cannot be thus limited is recognized even in Solomon's dedicatory prayer, 1 K. viii. 27. With *χειροποίητος* cf. the negative *ἀχειροποίητος*, used in Mk. xiv. 58 of a spiritual temple, in 2 Cor. v. 1 of the spiritual resurrection body, in Col. ii. 11 of spiritual circumcision.

vii. 49f.

καθὼς ὁ προφήτης λέγει κ.τ.λ.] The quotation is from Isa. lxvi. 1 f. Isa. lxvi. 1 is quoted in Ep. Barn. xvi. 2 in reference to the destruction of the Temple in A.D. 70, and with the same variation from LXX as here (*ἢ τίς τόπος* for *καὶ ποῖος τόπος*). Justin (*Dial. c. Tryph.* 22) brings together Amos v. 25 ff. and Isa. lxvi. 1 f. as Stephen does here. It is possible that Luke, Barnabas, and Justin all drew upon a collection of 'Testimonies', in which these two passages occurred in juxtaposition (see on i. 20; iii. 22), but it is equally likely that Barnabas and Justin were dependent on Ac.

οἰκοδομήσετε] *οἰκοδομήσατε* B.

vii. 50

οὐχὶ ἡ χείρ μου ἐποίησεν ταῦτα πάντα;] LXX, following Heb., puts this in the form of a statement, *πάντα γὰρ ταῦτα ἐποίησεν ἡ χείρ μου.*

vii. 51

σκληροτράχηλοι καὶ ἀπερίτμητοι καρδίαις καὶ τοῖς ὠσίν] This sudden invective may have been occasioned by an angry outburst against what he had just said. It was clear that he was attacking some of their most cherished beliefs about the Temple. The charge made in vi. 13 f. is easily explained by the argument of his reply. Real or imagined belittling of the Temple was certain to rouse to fury both the city populace and the priestly party with their vested interests in the building and in its cultus : cf. the charges brought against Jesus (Mk. xiv. 58) and against Paul (Ac. xxi. 28). The language of the invective is thoroughly OT ; for σκληροτράχηλοι cf. Ex. xxxiii. 5 ; for ἀπερίτμητοι καρδίαις cf. Lev. xxvi. 41 ; Dt. x. 16 ; Jer. iv. 4 ; ix. 26 ; Ezek. xliv. 7 ; for ἀπερίτμητοι . . . τοῖς ὠσίν cf. Jer. vi. 10.

τῷ πνεύματι τῷ ἁγίῳ ἀντιπίπτετε] Cf. Isa. lxiii. 10 (αὐτοὶ δὲ ἠπείθησαν καὶ παρώξυναν τὸ πνεῦμα τὸ ἅγιον αὐτοῦ) and Num. xxvii. 14 (ἐν τῷ ἀντιπίπτειν τὴν συναγωγὴν ἁγιάσαι με). They resisted Him as He spoke through Moses and the prophets.

vii. 52

The argument that they were following in the steps of their forefathers who had killed the prophets is very similar to our Lord's accusation in Mt. xxiii. 29-37.

περὶ τῆς ἐλεύσεως] G. D. Kilpatrick has pointed out that ἔλευσις was already a messianic term, denoting Messiah's advent (*JTS* xlvi [1945], pp. 136 ff.).

τοῦ δικαίου] For this title see on iii. 14 (cf. xxii. 14).

οὗ νῦν ὑμεῖς προδόται καὶ φονεῖς ἐγένεσθε] He does not mitigate their offence by ascribing it to ignorance, as Peter did when addressing the populace (iii. 17). The priestly Sadducees had acted with their eyes open (cf. Jn. xi. 49 f. ; xix. 11).

vii. 53

εἰς διαταγὰς ἀγγέλων] Another example of the encroaching of εἰς on ἐν, used here instrumentally, 'by the ordinances of angels'. Torrey (*CDA*, p. 33) sees behind this phrase the Aram. *lĕ-phuqdānē mal'ākhīn*, with the preposition *lĕ* in the sense 'according to', 'by'. διαταγή (also in Rom. xiii. 2 ; Ezra iv. 11 ; cf. *ver.* 44 above, διετάξατο) is freq. in papyri, inscriptions, and secular literature. Deissmann mentions its use by the physician Ruphus of Ephesus (fl. A.D. 100) to mean 'ordered way of living', and by Vettius Valens (342. 7 ; 355. 18) in the sense 'disposition' (*LAE*, pp. 89 f.).

The mediation of the Law by angels is referred to in Gal. iii. 19 (ὁ νόμος . . . διαταγεὶς δι' ἀγγέλων), and is used there as a proof that the Law is inferior to the promise made to Abraham by God Himself. Stephen's emphasis is different : they had failed to keep the Law even though it had been communicated to them by more than human agency. Cf. Heb. ii. 2, ὁ δι' ἀγγέλων λαληθεὶς λόγος, referring to the Mosaic Law, in contrast to the Gospel, which was brought to earth by the Lord Himself. This angelic mediation of the Law does not appear in OT, but is mentioned in Jos. *Ant.* xv. 5. 3 (ἡμῶν δὲ τὰ κάλλιστα τῶν δογμάτων καὶ τὰ ὁσιώτατα τῶν ἐν τοῖς νόμοις δι' ἀγγέλων παρὰ τοῦ θεοῦ μαθόντων); Philo (*De somniis* i. 141 ff.), the 'Testaments of the Twelve Patriarchs' (*Test. Dan* vi. 2), and Jubilees i. 29. See also on *ver.* 38 above.

(e) Martyrdom of Stephen, vii. 54-viii. 1a

Ἀκούοντες δὲ ταῦτα διεπρίοντο ταῖς καρδίαις αὐτῶν καὶ ἔβρυχον τοὺς 54
ὀδόντας ἐπ' αὐτόν. ὑπάρχων δὲ πλήρης πνεύματος ἁγίου ἀτενίσας εἰς τὸν 55
οὐρανὸν εἶδεν δόξαν θεοῦ καὶ Ἰησοῦν ἑστῶτα ἐκ δεξιῶν τοῦ θεοῦ, καὶ 56
εἶπεν Ἰδοὺ θεωρῶ τοὺς οὐρανοὺς διηνοιγμένους καὶ τὸν υἱὸν τοῦ ἀνθρώπου ἐκ δεξιῶν ἑστῶτα τοῦ θεοῦ. κράξαντες δὲ φωνῇ μεγάλῃ συνέσχον 57
τὰ ὦτα αὐτῶν, καὶ ὥρμησαν ὁμοθυμαδὸν ἐπ' αὐτόν, καὶ ἐκβαλόντες ἔξω 58
τῆς πόλεως ἐλιθοβόλουν. καὶ οἱ μάρτυρες ἀπέθεντο τὰ ἱμάτια αὐτῶν
παρὰ τοὺς πόδας νεανίου καλουμένου Σαύλου. καί ἐλιθοβόλουν 59
τὸν Στέφανον ἐπικαλούμενον καὶ λέγοντα Κύριε Ἰησοῦ, δέξαι τὸ
πνεῦμά μου· θεὶς δὲ τὰ γόνατα ἔκραξεν φωνῇ μεγάλῃ Κύριε, μὴ 60
στήσῃς αὐτοῖς ταύτην τὴν ἁμαρτίαν· καὶ τοῦτο εἰπὼν ἐκοιμήθη.
Σαῦλος δὲ ἦν συνευδοκῶν τῇ ἀναιρέσει αὐτοῦ. 61

vii. 54

διεπρίοντο] See on v. 33.

ἔβρυχον] Cf. Job xvi. 9; Ps. xxxv. 16 (LXX xxxiv), ἔβρυξαν ἐπ' ἐμὲ τοὺς ὀδόντας αὐτῶν. Stephen's sudden turning of his argument against themselves, added to the clear implication of his references to the Temple, proved more than they could bear; probably they cut his speech short.

vii. 55

ὑπάρχων δὲ πλήρης πνεύματος ἁγίου] See on vi. 5.

Ἰησοῦν] δ characteristically adds τὸν κύριον (cf. xviii. 5; see also on i. 22; ii. 38; iii. 31; xiii. 32).

ἑστῶτα] We should discount such fanciful 'dispensational' theories as that Christ had not yet sat down (cf. ii. 34) because He was waiting till He should be finally rejected by the Jewish nation. According to G. Dalman, ἑστῶτα 'is merely a verbal change' for καθήμενον in the words of Christ, Mk. xiv. 62. 'There is, of course, no thought of a "rising up" after being seated', he adds (*Words of Jesus*, p. 311), probably in reference to the interpretation which pictures Christ as rising to welcome His proto-martyr.

vii. 56

ἰδοὺ θεωρῶ τοὺς οὐρανοὺς διηνοιγμένους κ.τ.λ.] Cf. the similar language which resulted in a verdict of blasphemy against our Lord (Mt. xxvi. 64 = Mk. xiv. 62 = Lk. xxii. 69); also His words to Nathanael (Jn. i. 51). Hegesippus (*ap*. Euseb. *HE* ii. 23) ascribes similar language to James the Just at his martyrdom. The description in Hegesippus has been obviously coloured by Luke's account of the death of Stephen.

τὸν υἱὸν τοῦ ἀνθρώπου] The last NT occurrence of this title of Christ, and the only one outside the Gospels. (The phrase *ὅμοιον υἱὸν ἀνθρώπου* in Rev. i. 13; xiv. 14 is different.) The title as used by Jesus of Himself (Aram. *bar 'ĕnāshā*) identifies Him with the 'one like unto a son of man' (Aram. *kĕ-bar 'ĕnāsh*) who receives eternal and universal dominion in Dan. vii. 13, and with the pre-existent 'Son of Man' of 1 Enoch. This identification is explicit in our Lord's reply to the Sanhedrin (Mk. xiv. 62, etc.), which is here echoed by Stephen. Cf. G. Dalman, *Words of Jesus*, pp. 234 ff.; L. A. Muirhead in *ET* xi (1899), pp. 62 ff.; R. Otto, *The Kingdom of God and the Son of Man*, pp. 159 ff.; T. W. Manson, *The Teaching of Jesus*, pp. 211 ff., and *A. Fridrichsen FS* (1947), pp. 138 ff.; G. S. Duncan, *Jesus, Son of Man* (1947); J. Bowman in *ET* lix (1947-8), pp. 283 ff.; M. Black in *ET* lx (1948-9), pp. 11 ff., 32 ff.

ἐκ δεξιῶν] As in previous verse: from Ps. cx. 1 (cf. ii. 34).

ἑστῶτα appears after *ἐκ δεξιῶν* in ℵ[c] BD 81 byz, before it in ℵ* ACE 69 al *P*[45], probably by assimilation with *ver*. 55.

vii. 57

κράξαντες] *tunc populus exclamauit* h. It is difficult to decide whether we are to understand Stephen's execution as an instance of lynch-law or as an excess of jurisdiction on the part of the Sanhedrin. In this respect also the narrative resembles the story of the martyrdom of James as told by Hegesippus. For a legal execution the procurator's consent was necessary. But Pilate had good reason for conciliating the priestly party, and had apparently established a *modus vivendi* with Caiaphas (see on iv. 6). Besides, he lived normally in Caesarea, and when once strong feelings were stirred up in Jerusalem, they were not easily curbed. The later years of Pilate's administration were full of trouble.

vii. 58

καὶ οἱ μάρτυρες] *οἱ δὲ μ. P*[45]. It was their duty to play a prominent part in the execution (Lev. xxiv. 14; cf. Dt. xvii. 7).

αὐτῶν] *ἑαυτῶν* B. The *prisoner's* clothes were laid down a short distance from the place of stoning (Mishna, *Sanh.* vi. 3).[1] F. C. Conybeare therefore suggested the emendation *αὐτοῦ* (*Exp.* VIII. vi [1913], pp. 466 ff.). But xxii. 20 confirms that it was the clothes of the chief executioners (the witnesses) that Saul held.

vii. 59

ἐλιθοβόλουν] Imperfect, as in the previous verse, emphasizing the process of stoning, or the fact that several took part in it, thus making it a repeated action.

ἐπικαλούμενον] Without an object; the Person whom he invoked is made sufficiently clear by the words he uttered.

κύριε Ἰησοῦ, δέξαι τὸ πνεῦμά μου] Cf. Lk. xxiii. 46, *πάτερ, εἰς χεῖράς σου παρατίθεμαι τὸ πνεῦμά μου.* That the request made by our Lord to the Father should so soon be repeated to Himself by Stephen is evidence of the early date of the belief in the essential deity of Christ.

vii. 60

θεὶς δὲ τὰ γόνατα] This phrase is also found in ix. 40; xx. 36; xxi. 5; Mk. xv. 19; Lk. xxii. 41. Cf. Lat. *genua ponere.*

κύριε, μὴ στήσῃς αὐτοῖς ταύτην τὴν ἁμαρτίαν] Reminiscent of another Word from the Cross, Lk. xxiii. 34 (see on iii. 17). As in the previous verse, *κύριε* is probably addressed to Jesus. For a dying prayer in a different spirit we may compare the words of Zechariah in 2 Chr. xxiv. 22. Tr. *μὴ στήσῃς αὐτοῖς* 'do not reckon to them', 'do not put to their account'.

ταύτην τὴν ἁμαρτίαν] A B C D; *τὴν ἁμαρτίαν ταύτην* ℵ 81 byz.

ἐκοιμήθη] An unexpectedly beautiful word for so brutal a death. Cf. xiii. 36; Jn. xi. 11 ff.; 1 Th. iv. 14.

viii. 1

Σαῦλος δὲ ἦν συνευδοκῶν τῇ ἀναιρέσει αὐτοῦ] We need not take *συνευδοκῶν* to mean that Saul was a member of the Sanhedrin, though this is possible. Cf. the same word in xxii. 20. In xxvi. 10 more official action is implied, yet not necessarily membership of the Sanhedrin.

[1] The regulations for stoning, as given in the Mishna, may be partly the idealistic reconstruction of a later period. 'Four cubits from the stoning-place the criminal is stripped. . . . The drop from the stoning-place was twice the height of a man. One of the witnesses pushes the criminal from behind, so that he falls face downward. He is then turned over on his back. If he die from this fall, that is sufficient. If not, the second witness takes the stone and drops it on his heart. If this cause death that is sufficient; if not, he is stoned by all the congregation of Israel, for it is written: "The hand of the witnesses shall be against him first to put him to death, and afterwards the hand of all the people" (Dt. xvii. 7)' (*Sanhedrin* vi. 3 f.).

τῇ ἀναιρέσει] The only NT occurrence of the noun; the verb *ἀναιρέω* is similarly used in Paul's speeches, xxii. 20; xxvi. 10.

2. PHILIP, viii. 1*b*-40

(a) Persecution and Dispersion, viii. 1b-3

'Εγένετο δὲ ἐν ἐκείνῃ τῇ ἡμέρᾳ διωγμὸς μέγας ἐπὶ τὴν ἐκκλησίαν
τὴν ἐν 'Ιεροσολύμοις· πάντες δὲ διεσπάρησαν κατὰ τὰς χώρας τῆς
'Ιουδαίας καὶ Σαμαρίας πλὴν τῶν ἀποστόλων. συνεκόμισαν δὲ τὸν 2
Στέφανον ἄνδρες εὐλαβεῖς καὶ ἐποίησαν κοπετὸν μέγαν ἐπ' αὐτῷ.
Σαῦλος δὲ ἐλυμαίνετο τὴν ἐκκλησίαν κατὰ τοὺς οἴκους εἰσπορευόμε- 3
νος, σύρων τε ἄνδρας καὶ γυναῖκας παρεδίδου εἰς φυλακήν.

διωγμὸς μέγας] δ adds *καὶ θλίψις* (cf. xi. 19). The persecution was no doubt instituted by the priestly party; the believers had enjoyed popular favour hitherto (ii. 47; v. 13), but such revolutionary teaching as Stephen's gave their opponents an opportunity of stirring up the people against them. After Stephen's activity the new movement could easily be represented as hostile to the Temple prerogatives, which were protected by the law of the Empire, and the safeguarding of which belonged to the High Priest.

διεσπάρησαν] Cf. *ver.* 4; xi. 19: the new Ecclesia, like the old, was to have its Diaspora (cf. 1 Pet. i. 1). Chase (*Credibility*, p. 65) compares 2 Baruch i. 4, 'I will scatter this people among the Gentiles, that they may do good to the Gentiles'.

χώρας] Probably 'districts' in a non-technical sense, though the word might possibly be taken as referring to Judaea (in the narrower sense) and Samaria, as *regiones* (Gk. *χῶραι*) of the province of Judaea (see on xvi. 6; xviii. 23). The persecution led them to carry out further the terms of their Lord's commission in i. 8.

πλὴν τῶν ἀποστόλων] Not necessarily that they were exempt from persecution, though the popular resentment was not yet so hot against them as later (cf. xii. 2 f.), but they probably conceived it their duty to remain at their post. δ adds *οἳ ἔμειναν ἐν 'Ιερουσαλήμ* (another glimpse of the obvious).

viii. 2

συνεκόμισαν] 'took up for burial': cf. *ἐκκομίζω* in Lk. vii. 12 and *συστέλλω* in Ac. v. 6; also *ἐκφέρω* in v. 6, 10.

ἄνδρες εὐλαβεῖς] The adj. in NT is used particularly of Jews. These were probably Jewish Christians; at any rate, they disapproved of the Sanhedrin's action. *εὐλαβής* is used in xxii. 12 of Ananias, in Lk. ii. 25 of Simeon. Cf. Joseph of Arimathaea, *ἀνὴρ ἀγαθὸς καὶ δίκαιος* (Lk. xxiii. 50), who performed a like service for Jesus.

κοπετὸν] Connected with *κόπτω*, ' to beat the breast ' in mourning. The Law prescribed the duty of burying executed criminals (Dt. xxi. 22 f. ; Jos. *BJ* iv. 5. 2), but according to the Mishna there was no open (i.e. ceremonial) lamentation for them (*Sanh.* vi. 6).

viii. 3

Σαῦλος δὲ ἐλυμαίνετο τὴν ἐκκλησίαν] ' But Saul ravaged the church '. This is the only NT example of *λυμαίνομαι*, which is found in LXX, Hermas, papyri, etc. Philo (*Leg. ad Gai.* 134) uses it of anti-Jewish excesses in Alexandria. It refers especially to the ravaging of a body by a wild beast (LC). For Saul's persecuting zeal cf. ix. 1 ff. ; xxii. 4 ff. ; xxvi. 10 f. ; 1 Cor. xv. 9 ; Gal. i. 13, 22 ff. ; Phil. iii. 6 ; 1 Tim. i. 13.

(b) Philip in Samaria, viii. 4-8

Οἱ μὲν οὖν διασπαρέντες διῆλθον εὐαγγελιζόμενοι τὸν λόγον. 4
Φίλιππος δὲ κατελθὼν εἰς τὴν πόλιν τῆς Σαμαρίας ἐκήρυσσεν αὐτοῖς 5
τὸν χριστόν. προσεῖχον δὲ οἱ ὄχλοι τοῖς λεγομένοις ὑπὸ τοῦ Φιλίππου 6
ὁμοθυμαδὸν ἐν τῷ ἀκούειν αὐτοὺς καὶ βλέπειν τὰ σημεῖα ἃ ἐποίει·
πολλοὶ γὰρ τῶν ἐχόντων πνεύματα ἀκάθαρτα βοῶντα φωνῇ μεγάλῃ 7
ἐξήρχοντο, πολλοὶ δὲ παραλελυμένοι καὶ χωλοὶ ἐθεραπεύθησαν· ἐγένετο 8
δὲ πολλὴ χαρὰ ἐν τῇ πόλει ἐκείνῃ.

viii. 4

Οἱ μὲν οὖν διασπαρέντες] Either ' they, therefore, having been scattered ' or ' they, therefore, who were scattered '. For *μὲν οὖν* introducing a new section of the narrative, see on i. 6. Cf. also xi. 19, where the same phrase begins the story of others of this dispersion.

διῆλθον] Ramsay thought that this verb always meant missionary itineration in Ac. There is nothing in the verb itself to require this special sense, but naturally the context frequently requires it in Ac.

viii. 5

Φίλιππος] That Philip the Hellenist (cf. vi. 5 ; xxi. 8) should take the initiative in evangelizing outside Judaea is significant.

κατελθὼν] The context in Ac. frequently indicates that this verb, as here, is used of going down from Jerusalem to evangelize some district.

εἰς τὴν πόλιν τῆς Σαμαρίας] The city called Samaria in OT times was called Sebaste (after Augustus) after its restoration by Herod the Great (whence mod. Sebastiyeh). If this be the city referred to, it is strange to find it called by an archaic name. The phrase cannot easily be understood as 'the (capital) city of (the region) Samaria'. Justin Martyr, himself a native of Samaria, says that Simon Magus was born at Gitta (*Apol.* i. 26), and this may be the city in question here if, with Soden and Ropes, we adopt the less well attested reading which omits *τήν* (C D 81 byz sah boh). (א has the aberrant reading *τὴν πόλιν τῆς Καισαρίας*.)

ἐκήρυσσεν] Observe the imperfect; he was doing so when the following events happened.

αὐτοῖς] The pronoun sufficiently denotes the inhabitants of a place which has already been referred to (cf. xvi. 10; xx. 2).

τὸν χριστόν] For the Samaritans' expectation of Messiah cf. Jn. iv. 25, 29. They called him the *Taheb* ('Restorer'), and identified him with the Prophet of Dt. xviii. 15 ff.

viii. 6

προσεῖχον] In a full sense, of paying attention and giving a favourable response (with little difference from *ἐπίστευσαν* in *ver.* 12): cf. *vv.* 10, 11; xvi. 14. In v. 35; xx. 28 it has the different sense 'take care'.

ἐν τῷ ἀκούειν] In a temporal sense: for the construction see on ii. 1.

τὰ σημεῖα ἃ ἐποίει] A further example of such activity in one not an apostle: cf. Stephen, vi. 8.

viii. 7

πολλοὶ γὰρ τῶν ἐχόντων πνεύματα ἀκάθαρτα . . . ἐξήρχοντο] Actually, of course, it was the spirits that 'came out', not those who were possessed by them. Torrey (*CDA*, pp. 32 f.) explains the construction by the aid of an Aram. retroversion; Blass would insert *ἃ* after *ἀκάθαρτα*, in which case *ἐθεραπεύθησαν* would have the first *πολλοί* as well as the second for its subject; but probably we should simply take the construction, with LC, as a case of 'mental telescoping'.

πνεύματα ἀκάθαρτα] Cf. v. 16, where the apostles deal with these.

βοῶντα φωνῇ μεγάλῃ] As freq. in the Gospels, e.g., Mk. i. 26.

πολλοὶ δὲ παραλελυμένοι καὶ χωλοὶ] Paralysis and lameness are the troubles most commonly healed in Ac.: cf. iii. 2; ix. 33; xiv. 8.

(c) Simon Magus believes and is baptized, viii. 9-13

Ἀνὴρ δέ τις ὀνόματι Σίμων προϋπῆρχεν ἐν τῇ πόλει μαγεύων καὶ 9
ἐξιστάνων τὸ ἔθνος τῆς Σαμαρίας, λέγων εἶναί τινα ἑαυτὸν μέγαν, ᾧ 10
προσεῖχον πάντες ἀπὸ μικροῦ ἕως μεγάλου λέγοντες Οὗτός ἐστιν ἡ
Δύναμις τοῦ θεοῦ ἡ καλουμένη Μεγάλη. προσεῖχον δὲ αὐτῷ διὰ 11
τὸ ἱκανῷ χρόνῳ ταῖς μαγίαις ἐξεστακέναι αὐτούς. ὅτε δὲ ἐπίστευσαν 12
τῷ Φιλίππῳ εὐαγγελιζομένῳ περὶ τῆς βασιλείας τοῦ θεοῦ καὶ τοῦ
ὀνόματος Ἰησοῦ Χριστοῦ, ἐβαπτίζοντο ἄνδρες τε καὶ γυναῖκες. ὁ 13
δὲ Σίμων καὶ αὐτὸς ἐπίστευσεν, καὶ βαπτισθεὶς ἦν προσκαρτερῶν
τῷ Φιλίππῳ, θεωρῶν τε σημεῖα καὶ δυνάμεις μεγάλας γινομένας
ἐξίστατο.

viii. 9

Σίμων] Simon Magus plays a prominent part in post-apostolic Christian literature as the first heretic, the father of Gnosticism, and the untiring adversary of Peter, not only in Samaria, but also at Antioch and Rome. Justin tells how by his magic power he secured a large following even outside his native land, though his statement that he was honoured in Rome with a statue dedicated SIMONI DEO SANCTO seems due to the misreading of an inscription to an ancient Italian deity.[1] Simon's followers, the Simonians, survived to the middle of the third century at least (Origen, *c. Cels.* i. 57).

μαγεύων] The *μάγοι* were originally a Median caste, a pre-Zoroastrian priestly class (Herodotus i. 101, 140), but the word is used in an extended sense of practitioners of various kinds of sorcery and even quackery. The *μάγοι* of Mt. ii. 1 ff. were probably astrologers. For the verb *μαγεύω* (only here in NT), cf. Didaché ii. 2, *οὐ μαγεύσεις*. MM also quote from an inscription, *ἐμάγευσε Μίθρῃ*. In Mod. Gk. the verb means 'bewitch'.

ἐξιστάνων] 'amazing', 'making beside themselves': cf. *ἐξεστακέναι*, *ver.* 11; a like effect was produced on Simon himself by the apostles (*ἐξίστατο*, *ver.* 13).

μέγαν] LC would like to emend to *μάγον*, comparing the common emendation *μάγον* for *μέγαν* in Lucian's reference to Christ in *De morte peregrini* 11, *τὸν μάγον* (codd. *μέγαν*) *γοῦν ἐκεῖνον ἔτι σέβουσι, τὸν ἄνθρωπον τὸν ἐν τῇ Παλαιστίνῃ ἀποσκολοπισθέντα.*

[1] Justin's statement (*Apol.* i. 26) is probably due to the misreading of an inscription commencing SEMONI SANCO DEO FIDIO, 'to Semo Sancus the god of oaths' (*CIL* vi. 567). But it is quite possible that the error was not Justin's, but that the Simonians in Rome regarded this or a similar inscription as providentially applicable to Simon, and used it for their worship. Cf. Tertullian, *Apol.* xiii. 9: '*cum Simonem Magum statua et inscriptione Sancti Dei inauguratis*'. See the essay on 'Simon Magus' by R. P. Casey in *BC* v, pp. 151 ff.

viii. 10

ἀπὸ μικροῦ ἕως μεγάλου] The construction 'is LXX and even Greek' (J. de Zwaan). In LXX (Gen. xix. 11, etc.) it represents Heb. *min . . . wĕ-'ad*. For a commoner Gk. construction cf. xxvi. 22, *μικρῷ τε καὶ μεγάλῳ*.

ἡ Δύναμις τοῦ θεοῦ] Cf. Lk. xxii. 69, *τῆς δυνάμεως τοῦ θεοῦ*, an explanatory expansion of *τῆς δυνάμεως* (Mk. xiv. 62). The Rabbis used *ha-gĕbūrāh* (' the Power ') as a name of God. ' The sorcerer was really spoken of as " God ", and *τοῦ θεοῦ* as well as *καλουμένη* are additions due to Luke ', says Dalman (*Words of Jesus*, p. 200).

ἡ καλουμένη Μεγάλη] Ramsay (*BRD*, p. 117) quotes an inscription from Lydia, *εἷς θεὸς ἐν οὐρανοῖς Μὴν οὐράνιος μεγάλη δύναμις τοῦ ἀθανάτου θεοῦ*. Deissmann (*BS*, p. 336) quotes from the Paris magical papyrus (ll. 1275 ff.) *ἐπικαλοῦμαί σε τὴν μεγίστην δύναμιν τὴν ἐν τῷ οὐρανῷ ὑπὸ κυρίου θεοῦ τεταγμένην*. For *μέγας* in a divine title cf. xix. 28, 34. In Jubilees xl. 7 the Egyptians cry before Joseph *'Êl 'Êl wa 'Abîrĕr* (a corruption of Heb. *'Ēl 'Ēl wa-'ăbīr 'Ēl*, ' God, God, and the Mighty One of God '), which is explained by R. H. Charles as ' the title of a great magician '. J. de Zwaan (*BC* ii, p. 58) suggests that Simon claimed to be the Grand Vizier (*Ba'al Zĕbūl*) of the Lord of Heaven (*Ba'al Shāmīn*). A. Klostermann (*Probleme im Aposteltexte*, pp. 15 ff.) thought that *Μεγάλη* was a transliteration of Aram. *mĕgallē*, ' revealer ', in which case *καλουμένη* would apologize for the foreign term (cf. i. 12; iii. 2, 11; vi. 9). C. C. Torrey (*CDA*, pp. 18 ff.) turns the sentence back into Aram., *dēn ḥēlēh dī 'Elāhā dī mithqĕrē rab*, which can also mean ' this is the power of the God who is called Great ', this ' Great God ' being *Θεὸς Ὕψιστος*, a syncretism of Zeus and the God of Israel. It is plain at least that Simon was acclaimed as the one in whom the power of the supreme God resided.

viii. 12

εὐαγγελιζομένῳ περὶ τῆς βασιλείας τοῦ θεοῦ καὶ τοῦ ὀνόματος Ἰησοῦ Χριστοῦ] The sovereignty of God and the Name or Person of Jesus are associated in Philip's good news: cf. xxviii. 31. This was not a different Gospel from that which our Lord and His apostles proclaimed before the Cross. Its keynotes were still repentance, faith, and the remission of sins, accompanied by baptism, the gift of the Spirit, and evidential works, although all these things had naturally acquired a much deeper significance since the great events of the Crucifixion, the Resurrection, the Ascension and Pentecost. It was the same Gospel as our Lord foretold would be preached among all the nations, and which before His ascension He charged His disciples to make known (Mt. xxiv. 14; xxviii. 19 f.). It is identical with 'the gospel of the grace of God' (see on xx. 24 f.). See further on i. 3.

viii. 13

ἐπίστευσεν] The nature of Simon's belief is a matter of dispute. 'We must think of the Simon of Acts as a convert whose conversion was sincere as far as it went, but was very superficial' (J. E. Roberts, in *DAC*). No doubt he was convinced of the power of the Name which Philip proclaimed when he saw the mighty works wrought by it. A parallel is found in Jn. ii. 23, where it is implied that the faith that depends on seeing miracles is not the most satisfactory kind.

(d) Peter and John visit Samaria, viii. 14-24

Ἀκούσαντες δὲ οἱ ἐν Ἰεροσολύμοις ἀπόστολοι ὅτι δέδεκται ἡ 14
Σαμαρία τὸν λόγον τοῦ θεοῦ ἀπέστειλαν πρὸς αὐτοὺς Πέτρον καὶ
Ἰωάνην, οἵτινες καταβάντες προσηύξαντο περὶ αὐτῶν ὅπως λάβωσιν 15
πνεῦμα ἅγιον· οὐδέπω γὰρ ἦν ἐπ' οὐδενὶ αὐτῶν ἐπιπεπτωκός, μόνον 16
δὲ βεβαπτισμένοι ὑπῆρχον εἰς τὸ ὄνομα τοῦ κυρίου Ἰησοῦ. τότε 17
ἐπετίθεσαν τὰς χεῖρας ἐπ' αὐτούς, καὶ ἐλάμβανον πνεῦμα ἅγιον.
Ἰδὼν δὲ ὁ Σίμων ὅτι διὰ τῆς ἐπιθέσεως τῶν χειρῶν τῶν ἀποστόλων 18
δίδοται τὸ πνεῦμα προσήνεγκεν αὐτοῖς χρήματα λέγων Δότε κἀμοὶ 19
τὴν ἐξουσίαν ταύτην ἵνα ᾧ ἐὰν ἐπιθῶ τὰς χεῖρας λαμβάνῃ πνεῦμα ἅγιον.
Πέτρος δὲ εἶπεν πρὸς αὐτόν Τὸ ἀργύριόν σου σὺν σοὶ εἴη εἰς ἀπώ- 20
λειαν, ὅτι τὴν δωρεὰν τοῦ θεοῦ ἐνόμισας διὰ χρημάτων κτᾶσθαι.
οὐκ ἔστιν σοι μερὶς οὐδὲ κλῆρος ἐν τῷ λόγῳ τούτῳ, ἡ γὰρ καρδία 21
σου οὐκ ἔστιν εὐθεῖα ἔναντι τοῦ θεοῦ. μετανόησον οὖν ἀπὸ τῆς κακίας 22
σου ταύτης, καὶ δεήθητι τοῦ κυρίου εἰ ἄρα ἀφεθήσεταί σοι ἡ ἐπίνοια
τῆς καρδίας σου· εἰς γὰρ χολὴν πικρίας καὶ σύνδεσμον ἀδικίας ὁρῶ 23
σε ὄντα. ἀποκριθεὶς δὲ ὁ Σίμων εἶπεν Δεήθητε ὑμεῖς ὑπὲρ ἐμοῦ 24
πρὸς τὸν κύριον ὅπως μηδὲν ἐπέλθῃ ἐπ' ἐμὲ ὧν εἰρήκατε.

viii. 14

Πέτρον καὶ Ἰωάνην] Acting together as in iii. 1 ff. This is the last appearance of John in Ac. (his name is mentioned in xii. 2). His last recorded connection with Jerusalem is in Gal. ii. 9 (*c.* A.D. 46). Along with his brother James he had once wished to call down fire from heaven on the Samaritans (Lk. ix. 54). The Twelve had previously been forbidden to preach to the Samaritans (Mt. x. 5); this ban had since been rescinded (Ac. i. 8).

viii. 15

ὅπως λάβωσιν πνεῦμα ἅγιον] Although these Samaritan believers had received Christian baptism, they did not receive the Spirit until the laying on of the apostles' hands. The receiving of the Holy Spirit in Ac. is connected with the manifestation of some spiritual gift. The order of events varied; the Gentiles in x. 44 ff. were baptized because their glossolalia showed that they had already received the Spirit; the disciples at Ephesus in xix. 5 f. received Him thus as the immediate sequel to Christian baptism (cf. ii. 38) and the imposition of apostolic hands.

viii. 16

ἐπ' οὐδένι] *ἐπὶ οὐδένα* D.

βεβαπτισμένοι ὑπῆρχον] 'they had already been baptized'.

εἰς τὸ ὄνομα τοῦ κυρίου Ἰησοῦ] So in xix. 5; the phrase *ἐν τῷ ὀνόματι Ἰησου Χριστοῦ* in ii. 38 and x. 48 has a somewhat different force (see on ii. 38). The expression *εἰς τὸ ὄνομα* is common in a commercial context: some property is paid or transferred 'into the name' of someone, i.e., into his account. So the person baptized *εἰς τὸ ὄνομα τοῦ κυρίου Ἰησοῦ* bears public testimony that he has become Christ's property. These words may have been used regularly in a formula by the baptizer.[1] Cf. 1 Cor. i. 13 ff.

viii. 17

ἐπετίθεσαν] B has *ἐπετίθοσαν*, a sign of the tendency to assimilate non-thematic to thematic verbs.

ἐπετίθεσαν τὰς χεῖρας] A sign of the impartation of something possessed by the one who imposes his hands, here of the gift of the Spirit (as also in xix. 6). See also on vi. 6; ix. 17; xiii. 3.

viii. 18

τὸ πνεῦμα] ℵ B sah; A C 81 P^{45} δ byz add *τὸ ἅγιον*.

προσήνεγκεν αὐτοῖς χρήματα] From this action of Simon has come the term 'simony', the buying or selling of spiritual office with material means.

viii. 20

εἴη εἰς ἀπώλειαν] Cf. *εἰς ἀπώλειαν ἔσεσθε*, Dan. ii. 5 (Theodotion). In *εἴη* we have a real optative, expressing a wish (cf. Lk. i. 38;

[1] The trinitarian baptismal formula of Mt. xxviii. 19 and *Didaché* vii. 1 does not appear in Ac. The reason may be, as suggested by G. F. Moore (*Judaism* i., pp. 188 f.), that while the trinitarian formula was appropriate for Gentiles turning to the true God from idols, baptism into the name of the Lord Jesus as Messiah was sufficient in the case of Jews or Samaritans, who had no need to profess monotheism. The same consideration would hold good for the 'disciples' of Ac. xix. 1 ff., who had already submitted to the baptism of John. Cf. 'The End of the First Gospel', by F. F. Bruce, in *EQ* xii. (1940), pp. 203 ff.

Mk. xi. 14, etc.). There are thirty-eight such proper optatives in NT, fifteen of them being accounted for by the phrase *μὴ γένοιτο*. Of the remaining twenty-three, Paul is responsible for fifteen. The optative was dying out in Hellenistic Gk., and has disappeared in Mod. Gk., except in *μὴ γένοιτο*, which is of literary origin.

τὴν δωρεὰν τοῦ θεοῦ ἐνόμισας διὰ χρημάτων κτᾶσθαι] 'you thought you could obtain the gift of God by means of money'. For *τὴν δωρεὰν τοῦ θεοῦ* cf. ii. 38; Jn. iv. 10. For the sense cf. 1 Tim. vi. 5; 2 Clem. xx. 4 (*οὐ τὸ εὐσεβὲς ἀλλὰ τὸ κερδαλέον διώκοντες*).

viii. 21

οὐκ ἔστιν σοι μερὶς οὐδὲ κλῆρος] Cf. Dt. xii. 12, *ὅτι οὐκ ἔστιν αὐτῷ μερὶς οὐδὲ κλῆρος μεθ' ὑμῶν*.

ἡ γὰρ καρδία σου οὐκ ἔστιν εὐθεῖα ἔναντι τοῦ θεοῦ] Cf. Ps. lxxviii. 37 (LXX lxxvii), *ἡ δὲ καρδία αὐτῶν οὐκ εὐθεῖα*.

viii. 22

εἰ ἄρα ἀφεθήσεταί] A mixed conditional and final construction: 'beseech the Lord (in order that), if indeed (it may be so), the thought of your heart shall be forgiven'. Cf. xxvii. 12, where the construction is classical.

ἐπίνοια] Here only in NT; here, as frequently, of an evil thought or intent.

viii. 23

εἰς γὰρ χολὴν πικρίας καὶ σύνδεσμον ἀδικίας ὁρῶ σε ὄντα] For *εἶναι* followed by *εἰς* cf. *ver.* 20. In the papyri *εἰς* used thus after *εἶναι* expresses destination. D has *ἐν*, as in vii. 12.

χολὴν πικρίας] Cf. Dt. xxix. 18, *μή τίς ἐστιν ἐν ὑμῖν ῥίζα* (A F add *πικρίας*) *ἄνω φύουσα ἐν χολῇ καὶ πικρίᾳ* (quoted Heb. xii. 15); also Lam. iii. 19, *πικρία καὶ χολή μου μνησθήσεται*. In *χολὴ πικρίας* we probably have a Hebraic genitive ('gall of bitterness' = 'bitter gall'): cf. *ῥήματα βλασφημίας* (vi. 11 א* D); *σκεῦος ἐκλογῆς* (ix. 15).

σύνδεσμον ἀδικίας] Cf. Isa. lviii. 6, *ἀλλὰ λῦε πάντα σύνδεσμον ἀδικίας*.

viii. 24

ἀποκριθεὶς . . . εἶπεν] See on iv. 19.

εἰρήκατε] δ repeats *μοι* after *εἰρήκατε*, and adds *ὃς πολλὰ κλαίων οὐ διελίμπανεν*, 'who never stopped weeping copiously' (D hcl. mg. Tert.). The clause comes awkwardly at the end of the sentence and has probably been tacked on to the original text; the description may be true enough to life, if we picture Simon as the emotionally unstable type of ' medium ', though it does not accord so well with the Simon of later tradition. διαλιμπάνω occurs again in the δ text of xvii. 13.

(e) The Preachers return to Jerusalem, viii. 25

Οἱ μὲν οὖν διαμαρτυράμενοι καὶ λαλήσαντες τὸν λόγον τοῦ κυρίου 25
ὑπέστρεφον εἰς Ἱεροσόλυμα, πολλάς τε κώμας τῶν Σαμαρειτῶν
εὐηγγελίζοντο.

viii. 25

Οἱ μὲν οὖν] Indicating the commencement of a new paragraph (see on i. 6). That Philip returned with Peter and John is suggested by the next verse (*ἀπὸ Ἰερουσαλήμ*).

πολλάς τε κώμας τῶν Σαμαρειτῶν εὐηγγελίζοντο] Notice the variety of constructions after *εὐαγγελίζομαι*: it may take the accusative of the people evangelized (as here), the acc. of the person proclaimed (*ver.* 35), the acc. of the thing proclaimed (*ver.* 4); the persons evangelized may also be expressed by the dat. (Rom. i. 15) or by a prepositional phrase (*εἰς ὑμᾶς*, 1 Pet. i. 25); the substance of the message may also be expressed by a prepositional phrase (*ver.* 12).

(f) Philip and the Ethiopian, viii. 26-40

Ἄγγελος δὲ Κυρίου ἐλάλησεν πρὸς Φίλιππον λέγων Ἀνάστηθι 26
καὶ πορεύου κατὰ μεσημβρίαν ἐπὶ τὴν ὁδὸν τὴν καταβαίνουσαν ἀπὸ
Ἰερουσαλὴμ εἰς Γάζαν· αὕτη ἐστὶν ἔρημος. καὶ ἀναστὰς ἐπορεύθη, 27
καὶ ἰδοὺ ἀνὴρ Αἰθίοψ εὐνοῦχος δυνάστης Κανδάκης βασιλίσσης Αἰθιό-
πων, ὃς ἦν ἐπὶ πάσης τῆς γάζης αὐτῆς, ὃς ἐληλύθει προσκυνήσων εἰς
Ἰερουσαλήμ, ἦν δὲ ὑποστρέφων καὶ καθήμενος ἐπὶ τοῦ ἅρματος αὐτοῦ 28
καὶ ἀνεγίνωσκεν τὸν προφήτην Ἠσαίαν. εἶπεν δὲ τὸ πνεῦμα τῷ 29
Φιλίππῳ Πρόσελθε καὶ κολλήθητι τῷ ἅρματι τούτῳ. προσδραμὼν 30
δὲ ὁ Φίλιππος ἤκουσεν αὐτοῦ ἀναγινώσκοντος Ἠσαίαν τὸν προφήτην,
καὶ εἶπεν Ἆρά γε γινώσκεις ἃ ἀναγινώσκεις; ὁ δὲ εἶπεν Πῶς γὰρ 31
ἂν δυναίμην ἐὰν μή τις ὁδηγήσει με; παρεκάλεσέν τε τὸν Φίλιππον ἀνα-
βάντα καθίσαι σὺν αὐτῷ. ἡ δὲ περιοχὴ τῆς γραφῆς ἣν ἀνεγίνωσκεν 32
ἦν αὕτη

> *Ὡς πρόβατον ἐπὶ σφαγὴν ἤχθη,*
> *καὶ ὡς ἀμνὸς ἐναντίον τοῦ κείροντος αὐτὸν ἄφωνος,*
> *οὕτως οὐκ ἀνοίγει τὸ στόμα αὐτοῦ.*
> *Ἐν τῇ ταπεινώσει ἡ κρίσις αὐτοῦ ἤρθη·* 33
> *τὴν γενεὰν αὐτοῦ τίς διηγήσεται;*
> *ὅτι αἴρεται ἀπὸ τῆς γῆς ἡ ζωὴ αὐτοῦ.*

ἀποκριθεὶς δὲ ὁ εὐνοῦχος τῷ Φιλίππῳ εἶπεν Δέομαί σου, περὶ τίνος 34
ὁ προφήτης λέγει τοῦτο; περὶ ἑαυτοῦ ἢ περὶ ἑτέρου τινός; ἀνοίξας 35
δὲ ὁ Φίλιππος τὸ στόμα αὐτοῦ καὶ ἀρξάμενος ἀπὸ τῆς γραφῆς ταύτης

εὐηγγελίσατο αὐτῷ τὸν Ἰησοῦν. ὡς δὲ ἐπορεύοντο κατὰ τὴν ὁδόν, 36
ἦλθον ἐπί τι ὕδωρ, καί φησιν ὁ εὐνοῦχος Ἰδοὺ ὕδωρ· τί κωλύει με
βαπτισθῆναι; καὶ ἐκέλευσεν στῆναι τὸ ἅρμα, καὶ κατέβησαν ἀμφότεροι 38
εἰς τὸ ὕδωρ ὅ τε Φίλιππος καὶ ὁ εὐνοῦχος, καὶ ἐβάπτισεν αὐτόν.
ὅτε δὲ ἀνέβησαν ἐκ τοῦ ὕδατος, πνεῦμα Κυρίου ἥρπασεν τὸν Φίλιπ- 39
πον, καὶ οὐκ εἶδεν αὐτὸν οὐκέτι ὁ εὐνοῦχος, ἐπορεύετο γὰρ τὴν ὁδὸν
αὐτοῦ χαίρων. Φίλιππος δὲ εὑρέθη εἰς Ἄζωτον, καὶ διερχόμενος 40
εὐηγγελίζετο τὰς πόλεις πάσας ἕως τοῦ ἐλθεῖν αὐτὸν εἰς Καισαρίαν.

The language of this section is reminiscent here and there of the story of Elijah: cf. 1 K. xvii. 2, 9 f.; 2 K. i. 3, 15 (LXX 3 K., 4 K.); cf. also Jonah i. 2; iii. 2.

viii. 26

Ἄγγελος δὲ Κυρίου] See on v. 19; vii. 30. In this narrative it is difficult to distinguish the angel from the Spirit of the Lord (*vv.* 29, 39), though δ does so in *ver.* 39.

ἐλάλησεν . . . λέγων] Cf. xxvi. 31. The addition of the ptc. is a Hebraistic pleonasm, frequent in OT and in the Gospels. Cf. also *ἀποκριθεὶς εἶπεν*, *vv.* 24, 34.

ἀνάστηθι καὶ πορεύου] Note the different tenses; rising up is a momentary action, taking a journey a continuous one. Such a parataxis is unusual; D has *ἀναστὰς πορεύθητι*.

κατὰ μεσημβρίαν] In LXX *μεσημβρία* regularly means 'noon' (cf. *περὶ μεσημβρίαν*, xxii. 6) except Dan. viii. 4, 9, 'south'; so here more probably 'southwards'.

ἐπὶ τὴν ὁδὸν] One road from Jerusalem joined the main road to Egypt at Lydda. But Philip probably took the road going via Bethlehem and Hebron, which joined the main road south of Gaza.

εἰς Γάζαν] Gaza (mod. Ghuzzeh), in earlier days one of the five cities of the Philistines (called Kadytis by Herodotus, ii. 159; iii. 5), was taken by Alexander the Great after a five months' siege in 332 B.C., captured and destroyed by Alexander Jannaeus in 93 B.C., rebuilt under Gabinius 57 B.C., the new town being by the sea, a little south of Old Gaza.

αὕτη ἐστὶν ἔρημος] Old Gaza was also called Desert Gaza after its destruction; this clause is added here to distinguish it from the new city. Old Gaza was some 2½ miles inland. On Gaza, apart from OT references, cf. Jos. *BJ* i. 20. 3; ii. 6. 3; 18. 1; *Ant.* xiv. 5. 3; xv. 7. 3; xvii. 11. 4.

viii. 27

ἀναστὰς ἐπορεύθη] Cf. *ver.* 26; for the Semitic idiom see on v. 6.

Αἰθίοψ] The kingdom of Ethiopia, between Assuan and Khartoum, had existed since *c.* 750 B.C. Its two chief cities were Meroe and Napata. In the conversion of this Ethiopian some have seen a fulfilment of Ps. lxviii. 31; Zeph. iii. 10.

εὐνοῦχος] Eunuchs were commonly employed as court officials in Oriental lands until within recent times. They had at an earlier time been excluded from the religious privileges of Israel (Dt. xxiii. 1), but the removal of this ban is announced in Isa. lvi. 3 ff.

Κανδάκης βασιλίσσης] Candace was a hereditary title of the Ethiopian queens, who reigned in Meroe. An inscription from Pselchis (Dakkeh) in Nubia (13 B.C.) gives the title *τὴν κυρίαν βασίλισσαν* to an earlier Candace (Deissmann, *LAE*, p. 352). The 'queen' seems actually to have been the queen-mother, the real head of the government; the king her son was regarded as the child of the sun. So Bion of Soli, *Aethiopica* i. (in C. Müller's *Fragm. Hist. Graec.* iv, p. 351), *Αἰθίοπες τοὺς βασιλέων πατέρας οὐκ ἐκφαίνουσιν, ἀλλ' ὡς ὄντας υἱοὺς ἡλίου παραδιδόασιν· ἑκάστῳ δὲ τὴν μητέρα καλοῦσι Κανδάκην.* Cf. also Strabo xvii. i. 54; Pliny *NH* vi. 186; Dio Cass. liv. 5. 4; Euseb. *HE* ii. 1. 13.

γάζης] A Persian word by origin. Cf. Plutarch, *Demetrius* xxv. 5, *ἐπιεικῶς γὰρ εἰώθεσαν εὐνούχους ἔχειν γαζοφύλακας.*

προσκυνήσων] Fut. ptc. indicating purpose, rare in NT outside Lk.-Ac. Cf. xxiv. 11, 17. In Mod. Gk. *προσκυνητής* means 'pilgrim'. The Ethiopian, if not a proselyte, was perhaps one of the class of 'God-fearers' or 'devout persons', loosely attached to Judaism (see on ii. 10; x. 2).

viii. 28

ἅρματος] Probably an ox-waggon.

ἀνεγίνωσκεν] 'was reading'—and reading aloud, as is evident from *ver.* 30. Reading in ancient times was almost invariably aloud; the reason will be apparent to anyone who tries to read a copy of some ancient MS. The words require to be spelt out, and this is done much more easily aloud than silently. To illustrate the ancient practice it is customary to refer to the way in which Augustine describes, as something noteworthy, how Ambrose read in silence (*Confessions* vi. 3).

viii. 29

εἶπεν δὲ τὸ πνεῦμα] For such instances of direction by the Spirit in Ac. cf. x. 19; xiii. 2; xvi. 6 f.; xix. 1 D.

viii. 30

ἆρά γε γινώσκεις ἃ ἀναγινώσκεις;] Note the literary *ἆρά γε*, and the word-play in *γινώσκεις . . . ἀναγινώσκεις*, reproduced in vg. *intellegis quae legis?*

viii. 31

πῶς γὰρ ἂν δυναίμην ἐὰν μή τις ὁδηγήσει με;] The only Lukan example of *ἄν* with opt. in the apodosis where the protasis expressing a future condition has a more vivid form. For *ἐάν* with fut. indic. cf. Mt. xviii. 19; Lk. xix. 40; Rev. ii. 22. In NT Gk. there was no difference in pronunciation between fut. indic. *ὁδηγήσει* and aor. subj. *ὁδηγήσῃ*, which would be the classical construction here.

viii. 32

περιοχὴ] 'contents', 'passage'; in later ecclesiastical usage the word means 'lection'. Cf. Cic. *Att.* xiii. 25. 3, '*ergo ne Tironi quidem dictaui, qui totas περιοχάς persequi solet, sed Spintharo syllabatim*'.

ὡς πρόβατον ἐπὶ σφαγὴν ἤχθη κ.τ.λ.] From Isa. liii. 7 f., LXX. The Ethiopian was no doubt reading a roll containing part of Isa. in the Gk. version.

ἀμνὸς] Only in three other places in NT (Jn. i. 29, 36; 1 Pet. i. 19), each time with the sacrificial sense so common in OT.

κείροντος αὐτὸν] B 81 byz; *κείραντος αὐτόν* ℵ A C H L. In LXX *αὐτόν* is omitted in ℵ*cb B; and ℵca A have *κείραντος* for *κείροντος*.

οὕτως οὐκ ἀνοίγει τὸ στόμα αὐτοῦ] Cf. Mk. xiv. 61; xv. 5; Jn. xix. 9.

viii. 33

ἐν τῇ ταπεινώσει ἡ κρίσις αὐτοῦ ἤρθη κ.τ.λ.] Both Gk. and Heb. are difficult; but cf. RV of Isa. liii. 8 for the best sense, which also accords well with the application of the prophecy to Jesus.

viii. 34

ἀποκριθεὶς . . . εἶπεν] As in *ver.* 24: see on iv. 19.

δέομαί σου] 'Please'; a polite way of introducing a request: cf. xxi. 39; Lk. viii. 38; Gal. iv. 12.

viii. 35

εὐηγγελίσατο αὐτῷ τὸν Ἰησοῦν] The first explicit identification of the Suffering Servant with Jesus in Ac., though it has already been hinted in the use of the word *παῖς* (iii. 13, 26; iv. 27, 30). Our Lord Himself interpreted His mission in terms of this prophecy (see on iii. 13); and this interpretation can be traced in the words of John the Baptist in Jn. i. 29—in a twofold way if, with C. J. Ball[1] and C. F. Burney,[2] we take the underlying Aram. *ṭalyā d'Elāhā* to signify not merely 'Lamb of God', but 'Servant of God' (*παῖς θεοῦ*).

[1] *ET* xxi. (1909-10), pp. 92 f.

[2] *Aramaic Origin of the Fourth Gospel* (1922), pp. 107 f.

The Targum of Jonathan interprets those passages which speak of the Servant's prosperity of Messiah (e.g., Isa. lii. 13 is rendered, 'Behold my servant Messiah shall prosper'), but it refers the passages which speak of the Servant suffering to Israel (e.g., in Isa. lii. 14, it is they 'whose aspect, as they long for His coming, is dark among the nations, and their glory inferior to that of the sons of men'). A Messianic interpretation of Isa. liii. 4 is quoted in T. B. *Sanh.* 98*b*. and it was because of the word *nāgūa'* ('stricken') in this verse that some Rabbis gave Messiah the title 'the leprous one'.

'The older Jewish exegesis, in Targum and Talmud, interpreted Isa. liii. of the Messiah, with a hint of application (at least of Isa. vii.) to Hezekiah (T. B. Sanh., 94*a*). But, as the centuries advanced, many Jewish expositors abandoned the Messianic theory. . . . Though, however, the Messianic interpretation persisted, it became very popular to interpret the prophecy as applying to Israel. Rashi, Ibn Ezra, Qimhi, Isaac Abarbanel, and many others adopted this view. Naḥmanides allowed his readers to choose freely between the Messiah or Israel; Solomon de Marini offered both alternatives —Israel *and* the Messiah being both intended' (I. Abrahams, 'Jewish Interpretation of the Old Testament' in *The People and the Book*, ed. A. S. Peake [1925], pp. 408 f.).

The gradual abandonment of the Messianic interpretation by Jewish writers was no doubt due to the Christian application of the prophecy to Jesus; according to H. Loewe, it was for the same reason that Isa. lii. 13-liii. 12 was not included in the Haphtaroth, or public readings from the Prophets, though the passages immediately preceding and following were included (C. G. Montefiore and H. Loewe, *A Rabbinic Anthology* [1938], p. 544).

One of the most striking Messianic interpretations of the prophecy in Jewish literature is the hymn *'Az milliphnē bĕrēshīth* by Eleazar ha-Qalir (ninth century), which appears in the service for the Day of Atonement; it contains these lines :—

Messiah our righteousness has departed from us;
  We are horror-stricken, and there is none to justify us.
Our iniquities and the yoke of our transgressions
  He carries, and he is wounded for our transgressions.
He bears on his shoulders our sins,
  To find pardon for our iniquities;
We are healed by his stripes.[1]

[1] See also S. R. Driver and A. Neubauer, *The Fifty-third Chapter of Isaiah according to the Jewish Interpreters* (Oxford, 1877); G. H. Dalman, *Der leidende und der sterbende Messias der Synagoge im ersten nachchristlichen Jahrtausend* (Berlin, 1888) and *Jesaja 53, das Prophetenwort vom Sühnleiden des Heilsmittlers mit besonderer Berücksichtigung der synagogalen Litteratur* ² (Berlin, 1914); V. Taylor, *Jesus and His Sacrifice* (1937); J. J. Brierre-Narbonne, *Le Messie souffrant dans la littérature rabbinique* (1940); I. Engnell, *The 'Ebed Yahweh Songs and the Suffering Messiah in 'Deutero-Isaiah'* (1948); C. R. North, *The Suffering Servant in Deutero-Isaiah* (1948).

'It looks', wrote Franz Delitzsch of this prophecy, 'as if it had been written beneath the cross of Golgotha and was illuminated by the heavenly brightness of the *Sheb Limini* (= Sit at my right hand)'.

Of its application to our Lord, Sir G. A. Smith wrote:

'In every essential of consciousness and of experience He was the counterpart, embodiment, and fulfilment of this Suffering Servant and his Service. Jesus Christ answers the questions, which the prophecy raises and leaves unanswered. In the prophecy we see one, who is only a spectre, a dream, a conscience without a voice, without a name, without a place in history. But in Jesus Christ of Nazareth the dream becomes a reality; He, whom we have seen in this chapter only as the purpose of God, only through the eyes and consciences of a generation yet unborn,—He comes forward in flesh and blood; He speaks, He explains Himself, He accomplishes, almost to the last detail, the work, the patience, and the death which are here described as Ideal and Representative.'

viii. 36

ἐπί τι ὕδωρ] At the Wady el-Hasy north of Gaza this place is still pointed out, whether rightly or wrongly who shall say?

ἰδοὺ ὕδωρ] om *P*45.

τί κωλύει με βαπτισθῆναι;] Baptism was not a novelty in the Judaism of NT days. Either the eunuch had learned something of the Christian movement at Jerusalem, or Philip had wound up his exposition with words such as Peter used at Pentecost (ii. 38).

viii. 37 (not in WH)

εἶπεν δὲ ὁ Φίλιππος Εἰ πιστεύεις ἐξ ὅλης τῆς καρδίας, ἔξεστιν. ἀποκριθεὶς δὲ εἶπεν Πιστεύω τὸν υἱὸν τοῦ θεοῦ εἶναι τὸν Ἰησοῦν Χριστόν] This verse is wanting in *β P*45 byz and in the best texts of vg pesh sah boh. It is a characteristic addition of δ (represented by E 2298 minn g p hcl* arm Cypr Iren.lat; D is lacking from viii. 29 to x. 14). It reflects common Christian practice, and its insertion seems due to a feeling that Philip could not have baptized the Ethiopian without so much as a confession of faith. In such a construction as this, *τὸν Ἰησοῦν Χριστόν* is not a Lukan expression. Though not in byz, the verse found its way into TR from the editions of Erasmus, who thought it had been omitted through scribal carelessness.

viii. 38

κατέβησαν ἀμφότεροι εἰς τὸ ὕδωρ] For the primitive method of baptism cf. the account of our Lord's baptism (Mk. i. 9 f.), and the direction in *Didaché* vii. 1 that baptism should be performed if possible in running water (*ἐν ὕδατι ζῶντι*).

viii. 39

ἀνέβησαν ἐκ τοῦ ὕδατος] Cf. Mt. iii. 16, ἀνέβη ἀπὸ τοῦ ὕδατος.

πνεῦμα Κυρίου ἥρπασεν τὸν Φίλιππον] A minn p hcl* arm (repr. δ) have πνεῦμα ἅγιον ἐπέπεσεν ἐπὶ τὸν εὐνοῦχον, ἄγγελος δὲ Κυρίου ἥρπασεν τὸν Φίλιππον. The point of the δ reading (which is attested by Ephrem, Jerome, Augustine, Didymus, Cyril of Jerusalem) is to show that (as in ii. 38) the baptism was followed by the gift of the Holy Spirit (see on *ver.* 15 above). For the Spirit's action cf. 1 K. xviii. 12 ; 2 K. ii. 16 ; Ezek. iii. 14 ; viii. 3, etc.

οὐκ εἶδεν αὐτὸν οὐκέτι] Cf. οὐκ εἶδεν αὐτὸν ἔτι, 4 K. ii. 12 ; cf. also εὗρον in 4 K. ii. 17 with εὑρέθη in *ver.* 40.

ὁ εὐνοῦχος] Irenaeus (*Adu. Haer.* iii. 12. 8) says he became a missionary to the Ethiopians. The records of the Ethiopian church do not go farther back than the fourth century. Whether the eunuch was a proselyte or not, his conversion marks a step forward in the evangelization of Gentiles.

ἐπορεύετο . . . χαίρων] A contrast to the rich young ruler who 'went away sorrowful' (ἀπῆλθεν λυπούμενος), Mt. xix. 22 = Mk. x. 22.

viii. 40

εὑρέθη εἰς Ἄζωτον] The replacement of ἐν by εἰς is most marked before names of towns.

Ἄζωτον] The OT Ashdod, another of the five Philistine cities, 20 miles north of Gaza and 35 miles west of Jerusalem. The use of ζ to transliterate *shd* illustrates the original pronunciation of ζ, which was *zd*, not *dz*.

εὐηγγελίζετο τὰς πόλεις πάσας] It may have been due to his activity that disciples are found in Lydda and Joppa in ix. 32 ff., although some of the dispersed believers from Jerusalem may have found their way there already.

ἕως τοῦ ἐλθεῖν] Post-classical : cf. Gen. xxiv. 33, ἕως τοῦ λαλῆσαι. The Attic ἄχρι or μέχρι with τοῦ and the infin. does not appear in NT.

Καισαρίαν] Where we find him when next he appears in the story, xxi. 8, in a 'we' section : one of several indications that the 'we' sections form an integral part of Ac.

Caesarea (mod. Kaisariyeh) was built by Herod the Great on the site of Straton's Tower, between Joppa and Dora, and completed *c.* 13 B.C. It was intended to be the chief Mediterranean port of Palestine, and from the beginning was a thoroughly Gentile city. It was named Caesarea Sebaste, after Augustus. It became the official residence of the procurators of Judaea. During the Jewish War it was the headquarters of Vespasian (who was proclaimed Emperor there in A.D. 69) and of Titus; and after the fall of Jerusalem it was recognized beyond dispute as the capital of Palestine, with a new status as a Roman colony (*Colonia Flavia Augusta Caesariensis*) and freedom from taxation. Cf. Jos. *BJ* i. 3. 5; 21. 5 ff.; iii. 9. 1; *Ant.* xiii. 11. 2; xv. 9. 6; xvi. 5. 1.

3. Conversion of Saul of Tarsus, ix. 1-31

The event narrated in this chapter is without doubt the most important that has taken place in the history of Christianity—or of the world—since Pentecost. Luke's own estimate of its importance is sufficiently indicated by his devoting enough of his precious space to three accounts of it. Apart from the present account in the third person, we have two accounts by Paul himself, one to a Jerusalem audience (xxii. 3-21), the other before Agrippa (ch. xxvi). The different accounts are subtly adapted to their varying circumstances. As might be expected, the text of the three versions has suffered from harmonization and conflation.

(a) Saul's Expedition to Damascus, ix. 1-2

Ὁ δὲ Σαῦλος, ἔτι ἐνπνέων ἀπειλῆς καὶ φόνου εἰς τοὺς μαθητὰς 1
τοῦ κυρίου, προσελθὼν τῷ ἀρχιερεῖ ᾐτήσατο παρ' αὐτοῦ ἐπιστολὰς 2
εἰς Δαμασκὸν πρὸς τὰς συναγωγάς, ὅπως ἐάν τινας εὕρῃ τῆς ὁδοῦ
ὄντας, ἄνδρας τε καὶ γυναῖκας, δεδεμένους ἀγάγῃ εἰς Ἰερουσαλήμ.

ix. 1

ὁ δὲ Σαῦλος] The article points back to the earlier mention of Saul's persecuting zeal (viii. 3), the narrative of which is here resumed.

ἐνπνέων ἀπειλῆς καὶ φόνου] The idea of breathing anger is found in OT (e.g., Ps. xviii. 15,[1] ἀπὸ ἐνπνεύσεως πνεύματος ὀργῆς σου); the genitive after ἐνπνέω is on the analogy of its use after this and synonymous verbs in the sense 'to smell of': cf. also Josh. x. 40, καὶ πᾶν ἐνπνέον ζωῆς ἐξωλέθρευσεν.

τῷ ἀρχιερεῖ] Caiaphas was probably still in office: see on iv. 6.

ix. 2

ᾐτήσατο παρ' αὐτοῦ ἐπιστολὰς εἰς Δαμασκὸν πρὸς τὰς συναγωγάς] The decrees of the Sanhedrin were regarded as valid throughout Judaism. Within Judaea (and even, to some extent, outside it), the High Priest's privileges were generally upheld by the Roman power, and if we understand that the disciples at Damascus were some of those who had fled from Jerusalem, he apparently could

[1] xvii. 16 LXX.

demand their extradition as offenders against Jewish law (cf. 1 Macc. xv. 15 ff.; Jos. *Ant.* xiv. 10. 2). The size of the Jewish community at Damascus may be judged from the number of Jews slain there at the beginning of the Jewish War (10,000, according to *BJ* ii. 20. 2; 18,000, according to vii. 8. 7). The 'Zadokite Fragment' (ed. by S. Schechter; cf. also Charles's *Apocrypha and Pseudepigrapha* ii, pp. 785 ff.) reveals the existence at Damascus of a strict Jewish group, the 'Covenanters of Damascus', intensely loyal to the Mosaic Law, who migrated thither from Jerusalem some time before the commencement of the Christian era.

Δαμασκὸν] The history of Damascus, the chief city of Syria, goes back to a remote antiquity, as the records of the Egyptians, Assyrians and Hebrews bear witness. It lies on the main route from Egypt to Mesopotamia. From 64 B.C. onwards it belonged to the Roman province of Syria, though the absence of Roman coins at Damascus between A.D. 34 and 62 has been taken by some to indicate that it was held during these years by the Nabataean king (see on *ver.* 24; ii. 11).

τῆς ὁδοῦ] This name is applied to the Christian movement in xix. 9, 23; xxii. 4; xxiv. 14, 22; cf. also xvi. 17; xviii. 25 f. It probably corresponds to Heb. *hălākhāh* ('walk', 'rule of life'). Similar words are used in a religious sense elsewhere, e.g., Syr. *'urḥā*, 'religion'; Arab. *as-sabīl*, 'the way' (of Islam); Indian *pathin*, *mārga*; Chinese *tao*, etc.

(b) The Voice from Heaven, ix. 3-9

'Εν δὲ τῷ πορεύεσθαι ἐγένετο αὐτὸν ἐγγίζειν τῇ Δαμασκῷ, ἐξέ- 3
φνης τε αὐτὸν περιήστραψεν φῶς ἐκ τοῦ οὐρανοῦ, καὶ πεσὼν ἐπὶ τὴν 4
γῆν ἤκουσεν φωνὴν λέγουσαν αὐτῷ Σαούλ Σαούλ, τί με διώκεις; εἶπεν 5
δέ Τίς εἶ, κύριε; ὁ δέ 'Εγώ εἰμι 'Ιησοῦς ὃν σὺ διώκεις· ἀλλὰ ἀνάστηθι, 6
καὶ εἴσελθε εἰς τὴν πόλιν, καὶ λαληθήσεταί σοι ὅτι σε δεῖ ποιεῖν. οἱ 7
δὲ ἄνδρες οἱ συνοδεύοντες αὐτῷ ἱστήκεισαν ἐνεοί, ἀκούοντες μὲν τῆς
φωνῆς μηδένα δὲ θεωροῦντες. ἠγέρθη δὲ Σαῦλος ἀπὸ τῆς γῆς, ἀνεῳγ- 8
μένων δὲ τῶν ὀφθαλμῶν αὐτοῦ οὐδὲν ἔβλεπεν· χειραγωγοῦντες δὲ
αὐτὸν εἰσήγαγον εἰς Δαμασκόν. καὶ ἦν ἡμέρας τρεῖς μὴ βλέπων, 9
καὶ οὐκ ἔφαγεν οὐδὲ ἔπιεν.

ix. 3

ἐν δὲ τῷ πορεύεσθαι ἐγένετο αὐτὸν ἐγγίζειν] Temporal use of *ἐν τῷ* with infin. (see on ii. 1); for *ἐγένετο αὐτὸν ἐγγίζειν* see on iv. 5; for the combination of the two constructions cf. xix. 1.

τῇ Δαμασκῷ] Note the article; it points out the town as being that previously mentioned (in *ver.* 2). Cf. *ver.* 1; xx. 7, 11.

περιήστραψεν] 'flashed round'; the word is originally used of the flashing of lightning. For the more general sense cf. Lk. xi. 36, where *ἀστραπή* is used of the 'bright shining' of a lamp. Cf. *περιαστράψαι*, xxii. 6; the word used in xxvi. 13 is *περιλάμπω*. The time was about midday (xxii. 6; xxvi. 13). Paul no doubt had this light in mind in later years in many of his references to light and glory, e.g., 2 Cor. iii. 18; iv. 4, 6. Cf. 4 Macc. iv. 10, *οὐρανόθεν προὐφάνησαν ἔφιπποι ἄγγελοι περιαστράπτοντες τοῖς ὅπλοις*.

ix. 4

πεσὼν ἐπὶ τὴν γῆν] Cf. Ezek. i. 28; Dan. viii. 17.

ἤκουσεν φωνὴν] For a similar Voice from heaven cf. vii. 31; x. 13; Lk. iii. 22; ix. 35; Jn. xii. 28: the Rabbis have much to say of this phenomenon under the name *Bath Qōl* (lit., 'Daughter of the Voice').

Σαούλ] So in *ver.* 17; xxii. 7, 13; xxvi. 14, representing the Heb. form *Shā'ūl* ('asked for'), and used whenever we are intended to understand that Heb. or Aram. was the language spoken (on this occasion the Voice spoke *τῇ 'Εβραΐδι διαλέκτῳ*, xxvi. 14). *Σαούλ* is also used of King Saul, xiii. 21. The solemn repetition of the name is common in divine allocutions: cf. Gen. xxii. 11; xlvi. 2; Ex. iii. 4; 1 Sam. iii. 10; Lk. x. 41; xxii. 31; 4 Ezra xiv. 1 ('Ezra, Ezra'); 2 Baruch xxii. 2 ('Baruch, Baruch'); Dalman gives further references in Rabbinical literature (*Jesus-Jeshua*, p. 18).

τί με διώκεις;] Dalman (*loc. cit.*) reconstructs the Aram., *mā 'att rādĕphinnī*. '*Caput pro membris clamabat*', as Augustine finely says (for the thought cf. Mt. xxv. 40, 45).[1] The addition *σκληρόν σοι πρὸς κέντρα λακτίζειν* (E 431 e vg.codd pesh hcl*) is part of the longer δ text of *ver.* 5 transferred here to harmonize with xxvi. 14.

ix. 5

κύριε] 'Sir', 'my lord'; a title of respect, as Saul did not yet know who was speaking to him; when later he used this title of Jesus, it had a much fuller significance.

ὁ δέ] For omission of the verb of saying, cf. *ver.* 11; ii. 38. ℵ 81 add *εἶπεν*, byz adds *κύριος εἶπεν*.

'Ιησοῦς] A C E minn h pesh hcl* eth Hil Amb Aug add *ὁ Ναζωραῖος* from xxii. 8.

[1] Cf. Sadhu Sundar Singh's account of his vision of Christ: 'I heard a voice saying in Hindustani, "How long will you persecute me? . . ."' L. E. Browne (Comm., *ad. loc.*) aptly quotes the complete account as a parallel to Luke's narrative.

διώκεις] The added words (replacing ἀλλά), σκληρόν σοι πρὸς κέντρα λακτίζειν. τρέμων δὲ καὶ θαμβῶν εἶπε Κύριε, τί με θέλεις ποιῆσαι; καὶ ὁ κύριος πρὸς αὐτόν, are found in no Gk. MS., but occur with variations in some versions representing δ, notably h p vg. codd. mult; g has σκληρόν . . . λακτίζειν; hcl* has τρέμων . . . πρὸς αὐτόν (see on *ver.* 4). Erasmus translated them into Gk. from vg and hence they found their way into TR (cf. AV). Parts of the addition come from xxii. 10*a*; xxvi. 14*b*.

ix. 6

ὅτι] The indirect interrogative pronoun, more commonly written ὅ τι. The direct form τί is more frequent, even when introducing an indirect question.

ix. 7

συνοδεύοντες] Cf. συνοδία in Lk. ii. 44.

ἱστήκεισαν ἐνεοί] In xxvi. 14 Paul says πάντων τε καταπεσόντων ἡμῶν εἰς τὴν γῆν. Note the form ἱστήκεισαν (there was no difference of pronunciation between this and the regular form εἱστήκεισαν). Cf. i. 10.

ἐνεοί] The only NT occurrence of this classical word. Cf. κύνες ἐνεοί, Isa. lvi. 10; ἐνεὸν δέ τις ἑαυτὸν ποιήσας δόξει φρόνιμος εἶναι, Prov. xvii. 28.

ἀκούοντες . . . τῆς φωνῆς] Apparently contradicting xxii. 9, τὴν δὲ φωνὴν οὐκ ἤκουσαν τοῦ λαλοῦντός μοι. 'The fact that the maintenance of an old and well-known distinction between the acc. and the gen. with ἀκούω saves the author of Ac. ix. 7 and xxii. 9 from a patent self-contradiction, should by itself be enough to make us recognize it for Luke, and for other writers until it is proved wrong' (Moulton, *Proleg.*, p. 66). They heard the sound, that is, but did not distinguish the words. But a better suggestion was made in *ET* vi (1894-5), pp. 238 f., that τῆς φωνῆς here refers to *Paul's* voice; his companions heard him speaking, but saw no one to whom the speaking could be addressed.

θεωροῦντες] h, representing δ, adds *cum loqueretur. sed ait ad* [*eos, leua*]*te me de terra.*

ix. 8

ἠγέρθη δὲ Σαῦλος ἀπὸ τῆς γῆς] h, representing δ, has *et cum lebassent* (= *leuassent*) *illum.*

χειραγωγοῦντες] Cf. χειραγωγούς, xiii. 11. The only other NT occurrence of the verb is at xxii. 11; cf. Tobit xi. 16 ℵ (ὑπὸ μηδένος χειραγωγούμενον); Judg. xvi. 26 A, followed by Jos. *Ant.* v. 8. 12 (of Samson's being so led).

ix. 9

ἦν . . . μὴ βλέπων] 'he was . . . sightless'. For the construction see on i. 10. The periphrastic form here has a slightly different force from *οὐκ ἔβλεπεν*, as *μὴ βλέπων* is adjectival. The negative with participles is usually *μή* in Hellenistic Gk., though we might have expected *οὐ* here. Cf. *μὴ πιστεύοντες*, *ver.* 26.

οὐκ ἔφαγεν οὐδὲ ἔπιεν] Probably from shock. There is no need to understand his abstinence as penance or as fasting before baptism (a practice first attested in *Didaché* vii. 4; Justin, *Apol.* i. 61).

(c) Ananias sent to Saul, ix. 10-19a

Ἦν δέ τις μαθητὴς ἐν Δαμασκῷ ὀνόματι Ἁνανίας, καὶ εἶπεν 10
πρὸς αὐτὸν ἐν ὁράματι ὁ κύριος Ἁνανία. ὁ δὲ εἶπεν Ἰδοὺ ἐγώ, κύριε.
ὁ δὲ κύριος πρὸς αὐτόν Ἀνάστα πορεύθητι ἐπὶ τὴν ῥύμην τὴν καλου- 11
μένην Εὐθεῖαν καὶ ζήτησον ἐν οἰκίᾳ Ἰούδα Σαῦλον ὀνόματι Ταρσέα,
ἰδοὺ γὰρ προσεύχεται, καὶ εἶδεν ἄνδρα ἐν ὁράματι Ἁνανίαν ὀνό- 12
ματι εἰσελθόντα καὶ ἐπιθέντα αὐτῷ τὰς χεῖρας ὅπως ἀναβλέψῃ.
ἀπεκρίθη δὲ Ἁνανίας Κύριε, ἤκουσα ἀπὸ πολλῶν περὶ τοῦ ἀνδρὸς 13
τούτου, ὅσα κακὰ τοῖς ἁγίοις σου ἐποίησεν ἐν Ἰερουσαλήμ· καὶ ὧδε 14
ἔχει ἐξουσίαν παρὰ τῶν ἀρχιερέων δῆσαι πάντας τοὺς ἐπικαλουμένους
τὸ ὄνομά σου. εἶπεν δὲ πρὸς αὐτὸν ὁ κύριος Πορεύου, ὅτι σκεῦος 15
ἐκλογῆς ἐστίν μοι οὗτος τοῦ βαστάσαι τὸ ὄνομά μου ἐνώπιον τῶν
ἐθνῶν τε καὶ βασιλέων υἱῶν τε Ἰσραήλ, ἐγὼ γὰρ ὑποδείξω αὐτῷ ὅσα 16
δεῖ αὐτὸν ὑπὲρ τοῦ ὀνόματός μου παθεῖν. Ἀπῆλθεν δὲ Ἁνανίας 17
καὶ εἰσῆλθεν εἰς τὴν οἰκίαν, καὶ ἐπιθεὶς ἐπ' αὐτὸν τὰς χεῖρας εἶπεν
Σαοὺλ ἀδελφέ, ὁ κύριος ἀπέσταλκέν με, Ἰησοῦς ὁ ὀφθείς σοι ἐν τῇ
ὁδῷ ᾗ ἤρχου, ὅπως ἀναβλέψῃς καὶ πλησθῇς πνεύματος ἁγίου. καὶ 18
εὐθέως ἀπέπεσαν αὐτοῦ ἀπὸ τῶν ὀφθαλμῶν ὡς λεπίδες, ἀνέβλεψέν
τε, καὶ ἀναστὰς ἐβαπτίσθη, καὶ λαβὼν τροφὴν ἐνισχύθη. 19

ix. 10

Ἁνανίας] See his character described in xxii. 12. No account is given of the establishment of Christianity in Damascus; no doubt fugitive disciples from Jerusalem had arrived there, and these may have been the object of Saul's quest (cf. *ἐκεῖσε*, xxii. 5), but there is no reason why there should not have been Christians there earlier. *Ver.* 13 suggests that Ananias belonged to Damascus, and had learned of the Jerusalem persecution only by hearsay. The part played by Ananias is not really at variance with the argument of Gal. i. 12, 16, etc., where Paul is chiefly concerned to prove his independence of the Jerusalem apostles.

ἰδοὺ ἐγώ] Frequent in LXX for Heb. *hinnĕnī*, 'behold me', 'here am I' (e.g., Gen. xxii. 1).

ix. 11

ἀνάστα] B (a variant form for ἀνάστηθι, cf. xii. 7); ἀναστάς ℵ A C 81 byz.

ἐπὶ τὴν ῥύμην τὴν καλουμένην Εὐθεῖαν] Still one of the chief thoroughfares of Damascus, the *Derb el-Mustaqīm.* The house of Judas is traditionally located near the west end.

ἐν οἰκίᾳ Ἰούδα] Luke was interested in the hosts of his principal characters: cf. Simon the tanner (whose address, like Judas's, is given in a vision, x. 6), Mnason (xxi. 16).

Ταρσέα] The first indication of Saul's birthplace: see on *ver.* 30.

προσεύχεται] For the association of prayer and vision cf. x. 9 f.; xxii. 17; Lk. i. 10 f.; iii. 21; ix. 28; xxii. 43.

ix. 12

ἐν ὁράματι] B C; byz pesh hcl place it before ἄνδρα, ℵ A 81 g p vg sah boh omit it, probably rightly. It may have been introduced from the previous verse. Even if it is an addition here, it is exegetically sound. We can distinguish three early visions of Saul, (1) *vv.* 4 ff., on the way to Damascus, (2) *ver.* 12, presumably in Damascus, (3) xxii. 17 ff., after returning to Jerusalem.

ix. 13

ἤκουσα] Probably indicating that Ananias was not himself one of the fugitives from Jerusalem. For ἀπό after ἀκούω cf. 1 Jn. i. 5.

τοῖς ἁγίοις] This became a common name for Christians, the favourite name in Paul's writings. In Ac. it also occurs in *vv.* 32, 41; xxvi. 10. (For other names see on xi. 26.)

ix. 14

παρὰ τῶν ἀρχιερέων] For the plur. see on iv. 5. In *ver.* 1 the High Priest in office is alone mentioned, as the authority was formally vested in him, but the high-priestly families took a common line in defence of common interests. Cf. xxvi. 12.

τοὺς ἐπικαλουμένους τὸ ὄνομά σου] See on ii. 21, 38; xxii. 16; in practice the expression refers to those who address Jesus as Lord.

ix. 15

σκεῦος ἐκλογῆς] Hebraic genitive, lit., 'instrument of choice', i.e., 'chosen vessel'; Lat. *uas electionis:* cf. Dante, *vas d'elezione* (*Inferno*, ii. 28).[1] For Paul's own sense of this election cf. Gal. i. 15 f.; Rom. i. 1 ff.

[1] Cf. also *Paradiso* xxi. 127 f., *il gran vasello dello Spirito Santo.*

τοῦ βαστάσαι] For *τοῦ* with infin., see on iii. 12 (cf. xiv. 18; xv. 20; xx. 3, 27; xxvii. 1). Luke accounts for two-thirds of the NT examples of this construction; Luke and Paul together for five-sixths. It is evenly distributed throughout the Lukan writings, including the 'we' sections (see *Proleg.*, p. 217). Its force here is final.

βασιλέων] Including at least Agrippa II (xxv. 23 ff.) and Nero (xxvii. 24).

ix. 16

ὅσα] The implied antecedent is *πάντα*, so xiv. 27.

δεῖ αὐτὸν ὑπὲρ τοῦ ὀνόματός μου παθεῖν] Cf. v. 41; xxi. 13. He was to endure many times over (cf. 2 Cor. xi. 23 ff.) what he had made others suffer, and that for the sake of the same Name. But in the Kingdom of Heaven suffering for the King is a sure sign of His favour and an earnest of His reward (Mt. v. 11 f.; Rom. viii. 17; 2 Tim. ii. 12).

ix. 17

ἐπιθεὶς ἐπ' αὐτὸν τὰς χεῖρας] C *P*[45] have *ἐπιθεὶς τὰς χεῖρας ἐπ' αὐτόν*. Cf. *ver.* 12. We should probably connect the laying on of Ananias's hands with Saul's reception of the Holy Spirit (see on viii. 17) as well as with the recovery of his sight.

Σαοὺλ ἀδελφέ] Addressing him in Aram. (see on *ver.* 4). In calling him 'brother', Ananias not only addressed him as a fellow-Israelite, but welcomed him into the new fellowship. The first words of Ananias to the late persecutor are full of significance. Cf. xxii. 13, where the same words introduce a longer version of what Ananias said.

ὁ κύριος . . . Ἰησοῦς] 'the Lord, even Jesus': note the added words of identification: Jesus is Lord.

ὀφθείς] 'appeared'; intransitive use: cf. *ὀπτανόμενος* i. 3.

ἀναβλέψῃς] The regular word for recovery of sight, freq. in the Gospels, even in the case of those born blind (e.g., Jn. ix. 11 ff.).

πλησθῇς πνεύματος ἁγίου] Such filling was necessary for the prophetic service indicated in *ver.* 15 (cf. Mk. xiii. 11).

ix. 18

ἀπέπεσαν . . . ὡς λεπίδες] 'a flaky substance fell off': cf. Tob. iii. 17 (*τοῦ Τωβεὶτ λεπίσαι τὰ λευκώματα*); xi. 13 (*καὶ ἐλεπίσθη ἀπὸ τῶν κανθῶν τῶν ὀφθαλμῶν αὐτοῦ τὰ λευκώματα*). Hobart (pp. 39 f.) quotes instances from Hippocrates, Galen and Dioscorides for *ἀποπίπτω* used of the falling off of *λεπίδες*, though in connection with skin troubles, not eye diseases.

ἀνέβλεψέν τε] AB byz ; *ἀνέβλεψεν δέ* ℵC² ; *καὶ ἀνέβλεψεν* 431 *P*⁴⁵. C² E L 614 minn add *παραχρῆμα*.

ix. 19a.

λαβὼν τροφὴν ἐνισχύθη] Luke knows the importance of nourishment for convalescents (cf. Lk. viii. 55), but this is no necessary indication of medical authorship, as may be seen from Mk. v. 43 (*εἶπεν δοθῆναι αὐτῇ φαγεῖν*), the parallel to Lk. viii. 55.

ἐνισχύθη] BC ; *ἐνίσχυσεν* ℵAC² 81 byz ; *ἐνισχύσθη* *P*⁴⁵. Outside LXX, the transitive use of *ἐνισχύω*, according to Hobart (pp. 80 f.), is confined to Hippocrates and Luke (cf. Lk. xxii. 43). LS⁹ add an example in the passive from Julian the Apostate. Elsewhere it has the intrans. sense ' be strong '.

(d) Saul Preaches in Damascus, ix. 19b-22

Ἐγένετο δὲ μετὰ τῶν ἐν Δαμασκῷ μαθητῶν ἡμέρας τινάς, καὶ 20
εὐθέως ἐν ταῖς συναγωγαῖς ἐκήρυσσεν τὸν Ἰησοῦν ὅτι οὗτός ἐστιν ὁ
υἱὸς τοῦ θεοῦ. ἐξίσταντο δὲ πάντες οἱ ἀκούοντες καὶ ἔλεγον Οὐχ 21
οὗτός ἐστιν ὁ πορθήσας ἐν Ἰερουσαλὴμ τοὺς ἐπικαλουμένους τὸ ὄνομα
τοῦτο, καὶ ὧδε εἰς τοῦτο ἐληλύθει ἵνα δεδεμένους αὐτοὺς ἀγάγῃ ἐπὶ
τοὺς ἀρχιερεῖς; Σαῦλος δὲ μᾶλλον ἐνεδυναμοῦτο καὶ συνέχυννεν 22
Ἰουδαίους τοὺς κατοικοῦντας ἐν Δαμασκῷ, συνβιβάζων ὅτι οὗτός
ἐστιν ὁ χριστός.

ix. 19b.

ἡμέρας τινάς] *ἡμέρας ἱκανάς* *P*⁴⁵. Vague : cf. *ἡμέραι ἱκαναί*, *ver.* 23. According to Gal. i. 15 ff., after the revelation of Christ he did not confer with flesh and blood, but went away to Arabia ; this may not exclude a short period of such activity as is described in *vv.* 19-22. Or his preaching at Damascus may have followed his return from Arabia, though *εὐθέως* (*ver.* 20) makes this less likely. See on *ver.* 23.

ix. 20

ἐν ταῖς συναγωγαῖς] It is evident here and in *ver.* 2 that there were several synagogues in Damascus. There were many in some large towns (see on vi. 9) and the Jewish community in Damascus was very large (see on *ver.* 2).

ὁ υἱὸς τοῦ θεοῦ] It is significant that the only occurrence of this title in Ac. should be in a report of Paul's first preaching (cf. Gal. i. 16, *τὸν υἱὸν αὐτοῦ*). The title ' Son of God ' or its equivalent is used in OT (1) of the nation of Israel (e.g., Ex. iv. 22 ; Dt. xxxii. 6 ; Jer. xxxi. 9 ; Hos. xi. 1), (2) of the anointed king of

Israel (e.g. 2 Sam. vii. 14; Ps. ii. 7; lxxxix. 26 ff.); this use, especially in the passages in Pss. (see on iv. 25 f.; xiii. 33), merges into its application (3) to the ideal King, the Messiah (cf. 1 Enoch cv. 2; 4 Ezra vii. 28 f.; xiii. 32, 37, 52; xiv. 9). That our Lord's contemporaries believed that Messiah was God's Son is evident from the High Priest's question *σὺ εἶ ὁ χριστός, ὁ υἱὸς τοῦ εὐλογητοῦ;* (Mk. xiv. 61). As applied to Christ, the title 'Son of God' denotes Him as the true representative of the Israel of God (cf. the True Vine, Jn. xv. 1 ff.; and the development of the conception of the Servant of Jehovah), and as God's anointed King, as well as expressing that unique relationship to the Father which is His in the Triune Godhead. Here probably the Messianic sense of the title is uppermost (cf. *ver.* 22). δ (h Iren) adds *ὁ χριστός* before *ὁ υἱὸς τοῦ θεοῦ.*

ix. 21

ὁ πορθήσας] lit., 'he who sacked'; Paul himself uses this verb in the same sense in Gal. i. 13, 23.

ἐν Ἰερουσαλὴμ] B C 81 byz; *εἰς Ἰερουσαλήμ* ℵ A minn. See on ii. 5.

τὸ ὄνομα τοῦτο] If the speakers were Jews, we may compare iv. 17; v. 28 for the studied vagueness of reference.

ἐληλύθει] Pluperfect; as his original purpose in coming no longer existed, the perf. is no longer applicable.

ἀγάγῃ] *ἀναγάγῃ* P 69 105 P^{45} Chr; *ἀπαγάγῃ* 1739.

ix. 22

ἐνεδυναμοῦτο] Cf. *ἐνισχύθη*, *ver.* 19. δ (C 467 h) adds *τῷ λόγῳ*. For *ἐνδυναμόω* cf. LXX, Judg. vi. 34; Ps. li. 9 (EV lii. 7).

συνέχυννεν] Cf. ii. 6.

συνβιβάζων] lit., 'putting together', hence 'proving', here by putting the prophetic Scriptures alongside their fulfilment (cf. xvii. 2 f.; xviii. 28; xxvi. 22 f.). See on xvi. 10; xix. 33. He had previously been acquainted with these arguments, but had hitherto fought against them.

ὁ χριστός] The original δ text seems to have added *εἰς ὃν εὐδόκησεν ὁ θεός* (*in quem* [*bene se*]*nsit deus* h): cf. Mt. iii. 17; Lk. xxiii. 35.

(e) Saul Escapes from Damascus, ix. 23-25

Ὡς δὲ ἐπληροῦντο ἡμέραι ἱκαναί, συνεβουλεύσαντο οἱ Ἰουδαῖοι 23
ἀνελεῖν αὐτόν· ἐγνώσθη δὲ τῷ Σαύλῳ ἡ ἐπιβουλὴ αὐτῶν. παρετηρ- 24
οῦντο δὲ καὶ τὰς πύλας ἡμέρας τε καὶ νυκτὸς ὅπως αὐτὸν ἀνέλωσιν·
λαβόντες δὲ οἱ μαθηταὶ αὐτοῦ νυκτὸς διὰ τοῦ τείχους καθῆκαν αὐτὸν 25
χαλάσαντες ἐν σφυρίδι.

ix. 23

ὡς δὲ ἐπληροῦντο ἡμέραι ἱκαναί] 'as many days were drawing to an end'. Actually two full years at least elapsed from his conversion to his return to Jerusalem (Gal. i. 18, where 'three years' may be reckoned inclusively, as in xx. 31 below). During this time he visited Arabia, the country east of Damascus, and returned from there to Damascus (Gal. i. 17). By Arabia we should understand the Nabataean kingdom (see on ii. 11). His activity in this region seems to have excited the annoyance of Aretas, the Nabataean king (see below).

ix. 24

Σαύλῳ] Σαούλ P^{45}.

παρετηροῦντο δὲ καὶ τὰς πύλας] With this verse and the following we must compare 2 Cor. xi. 32 f., 'In Damascus the ethnarch of King Aretas was watching the city of the Damascenes to take me, and I was let down in a basket through a window in the wall, and escaped his hands.'

That the Damascene Jews should have enlisted the ethnarch's support is not unlikely (this kind of action can be paralleled elsewhere in Ac.); the ethnarch would be the more ready to lend his aid if Saul had annoyed Aretas by preaching in the Nabataean kingdom. The status of the ethnarch is uncertain; he may have been a viceroy, if Aretas was ruler of Damascus at this time, as Schürer (II. i. 98) and others have inferred from the absence of Roman coins in Damascus between A.D. 34 and 62. This inference, however, is precarious. The ethnarch's jurisdiction may have been outside the city (so K. Lake, *BC* v, p. 193) or, more probably, he was Aretas's representative in Damascus, who looked after the interests of the many Nabataean subjects in the city while it was under Roman rule (cf. E. Meyer, *Ursprung und Anfänge des Christentums* iii, p. 346; he calls him 'das Oberhaupt der nabataeischen Kolonie in Damaskus' and refers with approval to the statement of this view by E. Schwartz in *Nachr. Gött. Ges.*, 1906, pp. 367 f.). Aretas IV (*Ḥarethath*) reigned over the Nabataeans from 9 B.C. to A.D. 40; he was father-in-law of Antipas (see on iv. 27).

ix. 25

διὰ τοῦ τείχους] The same words occur in 2 Cor. xi. 33 (as also does the verb χαλάω), where it is made clear that he was lowered through a window in the wall.

ἐν σφυρίδι] In 2 Cor. xi. 33 it is called a σαργάνη, 'a large woven or network bag or basket suitable for hay, straw . . . or for bales of wool' (LC). σφυρίς (otherwise spelt σπυρίς) is also used in the narrative of the feeding of the 4,000 (Mk. viii. 8); in the story of the feeding of the 5,000 the word used is *κόφινος*, a smaller basket (Mk. vi. 43).

(f) Saul in Jerusalem; he is sent to Tarsus, ix. 26-30

Παραγενόμενος δὲ εἰς Ἰερουσαλὴμ ἐπείραζεν κολλᾶσθαι τοῖς 26
μαθηταῖς· καὶ πάντες ἐφοβοῦντο αὐτόν, μὴ πιστεύοντες ὅτι ἐστὶν
μαθητής. Βαρνάβας δὲ ἐπιλαβόμενος αὐτὸν ἤγαγεν πρὸς τοὺς ἀπο- 27
στόλους, καὶ διηγήσατο αὐτοῖς πῶς ἐν τῇ ὁδῷ εἶδεν τὸν κύριον καὶ ὅτι
ἐλάλησεν αὐτῷ, καὶ πῶς ἐν Δαμασκῷ ἐπαρρησιάσατο ἐν τῷ ὀνόματι
Ἰησοῦ. καὶ ἦν μετ' αὐτῶν εἰσπορευόμενος καὶ ἐκπορευόμενος εἰς 28
Ἰερουσαλήμ, παρρησιαζόμενος ἐν τῷ ὀνόματι τοῦ κυρίου, ἐλάλει 29
τε καὶ συνεζήτει πρὸς τοὺς Ἑλληνιστάς· οἱ δὲ ἐπεχείρουν ἀνελεῖν
αὐτόν. ἐπιγνόντες δὲ οἱ ἀδελφοὶ κατήγαγον αὐτὸν εἰς Καισαρίαν 30
καὶ ἐξαπέστειλαν αὐτὸν εἰς Ταρσόν.

ix. 26

παραγενόμενος] 'having arrived'. For his own account of this visit to Jerusalem cf. Gal. i. 18 f., and see further on next verse.

κολλᾶσθαι] Cf. v. 13.

τοῖς μαθηταῖς] i.e., to the few who were left in Jerusalem; the majority had been dispersed (viii. 1), and now formed the 'churches of Judaea', to which Paul says he was unknown by face (Gal. i. 22).

καὶ πάντες ἐφοβοῦντο αὐτόν] Not unnaturally; for all they knew, he might be an *agent provocateur*.

ix. 27

Βαρνάβας] See on iv. 36. The action of Barnabas implies that he was previously acquainted with Saul, and knew that the sincerity of his character left no room for doubting the reality of his conversion.

αὐτὸν] Grammatically dependent not on *ἐπιλαβόμενος* (which would take the gen.), but on *ἤγαγεν*.

πρὸς τοὺς ἀποστόλους] In view of Gal. i. 18 f., this may be the generalizing plural (so *μετ' αὐτῶν, ver.* 28). Of the leaders in the church he saw only Peter (with whom he spent a fortnight) and James the Lord's brother. In a certain sense James was also an apostle, being a witness of the Resurrection (1 Cor. xv. 7); Gal. i. 19 is ambiguous, but probably implies his apostleship (see Lightfoot *ad loc.*). The differences between the accounts of Ac. and Gal. will not appear insuperable if we bear in mind the quite different objects in view in the two works.

ὅτι ἐλάλησεν αὐτῷ] Probably 'what He said to him' rather than 'that He spoke to him'; this clause, coming between two indirect questions, is more likely to be another of the same than an indirect statement: for this use of ὅτι see on *ver.* 6.

ἐπαρρησιάσατο] A favourite word of our author, suggesting bold and frank utterance, perhaps under the Holy Spirit's impulsion (so *ver.* 29; xiii. 46; xiv. 3; xviii. 26; xix. 8; xxvi. 26; its only other NT occurrences are 1 Th. ii. 2; Eph. vi. 20). Cf. παρρησία, ii. 29; iv. 13, 29, 31; xxviii. 31.

ix. 28

εἰσπορευόμενος καὶ ἐκπορευόμενος] See on i. 21.

εἰς Ἰερουσαλήμ] Not in the sense of motion after εἰσπορευόμενος: outside Jerusalem he remained unknown by face to the Christians in Judaea (Gal. i. 22 ff.); εἰς is here definitely equivalent to ἐν, as in ii. 5. L. E. Browne avoids the discrepancy with Gal. i. 22 ff. by regarding εἰς Ἰερουσαλήμ as a gloss (as in xii. 25): *vv.* 27-29 will then form Barnabas's report of Saul's experiences at Damascus (Comm. *ad loc.*).

ix. 29

ἐν τῷ ὀνόματι τοῦ κυρίου] Cf. *ver.* 27, ἐν τῷ ὀνόματι Ἰησοῦ, i.e., by His authority, as His witness or 'ambassador' (2 Cor. v. 20).

πρὸς τοὺς Ἑλληνιστάς] As Stephen had done (vi. 9), and likely among the same people. Notice that συνζητέω is used there, as here. We should understand Ἑλληνιστάς here of Greek-speaking Jews, as in vi. 1. A has Ἕλληνας (cf. xi. 20). Saul himself, though a Hellenist by virtue of his Tarsian birth and citizenship, was also by ancestry, upbringing, and education 'a Hebrew of Hebrews' (Phil. iii. 5).

οἱ δὲ ἐπεχείρουν ἀνελεῖν αὐτόν] i.e., the Hellenists: cf. their action against Stephen (vi. 10 ff.).

ix. 30

ἐπιγνόντες] F. Field (*Notes on Trans. of NT*, pp. 117 f.) takes this as the equivalent of *re cognita*. Cf. συνιδόντες in the same sense in xiv. 6.

οἱ ἀδελφοὶ] Yet another name for members of the new community, as it was for members of the old Israel.

κατήγαγον αὐτὸν εἰς Καισαρίαν] The first, but not the last time that he had to be taken to Caesarea because of danger in Jerusalem (cf. xxiii. 23 ff.).

εἰς Ταρσόν] From Caesarea to Tarsus he probably went by sea. Tarsus was in the province of Syro-Cilicia (cf. Gal. i. 21, ἔπειτα ἦλθον εἰς τὰ κλίματα τῆς Συρίας καὶ Κιλικίας). For the period between ix. 30 and xi. 25 we have no authority for Saul's life. Probably during this period he 'suffered the loss of all things' (Phil. iii. 8) and endured some of the trials enumerated in 2 Cor. xi. 23 ff.

Tarsus, of which the Apostle was a native and citizen (*ver.* 11; xxi. 39), was the capital of Cilicia. In Gk. legend its foundation is associated with Perseus. Cf. A. H. Sayce in *JHS* xlv (1925), pp. 161 ff. At a very early date (*c.* 1000 B.C. or earlier) Greeks began to mingle with its Anatolian population. It was taken by Shalmaneser III of Assyria (858-824 B.C.); later it was subject in turn to the Persians, Alexander the Great, and the Seleucids. Antiochus Epiphanes gave it an autonomous constitution (*c.* 170 B.C.) and, in accordance with Seleucid practice, probably added a number of Jews to the population, incorporating them as citizens in a new tribe by themselves. About 83 B.C. it fell under the power of Tigranes of Armenia, but became part of the Roman Empire when Pompey reorganized the East in 64 B.C. In the Empire it ranked as a free city. In 15 B.C., Athenodorus the Stoic, the teacher of Augustus, who was a native of Tarsus, returned there and reformed the administration, a property qualification now being required in citizens, among whom those who were also Roman citizens formed an aristocracy. Athenodorus and his successor, Nestor the Academic, had also great educational influence in Tarsus, which ranked in those days as one of the three chief centres of learning in the world, the other two being Athens and Alexandria. Its schools were devoted to philosophy, rhetoric, and 'the whole round of education in general' (*τὴν ἄλλην παιδείαν ἐγκύκλιον ἅπασαν*, Strabo xiv. 5. 13)—in short, it was what we should call a University city. But the cultural influence of Tarsus on Paul has often been greatly exaggerated.

(g) The Church enjoys Peace and Prosperity, ix. 31

'Η μὲν οὖν ἐκκλησία καθ' ὅλης τῆς 'Ιουδαίας καὶ Γαλιλαίας καὶ 31
Σαμαρίας εἶχεν εἰρήνην οἰκοδομουμένη, καὶ πορευομένη τῷ φόβῳ τοῦ
κυρίου καὶ τῇ παρακλήσει τοῦ ἁγίου πνεύματος ἐπληθύνετο.

ix. 31

'Η μὲν οὖν ἐκκλησία κ.τ.λ.] As usual, *μὲν οὖν* commences a new paragraph; here, another report of progress such as we saw in vi. 7.

In place of the sing., which is maintained in β throughout this sentence, δ (g p Aug.unit vg.codd) and byz have the plur., *αἱ μὲν οὖν ἐκκλησίαι κ.τ.λ.* The plural is in accordance with NT usage elsewhere, where the singular is used only either of the Church in its entirety as the Body of Christ, or of that Body seen in miniature in each individual Christian community. So what is here called 'the church' (β text) is by Paul referred to as 'the churches of Judaea which were in Christ' (Gal. i. 22); 'the churches of God which are in Judaea in Christ Jesus' (1 Th. ii. 14). But these churches represented the original Jerusalem church, now in dispersion.

'The Ecclesia was still confined to Jewish or semi-Jewish populations and to ancient Jewish soil; but it was no longer the Ecclesia of a single city, and yet it was *one:* probably as corresponding, by these three modern representative districts of Judaea, Galilee and Samaria, to the ancient Ecclesia which had its home in the whole land of Israel' (Hort, *CE*, pp. 55 f.).

καὶ Γαλιλαίας] Galilee has not been mentioned in the narrative of evangelization so far; its mention here is noteworthy in view of our Lord's activity there, and the number of disciples who remained there (see on i. 15).

πορευομένη] Probably indicating manner of life ('living in the fear of the Lord'); so Heb. *hālakh* (whence *hălākhāh:* see on ὁδοῦ, *ver.* 2). Torrey, however, thinks it represents the continuous sense of Aram. *'ăzal,* 'to go', as in the corresponding Eng. idiom, 'it went on being multiplied in the fear of the Lord', etc.

τῇ παρακλήσει τοῦ ἁγίου πνεύματος] Cf. Παράκλητος as a title of the Holy Spirit (Jn. xiv. 26, etc.). The gen. may be subjective, 'the consolation given by the Holy Spirit', or objective, 'the invoking His guidance as Paraclete to the Ecclesia' (Hort, *op. cit.*, p. 55).

III. ACTS OF PETER: THE GENTILES BROUGHT IN, ix. 32-xii. 24

1. PETER IN WESTERN PALESTINE, ix. 32-43.

(a) Peter at Lydda; the Healing of Aeneas, ix. 32-35

Ἐγένετο δὲ Πέτρον διερχόμενον διὰ πάντων κατελθεῖν καὶ πρὸς 32
τοὺς ἁγίους τοὺς κατοικοῦντας Λύδδα. εὗρεν δὲ ἐκεῖ ἄνθρωπόν τινα 33
ὀνόματι Αἰνέαν ἐξ ἐτῶν ὀκτὼ κατακείμενον ἐπὶ κραβάττου, ὃς ἦν
παραλελυμένος. καὶ εἶπεν αὐτῷ ὁ Πέτρος Αἰνέα, ἰᾶταί σε Ἰησοῦς 34
Χριστός· ἀνάστηθι καὶ στρῶσον σεαυτῷ· καὶ εὐθέως ἀνέστη. καὶ 35
εἶδαν αὐτὸν πάντες οἱ κατοικοῦντες Λύδδα καὶ τὸν Σαρῶνα, οἵτινες
ἐπέστρεψαν ἐπὶ τὸν κύριον.

We now revert to the narrative of Peter, which was broken off at viii. 25 with his return from Samaria to Jerusalem.

ix. 32

ἐγένετο δὲ Πέτρον . . . κατελθεῖν] For the construction see on iv. 5.

διερχόμενον . . . κατελθεῖν] Not technical terms, but see on viii. 4 f. In Ac. they usually appear, as here, in a context of evangelization.

διὰ πάντων] i.e., through the whole region, or through all the places between Jerusalem and Lydda: cf. pesh *ba-mĕdīnāthā* ('through the cities'). Perhaps we are to understand that he went by a circuitous route, visiting the Samaritan villages of viii. 25.

τοὺς ἁγίους τοὺς κατοικοῦντας Λύδδα] These 'saints' (see on *ver.* 13) may have come from Jerusalem; Philip also evangelized these parts on his way from Ashdod to Caesarea (viii. 40).

Λύδδα] Lydda (OT Lod, 1 Chr. viii. 12; Ezra ii. 33; Neh. xi. 35; in Byzantine times Diospolis; mod. Ludd) was the capital of a Jewish toparchy. Here in Christian tradition the dragon was slain by St. George (the scene of the similar Gk. legend of Perseus and Andromeda was nearby); here, too, in local belief, Antichrist will be slain by Messiah. After A.D. 70, it was a centre of Rabbinical learning, and in the Middle Ages it was an episcopal see. A trade in purple dye-stuffs was carried on in the town. Cf. 1 Macc. xi. 34; Jos. *BJ* ii. 19. 1; iii. 3. 5; iv. 8. 1; *Ant.* xx. 6. 2; Pliny *NH* v. 70. Note the mixed declension of Λύδδα: here and in *ver.* 35 it is neut. plur.; in *ver.* 38 the gen. Λύδδας is fem. sing. Cf. xiv. 6, 8.

ix. 33

Αἰνέαν] He is usually supposed to have been a Christian (LC think not), but we are not told so explicitly.

ἐξ ἐτῶν ὀκτώ] Either 'for 8 years' or 'since 8 years old', probably the former. See on iii. 2; iv. 22 for Luke's notes of time in such cases.

κραβάττου] See on v. 15.

παραλελυμένος] Cf. Lk. v. 18. Luke's preference for this form over παραλυτικός, which other NT writers use, 'is in strict agreement with that of the medical writers' (Hobart, p. 6).

ix. 34

ἰᾶταί σε Ἰησοῦς Χριστός] The paronomasia ἰᾶται . . . Ἰησοῦς is to be noted: see on xvii. 18. Note that ἰᾶται is present (contrast the accentually different perfect ἴαται, Mk. v. 29); not a durative ('He is engaged in healing') but an aoristic present ('He effects the cure this moment'): cf. παραγγέλλω, xvi. 18; ἀφιένται, Mk. ii. 5. (But see H. J. Cadbury in *JTS* xlix [1948], pp. 57 f.)

στρῶσον σεαυτῷ] With στρῶσον sc. κλίνην. The meaning may be either 'make your bed' or 'get ready to eat' (cf. sense of στρώννυμι in Mk. xiv. 15), the κλίνη being in the latter case the couch on which one reclined at table. This would accord well with the interest shown by Luke and other NT writers in nourishment for convalescents (see on *ver.* 19*a*).

ix. 35

Λύδδα καὶ τὸν Σαρῶνα] This was not an entirely Jewish district. We can see the gradual widening of the circle from its native Palestinian beginnings: (1) Jews of the Dispersion and proselytes at Pentecost (ii. 9 ff.: cf. the Hellenists of vi. 1); (2) Samaritans (viii. 5 ff.); (3) the Ethiopian (viii. 27 ff.); (4) semi-Gentile towns (viii. 40; ix. 32 ff.). Then there follow (5) Cornelius (x. 1 ff.), and (6) the Greeks of Antioch (see on xi. 20).

τὸν Σαρῶνα] The coastal plain of Sharon (cf. *ὁ Σαρών*, Isa. xxxiii. 9 LXX). It stretched from Lydda to Mount Carmel, and was famed for its fertility.

οἵτινες] 'and they', introducing a subsequent action (cf. i. 11; viii. 15; xi. 20). A mass-movement to Christianity in this district is implied.

(b) Peter at Joppa; the Raising of Tabitha, ix. 36-43

Ἐν Ἰόππῃ δέ τις ἦν μαθήτρια ὀνόματι Ταβειθά, ἣ διερμηνευομένη 36
λέγεται Δορκάς· αὕτη ἦν πλήρης ἔργων ἀγαθῶν καὶ ἐλεημοσυνῶν ὧν
ἐποίει. ἐγένετο δὲ ἐν ταῖς ἡμέραις ἐκείναις ἀσθενήσασαν αὐτὴν ἀπο- 37
θανεῖν· λούσαντες δὲ ἔθηκαν ἐν ὑπερῴῳ. ἐγγὺς δὲ οὔσης Λύδδας 38
τῇ Ἰόππῃ οἱ μαθηταὶ ἀκούσαντες ὅτι Πέτρος ἐστὶν ἐν αὐτῇ ἀπέστει-
λαν δύο ἄνδρας πρὸς αὐτὸν παρακαλοῦντες Μὴ ὀκνήσῃς διελθεῖν
ἕως ἡμῶν· ἀναστὰς δὲ Πέτρος συνῆλθεν αὐτοῖς· ὃν παραγενόμενον 39
ἀνήγαγον εἰς τὸ ὑπερῷον, καὶ παρέστησαν αὐτῷ πᾶσαι αἱ χῆραι κλαίουσαι
καὶ ἐπιδεικνύμεναι χιτῶνας καὶ ἱμάτια ὅσα ἐποίει μετ' αὐτῶν οὖσα ἡ
Δορκάς. ἐκβαλὼν δὲ ἔξω πάντας ὁ Πέτρος καὶ θεὶς τὰ γόνατα προσ- 40
ηύξατο, καὶ ἐπιστρέψας πρὸς τὸ σῶμα εἶπεν Ταβειθά, ἀνάστηθι. ἡ
δὲ ἤνοιξεν τοὺς ὀφθαλμοὺς αὐτῆς, καὶ ἰδοῦσα τὸν Πέτρον ἀνεκάθισεν.
δοὺς δὲ αὐτῇ χεῖρα ἀνέστησεν αὐτήν, φωνήσας δὲ τοὺς ἁγίους καὶ τὰς 41
χήρας παρέστησεν αὐτὴν ζῶσαν. γνωστὸν δὲ ἐγένετο καθ' ὅλης Ἰόππης, 42
καὶ ἐπίστευσαν πολλοὶ ἐπὶ τὸν κύριον. Ἐγένετο δὲ ἡμέρας ἱκανὰς 43
μεῖναι ἐν Ἰόππῃ παρά τινι Σίμωνι βυρσεῖ.

ix. 36

Ἰόππῃ] Mod. Jaffa. It is mentioned in the tribute-lists of Thothmes III (1490-1436 B.C.); in OT, Josh. xix. 46; 2 Chr. ii. 16; Ezra iii. 7; Jonah i. 3. It belonged for long to the Philistines. Jonathan Maccabaeus conquered it from the Syrians (148 B.C.); Pompey restored it to them; in 47 B.C. it was given again to Hyrcanus II, the Jewish priest-king. Its population contained a high proportion of Greeks. Vespasian destroyed it in A.D. 68. It was, and is, the principal port of South Palestine. Cf. 1 Macc. x. 74 ff.; xii. 33; xiii. 11; Jos. *Ant.* xiv. 4. 4; 10. 6.

μαθήτρια] Only here in NT; a good Hellenistic word, found in Diodorus Siculus and Diogenes Laertius. Tabitha is explicitly called a disciple; it is not said whether Aeneas was one or not.

Ταβειθά] Aram. *ṭabyĕthā*, 'gazelle', cognate with Zibiah (Heb. *ṣibyāh*), 2 Kings xii. 1.

ἥ] Elsewhere in Ac. *ἥτις* is used for the relative *ἥ*.

Δορκάς] The Gk. equivalent of Tabitha; it occurs as a Gk. proper name, e.g. in Jos. *BJ* iv. 3. 5; cf. the similar name Damaris (or Damalis), xvii. 34.

πλήρης ἔργων ἀγαθῶν καὶ ἐλεημοσυνῶν] For similar uses of words meaning 'full' cf. Rom. xv. 14 (*μεστοί ἐστε ἀγαθωσύνης, πεπληρωμένοι πάσης τῆς γνώσεως*); Jas. iii. 17 (*μεστὴ ἐλέους καὶ καρπῶν ἀγαθῶν*); Plato, *Repub.* 563 D (*μεστὰ ἐλευθερίας*).

ix. 37

ἐγένετο . . . αὐτὴν ἀποθανεῖν] For the construction (the same as in *ver.* 32) see on iv. 5.

ἀσθενήσασαν] Ingressive aorist: 'fell sick'.

λούσαντες] A reference to the Jewish custom of 'purification of the dead' (cf. Mishna, *Shabbāth* xxiii. 5).

ἔθηκαν] *αὐτήν*, omitted by B, is added by ℵ A 81 after *ἔθηκαν*, by ℵ[c] C 33 P^{45} byz before *ἔθηκαν*.

ix. 38

ἐγγὺς] Joppa is about 10 miles N.W. of Lydda.

δύο ἄνδρας] For the sending of two messengers cf. viii. 14; xi. 30; xiii. 3; xv. 27; xix. 22; xxiii. 23: cf. our Lord's practice, Lk. x. 1.

μὴ ὀκνήσῃς διελθεῖν ἕως ἡμῶν] 'Don't fail to come to us': a polite request, equal to 'please come'. *ὀκνέω* is regularly used thus with a negative: cf. Num. xxii. 16 (*μὴ ὀκνήσῃς ἐλθεῖν πρός με*); Sir. vii. 35 (*μὴ ὄκνει ἐπισκέπτεσθαι ἄρρωστον*). For *ὀκνήσῃς . . . ἡμῶν* P^{45} byz have indirect *ὀκνῆσαι . . . αὐτῶν*.

ix. 39

ἀναστὰς κ.τ.λ.] For the idiom see on v. 6.

ὃν . . . ἀνήγαγον] Grammatically a relative clause; logically more important than the principal clause. P^{45} has *ἤγαγον* for *ἀνήγαγον*.

πᾶσαι αἱ χῆραι] As in vi. 1, widows are mentioned, not as members of an organization or ecclesiastical order, but as the natural recipients of charity.

ἐπιδεικνύμεναι] As this verb is used in the active elsewhere in NT, the middle here may mean 'showing on themselves'.

χιτῶνας καὶ ἱμάτια] The ἱμάτιον ('cloak') was worn above the χιτών ('tunic').

ἐποίει] ἐποίησεν αὐταῖς P^{45}.

ix. 40

ἐκβαλὼν δὲ ἔξω] As he had seen his Master do at the raising of Jairus's daughter (Mk. v. 40; this detail is missing from the parallel passage in Lk. viii. 54, but Luke in his Gospel frequently omits a Markan phrase which he introduces in Ac.: cf. i. 7; vi. 11 f.; xii. 4 with Mk. xiii. 32; xiv. 58; xiv. 2 respectively).

πάντας] The masc. is used as the generalizing gender; it includes the two messengers, the widows, and anyone else there (cf. τοὺς ἁγίους, *ver.* 41).

Ταβειθά, ἀνάστηθι] What he said was probably *Tabyĕthā qūmī*: cf. Mk. v. 41, where δ (mistakenly, as the following interpretation shows) has Ταβειθά for ταλειθά ('maiden'). There are a few parallels in this narrative to the story of Jairus's daughter, which may illustrate the principles of Form Criticism. After ἀνάστηθι g m p vg. codd Cypr Ambr hcl* sah (representing δ) add 'in the name of the Lord Jesus Christ'.

ἀνεκάθισεν] Cf. Lk. vii. 15. This verb used intransitively seems confined to a medical context (cf. MM *s.v.*; Harnack, *LP* p. 188; Hobart, pp. 11 f.). 'The circumstantial details of the gradual recovery of Tabitha . . . are quite in the style of medical description' (Hobart, p. 41).

ix. 41

δοὺς δὲ αὐτῇ χεῖρα] Cf. Mk. v. 41 = Lk. viii. 54.

τοὺς ἁγίους καὶ τὰς χήρας] Cf. *vv.* 13, 39; it is not necessarily implied that the widows were not saints.

παρέστησεν] The trans. 1st aor. (1 sg. παρέστησα); contrast παρέστησαν, *ver.* 39, the intrans. 2nd aor. (1 sg. παρέστην).

ix. 42

γνωστὸν δὲ ἐγένετο] Cf. i. 19; xix. 17.

Ἰόππης] א A 33 81 byz prefix τῆς, B C omit it.

ἐπίστευσαν πολλοὶ ἐπὶ τὸν κύριον] For πιστεύω ἐπὶ ('believe on') cf. xi. 17; xvi. 31; xxii. 19.

ix. 43

ἐγένετο κ.τ.λ.] See on iv. 5.

ἡμέρας ἱκανάς] Cf. *ver.* 23. How long Peter's stay in Joppa lasted we cannot say.

παρά τινι Σίμωνι βυρσεῖ] See on *ver.* 11 for Luke's interest in lodgings; cf. xvi. 14; xviii. 3; xix. 24 for notes of people's occupations. Already Peter has taken a step forward in liberalism, in lodging with a man who followed an unclean occupation. As Simon lived by the sea (x. 6), Peter's own occupation of fisherman may have influenced his choice of a lodging in this part of Joppa (cf. Harnack, *The Acts of the Apostles*, p. 85).

2. The Story of Cornelius, x. 1-48

The story of Cornelius, which 'bears the stamp both of probability and truth' (Foakes Jackson), is of great importance not only because it describes how 'a door of faith was opened to the Gentiles', but also because it introduces the fundamental questions of the social intercourse of Jewish Christians with Gentiles and of the admission of Gentiles to the Christian fellowship without circumcision. These were the questions later debated at the Jerusalem Council (see on ch. xv.). Luke's sense of the importance of the Cornelius story appears in his devoting a good part of ch. xi to Peter's rehearsal of it, and in the crucial part which Peter's reference to it plays in the account of the apostolic debate of ch. xv.

(a) Cornelius the Centurion's Vision, x. 1-8

Ἀνὴρ δέ τις ἐν Καισαρίᾳ ὀνόματι Κορνήλιος, ἑκατοντάρχης ἐκ 1
σπείρης τῆς καλουμένης Ἰταλικῆς, εὐσεβὴς καὶ φοβούμενος τὸν θεὸν 2
σὺν παντὶ τῷ οἴκῳ αὐτοῦ, ποιῶν ἐλεημοσύνας πολλὰς τῷ λαῷ καὶ δεό-
μενος τοῦ θεοῦ διὰ παντός, εἶδεν ἐν ὁράματι φανερῶς ὡσεὶ περὶ ὥραν 3
ἐνάτην τῆς ἡμέρας ἄγγελον τοῦ θεοῦ εἰσελθόντα πρὸς αὐτὸν καὶ εἰπόντα
αὐτῷ Κορνήλιε. ὁ δὲ ἀτενίσας αὐτῷ καὶ ἔμφοβος γενόμενος εἶπεν 4
Τί ἐστιν, κύριε; εἶπεν δὲ αὐτῷ Αἱ προσευχαί σου καὶ αἱ ἐλεημοσύναι
σου ἀνέβησαν εἰς μνημόσυνον ἔμπροσθεν τοῦ θεοῦ· καὶ νῦν πέμψον 5
ἄνδρας εἰς Ἰόππην καὶ μετάπεμψαι Σίμωνά τινα ὃς ἐπικαλεῖται
Πέτρος· οὗτος ξενίζεται παρά τινι Σίμωνι βυρσεῖ, ᾧ ἐστὶν οἰκία παρὰ 6
θάλασσαν. ὡς δὲ ἀπῆλθεν ὁ ἄγγελος ὁ λαλῶν αὐτῷ, φωνήσας δύο 7
τῶν οἰκετῶν καὶ στρατιώτην εὐσεβῆ τῶν προσκαρτερούντων αὐτῷ
καὶ ἐξηγησάμενος ἅπαντα αὐτοῖς ἀπέστειλεν αὐτοὺς εἰς τὴν Ἰόππην. 8

x. 1

Κορνήλιος] A frequent name in the Roman world since P. Cornelius Sulla's liberation in 82 B.C. of 10,000 slaves, who attached themselves to his *gens*.

ἑκατοντάρχης] An officer in the Roman army in command of 100 men. In status he corresponded to a non-commissioned officer of to-day. It is remarkable that the first Gentile with whom Jesus came into touch (so far as we know) was a centurion, with reference to whose faith He said, 'Many shall come from the east and the west, and shall sit down with Abraham and Isaac and Jacob in the kingdom of heaven' (Mt. viii. 11). These words now began to be fulfilled in another centurion. Other centurions mentioned in NT are the one in command at the Cross, and Julius, under whose charge Paul sailed to Rome (xxvii. 1, etc.). They all appear in a favourable light; centurions were, indeed, the salt of the Roman army. Polybius (*Hist.* vi. 24) enumerates the various grades of centurions (ταξίαρχοι) and describes their character thus: 'Centurions are desired not to be bold and adventurous so much as good leaders, of steady and prudent mind, not prone to take the offensive or start fighting wantonly, but able when overwhelmed and hard-pressed to stand fast and die at their post.'

ἐκ σπείρης τῆς καλουμένης Ἰταλικῆς] A *σπεῖρα* was a cohort (Lat. *cohors*), the tenth part of a legion, and had a paper strength of 600 men. We have inscriptional evidence of the presence in Syria in A.D. 69 of the auxiliary *cohors II Italica ciuium Romanorum* (Dessau *ILS* 9168), and it may have been there or near there at an earlier date. From A.D. 6 to 41 we have no direct evidence of the identity of the military units in Palestine. From 41 to 44, when Agrippa I reigned (see on xii. 1), his troops at Caesarea seem to have consisted mainly of *Καισαρεῖς καὶ Σεβαστηνοί* (Jos. *Ant.* xix. 9. 1 f.). The events of this chapter are probably to be dated before 41. See further on xxvii. 1, *σπείρης Σεβαστῆς*.

x. 2

εὐσεβὴς καὶ φοβούμενος τὸν θεὸν] 'pious and God-fearing'. Cornelius has every qualification, short of circumcision, which could satisfy the Jews. The expression *φοβούμενος τὸν θεόν* (cf. *ver.* 22; xiii. 16, 26), and the similar *σεβόμενοι τὸν θεόν* (xvi. 14; xviii. 7; cf. Jos. *Ant.* xiv. 7. 2) or simply *σεβόμενοι* (xiii. 50; xvii. 4, 17), though not strictly technical terms (see on xiii. 43), are generally used in Ac. to denote those Gentiles who, though not full proselytes (see on ii. 10), attached themselves to the Jewish religion, practising its monotheistic and imageless worship, attending the synagogue, observing the Sabbath and food-laws, etc. Juvenal (*Sat.* xiv. 96-106) satirizes this tendency in some Roman circles; the father keeps the Sabbath and avoids pork, the son goes farther and becomes a complete proselyte. Cf. Schürer, II. ii. 314 ff.

σὺν παντὶ τῷ οἴκῳ αὐτοῦ] Cf. xvi. 15, 32, 34.

ποιῶν ἐλεημοσύνας . . . καὶ δεόμενος] The association of prayer with almsgiving is common: cf. Mt. vi. 2 ff.; 1 Pet. iv. 7 f.; Tob. xii. 8; *Didaché* xv. 4; 2 Clem. xvi. 4.

τῷ λαῷ] i.e. the people of Israel.

x. 3

ἐν ὁράματι] Cf. ix. 10, 12.

ὡσεὶ περὶ ὥραν ἐνάτην τῆς ἡμέρας] Luke likes to qualify his numerical data with a cautious *ὡς* or *ὡσεί* (see on i. 15). For the ninth hour (about 3 p.m.), the hour of the evening oblation, see on iii. 1.

ἄγγελος τοῦ θεοῦ] For angelic activity in Ac. cf. v. 19; viii. 26; xii. 7 ff., 23; xxvii. 23.

x. 4

ἀτενίσας] See on i. 10.

κύριε] 'Sir', 'my lord'; no theological significance here.

ἀνέβησαν] 'have ascended', like the smoke of a sacrifice. The Heb. word for a burnt-offering is *'ōlāh*, lit., 'an ascending'.

εἰς μνημόσυνον] Cf. Lev. ii. 2, 9, 16 LXX, where *μνημόσυνον* is used of that part of the 'meal-offering' (*minḥāh*) which was burnt, i.e. presented to God. For the sacrificial efficacy of such conduct as that of Cornelius cf. Ps. cxli. 2; Phil. iv. 18; Heb. xiii. 15 f.; Tob. xii. 12 (*ἐγὼ προσήγαγον τὸ μνημόσυνον τῆς προσευχῆς ὑμῶν ἐνώπιον τοῦ ἁγίου*). In *ver.* 31 *ἐμνήσθησαν* is substituted for *ἀνέβησαν εἰς μνημόσυνον*.

x. 6

παρὰ θάλασσαν] See on ix. 43. A tanner lived outside the town, since his trade was regarded by the Jews as unclean. He doubtless used sea-water in his work.

x. 7

τῶν προσκαρτερούντων αὐτῷ] A classical expression: cf. Ps.-Demosthenes, *In Neaeram* 120, *θεραπαίνας τὰς Νεαίρᾳ τότε προσκαρτερούσας*. His *προσκαρτεροῦντες* were 'probably the equivalent of "his orderlies"' (LC), and, like his *οἰκέται*, reckoned in his *οἶκος* ('household': cf. *ver.* 2); it is significant, therefore, that this man, like his officer, is called 'pious'.

(b) Peter's Vision, x. 9-16

Τῇ δὲ ἐπαύριον ὁδοιπορούντων ἐκείνων καὶ τῇ πόλει ἐγγιζόντων 9
ἀνέβη Πέτρος ἐπὶ τὸ δῶμα προσεύξασθαι περὶ ὥραν ἕκτην. ἐγένετο 10
δὲ πρόσπεινος καὶ ἤθελεν γεύσασθαι· παρασκευαζόντων δὲ αὐτῶν
ἐγένετο ἐπ' αὐτὸν ἔκστασις, καὶ θεωρεῖ τὸν οὐρανὸν ἀνεῳγμένον καὶ 11
καταβαῖνον σκεῦός τι ὡς ὀθόνην μεγάλην τέσσαρσιν ἀρχαῖς καθιέμενον
ἐπὶ τῆς γῆς, ἐν ᾧ ὑπῆρχεν πάντα τὰ τετράποδα καὶ ἑρπετὰ τῆς γῆς καὶ 12
πετεινὰ τοῦ οὐρανοῦ. καὶ ἐγένετο φωνὴ πρὸς αὐτόν Ἀναστάς, 13
Πέτρε, θῦσον καὶ φάγε. ὁ δὲ Πέτρος εἶπεν Μηδαμῶς, κύριε, ὅτι 14

οὐδέποτε ἔφαγον πᾶν κοινὸν καὶ ἀκάθαρτον. καὶ φωνὴ πάλιν ἐκ 15
δευτέρου πρὸς αὐτὸν Ἃ ὁ θεὸς ἐκαθάρισεν σὺ μὴ κοίνου. τοῦτο 16
δὲ ἐγένετο ἐπὶ τρίς, καὶ εὐθὺς ἀνελήμφθη τὸ σκεῦος εἰς τὸν οὐρανόν.

x. 9

τῇ δὲ ἐπαύριον κ.τ.λ.] Cornelius saw the angel in the afternoon of the first day, and gave the three messengers their instructions. If they set off early next morning on horseback, they would arrive at Joppa (about 30 miles from Caesarea) about noon (περὶ ὥραν ἕκτην), the time of Peter's vision. See further on *vv.* 23, 24, 30.

ἐπὶ τὸ δῶμα] Probably there was an awning over the roof, and that may have had something to do with the vision of the great sheet. (Another suggestion is that a sail on the horizon, the last thing seen by Peter before he fell asleep, became the sheet of his dream.) Peter probably went up to the roof for quietness and privacy. For visions during prayer cf. *ver.* 30 ; ix. 11 f.

περὶ ὥραν ἕκτην] Noontide was not one of the set seasons for public prayer, according to Schürer (see on iii. 1), but those who prayed privately three times a day (cf. Ps. lv. 17 ; Dan. vi. 10 ; *Didaché* viii. 3, τρὶς τῆς ἡμέρας οὕτω προσεύχεσθε) probably prayed then.

x. 10

πρόσπεινος] The only other known occurrence of this word is in a passage of Demosthenes, a first-century eye-doctor, quoted by the sixth-century medical writer Aëtius (vii. 33). In *ET* xlvi (1934-5), p. 380, F. W. Dillistone suggests that Luke had special knowledge of eye-diseases, and that he attended the lectures of this Demosthenes or read his book.

γεύσασθαι] Noon was the usual time for the ***prandium*** at Rome. In Mod. Gk. γεῦμα is the midday meal.

ἐγένετο] ℵABC ; ἦλθεν P^{45} eth ; ἐπέπεσεν byz.

ἔκστασις] lit., a state in which a man stands outside himself (ἐξίσταται, cf. *ver.* 45 ; ii. 7, 12 ; viii. 9, 11, 13 ; ix. 21 ; xii. 16), a 'trance' : cf. xi. 5 ; xxii. 17, and see on xii. 11. 'As a medical term its use is frequent' (Hobart, p. 41). Elsewhere it has the more general sense of 'amazement' (cf. iii. 10).

x. 11

θεωρεῖ] The historic present is rare in Luke : cf. *ver.* 27.

καταβαῖνον . . . ἀρχαῖς] P^{45} has τέσσαρσιν ἀρχαῖς δεδεμένον σκεῦός τι.

σκεῦός τι] 'a certain object'.

ὀθόνην μεγάλην τέσσαρσιν ἀρχαῖς] 'If Galen expressly comments on the customary use of ἀρχαί, by himself as previously by

Hippocrates, to denote the ends (πέρατα) of a bandage (οἱ ἐπίδεσμοι, and often ὀθόνια and ὀθόνη), it is clear that Acts x. 11, xi. 5 were written by a physician' (Th. Zahn, *INT* iii, p. 162). Hobart has the same argument (p. 218). A less probable suggestion is that ἀρχαί means 'ropes' as, e.g., in Diodorus i. 35. 10 (on harpooning a hippopotamus, εἶθ' ἐνὶ τῶν ἐμπαγέντων ἐνάπτοντες ἀρχὰς στυππινὰς ἀφιᾶσι μέχρι ἂν ὅτου παραλυθῇ) : cf. our expression 'rope-ends'.

x. 12

πάντα τὰ τετράποδα καὶ ἑρπετὰ τῆς γῆς καὶ πετεινὰ τοῦ οὐρανοῦ] For this threefold division of the animal world cf. Gen. vi. 20 LXX, where κτήνη corresponds to τετράποδα here. After τετράποδα byz continues: τῆς γῆς καὶ τὰ θηρία καὶ τὰ ἑρπετὰ καὶ τὰ πετεινὰ τοῦ οὐρανοῦ (cf. xi. 6).

x. 13

Πέτρε] om P^{45}.

θῦσον καὶ φάγε] Cf. Dt. xii. 15, θύσεις καὶ φάγῃ. In this sense θύω has lost its original force 'to sacrifice': cf. Mt. xxii. 4; Lk. xv. 23; Jn. x. 10; 1 Macc. vii. 19.

x. 14

Μηδαμῶς, κύριε κ.τ.λ.] Cf. Ezekiel's protest, μηδαμῶς, κύριε θεὲ τοῦ Ἰσραήλ· εἰ ἡ ψυχή μου οὐ μεμίανται ἐν ἀκαθαρσίᾳ, καὶ θηριάλωτον καὶ θνησιμαῖον οὐ βέβρωκα ἀπὸ γενέσεώς μου ἕως τοῦ νῦν, οὐδὲ εἰσελήλυθεν εἰς τὸ στόμα μου πᾶν κρέας ἕωλον (Ezek. iv. 14).

οὐδέποτε . . . πᾶν] This construction is a characteristic Semitism, being frequent in OT and thence in LXX (cf. Ezek. iv. 14 quoted above); but it can also be paralleled from the vernacular of the papyri; cf. also Aristophanes, *Wasps* 1091, πάντα μὴ δεδοικέναι ('to fear nothing').

κοινὸν καὶ ἀκάθαρτον] Cf. Lev. xi for the Jewish food-laws. Those animals were clean which both chewed the cud and had cloven hooves; many of those on the sheet were thus disqualified.

x. 15

πάλιν ἐκ δευτέρου] Pleonasm; so Mt. xxvi. 42; cf. Jn. iv. 54; xxi. 16, πάλιν δεύτερον. For ἐκ δευτέρου cf. xi. 9; it occurs also in LXX (7 times) and papyri.

ἐκαθάρισεν] Cf. Mk. vii. 14 ff., especially *ver.* 19, where καθαρίζων πάντα τὰ βρώματα may reflect Peter's own comment.

σὺ μὴ κοίνου] The *present* imperative implies that he is not to go on doing what he is already doing. Cf. xviii. 9; xx. 10. For this sense of *κοινόω*, 'reckon common' (= *κοινὸν . . . λέγειν*, *ver.* 28), cf. other verbs in *-όω*, e.g., *δικαιόω*, 'justify', i.e., to pronounce or reckon righteous (xiii. 39). Elsewhere *κοινόω* means 'defile', 'profane', like classical *βεβηλόω* (xxiv. 6).

x. 16

καὶ εὐθὺς] ℵ A B C E 81 vg ; *καὶ πάλιν* byz ; *καὶ* (*ἀνελήμφθη*) *πάλιν* D ; *καί* 36 307 P^{45} d p sah boh arm Orig Ambr.

(c) The Messengers of Cornelius arrive at Joppa, x. 17-23a

Ὡς δὲ ἐν ἑαυτῷ διηπόρει ὁ Πέτρος τί ἂν εἴη τὸ ὅραμα ὃ εἶδεν, 17
ἰδοὺ οἱ ἄνδρες οἱ ἀπεσταλμένοι ὑπὸ τοῦ Κορνηλίου διερωτήσαντες
τὴν οἰκίαν τοῦ Σίμωνος ἐπέστησαν ἐπὶ τὸν πυλῶνα, καὶ φωνήσαντες 18
ἐπύθοντο εἰ Σίμων ὁ ἐπικαλούμενος Πέτρος ἐνθάδε ξενίζεται. Τοῦ 19
δὲ Πέτρου διενθυμουμένου περὶ τοῦ ὁράματος εἶπεν τὸ πνεῦμα Ἰδοὺ
ἄνδρες δύο ζητοῦντές σε· ἀλλὰ ἀναστὰς κατάβηθι καὶ πορεύου σὺν 20
αὐτοῖς μηδὲν διακρινόμενος, ὅτι ἐγὼ ἀπέσταλκα αὐτούς. καταβὰς 21
δὲ Πέτρος πρὸς τοὺς ἄνδρας εἶπεν Ἰδοὺ ἐγώ εἰμι ὃν ζητεῖτε· τίς
ἡ αἰτία δι' ἣν πάρεστε; οἱ δὲ εἶπαν Κορνήλιος ἑκατοντάρχης, ἀνὴρ 22
δίκαιος καὶ φοβούμενος τὸν θεὸν μαρτυρούμενός τε ὑπὸ ὅλου τοῦ
ἔθνους τῶν Ἰουδαίων ἐχρηματίσθη ὑπὸ ἀγγέλου ἁγίου μεταπέμψασθαί
σε εἰς τὸν οἶκον αὐτοῦ καὶ ἀκοῦσαι ῥήματα παρὰ σοῦ. εἰσκαλεσάμενος 23
οὖν αὐτοὺς ἐξένισεν.

x. 17

διηπόρει] Cf. ii. 12. Luke is fond of compounds with *διά*, cf. also *διερωτήσαντες* in this verse.

τί ἂν εἴη] Potential construction in an indirect question, as in v. 24. There is practically no difference in force between this and *τίς εἴη* (xxi. 33).

x. 18

ἐπύθοντο] B C ; *ἐπυνθάνοντο* ℵ A D 81 P^{45} al (followed by Soden).

εἰ] Probably introducing direct question (cf. i. 6 ; vii. 1 ; xix. 2 ; xxi. 37 ; xxii. 25). For direct questions after *πυνθάνομαι* cf. iv. 7 ; xxiii. 19.

x. 19

εἶπεν τὸ πνεῦμα] Cf. viii. 26 ; xvi. 7 ; xix. 21 ; xx. 23 for such direction. After *πνεῦμα* ℵ A C 81 al add *αὐτῷ*, which is omitted in B boh (D 33 P^{45} byz al put it before *τὸ πνεῦμα*).

δύο] B ; *τρεῖς* ℵ A C E 33 81 e g vg pesh hcl.mg. sah boh al ; om δ byz. The reading of B, being the most difficult, because of the discrepancy with *ver.* 7 and xi. 11, is preferred by Ropes, who suggests that the two servants alone (*ver.* 7) may be thought of as responsible messengers, the soldier acting as a guard. Cf. Homer, *Odyssey* ix. 90, x. 102, ἄνδρε δύω κρίνας, τρίτατον κήρυχ' ἅμ' ὀπάσσας.

x. 20

ἀναστὰς] D has ἀνάστα (cf. ix. 11). For ἀναστάς see on v. 6.

ἐγὼ] The Holy Spirit. What was the connection between the Spirit and the angel who appeared to Cornelius? For a similar problem see on viii. 26. And whose voice did Peter hear in *vv.* 13, 15? The voice of one whom he recognized as 'Lord'. As it was by the Holy Spirit that the risen Christ imparted His presence to the disciples after His ascension, it is often very difficult to distinguish between the risen Christ and the Spirit (cf. xvi. 7, τὸ πνεῦμα Ἰησοῦ).

x. 21

ἄνδρας] byz adds τοὺς ἀπεσταλμένους ἀπὸ (τοῦ) Κορνηλίου πρὸς αὐτόν.

x. 22

ἔθνος] For ἔθνος used of the Jewish nation cf. xxiv. 2, 10, 17; xxvi. 4; xxviii. 19.

ἐχρηματίσθη] 'was instructed (divinely)': cf. Mt. ii. 12, 22; Lk. ii. 26; Heb. viii. 5; xi. 7; xii. 25 (cf. Rom. xi. 4, χρηματισμός); Jer. xxxii. (xxv.) 30; xxxvi. (xxix.) 23; xxxvii. (xxx.) 2; xliii. (xxxvi.) 2, 4. (The verb in xi. 26 is different: see note *ad loc.*) The sense 'to give a divine warning' is paralleled in papyri (cf. MM) and in inscriptions (*Syll.* 1173).

ῥήματα παρὰ σοῦ] Amplified in xi. 14.

(d) Peter enters the House of Cornelius, x. 23b-33

Τῇ δὲ ἐπαύριον ἀναστὰς ἐξῆλθεν σὺν αὐτοῖς, καί τινες τῶν ἀδελφῶν 23
τῶν ἀπὸ Ἰόππης συνῆλθαν αὐτῷ. τῇ δὲ ἐπαύριον εἰσῆλθεν εἰς τὴν 24
Καισαρίαν· ὁ δὲ Κορνήλιος ἦν προσδοκῶν αὐτοὺς συνκαλεσάμενος
τοὺς συγγενεῖς αὐτοῦ καὶ τοὺς ἀναγκαίους φίλους. Ὡς δὲ ἐγένετο 25
τοῦ εἰσελθεῖν τὸν Πέτρον, συναντήσας αὐτῷ ὁ Κορνήλιος πεσὼν ἐπὶ
τοὺς πόδας προσεκύνησεν. ὁ δὲ Πέτρος ἤγειρεν αὐτὸν λέγων 26
Ἀνάστηθι· καὶ ἐγὼ αὐτὸς ἄνθρωπός εἰμι. καὶ συνομιλῶν αὐτῷ 27
εἰσῆλθεν, καὶ εὑρίσκει συνεληλυθότας πολλούς, ἔφη τε πρὸς αὐτούς 28
Ὑμεῖς ἐπίστασθε ὡς ἀθέμιτόν ἐστιν ἀνδρὶ Ἰουδαίῳ κολλᾶσθαι ἢ
προσέρχεσθαι ἀλλοφύλῳ· κἀμοὶ ὁ θεὸς ἔδειξεν μηδένα κοινὸν ἢ ἀκά- 29
θαρτον λέγειν ἄνθρωπον· διὸ καὶ ἀναντιρήτως ἦλθον μεταπεμφθείς.

πυνθάνομαι οὖν τίνι λόγῳ μετεπέμψασθέ με. καὶ ὁ Κορνήλιος ἔφη 30
Ἀπὸ τετάρτης ἡμέρας μέχρι ταύτης τῆς ὥρας ἤμην τὴν ἐνάτην προσευχόμενος ἐν τῷ οἴκῳ μου, καὶ ἰδοὺ ἀνὴρ ἔστη ἐνώπιόν μου ἐν ἐσθῆτι
λαμπρᾷ καί φησι Κορνήλιε, εἰσηκούσθη σου ἡ προσευχὴ καὶ αἱ 31
ἐλεημοσύναι σου ἐμνήσθησαν ἐνώπιον τοῦ θεοῦ· πέμψον οὖν εἰς 32
Ἰόππην καί μετακάλεσαι Σίμωνα ὃς ἐπικαλεῖται Πέτρος· οὗτος
ξενίζεται ἐν οἰκίᾳ Σίμωνος βυρσέως παρὰ θάλασσαν. ἐξαυτῆς οὖν 33
ἔπεμψα πρὸς σέ, σύ τε καλῶς ἐποίησας παραγενόμενος. νῦν οὖν
πάντες ἡμεῖς ἐνώπιον τοῦ θεοῦ πάρεσμεν ἀκοῦσαι πάντα τὰ προσ-
τεταγμένα σοι ὑπὸ τοῦ κυρίου.

x. 23

τῇ δὲ ἐπαύριον] It was midday on the second day (cf. *ver.* 9) before the messengers arrived at Joppa; by the time Peter had entertained them, it was too late to travel to Caesarea, and so they set out on the third day.

τινες τῶν ἀδελφῶν] Six in number, according to xi. 12.

x. 24

τῇ δὲ ἐπαύριον] They set out for Caesarea on the third day; there were ten altogether, and, travelling more slowly than the three messengers had done on the second day, they arrived at Caesarea on the fourth day: cf. *ver.* 30, *ἀπὸ τετάρτης ἡμέρας* (but see note on text *ad loc.*).

συνκαλεσάμενος τοὺς συγγενεῖς αὐτοῦ καὶ τοὺς ἀναγκαίους φίλους] δ (D p hcl.mg al) adds *καὶ* before *συνκαλεσάμενος* and *περιέμεινεν* after *φίλους*.

ἀναγκαίους] 'intimate', 'familiar'.

x. 25

ὡς δὲ ἐγένετο κ.τ.λ.] δ, continuing its reconstruction from *ver.* 24, gives this verse thus: *προσεγγίζοντος δὲ τοῦ Πέτρου εἰς τὴν Καισαρίαν, προδραμὼν εἷς τῶν δούλων διεσάφησεν παραγεγονέναι αὐτόν. ὁ δὲ Κορνήλιος ἐκπηδήσας καὶ συναντήσας αὐτῷ πεσὼν πρὸς τοὺς πόδας προσεκύνησεν αὐτόν* (D g hcl.mg). This no doubt represents what actually took place.

ὡς δὲ ἐγένετο τοῦ εἰσελθεῖν] In NT this construction is found only here and at ii. 1 D (see *ad loc.*); cf. *Acta Barnabae* vii, *ὡς δὲ ἐγένετο τοῦ τελέσαι αὐτοὺς διδάσκοντας* (quoted by LC). For similar constructions with *τοῦ* and the infin., cf. iii. 12; xxvii. 1; Lk. xvii. 1. The plain infin. would have sufficed, or the infin. preceded by *τό*.

προσεκύνησεν] The verb is used of paying homage to someone of whom a favour is being asked: cf. Mt. viii. 2; ix. 18; xv. 25; xviii. 26; xx. 20.

x. 26

Ἀνάστηθι· καὶ ἐγὼ αὐτὸς ἄνθρωπός εἰμι] For the protest of Peter cf. xiv. 14 f.; Rev. xix. 10; xxii. 9.

x. 27

συνομιλῶν αὐτῷ] 'talking to him': see on *ὁμιλήσας*, xx. 11.

εὑρίσκει] Historic present: see on *θεωρεῖ*, *ver.* 11.

x. 28

ἐπίστασθε] D prefixes *βέλτιον* (cf. *κάλλιον*, xxv. 10).

ἀθέμιτον] Not that all intercourse with Gentiles was absolutely prohibited, but all such intercourse rendered a Jew ceremonially unclean, as did even the entering of a Gentile house (cf. Jn. xviii. 28) or the handling of articles belonging to Gentiles. The most ordinary kinds of food, such as bread, oil, or milk, coming from Gentiles, could not be eaten by a strict Jew, not to speak of flesh, which might have been offered in sacrifice to idols (see on xv. 20, 29), and which in any case still contained blood. It was thus a very difficult thing for Jews to travel in foreign lands (cf. Jos. *Vita* 3). And of all intercourse with Gentiles, the most intolerable was sitting at meat with them (cf. xi. 3). In this context *ἀθέμιτον* (cf. 1 Pet. iv. 3) might almost be rendered 'tabu'.

ἀλλοφύλῳ] Common in classical and vernacular Gk. in the sense 'foreigner'; but its use here may reflect its frequent LXX usage as the equivalent of 'Philistine', i.e., 'uncircumcised'. Cf. *ἀλλογενής* in the Temple inscription quoted in the note on xxi. 28; Josephus (*BJ* v. 5. 2), alluding to this inscription, replaces *ἀλλογενής* by *ἀλλόφυλος*.

x. 29

ἀναντιρήτως] 'without demur': practically equivalent to *μηδὲν διακρινάμενος* (*ver.* 20), *μηδὲν διακρίναντα* (xi. 12, *q.v.*).

τίνι λόγῳ] 'why'; lit., 'with what reason'.

x. 30

ἀπὸ τετάρτης ἡμέρας] Inclusive reckoning; we should say 'three days ago'. D has *ἀπὸ τῆς τρίτης ἡμέρας*, thus shortening the time taken for the journey to Caesarea (see on *vv.* 23, 24). Torrey explains this use of *ἀπό* as an Aramaism.

μέχρι ταύτης τῆς ὥρας] It looks as if it was again 'the ninth hour' (cf. *ver.* 3). D has *μέχρι τῆς ἄρτι ὥρας*.

ἤμην τὴν ἐνάτην προσευχόμενος] δ has *ἤμην νηστεύων τὴν ἐνάτην τε προσευχόμενος*. Notice the pietistic addition of 'fasting'. It may be true enough, but the δ editor refuses to leave anything to the reader's imagination (cf. *ver.* 25).

ἐν ἐσθῆτι λαμπρᾷ] For angelic garb see on i. 10.

x. 31

ἐμνήσθησαν] Representing ἀνέβησαν εἰς μνημόσυνον of *ver.* 4.

x. 32

παρὰ θάλασσαν] δ byz add ὃς παραγενόμενος λαλήσει σοι, amplifying from xi. 14.

x. 33

ἔπεμψα πρὸς σέ] δ adds unnecessarily παρακαλῶν ἐλθεῖν πρὸς ἡμᾶς, as after καλῶς ἐποίησας it adds ἐν τάχει.

σὺ δὲ καλῶς ἐποίησας παραγενόμενος] 'you were so kind as to come'; an expression of thanks. The aor. ptc. must be regarded as having simultaneous force. καλῶς ποιήσεις with the aor. ptc. is a means of expressing a polite request, 'please do so and so' (cf. Phil. iv. 14; 3 Jn. 6). The meaning of εὖ πράξετε in xv. 29 (*q.v.*) is different.

πάντες] om P^{45}.

ἐνώπιον τοῦ θεοῦ] om P^{45}.

(e) The Good News First Preached to Gentiles, x. 34-43

ἀνοίξας δὲ Πέτρος τὸ στόμα εἶπεν Ἐπ' ἀληθείας καταλαμβάνομαι 34
ὅτι οὐκ ἔστιν προσωπολήμπτης ὁ θεός, ἀλλ' ἐν παντὶ ἔθνει ὁ φοβού- 35
μενος αὐτὸν καὶ ἐργαζόμενος δικαιοσύνην δεκτὸς αὐτῷ ἐστίν. τὸν 36
λόγον ἀπέστειλεν τοῖς υἱοῖς Ἰσραὴλ εὐαγγελιζόμενος εἰρήνην διὰ
Ἰησοῦ Χριστοῦ· οὗτός ἐστιν πάντων κύριος. ὑμεῖς οἴδατε τὸ γενό- 37
μενον ῥῆμα καθ' ὅλης τῆς Ἰουδαίας, ἀρξάμενος ἀπὸ τῆς Γαλιλαίας
μετὰ τὸ βάπτισμα ὃ ἐκήρυξεν Ἰωάνης, Ἰησοῦν τὸν ἀπὸ Ναζαρέθ, 38
ὡς ἔχρισεν αὐτὸν ὁ θεὸς πνεύματι ἁγίῳ καὶ δυνάμει, ὃς διῆλθεν εὐερ-
γετῶν καὶ ἰώμενος πάντας τοὺς καταδυναστευομένους ὑπὸ τοῦ διαβόλου,
ὅτι ὁ θεὸς ἦν μετ' αὐτοῦ· καὶ ἡμεῖς μάρτυρες πάντων ὧν ἐποίησεν ἔν 39
τε τῇ χώρᾳ τῶν Ἰουδαίων καὶ Ἰερουσαλήμ· ὃν καὶ ἀνεῖλαν κρεμάσαντες ἐπὶ ξύλου. τοῦτον ὁ θεὸς ἤγειρεν τῇ τρίτῃ ἡμέρᾳ καὶ ἔδωκεν 40
αὐτὸν ἐμφανῆ γενέσθαι, οὐ παντὶ τῷ λαῷ ἀλλὰ μάρτυσι τοῖς προκεχει- 41
ροτονημένοις ὑπὸ τοῦ θεοῦ, ἡμῖν, οἵτινες συνεφάγομεν καὶ συνεπίομεν
αὐτῷ μετὰ τὸ ἀναστῆναι αὐτὸν ἐκ νεκρῶν· καὶ παρήγγειλεν ἡμῖν 42
κηρύξαι τῷ λαῷ καὶ διαμαρτύρασθαι ὅτι οὗτός ἐστιν ὁ ὡρισμένος ὑπο
τοῦ θεοῦ κριτὴς ζώντων καὶ νεκρῶν. τούτῳ πάντες οἱ προφῆται μαρ- 43
τυροῦσιν, ἄφεσιν ἁμαρτιῶν λαβεῖν διὰ τοῦ ὀνόματος αὐτοῦ πάντα τὸν
πιστεύοντα εἰς αὐτόν.

x. 34

ἀνοίξας δὲ Πέτρος τὸ στόμα] D P^{45} g have τὸ στόμα before Πέτρος. The phrase is used to introduce some weighty utterance: cf. viii. 35; Mt. v. 2. 'The address of Peter to Cornelius is peculiarly appropriate to the occasion' (Foakes Jackson).

οὐκ ἔστιν προσωπολήμπτης ὁ θεός] The only NT example of προσωπολήμπτης, and its earliest known occurrence in Greek literature. This and kindred words are confined to Biblical and ecclesiastical Gk.: cf. Rom. ii. 11; Eph. vi. 9; Col. iii. 25; Jas. ii. 1; 1 Pet. i. 17; Ps. Sol. ii. 19; 1 Clem. i. 3; Ep. Barnab. iv. 12; Ep. Polycarp. vi. 1. They represent Heb. *nāsā pānīm*, 'to lift (someone's) face', i.e., to show favour, and hence in a bad sense, to show favouritism. This was literally rendered πρόσωπον λαμβάνω, cf. Lk. xx. 21; Gal. ii. 6; and in LXX cf. Dt. x. 17 (ὁ θεὸς . . . ὅστις οὐ θαυμάζει πρόσωπον); Ps. lxxxii. 2 (LXX lxxxi), πρόσωπα ἁμαρτωλῶν λαμβάνετε.

x. 35

δικαιοσύνην] Primarily, no doubt, 'righteousness' in the widest sense; but it is specially relevant in the case of Cornelius to remember that, as in Mt. vi. 1, the word was commonly used among the Jews to denote almsgiving (see Jastrow's dictionary s.v. צְדָקָה *ṣĕdāqāh*).

δεκτὸς] Primarily 'acceptable' but also 'accepted': cf. Lk. iv. 19, 24. The undeviating principle in divine judgment is 'To every man according to his works' (cf. Rom. ii. 6; Rev. xx. 12 f., etc.), and is so stated throughout the Bible, from Gen. iv. 7 ('If thou doest well, shalt thou not be accepted?') to Rev. xxii. 12 ('to each man according as his work is').

x. 36

The summary of Peter's address (*vv.* 36-43) gives the apostolic Kerygma in a nutshell. It contains more information about the life and work of Jesus before the Cross than Peter's previous sermons have given, because Gentiles might not be expected to have so much knowledge of these as a Palestinian Jewish audience had. The scope of the Kerygma, as outlined here and elsewhere, corresponds to that of Mk. In *ET* xliii (1931-2), pp. 396 ff., Prof. C. H. Dodd, examining K. L. Schmidt's thesis that Mk. consists of independent *pericopae* connected by short editorial generalizing summaries (*Sammelberichte*) which have no historical value, finds that these connecting summaries when put together form a coherent outline of the life and work of Jesus, such as formed the substance of apostolic preaching. This Markan outline, summarizing the events from the preaching of the Baptist to the Resurrection, corresponds closely to the outlines in Ac. x. 36 ff.; xiii. 23 ff.; and fragments of such an outline may be recognized in ii. 14 ff.; iii. 13 ff.; iv. 10 ff.; v. 30 ff.; 1 Cor. xi. 23-5; xv. 3-7. Cf. also C. H. Dodd's *The Apostolic Preaching and its Developments.*

τὸν λόγον ἀπέστειλεν] Cf. Ps. cvii. 20 (LXX cvi), *ἀπέστειλεν τὸν λόγον αὐτοῦ*, and Ps. cxlvii. 18 (LXX 7), *ἀποστελεῖ τὸν λόγον αὐτοῦ.*

εὐαγγελιζόμενος εἰρήνην] Cf. *ὡς πόδες εὐαγγελιζομένου ἀκοὴν εἰρήνης*, Isa. lii. 7; *οἱ πόδες εὐαγγελιζομένου καὶ ἀπαγγέλλοντος εἰρήνην*, Nah. i. 15 (LXX ii. 1).

x. 36ff.

τὸν λόγον ἀπέστειλεν . . . Ἰησοῦν τὸν ἀπὸ Ναζαρέθ] WH follow B (except in so far as B omits *ὑμεῖς* and has *κήρυγμα* for *βάπτισμα*). This text makes good sense if it is rendered, 'He sent His Word to the children of Israel, telling the good news of peace through Jesus Christ—He is Lord of all. You know what took place throughout the whole of Judaea, beginning from Galilee, after the baptism which John proclaimed, concerning Jesus of Nazareth, how God anointed Him. . . .' The construction is difficult, however, and shows signs of translation from Aram. Torrey shows (*CDA*, pp. 27, 35 f.) that if, following ℵ C D E byz e pesh hcl* (as we should), we read *ὅν* after *τὸν λόγον*, the whole passage can be literally translated into grammatical and intelligible Aram., which may be rendered, 'As for the Word which the Lord of All sent to the children of Israel, proclaiming good tidings of peace through Jesus Christ, you know what took place . . . .' Peter no doubt addressed his audience in Gk., or spoke through an interpreter, but the narrative was possibly preserved in an Aram. document. The Greek is certainly not Luke's free composition; if it were, it would be much clearer. The construction is recast in δ so as to read more fluently: *τὸν γὰρ λόγον ὃν ἀπέστειλεν τοῖς υἱοῖς Ἰσραὴλ εὐαγγελιζόμενος εἰρήνην διὰ Ἰησοῦ Χριστοῦ (οὗτός ἐστιν πάντων κύριος) ὑμεῖς οἴδατε, τὸ γενόμενον καθ' ὅλης Ἰουδαίας· ἀρξάμενος γὰρ ἀπὸ τῆς Γαλιλαίας, μετὰ τὸ βάπτισμα ὃ ἐκήρυξεν Ἰωάνης, Ἰησοῦς ὁ ἀπὸ Ναζαρέθ, ὃν ἔχρισεν ὁ θεὸς ἁγίῳ πνεύματι καὶ δυνάμει, οὗτος διῆλθεν κ.τ.λ.* (D has signs of contamination with the β text; for the restoration of the δ text cf. Moulton, *Proleg.*, p. 240.)

οὗτός ἐστιν πάντων κύριος] Parenthetic but none the less emphatic.

x. 37

τὸ γενόμενον ῥῆμα] 'the thing that took place': for this sense of *ῥῆμα* cf. v. 32.

Ἰουδαίας] In the wider sense, including Galilee—in short, what we understand by 'Palestine'.

ἀρξάμενος] A *nominativus pendens*, to be taken adverbially. See on i. 22, where ἀρξάμενος, though grammatically it could agree with Ἰησοῦς, is probably adverbial, representing Aram. *mĕshārē*. Here A D e p vg Iren.lat add γάρ, while 81 P^{45} byz have ἀρξάμενον for ἀρξάμενος.

x. 38

Ἰησοῦν τὸν ἀπὸ Ναζαρέθ] These words, the logical object of ἔχρισεν, are placed in front of their clause for reasons of emphasis (see on ii. 22) and caught up in the clause to which they properly belong by αὐτόν.

ὡς ἔχρισεν αὐτὸν κ.τ.λ.] This noun clause is parallel to τὸ γενόμενον ῥῆμα and is subordinate to οἴδατε. The anointing was at His baptism. Cf. iv. 27 and Isa. lxi. 1 (quoted in Lk. iv. 18 f.). The Christology of this sermon, like that of the earlier speeches in Ac., is the primitive Christology of Mk. rather than the more developed Christology of Paul; this is significant in view of the traditional dependence of Mk. on Peter.

πνεύματι ἁγίῳ καὶ δυνάμει] Cf. Ps. Sol. xvii. 42, ὁ θεὸς κατηργάσατο αὐτὸν δυνατὸν ἐν πνεύματι ἁγίῳ.

διῆλθεν] περιῆλθεν P^{45}.

εὐεργετῶν] Cf. the royal title εὐεργέτης (Lk. xxii. 25).

καταδυναστευομένους] The word has one other occurrence in NT (Jas. ii. 6); it appears in Greek literature from Xenophon onwards.

διαβόλου] lit., 'slanderer': Gk. equivalent of Satan (see on v. 3). In the Gospels not only demon-possession, but certain other ailments as well, are attributed to Satanic agency (cf. Lk. xiii. 16), not to mention unbelief and falsehood (cf. Mt. xiii. 19, 39; Jn. viii. 44).

x. 39

ἡμεῖς μάρτυρες] Cf. i. 8, 22; ii. 32, etc., for this emphasis on personal testimony.

ἐν . . . τῇ χώρᾳ τῶν Ἰουδαίων] In the same sense as Ἰουδαία, *ver.* 37.

κρεμάσαντες ἐπὶ ξύλου] See on v. 30, where the same phrase occurs.

x. 40

τοῦτον] Emphatic as in ii. 32; v. 31.

τῇ τρίτῃ ἡμέρᾳ] μετὰ τὴν τρίτην ἡμέραν D (an attempt at harmonization with Mt. xxvii. 63, etc.).

ἔδωκεν αὐτὸν ἐμφανῆ γενέσθαι] For *δίδωμι* followed by acc. and infin., cf. ii. 27 ; xiv. 3.

x. 41

συνεφάγομεν καὶ συνεπίομεν αὐτῷ] The eating and drinking were very important, being among the most convincing of the many proofs of His bodily resurrection. Cf. Lk. xxiv. 41, 43. δ adds *καὶ συνανεστράφημεν μετὰ τὸ ἀναστῆναι ἐκ νεκρῶν ἡμέρας τεσσεράκοντα*, harmonizing with i. 3.

x. 42

παρήγγειλεν] *ἐνετείλατο* D (cf. i. 2).

ὡρισμένος] Cf. ii. 23 ; iii. 20, and especially xvii. 31 (*ἐν ἀνδρὶ ᾧ ὥρισεν*), where the verb is used, as here, of His appointment as Judge.

κριτὴς ζώντων καὶ νεκρῶν] Cf. 1 Pet. iv. 5 ; 2 Tim. iv. 1.

x. 43

ἄφεσιν ἁμαρτιῶν] For this as a subject of prophecy, cf. iii. 18 ff. ; Lk. xxiv. 46 f. The prophets included those who are quoted throughout Ac. For remission of sins through faith in Christ, cf. xiii. 38 f. (There Paul adds justification to forgiveness, but the Gospel is the same, whether preached by Peter or Paul, and that not only on Luke's testimony, but on Paul's own, 1 Cor. xv. 11.)

πιστεύοντα εἰς αὐτόν] Cf. xiv. 23 ; xix. 4. Cf. also ix. 42 ; xi. 17 ; xvi. 31 for *πιστεύω ἐπί* ('believe on') ; and v. 14 ; viii. 12 ; xvi. 34 ; xviii. 8 ; xxiv. 14 ; xxvi. 27 ; xxvii. 25 for *πιστεύω* with the dat. See on v. 14.

(f) The Gentiles, receiving the Holy Spirit, are baptized, x. 44-48

Ἔτι λαλοῦντος τοῦ Πέτρου τὰ ῥήματα ταῦτα ἐπέπεσε τὸ πνεῦμα 44
τὸ ἅγιον ἐπὶ πάντας τοὺς ἀκούοντας τὸν λόγον. καὶ ἐξέστησαν οἱ 45
ἐκ περιτομῆς πιστοὶ οἳ συνῆλθαν τῷ Πέτρῳ, ὅτι καὶ ἐπὶ τὰ ἔθνη ἡ
δωρεὰ τοῦ πνεύματος τοῦ ἁγίου ἐκκέχυται· ἤκουον γὰρ αὐτῶν 46
λαλούντων γλώσσαις καὶ μεγαλυνόντων τὸν θεόν. τότε ἀπεκρίθη
Πέτρος Μήτι τὸ ὕδωρ δύναται κωλῦσαί τις τοῦ μὴ βαπτισθῆναι 47
τούτους οἵτινες τὸ πνεῦμα τὸ ἅγιον ἔλαβον ὡς καὶ ἡμεῖς; προσέταξεν 48
δὲ αὐτοὺς ἐν τῷ ὀνόματι Ἰησοῦ Χριστοῦ βαπτισθῆναι. τότε ἠρώτησαν
αὐτὸν ἐπιμεῖναι ἡμέρας τινάς.

x. 44

ἐπέπεσε τὸ πνεῦμα τὸ ἅγιον] Chase fittingly calls this day 'the Pentecost of the Gentile world' (*Credibility*, p. 79). As at Pentecost Peter had used the keys of the kingdom of heaven to admit

Jewish believers, so now he used them to open a door of faith to Gentiles. The coming of the Spirit upon them was manifested by outward signs, as at Pentecost.

x. 45

ἐξέστησαν] Cf. ii. 12, *ἐξίσταντο*, of those who saw the first manifestation of the Spirit's descent.

οἱ ἐκ περιτομῆς πιστοὶ] i.e., the Jewish believers: cf. xi. 2; Gal. ii. 12; Col. iv. 11; Tit. i. 10. Outside Ac., the expression denotes Jewish believers who insisted on the observance by Gentile Christians of circumcision and the Mosaic Law. For the construction, cf. xii. 1 (*τινας τῶν ἀπὸ τῆς ἐκκλησίας*); also Aeschines, *Timarch.* 54, *τῶν δὲ ἐκ τῆς διατριβῆς ταύτης*.

οἱ] B; *ὅσοι* ℵ A D 81 byz (so Soden and Ropes).

x. 46

γλώσσαις] δ adds *ἑτέραις* (cf. ii. 4; xix. 6).

μεγαλυνόντων τὸν θεόν] Equivalent to *λαλούντων τὰ μεγαλεῖα τοῦ θεοῦ*, ii. 11.

x. 47

ἀπεκρίθη] Cf. v. 8 for this use of *ἀποκρίνομαι* where apparently nothing has been said which could require an answer. Simply translate, 'said'.

κωλῦσαι . . . τοῦ μὴ βαπτισθῆναι] In classical Gk. *κωλύω* normally takes the plain infin., as in viii. 36. The longer construction is apparently due to the fact that *κωλῦσαι* has two objects here. Cf. xiv. 18; xx. 20, 27, and for *τοῦ* with infin. see on *ver.* 25.

x. 48

προσέταξεν δὲ] δ has *τότε προσέταξεν*. (The δ editor is fond of *τότε*, using it about twice as often as the β text.) Was the order given to the Gentiles ('Be baptized') or to Peter's companions ('Baptize them')? On the analogy of ii. 38; xxii. 16, the former is more likely.

ἐν τῷ ὀνόματι Ἰησοῦ Χριστοῦ] As in ii. 38 (*q.v.*); see also on viii. 16. Grammatically these words might be taken with *προσέταξεν*, but the analogy of ii. 38, etc., makes it fairly certain that they go with *βαπτισθῆναι*. There is no suggestion that Cornelius became circumcised. δ adds *τοῦ κυρίου* before *Ἰησοῦ Χριστοῦ*, as in ii. 38; v. 42; see also on i. 21.

3. Peter Defends his Action, xi. 1-18

(a) Peter accused of Intercourse with Gentiles, xi. 1-3

Ἤκουσαν δὲ οἱ ἀπόστολοι καὶ οἱ ἀδελφοὶ οἱ ὄντες κατὰ τὴν Ἰουδαίαν 1
ὅτι καὶ τὰ ἔθνη ἐδέξαντο τὸν λόγον τοῦ θεοῦ. Ὅτε δὲ ἀνέβη Πέτρος 2
εἰς Ἰερουσαλήμ, διεκρίνοντο πρὸς αὐτὸν οἱ ἐκ περιτομῆς λέγοντες ὅτι 3
εἰσῆλθεν πρὸς ἄνδρας ἀκροβυστίαν ἔχοντας καὶ συνέφαγεν αὐτοῖς.

xi. 1

ἤκουσαν . . . Ἰουδαίαν] δ (D pesh) has *ἀκουστὸν δὲ ἐγένετο τοῖς ἀποστόλοις καὶ τοῖς ἀδελφοῖς τοῖς ἐν τῇ Ἰουδαίᾳ.*

τὰ ἔθνη ἐδέξαντο] *τὰ ἔθνη ἐδέξατο* D. The classical rule that neut. plur. subjects take their verbs in the sing. is not always observed in NT Gk., especially when, as here, the noun denotes persons.

τὸν λόγον τοῦ θεοῦ] δ (g p^{corr} vg.codd hcl*) adds *καὶ ἐδόξαζον τὸν θεόν.*

xi. 2

Ὅτε δὲ ἀνέβη Πέτρος κ.τ.λ.] In δ (D and, as far as *διδάσκων αὐτούς*, hcl*) this verse is recast as follows: *ὁ μὲν οὖν Πέτρος διὰ ἱκανοῦ χρόνου ἠθέλησεν πορευθῆναι εἰς Ἱεροσόλυμα· καὶ προσφωνήσας τοὺς ἀδελφοὺς καὶ ἐπιστηρίξας αὐτοὺς* <*ἐξῆλθεν*>, *πολὺν λόγον ποιούμενος διὰ τῶν χωρῶν, διδάσκων αὐτούς· ὃς καὶ κατήντησεν αὐτοῖς καὶ ἀπήγγειλεν αὐτοῖς τὴν χάριν τοῦ θεοῦ. οἱ δὲ ἐκ περιτομῆς ἀδελφοὶ διεκρίνοντο πρὸς αὐτόν.* Perhaps the reviser, shocked at the controversy following so closely on the conversion of Cornelius, contrived to make the transition less abrupt by introducing a passage in the style of viii. 25; xv. 3. With this statement in δ that Peter taught in the districts between Caesarea and Jerusalem, Blass and others have connected the appearance of the early disciple Mnason in xxi. 16 (*q.v.*), who, according to δ there, lived in a village between Caesarea and Jerusalem. 'It is a natural combination that Mnason was one of his converts' (G. Salmon, quoted with approval by Blass, *PG*, p. 129).

διεκρίνοντο] 'were divided (from him in opinion)', and so 'disputed (with him)'. See on *ver.* 12.

οἱ ἐκ περιτομῆς] See on x. 45. It is possible that the expression here does not simply mean 'Jews' (as in x. 45), but denotes those Jewish Christians who were specially zealous for the law and sticklers for circumcision, those mentioned in xv. 5; xxi. 20. Cf. Gal. ii. 12.

xi. 3

ὅτι] om P^{45}. If the following verbs are read in the second person, *ὅτι* is indirect interrogative ('Why . . . ?').

εἰσῆλθεν . . . συνέφαγεν] B 33 81 431 614 P^{45} pesh al ; ℵ A D byz vg al have *εἰσῆλθες . . . συνέφαγες* (so WH mg., Soden, Ropes).

ἀκροβυστίαν ἔχοντας] 'uncircumcised': cf. *ἀπερίτμητοι* (vii. 51). *ἀκροβυστία* (Heb. *'orlāh*), used in LXX (e.g., Gen. xxxiv. 14, etc.), is probably a disguised form of the etymologically clear *ἀκροποσθία*, which is found in Hippocrates. Cf. MH ii, p. 277.

συνέφαγεν] Entering a Gentile house was bad enough (see on x. 28), but eating with them was the last straw. The favour which the apostles had enjoyed in Jerusalem was no doubt largely due to their strict adherence to the law; Stephen's attitude had gravely imperilled this favour, but it was just too bad that the leader of the Twelve should thus compromise their position. (It is probably no accident that shortly after this Agrippa I killed James the Zebedaean and imprisoned Peter to please the Jews [xii. 1 ff.].) There were many Jews in Caesarea, despite their unpopularity there, and the story of Peter's action soon got about, and preceded him to Jerusalem. While eating with Gentiles was the main subject of inquiry on this occasion, at the Jerusalem Council, where wider issues were debated, Peter uses the Cornelius episode as an argument against requiring Gentile converts to be circumcised (xv. 7 ff.).

(b) Peter's Defence, xi. 4-17

ἀρξάμενος δὲ Πέτρος ἐξετίθετο αὐτοῖς καθεξῆς λέγων Ἐγὼ 4,5
ἤμην ἐν πόλει Ἰόππῃ προσευχόμενος καὶ εἶδον ἐν ἐκστάσει ὅραμα,
καταβαῖνον σκεῦός τι ὡς ὀθόνην μεγάλην τέσσαρσιν ἀρχαῖς καθι-
εμένην ἐκ τοῦ οὐρανοῦ, καὶ ἦλθεν ἄχρι ἐμοῦ· εἰς ἣν ἀτενίσας κατε- 6
νόουν καὶ εἶδον τὰ τετράποδα τῆς γῆς καὶ τὰ θηρία καὶ τὰ ἑρπετὰ καὶ
τὰ πετεινὰ τοῦ οὐρανοῦ· ἤκουσα δὲ καὶ φωνῆς λεγούσης μοι Ἀναστάς, 7
Πέτρε, θῦσον καὶ φάγε. εἶπον δέ Μηδαμῶς, κύριε, ὅτι κοινὸν ἢ 8
ἀκάθαρτον οὐδέποτε εἰσῆλθεν εἰς τὸ στόμα μου. ἀπεκρίθη δὲ ἐκ 9
δευτέρου φωνὴ ἐκ τοῦ οὐρανοῦ Ἃ ὁ θεὸς ἐκαθάρισεν σὺ μὴ κοίνου.
τοῦτο δὲ ἐγένετο ἐπὶ τρίς, καὶ ἀνεσπάσθη πάλιν ἅπαντα εἰς τὸν οὐρανόν. 10
καὶ ἰδοὺ ἐξαυτῆς τρεῖς ἄνδρες ἐπέστησαν ἐπὶ τὴν οἰκίαν ἐν ᾗ ἦμεν, 11
ἀπεσταλμένοι ἀπὸ Καισαρίας πρός με. εἶπεν δὲ τὸ πνεῦμά μοι 12
συνελθεῖν αὐτοῖς μηδὲν διακρίναντα. ἦλθον δὲ σὺν ἐμοὶ καὶ οἱ ἓξ
ἀδελφοὶ οὗτοι, καὶ εἰσήλθομεν εἰς τὸν οἶκον τοῦ ἀνδρός. ἀπήγγειλεν 13
δὲ ἡμῖν πῶς εἶδεν τὸν ἄγγελον ἐν τῷ οἴκῳ αὐτοῦ σταθέντα καὶ εἰπόντα
Ἀπόστειλον εἰς Ἰόππην καὶ μετάπεμψαι Σίμωνα τὸν ἐπικαλούμενον
Πέτρον, ὃς λαλήσει ῥήματα πρὸς σὲ ἐν οἷς σωθήσῃ σὺ καὶ πᾶς ὁ οἶκός 14
σου. ἐν δὲ τῷ ἄρξασθαί με λαλεῖν ἐπέπεσεν τὸ πνεῦμα τὸ ἅγιον ἐπ' 15
αὐτοὺς ὥσπερ καὶ ἐφ' ἡμᾶς ἐν ἀρχῇ. ἐμνήσθην δὲ τοῦ ῥήματος τοῦ 16
κυρίου ὡς ἔλεγεν Ἰωάνης μὲν ἐβάπτισεν ὕδατι ὑμεῖς δὲ βαπτισθήσεσθε

ἐν πνεύματι ἁγίῳ. εἰ οὖν τὴν ἴσην δωρεὰν ἔδωκεν αὐτοῖς ὁ θεὸς ὡς 17
καὶ ἡμῖν πιστεύσασιν ἐπὶ τὸν κύριον Ἰησοῦν Χριστόν, ἐγὼ τίς ἤμην
δυνατὸς κωλῦσαι τὸν θεόν;

This section is a repetition of the story already told in the previous chapter. Indeed, Cornelius himself in x. 30-33 has already retold the narrative of x. 3-8 (it is still more succinctly summarized by his messengers in x. 22). It is therefore clear that Luke regards the Cornelius incident as epoch-making in his history. In the retelling of the story we should observe the masterly union of variety in expression with similarity in construction. Cf. the threefold account of the conversion of Saul (chs. ix, xxii, xxvi).

xi. 4

ἀρξάμενος] Semitizing redundant ptc. (see on i. 22; ii. 4; iv. 19; v. 6). According to Blass, it is used 'with a certain reference to *καθεξῆς* and occasioned by that word'. That is to say, he told the whole story in order from the beginning.

xi. 5

καὶ ἦλθεν ἄχρι ἐμοῦ· εἰς ἣν ἀτενίσας κατενόουν καὶ εἶδον] Observe the vividness of Peter's personal narrative contrasted with the comparative colourlessness of x. 11 f.

xi. 6

τετράποδα τῆς γῆς] In x. 12 *τῆς γῆς* is attached not to *τετράποδα* but to *ἑρπετά*.

θηρία] Not in x. 12; these are to be distinguished from *τετράποδα* as in Gen. i. 24 f., where *θηρία* (Heb. *ḥayyāh*) are apparently the wild animals as distinct from *τετράποδα* or *κτήνη* (Heb. *bĕhēmāh*), the domesticated ones.

xi. 7

ἤκουσα . . . φωνῆς λεγούσης] Cf. xxii. 7. D *P*[45] have *φωνὴν λέγουσαν*.

ἀναστάς] Cf. x. 13. D has *ἀνάστα*.

xi. 8

οὐδέποτε εἰσῆλθεν εἰς τὸ στόμα μου] Differently expressed from x. 14; but cf. the quotation *ad loc.* from Ezek. iv. 14, *οὐδὲ εἰσελήλυθεν εἰς τὸ στόμα μου πᾶν κρέας ἕωλον*. *P*[45] omits *μου*.

xi. 9

ἐκ δευτέρου φωνὴ] B E al ; φωνὴ ἐκ δευτέρου ℵ A 33 81 P^{45} byz (cf. WH mg.). D recasts, ἐγένετο φωνὴ ἐκ τοῦ οὐρανοῦ πρός με. For ἐκ δευτέρου cf. x. 15.

xi. 10

δὲ] om P^{45}.

ἀνεσπάσθη] 'was drawn up': more expressive than ἀνελήμφθη (x. 16).

xi. 11

ἐπέστησαν] + μοι P^{45}.

ἐπὶ τὴν οἰκίαν] The expression in x. 17 is ἐπὶ τὸν πυλῶνα, 'at the outside gate'.

ἦμεν] ℵ A B D ; ἤμην 33 81 P^{45} byz vers.omn (so WH mg., Soden, Ropes).

xi. 12

μηδὲν διακρίναντα] (om D) 'making no distinction': cf. x. 20, μηδὲν διακρινόμενος, 'without any doubting' (and also ἀναντιρρήτως, x. 29). ℵ* has μηδὲν διακρίνοντα.

οἱ ἓξ ἀδελφοὶ οὗτοι] They were present while Peter was making his defence, as witnesses to the accuracy of his account. There were thus seven witnesses in all, including Peter himself. LC compare the seven witnesses sometimes required in Egyptian documents, and the seven seals attached to a will in Roman law (cf. Rev. v. 1).

xi. 13

τὸν ἄγγελον] The art. (om D P^{45}) presupposes the previous mention of the angel in x. 3, so far as the readers of Ac. are concerned ; but so far as Peter's hearers are concerned, the implication is that the story in some form had already come to their ears, although they were now for the first time hearing a full and trustworthy account. Cf. the art. in τοῦ ἀνδρός, *ver.* 12.

ἀπόστειλον] B has the unsupported πέμψον, from x. 5, 32.

xi. 14

ὃς λαλήσει ῥήματα πρὸς σὲ] Cf. x. 22, ἀκοῦσαι ῥήματα παρὰ σοῦ.

σωθήσῃ σὺ καὶ πᾶς ὁ οἶκός σου] Cf. the same words in xvi. 31 (with the exception of πᾶς). The 'house' included not only the family, but all who were under the authority of the master of the house—slaves, attendants, etc. See on x. 7.

xi. 15

ἐν δὲ τῷ ἄρξασθαί με λαλεῖν] Cf. x. 44, *ἔτι λαλοῦντος τοῦ Πέτρου* (he had been speaking from *ver.* 34 to *ver.* 43): *ἄρξασθαι* is not to be pressed, being probably the Semitizing redundant auxiliary (see on ii. 4).

ἐν ἀρχῇ] i.e. on the Day of Pentecost. In ch. x. there is no explicit statement such as we have here (*ὥσπερ καὶ ἐφ' ἡμᾶς ἐν ἀρχῇ*), but the language of ch. ii. is recalled in x. 46, which is not repeated here.

xi. 16

ἐμνήσθην κ.τ.λ.] Cf. xx. 35, of remembering the words of Jesus.

'Ιωάνης μὲν κ.τ.λ.] The words ascribed to our Lord in i. 5 (*q.v.*): cf. xix. 4. The words *οὐ μετὰ πολλὰς ταύτας ἡμέρας* of i. 5 are omitted here, as they referred to Pentecost. Whereas *ὕδατι* and *πνεύματι* are contrasted here, they are combined in Jn. iii. 5, where there seems to be an allusion to the water of Ezek. xxxvi. 25 and the wind of Ezek. xxxvii. 9. It is remarkable that nothing is said here of the baptism of Gentiles in water (cf. x. 47 f.), though it is no doubt implied in *ver.* 17.

xi. 17

πιστεύσασιν] Probably agrees with both *αὐτοῖς* and *ἡμῖν*. For *πιστεύω ἐπί* see on ix. 42 (see also on x. 43).

ἐγὼ τίς ἤμην δυνατὸς] Double construction: (1) 'Who was I that I should hinder God?' (cf. Ex. iii. 11, *τίς εἰμι ἐγὼ ὅτι πορεύσομαι;*), (2) 'Was *I* able to hinder God?' Note the emphatic position of *ἐγώ*.

τὸν θεόν] δ (D vg.codd hcl*) adds *τοῦ μὴ δοῦναι αὐτοῖς πνεῦμα ἅγιον πιστεύσασιν ἐπ' αὐτῷ*—inappropriately, as they had already received the Holy Spirit.

(c) Peter's Defence accepted—for the Present at least, xi. 18

ἀκούσαντες δὲ ταῦτα ἡσύχασαν καὶ ἐδόξασαν τὸν θεὸν λέγοντες 18
Ἄρα καὶ τοῖς ἔθνεσιν ὁ θεὸς τὴν μετάνοιαν εἰς ζωὴν ἔδωκεν.

xi. 18

ἡσύχασαν καὶ ἐδόξασαν τὸν θεὸν] Note the aorists, '*ἡσύχασαν*, negative: their opposition ceased; *ἐδόξασαν*, positive: their praise began' (T. E. Page). Giving glory to God also involved a confession that Peter was right (cf. Jn. ix. 24; Rev. xvi. 9; Josh. vii. 19).

ἄρα] 'So then': inferential particle.

τὴν μετάνοιαν εἰς ζωὴν ἔδωκεν] i.e., has given them the change of heart and mind which results in spiritual and eternal life. See on ii. 38. Grammatically, *εἰς ζωήν* goes with *ἔδωκεν*, not with *τὴν μετάνοιαν*.

They accepted Peter's report and made no attempt to avoid the conclusion that Gentiles were not outside the scope of the Gospel. The resulting questions of the terms on which Jewish and Gentile believers were to associate and the obligation on Gentile believers to observe the Jewish law were not pressed at the moment, but they were by no means solved. Even Peter on a later occasion wavered in faithfulness to the lesson that he had learned on the housetop at Joppa (Gal. ii. 11 ff.). The question became more acute than ever after the return of Paul and Barnabas from h eir first missionary journey (cf. xv. 1 ff.).

4. ANTIOCH, xi. 19-30

(a) The First Gentile Church, xi. 19-26

Οἱ μὲν οὖν διασπαρέντες ἀπὸ τῆς θλίψεως τῆς γενομένης ἐπὶ 19
Στεφάνῳ διῆλθον ἕως Φοινίκης καὶ Κύπρου καὶ Ἀντιοχείας, μηδενὶ
λαλοῦντες τὸν λόγον εἰ μὴ μόνον Ἰουδαίοις. Ἦσαν δέ τινες ἐξ αὐτῶν 20
ἄνδρες Κύπριοι καὶ Κυρηναῖοι, οἵτινες ἐλθόντες εἰς Ἀντιόχειαν
ἐλάλουν καὶ πρὸς τοὺς Ἑλληνιστάς, εὐαγγελιζόμενοι τὸν κύριον
Ἰησοῦν. καὶ ἦν χεὶρ Κυρίου μετ' αὐτῶν, πολύς τε ἀριθμὸς ὁ πιστεύ- 21
σας ἐπέστρεψεν ἐπὶ τὸν κύριον. Ἠκούσθη δὲ ὁ λόγος εἰς τὰ ὦτα 22
τῆς ἐκκλησίας τῆς οὔσης ἐν Ἰερουσαλὴμ περὶ αὐτῶν, καὶ ἐξαπέστειλαν
Βαρνάβαν ἕως Ἀντιοχείας· ὃς παραγενόμενος καὶ ἰδὼν τὴν χάριν 23
τὴν τοῦ θεοῦ ἐχάρη καὶ παρεκάλει πάντας τῇ προθέσει τῆς καρδίας
προσμένειν ἐν τῷ κυρίῳ; ὅτι ἦν ἀνὴρ ἀγαθὸς καὶ πλήρης πνεύματος 24
ἁγίου καὶ πίστεως. καὶ προσετέθη ὄχλος ἱκανὸς τῷ κυρίῳ. ἐξῆλθεν 25
δὲ εἰς Ταρσὸν ἀναζητῆσαι Σαῦλον, καὶ εὑρὼν ἤγαγεν εἰς Ἀντιόχειαν. 26
ἐγένετο δὲ αὐτοῖς καὶ ἐνιαυτὸν ὅλον συναχθῆναι ἐν τῇ ἐκκλησίᾳ καὶ
διδάξαι ὄχλον ἱκανόν, χρηματίσαι τε πρώτως ἐν Ἀντιοχείᾳ τοὺς μαθητὰς
Χριστιανούς.

xi. 19

Οἱ μὲν οὖν διασπαρέντες] We revert to same point of departure as viii. 4, which commences with the same words: here, as there, *μὲν οὖν* indicates the beginning of a new section. From here onwards we have a narrative with Syrian Antioch as its centre of interest, containing three episodes, (1) the evangelization of Antioch (xi. 19-26), (2) the famine-relief delegation to Judaea (xi. 27-30 and, after an interlude, xii. 25), (3) the first missionary journey of Paul and Barnabas, based on Antioch (xiii. 1-xiv. 28).

ἀπὸ τῆς θλίψεως] The causal sense of *ἀπό* is both classical and vernacular: cf. xii. 14; xxii. 11. The *θλίψις* is the *διωγμός* of viii. 1 (where δ adds *καὶ θλίψις*, perhaps from here).

Φοινίκης] Phoenicia, the coastal strip containing Tyre and Sidon, 120 miles long by 15 broad.

Ἀντιοχείας] Antioch on the Orontes, a chief centre of the Jewish diaspora, now to become the metropolis of Gentile Christianity. It was 15 miles from the coast, its port being Seleucia (xiii. 4). It was founded by Seleucus Nicator in 300 B.C. Pompey, in his reorganization of the east (64 B.C.), made it a free city. It became the capital of the imperial province of Syria. Like some other busy commercial centres, its immorality was proverbial (cf. Juvenal, *Sat.* iii. 62, '*iam pridem Syrus in Tiberim defluxit Orontes*'). It was 5 miles from Daphne, the seat of a cult of Artemis and Apollo (a semi-Hellenized version of the Syrian goddess Astarte and her consort: see on xiii. 6), whence *Daphnici mores* became a by-word for loose-living. Antioch itself was called *ἡ ἐπὶ Δάφνῃ*, whence Epidaphna (Tac. *Ann.* ii. 83). Cf. Jos. *BJ* iii. 2. 4; vii. 3. 3; *Ap.* ii. 4; Strabo xvi. 2. 4 ff.

Notice that Luke gives no account of evangelization east and south of Palestine; he is concerned with the movement of the Gospel towards the heart of the Empire.

xi. 20

Κύπριοι] As Barnabas was (iv. 36).

Κυρηναῖοι] Cf. ii. 10; vi. 9; xiii. 1; the sons of Simon of Cyrene were well-known in the early church (Mk. xv. 21).

καὶ πρὸς τοὺς Ἑλληνιστάς] *καί* (א* A B 81 al) is omitted by א[c] D 33 byz. *Ἑλληνιστάς* is the reading of B D[2] E 33 81 byz, and it lies behind the erroneous *εὐαγγελιστάς* of א*; *Ἕλληνας* is the reading of א[c] A D* 1518 Euseb Chrys and *prima facie* of all the versions (but 'Greeks' in the versions is the equivalent of both *Ἕλληνας* and *Ἑλληνιστάς*). It is difficult to decide between the two readings; perhaps *Ἑλληνιστάς*, being the more difficult, ought to be accepted. Its previous occurrences in Ac. (vi. 1; ix. 29, *q.v.*) have referred to Greek-speaking Jews, and obviously non-Jews are meant here; *Ἕλληνας* is thus the easier reading, and the tendency would be to write it in place of an original *Ἑλληνιστάς*. We should not, however, regard *Ἑλληνισταί* as a technical term in the sense 'Greek-speaking Jews'; if, as it seems, it is connected with *ἑλληνίζω*, it may simply mean 'Greek speakers', and further information about the persons concerned must be gathered from the context. In vi. 1 and ix. 29, the context implies that the Greek speakers were Jews; here the contrast with *Ἰουδαῖοι* in *ver.* 19 (which probably refers to Greek-speaking Jews) plainly implies that the Greek speakers of *ver.* 20 are Gentiles. (See further on vi. 1.)

εὐαγγελιζόμενοι τὸν κύριον Ἰησοῦν] 'telling the good news of the Lord Jesus'. That Jesus is Lord is emphasized as in ii. 36; x. 36; but to Gentiles, naturally, He is not presented as the Christ (as He is in ii. 36; v. 42; viii. 5; ix. 22; etc.). (Peter, it is true, used the title 'Christ' in addressing Cornelius, x. 36; but Cornelius was well acquainted with the Jewish outlook.)

xi. 21

χεὶρ Κυρίου] i.e., His power; the expression can sometimes be taken as a metaphor for the Spirit of God. Cf. iv. 30; xiii. 11; Lk. i. 66: it is common in OT, e.g., Ex. ix. 3; 1 Sam. v. 3, 6, 9; Isa. lix. 1; lxvi. 14; Ezek. i. 3 (and cf. Mt. xii. 28 with Lk. xi. 20).

ἐπέστρεψεν] Here, as in iii. 19, etc., of turning to the Lord for the first time; elsewhere also of the recovery of a believer (e.g., Jas. v. 19 f.), even of an apostle (Lk. xxii. 32).

xi. 22

ἠκούσθη . . . εἰς τὰ ὦτα] εἰς τὰ ὦτα is a phrase quite common in LXX, e.g., Gen. xx. 8; l. 4 (λαλήσατε περὶ ἐμοῦ εἰς τὰ ὦτα Φαραώ); 3 K. xii. 24; Isa. v. 9 (quoted Jas. v. 4). Cf. εἰς τὰς ἀκοάς, xvii. 20; εἰς τὸ οὖς, Mt. x. 27 (of a whispered report). But of its use here after ἠκούσθη, Torrey says: 'No Greek writer would ever have perpetrated this—unless he had wished to create the impression that he was using a Semitic "source"' (*CDA*, p. 36).

τῆς ἐκκλησίας τῆς οὔσης] 'of the local church'; for this use of ὤν see on v. 17; xiii. 1.

ἐξαπέστειλαν Βαρνάβαν] Barnabas was to play in Antioch the part that Peter and John played in Samaria (viii. 14). A better man could not have been chosen for this delicate work; apart from his character (described in *ver.* 24), he was himself a Cyprian Jew, like some of those who had taken the initiative in this Gentile evangelization, and therefore much more likely to be sympathetic than a more rigid Jerusalem disciple might have been.

xi. 23

χάριν . . . ἐχάρη] Probably an intentional play on words: cf. Lk. i. 28, χαῖρε, κεχαριτωμένη. God's grace (χάρις) brings joy (χαρά). What made Barnabas glad was the evidence of the free favour of God, unlimited by racial or religious frontiers, extended to all men without distinction.

παρεκάλει] Perhaps with reference to the meaning of his name: see on iv. 36.

τῇ προθέσει τῆς καρδίας] 'with purpose of heart', i.e., with determination; the only other occurrence of the phrase in Bib. Gk. is in Ps. x. 17 (Symmachus's version [ix. 38 in LXX arrangement]).

προσμένειν ἐν τῷ κυρίῳ] B Ψ 181 vg hcl sah boh are our witnesses for *ἐν*, which is elsewhere omitted. The sense is in any case 'to abide in the Lord' or 'to cleave to the Lord': cf. xiii. 43, *προσμένειν τῇ χάριτι τοῦ θεοῦ*.

xi. 24

ἀνὴρ ἀγαθὸς] So another Joseph (of Arimathaea) is also described, Lk. xxiii. 50.

πλήρης πνεύματος ἁγίου καὶ πίστεως] Cf. Stephen, vi. 5.

προσετέθη ὄχλος ἱκανὸς τῷ κυρίῳ] B* omits *τῷ κυρίῳ*: cf. the absolute use of *προστίθημι* in ii. 41, 47; v. 14 (i.e., if we take *τῷ κυρίῳ* with *πιστεύοντες*: if we take it with *προσετίθεντο* we have a parallel to *προσετέθη . . . τῷ κυρίῳ*, the reading of all our authorities here except B).

xi. 25

ἐξῆλθεν δὲ εἰς Ταρσὸν ἀναζητῆσαι Σαῦλον] This reinforces the impression received from ix. 27, that Barnabas was previously acquainted with Saul. He evidently knew that Saul was just the man required for this work at Antioch. So he fetches him from Tarsus, where we left him in ix. 30. For *Σαῦλον* P^{45} has *Σαούλ*. In δ this sentence is recast, *ἀκούσας δὲ ὅτι Σαῦλός ἐστιν εἰς Ταρσὸν ἐξῆλθεν ἀναζητῶν αὐτόν, καὶ συντυχὼν παρεκάλεσεν ἐλθεῖν εἰς Ἀντιόχειαν.*

ἀναζητῆσαι] B has the unsupported and clearly erroneous reading *ἀναστῆσαι*. In the papyri, *ἀναζητέω* 'is specially used of searching for human beings, with an implication of difficulty, as in the NT passages' (MM). Cf. Lk. ii. 44.

xi. 26

ἐγένετο κ.τ.λ.] A twofold construction after *ἐγένετο*, (1) dat. and infin., *αὐτοῖς . . . συναχθῆναι . . . καὶ διδάξαι*, (2) acc. and infin., *χρηματίσαι τοὺς μαθητάς*. The former may literally be rendered, 'It happened to them to be gathered'.

συναχθῆναι] For repeated action we might expect *συνάγεσθαι*, but the meaning is made plain here by the addition of the note of time *ἐνιαυτὸν ὅλον*.

ἐν τῇ ἐκκλησίᾳ] The first use of *ἐκκλησία* in Ac. for a community other than the original Jerusalem church either in its pristine unity (see on v. 11) or in dispersion (see on ix. 31). Henceforth in Ac. the word is regularly used of individual communities of Christians.

ὄχλον ἱκανόν] As in *ver.* 24, *ὄχλος ἱκανός*.

χρηματίσαι] lit., ' transacted business ' under the name Christians, i.e., were commonly known as such. Cf. Rom. vii. 3. This *χρηματίζω*, from *χρήματα*, ' business ', must be distinguished from the *χρηματίζω* of x. 22, etc., which in sense is akin to *χράομαι*, ' give an oracular response '. Cf. MH ii. p. 265.

πρώτως] ℵ B 36 P^{45} ; *πρῶτον* A D 81 byz.

ἐν Ἀντιοχείᾳ τοὺς μαθητὰς] *τοὺς μαθητὰς ἐν Ἀντιοχείᾳ* P^{45}.

Χριστιανούς] It was naturally in Gentile circles that *Χριστός* first came to be used as a personal name rather than as a title. The populace of Antioch, hearing the disciples use this name frequently, added a colloquial suffix (originally Latin) to it, and called those who so often named the name of Christ Christians. *Χριστός* meant nothing to the unbelieving Gentiles, who confused it with the identically pronounced *χρηστός*, ' kindly ', ' useful ' (hence, e.g., the variant *Chrestus* in Suet. *Claud.* xxv. 4 : see on xviii. 2). The variant spelling *Χρηστιανούς* occurs here in ℵ 81. The name *Χριστιανοί* is not used by Christians of themselves in NT ; in xxvi. 28 Agrippa II uses it ; in 1 Pet. iv. 16, *ὡς Χριστιανός* represents the language of the accusation. Cf. Tac. *Ann.* xv. 44, ' . . . *quos per flagitia inuisos uulgus Christianos appellabat. auctor nominis eius Christus Tiberio imperitante per procuratorem Pontium Pilatum supplicio adfectus erat* '.

Other names for Christians in Ac. are *οἱ σωζόμενοι* (ii. 47) ; *μαθηταί* (vi. 1), *ἅγιοι* (ix. 13), *ἀδελφοί* (ix. 30), *πιστοί* (x. 45) ; *Ναζωραῖοι* (xxiv. 5), and perhaps *φίλοι* (xxvii. 3, *q.v.*). See *BC* v, Note 30.

After *Ἀντιόχειαν* the sentence is continued thus by δ : *οἵτινες παραγενόμενοι ἐνιαυτὸν ὅλον συνεχύθησαν* <*τῇ ἐκκλησίᾳ καὶ ἐδίδασκον*> *ὄχλον ἱκανόν, καὶ τότε πρῶτον ἐχρημάτισαν ἐν Ἀντιοχείᾳ οἱ μαθηταὶ Χριστιανοί* (reconstructed by Ropes).

(b) Famine-Relief Expedition to Judaea, xi. 27-30

Ἐν ταύταις δὲ ταῖς ἡμέραις κατῆλθον ἀπὸ Ἱεροσολύμων προφῆται 27
εἰς Ἀντιόχειαν· ἀναστὰς δὲ εἷς ἐξ αὐτῶν ὀνόματι Ἄγαβος ἐσήμαινεν διὰ 28
τοῦ πνεύματος λιμὸν μεγάλην μέλλειν ἔσεσθαι ἐφ' ὅλην τὴν οἰκουμένην·
ἥτις ἐγένετο ἐπὶ Κλαυδίου. τῶν δὲ μαθητῶν καθὼς εὐπορεῖτό τις 29
ὥρισαν ἕκαστος αὐτῶν εἰς διακονίαν πέμψαι τοῖς κατοικοῦσιν ἐν τῇ
Ἰουδαίᾳ ἀδελφοῖς· ὃ καὶ ἐποίησαν ἀποστείλαντες πρὸς τοὺς πρεσ- 30
βυτέρους διὰ χειρὸς Βαρνάβα καὶ Σαύλου.

xi. 27

Ἐν ταύταις δὲ ταῖς ἡμέραις] For the use of this phrase to mark a fresh beginning cf. i. 15 ; vi. 1. The 'days' referred to are those during which Barnabas and Saul were at Antioch.

προφῆται] For the presence of prophets in the church cf. xiii. 1 ; xv. 32 ; xxi. 9, 10. It was believed that prophecy had ceased in Israel soon after the Babylonian exile (cf. 1 Macc. iv. 46 ; ix. 27 ; xiv. 41).[1] It appeared again with John the Baptist, the title 'prophet' is frequently given to Jesus (cf. iii. 22 ; vii. 37), and in the church prophets ranked next to apostles (1 Cor. xii. 28 ; Eph. iv. 11).

xi. 28

ἀναστὰς . . . ἐσήμαινεν] δ (D p Aug al) reads : ἦν δὲ πολλὴ ἀγαλλίασις· συνεστραμμένων δὲ ἡμῶν ἔφη εἷς ἐξ αὐτῶν ὀνόματι Ἄγαβος σημαίνων. This is chiefly important as giving us a 'we' passage earlier than any in the β text. The presence of ἡμῶν here is probably due to the δ reviser's acquaintance with the tradition that Luke was a native of Antioch. See pp. 6 f., and cf. Ramsay, *SPT*[14], p. xxxviii.

Ἄγαβος] He reappears at Caesarea in xxi. 10 (*q.v.*), in a 'we' section. The name is apparently the OT Hagab, Hagaba (Ezra ii. 46 ; Neh. vii. 48).

ἐσήμαινεν] B vg (*significabat*) ; ἐσήμανεν ℵ A 81 byz (so WH mg., Soden, Ropes). For σημαίνω cf. xxv. 27 ; Jn. xii. 33 ; xviii. 32 ; xxi. 19 ; Rev. i. 1 : here probably of oracular utterance.

διὰ τοῦ πνεύματος] Cf. xxi. 4, of similar inspired prediction.

λιμὸν μεγάλην] The gender of λιμός varies in NT. Here and in Lk. xv. 14 it is fem. ; in Lk. iv. 25 masc.

ἔσεσθαι] Cf. xxiii. 30 ; xxiv. 15 ; xxvi. 7 (?) ; xxvii. 10. Apart from εἰσελεύσεσθαι (Heb. iii. 18) and χωρήσειν (Jn. xxi. 25), the fut. infin. in NT is limited to Ac.

ἐφ' ὅλην τὴν οἰκουμένην] Here, as in Lk. ii. 1, οἰκουμένη is to be understood of the Roman world, the *orbis terrarum*. There was no single famine throughout the whole Empire under Claudius ; his rule, however, was marked by *assiduae sterilitates* (Suet., *Claud.* xviii. 2). We may thus translate with AV 'great dearth' rather than, with RV, 'a great famine'. But Torrey thinks that ὅλην τὴν οἰκουμένην represents Aram. *kōl 'arʿā*, 'all the land', i.e., Palestine (similarly he regards πᾶσαν τὴν οἰκουμένην in Lk. ii. 1 as representing Heb. *kōl hā-'āreṣ*). Josephus (*Ant.* iii. 15. 3 ; xx. 2. 5 ; 5. 2) tells of a famine in Judaea about this time, under the procurators Cuspius Fadus and Tiberius Alexander, i.e.,

[1] Cf. also Jos. *Ap.* i. 8.

between A.D. 44 and 48 (*ἐπὶ τούτοις δὴ καὶ τὸν μέγαν λιμὸν κατὰ τὴν Ἰουδαίαν συνέβη γενέσθαι*). He relates how Queen Helena of Adiabene, a Jewish proselyte, bought corn in Egypt and figs in Cyprus, and brought them to Jerusalem for distribution in this famine.

ἥτις] Regularly in NT for *ἥ*: cf. ix. 36 for an exception.

ἐπὶ Κλαυδίου] The fourth Emperor, grandson of Livia (the wife of Augustus), and nephew of Tiberius, succeeded his own nephew Gaius in A.D. 41 and ruled till 54. He paid great attention to the administration of the Empire, introducing several changes, especially in the east. During his principate Britain was conquered and made a Roman province. Other famines in his reign occurred in Rome, at the beginning of his rule (Dio Cassius lx. 11), in Greece, in his eighth or ninth year (Eusebius, *Chron.-Canon*), and again in Rome between his ninth and eleventh years (Tac. *Ann.* xii. 43; Orosius vii. 6. 17). See further on xviii. 2.

The words here may imply that the prophecy itself was made before his accession in 41, but this inference is not certain.

xi. 29

εὐπορεῖτο] 'had plenty'. Here only in NT: cf. *εὐπορία*, xix. 25. The passive in this sense occurs in Aristotle and Polybius; and cf. Lev. xxv. 26, 49 LXX. Cf. also 1 Cor. xvi. 2, *ὅτι ἐὰν εὐοδῶται*.

ὥρισαν] 'they arranged': perhaps the meaning is that each one set aside a fixed sum out of his property or income as a contribution to the fund, much as the Corinthian Christians were later advised to do (1 Cor. xvi. 1 ff.).

ὥρισαν ἕκαστος αὐτῶν] *ἕκαστος ὥρισαν* P^{45}.

εἰς διακονίαν] Cf. xii. 25, *πληρώσαντες τὴν διακονίαν*. For this sense of *διακονία* cf. also vi. 1; Rom. xv. 31; 2 Cor. viii. 4, 19 f. It is not necessary to suppose, with Ramsay, that Barnabas and Saul actually *administered* the gifts in Jerusalem (*SPT*, p. 51).

xi. 30

ἀποστείλαντες] Aor. ptc. with simultaneous force.

πρὸς τοὺς πρεσβυτέρους] Why are the apostles not mentioned? Probably because the business of the Twelve was not this *διακονία* but the *διακονία τοῦ λόγου* (vi. 2 ff.).

διὰ χειρὸς] Semitic *bĕ-yad*: cf. v. 12; vii. 25, 35.

Βαρνάβα καὶ Σαύλου] (For *Σαύλου* P^{45} has *Σαούλ*: cf. *ver.* 25; ix. 24; xii. 7.) Two delegates again, as in viii. 14; ix. 38, etc. If Agabus made his prediction a good while before the famine, it may be that the delegation went to Jerusalem before the necessity arose; on the other hand, the Antiochians may have started collecting when the prophecy was made and continued doing so until the famine came. It is therefore difficult to fix the date of this visit to Jerusalem. If it is to be identified with Paul's second Jerusalem visit according to his own account in Gal. ii. 1 ff. (the most satisfactory identification, in my opinion), we should connect *ἀνέβην δὲ κατὰ ἀποκάλυψιν* (Gal. ii. 2) with the prophecy of Agabus, and Gal. ii. 10 (*μόνον τῶν πτωχῶν ἵνα μνημονεύωμεν, ὃ καὶ ἐσπούδασα*[1] *αὐτὸ τοῦτο ποιῆσαι*) with the object of the visit according to Ac. The visit of Gal. ii. 1 ff. took place about A.D. 46 (if we reckon the fourteen years of Gal. ii. 1 from Paul's conversion, not from his first Jerusalem visit); this agrees quite well with the date of the famine, between 44 and 48 (if, as is most likely, it is the same as that recorded by Josephus). See pp. 38 f.

5. Herod Agrippa I and the Church, xii. 1-24

(a) Martyrdom of James; Imprisonment and Escape of Peter, xii. 1-19

Κατ' ἐκεῖνον δὲ τὸν καιρὸν ἐπέβαλεν Ἡρῴδης ὁ βασιλεὺς τὰς 1
χεῖρας κακῶσαί τινας τῶν ἀπὸ τῆς ἐκκλησίας. ἀνεῖλεν δὲ Ἰάκωβον 2
τὸν ἀδελφὸν Ἰωάνου μαχαίρῃ. ἰδὼν δὲ ὅτι ἀρεστόν ἐστιν τοῖς Ἰου- 3
δαίοις προσέθετο συλλαβεῖν καὶ Πέτρον, (ἦσαν δὲ ἡμέραι τῶν ἀζύμων,)
ὃν καὶ πιάσας ἔθετο εἰς φυλακήν, παραδοὺς τέσσαρσιν τετραδίοις 4
στρατιωτῶν φυλάσσειν αὐτόν, βουλόμενος μετὰ τὸ πάσχα ἀναγαγεῖν
αὐτὸν τῷ λαῷ. ὁ μὲν οὖν Πέτρος ἐτηρεῖτο ἐν τῇ φυλακῇ· προσευχὴ 5
δὲ ἦν ἐκτενῶς γινομένη ὑπὸ τῆς ἐκκλησίας πρὸς τὸν θεὸν περὶ αὐτοῦ.
Ὅτε δὲ ἤμελλεν προσαγαγεῖν αὐτὸν ὁ Ἡρῴδης, τῇ νυκτὶ ἐκείνῃ ἦν 6
ὁ Πέτρος κοιμώμενος μεταξὺ δύο στρατιωτῶν δεδεμένος ἁλύσεσιν
δυσίν, φύλακές τε πρὸ τῆς θύρας ἐτήρουν τὴν φυλακήν. καὶ ἰδοὺ 7
ἄγγελος Κυρίου ἐπέστη, καὶ φῶς ἔλαμψεν ἐν τῷ οἰκήματι· πατάξας
δὲ τὴν πλευρὰν τοῦ Πέτρου ἤγειρεν αὐτὸν λέγων Ἀνάστα ἐν τάχει·
καὶ ἐξέπεσαν αὐτοῦ αἱ ἁλύσεις ἐκ τῶν χειρῶν. εἶπεν δὲ ὁ ἄγγελος 8
πρὸς αὐτόν Ζῶσαι καὶ ὑπόδησαι τὰ σανδάλιά σου· ἐποίησεν δὲ οὕτως.
καὶ λέγει αὐτῷ Περιβαλοῦ τὸ ἱμάτιόν σου καὶ ἀκολούθει μοι· καὶ 9
ἐξελθὼν ἠκολούθει, καὶ οὐκ ᾔδει ὅτι ἀληθές ἐστιν τὸ γινόμενον διὰ
τοῦ ἀγγέλου, ἐδόκει δὲ ὅραμα βλέπειν. διελθόντες δὲ πρώτην 10
φυλακὴν καὶ δευτέραν ἦλθαν ἐπὶ τὴν πύλην τὴν σιδηρᾶν τὴν φέρουσαν
εἰς τὴν πόλιν, ἥτις αὐτομάτη ἠνοίγη αὐτοῖς, καὶ ἐξελθόντες προῆλθον
ῥύμην μίαν, καὶ εὐθέως ἀπέστη ὁ ἄγγελος ἀπ' αὐτοῦ. καὶ ὁ Πέτρος 11
ἐν ἑαυτῷ γενόμενος εἶπεν Νῦν οἶδα ἀληθῶς ὅτι ἐξαπέστειλεν ὁ κύριος
τὸν ἄγγελον αὐτοῦ καὶ ἐξείλατό με ἐκ χειρὸς Ἡρῴδου καὶ πάσης
τῆς προσδοκίας τοῦ λαοῦ τῶν Ἰουδαίων. συνιδών τε ἦλθεν ἐπὶ τὴν 12

[1] 'The aorist *ἐσπούδασα* fits in well with the fact that Paul had actually just brought alms to Jerusalem: it is almost a pluperfect' (C. W. Emmet, *BC* ii. p. 279).

οἰκίαν τῆς Μαρίας τῆς μητρὸς Ἰωάνου τοῦ ἐπικαλουμένου Μάρκου,
οὗ ἦσαν ἱκανοὶ συνηθροισμένοι καὶ προσευχόμενοι. κρούσαντος 13
δὲ αὐτοῦ τὴν θύραν τοῦ πυλῶνος προσῆλθε παιδίσκη ὑπακοῦσαι
ὀνόματι Ῥόδη, καὶ ἐπιγνοῦσα τὴν φωνὴν τοῦ Πέτρου ἀπὸ τῆς χαρᾶς 14
οὐκ ἤνοιξεν τὸν πυλῶνα, εἰσδραμοῦσα δὲ ἀπήγγειλεν ἑστάναι τὸν
Πέτρον πρὸ τοῦ πυλῶνος. οἱ δὲ πρὸς αὐτὴν εἶπαν Μαίνῃ. ἡ δὲ 15
διισχυρίζετο οὕτως ἔχειν. οἱ δὲ ἔλεγον Ὁ ἄγγελός ἐστιν αὐτοῦ.
ὁ δὲ Πέτρος ἐπέμενεν κρούων· ἀνοίξαντες δὲ εἶδαν αὐτὸν καὶ ἐξέστησαν. 16
κατασείσας δὲ αὐτοῖς τῇ χειρὶ σιγᾶν διηγήσατο αὐτοῖς πῶς ὁ κύριος 17
αὐτὸν ἐξήγαγεν ἐκ τῆς φυλακῆς, εἶπέν τε Ἀπαγγείλατε Ἰακώβῳ
καὶ τοῖς ἀδελφοῖς ταῦτα. καὶ ἐξελθὼν ἐπορεύθη εἰς ἕτερον τόπον.
Γενομένης δὲ ἡμέρας ἦν τάραχος οὐκ ὀλίγος ἐν τοῖς στρατιώταις, τί 18
ἄρα ὁ Πέτρος ἐγένετο. Ἡρῴδης δὲ ἐπιζητήσας αὐτὸν καὶ μὴ εὑρὼν 19
ἀνακρίνας τοὺς φύλακας ἐκέλευσεν ἀπαχθῆναι, καὶ κατελθὼν ἀπὸ
τῆς Ἰουδαίας εἰς Καισαρίαν διέτριβεν.

xii. 1

Κατ' ἐκεῖνον δὲ τὸν καιρὸν] About the time of the events of xi. 27-30; after the prophecy of Agabus, and before the famine. For the phrase cf. xix. 23, where also it introduces a new episode.

ἐπέβαλεν . . . τὰς χεῖρας] This phrase is used of hostile action in iv. 3; v. 18; xxi. 27 (as elsewhere in NT, LXX, Polybius and papyri); but this use with infin. is peculiar. For its use with *κακῶσαι* here cf. xviii. 10, *ἐπιθήσεταί σοι τοῦ κακῶσαί σε*.

Ἡρῴδης ὁ βασιλεὺς] Herod Agrippa I, born 11 B.C., son of Aristobulus and grandson of Herod the Great. His title as a Roman citizen was M. Julius Agrippa, no doubt because of his father's friendship with the Roman statesman of that name, who died in 12 B.C. (cf. xxv. 13). After his father's execution in 7 B.C., he was sent with his mother Berenice to Rome, where he grew up on terms of intimacy with the Imperial family. He became so heavily involved in debt that in A.D. 23 he had to retire to Idumaea. Through the influence of his sister Herodias he received an asylum and pension at Tiberias from his uncle Antipas (see on iv. 27), with whom, however, he eventually quarrelled. In 36 he returned to Rome, but offended Tiberius and was imprisoned. He was released the following year by Gaius, the successor of Tiberius, and received from him the title of king, the tetrarchies of Philip and Lysanias (cf. Lk. iii. 1), and a gold chain equal in weight to the iron one which he had worn in prison. When Antipas was banished in 39, Agrippa received his tetrarchy as well. He was able in 40 to dissuade Gaius from his intention to have his statue set up in the Temple at Jerusalem. He continued to enjoy the imperial favour under Claudius, who added Judaea and Samaria to his territory, so that his kingdom (41-44) was comparable to his grandfather's. In Palestine he sedulously cultivated the good will of the Jews, observing their customs and preferring their company, so that even the Pharisees thought well of him. On one occasion, at the Feast of Tabernacles, he is said to have wept as he read Dt. xvii. 15, remembering his Edomite ancestry, whereupon the people called out repeatedly, 'You are our brother!' (Mishna, *Soṭa*, vii. 8). Cf. Jos. *Ant.* xviii. 6, 7, 8; xix. 4. 1–8. 2. For his death see on *vv.* 20 ff.

τινας τῶν ἀπὸ τῆς ἐκκλησίας] cf. *οἱ ἐκ τῆς περιτομῆς*, x. 45; xi. 2.

xii. 2

ἀνεῖλεν δὲ Ἰάκωβον] Thus was fulfilled, so far as James was concerned, his Master's prophecy of Mk. x. 39. E. Schwartz (*ZNTW* xi [1910], pp. 89 ff.), followed by A. Loisy and R. Eisler, unwarrantably assumed that the original text said 'James and John his brother', or words to that effect. The theory, so strongly advocated by some, that John the son of Zebedee also suffered martyrdom either now or at some later time before the destruction of Jerusalem rests on the flimsiest evidence, which, in the words of A. S. Peake, 'would have provoked derision if it had been adduced in favour of a conservative conclusion' (quoted by W. F. Howard in *The Fourth Gospel in Recent Criticism and Interpretation*, p. 234). Anyone who wishes to see it satisfactorily disposed of may consult J. H. Bernard in *Studia Sacra*, pp. 260 ff., and in his commentary on Jn. in *ICC*, pp. xxxvii ff.; the conclusion reached is that 'no inference can be drawn from a corrupt sentence in a late epitome of a work of a careless historian'. Eusebius (*HE* ii. 9) quotes from Clement of Alexandria's *Hypotyposes* vii the tradition that the officer who guarded James was so impressed by his demeanour that he professed himself a Christian and both were beheaded together.

xii. 3

ὅτι ἀρεστόν ἐστιν τοῖς Ἰουδαίοις] This is in accordance with Herod's consistent policy of conciliating Jewish opinion. The δ text adds *ἡ ἐπιχείρησις αὐτοῦ ἐπὶ τοὺς πιστούς*.

προσέθετο συλλαβεῖν] lit., 'he added to seize', i.e., 'he also seized'. A Semitic construction, common in OT. Cf. Lk. xix. 11; xx 11 f. (where *προσέθετο . . . πέμψαι* = *πάλιν ἀπέστειλεν* of Mt. xxi. 36; Mk. xii. 4). This is frequently said to be the only Semitism found in the Gk. of Josephus (cf. *BC* ii, p. 63 n.), but H. St. J. Thackeray, in *JTS* xxx (1929), pp. 361 ff., points out that the examples of προστίθεσθαι with infin. in Josephus have a different meaning, and are not Semitisms.[1]

καὶ Πέτρον] Probably because Peter was the recognized leader of the Twelve.

ἦσαν δὲ ἡμέραι τῶν ἀζύμων] The days of unleavened bread commenced on Passover Eve, 14th Nisan, and lasted till 21st Nisan (Ex. xii. 18, etc.).[2] Cf. xx. 6. Observe how the parenthesis commences with δέ, after which the relative ὅν catches up the antecedent Πέτρον.

xii. 4

ἔθετο εἰς φυλακήν] ἔθετο ἐν φυλακῇ E P^{45}. Cf. iv. 3; v. 18, 25 for similar phrases with the middle of τίθημι (cf. also i. 7).

παραδοὺς . . . φυλάσσειν] For the infin. cf. xvi. 4, παρεδίδοσαν . . . φυλάσσειν.

τέσσαρσιν τετραδίοις στρατιωτῶν] One quaternion (company of four soldiers) for each watch of the night. Cf. Vegetius, *de re militari* iii. 8, '*in quattuor partes ad clepsydram sunt diuisae uigiliae ut non amplius quam tribus horis nocturnis necesse sit uigilare*'.

μετὰ τὸ πάσχα] Cf. Mk. xiv. 2, μὴ ἐν τῇ ἑορτῇ, omitted in Lk. xxii. 2. Cf. i. 7; vi. 11 ff.; ix. 40 for Markan ideas omitted in Lk. but used in a new context in Ac.[3] The Passover strictly speaking was the feast of 14th Nisan, but Luke uses πάσχα in a wider sense, of the whole festal season: cf. Lk. xxii. 1 (ἡ ἑορτὴ τῶν ἀζύμων ἡ λεγομένη πάσχα) and 7 (ἡ ἡμέρα τῶν ἀζύμων ᾗ ἔδει θύεσθαι τὸ πάσχα) in contrast with Mk. xiv. 1, τὸ πάσχα καὶ τὰ ἄζυμα.

ἀναγαγεῖν αὐτὸν τῷ λαῷ] MM quote from an inscription of the first century A.D. the phrase ἀναχθέντα εἰς τὸν δῆμον.

xii. 5

ἐν τῇ φυλακῇ] Some forms of δ (p vg.cod hcl*) add *a cohorte regis*, which Blass, Zahn and Clark restore as ὑπὸ τῆς σπείρης τοῦ βασιλέως. See further on x. 1 for Herod's armed forces.

[1] But Thackeray did trace in Josephus's use of the otiose ἄρχεσθαι with infin. of verbs of speaking in *Ant.* i.-xiii. and *BJ* iii. 8. 5, 'an instance of unconscious and involuntary retention of the author's native Aramaic phraseology'.

[2] According to R. A. Parker and W. H. Dubberstein (*Babylonian Chronology* [1946], p. 46), 14th Nisan in A.D. 44 fell on 1st May—an unusually late date owing to the intercalation of a second Adar that year from 19th March to 17th April (inclusive).

[3] The chief instance of this Lukan procedure may be found in the 'Great Omission', i.e. Mk. vi. 45-viii. 26, which has no parallel in Lk., possibly because it adumbrates Christ's communication of himself to the Gentiles, a subject fully developed in Ac.

ἦν . . . γινομένη] A curious example of the periphrasis commented on in the note on i. 10 ; if it differs from ἐγίνετο, it must be as laying special emphasis on the continuousness of the praying.

ἐκτενῶς] 'earnestly' : cf. xxvi. 7 (ἐν ἐκτενείᾳ) ; Lk. xxii. 44 (ἐκτενέστερον) ; Judith iv. 9 (καὶ ἀνεβόησαν πᾶς ἀνὴρ Ἰσραὴλ πρὸς τὸν θεὸν ἐν ἐκτενείᾳ μεγάλῃ, καὶ ἐταπεινοῦσαν τὰς ψυχὰς αὐτῶν ἐν ἐκτενείᾳ μεγάλῃ).

xii. 6

προσαγαγεῖν] B 33 ; προαγαγεῖν A 36 81 ; προσάγειν א ; προάγειν D byz. With aor. infin. μέλλω is used six times in NT (here and in Rom. viii. 18 ; Gal. iii. 23 ; Rev. iii. 2, 16 ; xii. 4 ; also Lk. xx. 36 D W Θ Marcion) ; with pres. infin. eighty-four times ; with fut. infin. three times (all in Ac. : xi. 28 ; xxiv. 15 ; xxvii. 10). See *Proleg.*, p. 114 n.

δεδεμένος] Cf. xxi. 33 ; xxvi. 7, 29 ; Ignatius, *Rom.* v. i (δεδεμένος δέκα λεοπάρδοις, ὅ ἐστιν στρατιωτικὸν τάγμα). Herod had himself been so bound during his imprisonment in Rome, συνδεδεμένον αὐτῷ στρατιώτην (Jos. *Ant.* xviii. 6. 7).

φύλακές τε πρὸ τῆς θύρας] Two members of the quaternion were on either side of Peter ; the other two probably acted as guards at the door. Cf. v. 23, τοὺς φύλακας ἑστῶτας ἐπὶ τῶν θυρῶν.

xii. 7

καὶ ἰδοὺ ἄγγελος Κυρίου ἐπέστη] Cf. Lk. ii. 9, καὶ ἄγγελος Κυρίου ἐπέστη. The expression used, and the name ἄγγελος Κυρίου (see on v. 19 ; viii. 26) seem to exclude the idea that a human messenger is meant. A certain parallelism of form and language can be observed in both Biblical and extra-Biblical accounts of escapes from prison : with this passage cf. v. 17 ff. (where also the angel of the Lord opens the prison) ; xvi. 25 f. ; cf. also Euripides, *Bacchae* 443 ff. ; Ovid, *Metamorphoses* iii. 696 ff. Cf. R. Reitzenstein, *Hellenistische Wundererzählungen*, pp. 120 ff., who compares similar language in the 'Acts of Thomas', 118 ff.

ἐπέστη] Of superhuman appearances in xxiii. 11 ; Lk. ii. 9 (cf. previous note) ; xxiv. 4.

φῶς ἔλαμψεν] Cf. the continuation of the passage quoted above from Lk. ii. 9, δόξα Κυρίου περιέλαμψεν αὐτούς.

οἰκήματι] For the Attic use of οἴκημα euphemistically for prison cf. Demosthenes, *Zenothemis* 29.

ἀνάστα] See on ix. 11.

xii. 9

διὰ τοῦ ἀγγέλου] 'by the agency of the angel' : it was the work of God.

ὅραμα] Cf. ix. 10, 12; x. 3, 17. Sadhu Sundar Singh's escape from a well in Tibet, which presents remarkable parallels to this narrative, is quoted by L. E. Browne (Comm., *ad loc.*). But 'Peter thought it was all a vision until he found himself safe and sound. The Sadhu thought the rescuer was a man until he disappeared.'

xii. 10

διελθόντες κ.τ.λ.] The description seems to reflect the account of an eyewitness. Peter's prison was probably the Tower of Antonia, where Paul also was detained (xxi. 34-xxiii. 30).

πρώτην κ.τ.λ.] 'There were obviously three gates and three wards to pass (Peter was allowed to pass the first and the second, being taken presumably as a servant; but no servant would be expected to pass beyond the outermost ward at night, and a different course was needed there)' (Ramsay, *SPT*, p. 28).

αὐτομάτη] Such automatic opening of doors can be traced in Gk. literature from Homer downwards. Cf. the account in Jos. *BJ* vi. 5. 3 of how the heavy east gate of the inner court of the Temple opened *αὐτομάτως*. LC quote Artapanus, *de Iudaeis* (*ap.* Euseb. *Praep. Evang.* ix. 27, 23), *νυκτὸς δὲ ἐπιγενομένης τάς τε θύρας πάσας αὐτομάτως ἀνοιχθῆναι τοῦ δεσμωτηρίου καὶ τῶν φυλάκων οὓς μὲν τελευτῆσαι, τινὰς δὲ ὑπὸ τοῦ ὕπνου παρεθῆναι τά τε ὅπλα κατεαγῆναι.* Cf. also the opening of the doors by earthquake action in xvi. 26, and by angelic action in v. 19.

ἐξελθόντες] δ (D p) adds *κατέβησαν τοὺς ἑπτὰ βαθμοὺς καί*, an addition so circumstantial that it looks like a genuine piece of local colour depending on the information of someone who saw Jerusalem before its fall in A.D. 70. (N.B. p omits *ἑπτά*.)

ῥύμην μίαν] Another detail depending on local knowledge. The use of *μίαν* practically as an indefinite art. is a mark of Koiné.

xii. 11

ἐν ἑαυτῷ γενόμενος] 'coming to himself' (lit., 'in himself'); hitherto he had been 'outside himself', i.e., *ἐν ἐκστάσει*, as on the housetop in Joppa (see on x. 10). The angel and the 'trance' left him together. With the phrase here cf. Lk. xv. 17, *εἰς ἑαυτὸν δὲ ἐλθών*.

ὁ κύριος] B Ψ 614 Chrys; *Κύριος* ℵ A D 81 byz.

προσδοκίας] Objective, not subjective. Torrey (*CDA*, pp. 36 f.) sees behind it Aram. *maḥshabtā*, which can mean 'plot', 'machination' as well as 'thought', 'opinion', 'calculation'.

xii. 12

συνιδών] 'having realized the position': cf. xiv. 6.

ἐπὶ τὴν οἰκίαν τῆς Μαρίας τῆς μητρὸς Ἰωάνου τοῦ ἐπικαλουμένου Μάρκου] This house seems to have been a meeting-place of disciples in Jerusalem; it was, perhaps, the house in which the Last Supper took place. If we put this conjecture alongside the usual interpretation of Mk. xiv. 51, we have an attractive and not improbable picture of Mark's first appearance in the NT narrative. His subsequent history may be gathered from xii. 25; xiii. 5-13; xv. 37 ff.; Col. iv. 10 with Philm. 24; 2 Tim. iv. 11; 1 Pet. v. 13. According to later writers, he acted as Peter's interpreter in Rome and reproduced his preaching in the Second Gospel, and afterwards went to Egypt and founded the church in Alexandria (cf. the traditions of Papias, Irenaeus, Clement of Alexandria and others preserved in Euseb. *HE* ii. 15 f.; iii. 39; v. 8; vi. 14). He is one of many Jews in Ac. who have a Gentile as well as a Jewish name. He may well have been Luke's informant for this and other Jerusalem narratives. B. Weiss, F. Blass and others have supposed that Mark wrote a continuation of his Gospel, which was used by Luke as a source for the early history of the Jerusalem church (cf. p. 22). Blass argues that this continuation must have been written in Aram. (*PG*, pp. 141, 193), as indeed his Gospel seems to him originally to have been.

Notice how Mary is identified by the addition of her son's name (cf. Mk. xv. 21, 40); the readers of Ac. were better acquainted with the second than with the first generation of disciples.

xii. 13

ὑπακοῦσαι] 'to answer the door': cf. Plato, *Phaedo* 59E, *ὁ θυρωρός, ὅσπερ εἰώθει ὑπακούειν.*

Ῥόδη] Gk. name (*ῥόδος*, 'rose'); the name is common, appearing, e.g., in the *Shepherd* of Hermas, i. 1. Cf. Ramsay's chapter, 'Rhoda the Slave-Girl', in *BRD*, pp. 209 ff.

xii. 14

ἀπὸ τῆς χαρᾶς] Causal *ἀπό* as in xi. 19; xxii. 11.

xii. 15

πρὸς αὐτὴν εἶπαν] *εἶπον πρὸς αὐτήν* 33 P^{45}.

ἔλεγον] B has *εἶπαν*. The imperf. implies repetition.

ὁ ἄγγελός ἐστιν αὐτοῦ] Cf. Mt. xviii. 10; Heb. i. 14; Gen. xlviii. 16; Dan. iii. 28; vi. 22; Tobit v. 4 ff. The angel is here conceived of as a man's spiritual counterpart, capable of assuming his appearance and being mistaken for him. Cf. J. H. Moulton in *JTS* iii (1902), pp. 516 f. ℵ* P^{45} omit *ὁ*.

xii. 17

κατασείσας δὲ αὐτοῖς τῇ χειρὶ σιγᾶν] Again the evident touch of an eye-witness, as indeed the whole scene is—the delightful description of Rhoda's excitement, which made her forget to open the door; the incredulous reply of those within, too surprised to believe that their own prayers had been answered so quickly; Rhoda's insistence that it really was Peter—while all the time the poor man himself stands anxiously knocking for admission! Now we picture him entering and hushing with a gesture the Babel of excited questions about to burst forth; for all he knew, his enemies might already be on his track.

For *σιγᾶν* the δ text has *ἵνα σιγάσωσιν*, as in xvi. 18 it has *ἵνα ἐξέλθῃς* for *ἐξελθεῖν*, in both places after a verb of command or its equivalent. This infinitival use of *ἵνα* with subjunctive is a step in the direction of Mod. Gk.

Ἰακώβῳ] James gets separate mention as a recognized leader; no mention is made of the other apostles. See on xv. 13.

εἰς ἕτερον τόπον] The tradition, recorded in Eusebius's *Chronicon* under the year 42, that Peter went to Rome at this time, is contradicted by the evidence of the NT (he is still in Jerusalem at the time of Paul's visits recorded in Gal. ii. 1 ff. and Ac. xv. 2 ff.), and is due to the fictions in the 'Acts of Peter' and the *Clementine Recognitions* and *Homilies* which brought him to Rome at that time to contend with Simon Magus, who, according to Justin, came to Rome in the time of Claudius (see on viii. 9). Cf. B. H. Streeter, *The Primitive Church*, pp. 7 ff. We cannot say where the 'other place' was to which Peter now went; probably he did not say where he was going, for very good reasons.[1]

xii. 18

οὐκ ὀλίγος] This particular litotes is characteristic of Luke, as it was of Thucydides. It recurs in xiv. 28; xv. 2; xvii. 4, 12; xix. 23 f.; xxvii. 20. For other examples of litotes cf. xiv. 17; xvii. 27; xix. 11; xx. 12; xxi. 39; xxvi. 19, 26; xxviii. 2.

τί ἄρα ὁ Πέτρος ἐγένετο] 'what had become of Peter': *ἄρα* is inferential (cf. xi. 18); he was clearly not in the prison, so what had happened to him? Cf. Lk. i. 66, *Τί ἄρα τὸ παιδίον τοῦτο ἔσται;*

xii. 19

μὴ εὑρὼν] *μή* with ptc., as regularly (cf. ix. 9, 26).

ἀνακρίνας] Cf. iv. 9; xxiv. 8; xxviii. 18.

ἀπαχθῆναι] Probably in the Attic sense, to be led away to execution, as in Lk. xxiii. 26. D has *ἀποκτανθῆναι*, d *obduci*. There is, however, papyrus evidence for *ἀπάγω* as the ordinary word meaning

[1] We should probably accept the statement of Lactantius (*de mort. persec.* ii. 5) that Nero was already Emperor when Peter came to Rome. For dating Peter's first Roman visit *c.* A.D. 55 see T. W. Manson in *BJRL* xxviii (1944), pp. 130 f.

'to arrest', 'to lead off to prison': cf. Gen. xxxix. 22; xl. 3; xlii. 16 LXX. According to Justinian's Code (ix. 4. 4) a guard who allowed a prisoner to escape became liable to the same penalty as had awaited the prisoner.

κατελθὼν ἀπὸ τῆς Ἰουδαίας εἰς Καισαρίαν διέτριβεν] Judaea is here used in the narrowest sense; politically Caesarea was in Judaea, being the Roman capital of the province; but as a thoroughly Gentile city it was not in the country of the Jews.

(b) Death of Herod Agrippa I, xii. 20-23

Ἦν δὲ θυμομαχῶν Τυρίοις καὶ Σιδωνίοις· ὁμοθυμαδὸν δὲ παρῆσαν 20
πρὸς αὐτόν, καὶ πείσαντες Βλάστον τὸν ἐπὶ τοῦ κοιτῶνος τοῦ βασιλέως
ᾐτοῦντο εἰρήνην διὰ τὸ τρέφεσθαι αὐτῶν τὴν χώραν ἀπὸ τῆς βασιλικῆς.
τακτῇ δὲ ἡμέρᾳ ὁ Ἡρῴδης ἐνδυσάμενος ἐσθῆτα βασιλικὴν καθίσας 21
ἐπὶ τοῦ βήματος ἐδημηγόρει πρὸς αὐτούς· ὁ δὲ δῆμος ἐπεφώνει Θεοῦ 22
φωνὴ καὶ οὐκ ἀνθρώπου. παραχρῆμα δὲ ἐπάταξεν αὐτὸν ἄγγελος Κυρίου 23
ἀνθ' ὧν οὐκ ἔδωκεν τὴν δόξαν τῷ θεῷ, καὶ γενόμενος σκωληκόβρωτος
ἐξέψυξεν.

xii. 20

θυμομαχῶν] 'furious', 'exasperated'; so in Polybius ix. 40. 4; xxvii. 8. 4; Plutarch, *Demetrius* 22.

Τυρίοις καὶ Σιδωνίοις] Tyre and Sidon were from ancient times the chief cities of the Phoenician coast. Under the Romans they were free cities, but their economic dependence on Herod's territory made it a matter of prudence to keep on friendly terms with him. The cause of his anger is unknown. It was at Tyre that he quarrelled with Antipas (see on *ver.* 1).

ὁμοθυμαδὸν δὲ] *καὶ ὁμοθυμαδόν* P^{45}.

πείσαντες] 'having persuaded'; i.e., having procured his good offices.

Βλάστον] This Blastus is otherwise unknown; the name is common.

τὸν ἐπὶ τοῦ κοιτῶνος τοῦ βασιλέως] lit., 'who was over the king's bedchamber', i.e., 'the king's chamberlain'; the title is common in inscriptions and in the Byzantine period.

ᾐτοῦντο] Middle voice; what they sought was something in their own interest.

διὰ τὸ τρέφεσθαι κ.τ.λ.] As in the days of Hiram, Phoenicia depended on Galilee for its food supply (cf. 1 K. v. 9 ff. [LXX, 3 K.]).

xii. 21

τακτῇ δὲ ἡμέρᾳ] According to Jos. *Ant.* xix. 8. 2, it was a festival in honour of the Emperor, possibly on 1st August, the anniversary of his birthday (cf. Suet., *Claud.* ii. 1). This may well have been utilized as an opportunity for public reconciliation.

ἐνδυσάμενος ἐσθῆτα βασιλικὴν] Cf. Josephus (*loc. cit.*). στολὴν ἐνδυσάμενος ἐξ ἀργύρου πεποιημένην πᾶσαν, ὡς θαυμάσιον τὴν ὑφὴν εἶναι.

πρὸς αὐτούς] δ adds καταλλαγέντος δὲ αὐτοῦ τοῖς Τυρίοις.

xii. 22

δῆμος] The populace of a Greek city, here of Caesarea.

Θεοῦ φωνὴ καὶ οὐκ ἀνθρώπου] According to Josephus, his flatterers, addressing him as a god (θεὸν προσαγορεύοντες), said, 'Be gracious to us; if hitherto we have reverenced thee as a human being, yet henceforth we acknowledge thee to be of more than mortal nature'.

xii. 23

ἐπάταξεν αὐτὸν ἄγγελος Κυρίου] Cf. *ver.* 7, ἄγγελος Κυρίου . . . πατάξας, a different kind of smiting! For this sense, cf. xxiii. 3; 1 Sam. xxv. 38; 2 Sam. xii. 15; 2 K. xix. 35; 2 Chr. xiii. 20; 2 Macc. ix. 5.

ἀνθ' ὧν] Cf. Lk. i. 20; xix. 44; 2 Th. ii. 10.

οὐκ ἔδωκεν τὴν δόξαν τῷ θεῷ] See on xi. 18. Here the sense seems to be that he did not give God the glory that had been improperly ascribed to himself; contrast the action of Paul and Barnabas in xiv. 14 ff. The δ text (D Eph) adds καὶ καταβὰς ἀπὸ τοῦ βήματος, γενόμενος σκωληκόβρωτος ἔτι ζῶν καὶ οὕτως ἐξέψυξεν. The addition ἔτι ζῶν emphasizes the unpleasantness of his disease (cf. Herodotus iv. 205; Pausanias ix. 7. 2; Tert., *ad Scap.* 3).

σκωληκόβρωτος] Theophrastus (*History of Plants*, iii. 12. 6) uses this word of diseased grain, a use which can be paralleled from the papyri (cf. MM). This kind of death is frequently mentioned by ancient writers, especially as having been endured by people who were considered to have richly deserved it (see on i. 18): cf. 2 Macc. ix. 5 ff. (of Antiochus IV); Jos. *Ant.* vii. 6. 5 (of Herod the Great); Papias, fragment referred to on i. 18 (of Judas); Lucian, *Alexander* 59 (of Alexander the impostor); Euseb. *HE* viii. 16 (of Galerius); Theodoretus *HE* iii. 9 (of the uncle and namesake of Julian the Apostate).

ἐξέψυξεν] Cf. v. 5, 10.

While there is substantial agreement between Luke and Josephus on the manner of Agrippa's death, there is so great a difference in the details as to exclude the possibility that the one account is dependent on the other. According to Josephus, early on the second morning of the festival at Caesarea the king entered the theatre, when the rays of the rising sun made his silver robe shine so brightly that those who saw it were dazzled and cried out that he was a god. He neither repudiated the title nor rebuked their flattery, but soon afterwards, seeing an owl sitting above his head, he recognized it to be a messenger of evil (ἄγγελον κακῶν εἶναι), in accordance with a prophecy once made to him, and, being immediately seized with violent internal pains, was carried home and died five days later (see p. 18 n.).

(c) The Gospel continues to progress, xii. 24

Ὁ δὲ λόγος τοῦ κυρίου ηὔξανεν καὶ ἐπληθύνετο. 24

xii. 24

ὁ δὲ λόγος κ.τ.λ.] This is the third of the brief reports of progress by which the book is punctuated (cf. vi. 7 ; ix. 31), the prosperity of the work of God being emphasized by contrast with the persecutor's miserable end.

κυρίου] B vg ; θεοῦ cett.

IV. PAUL'S FIRST MISSIONARY JOURNEY AND THE APOSTOLIC DECREE, xii. 25-xvi. 5

1. Barnabas and Saul, xii. 25-xiii. 3

(a) Return of the Famine-Relief Delegation, xii. 25

Βαρνάβας δὲ καὶ Σαῦλος ὑπέστρεψαν εἰς Ἰερουσαλὴμ πληρώσαντες 25
τὴν διακονίαν, συνπαραλαβόντες Ἰωάνην τὸν ἐπικληθέντα Μάρκον.

xii. 25

Βαρνάβας δὲ καὶ Σαῦλος] δ (614 p hcl*) adds ὃς ἐπεκλήθη Παῦλος.

ὑπέστρεψαν εἰς Ἰερουσαλὴμ πληρώσαντες τὴν διακονίαν] This, the reading of ℵ B 81 byz hcl.mg. eth, might possibly be translated, 'Barnabas and Saul returned [to Antioch], having fulfilled their ministry at Jerusalem'. But this rendering, though it undoubtedly gives the true sense, supposes an unnatural order of the Gk. words. K. Lake (*EEP*, pp. 317 ff.) takes εἰς Ἰερουσαλήμ with ὑπέστρεψαν, and the aor. ptc. πληρώσαντες in the sense 'in fulfilment of' (cf. xxv. 13, ἀσπασάμενοι). We should then translate, 'But Barnabas and Saul returned [from Antioch] to Jerusalem in fulfilment of their ministry'. The attractiveness of this rendering, which takes ὑπέστρεψαν εἰς Ἰερουσαλήμ in the most natural way, is offset by the difficulty of getting at the same time a satisfactory sense for συνπαραλαβόντες. The difficulty of the reading led to various early attempts at correction ; thus A 33 minn boh arm have ἐξ Ἰερουσαλήμ, D 181 431 614 g vg have ἀπὸ Ἰερουσαλήμ, some minn have εἰς Ἀντιόχειαν, while E 1898 minn e p pesh sah have the conflate ἐξ (or ἀπὸ) Ἰερουσαλὴμ εἰς Ἀντιόχειαν. WH suggest a change of order τὴν εἰς Ἰερουσαλὴμ πληρώσαντες διακονίαν, which is much neater and more intelligible than the reading in their text, but for that very reason not likely to have been replaced by it. J. V. Bartlet (Cent. Bib.) regards εἰς Ἰερουσαλήμ as a gloss, inserted by a scribe in imitation of the expression in i. 12 ; viii. 25 ; xiii. 13 ; xxii. 17 ; Lk. ii. 45 ; xxiv. 33, 52. In view of the variety of readings, this solution has claims to be regarded as the most satisfactory one, even though it cuts the knot instead of untying it. L. E. Browne agrees (see on ix. 28).

διακονίαν] The διακονία of xi. 29 (*q.v.*).

Μάρκον] Ephrem Syrus adds 'and Luke the Cyrenean', with the comment, 'And these were both evangelists, and wrote before the discipleship of Paul'. The comment has interest mainly as indicating a belief that Luke the evangelist was Lucius of Cyrene (cf. xiii. 1).

(b) Barnabas and Saul sent from Antioch to Evangelize, xiii. 1-3

Ἦσαν δὲ ἐν Ἀντιοχείᾳ κατὰ τὴν οὖσαν ἐκκλησίαν προφῆται καὶ 1
διδάσκαλοι ὅ τε Βαρνάβας καὶ Συμεὼν ὁ καλούμενος Νίγερ, καὶ
Λούκιος ὁ Κυρηναῖος, Μαναήν τε Ἡρῴδου τοῦ τετραάρχου σύντροφος
καὶ Σαῦλος. Λειτουργούντων δὲ αὐτῶν τῷ κυρίῳ καὶ νηστευόντων 2
εἶπεν τὸ πνεῦμα τὸ ἅγιον Ἀφορίσατε δή μοι τὸν Βαρνάβαν καὶ Σαῦλον
εἰς τὸ ἔργον ὃ προσκέκλημαι αὐτούς. τότε νηστεύσαντες καὶ προσ- 3
ευξάμενοι καὶ ἐπιθέντες τὰς χεῖρας αὐτοῖς ἀπέλυσαν.

xiii. 1

κατὰ τὴν οὖσαν ἐκκλησίαν] 'in the local church': cf. xi. 22, and see on v. 17.

προφῆται] In addition to those who came down from Jerusalem, xi. 27 (*q.v.*) ; those were temporary visitors, while these in this verse belonged to the Antiochene church.

διδάσκαλοι] Cf. 1 Cor. xii. 28 f. ; Eph. iv. 11 for their place in the church ; for the nature of their activity cf. xi. 26 ; xv. 35 ; xviii. 11 ; xx. 20 ; xxviii. 31.

Συμεὼν ὁ καλούμενος Νίγερ] Another example of a Jew with a Latin name as well as a Hebrew one (cf. xii. 12). His Latin name probably indicates that he was an African ; but his identity with Simon of Cyrene (Lk. xxiii. 26, etc.) is not proven.

Λούκιος ὁ Κυρηναῖος] Perhaps one of the men of Cyrene mentioned in xi. 20. There is no evidence to connect him with the

Lucius of Rom. xvi. 21. and the suggestion that he was Luke the evangelist is improbable (see on xii. 25 *fin.*).[1]

Μαναήν τε Ἡρῴδου τοῦ τετραάρχου σύντροφος] D has *καί* for *τοῦ*. Manaen is the OT name Menaḥem ('comforter'). The title *σύντροφος* was given to boys of the same age as princes, who were brought up with them at court. (Here MM prefer the more general sense 'courtier', 'intimate friend', found in inscriptions.) 'Herod the tetrarch' is Antipas (see on iv. 27). In Jos. *Ant.* xv. 10. 5 we read of another Manaen, an Essene, honoured by Herod the Great for having foretold his rise to royal estate; he could have been the grandfather of this Manaen. Luke shows a special interest in Antipas and his entourage (cf. Lk. viii. 3; xiii. 32; xxiii. 7 ff.). Some of his information may well have been derived from Manaen, especially if Luke himself was an Antiochene.

xiii. 2

λειτουργούντων] This verb was used in Attic Gk. of performing an unpaid public service, e.g., helping to equip naval units or training choruses (dancing choirs) for the state festivals. In NT it is used of service in the Christian community, in a much wider sense than that represented by the later ecclesiastical use of 'liturgy'.

νηστευόντων] For spiritual communications received during hunger or fasting, cf. ix. 12; x. 10 ff., 30 (δ).

εἶπεν τὸ πνεῦμα τὸ ἅγιον] Presumably through a prophet.

ἀφορίσατε δή] The addition of *δή* emphasizes the imperative: cf. xv. 36; Lk. ii. 15.

Βαρνάβαν καὶ Σαῦλον] It is worth noting that the two men to be released for missionary service were the most gifted and outstanding in the church.

[1] A remarkable reading of this verse is given in a work apparently entitled *Prophetiae ex omnibus libris collectae*, described by Zahn as a compendium of Biblical prophecy, originating in the African Church *c.* 305-25: '*erant etiam in ecclesia prophetae et doctores Barnabas et Saulus, quibus imposuerunt manus prophetae Symeon qui appellatus est Niger, et Lucius Cirenensis, qui manet usque adhuc et Ticius conlactaneus, qui acceperant responsum ab spiritu sancto, unde dixerunt Segregate' et sqq.* On the basis of this reading Zahn (*Urausgabe*) reconstructs the original Greek text: *ἦσαν δὲ ἐν τῇ ἐκκλησίᾳ προφῆται καὶ διδάσκαλοι Βαρνάβας καὶ Σαῦλος οἷς ἐπέθηκαν τὰς χεῖρας οἱ προφῆται Συμεὼν ὁ καλούμενος Νίγερ καὶ Λούκιος Κυρηναῖος ὃς μένει ἕως ἄρτι, καὶ Τίτος ⟨Ἀντιοχεὺς⟩ Μαναήν τε Ἡρῴδου τοῦ τετράρχου σύντροφος, οἵτινες ἐχρηματίσθησαν ὑπὸ τοῦ πνεύματος τοῦ ἁγίου, ὅθεν εἶπον Ἀφορίσατε κ.τ.λ.* As this document is also a witness for the δ reading at xi. 27 f., it suggests that here Lucius of Cyrene was understood as Luke the evangelist, and that Titus was his brother. (For the connection of Titus with Antioch see Gal. ii. 1.) Lucius was a common Roman praenomen. See H. J. Cadbury's note 'Lucius of Cyrene' in *BC* v, pp. 489 ff.

ἔργον] Cf. *ver.* 41; xiv. 26; xv. 38; the work was the evangelizing of the routes to the west.

ὅ] Acc., governed by πρός in προσκέκλημαι.

προσκέκλημαι αὐτούς] The call came from God; the church's responsibility was to recognize the divine appointment and act accordingly. This verb in NT appears in the middle voice only ('call to oneself'); the force here may be 'call to one's service'.

xiii. 3

νηστεύσαντες καὶ προσευξάμενοι] For the combination of fasting and praying cf. xiv. 23; Lk. ii. 37. After προσευξάμενοι D adds πάντες, which is probably the proper interpretation. The whole church sent them forth, and it was to the whole church that they gave their report when they returned. Cf. xiv. 26 f.

ἐπιθέντες τὰς χεῖρας αὐτοῖς] Not that they could by this act qualify Barnabas and Saul for the work to which God had called them; but by this means they expressed their fellowship with the two and their recognition of the divine call. Cf. Gal. i. 1 ff. for Paul's claim to have been an apostle since his conversion.

ἀπέλυσαν] 'let them go': cf. iv. 23; xv. 33.

2. CYPRUS, xiii. 4-12

(a) The Missionaries arrive in Cyprus, xiii. 4-5

Αὐτοὶ μὲν οὖν ἐκπεμφθέντες ὑπὸ τοῦ ἁγίου πνεύματος κατῆλθον 4
εἰς Σελευκίαν, ἐκεῖθέν τε ἀπέπλευσαν εἰς Κύπρον, καὶ γενόμενοι ἐν 5
Σαλαμῖνι κατήγγελλον τὸν λόγον τοῦ θεοῦ ἐν ταῖς συναγωγαῖς τῶν
Ἰουδαίων· εἶχον δὲ καὶ Ἰωάννην ὑπηρέτην.

xiii. 4

κατῆλθον] Compounds in κατά are regularly used of movement towards the coast, either from inland (as here) or from the high seas; conversely, compounds in ἀνά are used of movement either out to sea or inland from the coast (cf. ἀναχθέντες, *ver.* 13).

Σελευκίαν] The port of Antioch, founded by Seleucus Nicator. It was 16 miles west of Antioch and 5 miles north of the mouth of the Orontes. Luke is usually careful to note the ports of departure and arrival: cf. xiv. 25; xvi. 11; xviii. 18.

Κύπρον] Cyprus (OT Kittim; cf. its Phoenician town Kition, mod. Larnaka) was an important island in very early times, especially for its export of copper, to which it gave its name. The Romans annexed it in 57 B.C. In 55 B.C. it was incorporated in the province of Cilicia. After various changes, it was made an imperial province, governed by a *legatus pro praetore*, in 27 B.C. Five years later Augustus gave it (and Gallia Narbonensis) to the

Senate, in exchange for Dalmatia, and from that date it was, like other senatorial provinces, governed by a proconsul (Gk. ἀνθύπατος), as Luke correctly indicates in *ver.* 7.

xiii. 5

Σαλαμῖνι] Salamis, a Greek city on the east coast of Cyprus, dating from the sixth century B.C., was the chief town of the island and seat of government of the eastern half, though the provincial capital was New Paphos. It was a flourishing commercial centre, and its Jewish colony was large enough to require more than one synagogue.

ἐν ταῖς συναγωγαῖς] Cf. ix. 20. Throughout his journeys, Paul's settled policy was to visit the synagogues first (cf. *ver.* 14), that the good news might be preached 'to the Jew first' (ὑμῖν . . . πρῶτον, *ver.* 46). Besides, 'he was always sure of a good opening for his Gentile mission among the "God-fearing", who formed part of his audience in every synagogue' (Ramsay, *SPT*, p. 72).

εἶχον δὲ καὶ Ἰωάννην ὑπηρέτην] For δὲ καί cf. ii. 26; v. 16. 'John' is the John Mark of xii. 12, 25, who was cousin to Barnabas (Col. iv. 10). With ὑπηρέτην cf. Lk. i. 2, ὑπηρέται τοῦ λόγου, among whom perhaps Mark is included. A. Wright (*Composition of the Four Gospels* [1890], pp. 15 f.) argues that he attended them as a duly authorized catechist. Even at this early stage he may have begun to take notes of the Kerygma, especially as proclaimed by Peter, who was a welcome guest in his home; this would make him a useful companion to the missionaries. He may also have had first-hand knowledge of some of the momentous events of Passion Week (see on xii. 12).

(b) The Incident at Paphos, xiii. 6-12

Διελθόντες δὲ ὅλην τὴν νῆσον ἄχρι Πάφου εὗρον ἄνδρα τινὰ μάγον 6
ψευδοπροφήτην Ἰουδαῖον ᾧ ὄνομα Βαριησοῦς, ὃς ἦν σὺν τῷ ἀνθυπάτῳ 7
Σεργίῳ Παύλῳ, ἀνδρὶ συνετῷ. οὗτος προσκαλεσάμενος Βαρνάβαν
καὶ Σαῦλον ἐπεζήτησεν ἀκοῦσαι τὸν λόγον τοῦ θεοῦ· ἀνθίστατο δὲ 8
αὐτοῖς Ἐλύμας ὁ μάγος, οὕτως γὰρ μεθερμηνεύεται τὸ ὄνομα αὐτοῦ,
ζητῶν διαστρέψαι τὸν ἀνθύπατον ἀπὸ τῆς πίστεως. Σαῦλος δέ, ὁ καὶ 9
Παῦλος, πλησθεὶς πνεύματος ἁγίου ἀτενίσας εἰς αὐτὸν εἶπεν Ὦ 10
πλήρης παντὸς δόλου καὶ πάσης ῥᾳδιουργίας, υἱὲ διαβόλου, ἐχθρὲ
πάσης δικαιοσύνης, οὐ παύσῃ διαστρέφων τὰς ὁδοὺς τοῦ κυρίου
τὰς εὐθείας; καὶ νῦν ἰδοὺ χεὶρ Κυρίου ἐπὶ σέ, καὶ ἔσῃ τυφλὸς μὴ 11
βλέπων τὸν ἥλιον ἄχρι καιροῦ. παραχρῆμα δὲ ἔπεσεν ἐπ' αὐτὸν
ἀχλὺς καὶ σκότος, καὶ περιάγων ἐζήτει χειραγωγούς. τότε ἰδὼν ὁ 12
ἀνθύπατος τὸ γεγονὸς ἐπίστευσεν ἐκπληττόμενος ἐπὶ τῇ διδαχῇ τοῦ
κυρίου.

xiii. 6

Πάφου] i.e., New Paphos, the official capital, in the west of the island, by tradition a Greek settlement. Old Paphos, of Phoenician origin, lay about 7 miles S.E. In both towns the chief object of worship was the goddess of Syrian origin commonly called 'the Paphian', and identified with the Gk. Aphrodite (see also on xi. 19).

εὗρον ἄνδρα τινὰ μάγον] Cf. viii. 9 ff. Luke is fond of pointing parallels between Peter's work and Paul's, perhaps to show that the latter's apostleship was as well attested as the former's (see pp. 32 f.). As this man was a Jew, *μάγος* is not used here in its original or technical sense (see on viii. 9), but in the sense of 'magician'.

ψευδοπροφήτην] Not here one who foretells things which do not come to pass, but one who claims falsely to be a medium of divine revelations.

ᾧ ὄνομα] *ὀνόματι* 431 P[45] p ; *ὀνόματι καλούμενον* D.

Βαριησοῦς] i.e., son of Joshua. *Βαρ- Ἰησοῦα*, the reading of D, represents an attempt to transliterate more accurately the Semitic *Yēshūa'* ('Joshua, Jesus').

xiii. 7

ἀνθυπάτῳ] 'proconsul' (*ἀντί*, 'instead of'; *ὕπατος*, lit. 'highest', used as the equivalent of Lat. *consul*). See on *ver.* 4; and cf. xviii. 12; xix. 38.

Σεργίῳ Παύλῳ] He may be the Lucius Sergius Paullus referred to in *CIL* vi. 31545 as one of the curators of the Tiber in the reign of Claudius. If he went to Cyprus after this curatorship, the date would fit well with his appearance in Ac. Others of the same name, and probably of the same family, are mentioned elsewhere, e.g., L. Sergius Paullus who was propraetor of Galatia in A.D. 72-74, and another namesake who was consul in 152 and 168. In a chapter entitled 'Sergius Paullus and his Relation to Christian Faith' (*BRD*, pp. 150 ff.), Ramsay argues that Sergius Paullus became a well-known name in Christian circles, and that Sergia Paulla, the daughter of our proconsul, was a Christian, together with her son C. Caristanius Fronto, member of a prominent family of Pisidian Antioch.

οὗτος] i.e., Sergius Paullus.

Σαῦλον] *Σαούλ* P[45] (cf. ix. 24; xi. 30).

xiii. 8

Ἐλύμας ὁ μάγος, οὕτως γὰρ μεθερμηνεύεται τὸ ὄνομα αὐτοῦ] Elymas is probably a Semitic word, akin to Arabic *'alīm*, 'wise', 'learned'. Luke explains the name Elymas by adding 'the magician (for thus his name is translated) '. The meaning cannot be that Elymas is the translation of Bar-Jesus, for the two names have quite different meanings, and even if they had the same meaning, it would be a case of explaining *ignotum per ignotius*. The original reading of δ seems to have been Ἐτυμᾶς or Ἑτοιμᾶς, the latter of which forms (cf. ἕτοιμος, 'ready') Klostermann and Zahn tried to connect with Βαρ-Ἰησοῦα, as if Ἰησοῦα were from the Heb. root *shāwāh* ('be equal', and hence, in a derived sense, 'be ready') : cf. the name Ishvah in Gen. xlvi. 17 ; 1 Chr. vii. 30. The variants with *t* instead of *l* may be influenced by the name of Atomos, a Jewish magician who lived in Cyprus about this time, according to Jos. *Ant.* xx. 7. 2 (see on xxiv. 24).

διαστρέψαι] 'to pervert' : cf. *ver.* 9.

ἀπὸ τῆς πίστεως] 'from his faith', the subjective *fides quâ creditur*, rather than the objective *fides quae creditur*. After πίστεως the δ text adds ἐπειδὴ ἥδιστα ἤκουεν αὐτῶν, which is obviously true, but hardly worth saying. Elymas seems to have been one of the pet magicians whom great men sometimes kept in their entourage (cf. *ver.* 7, ὃς ἦν σὺν τῷ ἀνθυπάτῳ), and he had a shrewd suspicion that if the proconsul paid heed to Barnabas and Saul, his own services were likely to be dispensed with.

xiii. 9

Σαῦλος δέ, ὁ καὶ Παῦλος] Here both his Jewish and Gentile names are given, and henceforth, as the environment is now mainly Gentile, he is known by his Roman name. As he was a Roman citizen, Paul (Paullus) must have been his *cognomen;* what his *praenomen* and *nomen* may have been we cannot say. (For an example of a Roman citizen's full name—*praenomen, nomen* and *cognomen*—cf. 'Lucius Sergius Paullus' in the note on *ver.* 7 above.) ὁ καί is the regular way in Gk. of introducing a person's alternative name ; we might almost translate it 'alias'. Ignatius begins each of his letters with Ἰγνάτιος ὁ καὶ Θεοφόρος, and there are many other examples, especially in inscriptions and papyri. The Latin equivalent is *qui et,* also frequent in inscriptions ; so here the Latin versions have *Saulus qui et Paulus.*

xiii. 10

εἶπεν] P^{45} has this after δόλου.

υἱὲ διαβόλου] Cf. Jn. viii. 44 ; 1 Jn. iii. 10. Some have seen here an antithesis to the name Bar-Jesus. For other instances of Paul's use of διάβολος cf. Eph. iv. 27 ; vi. 11 ; 1 Tim. iii. 6 f. ; 2 Tim. ii. 26. See also on x. 38.

οὐ παύσῃ διαστρέφων] 'will you not stop perverting ?'—the 'volitive future', slightly imperative, with an implied reproach.

τὰς ὁδοὺς τοῦ κυρίου τὰς εὐθείας] ℵ[c] C D 81 byz omit τοῦ. Cf. ὁ δὲ διαστρέφων τὰς ὁδοὺς αὐτοῦ γνωσθήσεται, Prov. x. 9; also διότι εὐθεῖαι αἱ ὁδοὶ τοῦ κυρίου, Hos. xiv. 9 (10 LXX).

xiii. 11

καὶ νῦν ἰδοὺ] Cf. xx. 22, 25, where Paul is the speaker.

χεὶρ *Κυρίου*] See on xi. 21; there of blessing, here of judgment.

ἐπὶ σέ] 'against you'.

καὶ ἔσῃ τυφλὸς] 'The apostle, remembering his own example, knew that from the darkness of the eyes the mind's darkness might be restored to light' (Bede). Similarly Chrysostom, *Hom.* xxviii.

μὴ βλέπων] As in ix. 9.

ἄχρι καιροῦ] Cf. Lk. iv. 13; cf. also Ac. xxii. 22, ἄχρι τούτου τοῦ λόγου.

παραχρῆμα δὲ] παραχρῆμά τε ℵ C 81 P^{45}; καὶ εὐθέως D.

ἔπεσεν] ἐπέπεσεν C byz. B omits the following ἐπ' αὐτόν.

ἀχλὺς] Used in medical writers of an inflammation which gives the eye a cloudy appearance; Hobart (pp. 44 f.) gives examples from Hippocrates, Galen and Dioscorides. In Jos. *Ant.* ix. 4. 3 it is used in the same sense as here, of the Syrian army blinded at Elisha's request, τὰς τῶν πολεμίων ὄψεις ἀμαυρῶσαι τὸν θεὸν παρεκάλει, ἀχλὺν αὐταῖς ἐπιβαλόντα ἀφ' ἧς ἀγνοήσειν αὐτὸν ἔμελλον (cf. 2 K. vi. 18 [LXX, 4 K.]).

σκότος] It is unnecessary to find medical parallels for a word so naturally associated with blindness, though Hobart quotes Hippocrates for this use.

> 'The indication of the several stages of the coming on of the blindness, first a dimness, which is succeeded by total darkness, bears traces of medical writing. Compare the description of the healing of the lame man at the temple, ch. iii. 8' (Hobart, p. 45).

περιάγων] 'moving round' (intrans.).

χειραγωγούς] Occurs in Plutarch, *De Fortuna* 98 B; *An seni respublica gerenda sit* 794 D. Cf. χειραγωγοῦντες, ix. 8.

xiii. 12

ἐπίστευσεν] The nature of his belief has been debated, Ramsay suggesting that for Luke belief is the first stage in the process of which the second stage is 'turning to the Lord' (cf. xi. 21), with accompanying baptism; while LC thinks the apostles 'may have mistaken courtesy for conversion'! But a matter-of-fact Roman official was the very person to be convinced by the miracle he had witnessed (seeing is believing!), especially as he was also impressed by their message. Before ἐπίστευσεν the δ text adds ἐθαύμασεν καί.

ἐκπληττόμενος ἐπὶ τῇ διδαχῇ τοῦ κυρίου] Cf. ἐξεπλήσσοντο ἐπὶ τῇ διδαχῇ αὐτοῦ, Mt. vii. 28 ; xxii. 33 ; Mk. i. 22 ; xi. 18 ; Lk. iv. 32 ; also Mt. xiii. 54 ; Mk. vi. 2 ; Lk. ii. 48. ἐπί is common in Koiné after verbs of emotion. The authoritative teaching is accompanied by the power, which is manifested in miracles (cf. Mk. i. 22, 27).

3. Pisidian Antioch, xiii. 13-52

(a) Arrival at Pisidian Antioch, xiii. 13-15

Ἀναχθέντες δὲ ἀπὸ τῆς Πάφου οἱ περὶ Παῦλον ἦλθον εἰς Πέργην 13
τῆς Παμφυλίας· Ἰωάνης δὲ ἀποχωρήσας ἀπ' αὐτῶν ὑπέστρεψεν εἰς
Ἰεροσόλυμα. Αὐτοὶ δὲ διελθόντες ἀπὸ τῆς Πέργης παρεγένοντο εἰς 14
Ἀντιόχειαν τὴν Πισιδίαν, καὶ ἐλθόντες εἰς τὴν συναγωγὴν τῇ ἡμέρᾳ
τῶν σαββάτων ἐκάθισαν. μετὰ δὲ τὴν ἀνάγνωσιν τοῦ νόμου καὶ τῶν 15
προφητῶν ἀπέστειλαν οἱ ἀρχισυνάγωγοι πρὸς αὐτοὺς λέγοντες Ἄνδρες
ἀδελφοί, εἴ τις ἔστιν ἐν ὑμῖν λόγος παρακλήσεως πρὸς τὸν λαόν, λέγετε.

xiii. 13

ἀναχθέντες δὲ] (καὶ ἀν)αχθέντε P[45], 'and putting out to sea'; for compounds with ἀνά and κατά see on κατῆλθον, *ver.* 4.

οἱ περὶ Παῦλον] 'Paul and his company;' the expression, a classical Gk. idiom, includes Paul, and marks him out as leader of the company. Previously we have read of 'Barnabas and Saul'; now Barnabas is content with second place, a further light on his character.

Πέργην] Probably they landed at Attalia (cf. xiv. 25) and went by land to Perga, which was 12 miles distant, though it had a river-harbour of its own on the Cestrus 5 miles away.

Παμφυλίας] A district of Asia Minor between Taurus and the sea, bordered west and east by Lycia and Cilicia respectively. From A.D. 43 to *c.* 68 it formed part of the province Pamphylia-Lycia. Ramsay supposed that Paul caught malarial fever here, and went to recuperate in the high country at Pisidian Antioch (cf. Gal. iv. 13)—an interesting speculation, but only a speculation (*SPT*, pp. 94 ff.).

Ἰωάνης δὲ ἀποχωρήσας ἀπ' αὐτῶν ὑπέστρεψεν εἰς Ἰεροσόλυμα] We are not told the reason for his return. It may have been because there was an abandonment of the original itinerary, or because he resented his cousin's falling into the second place, or for some other cause—we do not know. See on xv. 37 ff.

xiii. 14

αὐτοὶ δὲ] 'But they themselves' (emphatic), i.e., Paul and Barnabas. For αὐτοί P[45] has οὗτοι.

διελθόντες] Crossing the Taurus range.

εἰς Ἀντιόχειαν τὴν Πισιδίαν] א A B C P^{45} have τὴν Πισιδίαν, rightly; D 33 81 byz have τῆς Πισιδίας, implying that Antioch was in Pisidia, which at this time it was not. It was near Pisidia, and its full name is given by Strabo (xii. 6. 4) as τὴν . . . Ἀντιόχειαν . . . τὴν πρὸς τῇ Πισιδίᾳ (' Antioch near Pisidia '); hence it was called ' Pisidian Antioch ', as here. Pisidia was one of the regions into which the Roman province of Galatia was divided (see further on *ver.* 49). Pisidian Antioch was actually in the region probably called Phrygia Galatica, and was the civil and military centre of that part of the province. It was 3600 feet above sea-level. Augustus made it a Roman colony (Colonia Caesarea). Paul obviously attached great importance to introducing the Gospel to Roman colonies—Lystra, Philippi, Corinth were among other colonies which he visited. See on xvi. 12. In A.D. 295 Antioch became the metropolis of the enlarged province of Pisidia; hence, no doubt, the variant τῆς Πισιδίας.

τῇ ἡμέρᾳ τῶν σαββάτων] So in xvi. 13. σάββατα is formed from Aram. *sabbĕthā*, where the final *ā*, the sign of the ' emphatic state ' in the sing., corresponds roughly to the definite article. Thus, though the Gk. form was declined as a neut. plur., its meaning was singular. From the plur. form was formed a sing. σάββατον, as in *vv.* 27, 42, 44; i. 12; xv. 21; xviii. 4. See also on xvii. 2; xx. 7.

xiii. 15

μετὰ δὲ τὴν ἀνάγνωσιν τοῦ νόμου καὶ τῶν προφητῶν] The synagogue service in the first century consisted of (1) the *Shĕma'* (' Hear, O Israel: the Lord our God the Lord is one '), (2) prayer by the leader, (3) reading of the Law (and, on Sabbath and feast days, of the Prophets), (4) a sermon by any suitable member of the congregation (cf. Lk. iv. 16; also Philo, *de spec. leg.* ii. 62, ἀναστὰς δέ τις τῶν ἐμπειροτάτων ὑφηγεῖται τὰ ἄριστα καὶ συνοίσοντα). The readings from the Prophets (*haphtārōth*) are in the modern synagogue service not continuous, but selected. In the Nazareth synagogue, our Lord was handed the roll of Isa. and read a *haphtārāh* from ch. lxi, and His sermon which followed took its cue from the reading. As we cannot be sure what portions of the Law and Prophets were read on the present occasion, we cannot say whether Paul's sermon was based on them or not.[1]

[1] If, as has been suggested, the lessons for this day were Dt. i. and Isa. i. (cf. ἐτροποφόρησεν of *ver.* 18 with Dt. i. 31 and ὕψωσεν of *ver.* 17 with ὕψωσα of Isa. i. 2), Paul's sermon may have been based on the historical retrospect in the former passage and the promise of remission of sins in the latter. Cf. *BC*, v, p. 409.

ἀρχισυνάγωγοι] The functions of an *ἀρχισυνάγωγος* (Heb. *rōsh ha-kĕnēseth*, 'head of the synagogue': cf. Lk. viii. 41, *ἄρχων τῆς συναγωγῆς*[1]) were to take charge of the building, see that nothing unseemly happened in it, make arrangements for public worship, appoint members of the congregation to read the prayers and lessons, and invite fit persons to speak. He was usually one of the elders of the congregation. There was generally one in each synagogue (cf. xviii. 8, 17), but sometimes more, as here. The office was sometimes held for life and by successive generations, as inscriptions testify. Sometimes the title was honorary, and might be held by women and children. The office and title also existed in some Jewish-Christian churches of Palestine: cf. Epiphanius, *Pan.* xxx. 18, *πρεσβυτέρους γὰρ οὗτοι ἔχουσι καὶ ἀρχισυναγώγους.*

λόγον παρακλήσεως] Cf. Heb. xiii. 22; also 1 Tim. iv. 13; probably a synagogue expression for the sermon which followed the Scripture lessons.

(b) Paul's Sermon in Pisidian Antioch, xiii. 16-41

ἀναστὰς δὲ Παῦλος καὶ κατασείσας τῇ χειρὶ εἶπεν Ἄνδρες Ἰσραηλ- 16
εῖται καὶ οἱ φοβούμενοι τὸν θεόν, ἀκούσατε. Ὁ θεὸς τοῦ λαοῦ τούτου 17
Ἰσραὴλ ἐξελέξατο τοὺς πατέρας ἡμῶν, καὶ τὸν λαὸν ὕψωσεν ἐν
τῇ παροικίᾳ ἐν γῇ Αἰγύπτου, καὶ μετὰ βραχίονος ὑψηλοῦ ἐξήγαγεν
αὐτοὺς ἐξ αὐτῆς, καί, ὡς τεσσερακονταετῆ χρόνον ἐτροποφόρησεν 18
αὐτοὺς ἐν τῇ ἐρήμῳ, καθελὼν ἔθνη ἑπτὰ ἐν γῇ Χαναὰν κατεκληρο- 19
νόμησεν τὴν γῆν αὐτῶν ὡς ἔτεσι τετρακοσίοις καὶ πεντήκοντα. καὶ 20
μετὰ ταῦτα ἔδωκεν κριτὰς ἕως Σαμουὴλ προφήτου. κἀκεῖθεν ᾐτήσαντο 21
βασιλέα, καὶ ἔδωκεν αὐτοῖς ὁ θεὸς τὸν Σαοὺλ υἱὸν Κείς, ἄνδρα ἐκ
φυλῆς Βενιαμείν, ἔτη τεσσεράκοντα· καὶ μεταστήσας αὐτὸν ἤγειρεν 22
τὸν Δαυεὶδ αὐτοῖς εἰς βασιλέα, ᾧ καὶ εἶπεν μαρτυρήσας Εὗρον Δαυεὶδ
τὸν τοῦ Ἰεσσαί, ἄνδρα κατὰ τὴν καρδίαν μου, ὃς ποιήσει πάντα τὰ
θελήματά μου. τούτου ὁ θεὸς ἀπὸ τοῦ σπέρματος κατ' ἐπαγγελίαν 23
ἤγαγεν τῷ Ἰσραὴλ σωτῆρα Ἰησοῦν, προκηρύξαντος Ἰωάνου πρὸ 24
προσώπου τῆς εἰσόδου αὐτοῦ βάπτισμα μετανοίας παντὶ τῷ λαῷ Ἰσραήλ.

[1] According to *CIG* 9906 (*Ἰουλιανὸς ἱερεὺς ἄρχων . . . υἱὸς Ἰουλιανοῦ ἀρχισυναγώγου*) and *CIL* x. 3905 (*Alfius Iuda arcon arcosynagogus*) the functions of *ἄρχων* and *ἀρχισυνάγωγος*, though distinct, might be united in the same person. The *ἄρχοντες* were the chief members of the congregation, the governing body in whose hands lay the general direction; their head was the *γερουσιάρχης* (cf. *CIG* 9902, *Κυντιανὸς γερουσιάρχης συναγωγῆς Αὐγοστησίων*). Cf. Lake, *EEP*, p. 104 *n*. Ramsay (*SPT*, p. 257) refers to S. Reinach as deducing from a Smyrnean inscription that *ἀρχισυνάγωγος* in Asia Minor did not indicate an office but was an expression of dignity, 'a leading person in the synagogue'. The distinction, however, cannot always be maintained; e.g., in Lk. viii. 41 *ἄρχων τῆς συναγωγῆς* corresponds to *εἷς τῶν ἀρχισυναγώγων* of Mk. v. 22: cf. Lk. viii. 49, *ἀρχισυναγώγου*.

ὡς δὲ ἐπλήρου Ἰωάνης τὸν δρόμον, ἔλεγεν Τί ἐμὲ ὑπονοεῖτε εἶναι; 25
οὐκ εἰμὶ ἐγώ· ἀλλ' ἰδοὺ ἔρχεται μετ' ἐμὲ οὗ οὐκ εἰμὶ ἄξιος τὸ
ὑπόδημα τῶν ποδῶν λῦσαι. Ἄνδρες ἀδελφοί, υἱοὶ γένους Ἀβραὰμ 26
καὶ οἱ ἐν ὑμῖν φοβούμενοι τὸν θεόν, ἡμῖν ὁ λόγος τῆς σωτηρίας ταύτης
ἐξαπεστάλη. οἱ γὰρ κατοικοῦντες ἐν Ἰερουσαλὴμ καὶ οἱ ἄρχοντες 27
αὐτῶν τοῦτον ἀγνοήσαντες καὶ τὰς φωνὰς τῶν προφητῶν τὰς κατὰ πᾶν
σάββατον ἀναγινωσκομένας κρίναντες ἐπλήρωσαν, καὶ μηδεμίαν αἰτίαν 28
θανάτου εὑρόντες ᾐτήσαντο Πειλᾶτον ἀναιρεθῆναι αὐτόν· ὡς δὲ ἐτέλεσαν 29
πάντα τὰ περὶ αὐτοῦ γεγραμμένα, καθελόντες ἀπὸ τοῦ ξύλου ἔθηκαν
εἰς μνημεῖον. ὁ δὲ θεὸς ἤγειρεν αὐτὸν ἐκ νεκρῶν· ὃς ὤφθη ἐπὶ ἡμέρας 30
πλείους τοῖς συναναβᾶσιν αὐτῷ ἀπὸ τῆς Γαλιλαίας εἰς Ἰερουσαλήμ, 31
οἵτινες νῦν εἰσὶ μάρτυρες αὐτοῦ πρὸς τὸν λαόν. καὶ ἡμεῖς ὑμᾶς 32
εὐαγγελιζόμεθα τὴν πρὸς τοὺς πατέρας ἐπαγγελίαν γενομένην ὅτι ταύτην 33
ὁ θεὸς ἐκπεπλήρωκεν τοῖς τέκνοις ἡμῶν ἀναστήσας Ἰησοῦν, ὡς
καὶ ἐν τῷ ψαλμῷ γέγραπται τῷ δευτέρῳ Υἱός μου εἶ σύ, ἐγὼ σήμερον
γεγέννηκά σε. ὅτι δὲ ἀνέστησεν αὐτὸν ἐκ νεκρῶν μηκέτι μέλλοντα 34
ὑποστρέφειν εἰς διαφθοράν, οὕτως εἴρηκεν ὅτι Δώσω ὑμῖν τὰ ὅσια
Δαυεὶδ τὰ πιστά. διότι καὶ ἐν ἑτέρῳ λέγει Οὐ δώσεις τὸν ὅσιόν σου 35
ἰδεῖν διαφθοράν· Δαυεὶδ μὲν γὰρ ἰδίᾳ γενεᾷ ὑπηρετήσας τῇ τοῦ θεοῦ 36
βουλῇ ἐκοιμήθη καὶ προσετέθη πρὸς τοὺς πατέρας αὐτοῦ καὶ εἶδεν
διαφθοράν, ὃν δὲ ὁ θεὸς ἤγειρεν οὐκ εἶδεν διαφθοράν. Γνωστὸν οὖν 37 38
ἔστω ὑμῖν, ἄνδρες ἀδελφοί, ὅτι διὰ τούτου ὑμῖν ἄφεσις ἁμαρτιῶν καταγ-
γέλλεται, καὶ ἀπὸ πάντων ὧν οὐκ ἠδυνήθητε ἐν νόμῳ Μωυσέως 39
δικαιωθῆναι ἐν τούτῳ πᾶς ὁ πιστεύων δικαιοῦται. βλέπετε οὖν μὴ 40
ἐπέλθῃ τὸ εἰρημένον ἐν τοῖς προφήταις

Ἴδετε, οἱ καταφρονηταί, καὶ θαυμάσατε καὶ ἀφανίσθητε, 41
ὅτι ἔργον ἐργάζομαι ἐγὼ ἐν ταῖς ἡμέραις ὑμῶν,
ἔργον ὃ οὐ μὴ πιστεύσητε ἐάν τις ἐκδιηγῆται ὑμῖν.

This sermon is given *in extenso* probably to give the reader a sample of Paul's synagogue addresses. Like Stephen's defence, it begins with a historical summary, which is by no means a repetition of Stephen's, but extends from the Exodus to David, and provides an introduction to the presentation of Christ as the Son of David.

xiii. 16

ἀναστὰς] Cf. the quotation from Philo in note on *ver.* 15. Jesus, after the manner of the Rabbis, *sat* while teaching (Lk. iv. 20; Mt. xxvi. 55).

κατασείσας τῇ χειρὶ] Cf. xii. 17; xxi. 40, also xxvi. 2. The gesture was an appeal for silence and attention.

ἄνδρες Ἰσραηλεῖται] Cf. ii. 22.

οἱ φοβούμενοι τὸν θεόν] Cf. *vv.* 26, 43, 50. For this class of Gentiles who attended Jewish worship see on x. 2. Josephus

(*Ap.* ii. 40) testifies to Gentile adherence to Jewish religious observances; cf. also Ac. xv. 21.

xiii. 17

παροικίᾳ] See on *πάροικος*, vii. 6, 29.

μετὰ βραχίονος ὑψηλοῦ ἐξήγαγεν αὐτοὺς ἐξ αὐτῆς] Cf. Ex. vi. 1 (*ἐν γὰρ χειρὶ κραταιᾷ ἐξαποστελεῖ αὐτοὺς καὶ ἐν βραχίονι ὑψηλῷ ἐκβαλεῖ αὐτοὺς ἐκ τῆς γῆς αὐτοῦ*); vi. 6 (*καὶ λυτρώσομαι ὑμᾶς ἐν βραχίονι ὑψηλῷ*); Ps. cxxxvi. 11 f. (cxxxv LXX), *καὶ ἐξαγαγόντι Ἰσραὴλ ἐκ μέσου αὐτῶν . . . ἐν χειρὶ κραταιᾷ καὶ ἐν βραχίονι ὑψηλῷ.*

xiii. 18

ὡς τεσσερακονταετῆ χρόνον] Again Luke's fondness for qualifying a number by *ὡς*, so in *ver.* 20. Here D sah boh omit *ὡς*.

ἐτροποφόρησεν αὐτοὺς ἐν τῇ ἐρήμῳ] In place of *ἐτροποφόρησεν* (the reading of ℵ B C[2] D 81 byz vg), *ἐτροφοφόρησεν* ('He carried them like a nurse') is found in A C* E 33 minn d e g sah boh pesh hcl arm eth. The latter may be the original δ reading (that of D seems due to contamination with the β text; contrast d *et annis xl ac si nutrix aluit eos in solitudine*). The same variation occurs in the LXX text of Dt. i. 31 (from which Paul is here quoting), though there the form with φ is much the better attested (*καὶ ἐν τῇ ἐρήμῳ ταύτῃ, ἣν εἴδετε, ὡς ἐτροφοφόρησέν* [*AB*] *σε Κύριος ὁ θεός σου, ὡς εἴ τις τροφοφορήσει* [*AB*[c]] *ἄνθρωπος τὸν υἱὸν αὐτοῦ*). The δ text of our verse was probably due to LXX influence. The Heb. word is *nāsā*, which may mean 'to carry' or 'to endure', and could be represented by either of the Gk. words.

xiii. 19

καθελὼν] ℵ A C D byz vg pesh al have *καί* before *καθελών*, no doubt rightly (so WH mg., Soden). It was easily dropped (as in B 81 sah) before a word commencing with the same two letters.

ἔθνη ἑπτὰ] They are enumerated in Dt. vii. 1, the wording of which is reflected here, *ἐὰν δὲ εἰσαγάγῃ σε Κύριος ὁ θεός σου εἰς τὴν γῆν εἰς ἣν εἰσπορεύῃ ἐκεῖ κληρονομῆσαι, καὶ ἐξαρεῖ ἔθνη μεγάλα ἀπὸ προσώπου σου, τὸν Χετταῖον καὶ Ἀμορραῖον καὶ Γεργεσαῖον καὶ Χαναναῖον καὶ Φερεζαῖον καὶ Εὐαῖον καὶ Ἰεβουσαῖον, ἑπτὰ ἔθνη πολλὰ καὶ ἰσχυρότερα ὑμῶν.*

ἐν γῇ Χαναὰν κατεκληρονόμησεν τὴν γῆν αὐτῶν] 'gave their land for a possession in the land of Canaan'. Cf. Josh. xiv. 1, *καὶ οὗτοι οἱ κατακληρονομήσαντες υἱῶν Ἰσραὴλ ἐν τῇ γῇ Χαναάν, οἷς κατεκληρονόμησεν αὐτοῖς Ἐλεαζὰρ κ.τ.λ.* Observe from the LXX passage how *κατακληρονομέω* is used with two meanings, 'take for a possession' and 'give for a possession', representing Heb. *nāḥal* in its normal (Qal) and causative (here Pi'el) forms respectively. In our verse in Ac. some minn have *κατεκληροδότησεν* (so TR).

xiii. 20

ὡς ἔτεσι τετρακοσίοις καὶ πεντήκοντα. καὶ μετὰ ταῦτα] According to this, the reading of ℵ A B C 33 81 vg arm sah (om *μετὰ ταῦτα*) boh (om *ὡς*), the period of about 450 years has some definite connection with the giving of the inheritance. It is best explained as covering the 400 years' sojourning (the *παροικία* of *ver.* 17 ; cf. vii. 6), the 40 years in the wilderness, and the time that elapsed between the entry into Canaan and the distribution of the land in Josh. xiv. The dat. implies point of time, not duration, though the sense would have been clearer had ordinal numerals been used and not cardinal. We are not surprised to find that attempts were made to simplify this rather complicated passage ; thus in δ *ver.* 20 runs *καὶ ὡς ἔτεσι τετρακοσίοις καὶ πεντήκοντα ἔδωκεν κριτὰς ἕως Σαμουὴλ τοῦ προφήτου* (so byz, with *μετὰ ταῦτα* from the β text before *ὡς ἔτεσι*). By this reading, if we take the dat. exceptionally to indicate duration, the judges are said to have judged for about 450 years. According to 1 K. vi. 1 the fourth year of Solomon was the 480th year since the Exodus, but if we take the data of δ byz here, it must have been at least the 574th year. Attempts to explain the difference by supposing that the years of foreign oppression in the period of the judges are omitted from the reckoning in 1 K. vi. 1 are not convincing. Comparative chronology supports the shorter against the longer reckoning. We should retain the β reading here ; though it is the more difficult (and has therefore claims to be regarded as the more probable), it yields good sense.

ἕως Σαμουὴλ προφήτου] Samuel was regarded as the last judge and as the first prophet (after Moses) : cf. iii. 24. He also discharged priestly functions.

xiii. 21

ᾐτήσαντο βασιλέα] Middle voice ; lit., 'they asked for themselves a king'. Cf. 1 Sam. viii. 6.

τὸν Σαοὺλ υἱὸν Κείς, ἄνδρα ἐκ φυλῆς Βενιαμείν] The Saul who was now speaking was also 'a man of the tribe of Benjamin' (cf. Phil. iii. 5). For the form *Σαούλ* see on ix. 4.

ἔτη τεσσεράκοντα] So Jos. *Ant.* vi. 14. 9 ; but in *Ant.* x. 8. 4 he says 20 years (either the 2 years of 1 Sam. xiii. 1 multiplied by 10, or the 20 years of 1 Sam. vii. 2). The length of Saul's reign is not given in OT (it was certainly longer than the 2 years of 1 Sam.

xiii. 1, the text of which is usually regarded as corrupt [1]). On the present passage J. A. Bengel (*Gnomon of NT*) says,

> 'Here the years of Samuel the prophet and Saul the king are brought into one sum: for between the anointing of King Saul and his death there were not *twenty*, much less *forty* years (1 Sam. vii. 2)'.

xiii. 22

μεταστήσας] This may refer to his deposition (cf. Lk. xvi. 4) or to his death; Josephus uses the word in both senses.

ἤγειρεν] Both *ἐγείρω* and *ἀνίστημι* are used in Ac. (1) of raising someone up to occupy a certain position (as here), (2) of raising from the dead (as in *ver.* 30): see further on *vv.* 33 f.

εἰς βασιλέα] Best explained here as a Hebraism from LXX. Cf. *ver.* 47; vii. 21; Mt. xxi. 46. The construction is found also in the Hellenistic vernacular, e.g., in a papyrus, *ἔσχον παρ' ὑμῶν εἰς δάνειον σπέρματα*, where *εἰς δάνειον* means 'as a loan'.

ᾧ καὶ εἶπεν μαρτυρήσας] Take *ᾧ* with *μαρτυρήσας*, not with *εἶπεν*, as the words were spoken to God's 'saints' (Ps. lxxxix. 19 RV). In *εἶπεν μαρτυρήσας* we have a further example of the simultaneous aor. ptc.; the meaning is the same as *ἐμαρτύρησεν λέγων* (Jn. i. 32) or *ἐμαρτύρησεν καὶ εἶπεν* (Jn. xiii. 21).

εὗρον Δαυεὶδ] From Ps. lxxxix. 20 (LXX lxxxviii. 21), *εὗρον Δαυεὶδ τὸν δοῦλόν μου.*

ἄνδρα κατὰ τὴν καρδίαν μου] From 1 Sam. xiii. 14 (LXX 1 K.), *ζητήσει Κύριος ἑαυτῷ ἄνθρωπον κατὰ τὴν καρδίαν αὐτοῦ.* These two quotations are also joined in this way in 1 Clem. xviii. 1, where also *ἄνδρα* takes the place of LXX *ἄνθρωπον*. The later writer has probably been influenced by Ac.; cf. also 1 Clem. ii. 1 with Ac. xx. 35 (*q.v.*). B omits *ἄνδρα*.

ὃς ποιήσει πάντα τὰ θελήματά μου] Cf. Isa. xliv. 28, *πάντα τὰ θελήματά μου ποιήσει*, in reference to Cyrus. For the plur. *θελήματα* cf. Mk. iii. 35 (WH mg.); Eph. ii. 3.

xiii. 23

τούτου] Taken from its natural position with *τοῦ σπέρματος* and placed at the beginning of the sentence for emphasis. For Paul's statement of the Davidic descent of Christ cf. Rom. i. 3.

κατ' ἐπαγγελίαν] Cf. ii. 30; 2 Sam. xxii. 51; Ps. cxxxii. 11, 17 for this promise.

ἤγαγεν] C D 33 pesh hcl sah arm al have *ἤγειρεν* (so TR): cf. v. 30 and Judg. iii. 9 (*καὶ ἤγειρε Κύριος σωτῆρα τῷ Ἰσραήλ*).

[1] But see E. Robertson, *The Old Testament Problem* (Manchester, 1950), pp. 150 ff., where it is ably maintained that Saul's two years' kingship, entered upon when he was 52 years old, followed a period of many years during which he was military commander (*nāgīd*).

σωτῆρα Ἰησοῦν] Cf. σωτῆρα in Judg. iii. 9 quoted in previous note; perhaps there is an allusion here to the etymology of the name Jesus ('Yahweh saves'): cf. Mt. i. 21.

xiii. 24

Verses 24-31 contain an outline of the Gospel story similar to that in x. 36-43, from the preaching of John to the appearances of the risen Christ. See on x. 36.

πρὸ προσώπου τῆς εἰσόδου αὐτοῦ] For the Semitic idiom πρὸ προσώπου (no different in force from the simple πρό) cf. Lk. i. 76; vii. 27; ix. 52; x. 1, and for the present context, Mal. iii. 1 f. (πρὸ προσώπου μου . . . ἡμέραν εἰσόδου αὐτοῦ). Cf. also ἀπὸ προσώπου, iii. 20; v. 41; vii. 45; ἐπὶ πρόσωπον, xvii. 26; κατὰ πρόσωπον, iii. 13.

βάπτισμα μετανοίας] The baptism was the 'outward and visible sign' of their repentance: cf. xix. 4.

xiii. 25

ἐπλήρου τὸν δρόμον] 'was completing his course': cf. xx. 24; 2 Tim. iv. 7. For the metaphor cf. Jer. viii. 6, διέλιπεν ὁ τρέχων ἀπὸ τοῦ δρόμου αὐτοῦ.

ἔλεγεν] Imperfect, implying iteration: 'he used to say'.

Τί ἐμὲ ὑπονοεῖτε εἶναι; οὐκ εἰμὶ ἐγώ] C δ P^{45} byz have τίνα for τί. If we replace the question-mark by a comma (as in WH mg.), the first clause becomes indirect: 'I am not what you think I am'. This use of the interrogative for relative is Hellenistic, as in Mt. x. 19*b*; Mk. xiv. 36; Lk. xvii. 8. It is better to retain the punctuation of WH text, in which case οὐκ εἰμὶ ἐγώ means 'I am not He (i.e., the Coming One)'; cf. Jn. i. 20, ἐγὼ οὐκ εἰμὶ ὁ χριστός.[1] (With the question τί ἐμὲ ὑπονοεῖτε εἶναι cf. our Lord's question in Mk. viii. 29, etc.)

ἀλλ' ἰδοὺ ἔρχεται μετ' ἐμὲ οὗ οὐκ εἰμὶ ἄξιος τὸ ὑπόδημα τῶν ποδῶν λῦσαι] Cf. Mt. iii. 11; Mk. i. 7; Lk. iii. 16; Jn. i. 27. This passage agrees with Jn. against the Synoptics in having ἄξιος for their ἱκανός and with Mt. against the other three in omitting τὸν ἱμάντα

[1] For other points of contact between Ac. and the Fourth Gospel in relation to the ministry of John the Baptist see on xix. 4. Cf. also *ET* lii. (1940-1), pp. 334 ff., where W. F. Lofthouse points out that the emphasis of the five passages in Jn. xiv.-xvi. where the Holy Spirit is mentioned 'is precisely that which underlies the conception of the Spirit in Ac. i.-xv.' Such considerations add weight to the opinion expressed, e.g., by J. V. Bartlet (in *Oxford Studies in the Synoptic Problem* [1911], pp. 352 f.), G. W. Broomfield (*John, Peter and the Fourth Gospel* [1934], pp. 108 ff.), and J. A. Findlay (*The Gospel according to St. Luke* [1937], p. 14), that John the son of Zebedee was, directly or indirectly, one of Luke's informants.

(' the thong ') and the final *αὐτοῦ* which in Mk., Lk., Jn. repeats the sense of the relative *οὗ* (for the construction see on xv. 17). For *οὐκ εἰμὶ ἄξιος* P^{45} has *ἄξιος οὐκ εἰμὶ ἐγώ*.

xiii. 26

ἄνδρες κ.τ.λ.] The words of address with which the sermon began are repeated with variations to emphasize the personal application of his message to the audience.

καὶ οἱ] om *καί* B P^{45}.

ἐν ὑμῖν] A D 81 have *ἐν ἡμῖν*.

ἡμῖν] ℵ A B D 33 81 minn.pauc hcl.mg sah; *ὑμῖν* C E P^{45} byz vg pesh hcl boh arm eth.

ὁ λόγος . . . ἐξαπεστάλη] See on x. 36.

τῆς σωτηρίας ταύτης] Cf. *σωτῆρα*, *ver*. 23. It has been pointed out that the Aram. equivalent of this phrase would be identical with the Aram. original of *τῆς ζωῆς ταύτης*, v. 20. But in Pisidian Antioch, of course, the language spoken was Gk.

xiii. 27

οἱ γὰρ κατοικοῦντες κ.τ.λ.] The δ text of this and the two following verses has been reconstructed as follows by Ropes (*BC* iii, p. 261): *οἱ γὰρ κατοικοῦντες ἐν Ἰερουσαλὴμ καὶ οἱ ἄρχοντες αὐτῆς, μὴ συνιέντες τὰς γραφὰς τῶν προφητῶν τὰς κατὰ πᾶν σάββατον ἀναγινωσκομένας ἐπλήρωσαν, καὶ μηδεμίαν αἰτίαν θανάτου εὑρόντες ἐν αὐτῷ, κρίναντες αὐτόν, παρέδωκαν Πιλάτῳ εἰς ἀναίρεσιν· ὡς δὲ ἐτέλουν πάντα τὰ περὶ αὐτοῦ γεγραμμένα, ἠτοῦντο τὸν Πιλᾶτον μετὰ τὸ σταυρωθῆναι αὐτὸν ἀπὸ τοῦ ξύλου καθαιρεθῆναι, καὶ ἐπιτυχόντες καθεῖλον καὶ ἔθηκαν εἰς μνημεῖον.* The text of D as it stands is corrupt and conflate; the δ text has to be reconstructed with the aid of hcl* and hcl. mg. The *β* text is difficult but intelligible,

> 'For the inhabitants of Jerusalem and their rulers, failing to recognize this Man and the voices of the prophets which are read every Sabbath day, fulfilled them by condemning Him', etc.

ἀγνοήσαντες] For this emphasis on their ignorance cf. iii. 17. They neither recognized Him as the fulfilment of the prophets, nor them as having foretold Him.

πᾶν σάββατον] *σάββατον πᾶν* P^{45}.

κρίναντες] Blass emended this to *μὴ ἀνακρίναντες*, 'not discerning'. Lachmann put it immediately after *ἀγνοήσαντες καί*, 'by condemning him in their ignorance' (Moffatt).

xiii. 28

μηδεμίαν αἰτίαν θανάτου εὑρόντες] With the emphasis on the innocence of Jesus, and its acknowledgement by the authorities, cf.

iii. 13; Lk. xxiii. 4. This is in keeping with the purpose of Ac.: cf. the emphasis on the civil authorities' explicit or implicit acknowledgement in various places of the innocence of the apostles (cf. xvi. 35 ff.; xviii. 14 ff.; xix. 31, 37; xxiii. 29; xxv. 14 ff.; xxvi. 31 f.).

xiii. 29

ὡς δὲ ἐτέλεσαν πάντα τὰ περὶ αὐτοῦ γεγραμμένα] Cf. Lk. xxii. 37; Jn. xix. 28.

καθελόντες . . . ἔθηκαν] Generalizing plur.; in the Gospels Joseph of Arimathaea and Nicodemus (members of the Sanhedrin) are mentioned in this connection (cf. Lk. xxiii. 50 ff.; Jn. xix. 38 ff.). But Gwilym O. Griffith's interpretation may be the right one: 'The suggestion is that it was His enemies who undertook to have Him removed from the cross. It agrees with the record of John xix. 31' (*St. Paul's Life of Christ* [1925], p. 150).

ξύλου] For this word for the Cross cf. v. 30; x. 39.

ἔθηκαν εἰς μνημεῖον] Note the early emphasis on the burial of Jesus, as helping to prove the reality of His death, and therefore of His resurrection (cf. 1 Cor. xv. 4, the 'Apostles' Creed', etc.). The burial as well as the hanging on a tree (*ξύλον*) is included in the context of Dt. xxi. 23 (see on v. 30).

xiii. 30

ὁ δὲ θεὸς κ.τ.λ.] In contrast to 'the inhabitants of Jerusalem and their rulers' (*ver.* 27). Contrast the force of *ἐγείρω* here and in *ver.* 22 (*q.v.*). In these verses, as in 1 Cor. xv. 3 ff., we have the elements of the Gospel preached by Paul—the death, burial and resurrection of Christ, with the evidence of His resurrection.

xiii. 31

ὅς] Demonstrative rather than relative.

ὤφθη] 'appeared'; intrans. use, followed by dat.: cf. ix. 17.

ἐπὶ ἡμέρας πλείους] Cf. i. 3, *δι' ἡμερῶν τεσσεράκοντα.*

τοῖς συναναβᾶσιν αὐτῷ] i.e., before His crucifixion. Luke does not mention the post-resurrection appearances in Galilee: contrast Lk. xxiv. 6 with Mk. xvi. 7.

νῦν] om B byz; *ἄχρι νῦν* D vg. Of the authorities which have *νῦν*, ℵ has it after *εἰσί*, A C 81 P^{45} before *εἰσί*.

μάρτυρες] Again the insistence on personal testimony (cf. ii. 32, etc.), but Paul does not here mention Christ's appearance to himself, as he does in 1 Cor. xv. 8.

λαόν] As usual, *λαός* is used of the Jewish nation (cf. x. 2).

xiii. 32

εὐαγγελιζόμεθα] With three objects, (1) ὑμᾶς, (2) τὴν . . . ἐπαγγελίαν, (3) the ὅτι clause : 'and we tell you the good news of the promise made to the fathers, that God has fulfilled it . . .'. The promise is that referred to in *ver.* 23. For constructions after εὐαγγελίζομαι see on viii. 25.

xiii. 33

ἡμῶν] This has the weighty authority of ℵ A B C* D vg eth, but 'to our children' gives an improbable sense. As the promise was made to the fathers, we expect to read that it was fulfilled 'to *their* children'; thus g sah replace ἡμῶν by αὐτῶν, C[3] E 81 byz pesh hcl arm by αὐτῶν ἡμῖν, while boh omits it. 'It can hardly be doubted that ἡμῶν is a primitive corruption of ἡμῖν' (WH). But a more probable emendation is suggested by F. H. Chase (*Credibility*, p. 187 *n.*), who would insert ἡμῖν καί before τοῖς, the reading 'to us and to our children' then falling into line with ii. 39 (cf. Ps. Sol. viii. 39, ἡμῖν καὶ τοῖς τέκνοις ἡμῶν ἡ εὐδοκία εἰς τὸν αἰῶνα).

ἀναστήσας] i.e., by raising Him up in the sense in which He raised up David (*ver.* 22, where the verb is ἐγείρω, but for ἀνίστημι in this sense cf. iii. 22 ; vii. 37). Cf. also *ver.* 23 (where δ has ἤγειρεν instead of ἤγαγεν) ; iii. 26 ; v. 30. The promise of *ver.* 23, the fulfilment of which is here described, has to do with the sending of Messiah, not His resurrection (for which cf. *ver.* 34).

'Ιησοῦν] δ has the reverential amplification τὸν κύριον 'Ιησοῦν Χριστόν (see also on i. 21 ; ii. 38 ; vii. 55).

ὡς καὶ ἐν τῷ ψαλμῷ γέγραπται τῷ δευτέρῳ] δ (D d g and Latin codd. known to Bede) has οὕτως γὰρ ἐν τῷ πρώτῳ ψαλμῷ γέγραπται. Origen on Ps. ii says he had seen two Heb. MSS., in one of which Pss. i and ii were given as one. Justin, Tertullian, Cyprian, Eusebius and Hilary also testify more or less explicitly to this practice of regarding the two Psalms as one. See *BC* iii, pp. 263 ff. This is not the δ text's only indication of knowledge of the Heb. Scriptures and language :[1] cf. Βαρ-'Ιησοῦα, *ver.* 6. P^{45} has ἐν τοῖς ψαλμοῖς.

Υἱός μου εἶ σύ, ἐγὼ σήμερον γεγέννηκά σε] Ps. ii. 7, quoted also in Heb. i. 5 ; v. 5 ; and in the δ text of Lk. iii. 22 as the words spoken from heaven at our Lord's baptism. See on iv. 25 f. for another quotation from this Ps. Ps. ii. is interpreted Messianically in Ps. Sol. xvii. 26 (first century B.C.) and in several early Rabbinical

[1] Thus, for the Aram. *shĕbaqtani* (σαβαχθανεί) of Mt. xxvii. 46 and Mk. xv. 34, the δ text, represented by D and various Old Latin texts, has ζαφθανεί, representing MT *'ăzabhtani* of Ps. xxii. 1.

texts (see Dalman, *Words of Jesus*, pp. 268 ff.). For Paul's presentation of Christ as the Son of God see on ix. 20, and cf. the many places in his Epp. (e.g., Rom. i. 3 f.; Col. i. 13 ff.) where this doctrine is developed.

ἐγὼ σήμερον γεγέννηκά σε] The day of the king's anointing 'was ideally the day in which he, the nation's representative, was born into a new relation of sonship towards Jehovah' (Chase, *op. cit.*, p. 126). After these words δ continues the quotation by adding *αἴτησαι παρ' ἐμοῦ καὶ δώσω σοι ἔθνη τὴν κληρονομίαν σου, καὶ τὴν κατάσχεσίν σου τὰ πέρατα τῆς γῆς.*

xiii. 34

ἀνέστησεν αὐτὸν ἐκ νεκρῶν] The addition of *ἐκ νεκρῶν* here differentiates this use of *ἀνίστημι* from that in *ver.* 33.

διαφθοράν] From Ps. xvi. 10, quoted in *ver.* 35.

ὅτι] *recitantis.*

δώσω ὑμῖν τὰ ὅσια Δαυεὶδ τὰ πιστά] Isa. lv. 3 LXX, *καὶ διαθήσομαι ὑμῖν διαθήκην αἰώνιον, τὰ ὅσια Δαυεὶδ τὰ πιστά.* The Heb. original of the last words is *ḥasdē Dāwīd ha-ne'ĕmānīm*, rendered in EV 'the sure mercies of David'; but *ḥesed* (sing. of *ḥasdē*) is radically connected with *ḥāsīd*, the word rendered *ὅσιος* in Ps. xvi. 10 (LXX xv), as in next verse. Paul regards the resurrection of Christ as the fulfilment of the 'sure mercies' or 'holy and sure blessings' (RV) promised to David. The substitution of *δώσω* for LXX *διαθήσομαι* may be due to the influence of *δώσεις* in the following quotation.

xiii. 35

ἐν ἑτέρῳ] 'in a second place'.

λέγει] The subject is *ἡ γραφή*, understood; not *ὁ θεός*, as it is to God that the words are spoken.

οὐ δώσεις τὸν ὅσιόν σου ἰδεῖν διαφθοράν] Ps. xvi. 10, also quoted in this sense in ii. 27 (*q.v.*). This and the previous quotation are connected by their common word *ὅσιος*.

xiii. 36

Δαυεὶδ μὲν γὰρ κ.τ.λ.] The argument is much the same as in ii. 29 ff. David died and was not raised; the prophecy therefore does not apply to him, but to the One who in actual historic fact did rise again and saw no corruption.

ἰδίᾳ γενεᾷ] Either 'his own generation' as object to *ὑπηρετήσας* or 'in his own generation', in which case the object to *ὑπηρετήσας* is *βουλῇ*. That David served the will of God is in accord with *ver.* 22, *ὃς ποιήσει πάντα τὰ θελήματά μου.*

ἐκοιμήθη καὶ προσετέθη πρὸς τοὺς πατέρας αὐτοῦ] Cf. 1 K. (LXX 3 K.) ii. 10 (καὶ ἐκοιμήθη Δαυεὶδ μετὰ τῶν πατέρων αὐτοῦ) and Judg. ii. 10 (καί γε πᾶσα ἡ γενεὰ ἐκείνη προσετέθησαν πρὸς τοὺς πατέρας αὐτῶν).

xiii. 37

ὃν δὲ] δέ is adversative to μέν in *ver.* 36 ; Christ is contrasted with David.

xiii. 38

γνωστὸν οὖν ἔστω ὑμῖν] Cf. ii. 14 ; iv. 10 ; xxviii. 28.

διὰ τούτου] 'through this Man' ; B has διὰ τοῦτο, 'for this reason'.

ἄφεσις ἁμαρτιῶν] As in ii. 38 ; x. 43.

xiii. 39

καὶ ἀπὸ πάντων κ.τ.λ.] To the Gospel as preached in the earlier chapters, offering remission of sins through Christ, there is now added the characteristically Pauline doctrine of justification. *Grammatically*, the sentence is capable of two meanings : (1) the Mosaic Law provided justification from *some* things, but from all those things from which it could not justify, Christ justifies those who believe in Him ; (2) the Law could never justify anyone from anything, for all have transgressed it, but complete justification from all sins is afforded by Christ to every believer. That the second meaning is to be preferred is suggested both by the context (at the climax of the argument we expect a complete and not a partial claim for the power of the Gospel) and by the teaching of Paul's epistles. In δ this verse is paraphrased καὶ μετάνοια ἀπὸ πάντων ὧν οὐκ ἠδυνήθητε ἐν νόμῳ Μωυσέως δικαιωθῆναι, ἐν τούτῳ οὖν πᾶς ὁ πιστεύων δικαιοῦται παρὰ θεῷ. With παρὰ θεῷ cf. Rom. ii. 13 ; Gal. iii. 11 (also of justification).

ἐν νόμῳ . . . ἐν τούτῳ] Instrumental ἐν, found elsewhere with δικαιόω, e.g., ἐν νόμῳ in Gal. iii. 11 ; v. 4. For the phrase ἐν νόμῳ δικαιωθῆναι cf. 2 Baruch li. 3, where God is represented as speaking of 'the glory of those who have now been justified in My law'. Contrast 4 Ezra viii. 32 ff., on the necessity of justification by grace for those who have no store of good works. But Paul goes far beyond this, seeing all men, irrespective of their works, as equally in need of justification.

xiii. 40

ἐν τοῖς προφήταις] i.e., in the Book of the Twelve Prophets (cf. vii. 42). The quotation is from Hab. i. 5. It was in Hab. that

Paul found one of the OT foreshadowings of justification by faith (Hab. ii. 4, quoted Rom. i. 17 and Gal. iii. 11, also in Heb. x. 38).

xiii. 41

ἴδετε κ.τ.λ.] The LXX runs, *ἴδετε, οἱ καταφρονηταί, καὶ ἐπιβλέψατε καὶ θαυμάσατε θαυμάσια, καὶ ἀφανίσθητε, διότι ἔργον ἐγὼ ἐργάζομαι ἐν ταῖς ἡμέραις ὑμῶν, ὃ οὐ μὴ πιστεύσητε ἐάν τις ἐκδιηγῆται.* MT has *ba-gōyīm* ('among the nations') for οἱ καταφρονηταί (which would represent Heb. *ha-bōzīm*). There is nothing in the Heb. corresponding to ἀφανίσθητε. The words as used by Habakkuk referred to the imminent Chaldaean invasion. Paul uses them in an eschatological sense, of the judgment about to fall (cf. ii. 40). After the quotation D adds καὶ ἐσίγησαν (καὶ ἐσίγησεν 614 hcl *).

Thus ends the first reported sermon of Paul. Its theology is definitely Pauline, though not so developed as his later teaching. It forms a bridge between the primitive preaching of the early chapters of Ac. and the mature doctrine of the Epistles.

(c) Paul's Sermon arouses Interest, xiii. 42-43

Ἐξιόντων δὲ αὐτῶν παρεκάλουν εἰς τὸ μεταξὺ σάββατον λαληθῆναι 42
αὐτοῖς τὰ ῥήματα ταῦτα. λυθείσης δὲ τῆς συναγωγῆς ἠκολούθησαν 43
πολλοὶ τῶν Ἰουδαίων καὶ τῶν σεβομένων προσηλύτων τῷ Παύλῳ καὶ
τῷ Βαρνάβᾳ, οἵτινες προσλαλοῦντες αὐτοῖς ἔπειθον αὐτοὺς προσμένειν
τῇ χάριτι τοῦ θεοῦ.

xiii. 42

παρεκάλουν] Omitted by B, which has ἠξίουν after σάββατον.

'Perhaps ἀξιούντων should replace ἐξιόντων, and παρεκάλουν and the stop at the end of the verse be omitted. The language of *vv.* 42 f. would then be natural if the requests for another discourse on the following sabbath were interrupted by the breaking up of the congregation by the ἀρχισυνάγωγοι (*ver.* 15), e.g. for prudential reasons (cf. *ver.* 45)' (Hort).

μεταξὺ] Originally 'between', but in common parlance came to mean 'next' (so Plut. *Instituta Laconica*, 240 B; Ep. Barn. xiii. 5; 1 Clem. xliv. 2; freq. in Josephus; cf. xxiii. 25 δ).

xiii. 43

τῶν σεβομένων προσηλύτων] 'of the worshipping proselytes'. While σεβόμενοι commonly refers to the class of people otherwise designated φοβούμενοι τὸν θεόν (see on x. 2) it is not a technical term restricted to them, and seems to be used here to characterize full proselytes (see on ii. 10). This is better than to suppose that Luke here describes as proselytes those who were not so in the proper and regular sense of the word. Cf. *BC* v. p. 88. There is no MS. evidence to warrant rejecting *προσηλύτων* as a gloss.

ἔπειθον] 'urged'; the imperf. does not mean 'persuaded', as the aor. does.

προσμένειν τῇ χάριτι τοῦ θεοῦ] See on xi. 23. After *θεοῦ* the δ text adds *ἐγένετο δὲ καθ' ὅλης τῆς πόλεως διελθεῖν τὸν λόγον τοῦ θεοῦ.*

(d) Gentile Interest arouses Jewish Envy, xiii. 44-52

Τῷ δὲ ἐρχομένῳ σαββάτῳ σχεδὸν πᾶσα ἡ πόλις συνήχθη ἀκοῦσαι 44
τὸν λόγον τοῦ θεοῦ. ἰδόντες δὲ οἱ Ἰουδαῖοι τοὺς ὄχλους ἐπλήσθησαν 45
ζήλου καὶ ἀντέλεγον τοῖς ὑπὸ Παύλου λαλουμένοις βλασφημοῦντες.
παρρησιασάμενοί τε ὁ Παῦλος καὶ ὁ Βαρνάβας εἶπαν Ὑμῖν ἦν ἀναγ- 46
καῖον πρῶτον λαληθῆναι τὸν λόγον τοῦ θεοῦ· ἐπειδὴ ἀπωθεῖσθε
αὐτὸν καὶ οὐκ ἀξίους κρίνετε ἑαυτοὺς τῆς αἰωνίου ζωῆς, ἰδοὺ στρεφό-
μεθα εἰς τὰ ἔθνη· οὕτω γὰρ ἐντέταλται ἡμῖν ὁ κύριος 47
Τέθεικά σε εἰς φῶς ἐθνῶν
τοῦ εἶναί σε εἰς σωτηρίαν ἕως ἐσχάτου τῆς γῆς.
ἀκούοντα δὲ τὰ ἔθνη ἔχαιρον καὶ ἐδόξαζον τὸν λόγον τοῦ θεοῦ, καὶ 48
ἐπίστευσαν ὅσοι ἦσαν τεταγμένοι εἰς ζωὴν αἰώνιον· διεφέρετο δὲ 49
ὁ λόγος τοῦ κυρίου δι' ὅλης τῆς χώρας. οἱ δὲ Ἰουδαῖοι παρώτρυναν 50
τὰς σεβομένας γυναῖκας τὰς εὐσχήμονας καὶ τοὺς πρώτους τῆς πόλεως
καὶ ἐπήγειραν διωγμὸν ἐπὶ τὸν Παῦλον καὶ Βαρνάβαν, καὶ ἐξέβαλον
αὐτοὺς ἀπὸ τῶν ὁρίων αὐτῶν. οἱ δὲ ἐκτιναξάμενοι τὸν κονιορτὸν τῶν 51
ποδῶν ἐπ' αὐτοὺς ἦλθον εἰς Ἰκόνιον, οἵ τε μαθηταὶ ἐπληροῦντο 52
χαρᾶς καὶ πνεύματος ἁγίου.

xiii. 44

δὲ] *τε* B E P minn.pauc.

ἐρχομένῳ] ℵ B C* D 81 byz. The variant *ἐχομένῳ*, 'next' (A C² E 33 minn), while more idiomatic Gk., is probably an emendation. The same variation occurs in the MSS. of Thuc. vi. 3; Jos. *Ant.* vi. 9. 1; vi. 11. 9. In xx. 15, D has *ἐρχομένῃ* for *ἐχομένῃ*.

σχεδὸν πᾶσα ἡ πόλις συνήχθη] The Gentiles who attended the synagogue had spread the news through the town. Cf. *ver.* 43 δ.

τὸν λόγον τοῦ θεοῦ] For *θεοῦ* (B C E byz vg.codd pesh hcl boh arm eth) we should perhaps read *κυρίου* (ℵ A B³ 33 81 g vg sah); the more frequent phrase was likely to be substituted for the less frequent one. Cf. *ver.* 48. After *ἀκοῦσαι* D has *Παύλου· πολύν τε λόγον ποιησαμένου περὶ τοῦ κυρίου.*

xiii. 45

λαλουμένοις] *λεγομένοις* C D byz.

βλασφημοῦντες] 'speaking evil', 'slandering', perhaps defaming the name of Jesus, which is probably the sense in xxvi. 11. Before *βλασφημοῦντες* D P S hcl add *ἀντιλέγοντες καὶ*, tautologically after *ἀντέλεγον*. For the tendency of δ to amplification cf. viii. 1.

xiii. 46

παρρησιασάμενοι] See on ix. 27.

ὑμῖν . . . πρῶτον] Cf. iii. 26; for the principle that the Jew should have the first offer cf. Rom. i. 16. Luke shows consistently how in nearly every place the Jews were told the good news first; only when they refused to believe did the apostles turn to the Gentiles. Had the Jews believed, they would have had the privilege of evangelizing the Gentiles. This order is maintained in Paul's epistles as much as in Ac., e.g., in Rom. xi. 11 ff. One of the subsidiary themes of Ac. is Israel's rejection of the Gospel as a nation: cf. xviii. 6; xxviii. 28.

ἐπειδὴ] ℵ* B D*. But we feel the need of an adversative particle; ℵ^{c} A D^{2} byz supply it by adding *δέ*, while C 81 P^{45} have *ἐπεὶ δέ* (probably the true reading; so WH mg.).

ἀπωθεῖσθε] Cf. vii. 27, 39; Rom. xi. 1 f.; 1 Tim. i. 19.

οὐκ ἀξίους . . . τῆς αἰωνίου ζωῆς] For *αἰωνίου* P^{45} has *αἰωνίας*. 'Eternal life' (in Ac. only here and *ver.* 48) is to be understood as in the Synoptic Gospels of 'the life of the age to come' (so it would be understood by Jewish hearers); since the coming of Christ, however, with the good news of the Kingdom of God, this life may be enjoyed in anticipation here and now by those who receive it by faith. Those who believe in Christ experience already in Him the life of the resurrection age (*συνεζωοποίησεν τῷ Χριστῷ . . . καὶ συνήγειρεν*, Eph. ii. 5 f.). With *οὐκ ἀξίους* cf. Mt. xxii. 8, *οἱ δὲ κεκλημένοι οὐκ ἦσαν ἄξιοι*, which also refers to the Jewish nation; those who *are* worthy are referred to in Lk. xx. 35, *οἱ δὲ καταξιωθέντες τοῦ αἰῶνος ἐκείνου τυχεῖν καὶ τῆς ἀναστάσεως τῆς ἐκ νεκρῶν*.

στρεφόμεθα εἰς τὰ ἔθνη] Presumably leaving the synagogue: cf. xviii. 6 f.; xix. 9; xxviii. 28.

xiii. 47

ἡμῖν] The words which follow (from Isa. xlix. 6) are addressed by God to His Servant, and alluded to in the words of Simeon (*φῶς εἰς ἀποκάλυψιν ἐθνῶν*, Lk. ii. 32), who applied them to our Lord. Here Paul uses them of the servants of Christ. Cf. *ἐγώ εἰμι τὸ φῶς τοῦ κόσμου* (Jn. viii. 12; cf. ix. 5) with *ὑμεῖς ἐστε τὸ φῶς τοῦ κόσμου* (Mt. v. 14).

τέθεικά σε εἰς φῶς ἐθνῶν] This clause is contracted from LXX ἰδοὺ τέθεικά [ℵ A] σε εἰς διαθήκην γένους, εἰς φῶς ἐθνῶν, omitting the LXX words which represent nothing in the Heb. text. The δ text has ἰδοὺ φῶς τέθεικά σε τοῖς ἔθνεσιν. The second clause (τοῦ εἶναί σε κ.τ.λ.) is quoted *verbatim* from LXX (P45 242 522 omit σε). This quotation is in the style of those in Rom. xv. 9 ff., where the evangelization of the Gentiles is foreshadowed. With ἕως ἐσχάτου τῆς γῆς cf. i. 8.

xiii. 48

ἐδόξαζον] ἐδέξαντο D (cf. viii. 14 ; xi. 1 ; xvii. 11).

θεοῦ] B D E minn.pauc Aug.unit boh arm ; κυρίου ℵ A C 33 81 P45 byz vg sah Chr. The latter reading is probably right (cf. *ver*. 44).

τεταγμένοι εἰς ζωὴν αἰώνιον] lit., 'appointed . . .', but here perhaps in the sense 'enrolled', 'inscribed', which is found in papyri: cf. Dan. vi. 12 (Theod.), ὁρισμὸν ἔταξας, 'thou hast signed a decree'. For this divine enrolment cf. Lk. x. 20 ; Phil. iv. 3 ; Rev. xiii. 8 ; xx. 12 ; xxi. 27 ; Ex. xxxii. 32 f. ; Ps. lxix. 28 ; Isa. iv. 3 ; Dan. xii. 1. The idea is found also in 1 Enoch xlvii. 3 ; civ. 1 ; cviii. 3 ; Jubilees xxx. 20, 22, and in the Talmud (e.g. TJ *Rōsh-ha-Shānāh* i. 9. 57*a* ; TB *Rōsh-ha-Shānāh* 16*b*). Targ. Isa. iv. 3 interprets the 'life' to which some are there written (οἱ γραφέντες εἰς ζωήν, LXX) as 'eternal life' (*ḥayyē 'ālmā*). Cf. Dalman, *Words of Jesus*, p. 209. Those here referred to showed by their believing that they had been so enrolled, in contrast to the unbelieving Jews of *ver*. 46.

xiii. 49

τοῦ κυρίου] om P45.

δι' ὅλης τῆς χώρας] Ramsay and others have regarded χώρα here as equivalent to Lat. *regio* in its technical sense (see on *ver*. 14), in which case the region Phrygia Galatica is meant (see also on xvi. 6 ; xviii. 23). It is unnecessary, however, to take the word in any technical sense here.

xiii. 50

τὰς σεβομένας γυναῖκας τὰς εὐσχήμονας] 'The influence attributed to the women . . . is in perfect accord with the manners of the country. In Athens or in an Ionian city, it would have been impossible' (Ramsay, *SPT*, p. 102). The women were more or less attached to the Jewish worship (σεβόμεναι) and well-to-do (for εὐσχήμων cf. Mk. xv. 43, where it corresponds to πλούσιος of Mt. xxvii. 57 ; cf. also Ac. xvii. 12).

τοὺς πρώτους τῆς πόλεως] i.e., the magistrates. Cf. xxviii. 7 (*q.v.*); Jos. *Vita* 34 (*τοὺς πολλοὺς τοῦ δήμου πρώτους ἄνδρας*). Luke carefully shows how throughout Paul's travels in the Roman world it was Jews who were foremost in stirring up opposition against him, not the authorities acting on their own initiative.

διωγμὸν] The δ text inserts *θλίψιν μεγαλὴν καὶ* before *διωγμόν* (cf. the similar insertion in viii. 1).

xiii. 51

ἐκτιναξάμενοι τὸν κονιορτὸν τῶν ποδῶν] For this gesture cf. Mt. x. 14 = Mk. vi. 11 = Lk. ix. 5; x. 11: for similar gestures in Ac. cf. xviii. 6; xxii. 22 f. It signified the breaking off of all intercourse, and was regarded as tantamount to calling a man a heathen.

'Ικόνιον] Modern Konia, in NT times the easternmost city of Phrygia Galatica (see on xiv. 6). Since the third century B.C., it had passed successively under the rule of the Seleucids, Galatians, and kings of Pontus, from whom the Roman conquest of Mithradates VI set it free. In 39 B.C. Antony gave it to Polemon of Cilicia, and three years later to Amyntas of Galatia. When the latter died in 25 B.C., he bequeathed his kingdom to the Romans, who made it the province of Galatia. Under Claudius the city was granted the honorary imperial prefix and became known as Claudiconium. In the reign of Hadrian (A.D. 117-138) it became a Roman colony.

xiii. 52

οἵ τε] A B 33 vg pesh eth; *οἱ δέ* ℵ C D E 81 byz hcl sah boh arm. The latter reading suits the sense better (so WH mg.). (P^{45} has *οἵ γε*.)

4. Iconium, Lystra, Derbe, xiv. 1-28

(a) Adventures in Iconium, xiv. 1-7

'Εγένετο δὲ ἐν 'Ικονίῳ κατὰ τὸ αὐτὸ εἰσελθεῖν αὐτοὺς εἰς τὴν 1
συναγωγὴν τῶν 'Ιουδαίων καὶ λαλῆσαι οὕτως ὥστε πιστεῦσαι 'Ιουδαίων
τε καὶ 'Ελλήνων πολὺ πλῆθος. οἱ δὲ ἀπειθήσαντες 'Ιουδαῖοι ἐπήγειραν 2
καὶ ἐκάκωσαν τὰς ψυχὰς τῶν ἐθνῶν κατὰ τῶν ἀδελφῶν. ἱκανὸν μὲν 3
οὖν χρόνον διέτριψαν παρρησιαζόμενοι ἐπὶ τῷ κυρίῳ τῷ μαρτυροῦντι
τῷ λόγῳ τῆς χάριτος αὐτοῦ, διδόντι σημεῖα καὶ τέρατα γίνεσθαι διὰ
τῶν χειρῶν αὐτῶν. ἐσχίσθη δὲ τὸ πλῆθος τῆς πόλεως, καὶ οἱ μὲν 4
ἦσαν σὺν τοῖς 'Ιουδαίοις οἱ δὲ σὺν τοῖς ἀποστόλοις. ὡς δὲ ἐγένετο 5
ὁρμὴ τῶν ἐθνῶν τε καὶ 'Ιουδαίων σὺν τοῖς ἄρχουσιν αὐτῶν ὑβρίσαι καὶ
λιθοβολῆσαι αὐτούς, συνιδόντες κατέφυγον εἰς τὰς πόλεις τῆς Λυ- 6
καονίας Λύστραν καὶ Δέρβην καὶ τὴν περίχωρον, κἀκεῖ εὐαγγελιζό- 7
μενοι ἦσαν.

xiv. 1

κατὰ τὸ αὐτὸ] 'after the same manner' as in Antioch. Cf. κατὰ τὸ εἰωθός, xvii. 2; κατὰ τὰ αὐτά, Lk. vi. 23, 26; xvii. 30. (Cf. Eb. Nestle in *ET* xxiv [1912-13], pp. 187 f.)

xiv. 2f.

οἱ δὲ ἀπειθήσαντες κ.τ.λ.] The sequence of these two verses has been felt to present difficulties. *Ver.* 2 appears to anticipate *ver.* 5; and after the Jews had stirred up the Gentiles against the apostles, why did the latter remain a 'considerable time' (*ver.* 3) instead of departing as they had done from Pisidian Antioch? Ramsay regarded *ver.* 3 as an early gloss (*SPT*, pp. 107 ff.); others, like Moffatt, transpose *vv.* 2 and 3. The δ text tries to mend matters by recasting *ver.* 2 as follows: οἱ δὲ ἀρχισυνάγωγοι τῶν Ἰουδαίων καὶ οἱ ἄρχοντες (τῆς συναγωγῆς) ἐπήγαγον αὐτοῖς[1] διωγμὸν κατὰ τῶν δικαίων, καὶ ἐκάκωσαν τὰς ψυχὰς τῶν ἐθνῶν κατὰ τῶν ἀδελφῶν. ὁ δὲ κύριος ἔδωκεν ταχὺ εἰρήνην. This reads more smoothly, when followed by *ver.* 3, but involves a double persecution, a brief one at the beginning of the visit (*ver.* 2), and a more violent one at the end (*ver.* 5). The greater smoothness of this reading is probably a mark of its secondary character. It requires no excess of imagination to suppose that the Jews of Pisidian Antioch communicated with those in Iconium, who proceeded at once to prejudice the authorities against Paul and Barnabas: *ver.* 2 will then indicate the immediate Jewish opposition, *ver.* 5 the success of the attempt to stir up the magistrates and populace. But until the Gentile opposition broke out, the apostles ignored the Jewish hostility and carried on the work of evangelization for a considerable time.

οἱ δὲ ἀπειθήσαντες Ἰουδαῖοι κ.τ.λ.] 'But the Jews who had disobeyed . . .': unbelief and disobedience are both involved in the rejection of the Gospel (cf. xix. 9; Jn. iii. 36; 2 Th. i. 8; Heb. iii. 18 f.; 1 Pet. ii. 7 f.). The words substituted in D (οἱ δὲ ἀρχισυνάγωγοι τῶν Ἰουδαίων καὶ οἱ ἄρχοντες τῆς συναγωγῆς) make the distinction between the ἀρχισυνάγωγοι and the ἄρχοντες noted on p. 261, n. 1.

ἐπήγειραν κ.τ.λ.] Cf. 1 Chr. v. 26 LXX, ἐπήγειρεν ὁ θεὸς τὸ πνεῦμα Φαλὼχ βασιλέως Ἀσσούρ. D has ἐπήγαγον (cf. xiii. 23, where δ has ἤγειρεν as against ἤγαγεν in β).

ἐκάκωσαν κ.τ.λ.] lit., 'made the minds of the Gentiles evil against the brethren'; for this sense cf. Ps. cvi. 32 (LXX cv), ἐκακώθη Μωυσῆς, 'Moses was enraged' (EV, 'it went ill with Moses').

[1] Perhaps ἐπήγαγον of D is a copyist's error for ἐπήγειραν. Torrey (*DPC*, pp. 125, 138, 147) suggests that αὐτοῖς is the rendering of the Aramaic ethical dative.

This sense of κακόω is also found in Josephus (*Ant.* xvi. 1. 2 ; 7. 3 ; 8. 6) and in the papyri. Elsewhere it means 'ill-treat', as in xii. 1 ; xviii. 10, and in classical Gk.

xiv. 3

μὲν οὖν] With resumptive force: 'so then', 'well, then', suggesting that *ver.* 2 is parenthetical, preparing the way for *ver.* 5.

παρρησιαζόμενοι ἐπὶ τῷ κυρίῳ] With this use of ἐπί cf. iv. 17, λαλεῖν ἐπὶ τῷ ὀνόματι τούτῳ. It is used of 'the ground or foundation upon which some feeling or act is based' (Page): cf. also iii. 10, 12, 16 ; iv. 9 ; v. 28, 40 ; xv. 31 ; xx. 38.

τῷ μαρτυροῦντι κ.τ.λ.] Cf. Mk. xvi. 20.

τῷ λόγῳ τῆς χάριτος αὐτοῦ] Cf. xx. 32 ; also xx. 24, τὸ εὐαγγέλιον τῆς χάριτος τοῦ θεοῦ. The gen. is objective: the message (λόγος) proclaims the grace of God.

σημεῖα καὶ τέρατα] See on ii. 22, 43.

xiv. 4

ἐσχίσθη δὲ] D has ἦν δὲ ἐσχισμένον, as if the populace had taken sides before the events of *ver.* 2.

σὺν τοῖς ἀποστόλοις] Barnabas is called an apostle; though not one of the Twelve, he was probably one of the 120 (i. 15) and a witness of the Resurrection. After ἀποστόλοις the δ text adds κολλώμενοι διὰ τὸν λόγον τοῦ θεοῦ.

xiv. 5

σὺν τοῖς ἄρχουσιν αὐτῶν] The leaders both of Gentiles and of Jews seem to be meant, the Gentile magistrates (cf. τοὺς πρώτους τῆς πόλεως, xiii. 50) and the leaders of the Jewish community (see on xiii. 15).

ὑβρίσαι καὶ λιθοβολῆσαι αὐτούς] 'to assault and stone them': not, of course, the legal Jewish stoning, but mob-violence. The impression made by Paul in Iconium is reflected in the 'Acts of Paul' (*c.* A.D. 150). The description of Paul's appearance in that work may rest upon a local tradition; it does not read like a later idealization:

> 'a man little of stature, thin-haired upon the head, crooked in the legs, of good state of body, with eyebrows joining, and a nose somewhat crooked; full of grace, for sometimes he appeared like a man, and sometimes had the face of an angel' (see Ramsay, *CRE*, pp. 31 f.).

xiv. 6

συνιδόντες] 'getting wind of it'. See on συνιδών, xii. 12 ; also ἐπιγνόντες, ix. 30. The previous verse probably refers to a plot to stone the apostles, the carrying out of which they prevented by escaping; and ὁρμή (*ver.* 5) means 'movement' (cf. Jas. iii. 4) rather than 'onset'. See on λιθάσαντες, *ver.* 19.

κατέφυγον] The classical sense is 'fled for refuge'.

εἰς τὰς πόλεις τῆς Λυκαονίας] The implication is that Iconium was not in Lycaonia. The region probably called Lycaonia Galatica lay east of Phrygia Galatica; it is to be distinguished from Lycaonia Antiochiana, which lay farther east, outside the province of Galatia, and formed part of the territory of Antiochus, king of Commagene. Xenophon (*Anabasis*, i. 2. 19) calls Iconium 'the last city of Phrygia' (τῆς Φρυγίας πόλιν ἐσχάτην). As it was a frontier town between Phrygia and Lycaonia, and commonly shared the fortune of the latter region, ancient writers (e.g. Cicero, *Fam.* xv. 4. 2; Pliny, *NH* v. 25) frequently call it a Lycaonian town. But this passage in Ac. is sufficient evidence that at this time it was on the Phrygian side of the border, at least in the linguistic sense and probably also in the political sense. For a full discussion cf. Ramsay, *BRD*, pp. 39 ff., where the mention of Iconium as Phrygian in the second-century *Acta Iustini* is adduced, together with epigraphic evidence of the use of the Phrygian language there in the third century.

Λύστραν] Lystra, along with Pisidian Antioch, was made a Roman colony by Augustus in A.D. 6. The two colonies were connected by a military road, which did not pass through Iconium. Lystra lay about 18 miles S.S.W. of Iconium. Its site was identified by J. R. S. Sterrett in 1885 at Zoldera, near Khatyn Serai.

Δέρβην] Sterrett thought it was situated at or near the modern Zosta; Ramsay at Gudelissin, 3 miles N.W. of Zosta. According to Stephanus of Byzantium, its name represents Lycaonian *delbeia*, 'juniper'. It was part of the territory of Amyntas of Galatia, whose kingdom passed to the Romans at his death in 25 B.C. From A.D. 41 to 72 Derbe was a frontier city of the province of Galatia, and from Claudius it received the honorary title Claudio-Derbe (cf. Claudiconium).

τὴν περίχωρον] Probably 'the surrounding district' in a general sense. Ramsay, however, suggested that it referred to the Roman region of Lycaonia Galatica, in which Lystra and Derbe were situated (*SPT*, pp. 110 f.).

xiv. 7

εὐαγγελιζόμενοι ἦσαν] For the construction see on i. 10. The δ text adds καὶ ἐκινήθη ὅλον τὸ πλῆθος ἐπὶ τῇ διδαχῇ. ὁ δὲ Παῦλος καὶ Βαρνάβας διέτριβον ἐν Λύστροις.

(b) The Miracle at Lystra, xiv. 8-18

Καί τις ἀνὴρ ἀδύνατος ἐν Λύστροις τοῖς ποσὶν ἐκάθητο, χωλὸς 8
ἐκ κοιλίας μητρὸς αὐτοῦ, ὃς οὐδέποτε περιεπάτησεν. οὗτος ἤκουεν 9
τοῦ Παύλου λαλοῦντος· ὃς ἀτενίσας αὐτῷ καὶ ἰδὼν ὅτι ἔχει πίστιν
τοῦ σωθῆναι εἶπεν μεγάλῃ φωνῇ Ἀνάστηθι ἐπὶ τοὺς πόδας σου ὀρθός· 10
καὶ ἥλατο καὶ περιεπάτει. οἵ τε ὄχλοι ἰδόντες ὃ ἐποίησεν Παῦλος 11
ἐπῆραν τὴν φωνὴν αὐτῶν Λυκαονιστὶ λέγοντες Οἱ θεοὶ ὁμοιωθέντες
ἀνθρώποις κατέβησαν πρὸς ἡμᾶς, ἐκάλουν τε τὸν Βαρνάβαν Δία, 12
τὸν δὲ Παῦλον Ἑρμῆν ἐπειδὴ αὐτὸς ἦν ὁ ἡγούμενος τοῦ λόγου.
ὅ τε ἱερεὺς τοῦ Διὸς τοῦ ὄντος πρὸ τῆς πόλεως ταύρους καὶ στέμματα 13
ἐπὶ τοὺς πυλῶνας ἐνέγκας σὺν τοῖς ὄχλοις ἤθελεν θύειν. ἀκούσαντες 14
δὲ οἱ ἀπόστολοι Βαρνάβας καὶ Παῦλος, διαρρήξαντες τὰ ἱμάτια
ἑαυτῶν ἐξεπήδησαν εἰς τὸν ὄχλον, κράζοντες καὶ λέγοντες Ἄνδρες, 15
τί ταῦτα ποιεῖτε; καὶ ἡμεῖς ὁμοιοπαθεῖς ἐσμὲν ὑμῖν ἄνθρωποι, εὐαγγε-
λιζόμενοι ὑμᾶς ἀπὸ τούτων τῶν ματαίων ἐπιστρέφειν ἐπὶ θεὸν ζῶντα
ὃς ἐποίησεν τὸν οὐρανὸν καὶ τὴν γῆν καὶ τὴν θάλασσαν καὶ πάντα
τὰ ἐν αὐτοῖς· ὃς ἐν ταῖς παρῳχημέναις γενεαῖς εἴασεν πάντα τὰ ἔθνη 16
πορεύεσθαι ταῖς ὁδοῖς αὐτῶν· καίτοι οὐκ ἀμάρτυρον αὑτὸν ἀφῆκεν 17
ἀγαθουργῶν, οὐρανόθεν ὑμῖν ὑετοὺς διδοὺς καὶ καιροὺς καρποφόρους,
ἐμπιπλῶν τροφῆς καὶ εὐφροσύνης τὰς καρδίας ὑμῶν. καὶ ταῦτα 18
λέγοντες μόλις κατέπαυσαν τοὺς ὄχλους τοῦ μὴ θύειν αὐτοῖς.

In this miracle, and in the language describing it, we find several parallels to the story of ch. iii. See pp. 32 f. for parallels between Peter's work and Paul's.

xiv. 8

ἀδύνατος] 'powerless', 'weak'. Cf. Rom. xv. 1, where, however, the word is not used in the physical sense, as here.

Λύστροις] As if from a neut. pl. *Λύστρα*, while *Λύστραν* (*ver.* 6) is from fem. sing. *Λύστρα*. For a similar heteroclite declension see on *Λύδδα*, ix. 32.

χωλὸς ἐκ κοιλίας μητρὸς αὐτοῦ] The same words are used in iii. 2 (*q.v.*). Here the three-fold emphasis, *ἀδύνατος . . . τοῖς ποσίν, χωλὸς ἐκ κοιλίας μητρὸς αὐτοῦ, ὃς οὐδέποτε περιεπάτησεν*, stresses the reality of his trouble and therefore of his cure.

xiv. 9

λαλοῦντος] δ adds *ὑπάρχων ἐν φόβῳ*.

ἀτενίσας] Cf. iii. 4, and for the word see on i. 10.

πίστιν τοῦ σωθῆναι] Primarily, *σωθῆναι* here means 'to be healed' in the bodily sense, but even when the word is used in a Gentile context 'there lies latent in it some undefined and hardly conscious thought of the spiritual and the moral, which made it suit Paul's purpose admirably' (Ramsay, *Teaching of Paul*, p. 95). See on ὁδὸν σωτηρίας, xvi. 17. For the element of faith in healing cf. iii. 16; also Lk. v. 20; vii. 50; viii. 48; xvii. 19; xviii. 42 (though in the Gospels the faith is frequently exercised by someone interested in the sick person).

xiv. 10

ἀνάστηθι] δ prefixes σοὶ λέγω ἐν τῷ ὀνόματι τοῦ κυρίου Ἰησοῦ Χριστοῦ, a pietistic addition which makes the parallelism with ch. iii more complete (cf. iii. 6).

ὀρθός] δ adds καὶ περιπάτει (cf. iii. 6).

καὶ ἥλατο καὶ περιεπάτει] Cf. iii. 8. δ continues its amplification of this verse by expanding these words to καὶ εὐθέως παραχρῆμα ἀνήλατο καὶ περιεπάτει (for παραχρῆμα cf. iii. 7). Observe that ἥλατο is aor. ('he jumped up') and περιεπάτει is imperf. ('he began to walk', 'he walked about').

xiv. 11

ἐπῆραν τὴν φωνὴν . . . λέγοντες] See on ii. 14.

Λυκαονιστί] These people were not the aristocracy of Lystra, the Roman colonists, whose language was Latin (as appears from funerary inscriptions), but the native inhabitants (the *incolae*). Their language was one of the many languages which had been spoken in Asia Minor since ancient times. The apostles evidently did not at first understand what the crowd was saying, and realized it only when they saw the preparations that followed.

Οἱ θεοὶ ὁμοιωθέντες ἀνθρώποις κατέβησαν πρὸς ἡμᾶς] Cf. the second reaction of the Maltese in xxviii. 6. For the identification of Barnabas and Paul with Zeus and Hermes respectively, we should compare the story of Philemon and Baucis, an aged and pious couple of that region who gave hospitality unawares to Jupiter and Mercury (Ovid, *Metamorphoses*, viii. 626 ff.).[1] Of two inscriptions of Sedasa, near Lystra, dating from *c.* A.D. 250, discovered by Prof. W. M. Calder, one records the dedication to Zeus of a statue of Hermes along with a sundial, by men with Lycaonian names, the other mentions 'priests of Zeus'. See *CR* xxiv (1910), pp. 76 ff., xxxviii (1924), p. 29, *n.* 1; *Expositor*, VII. x (1910), pp. 1 ff., 148 ff. A further indication of the joint worship of Zeus and Hermes in these parts is probably to be found in a stone altar discovered near Lystra by W. M. Calder and W. H. Buckler in 1926, dedicated to the 'Hearer of Prayer' (presumably Zeus)

[1] Cf. W. M. Calder, 'New Light on Ovid's Story of Philemon and Baucis' in *Discovery* iii. (1922), pp. 207 ff.

and Hermes. See *Discovery* vii (1926), p. 262; *ET* xxxvii (1925-6), p. 528.

xiv. 12

Δία . . . Ἑρμῆν] Zeus was the chief god in the Greek pantheon, Hermes was his son by Maia, and messenger of the gods. These names may represent native gods of Lycaonia identified with the Greek Zeus and Hermes. Jupiter and Mercury were the corresponding Roman gods.

ὁ ἡγούμενος τοῦ λόγου] lit., 'the leader of the speaking'. According to Iamblichus (*de mysteriis Aegyptiacis* i) Hermes was θεὸς ὁ τῶν λόγων ἡγεμών.

xiv. 13

ὅ τε ἱερεὺς τοῦ Διὸς τοῦ ὄντος πρὸ τῆς πόλεως] 'the priest of Zeus Propolis', lit., 'of the Zeus who was (i.e., whose temple was) in front of the city'. δ has οἱ δὲ ἱερεῖς τοῦ ὄντος Διὸς πρὸ πόλεως, which is idiomatic Greek and accords with the practice of having a college of priests at great temples (cf. Aeschylus, *Septem c. Thebas* 164; *CIG* 2963, τῆς μεγάλης θεᾶς [Ἀρτεμί]δος πρὸ πόλ[εω]ς ἱερεῖς). Ramsay (*CRE*, p. 51) quotes from the Isaurican Claudiopolis, S.E. of Lystra, a dedication Διῒ Προαστίῳ: cf. the phrase τοῦ πρὸ πόλεως Διονύσου in *IG XII*. iii. 420, 522. In the δ text τοῦ ὄντος κ.τ.λ. probably means 'the local Zeus Propolis': for this use of ὁ ὤν see on v. 17; xiii. 1.

στέμματα] Woollen wreaths or fillets for the sacrificial oxen.

πυλῶνας] It is not clear whether these portals were those of the temple, the city, or the house where the apostles were lodging (cf. x. 17). Perhaps, as in iii. 2, the lame man lay at the temple gates. But Ephrem Syrus thinks the ox was brought to the house-door where they were; this perhaps agrees better with ἐξεπήδησαν, *ver.* 14.

θύειν] D has ἐπιθύειν, which in Ramsay's opinion refers to a special sacrifice, in addition to (ἐπί) the regular ritual (*SPT*, p. 118). It is not clear that ἐπιθύειν has this meaning, and d h have simply *immolare*.

xiv. 14

διαρρήξαντες τὰ ἱμάτια ἑαυτῶν] For ἑαυτῶν (ℵ[c] A B 33), αὐτῶν (as in WH mg.) is the reading of ℵ C D 81 byz. The pronoun expresses the shade of meaning which in classical Gk. would be expressed by the use of the middle voice. The rending of their garments indicated horror at blasphemy (cf. Mk. xiv. 63). The action in xvi. 22 is quite different. For other gestures cf. xiii. 51.

ἐξεπήδησαν] εἰσεπήδησαν byz. Cf. Judith xiv. 16 f., διέρρηξεν τὰ ἱμάτια αὐτοῦ . . . καὶ ἐξεπήδησεν εἰς τὸν λαὸν κράζων.

xiv. 15

τί ταῦτα ποιεῖτε;] 'Why are you doing this?' or 'What's this you're doing?' Cf. Demosthenes, *ad Calliclem* 5, Τεισία, τί ταῦτα ποιεῖς; Cf. also Lk. xvi. 2, τί τοῦτο ἀκούω; 'What's this I hear?'

καὶ ἡμεῖς] om P^{45}.

ὁμοιοπαθεῖς] Cf. Jas. v. 17. Perhaps here in contrast to God, who is ἀπαθής (but Christ is παθητός, xxvi. 23). For the expostulation cf. x. 26; Rev. xix. 10; xxii. 9.

εὐαγγελιζόμενοι κ.τ.λ.] This is the first recorded Christian address to a pagan audience. The appeal is made to such knowledge of God as they might reasonably have, i.e., by 'natural revelation'. Cf. Rom. i. 19 ff.; ii. 14 f., and the longer address at Athens, Ac. xvii. 22 ff.

ἀπὸ τούτων τῶν ματαίων ἐπιστρέφειν ἐπὶ θεον ζῶντα] P^{45} has ἀποστῆναι before ἀπό, and καὶ before ἐπιστρέφειν. Cf. 1 Th. i. 9, ἐπεστρέψατε πρὸς τὸν θεὸν ἀπὸ τῶν εἰδώλων δουλεύειν θεῷ ζῶντι καὶ ἀληθινῷ. To Jews the Gospel proclaims 'Jesus is the Christ'; to Gentiles it begins by saying, 'God is one (cf. Dt. vi. 4), and has not left Himself without witness' (ἀμάρτυρος, *ver.* 17).

θεὸν ζῶντα] ℵ^{c} A B C D^{2}; θεὸν τὸν ζῶντα ℵ*; τὸν θεὸν ζῶντα D*; τὸν θεὸν τὸν ζῶντα P^{45} byz.

ὃς ἐποίησεν κ.τ.λ.] See on iv. 24; xvii. 24, and cf. references given in notes *ad loc.*

xiv. 16

ὃς ἐν ταῖς παρῳχημέναις γενεαῖς κ.τ.λ.] With the teaching of this verse cf. xvii. 30, where the meaning is similar; also Rom. i. 18 ff., where the meaning is somewhat different. Here and in ch. xvii. the point is that until the full revelation of God came to the Gentiles, He overlooked their errors in so far as these arose from ignorance of His will; in Rom. i. God's giving them up to their own devices is the penalty for their rejecting even the little light they had.

ἐν ταῖς παρῳχημέναις γενεαῖς] Cf. χρόνοις αἰωνίοις, Rom. xvi. 25; ἑτέραις γενεαῖς, Eph. iii. 5; these are the 'times of ignorance' of Ac. xvii. 30. The word παρῳχημένος is literary (cf. Jos. *Ant.* viii. 12. 3; in grammar, ὁ παρῳχημένος χρόνος is 'the past tense').

xiv. 17

καίτοι] 'and yet'. For this (the reading of ℵ^{c} A B C 33 81) D E P^{45} have καί γε (cf. xvii. 27), ℵ byz have καίτοιγε. Cf. xvii. 27.

οὐκ ἀμάρτυρον] Lukan litotes: cf. xii. 18, etc. (οὐκ ὀλίγος),

xxi. 39 (*οὐκ ἀσήμου*). Cf. Rom. i. 20 for Paul's insistence that the creation bears witness to God.

ἀγαθουργῶν] The literary contracted form is rare; for the uncontracted *ἀγαθοεργεῖν* cf. 1 Tim. vi. 18.

οὐρανόθεν] An early poetical form (cf. xxvi. 13), equivalent to *ἐξ οὐρανοῦ*.

καρποφόρους] Literary, from Pindar onwards.

ἐμπιπλῶν τροφῆς καὶ εὐφροσύνης τὰς καρδίας ὑμῶν] 'Filling your hearts with food' is a curious expression; but the use of *καρδία* in such a context is quite Lukan (cf. Lk. xxi. 34).

xiv. 18

τοῦ μὴ θύειν αὐτοῖς] For the construction cf. x. 47. C 33 81 431 614 2147 h hcl.mg arm add *ἀλλὰ πορεύεσθαι ἕκαστον εἰς τὰ ἴδια*. (This addition probably represents the δ text.[1]) The restraint of the speech speaks for its genuineness; an inventor would have introduced more distinctively Christian teaching.

(c) Persecution at Lystra; they visit Derbe and return to Syrian Antioch, xiv. 19-28

Ἐπῆλθαν δὲ ἀπὸ Ἀντιοχείας καὶ Ἰκονίου Ἰουδαῖοι, καὶ πείσ- 19
αντες τοὺς ὄχλους καὶ λιθάσαντες τὸν Παῦλον ἔσυρον ἔξω τῆς πόλεως,
νομίζοντες αὐτὸν τεθνηκέναι. κυκλωσάντων δὲ τῶν μαθητῶν αὐτὸν 20
ἀναστὰς εἰσῆλθεν εἰς τὴν πόλιν. καὶ τῇ ἐπαύριον ἐξῆλθεν σὺν τῷ
Βαρνάβᾳ εἰς Δέρβην. εὐαγγελισάμενοί τε τὴν πόλιν ἐκείνην καὶ 21
μαθητεύσαντες ἱκανοὺς ὑπέστρεψαν εἰς τὴν Λύστραν καὶ εἰς Ἰκόνιον
καὶ εἰς Ἀντιόχειαν, ἐπιστηρίζοντες τὰς ψυχὰς τῶν μαθητῶν, παρα- 22
καλοῦντες ἐμμένειν τῇ πίστει καὶ ὅτι διὰ πολλῶν θλίψεων δεῖ ἡμᾶς
εἰσελθεῖν εἰς τὴν βασιλείαν τοῦ θεοῦ. χειροτονήσαντες δὲ αὐτοῖς 23
κατ' ἐκκλησίαν πρεσβυτέρους προσευξάμενοι μετὰ νηστειῶν παρέθεντο
αὐτοὺς τῷ κυρίῳ εἰς ὃν πεπιστεύκεισαν. καὶ διελθόντες τὴν Πισιδίαν 24
ἦλθαν εἰς τὴν Παμφυλίαν, καὶ λαλήσαντες ἐν Πέργῃ τὸν λόγον 25
κατέβησαν εἰς Ἀτταλίαν, κἀκεῖθεν ἀπέπλευσαν εἰς Ἀντιόχειαν, ὅθεν 26
ἦσαν παραδεδομένοι τῇ χάριτι τοῦ θεοῦ εἰς τὸ ἔργον ὃ ἐπλήρωσαν.
Παραγενόμενοι δὲ καὶ συναγαγόντες τὴν ἐκκλησίαν ἀνήγγελλον ὅσα 27
ἐποίησεν ὁ θεὸς μετ' αὐτῶν καὶ ὅτι ἤνοιξεν τοῖς ἔθνεσιν θύραν πίστεως.
διέτριβον δὲ χρόνον οὐκ ὀλίγον σὺν τοῖς μαθηταῖς. 28

xiv. 19

ἐπῆλθαν δὲ ἀπὸ Ἀντιοχείας καὶ Ἰκονίου Ἰουδαῖοι] More than 100 miles separated Lystra from Pisidian Antioch, but the inter-

[1] More scholars than one have quoted P^{45} as an authority for this addition, possibly by a mistaken inference from Sir F. G. Kenyon's *apparatus criticus*; a study of the facsimile makes it certain that the added words were at no time in P^{45}.

course between them is indicated by the fact that the citizens of Lystra erected a statue in Antioch (*CRE*, pp. 47 ff.). D begins the verse, διατριβόντων αὐτῶν καὶ διδασκόντων ἐπῆλθόν τινες Ἰουδαῖοι ἀπὸ Ἰκονίου καὶ Ἀντιοχείας, καὶ ἐπισείσαντες τοὺς ὄχλους . . . .

πείσαντες τοὺς ὄχλους] The original δ text of this verse is probably preserved in the reading of C 81 minn h hcl.mg arm, καὶ διαλεγομένων αὐτῶν παρρησίᾳ ἔπεισαν (ἀνέπεισαν 81) τοὺς ὄχλους ἀποστῆναι ἀπ' αὐτῶν λέγοντες ὅτι οὐδὲν ἀληθὲς λέγουσιν ἀλλὰ πάντα ψεύδονται.

λιθάσαντες] This must be the occasion referred to in 2 Cor. xi. 25, where the words ἅπαξ ἐλιθάσθην support the view that the plot at Iconium (*ver.* 5) was not carried into effect. This was a riotous proceeding, not the judicial stoning of Jewish law. There is grim irony in the quick reversal of the inhabitants' attitude to the apostles (cf. xxviii. 4-6). This may have been the occasion when Paul received the στίγματα of Gal. vi. 17; for his remembrance many years later of what he endured at Antioch, Iconium and Lystra, cf. 2 Tim. iii. 11.

xiv. 20

μαθητῶν] D E P^{45} eth add αὐτοῦ.

ἀναστὰς] h sah add 'at evening', which is also implied in Ephrem's paraphrase.

xiv. 21

μαθητεύσαντες ἱκανοὺς] Cf. Mt. xxviii. 19, μαθητεύσατε πάντα τὰ ἔθνη.

εἰς Ἀντιόχειαν] The omission of this εἰς before Ἀντιόχειαν in B 81, implying a closer association between Iconium and Antioch, Ramsay supposed to be due to these cities being in the same region (Phrygia Galatica), while Lystra (in Lycaonia) is kept separate (*BRD*, p. 422). D P^{45} byz omit εἰς before Ἰκόνιον as well. Luke makes no comment on the courage shown by the apostles in returning so soon to the cities where they had been so shamefully treated; the bare statement that they visited these places again is eloquent enough.

xiv. 22

ἐπιστηρίζοντες τὰς ψυχὰς τῶν μαθητῶν] Cf. xviii. 23, στηρίζων πάντας τοὺς μαθητάς.

παρακαλοῦντες ἐμμένειν τῇ πίστει] Cf. xi. 23; xiii. 43.

ὅτι διὰ πολλῶν θλίψεων δεῖ ἡμᾶς εἰσελθεῖν εἰς τὴν βασιλείαν τοῦ θεοῦ] As ἡμᾶς indicates, this is direct speech, introduced by ὅτι *recitantis*. Translate: 'saying, "Through many tribulations we must enter the kingdom of God".' For the sense cf. 2 Th. i. 5.

The kingdom of God is to be understood here in the sense of a consummation yet future (cf. 2 Tim. iv. 18; 2 Pet. i. 11), not as something already realized (see on i. 3).

xiv. 23

χειροτονήσαντες δὲ αὐτοῖς κατ' ἐκκλησίαν πρεσβυτέρους] Although the etymological sense of *χειροτονέω* is 'to elect by show of hands', it came to be used in the sense 'designate', 'appoint': cf. the same word with prefix *πρό* in x. 41. The *πρεσβύτεροι* were appointed on the model of those in the Jerusalem church (cf. xi. 30); the background of the word is Jewish (see on *πρεσβυτέρους*, iv. 5). The 'elders' of a church are also called *ἐπίσκοποι* ('overseers'), as at Ephesus (xx. 28, cf. xx. 17) and Philippi (Phil. i. 1), *προϊστάμενοι* ('leaders'), as at Rome (Rom. xii. 8) and Thessalonica (1 Th. v. 12), *ἡγούμενοι* ('guides'), as in Heb. xiii. 17.

προσευξάμενοι μετὰ νηστειῶν] For this combination cf. xiii. 3.

πεπιστεύκεισαν] Pluperfect without augment: cf. iv. 22. D has the perf. *πεπιστεύκασιν* (cf. vg *crediderunt*). For *πιστεύω εἰς* cf. x. 43; xix. 4.

xiv. 24

διελθόντες τὴν Πισιδίαν] Pisidia was the southernmost 'region' of the province of Galatia; it lay across the northern boundary of Pamphylia. See on xiii. 14.

xiv. 25

ἐν Πέργῃ] ℵ^{c} B C D byz; *εἰς Πέργην* A; *εἰς τὴν Πέργην* ℵ 81 (so WH mg., Ropes). For this use of *εἰς* with names of towns cf. viii. 40.

Ἀτταλίαν] Mod. Andaliya. Situated at the mouth of the Cataractes, it was the chief port of Pamphylia. This is a further example of Luke's interest in ports of embarkation and disembarkation (see on xiii. 4), but δ improves the occasion by adding *εὐαγγελιζόμενοι αὐτούς*.

xiv. 26

ὅθεν ἦσαν παραδεδομένοι κ.τ.λ.] Cf. xiii. 2 f.

xiv. 27

ἀνήγγελλον] 'they reported' (cf. Attic *ἀπαγγέλλω*).

ὅσα ἐποίησεν ὁ θεὸς μετ' αὐτῶν] Cf. xv. 4. This construction has been regarded as translation-Gk. (cf. the Heb. idiom of Lk. i. 72), meaning 'all that God had done to (*or* for) them'; but more probably the idea is that they were God's co-workers (cf. 2 Cor. vi. 1), in which case the EV rendering is to be retained. For *μετ' αὐτῶν* the δ text has *μετὰ τῶν ψυχῶν αὐτῶν* [1] (cf. Ps. lxvi. 16 [LXX lxv.]).

θύραν πίστεως] A favourite Pauline metaphor : cf. 1 Cor. xvi. 9 ; 2 Cor. ii. 12 ; Col. iv. 3.

xiv. 28

χρόνον οὐκ ὀλίγον] For *οὐκ ὀλίγος* cf. xii. 18. It is in this period that we may most satisfactorily place the events of Gal. ii. 11 ff.

5. The Council at Jerusalem, xv. 1-29.

As time went on, the problems raised by the presence of Gentiles in the Church could not be avoided. For those to whom the Church was but another party within the Jewish fold, the answer was simple enough : Gentiles should be admitted into the Church in the usual manner in which proselytes were adopted into the Jewish commonwealth, by circumcision and obedience to the whole Mosaic law (see on ii. 10). It is clear, however, that outside Jerusalem these conditions had not been insisted on. Peter had learned the lesson that no man should be called common or unclean (x. 28) ; he had seen that God was as ready to accept believing Gentiles as believing Jews, and there is no suggestion that the necessity or even desirability of circumcision was urged upon Cornelius. The church at Antioch seems to have adopted the liberal attitude from the first, and the churches formed in Asia Minor during the missionary tour of Paul and Barnabas included not only Jews but an even greater number of Gentiles, who were not required to be circumcised or otherwise to observe the Mosaic law. There were, indeed, some Jews who thought that the actual rite of circumcision might be neglected, provided that its spiritual significance were appreciated, but the vast majority, including even so liberal a Jew as Philo, insisted on circumcision as indispensable ; [2] and this was no doubt the attitude of the rank and file of Jewish believers in Jerusalem. Unless, therefore, the problem were ventilated and

[1] In accordance with his theory about the origin of the δ text, C. C. Torrey supposes that *ἐποίησεν . . . μετ' αὐτῶν* was targumed into the Aram. idiom *'ăbad 'amhōn naphshĕhōn*, which was then turned back more literally into Gk., *ἐποίησεν . . . μετὰ τῶν ψυχῶν αὐτῶν* (*DPC*, p. 146).

[2] Philo (*migr. Abr.* 89-94) criticizes those who would give up the literal observance of ceremonial laws on the plea that it is enough to learn and practise their spiritual lessons : ' nor, because circumcision signifies the cutting away of pleasure and all passions and the destruction of ungodly glory . . ., let us do away with the law of circumcision ' (92). Cf. also Jos. *Ant.* xx. 2. 4, where Ananias, the Jewish instructor of King Izates of Adiabene, advises him to worship God according to the Jewish religion without being circumcised.

thoroughly discussed and decided, there was grave danger of a division between the churches of Jerusalem and Judaea on the one hand and the more liberal church of Antioch with its daughter-churches on the other.

The danger was increased by the action at Antioch of some emissaries from the Jerusalem church. These exceeded the terms of their commission and took matters into their own hands by insisting that circumcision and obedience to the Mosaic law were necessary to salvation. Such men would naturally refuse all social intercourse with uncircumcised persons, and this included common participation in the Eucharist. They thus introduced an awkward situation into the church at Antioch in regard both to the fundamental question of the way of salvation and to the practical question of fellowship between Jewish and Gentile believers. Some who would have refused to compromise on the fundamental question were disposed to give way on the other. Thus Peter, who (according to the view here taken of the relation between Ac. and Gal.) was in Antioch at the time, had eaten freely with Gentile Christians before the arrival of these Jerusalem emissaries, but after they came, he withdrew from Gentile society and ate with Jews only, thus appearing to forget the lesson he had learned at Joppa and Caesarea. The example of Peter's concession was bound to have a most disastrous effect on other Jewish Christians; even Barnabas, who had just returned with Paul from their first missionary journey, was inclined to follow his example. Paul was clear-sighted enough to see that in the long run the concession on the question of fellowship compromised the fundamental principle of salvation by grace. Ultimately, the only valid reason for making circumcision a condition of social intercourse was if it was necessary for salvation. Peter's concession was the thin end of the wedge; refusal to have fellowship at table with uncircumcised believers would be followed ere long by refusal to admit them to church fellowship or to regard them as really saved. No wonder, then, that Paul withstood Peter to his face, for his behaviour logically implied that circumcision, even if not a condition of salvation, was none the less necessary in practice.

This was the situation which the apostles and elders at Jerusalem met to discuss with the delegates from Antioch. It was decided that no such conditions were to be imposed on Gentile Christians, as necessary either for salvation or for fellowship with their Jewish brethren. Peter, on whom Paul's rebuke had evidently had the desired effect, reminded the council how God had shown His will in the conversion of Cornelius; Barnabas and Paul related how He had blessed Gentiles during their recent tour, and James, in his summing-up, agreed that as God had clearly chosen Gentiles as well as Jews, they must not impose on Gentile believers conditions which God had obviously not required of them.

There remained, however, the practical difficulty that in most of the churches Gentile believers had to live alongside Jews, who had been brought up to venerate certain food-laws and to refrain as far as possible from intercourse with Gentiles (see on x. 28). While there was no more question of requiring Gentile Christians to be circumcised and to keep the Mosaic law, these would do well to respect the scruples of their weaker Jewish brethren (all of whom could not be expected to become as emancipated as Peter or Paul), provided that there was no compromise on matters of principle. Hence the *modus vivendi* recommended to the Gentile Christians in the apostolic decree. Probably it was on much the same lines as the terms on which synagogues of the Dispersion found it possible to have some measure of intercourse with 'God-fearing' Gentiles—abstention from everything that savoured of idolatry and from meat from which the blood had not been completely drained, and conformity to the high Jewish code of relations between the sexes.

There is no good reason to suppose that Paul would have found the decree objectionable; where no compromise of principle was involved, he was the most conciliatory of men (cf. xvi. 3; xxi. 26; 1 Cor. ix. 19 ff.). In his epistles he himself urges that those who are strong in faith should voluntarily restrict their liberty in food and other matters, to avoid offending those with weaker consciences (cf. Rom. xiv. 1-xv. 6; 1 Cor. viii.).

The purpose of the apostolic decree is obscured by the widely-spread δ text, which substitutes ethical requirements for the food-regulations. This is certainly an alteration of the original text, and dates from a time after the Fall of Jerusalem in A.D. 70, when the relation between Jewish and Gentile Christians was no longer such a burning question in the churches, and such a *modus vivendi* as that contained in the apostolic decree was no longer required.[1]

(a) Judaizers visit Antioch, xv. 1-2

Καί τινες κατελθόντες ἀπὸ τῆς Ἰουδαίας ἐδίδασκον τοὺς ἀδελφοὺς 1
ὅτι Ἐὰν μὴ περιτμηθῆτε τῷ ἔθει τῷ Μωυσέως, οὐ δύνασθε σωθῆναι.
γενομένης δὲ στάσεως καὶ ζητήσεως οὐκ ὀλίγης τῷ Παύλῳ καὶ τῷ 2

[1] What is probably a relic of the Apostolic Decree appears in the second century as far west as Lyons in Gaul, where one of the martyrs in the persecution of A.D. 177 says: 'How could such people eat children, when they are not even permitted to eat the blood of irrational animals?' (Euseb. *HE* v. 1. 26). Gaul was probably evangelized from the province of Asia, where we find the terms of the decree approved later in the first century by the writer of the Apocalypse (Rev. ii. 14, 20).

Βαρνάβᾳ πρὸς αὐτοὺς ἔταξαν ἀναβαίνειν Παῦλον καὶ Βαρνάβαν καί τινας ἄλλους ἐξ αὐτῶν πρὸς τοὺς ἀποστόλους καὶ πρεσβυτέρους εἰς Ἰερουσαλὴμ περὶ τοῦ ζητήματος τούτου.

xv. 1

καί τινες κατελθόντες ἀπὸ τῆς Ἰουδαίας] We gather from *ver.* 24 and Gal. ii. 12 (*ἐλθεῖν τινας ἀπὸ Ἰακώβου*) that they had some commission from the Jerusalem church, the terms of which they exceeded in the conditions they tried to impose. No doubt they belonged to the class of believers described in xxi. 20 as 'zealots for the law'. In 383 614 minn hcl.mg (representing δ) *τῶν πεπιστευκότων ἀπὸ τῆς αἱρέσεως τῶν Φαρισαίων* is added (from *ver.* 5, *q.v.*).

ὅτι] *recitantis.*

τῷ ἔθει τῷ Μωυσέως] δ (D hcl.mg sah) expands to *καὶ τῷ ἔθει Μωυσέως περιπατῆτε.*

xv. 2

οὐκ ὀλίγης] See on xii. 18 for the litotes.

πρὸς αὐτοὺς] δ has *σὺν αὐτοῖς*, and continues, *ἔλεγεν γὰρ ὁ Παῦλος μένειν οὕτως καθὼς ἐπίστευσαν διισχυριζόμενος, οἱ δὲ ἐληλυθότες ἀπὸ Ἰερουσαλὴμ παρήγγειλαν αὐτοῖς*[1] *τῷ Παύλῳ καὶ Βαρνάβᾳ καί τισιν ἄλλοις ἀναβαίνειν πρὸς τοὺς ἀποστόλους καὶ πρεσβυτέρους εἰς Ἰερουσαλὴμ ὅπως κριθῶσιν ἐπ' αὐτοῖς περὶ τοῦ ζητήματος τούτου.* In β there is no explicit subject to *ἔταξαν*, but in all probability we are to understand that the Antiochene Christians sent them (cf. *ver.* 3). Note the joint mention of apostles and elders here in contrast with xi. 30 (*q.v.*).

(b) Paul and Barnabas go up to Jerusalem, xv. 3-5

Οἱ μὲν οὖν προπεμφθέντες ὑπὸ τῆς ἐκκλησίας διήρχοντο τήν τε 3
Φοινίκην καὶ Σαμαρίαν ἐκδιηγούμενοι τὴν ἐπιστροφὴν τῶν ἐθνῶν, καὶ
ἐποίουν χαρὰν μεγάλην πᾶσι τοῖς ἀδελφοῖς. παραγενόμενοι δὲ εἰς 4
Ἰεροσόλυμα παρεδέχθησαν ἀπὸ τῆς ἐκκλησίας καὶ τῶν ἀποστόλων
καὶ τῶν πρεσβυτέρων, ἀνήγγειλάν τε ὅσα ὁ θεὸς ἐποίησεν μετ' αὐτῶν.
Ἐξανέστησαν δέ τινες τῶν ἀπὸ τῆς αἱρέσεως τῶν Φαρισαίων πεπιστευ- 5
κότες, λέγοντες ὅτι δεῖ περιτέμνειν αὐτοὺς παραγγέλλειν τε τηρεῖν
τὸν νόμον Μωυσέως.

xv. 3

διήρχοντο] Imperft, because the manner of their journey is described: contrast the aor. *διῆλθον* in xvi. 6, where the bare fact is stated.

[1] Torrey regards this *αὐτοῖς* as the rendering of the Aramaic proleptic pronoun (*DPC*, p. 138).

Φοινίκην] For the evangelization of Phoenicia cf. xi. 19; the church of Tyre is mentioned in xxi. 3 ff.

xv. 4

ἀπὸ] B C minn; *ὑπό* ℵ A D 33 81 byz. For *ἀπό* of the agent cf. *ver.* 33; ii. 22; xx. 9.

τῆς ἐκκλησίας καὶ τῶν ἀποστόλων καὶ τῶν πρεσβυτέρων] For the special mention of the leaders after the reference to the whole community cf. Phil. i. 1, *τοῖς ἁγίοις . . . σὺν ἐπισκόποις καὶ διακόνοις*.

ἀνήγγειλάν τε ὅσα ὁ θεὸς ἐποίησεν μετ' αὐτῶν] See on xiv. 27, from which byz adds *καὶ ὅτι ἤνοιξεν τοῖς ἔθνεσιν θύραν πίστεως*. For *ἀνήγγειλάν τε* D* P^{45} have *ἀπαγγείλαντες*, and for *ὁ θεὸς ἐποίησεν* D 383 614 P^{45} vg pesh have *ἐποίησεν ὁ θεός*.

xv. 5

ἐξανέστησαν . . . λέγοντες] The δ text, identifying these with the men who visited Antioch, alters this to *οἱ δὲ παραγγείλαντες αὐτοῖς ἀναβαίνειν πρὸς τοὺς πρεσβυτέρους ἐξανέστησαν λέγοντες*, to which D, by an awkward conflation with β, adds *τινὲς ἀπὸ τῆς αἱρέσεως τῶν Φαρισαίων πεπιστευκότες*. The original δ text is probably represented by those authorities which transfer these last words to *ver.* 1 (*q.v.*). Note that these words added in D from β omit *τῶν* before *ἀπὸ τῆς αἱρέσεως*, an omission also found in P^{45}.

αἱρέσεως] See on v. 17.

Φαρισαίων] See on v. 34. These believing Pharisees were no doubt the chief among the 'zealots for the law' of xxi. 20.

αὐτοὺς] The Gentile converts; there is no explicit antecedent, unless we adopt the reading of byz at the end of *ver.* 4 (according to Blass, it is more appropriate there than in xiv. 27). It is not certain that these Pharisees went quite so far as the Judaizers of *ver.* 1; their meaning may have been that circumcision and observance of the law were necessary, not indeed for salvation, but for recognition by and fellowship with Jewish Christians.

(c) The Council Meets; Peter's Speech, xv. 6-11

Συνήχθησάν τε οἱ ἀπόστολοι καὶ οἱ πρεσβύτεροι ἰδεῖν περὶ τοῦ 6
λόγου τούτου. Πολλῆς δὲ ζητήσεως γενομένης ἀναστὰς Πέτρος 7
εἶπεν πρὸς αὐτούς Ἄνδρες ἀδελφοί, ὑμεῖς ἐπίστασθε ὅτι ἀφ' ἡμερῶν
ἀρχαίων ἐν ὑμῖν ἐξελέξατο ὁ θεὸς διὰ τοῦ στόματός μου ἀκοῦσαι
τὰ ἔθνη τὸν λόγον τοῦ εὐαγγελίου καὶ πιστεῦσαι, καὶ ὁ καρδιογνώστης 8
θεὸς ἐμαρτύρησεν αὐτοῖς δοὺς τὸ πνεῦμα τὸ ἅγιον καθὼς καὶ ἡμῖν,
καὶ οὐθὲν διέκρινεν μεταξὺ ἡμῶν τε καὶ αὐτῶν, τῇ πίστει καθαρίσας 9

τὰς καρδίας αὐτῶν. νῦν οὖν τί πειράζετε τὸν θεόν, ἐπιθεῖναι ζυγὸν 10
ἐπὶ τὸν τράχηλον τῶν μαθητῶν ὃν οὔτε οἱ πατέρες ἡμῶν οὔτε ἡμεῖς
ἰσχύσαμεν βαστάσαι; ἀλλὰ διὰ τῆς χάριτος τοῦ κυρίου Ἰησοῦ 11
πιστεύομεν σωθῆναι καθ᾽ ὃν τρόπον κἀκεῖνοι.

xv. 6

συνήχθησάν τε οἱ ἀπόστολοι καὶ οἱ πρεσβύτεροι] Apparently other members of the church were present (cf. *πᾶν τὸ πλῆθος*, *ver.* 12; *σὺν ὅλῃ τῇ ἐκκλησίᾳ*, *ver.* 22), although the deliberation and discussion rested with the leaders.

ἰδεῖν περὶ τοῦ λόγου τούτου] Cf. the colloquial Eng., 'to see about this matter'. The question was whether Gentile converts must conform, like proselytes, to the Jewish law in order to enjoy the privileges of church fellowship, or indeed to be saved at all, as the stricter sort insisted.

xv. 7

ζητήσεως γενομένης] Cf. *ver.* 2. P^{45} adds *τῷ Παύλῳ καὶ τῷ Βαρνάβᾳ πρὸς αὐτούς* and something else which is no longer intelligible.

ἀναστὰς] δ has *ἀνέστησεν ἐν πνεύματι* (cf. additions in *vv.* 29, 32).

Πέτρος] 'The figure of a Judaizing St. Peter is a figment of the Tübingen critics with no basis in history' (Lake, *EEP*, p. 116).

αὐτοὺς] (*τοὺς*) *ἀποστόλους* P^{45}.

ἀφ᾽ ἡμερῶν ἀρχαίων] The events of ch. x may have taken place some ten years earlier. We should keep in mind the connection between *ἀρχαῖος* and *ἀρχή* in translating; conformably to Eng. idiom we might render, 'in the early days' (i.e., of the Church). See on xxi. 16.

ἐν ὑμῖν ἐξελέξατο ὁ θεὸς] 'God made choice among you'. It is a little awkward here to follow Torrey (*CDA*, pp. 21 f.) in supposing that *ἐν ὑμῖν* (om. pesh sah) is a Semitism, representing the direct object, as in Neh. ix. 7 (LXX 2 Esdras xix. 7), *ἐξελέξω ἐν Ἀβραάμ*.

εὐαγγελίου] Only here and in xx. 24 (δ in i. 2) does Luke use the noun *εὐαγγέλιον*.

xv. 8

ὁ καρδιογνώστης θεὸς] Cf. the same adj. in i. 24.

αὐτοῖς] Probably, like its correlative *ἡμῖν*, to be taken with both *ἐμαρτύρησεν* and *δούς*.

δοὺς] Simultaneous or coincident aor. ptc., as *καθαρίσας* in *ver.* 9.

καθὼς καὶ ἡμῖν] Cf. xi. 17 (*ὡς καὶ ἡμῖν*) ; also x. 47, *ὡς καὶ ἡμεῖς*. Other reminiscences of the Cornelius episode in this speech are mentioned below.

xv. 9

οὐθὲν] B byz ; *οὐδέν* א A C D E 33 81 al. WH accept the form *οὐθ-* here and in xix. 27 ; xxvi. 26 ; Lk. xxii. 35 ; xxiii. 14 ; 1 Cor. xiii. 2 ; 2 Cor. xi. 9 (cf. *μηθέν*, xxvii. 33). As this form 'was obsolete long before our oldest MSS., we should incline towards accepting it as often as good uncials show it' (MH ii, p. 111, where this spelling is also suggested as the true reading in xx. 33 ; xxvii. 34 ; 1 Cor. xiii. 3).

οὐθὲν διέκρινεν] 'made no difference'. The only other examples of *διακρίνω* in Ac. are x. 20 ; xi. 2, 12, in connection, as here, with the Cornelius episode.

καθαρίσας] Simultaneous aor. ptc., as *δούς*, *ver.* 8. As with *διακρίνω* (above), the only other occurrences of *καθαρίζω* in Ac. are in connection with the Cornelius episode (x. 15 ; xi. 9). For the association between the giving of the Spirit and purification cf. the reading of the minuscules 162 and 700 in Lk. xi. 2 *fin.*, *ἐλθέτω τὸ ἅγιον πνεῦμά σου ἐφ' ἡμᾶς καὶ καθαρισάτω ἡμᾶς* (so also Marcion, Gregory of Nyssa, and Maximus of Turin). (B. H. Streeter, *The Four Gospels*, p. 277, considers it highly probable that this is what Luke wrote.) Cf. *καθαρὸς τῇ καρδίᾳ*, Ps. xxiv. 4 (LXX xxiii) ; *καρδίαν καθαρὰν κτίσον ἐν ἐμοί*, Ps. li. 12 (LXX l) ; *ἀπὸ πάσης ἁμαρτίας καθάρισον καρδίαν*, Sir. xxxviii. 10.

xv. 10

τί πειράζετε τὸν θεόν] An OT expression : cf. v. 9.

ἐπιθεῖναι] Epexegetic infin., explaining wherein their tempting God lay : 'why do you tempt God by putting . . . ?' God had declared His satisfaction with the Gentiles' faith by giving them the Spirit ; to impose conditions in addition to the one that satisfied God would be 'tempting' Him.

ζυγὸν] This word (Heb. *'ōl*) was used by Jewish writers in the sense of 'obligation' ; thus, 'to take up the yoke of the kingdom of heaven' meant to undertake to fulfil the law, i.e., to become a proselyte (later also to recite the *Shĕma'*). In the light of this idiom we are to understand the words of Christ in Mt. xi. 29 f., *ἄρατε τὸν ζυγόν μου ἐφ' ὑμᾶς . . . ὁ γὰρ ζυγός μου χρηστός*. But Peter here uses the word in the sense of a heavy weight (cf. Mt. xxiii. 4 ; Lk. xi. 46 ; Gal. v. 1). His attitude was probably not unusual, especially in Galilaean Jews, in the days preceding the fall of the Second Temple.[1]

xv. 11

διὰ τῆς χάριτος κ.τ.λ.] Salvation by the grace of God, to be received by men through faith, is of course characteristically Pauline teaching; but Paul insists (1 Cor. xv. 11) that his Gospel is the same as that preached by Peter and the other apostles. Cf. 1 Pet. i. 9 f.

πιστεύομεν σωθῆναι] Either (1) 'we believe we shall be saved' (for the aor. infin. in this future sense cf. ii. 30; iii. 18; vii. 5),

[1] With Peter's attitude we may compare the description of Schürer: 'It was a fearful burden which a spurious legalism had laid upon the shoulders of the people. . . . Nothing was left to free personality, everything was placed under the bondage of the letter. . . . A healthy moral life could not flourish under such a burden, action was nowhere the result of inward motive, all was, on the contrary, weighed and measured. Life was a continual torment to the earnest man, who felt at every moment that he was in danger of transgressing the law; and where so much depended on the external form, he was often left in uncertainty whether he had really fulfilled its requirements. On the other hand, pride and conceit were almost inevitable for one who had attained to mastership in the knowledge and treatment of the law. He could indeed say that he had done his duty, had neglected nothing, had fulfilled all righteousness. But all the more certain is it, that this righteousness of the scribes and Pharisees . . . was not that true righteousness which was well-pleasing to God' (II. ii. 124 f.).

The accuracy of Schürer's picture is frequently denied, as it is so manifestly at variance with the picture preserved in the Rabbinical writings, 'Schürer's verdict is only a *partial* presentation of *one* aspect of a *whole*', says Prof. H. Danby in *Studies in Judaism*, p. 5 (two lectures delivered at St. George's Cathedral, Jerusalem, in January 1922). According to Danby (*ib.*, p. 19), the extreme legal position which insisted on the fulfilment of every jot and tittle was characteristic of the school of Shammai as opposed to the school of Hillel. It must be remembered that the Rabbinical writings rarely reflect the conditions of the time of the Second Temple, or even of the first century A.D.; and there is some evidence that about A.D. 100 a change arose in the conception of one's duty to observe the whole law. This change may have been largely due to the influence of Rabbi Aqiba. He laid down the principle that 'the world is judged in mercy, and all is according to the amount of the work' (*Pirqe Aboth*, iii. 19), i.e., according to the preponderance of good or bad in human acts. 'Sometimes he asserted God's mercy to be such that a single meritorious act will win a man admission to the future world' (L. Finkelstein, *Akiba*, p. 185). That is to say, one righteous act suffices to weigh down the scale of merit, when the good and evil deeds are equally balanced, so that, in effect, a 51 per cent. righteousness sufficed to open the way to Paradise. This is a very different viewpoint from that quoted in Jas. ii. 10 (*c.* A.D. 50 ?): 'Whosoever shall keep the whole law, and yet stumble in one point, he is become guilty of all'. The relevant parts of the NT are among the best evidence we have for the attitude to the law in Palestine in the first 70 years of the Christian era. (Cf. B. S. Easton, *Christ in the Gospels* [1930], pp. 88 ff.; C. G. Montefiore and H. Loewe, *A Rabbinic Anthology*, p. 595 ff.; TJ *Qid.* i. 10, 61*d*; TB *Rosh-ha-Shanah* 16*b*, 17*a*.)

(2) 'we believe we have been saved', or (3) 'we believe (so as) to be saved' (epexegetic infin.), i.e., we are saved by faith. The last interpretation seems best.

καθ' ὃν τρόπον κἀκεῖνοι] 'even as they also' (i.e., the Gentiles), sc. are saved by faith.

Peter has quite recovered from his lapse at Antioch (Gal. ii. 11 ff.). To suppose that his lapse was later than the Council is to make him guilty, in Ramsay's words, of 'meaningless tergiversation' (*SPT*, p. 164). With his argument here cf. Paul's in Gal. ii. 15 ff.

(d) The Missionaries address the Council, xv. 12

Ἐσίγησεν δὲ πᾶν τὸ πλῆθος, καὶ ἤκουον Βαρνάβα καὶ Παύλου 12
ἐξηγουμένων ὅσα ἐποίησεν ὁ θεὸς σημεῖα καὶ τέρατα ἐν τοῖς ἔθνεσιν
δι' αὐτῶν.

The report of the missionary tour in Cyprus and Asia Minor was calculated to emphasize Peter's argument; to the example of Cornelius, adduced by Peter, Barnabas and Paul could add many more.

xv. 12

ἐσίγησεν δὲ] δ (D hcl*) has *συγκατατεθεμένων δὲ τῶν πρεσβυτέρων τοῖς ὑπὸ τοῦ Πέτρου εἰρημένοις ἐσίγησεν* . . . .

πᾶν τὸ πλῆθος] Perhaps simply the company gathered together on this occasion; but probably, as in iv. 32; vi. 2, 5, it refers to the Christian community: cf. *ver.* 30, of the church at Antioch. Cf. also xxiii. 7.

Βαρνάβα καὶ Παύλου] This is the natural order in a Jerusalem context (cf. *ver.* 25). The only other occurrence of this order after xiii. 7 is in xiv. 14, where it is probably due to the order Zeus-Hermes in xiv. 12.

ὅσα ἐποίησεν ὁ θεὸς κ.τ.λ.] Cf. *ver.* 4; xiv. 27; here the expression is more explicit.

σημεῖα καὶ τέρατα] See on ii. 22, 43.

(e) The Speech of James, xv. 13-21

Μετὰ δὲ τὸ σιγῆσαι αὐτοὺς ἀπεκρίθη Ἰάκωβος λέγων Ἄνδρες 13
ἀδελφοί, ἀκούσατέ μου. Συμεὼν ἐξηγήσατο καθὼς πρῶτον ὁ θεὸς 14
ἐπεσκέψατο λαβεῖν ἐξ ἐθνῶν λαὸν τῷ ὀνόματι αὐτοῦ. καὶ τούτῳ 15
συμφωνοῦσιν οἱ λόγοι τῶν προφητῶν, καθὼς γέγραπται

Μετὰ ταῦτα ἀναστρέψω 16
καὶ ἀνοικοδομήσω τὴν σκηνὴν Δαυεὶδ τὴν πεπτωκυῖαν
καὶ τὰ κατεστραμμένα αὐτῆς ἀνοικοδομήσω
καὶ ἀνορθώσω αὐτήν,
ὅπως ἂν ἐκζητήσωσιν οἱ κατάλοιποι τῶν ἀνθρώπων τὸν κύριον, 17
καὶ πάντα τὰ ἔθνη ἐφ' οὓς ἐπικέκληται τὸ ὄνομά μου ἐπ' αὐτούς,
λέγει Κύριος ποιῶν ταῦτα γνωστὰ ἀπ' αἰῶνος. 18

διὸ ἐγὼ κρίνω μὴ παρενοχλεῖν τοῖς ἀπὸ τῶν ἐθνῶν ἐπιστρέφουσιν 19
ἐπὶ τὸν θεόν, ἀλλὰ ἐπιστεῖλαι αὐτοῖς τοῦ ἀπέχεσθαι τῶν ἀλισγημάτων 20
τῶν εἰδώλων καὶ τῆς πορνείας καὶ πνικτοῦ καὶ τοῦ αἵματος· Μωυσῆς 21
γὰρ ἐκ γενεῶν ἀρχαίων κατὰ πόλιν τοὺς κηρύσσοντας αὐτὸν ἔχει ἐν
ταῖς συναγωγαῖς κατὰ πᾶν σάββατον ἀναγινωσκόμενος.

xv. 13

αὐτοὺς] Barnabas and Paul.

ἀπεκρίθη] Probably the Semitic pleonastic use, as in iii. 12; v. 8. Hort (*CE*, p. 80) says the reply was made to the speakers of *ver.* 5.

Ἰάκωβος] Cf. xii. 17; xxi. 18; 1 Cor. xv. 7; Gal. i. 19 (where he is called 'the Lord's brother': see on i. 14); Jas. i. 1. We can see here the prominent part played by James in the Jerusalem church. His arguments would prevail with the stricter sort much more than Barnabas and Paul's, or even Peter's. His relations with the stricter party are reflected in xxi. 18 ff. Whether he was counted an apostle or not is not quite clear from Gal. i. 19 (though it seems more likely that he was); although not one of the Twelve, and indeed not a believer until the Resurrection, he had apostolic qualifications as a witness of the risen Christ. According to Marius Victorinus (on Gal. i. 19, Migne *PL* viii. 1155B), the Symmachians (i.e., Ebionites, a Judaeo-Christian party) counted him as the twelfth apostle; and in the *Clementine Homilies* Clement is made to address him as 'bishop of bishops' and ruler both of the Jerusalem church and of all churches everywhere properly founded by Divine Providence. Hegesippus (*ap.* Euseb. *HE* ii. 23) relates how he was held in high respect by the people, who surnamed him 'the Just'; and how he suffered martyrdom in a manner similar to Stephen. Cf. also Jos. *Ant.* xx. 9. 1, where we learn that during the period between the death of Festus and the arrival of his successor Albinus (*c.* A.D. 61), the High Priest Ananus 'assembled a Sanhedrin, and brought before them the brother of Jesus, the so-called Christ, whose name was James, and some others, and having accused them as law-breakers, he delivered them over to be stoned'.

Ἄνδρες ἀδελφοί, ἀκούσατέ μου] Cf. Jas. ii. 5, ἀκούσατε, ἀδελφοί μου ἀγαπητοί. J. B. Mayor, in his *Commentary on the Epistle of*

James (pp. iii f.), enumerates what he calls some 'remarkable agreements' between that epistle and this speech.

xv. 14

Συμεὼν] i.e., Simon Peter. *Συμεών*, the LXX form of the name Simeon, approaches Heb. *Shim'ōn* more closely than does *Σίμων*, the *ε* representing the guttural sound of the Heb. letter ע (*'ayin*). Cf. 2 Pet. i. 1, *Συμεὼν Πέτρος*.

καθὼς] 'how'.

ἐπεσκέψατο] This verb is used of providential visitation in Lk. i. 68, 78; vii. 16.

λαβεῖν] Epexegetic infinitive (cf. *vv.* 10, 11).

ἐξ ἐθνῶν λαὸν] '*Egregium paradoxon*' (Bengel), for *λαός* is the word regularly used of the Jewish people, *ἔθνη* of the Gentiles. For *λαός* of the Christian community cf. xviii. 10; Tit. ii. 14; 1 Pet. ii. 9 f. The new community is taken from among the Gentiles as well as from among the Jews. Thus was fulfilled our Lord's saying about 'other sheep . . . not of this fold', which were to be united with the obedient sheep from the Jewish fold, so that all that heard His voice, both Jews and Gentiles, might together form 'one flock' (Jn. x. 16).

xv. 15

τῶν προφητῶν] i.e., the Book of the Twelve Prophets, which includes the prophecy of Amos. See on vii. 42; xiii. 40.

xv. 16ff.

μετὰ ταῦτα κ.τ.λ.] The quotation is from Amos ix. 11 f. LXX, *ἐν τῇ ἡμέρᾳ ἐκείνῃ ἀναστήσω τὴν σκηνὴν Δαυεὶδ τὴν πεπτωκυῖαν, καὶ ἀνοικοδομήσω τὰ πεπτωκότα αὐτῆς, καὶ τὰ κατεστραμμένα* (A^bQ^*; *κατεσκαμμένα* BQ^a) *αὐτῆς ἀναστήσω, καὶ ἀνοικοδομήσω αὐτὴν καθὼς αἱ ἡμέραι τοῦ αἰῶνος, ὅπως ἂν ἐκζητήσωσιν οἱ κατάλοιποι τῶν ἀνθρώπων, καὶ πάντα τὰ ἔθνη ἐφ' οὓς ἐπικέκληται τὸ ὄνομά μου ἐπ' αὐτούς, λέγει Κύριος ὁ ποιῶν ταῦτα.*

μετὰ ταῦτα ἀναστρέψω] These words do not appear in Amos; but cf. Jer. xii. 15, *καὶ ἔσται μετὰ τὸ ἐκβαλεῖν με αὐτοὺς ἐπιστρέψω κ.τ.λ.*

τὴν σκηνὴν Δαυεὶδ] The Church is the legitimate continuation and fulfilment of the old Church of Israel; this is implied in the use of the terms *λαός* (see on *ver.* 14) and *ἐκκλησία* (see on v. 11; vii. 38), and in Paul's metaphor of the olive-tree (Rom. xi. 13 ff.). The literal reference of the prophecy in Amos is to the restoration of the undivided kingdom of Israel, as in the reign of David.

xv. 17

ὅπως ἂν ἐκζητήσωσιν οἱ κατάλοιποι τῶν ἀνθρώπων τὸν κύριον] As the presence of believing Jews in the Church fulfilled the prediction of the rebuilding of the tabernacle of David, so the presence of believing Gentiles fulfilled the next part of the prophecy. But this application of the words of Amos depends on the LXX. MT gives a different meaning: 'that they (Israel) may possess the remnant of Edom and all the nations which are called by my name'—a prediction of the expansion of the kingdom to its Davidic limits. LXX presupposes ידרשו *yidrĕshū* ('will seek') for MT ייִרשו *yīrĕshū* ('will possess'), and אדם *'ādām* ('man') for אדום *'Ĕdōm*. Besides, שארית *shĕ'ērīth* ('remnant') is clearly the object in Heb., being preceded by את *'eth*, the *nota accusativi*. We need not be surprised to find James, a Galilaean, speaking Gk. and quoting from the LXX, especially in the presence of the 'certain others' from Antioch (*ver.* 2), whose language would be Gk. It has been pointed out in this connection that the OT quotations in the Epistle of James are nearly all from the LXX.[1]

καὶ πάντα τὰ ἔθνη] *καί* epexegetic: 'even'.

ἐφ' οὓς ἐπικέκληται τὸ ὄνομά μου ἐπ' αὐτούς] A Hebraism; Heb. repeats the personal or demonstrative pronoun after the relative *'ăsher* (cf. Mod. Gk. construction with *ποῦ*, and colloquial Eng., e.g., 'which her name is Mrs. Harris'). Cf. for the sense Jas. ii. 7, *τὸ καλὸν ὄνομα τὸ ἐπικληθὲν ἐφ' ὑμᾶς*.

xv. 18

λέγει Κύριος ποιῶν ταῦτα γνωστὰ ἀπ' αἰῶνος] The quotation, which ends with *ταῦτα*, is rounded off with language reminiscent of Isa. xlv. 21 (*ἵνα γνῶσιν ἅμα τίς ἀκουστὰ ἐποίησεν ταῦτα ἀπ' ἀρχῆς*). With *ἀπ' αἰῶνος* cf. iii. 21; also *αἱ ἡμέραι τοῦ αἰῶνος*, Amos ix. 11. The δ text (A D vg Iren.lat hcl.mg) commenced a new sentence after *ταῦτα*, thus: *γνωστὸν ἀπ' αἰῶνός ἐστιν τῷ κυρίῳ τὸ ἔργον αὐτοῦ* (A omits *ἐστιν*, hcl.mg omits *τῷ κυρίῳ*); similarly byz has *γνωστὰ*

[1] On this question of the text, C. C. Torrey writes: 'Luke always uses the Greek Bible for his Old Testament quotations; see my *Aramaic Gospels*, 298 ff. In this case, we do not know to what extent the Greek varied from the Aramaic—or rather, Hebrew—which actually lay before him. Rabbi Akiba and his fellows had not yet set up a "standard" text of the Prophets; the author of this Aramaic document was at liberty to select the reading which best suited his purpose; and the LXX rendering of Am. ix. 11 f. certainly represented a varying *Hebrew* text. But even our Massoretic Hebrew would have served the present purpose admirably, since it predicted that "the tabernacle of David", i.e. the church of the Messiah, would "gain possession of all the nations which are called by the name [of the God of Israel]"' (*CDA*, pp. 38 f.). The Targum of Jonathan and the Peshitta agree with MT.

ἀπ' αἰῶνός ἐστιν τῷ θεῷ πάντα τὰ ἔργα αὐτοῦ. According to the β text James insists that the inclusion of Gentiles in the Church was revealed of old (cf. Paul's arguments in Rom. xv. 8 ff.).

xv. 19

ἐγὼ κρίνω] 'I for my part judge' (cf. Iren.lat., *ego secundum me iudico*), 'this is my vote'. James acts more or less as chairman; he winds up the debate, and formulates the motion which he puts to the meeting.

μὴ παρενοχλεῖν] 'to stop troubling' (*N.B.* the force of the present tense).

xv. 20

ἐπιστεῖλαι] 'to send them a letter'.

τοῦ ἀπέχεσθαι τῶν ἀλισγημάτων τῶν εἰδώλων καὶ τῆς πορνείας καὶ πνικτοῦ καὶ τοῦ αἵματος] The four things from which they are to be asked to refrain are repeated, with slight variations, in *ver.* 29 and xxi. 25. δ (D g Iren.lat.) omits καὶ πνικτοῦ, and after αἵματος adds καὶ ὅσα μὴ θέλουσιν ἑαυτοῖς γίνεσθαι ἑτέροις μὴ ποιεῖν, a negative form of the Golden Rule (D 322 323 vg.codd. sah eth Iren.lat.).[1] This reading makes the decree a purely ethical one ('to abstain from idolatry, fornication and bloodshed, and not to do to others what they would not like done to themselves'). Idolatry, fornication and murder were the three cardinal sins in Jewish eyes. Abstinence from these is regarded in the Talmud as binding on the whole human race since the days of Noah. Cf. J. W. Hunkin in *JTS* xxvii. (1926), pp. 272 ff., H. J. Schonfield in *ET* xli. (1929-30),

[1] The best known instance of the negative Golden Rule is probably Hillel's: 'What is hateful to thee, do not to thy fellow: this is the whole law (*Torah*); all else is commentary (*pērūshā*)' (TB *Shabbath* 31*a*; cf. *Aboth de R. Nathan*, ii. 26). Cf. Tobit iv. 15, ὃ μισεῖς, μηδένι ποιήσῃς. C. G. Montefiore, commenting on the positive Golden Rule of Mt. vii. 12, makes the curious suggestion 'that if an undoubtedly authentic saying of Hillel were to be discovered in the positive form, every Jewish writer would, I fancy, be rather pleased, while every Christian writer would, I fancy, be rather sorry' (*The Synoptic Gospels*[1], p. 550). One Jew at any rate, Ahad Ha-Am, so far from approving of Montefiore's sentiment, declares that if such a positive form were found, it would be alien to the true spirit of Judaism (*'Al shtē-ha-sĕ'ippīm*, in *'Al pārāshath dĕrākhīm*[4], iv, p. 46). But the positive form is found in Jewish literature, e.g. in Maimonides' *Mishnēh Tōrāh* ii: *Hilĕkhōth 'Abēl* xiv. 1 (I am indebted to Prof. S. Rawidowicz for this reference); and Maimonides can hardly be accused of treason to the spirit of Judaism. But surely no Christian is *sorry* to find the positive form in Jewish or in any other literature. Among other examples of the negative form is *Didaché*, i. 2, πάντα δὲ ὅσα ἐὰν θελήσῃς μὴ γίνεσθαί σοι, καὶ σὺ ἄλλῳ μὴ ποίει, where it follows immediately the words of Lev. xix. 18, just as in the Jerusalem Targum on that verse.

pp. 128 f. Here as elsewhere the δ revision shows familiarity with Jewish thought. But the β text is to be preferred as original; it has already been decided that no additional conditions are to be laid down for the admission of Gentiles to the Church, and the question that remains is the practical one of social intercourse between Jewish and Gentile Christians (including joint participation in the Lord's Supper), and of concessions which Gentiles are to be invited to make to avoid scandalizing their weaker Jewish brethren.

ἀλισγημάτων τῶν εἰδώλων] 'pollutions of idols', explained in *ver.* 29 and xxi. 25 by εἰδωλόθυτα, 'things offered in sacrifice to idols'. As we know from Paul's epistles, this was a very live issue in the Gentile churches. ἀλίσγημα is a *hapax legomenon.* It is derived from a late verb ἀλισγέω, which occurs 6 times in LXX (Dan. i. 8; Mal. i. 7 *ter*, 12; Sir. xl. 29), each time in connection with food.

καὶ τῆς πορνείας] om P^{45} eth. It seems strange to find an injunction against fornication coupled with food regulations. Illicit sexual relations were, however, regarded very lightly by the Greeks, and πορνεία was closely associated with several of their religious festivals. Here the word should probably be taken in a special sense, of breaches of the Jewish marriage law (Lev. xviii.), which was taken over by the Church. W. K. Lowther Clarke (*New Testament Problems* [1929], pp. 59 ff.) finds the same meaning in Mt. v. 32; xix. 9. In 1 Cor. vi. 13 ff., etc., πορνεία is used, of course, in the widest sense. J. Halévy (*Revue Sémitique* x. [1902], pp. 238 f.) proposed πορκείας ('swine-flesh') for πορνείας here and in the parallel passages (cf. the emendation χοιρείας, ascribed by Wetstein to Bentley), but πορκεία is not found in Gk., and πόρκος only as a transliteration of Lat. *porcus* (Plutarch, *Publicola* 11).

καὶ πνικτοῦ καὶ τοῦ αἵματος] Eating flesh with blood in it (which is inevitable when the animal has died by strangulation) was expressly forbidden in the Jewish law (Lev. xvii. 10 ff.), because the life or soul (Heb. *nephesh*) resided in the blood. The prohibition goes back to Gen. ix. 4. Of πνικτόν F. C. Burkitt remarks: 'The word is technical and unfamiliar outside the poultry-shop and the kitchen' (*JTS* xxviii [1927], p. 199).

xv. 21

Μωυσῆς γὰρ κ.τ.λ.] The exact force of γάρ has been disputed. Possibly James means that since Jews are to be found everywhere, their scruples are to be respected. But other suggestions have been made, e.g., by Erasmus: '*nec est metuendum ne Moses antiquetur, habet enim ille . . .*' (similarly Rackham: 'Moses, so to speak, would suffer no loss, in failing to obtain the allegiance of those who never had been his '); LC refer to an article of J. H. Ropes in *JBL* xv. (1896), pp. 75 ff., where the words are taken to mean that since synagogues where Moses is proclaimed are to be found everywhere, the expression 'all the nations upon whom my name is called' evidently covers the whole known world.

ἐκ γενεῶν ἀρχαίων] Schürer (II. ii. 54) would place the commencement of synagogues as far back as Ezra's time (see also on vi. 9), but the thought here is rather the antiquity of Jewish colonies outside Palestine, which date back to the 6th century B.C.

κατὰ πόλιν] om P[45]. Cf. Philo, *τὰ . . . κατὰ πόλεις προσευκτήρια* (*Vit. Moys.* ii. 216); *κατὰ πᾶσαν πόλιν* (*spec. leg.* 62).

(f) The Letter to the Gentile Churches, xv. 22-29

Τότε ἔδοξε τοῖς ἀποστόλοις καὶ τοῖς πρεσβυτέροις σὺν ὅλῃ τῇ 22
ἐκκλησίᾳ ἐκλεξαμένους ἄνδρας ἐξ αὐτῶν πέμψαι εἰς Ἀντιόχειαν σὺν
τῷ Παύλῳ καὶ Βαρνάβᾳ, Ἰούδαν τὸν καλούμενον Βαρσαββᾶν καὶ
Σίλαν, ἄνδρας ἡγουμένους ἐν τοῖς ἀδελφοῖς, γράψαντες διὰ χειρὸς 23
αὐτῶν Οἱ ἀπόστολοι καὶ οἱ πρεσβύτεροι ἀδελφοὶ τοῖς κατὰ τὴν Ἀντιό-
χειαν καὶ Συρίαν καὶ Κιλικίαν ἀδελφοῖς τοῖς ἐξ ἐθνῶν χαίρειν.
Ἐπειδὴ ἠκούσαμεν ὅτι τινὲς ἐξ ἡμῶν ἐτάραξαν ὑμᾶς λόγοις ἀνασκευά- 24
ζοντες τὰς ψυχὰς ὑμῶν, οἷς οὐ διεστειλάμεθα, ἔδοξεν ἡμῖν γενομένοις 25
ὁμοθυμαδὸν ἐκλεξαμένοις ἄνδρας πέμψαι πρὸς ὑμᾶς σὺν τοῖς ἀγα-
πητοῖς ἡμῶν Βαρνάβᾳ καὶ Παύλῳ, ἀνθρώποις παραδεδωκόσι τὰς 26
ψυχὰς αὐτῶν ὑπὲρ τοῦ ὀνόματος τοῦ κυρίου ἡμῶν Ἰησοῦ Χριστοῦ.
ἀπεστάλκαμεν οὖν Ἰούδαν καὶ Σίλαν, καὶ αὐτοὺς διὰ λόγου ἀπαγ- 27
γέλλοντας τὰ αὐτά. ἔδοξεν γὰρ τῷ πνεύματι τῷ ἁγίῳ καὶ ἡμῖν μηδὲν 28
πλέον ἐπιτίθεσθαι ὑμῖν βάρος πλὴν τούτων τῶν ἐπάναγκες, ἀπέχεσθαι 29
εἰδωλοθύτων καὶ αἵματος καὶ πνικτῶν καὶ πορνείας· ἐξ ὧν διατηροῦντες
ἑαυτοὺς εὖ πράξετε. Ἔρρωσθε.

xv. 22

ἔδοξε τοῖς ἀποστόλοις . . . ἐκλεξαμένους . . . πέμψαι . . . γράψαντες] With this breach of concord cf. Thuc. iii. 36. 2, *ἔδοξεν αὐτοῖς . . . ἀποκτεῖναι, . . . ἐπικαλοῦντες.*

Ἰούδαν τὸν καλούμενον Βαρσαββᾶν] For the surname cf. Joseph Barsabbas, i. 23 (*q.v.*).

Σίλαν] Silas may be a Semitic name. Burkitt pointed out its equivalence to Talmudic *Shīlā*, Palmyrene *Sh'īlā* ('little wolf'?). This Silas was a Roman citizen (xvi. 37), and his Latin *cognomen* Silvanus (1 Th. i. 1; 2 Th. i. 1; 2 Cor. i. 19; 1 Pet. v. 12) may have been chosen because of its similarity to his Semitic name.

ἄνδρας ἡγουμένους] 'leaders': cf. Heb. xiii. 7, 17, 24.

xv. 23

οἱ πρεσβύτεροι ἀδελφοὶ] 'the elder brethren': the only NT occurrence of this phrase.[1] P^{45} omits *οἱ*.

διὰ χειρὸς] 'by': see on xi. 30. Before *διὰ χειρός* the δ text inserts *ἐπιστολήν*, and adds *περιέχουσαν τάδε* after *αὐτῶν*.

κατὰ τὴν Ἀντιόχειαν καὶ Συρίαν καὶ Κιλικίαν] Antioch was the chief town of the united province of Syria and Cilicia (cf. *ver.* 41; Gal. i. 21). Cf. i. 8 for the name of a town followed by that of the double province in which it was situated. P^{45} has *τήν* before *Συρίαν*.

χαίρειν] Infin. for imper.: cf. xxiii. 26; Jas. i. 1 for its epistolary use; cf. also Rom. xii. 15; Phil. iii. 16; Tit. ii. 2 ff. This construction is common in both classical and Hellenistic Gk.

xv. 24

τινὲς ἐξ ἡμῶν] Cf. Gal. ii. 12 (*τινας ἀπὸ Ἰακώβου*), and see on *ver.* 1.

ἀνασκευάζοντες] 'subverting': a military metaphor, of plundering a town. E. K. Simpson (*EQ* ii. p. 397) compares the phrase *ἀνασκευαὶ πραγμάτων*, 'ruination', in Vettius Valens 2. 7; 176. 9; 199. 33.

τὰς ψυχὰς ὑμῶν] C E byz e pesh hcl arm Chr add *λέγοντες περιτέμνεσθαι καὶ τηρεῖν τὸν νόμον*, which probably is part of the original δ text, though absent from D.

οἷς οὐ διεστειλάμεθα] If they went to Antioch on some official business, as Gal. ii. 12 suggests, they exceeded the terms of their commission by urging the necessity of circumcision.

xv. 25

ἐκλεξαμένοις] So A B 33 81 P^{45}; ℵ C D byz have the anacoluthic *ἐκλεξαμένους* as in *ver.* 22 (so WH mg., Soden).

γενομένοις ὁμοθυμαδὸν] 'having met together': see on i. 14.

ἀγαπητοῖς] Only here in Ac.; its occurrence in a letter is interesting, as it occurs in most of the NT epistles in a similar setting.

xv. 26

παραδεδωκόσι τὰς ψυχὰς αὐτῶν] 'who have devoted their lives': for this sense of *παραδίδωμι* cf. Gal. ii. 20.

ὑπὲρ τοῦ ὀνόματος] Cf. v. 41.

Χριστοῦ] δ (D E 383 614 hcl.mg) adds *εἰς πάντα πειρασμόν*.

[1] 'But it is faultless Aramaic idiom. In the phrase שְׁלִיחַיָּא וְקַשִּׁישַׁיָּא אַחַיָּא [*shĕlīḥayyā wĕqashshīshayyā 'aḥayyā*] the word "brethren" would naturally refer to *both* the nouns preceding' (C. C. Torrey, *CDA*, p. 39). LC also take *ἀδελφοί* in apposition with *οἱ ἀπόστολοι καὶ οἱ πρεσβύτεροι*.

xv. 27

ἀπεστάλκαμεν] Epistolary perfect; the tense indicates the viewpoint of the readers, not of the writers.

καὶ αὐτοὺς διὰ λόγου ἀπαγγέλλοντας τὰ αὐτά] 'who also will themselves deliver the same report by word of mouth': *ἀπαγγέλλοντας* is an example of the use of the pres. ptc. to denote purpose. In classical Gk. the fut. ptc. was used in this way, but it was decaying by this time.

xv. 28

ἔδοξεν γὰρ κ.τ.λ.] Deissmann compares a decree of Domitian beginning *uisum est mihi edicto significare* . . . (*LAE*, p. 444).

'The New Testament is not poor of words expressive of command . . . yet none of them is used. . . . The independence of the Ecclesia of Antioch had to be respected, and yet not in such a way as to encourage disregard either of the great mother Ecclesia, or of the Lord's own Apostles, or of the unity of the whole Christian body. Accordingly we do not find a word of a hint that the Antiochians would have done better to get sanction from Jerusalem before plunging into such grave responsibilities. But along with the cordial concurrence in the release of Gentile converts from legal requirements there goes a strong expression of opinion, more than advice and less than a command, respecting certain salutary restraints. A certain authority is thus implicitly claimed. There is no evidence that it was more than a moral authority; but that did not make it less real' (Hort, *CE*, p. 82 f.).

τῷ πνεύματι τῷ ἁγίῳ καὶ ἡμῖν] This assigning to the Holy Spirit of prior authority in issuing the recommendation is eloquent of the practical realization of His presence in the early Church: cf. v. 3, 9; xiii. 2; xvi. 6 f.

τούτων τῶν ἐπάναγκες] ℵ^c B C 81; *τούτων ἐπάναγκες* ℵ* D 33; *τῶν ἐπάναγκες* A; *τῶν ἐπάναγκες τούτων* byz. The *τῶν* may have been omitted after *τούτων* by haplography, or inserted by dittography. If we retain our text, *ἐπάναγκες* is an adv. here treated as a noun; if we omit *τῶν*, we should put a colon after *τούτων* and take *ἐπάναγκες* with *ἀπέχεσθαι* (' to lay no burden on you except these things: you must abstain from things sacrificed to idols, etc.'). This last construction is implied by Clem. Alex., *ἐμήνυσαν γὰρ ἐπάναγκες ἀπέχεσθαι δεῖν εἰδωλοθύτων κ.τ.λ.* (*Strom.* iv. 15. 97), and probably represents the original text.

xv. 29

ἀπέχεσθαι εἰδωλοθύτων καὶ αἵματος καὶ πνικτῶν καὶ πορνείας] δ omits *καὶ πνικτῶν* and adds *καὶ ὅσα μὴ θέλετε ἑαυτοῖς γίνεσθαι ἑτέρῳ μὴ ποιεῖν*. See on *ver.* 20 for the significance of the variant readings. Tertullian omits *καὶ πνικτῶν* but does not add the negative Golden Rule (*De pudicitia* 12, etc.). For *πνικτῶν*, ℵ^c A² E byz vet.

lat vg pesh hcl arm Did Chr al have *πνικτοῦ*, as in *ver.* 20. J. Rendel Harris (*ET* xxv. [1913-14], p. 200) compares with the terms of this decree the food-tabus in the Koran, *Sura* 5, § 3, where ' things strangled ' are included.

ἑαυτοὺς] In Hellenistic Gk. this serves as the reflexive of the 1st and 2nd persons as well as of the 3rd. Cf. v. 35; xiii. 46; xx. 28.

εὖ πράξετε] ' you will prosper ', according to the regular Gk. usage; but in Ignatius, *Eph.* iv. 2; *Smyrn.* xi. 3, and Justin, *Apol.* i. 28, *εὖ πράττω* can only mean ' do right ', which may be the sense here. Cf. *καλῶς ποιεῖτε*, Jas. ii. 8. δ adds *φερόμενοι ἐν τῷ ἁγίῳ πνεύματι* (for similar interpolated references to the Spirit cf. *vv.* 7, 32; xx. 3). Cf. 2 Pet. i. 21.

ἔρρωσθε] ' farewell ' (perf. imper. of *ῥώννυμαι*, ' be strong ': cf. Lat. *ualete*): cf. sing. *ἔρρωσο*, xxiii. 30 (א E 81 byz).

6. The Letter received in Antioch and the Anatolian Churches, xv. 30-xvi. 5

(a) The Church at Antioch receives the Letter, xv. 30-35

Οἱ μὲν οὖν ἀπολυθέντες κατῆλθον εἰς Ἀντιόχειαν, καὶ συναγαγόντες 30
τὸ πλῆθος ἐπέδωκαν τὴν ἐπιστολήν· ἀναγνόντες δὲ ἐχάρησαν ἐπὶ τῇ 31
παρακλήσει. Ἰούδας τε καὶ Σίλας, καὶ αὐτοὶ προφῆται ὄντες, διὰ 32
λόγου πολλοῦ παρεκάλεσαν τοὺς ἀδελφοὺς καὶ ἐπεστήριξαν· ποιή- 33
σαντες δὲ χρόνον ἀπελύθησαν μετ᾽ εἰρήνης ἀπὸ τῶν ἀδελφῶν πρὸς τοὺς
ἀποστείλαντας αὐτούς. Παῦλος δὲ καὶ Βαρνάβας διέτριβον ἐν 35
Ἀντιοχείᾳ διδάσκοντες καὶ εὐαγγελιζόμενοι μετὰ καὶ ἑτέρων πολλῶν
τὸν λόγον τοῦ κυρίου.

xv. 30

Οἱ μὲν οὖν] i.e., Paul, Barnabas, Judas, Silas, and the ' certain others ' of *ver.* 2.

ἀπολυθέντες] ' being sent off ' (lit. ' let go '): cf. *ver.* 33; xiii. 3. In iii. 13; iv. 21, 23; v. 40 it is used of the dismissal of accused persons.

τὸ πλῆθος] ' the community '; here the church at Antioch: see on *ver.* 12.

ἐπέδωκαν] ' handed over ': technical in later Gk. for sending in a report or handing over a letter (cf. *ἀναδόντες*, xxiii. 33).

xv. 31

παρακλήσει] For the twofold meaning of this word see on iv. 36. Here it may include the exhortation in the letter (cf. *παρεκάλεσαν* in next verse) and the relief felt at its contents.

xv. 32

καὶ αὐτοὶ προφῆται ὄντες] 'they themselves also being prophets', i.e., in addition to those mentioned in xiii. 1. Or we may regard *προφῆται ὄντες* as parenthetical, and take *καὶ αὐτοί* with *παρεκάλεσαν*, i.e., the exhortation of Judas and Silas was added to that contained in the letter. After *ὄντες*, D adds *πλήρεις πνεύματος ἁγίου*.

διὰ λόγου πολλοῦ] Cf. *διὰ λόγου*, *ver.* 27.

παρεκάλεσαν] For the connection between prophecy and exhortation cf. 1 Cor. xiv. 3.

xv. 33

ποιήσαντες δὲ χρόνον] 'having spent some time'. This use of *ποιέω* is classical (cf. xx. 3; Mt. xx. 12; 2 Cor. xi. 25). For *χρόνος* used thus cf. xix. 22, *ἐπέσχεν χρόνον*.

ἀπελύθησαν] See on *ver.* 30.

μετ' εἰρήνης] i.e., with the words 'Go in peace' (*ἔρχεσθε εἰς εἰρήνην*) or 'Peace to you' (*εἰρήνη ὑμῖν*).

xv. 34 (not in WH)

ἔδοξεν δὲ τῷ Σίλᾳ ἐπιμεῖναι αὐτοῦ, μόνος δὲ Ἰούδας ἐπορεύθη] This verse is inserted in the δ text, C D 33 614 al g hcl* sah arm eth being our authorities for *ἔδοξεν δὲ τῷ Σίλᾳ ἐπιμεῖναι αὐτοῦ* (C D have *αὐτούς* for *αὐτοῦ*), and D g w vg.codd Ephrem for *μόνος δὲ Ἰούδας ἐπορεύθη*. The insertion, which contradicts *ver.* 33, was no doubt intended to explain why Silas appears again at Antioch in *ver.* 40; as, however, the plain sense of *ver.* 33 is that both Judas and he returned to Jerusalem, we must infer that Silas later came back from Jerusalem to Antioch.

(b) Paul's second Missionary Journey commences, xv. 36-41

Μετὰ δέ τινας ἡμέρας εἶπεν πρὸς Βαρνάβαν Παῦλος Ἐπιστρέψαντες 36
δὴ ἐπισκεψώμεθα τοὺς ἀδελφοὺς κατὰ πόλιν πᾶσαν ἐν αἷς κατηγγείλαμεν
τὸν λόγον τοῦ κυρίου, πῶς ἔχουσιν. Βαρνάβας δὲ ἐβούλετο συνπαρα- 37
λαβεῖν καὶ τὸν Ἰωάνην τὸν καλούμενον Μάρκον· Παῦλος δὲ ἠξίου, 38
τὸν ἀποστάντα ἀπ' αὐτῶν ἀπὸ Παμφυλίας καὶ μὴ συνελθόντα αὐτοῖς
εἰς τὸ ἔργον, μὴ συνπαραλαμβάνειν τοῦτον. ἐγένετο δὲ παροξυσμὸς 39
ὥστε ἀποχωρισθῆναι αὐτοὺς ἀπ' ἀλλήλων, τόν τε Βαρνάβαν παρα-
λαβόντα τὸν Μάρκον ἐκπλεῦσαι εἰς Κύπρον. Παῦλος δὲ ἐπιλεξά- 40
μενος Σίλαν ἐξῆλθεν παραδοθεὶς τῇ χάριτι τοῦ κυρίου ὑπὸ τῶν ἀδελφῶν,
διήρχετο δὲ τὴν Συρίαν καὶ τὴν Κιλικίαν ἐπιστηρίζων τὰς ἐκκλησίας. 41

xv. 36

μετὰ δέ τινας ἡμέρας] *μετά* with a note of time, or *μετὰ ταῦτα*, is used in the second part of Ac. to begin a new section much as *μὲν οὖν* is in the earlier part (see on i. 6). Cf. xviii. 1; xxi. 15; xxiv. 1, 24; xxv. 1; xxviii. 11, 17.

δή] With hortative subjunctive *ἐπιστρεψώμεθα*, as in xiii. 2 with imperative (*q.v.*).

κατὰ πόλιν πᾶσαν ἐν αἷς] Although the antecedent is grammatically singular, the pronoun, by a sense construction, is plural; several cities are referred to. Cf. viii. 5; xvi. 10; xx. 2.

xv. 37f.

συνπαραλαβεῖν . . . συνπαραλαμβάνειν] Notice the variation of tenses, a 'delicate *nuance*' Moulton called it: 'Barnabas, with easy forgetfulness of risk, wishes *συνπαραλαβεῖν* Mark—Paul refuses *συνπαραλαμβάνειν*, to have with them day by day one who had shown himself unreliable' (*Proleg.*, p. 130). See on xiii. 13 for Mark's leaving the earlier expedition.

xv. 38

τοῦτον] om P^{45}. The position at the end of the sentence is very emphatic. D spoils the emphasis by adding *μὴ εἶναι σὺν αὐτοῖς*.

xv. 39

παροξυσμὸς] 'irritation', 'provocation' (in LXX Dt. xxix. 28; Jer. xxxii. 37): cf. *παρωξύνετο*, xvii. 16. (For another kind of *παροξυσμός* cf. Heb. x. 24.) It is a tribute to Luke's honesty that he should describe a quarrel between two apostles by so strong a term. Probably family-feeling influenced Barnabas to some extent; Mark was his cousin (Col. iv. 10). It is a mistake to connect this dispute with that of Gal. ii. 13, which probably belongs to an earlier date, and in which Barnabas played only a minor and temporary part, for which he is almost excused by Paul. The reason given by Luke is quite sufficient to account for the present quarrel. It is pleasant to know that Mark later redeemed himself in Paul's eyes and served as his fellow-worker (Col. iv. 10; Phm. 24; 2 Tim. iv. 11).

ἐκπλεῦσαι εἰς Κύπρον] Barnabas and Mark had visited Cyprus previously along with Paul (xiii. 4 ff.). It was Barnabas's native island (iv. 36), and there, according to the late *Periodi Barnabae*, Barnabas remained until his death. The quarrel had at least one good result, that two missionary expeditions set out instead of one.

xv. 40

Σίλαν] See on *vv.* 22, 32 ff. Paul no doubt had good reasons for taking a Jerusalem Christian as his companion—one who was also a Roman citizen (cf. xvi. 37). As Silas was mentioned by name in the apostolic decree, it was well that he should share with Paul the duty of handing it over to the Gentile churches.

παραδοθεὶς τῇ χάριτι τοῦ κυρίου] Cf. xiv. 26.

xv. 41

τὴν Συρίαν καὶ τὴν Κιλικίαν] Syria and Cilicia formed one administrative province (see on *ver.* 23). *τήν* before *Κιλικίαν* (B D) is omitted by ℵ A C 33 81 byz (so WH mg., Soden). P^{45} has the peculiar reading *διὰ τῆς Συρίας καὶ τῆς Κιλικίας*.

ἐπιστηρίζων τὰς ἐκκλησίας] Cf. *ver.* 32; xiv. 21. δ adds *παραδιδοὺς τὰς ἐντολὰς τῶν πρεσβυτέρων*, which is obviously true, being deduced from *ver.* 23 and xvi. 4.

(c) In the Province of Galatia; Timothy joins them, xvi. 1-4

Κατήντησεν δὲ καὶ εἰς Δέρβην καὶ εἰς Λύστραν. καὶ ἰδοὺ μαθητής 1
τις ἦν ἐκεῖ ὀνόματι Τιμόθεος, υἱὸς γυναικὸς Ἰουδαίας πιστῆς πατρὸς
δὲ Ἕλληνος, ὃς ἐμαρτυρεῖτο ὑπὸ τῶν ἐν Λύστροις καὶ Ἰκονίῳ ἀδελφῶν· 2
τοῦτον ἠθέλησεν ὁ Παῦλος σὺν αὐτῷ ἐξελθεῖν, καὶ λαβὼν περιέτεμεν 3
αὐτὸν διὰ τοὺς Ἰουδαίους τοὺς ὄντας ἐν τοῖς τόποις ἐκείνοις, ᾔδεισαν
γὰρ ἅπαντες ὅτι Ἕλλην ὁ πατὴρ αὐτοῦ ὑπῆρχεν. Ὡς δὲ διεπορεύοντο 4
τὰς πόλεις, παρεδίδοσαν αὐτοῖς φυλάσσειν τὰ δόγματα τὰ κεκριμένα
ὑπὸ τῶν ἀποστόλων καὶ πρεσβυτέρων τῶν ἐν Ἰεροσολύμοις.

xvi. 1

κατήντησεν] 'he arrived': cf. xviii. 19, 24; xxvii. 12. The singular indicates Paul as leader.

εἰς Δέρβην καὶ εἰς Λύστραν] See on xiv. 6, where they are named in the reverse order, as Paul then approached them from the opposite direction.

ἐκεῖ] Probably in Lystra, the common term in 'Derbe and Lystra' (*ver.* 1) and 'Lystra and Iconium' (*ver.* 2). But Orig. lat. on Rom. xvi. 21 calls him *Derbaeus ciuis* (see on xx. 4).

ὀνόματι] om P^{45}.

υἱὸς γυναικὸς Ἰουδαίας πιστῆς πατρὸς δὲ Ἕλληνος] That a Jewess married a Gentile reflects a less exclusive standard than in Palestine. In Phrygia 'there can be little doubt that the Jews married into the dominant families' (Ramsay, *BRD*, p. 357). We learn from 2 Tim. i. 5 that the name of Timothy's mother was Eunice; there Timothy is reminded of her faith and that of his grandmother Lois. Probably both women had believed on Paul's first visit to their city.

xvi. 2

ὃς ἐμαρτυρεῖτο] For Luke's interest in men's reputations cf. i. 21; vi. 3; x. 22; xxii. 12.

ἐν Λύστροις καὶ Ἰκονίῳ] Iconium was nearer to Lystra than was Derbe, although Iconium was in Phrygia Galatica, and Lystra and Derbe in Lycaonia Galatica. For the declension of Lystra see on xiv. 8.

xvi. 3

λαβὼν περιέτεμεν αὐτὸν] *ἔλαβεν καὶ περιτεμὼν αὐτόν* P^{45}. In the eyes of Jews Timothy ranked as a Gentile, because he had a Greek father and was uncircumcised. In the eyes of Gentiles, however, he was practically a Jew, having been brought up in his mother's religion (cf. 2 Tim. iii. 15). (For the position of proselytes whose mothers were Israelites, see p. 86, n.) Paul therefore regularized his status (and, in Jewish eyes, legitimized him) by circumcising him. That he did so is striking, in view of such passages as Gal. ii. 3; v. 3, etc., but Timothy's was an exceptional case. Paul's readiness to conciliate Jewish opinion is seen elsewhere in Ac., e.g., xxi. 26; cf. 1 Cor. ix. 19-22 for his justification of such action.

ὑπῆρχεν] The tense probably indicates that his father was dead; had he been alive, the present would have been more natural after *ᾔδεισαν*.

xvi. 4

Ὡς δὲ διεπορεύοντο τὰς πόλεις κ.τ.λ.] δ has *διερχόμενοι δὲ τὰς πόλεις ἐκήρυσσον μετὰ πάσης παρρησίας τὸν κύριον Ἰησοῦν Χριστόν, ἅμα παραδιδόντες καὶ τὰς ἐντολὰς ἀποστόλων καὶ πρεσβυτέρων τῶν ἐν Ἱεροσολύμοις*. The cities were those evangelized on the previous journey—Derbe, Lystra, Iconium and Pisidian Antioch.

παρεδίδοσαν κ.τ.λ.] The letter was not explicitly addressed to the Galatian churches, but they received it as well as those of Syria and Cilicia because (1) they had been evangelized from Antioch, (2) if, as seems more probable, Gal. was written before the Council, the Jerusalem letter confirmed Paul's argument in that epistle. In discussing the food question with the churches of Corinth and Rome, however, he makes no reference to the Jerusalem decree (1 Cor. viii; Rom. xiv). From Rev. ii. 14, 20 we may infer that the decree in due course reached the churches in the province of Asia, whence probably it was later carried to Gaul (see p. 289, n. 1).

τὰ δόγματα] 'the decisions'; *δόγμα* is derived from *δοκεῖν*, the verb used in the letter (xv. 28). The same noun is used of imperial decrees in xvii. 7; Lk. ii. 1.

(d) The Churches grow in Faith and Numbers, xvi. 5

Αἱ μὲν οὖν ἐκκλησίαι ἐστερεοῦντο τῇ πίστει καὶ ἐπερίσσευον τῷ 5
ἀριθμῷ καθ᾽ ἡμέραν.

xvi. 5

Αἱ μὲν οὖν ἐκκλησίαι κ.τ.λ.] The third of six brief reports of progress: cf. vi. 7; ix. 31. For *μὲν οὖν* see on i. 6. The record of the Council is now finished, with the last reference to the handing over of its recommendations.

V. EVANGELIZATION ON THE SHORES OF THE AEGEAN, xvi. 6-xix. 20

1. PHILIPPI, xvi. 6-40

(a) The Missionaries are called to Macedonia, xvi. 6-10

Διῆλθον δὲ τὴν Φρυγίαν καὶ Γαλατικὴν χώραν, κωλυθέντες ὑπὸ 6
τοῦ ἁγίου πνεύματος λαλῆσαι τὸν λόγον ἐν τῇ Ἀσίᾳ, ἐλθόντες δὲ κατὰ 7
τὴν Μυσίαν ἐπείραζον εἰς τὴν Βιθυνίαν πορευθῆναι καὶ οὐκ εἴασεν
αὐτοὺς τὸ πνεῦμα Ἰησοῦ· παρελθόντες δὲ τὴν Μυσίαν κατέβησαν 8
εἰς Τρῳάδα. καὶ ὅραμα διὰ νυκτὸς τῷ Παύλῳ ὤφθη, ἀνὴρ Μακεδών 9
τις ἦν ἑστὼς καὶ παρακαλῶν αὐτὸν καὶ λέγων Διαβὰς εἰς Μακεδονίαν
βοήθησον ἡμῖν. ὡς δὲ τὸ ὅραμα εἶδεν, εὐθέως ἐζητήσαμεν ἐξελθεῖν 10
εἰς Μακεδονίαν, συνβιβάζοντες ὅτι προσκέκληται ἡμᾶς ὁ θεὸς εὐαγ-
γελίσασθαι αὐτούς.

xvi. 6

Διῆλθον] *διελθόντες*, the reading of byz, alters the order of events (see below on *κωλυθέντες*).

τὴν Φρυγίαν καὶ Γαλατικὴν χώραν] 'the Phrygian and Galatian region', i.e., the region which is both Phrygian and Galatian. The phrase may be understood *either* (1) in the political sense, of that part of Phrygia which belonged to the Roman province of Galatia (the region apparently known as Phrygia Galatica, in which Pisidian Antioch and probably Iconium were situated: see on xiii. 14; xiv. 6), in which case these words are resumptive of *ver.* 4; *or* (2) in the ethnic or popular sense, of the border district between ethnic Phrygia and Galatia, where both the Phrygian and Celtic languages were to be heard. Although the former interpretation is supported by the weighty names of W. M. Ramsay, W. M. Calder, and others, yet the latter possibly suits the present context better.[1] See further on xviii. 23. There is no direct evidence elsewhere for the adjectival use of *Φρυγία*, but cf. the similar phrase *τῆς Ἰτουραίας καὶ Τραχωνίτιδος χώρας* in Lk. iii. 1, where *Ἰτουραία*, elsewhere a substantive, is used as an adj. The sense here is altered in byz by the insertion of *τήν* before *Γαλατικήν*. The weight of evidence is against the 'North Galatian' theory, according to which Paul on this occasion and later (xviii. 23) evangelized the Celtic population which had invaded Asia Minor in 278-7 B.C.[2]

κωλυθέντες] We naturally infer from the aor. ptc. that they had received this prohibition before journeying through the 'Phrygo-Galatian region'. The original plan had probably been to go on to Ephesus. When Paul was forbidden to preach in Asia, he turned northward from Pisidian Antioch and, crossing the Sultan Dagh range, went north until he arrived near the Bithynian border. Here he might either go north to Nicomedia, or turn west to Troas.

Ἀσίᾳ] The Roman province of Asia was formed in 133 B.C. from the kingdom of Attalus III of Pergamum, which he bequeathed to Rome. The name Asia was previously applied to a more restricted area, bounded on the north by Mysia, on the south by Caria, and on the east by Phrygia, and this popular sense may be the one intended here, the more so as Asia here seems to be distinct from Mysia (*vv.* 7 f.), which was included in Roman Asia.

xvi. 7

κατὰ τὴν Μυσίαν] i.e., opposite the eastern border of Mysia, at Cotiaeum or Dorylaeum. Mysia, the N.W. part of the province of Asia, had its name from the Mysi, a Thraco-Phrygian people who belonged originally to Europe, and also gave their name to Moesia, south of the lower Danube.

Βιθυνίαν] A senatorial province in N.W. Asia Minor, formed in 74 B.C., and usually reckoned along with Pontus for administrative purposes. Cf. 1 Pet. i. 1.

[1] See K. Lake in *BC* v. pp. 231 ff.; also K. and S. Lake, *INT* (1938), pp. 85 ff., 129 f. Paul uses 'Galatia' and 'Galatians' with reference to the Roman province; Luke, however, 'prefers in general the ancient district names to the new-fangled Roman nomenclature' (D. B. Knox, 'The Date of the Epistle to the Galatians', *EQ*, xiii. [1941], pp. 262 ff.)

[2] The kingdom of Galatia was taken over as a province by Augustus in 25 B.C., after the death in battle of Amyntas, the last Galatian king. It had been a client state of Rome since 64 B.C. The history of the kingdom and thereafter of the province is sketched by Ramsay in his *Historical Commentary on St. Paul's Epistle to the Galatians* (1899), pp. 45 ff. The Galatians to whom Paul's epistle was addressed were the Christians of Pisidian Antioch, Iconium, Lystra and Derbe; they are called Galatians not as being of Gaulish (Celtic) descent, but as members of the province of Galatia, which included much more than the territory where the ethnic Galatians lived.

οὐκ εἴασεν αὐτοὺς τὸ πνεῦμα Ἰησοῦ] om *Ἰησοῦ* byz. How was the prohibition conveyed? Perhaps by inward monition, perhaps by vision (cf. *ver.* 9), but more probably by prophetic utterance of one of the party (cf. xx. 23; xxi. 4, 11).

xvi. 8

παρελθόντες] lit., 'passing by'. They could not get to Troas without passing through Mysia; but *παρελθόντες* may be used here instead of *διελθόντες* to indicate that they did not stay to preach in Mysia. δ has *διελθόντες*. Cf. the similar use of *παρελθεῖν* in xvii. 15 δ.

κατέβησαν] D has *κατήντησαν* (cf. *ver.* 1).

Τρῳάδα] Troas (its full name was *Ἀλεξάνδρεια ἡ Τρῳάς*) was founded by Antigonus (323-301 B.C.) and refounded by Lysimachus (300 B.C.). It was a free city under the Seleucids, the Pergamene kings, and the Romans. Augustus made it a colony. It was a regular port of call on journeys from Asia to Macedonia and vice versa: cf. xx. 5.

xvi. 9

ὅραμα] Cf. ix. 10, 12; x. 3, 17; xviii. 9; xxii. 17 for other visions.

ἀνὴρ Μακεδών τις] Much has been written to explain how Paul knew that he was a Macedonian. The man's words indicated sufficiently where he came from.

The Macedonians, though the Greeks considered them barbarians in classical times, were Greeks linguistically. Macedonia became the dominant power in Greece under Philip (359-336 B.C.); and after his son Alexander's conquests Egypt and Syria were ruled by Macedonian dynasties. After three wars with the Romans, Macedonia was finally conquered by them in 168 B.C., and made a province in 146.

xvi. 10

ὡς δὲ τὸ ὅραμα εἶδεν κ.τ.λ.] δ recasts this verse, *διεγερθεὶς οὖν διηγήσατο τὸ ὅραμα ἡμῖν, καὶ ἐνοήσαμεν ὅτι προσκέκληται ἡμᾶς ὁ κύριος εὐαγγελίσασθαι τοὺς ἐν τῇ Μακεδονίᾳ.*

ἐζητήσαμεν] This verb indicates the commencement of the first 'we' section, which continues till *ver.* 17. We gather that Luke joined Paul, Silas, and Timothy in Troas, and accompanied them from there to Philippi.

συνβιβάζοντες] Cf. ix. 22; xix. 33. In LXX the word always means 'instruct' (cf. 1 Cor. ii. 16 from Isa. xl. 13). Its normal sense is 'put together' (Eph. iv. 16; Col. ii. 2, 19), from which is derived its sense 'infer' in this verse, a sense for which LS[9] gives seven examples from Aristotle (cf. the similar derivative use of Eng. 'gather', Lat. *colligo*).

(b) Troas to Philippi, xvi. 11-12a

Ἀναχθέντες οὖν ἀπὸ Τρῳάδος εὐθυδρομήσαμεν εἰς Σαμοθρᾴκην, 11
τῇ δὲ ἐπιούσῃ εἰς Νέαν Πόλιν, κἀκεῖθεν εἰς Φιλίππους, ἥτις ἐστὶν 12
πρώτη τῆς μερίδος Μακεδονίας πόλις, κολωνία.

xvi. 11

ἀναχθέντες οὖν] δ has *τῇ δὲ ἐπαύριον ἀχθέντες.*

εὐθυδρομήσαμεν] i.e., before a favourable wind. Samothrace was a good day's sail from Troas, as was Neapolis from Samothrace. In xx. 6 the reverse journey from Philippi to Troas took five days.

Σαμοθρᾴκην] This mountainous island, rising to 5000 feet, forms a conspicuous landmark.

Νέαν Πόλιν] This spelling of the name as two words (so ℵ A B; whereas C D 81 byz have *Νεάπολιν*) conforms to classical usage: cf. *Ἄρειος πάγος*, xvii. 19, 22; *Ἱερᾷ Πόλει*, Col. iv. 13, WH (the reading here is not easily determined, as there would be no difference in spelling in uncial MSS). Neapolis (mod. Kavalla) was the port of Philippi, and lay about 10 miles distant from it. The Via Egnatia from Dyrrhachium (mod. Durazzo) reached the sea here, after passing through Thessalonica, Amphipolis and Philippi. Luke likes to mention ports of arrival and departure (cf. xiii. 4), and the detailed account of this journey shows his interest in sea-itineraries, specially marked in the 'we' sections.

xvi. 12a

Φιλίππους] Philippi was originally the Thasian settlement of Crenides, founded in connection with the gold-mines of the neighbouring Mt. Pangaeus. Philip of Macedon seized the gold-mines and fortified the city, calling it after himself. With the rest of Macedonia it passed into the hands of the Romans in 168 B.C. In the vicinity was fought the battle where Brutus and Cassius were defeated by Antony and Octavian (later the Emperor Augustus) in 42 B.C. After the battle it was made a Roman colony, and the victors settled a number of veterans there; more colonists were settled after Actium, when Octavian defeated Antony and Cleopatra, in 31 B.C., and the city then received its full title Colonia Iulia Augusta Philippensis.

ἥτις ἐστὶν πρώτη τῆς μερίδος Μακεδονίας πόλις] So ℵ A C 81 byz. In B *τῆς* comes after *μερίδος*, not before it. In 167 B.C. Macedonia was divided by its conqueror Aemilius Paullus into four administrative districts. The chief town of the district which included Philippi was Amphipolis. Ramsay puts down the statement that Philippi was ‘ the leading city of its district of Macedonia ’ to Luke’s special interest in the place ; he need not have meant that it was technically the capital. Blass, like Field, attractively emends πρώτη to πρώτης, which is supported by *primae partis* of some Vulgate codices (Θ c Par.lat.11505²), but by no Gk. MS, and renders πρώτης μερίδος τῆς Μακεδονίας πόλις, ‘ a city of the first division of Macedonia ’.[1] That Philippi was in the first part of Macedonia we know from Livy xlv. 29 and inscriptions. D paraphrases the end of the verse ἥτις ἐστὶν κεφαλὴ τῆς Μακεδονίας, πόλις κολωνία. Pesh similarly has *rīshā dĕ Maqedôniya*. But Thessalonica, not Philippi, was the capital of Macedonia.

κολωνία] Transliteration of Lat. *colonia*. A Roman colony was like a piece of Rome or Italy transplanted abroad ; its citizens enjoyed the same rights as they would have had in Italy. They used Roman law, and their constitution was modelled on that at home (see on στρατηγοῖς, *ver.* 20). Their original purpose was military ; it was obviously an advantage to have settlements of Roman citizens at strategic points throughout the Empire. Other Roman colonies mentioned in Ac. are Pisidian Antioch, Lystra, Troas, Ptolemais, Corinth.

(c) The Conversion of Lydia, xvi. 12b-15

ʽΗμεν δὲ ἐν ταύτῃ τῇ πόλει διατρίβοντες ἡμέρας τινάς. τῇ τε 13
ἡμέρᾳ τῶν σαββάτων ἐξήλθομεν ἔξω τῆς πύλης παρὰ ποταμὸν οὗ
ἐνομίζομεν προσευχὴν εἶναι, καὶ καθίσαντες ἐλαλοῦμεν ταῖς συνελ-
θούσαις γυναιξίν. καί τις γυνὴ ὀνόματι Λυδία, πορφυρόπωλις πόλεως 14
Θυατείρων σεβομένη τὸν θεόν, ἤκουεν, ἧς ὁ κύριος διήνοιξεν τὴν
καρδίαν προσέχειν τοῖς λαλουμένοις ὑπὸ Παύλου. ὡς δὲ ἐβαπτίσθη 15
καὶ ὁ οἶκος αὐτῆς, παρεκάλεσεν λέγουσα Εἰ κεκρίκατέ με πιστὴν τῷ
κυρίῳ εἶναι, εἰσελθόντες εἰς τὸν οἶκόν μου μένετε· καὶ παρεβιάσατο
ἡμᾶς.

xvi. 12b

ἦμεν . . . διατρίβοντες] For the periphrasis see on i. 10.

xvi. 13

τῇ τε ἡμέρᾳ τῶν σαββάτων] See on xiii. 14.

παρὰ ποταμὸν] The Gangites or Angites, a tributary of the Strymon.

[1] Cf. vg.codd A Par.lat.342, *in* (om A) *prima parte Macedoniae ciuitas;* uersio prouincialis lugdunensis, *en la primiera part de Macedonia;* cod. tepl., *das do ist eine fremde stat in deme ersten teile zu Macedon.*

ἐνομίζομεν προσευχὴν εἶναι] C (-ζαμεν) 33 81 boh arm. There is no thought of a synagogue here, as women only are mentioned. A synagogue service traditionally requires a minimum (*minyān*) of ten men. But προσευχή when used of a building is simply a synonym for συναγωγή (see on vi. 9, and cf. Schürer II. ii. 72 f.). It is therefore more likely that the meaning here is 'prayer'. Our best authorities for β are corrupt here; A (rewritten) and B have ἐνομίζομεν προσευχὴ[1] εἶναι, ℵ has ἐνόμιζεν προσευχὴν εἶναι. The best text is probably given in byz (followed by Soden and Ropes), ἐνομίζετο προσευχὴ εἶναι (rightly translated in AV, 'prayer was wont to be made'). This is reflected in the paraphrase in δ, ἐδόκει προσευχὴ εἶναι, the result of misinterpreting ἐνομίζετο as 'it was thought'.

xvi. 14

Λυδία] lit., 'the Lydian woman' (Thyatira was in Lydia). Perhaps she had another personal name.

πορφυρόπωλις] A trader in that purple dye for which the Lydians were famed as early as Homer. Cf. *Iliad* iv. 141 f.,

ὡς δ' ὅτε τίς τ' ἐλέφαντα γυνὴ φοίνικι μιήνῃ
Μῃονὶς ἠὲ Κάειρα.

πόλεως Θυατείρων] Thyatira was founded by Seleucus Nicator early in the third century B.C. as a garrison city to defend his realm against Lysimachus. Its original settlers were Macedonians. It passed under Roman control in 190 B.C., and was included in the province of Asia after 133 B.C. Lydia may have become acquainted with the Jewish religion in Thyatira, where there was a Jewish colony. The church founded in Thyatira at some date subsequent to this was one of the seven addressed in the Apocalypse.

σεβομένη τὸν θεόν] See on x. 2.

διήνοιξεν τὴν καρδίαν] Cf. διήνοιξεν αὐτῶν τὸν νοῦν, Lk. xxiv. 45; διανοίξαι τὴν καρδίαν ὑμῶν, 2 Macc. i. 4.

προσέχειν τοῖς λαλουμένοις] Epexegetic infin. Cf. προσεῖχον . . . τοῖς λεγομένοις, viii. 6. Here at any rate the phrase signifies full belief.

xvi. 15

καὶ ὁ οἶκος αὐτῆς] Lydia appears to have been the head of the house; we may conclude that she was unmarried or a widow. In that case her household would include servants and other dependents, perhaps some of the women of *ver.* 13. For women in the Philippian church cf. Phil. iv. 2 f.

παρεβιάσατο] Cf. Lk. xxiv. 29, in a similar context; 2 K. ii. 17 (LXX 4 K.), καὶ παρεβιάσαντο αὐτὸν ἕως οὗ ᾔσχύνετο.

[1] Or προσευχῇ: thus sah renders 'we were accustomed to be at prayer'.

(d) The Pythoness, xvi. 16-18

Ἐγένετο δὲ πορευομένων ἡμῶν εἰς τὴν προσευχὴν παιδίσκην τινὰ 16
ἔχουσαν πνεῦμα πύθωνα ὑπαντῆσαι ἡμῖν, ἥτις ἐργασίαν πολλὴν παρεῖχεν
τοῖς κυρίοις αὐτῆς μαντευομένη· αὕτη κατακολουθοῦσα τῷ Παύλῳ 17
καὶ ἡμῖν ἔκραζεν λέγουσα Οὗτοι οἱ ἄνθρωποι δοῦλοι τοῦ θεοῦ τοῦ
ὑψίστου εἰσίν, οἵτινες καταγγέλλουσιν ὑμῖν ὁδὸν σωτηρίας. τοῦτο 18
δὲ ἐποίει ἐπὶ πολλὰς ἡμέρας. διαπονηθεὶς δὲ Παῦλος καὶ ἐπιστρέψας
τῷ πνεύματι εἶπεν Παραγγέλλω σοι ἐν ὀνόματι Ἰησοῦ Χριστοῦ
ἐξελθεῖν ἀπ' αὐτῆς· καὶ ἐξῆλθεν αὐτῇ τῇ ὥρᾳ.

xvi. 16

Ἐγένετο δὲ . . . ὑπαντῆσαι] For the construction see on iv. 5.

εἰς τὴν προσευχὴν] 'to prayer'; for the article cf. i. 14; ii. 42; iii. 1; vi. 4.

παιδίσκην] 'slave-girl', as in xii. 13.

ἔχουσαν πνεῦμα πύθωνα] . . . *πύθωνος* P^{45} byz. Here *πύθωνα* is in apposition to *πνεῦμα*. Usually it is used of the person possessed, which is just possible here. *πύθωνες* were inspired by Apollo, the Pythian god, who was regarded as embodied in a snake (the Python) at Delphi (also called Pytho). Plutarch (*de defectu oraculorum* ix. 414 E) calls them *ἐγγαστριμύθους*, 'ventriloquists'—ventriloquists who uttered words not only apparently, but actually, beyond their own control. In LXX *ἐγγαστρίμυθος* is used of one who has a familiar spirit (Heb. *'ōbh*), e.g., the witch of Endor, 1 Sam. xxviii. 7 ff. (LXX 1 K.).

ἐργασίαν] 'profit'; lit., 'work'; cf. our use of 'business': cf. *ver.* 19; xix. 24.

μαντευομένη] 'by her inspired speech'; only here in NT. The pagan connotation of the word made it unsuitable for use in Christian contexts.

xvi. 17

Παύλῳ καὶ ἡμῖν] Notice how Paul is distinguished from 'us' here and in xxi. 18, in both places at the end of a 'we' section.

ἔκραζεν] Imperf., because she did it many days (*ver.* 18).

δοῦλοι] om P^{45}.

τοῦ θεοῦ τοῦ ὑψίστου] *θεὸς ὕψιστος*, 'God most high', was a divine title current among both Jews and Greeks, and thus provided them with a common denominator in referring to the Deity. Cf. Mk. v. 7; Num. xxiv. 16; Isa. xiv. 14; Dan. iii. 26; 1 Esdras ii. 3. The Jewish title is a translation of Heb. *'Ēl 'Elyōn*. Here the word is used in its Gentile context (contrast the Jewish context of *ὁ ὕψιστος*, vii. 48).

ὑμῖν] ℵ B D E vg pesh hcl arm; ἡμῖν A C[2] 33 81 byz e sah boh.

ὁδὸν σωτηρίας] 'a way of salvation'; σωτηρία was a current term among Gentiles as well as Jews; as used by Gentiles it combined the idea of salvation in the more spiritual sense with that of bodily healing (see on σωθῆναι, xiv. 9). Cf. Harnack, *Mission and Expansion of Christianity*, i. pp. 101 ff.; Ramsay, *BRD*, pp. 173 ff. Among the Gentiles σωτηρία was the object of many vows and prayers to Θεὸς Ὕψιστος and other gods (θεοὶ σωτῆρες), and was the desired object set before initiates in the various Mysteries.

xvi. 18

ἐπὶ πολλὰς ἡμέρας] Cf. xiii. 31, ἐπὶ ἡμέρας πλείους.

διαπονηθεὶς] Cf. διαπονούμενοι, iv. 2.

παραγγέλλω] Aoristic present: cf. ἰᾶται, ix. 34.

ἐν ὀνόματι Ἰησοῦ Χριστοῦ] See on iii. 6. The authority with which Jesus Himself had commanded possessing spirits to leave their victims (e.g. Mk. i. 25) was now invoked by His apostle, and proved as potent in exorcism as in other forms of healing (cf. xix. 13).

ἐξελθεῖν] ἵνα ἐξέλθῃς D (cf. xii. 17).

αὐτῇ τῇ ὥρᾳ] Implying immediacy: cf. xxii. 13; Lk. ii. 38; x. 21; xii. 12; xx. 19; xxiv. 33. The idiom is characteristically Lukan. The first 'we' section now ends; the next one begins in xx. 5.

(e) Imprisonment of Paul and Silas, xvi. 19-24

Ἰδόντες δὲ οἱ κύριοι αὐτῆς ὅτι ἐξῆλθεν ἡ ἐλπὶς τῆς ἐργασίας 19
αὐτῶν ἐπιλαβόμενοι τὸν Παῦλον καὶ τὸν Σίλαν εἵλκυσαν εἰς τὴν ἀγορὰν
ἐπὶ τοὺς ἄρχοντας καὶ προσαγαγόντες αὐτοὺς τοῖς στρατηγοῖς εἶπαν 20
Οὗτοι οἱ ἄνθρωποι ἐκταράσσουσιν ἡμῶν τὴν πόλιν Ἰουδαῖοι ὑπάρχοντες,
καὶ καταγγέλλουσιν ἔθη ἃ οὐκ ἔξεστιν ἡμῖν παραδέχεσθαι οὐδὲ ποιεῖν 21
Ῥωμαίοις οὖσιν. καὶ συνεπέστη ὁ ὄχλος κατ' αὐτῶν, καὶ οἱ στρατηγοὶ 22
περιρήξαντες αὐτῶν τὰ ἱμάτια ἐκέλευον ῥαβδίζειν, πολλὰς δὲ ἐπι- 23
θέντες αὐτοῖς πληγὰς ἔβαλον εἰς φυλακήν, παραγγείλαντες τῷ δεσμοφύ-
λακι ἀσφαλῶς τηρεῖν αὐτούς· ὃς παραγγελίαν τοιαύτην λαβὼν 24
ἔβαλεν αὐτοὺς εἰς τὴν ἐσωτέραν φυλακὴν καὶ τοὺς πόδας ἠσφαλίσατο
αὐτῶν εἰς τὸ ξύλον.

xvi. 19

ἰδόντες δὲ] καὶ ἰδόντες B (cf. WH mg.).

ἐξῆλθεν ἡ ἐλπὶς τῆς ἐργασίας αὐτῶν] Luke's sense of humour appears in his choice of ἐξῆλθεν here after its use in *ver.* 18; their 'hope of profit' was in fact the expelled spirit itself. For ἐργασία see on *ver.* 16. On the two occasions where Luke records spontaneous opposition to the Gospel on the part of Gentiles, the reason lies in its threat to 'vested interests' (cf. xix. 23 ff.).[1]

τὸν Παῦλον καὶ τὸν Σίλαν] The two leaders of the company. Luke and Timothy were left alone; the one was a Greek, the other a half-Greek.

τοὺς ἄρχοντας] 'the magistrates'; this is the Gk. term for the supreme magistrates in any city. See on *τοῖς στρατηγοῖς, ver.* 20.

xvi. 20

προσαγαγόντες αὐτοὺς τοῖς στρατηγοῖς] This practically repeats *εἵλκυσαν . . . ἐπὶ τοὺς ἄρχοντας* (*ver.* 19). Gk. *στρατηγοί* represents Lat. *praetores*, the courtesy title of the chief magistrates of the colony. They were two in number, whence their official title *duouiri*, 'duumvirs'. Cicero's remark on the magistrates of Capua is apposite: '*cum ceteris in coloniis duouiri appellentur, hi se praetores appellari uolebant*' (*de leg. agr.* ii. 93). Cf. *CIL* iii. 633, 654, 7339, 14206[15] for titles of Philippian magistrates.

Ἰουδαῖοι ὑπάρχοντες] An appeal to anti-Jewish prejudice, emphasized by the contrasting *Ῥωμαίοις οὖσιν* (*ver.* 21), which again is neatly countered by Paul in *ver.* 37, *Ῥωμαίους ὑπάρχοντας*.

xvi. 21

ἃ οὐκ ἔξεστιν] Cf. xviii. 13, *παρὰ τὸν νόμον*. The magistrates took cognizance of such religious activity as tended to create a breach of the peace, or encouraged unlawful practices or organizations.

Ῥωμαίοις οὖσιν] The *coloni* were very conscious of the superiority of their Roman citizenship in contrast even with the status of the surrounding Greeks, not to speak of wandering Jews.

xvi. 22

περιρήξαντες αὐτῶν τὰ ἱμάτια] Not 'tearing off their own clothes' (as in xiv. 14), but the apostles' clothes. The magistrates need not have done this themselves: *qui facit per alium facit per se.* Cf. 2 Macc. iv. 38, *τοὺς χιτῶνας περιρήξας*.

ἐκέλευον ῥαβδίζειν] This beating with rods was carried out by the lictors, the *ῥαβδοῦχοι* of *ver.* 35 (*q.v.*). Cf. 2 Cor. xi. 25, *τρὶς ἐραβδίσθην*.

[1] It is possible that some of the Jewish opposition to Paul was due to similar considerations, as by detaching Jews, proselytes, and God-fearers from the synagogues, he was reducing the number of actual or potential payers of the Temple-tax. The fact that it was the chief priests whose hostility was bitterest against him in Jerusalem suggests that they, at least, may have been animated by economic as well as by religious motives.

xvi. 23

πολλὰς δὲ] B 81 boh; *πολλάς τε* ℵ A C D byz (WH mg.).

ἔβαλον εἰς φυλακήν] W. K. Lowther Clarke in *JTS* xv. (1914), p. 599 (cf. *BC* ii. pp. 77 f.) points out several linguistic parallels between this passage and the *Testament of Joseph* (in the *Testaments of the Twelve Patriarchs*) viii. 4 f. (recension α), *ἔβαλέ με εἰς φυλακὴν ἐν τῷ αὐτοῦ οἴκῳ, καὶ τῇ ἑξῆς μαστιγώσας ἐξέπεμψέ με εἰς τὴν τοῦ Φαραὼ εἱρκτήν. καὶ ὡς ἤμην ἐν δεσμοῖς ἡ Αἰγυπτία . . . ἐπηκροᾶτό μου πῶς εὐχαρίστουν τῷ κυρίῳ καὶ ὕμνουν ἐν οἴκῳ τοῦ σκότους καὶ ἔχαιρον ἐν ἱλαρᾷ φωνῇ δοξάζων τὸν θεόν μου.*

δεσμοφύλακι] This word occurs in the *Testament of Joseph*, ii. 3: cf. *ἀρχιδεσμόφυλαξ*, Gen. xxxix. 21 ff.

xvi. 24

εἰς τὴν ἐσωτέραν φυλακὴν] The comparative has perhaps superlative force, ' inmost '.

ξύλον] An instrument of torture similar to the stocks. It had more than two holes for the legs, which could thus be forced wide apart, causing great discomfort and pain. Cf. Euseb. *HE* v. 1. 27, *τὰς ἐν τῷ ξύλῳ διατάσεις τῶν ποδῶν, ἐπὶ πέμπτον διατεινομένων τρύπημα*, and vi. 39 (of Origen), *ἐπὶ πλείσταις ἡμέραις τοὺς πόδας ὑπὸ τέσσαρα τοῦ κολαστηρίου ξύλου παραταθεὶς διαστήματα κατασπώμενος.*

(f) Deliverance from Prison; Conversion of the Jailer, xvi. 25-34

Κατὰ δὲ τὸ μεσονύκτιον Παῦλος καὶ Σίλας προσευχόμενοι 25
ὕμνουν τὸν θεόν, ἐπηκροῶντο δὲ αὐτῶν οἱ δέσμιοι· ἄφνω δὲ σεισμὸς 26
ἐγένετο μέγας ὥστε σαλευθῆναι τὰ θεμέλια τοῦ δεσμωτηρίου, ἠνεῴ-
χθησαν δὲ παραχρῆμα αἱ θύραι πᾶσαι, καὶ πάντων τὰ δεσμὰ ἀνέθη.
ἔξυπνος δὲ γενόμενος ὁ δεσμοφύλαξ καὶ ἰδὼν ἀνεῳγμένας τὰς θύρας 27
τῆς φυλακῆς σπασάμενος τὴν μάχαιραν ἤμελλεν ἑαυτὸν ἀναιρεῖν,
νομίζων ἐκπεφευγέναι τοὺς δεσμίους. ἐφώνησεν δὲ Παῦλος μεγάλῃ 28
φωνῇ λέγων Μηδὲν πράξῃς σεαυτῷ κακόν, ἅπαντες γὰρ ἐσμεν ἐνθάδε.
αἰτήσας δὲ φῶτα εἰσεπήδησεν, καὶ ἔντρομος γενόμενος προσέπεσεν 29
τῷ Παύλῳ καὶ Σίλᾳ, καὶ προαγαγὼν αὐτοὺς ἔξω ἔφη Κύριοι, τί με 30
δεῖ ποιεῖν ἵνα σωθῶ; οἱ δὲ εἶπαν Πίστευσον ἐπὶ τὸν κύριον Ἰησοῦν, 31
καὶ σωθήσῃ σὺ καὶ ὁ οἶκός σου. καὶ ἐλάλησαν αὐτῷ τὸν λόγον τοῦ 32
θεοῦ σὺν πᾶσι τοῖς ἐν τῇ οἰκίᾳ αὐτοῦ. καὶ παραλαβὼν αὐτοὺς ἐν 33
ἐκείνῃ τῇ ὥρᾳ τῆς νυκτὸς ἔλουσεν ἀπὸ τῶν πληγῶν, καὶ ἐβαπτίσθη
αὐτὸς καὶ οἱ αὐτοῦ ἅπαντες παραχρῆμα, ἀναγαγών τε αὐτοὺς εἰς τὸν 34
οἶκον παρέθηκεν τράπεζαν, καὶ ἠγαλλιάσατο πανοικεὶ πεπιστευκὼς
τῷ θεῷ.

xvi. 25

Κατὰ δὲ τὸ μεσονύκτιον] For the originally Ionic *μεσονύκτιον* cf. xx. 7; Lk. xi. 5; Mk. xiii. 35. Cf. *κατὰ μέσον τῆς νυκτός*, xxvii. 27. See W. G. Rutherford, *The New Phrynichus*, p. 126.

προσευχόμενοι ὕμνουν τὸν θεόν, ἐπηκροῶντο δὲ αὐτῶν οἱ δέσμιοι] Cf. the quotation from *Test. Jos.* on *ver.* 23, and *ib.* ix. 4, *ἤκουσε τῆς φωνῆς μου προσευχομένου.* '*Nihil crus sentit in neruo cum animus in caelo est*', says Tertullian (*Ad martyras* 2); and cf. Epictetus ii. 6. 26, *καὶ τότ' ἐσόμεθα ζηλωταὶ Σωκράτους, ὅταν ἐν φυλακῇ δυνώμεθα παιᾶνας γράφειν.*

xvi. 26

ἄφνω δὲ σεισμὸς ἐγένετο κ.τ.λ.] R. Reitzenstein, *Die Hellenistischen Wundererzählungen*, pp. 120 ff., points out a recurring pattern followed by stories of escapes from prison in Gk. literature. Celsus suggested a parallel between this narrative and the description of the deliverance of the Bacchanals and of Dionysus in the *Bacchae* of Euripides, 443 ff., 586 ff. (Orig. *c. Cels.* ii. 34). Cf. v. 19; xii. 6 ff.

ὥστε σαλευθῆναι τὰ θεμέλια] Cf. Ps. lxxxii. 5 (LXX lxxxi), *σαλευθήσονται πάντα τὰ θεμέλια τῆς γῆς.* The neut. plur. regards the foundations collectively; the masc. plur. (sc. *λίθοι*) shows that the actual foundation-stones are in view (cf. Rev. xxi. 19).

παραχρῆμα] ℵ A C D 81 byz; om B.

τὰ δεσμὰ ἀνέθη] The neut. plur. *δεσμά* occurs in xx. 23; Lk. viii. 29; the masc. plur. *δεσμοί* in Phil. i. 13. W. G. Rutherford (*Gram.*, p. 9; *The New Phrynichus*, p. 353), following Cobet, says that *δεσμά* means actual bonds, *δεσμοί* bondage or imprisonment. With the description cf. Eurip. *Bacchae*, 447 f.,

αὐτόματα δ' αὐταῖς δεσμὰ διελύθη ποδῶν
κλῇδές τ' ἀνῆκαν θύρετρ' ἄνευ θνητῆς χερός.

xvi. 27

ἔξυπνος δὲ γενόμενος] Cf. 1 Esdr. iii. 3; 1 Enoch xiii. 9; *Test. Levi* v. 7; Jos. *Ant.* xi. 3. 2.

ἤμελλεν ἑαυτὸν ἀναιρεῖν] Either as a sort of hara-kiri, as he had failed in his duty; or to avoid the penalty for letting the prisoners escape, since he was answerable for their safe keeping (see on xii. 19).

xvi. 28

ἐφώνησεν δὲ Παῦλος κ.τ.λ.] Paul may have judged by sounds what the jailer was about; or, if there was moonlight or even starlight, he might from the inner cell see the jailer in the doorway while the jailer could see only darkness inside. Whether Paul's influence restrained the other prisoners from escaping, or they were stunned by the violence and suddenness of the earthquake, we can only guess.

xvi. 29

φῶτα] 'lights' (neut. plur.).

εἰσεπήδησεν] Only here in NT, and once in LXX (Amos v. 19).[1] It is common in literature and papyri for violent action. Cf. *ἐκπηδάω*, xiv. 14.

ἔντρομος γενόμενος] Cf. vii. 32; also Heb. xii. 21.

xvi. 30

ἔξω] δ adds *τοὺς λοιποὺς ἀσφαλισάμενος*, a vivid touch which no doubt represents what actually happened. Ramsay is inclined to accept its authenticity as 'suggestive of the orderly well-disciplined character of the jailor' (*SPT*, p. 222); W. L. Knox, on the other hand, calls it 'an amusing insertion' (*St. Paul and the Church of Jerusalem*, p. xxiv). So differently does the δ text impress different people!

Κύριοι] 'Sirs': see on i. 6.

ἵνα σωθῶ] The jailer may have heard of the soothsayer's witness to the apostles as preachers of 'a way of salvation' (see on *ver.* 17); doubtless he regarded the earthquake as a supernatural vindication of their right to be so described.

xvi. 31

πίστευσον ἐπὶ τὸν κύριον Ἰησοῦν] For *πιστεύω ἐπί* cf. ix. 42; xi. 17. The δ text (followed by byz) characteristically adds *Χριστόν*.

σὺ καὶ ὁ οἶκός σου] Cf. xi. 14, *σὺ καὶ πᾶς ὁ οἶκός σου*. Logically these words are to be understood with *πίστευσον* as well as with *σωθήσῃ*.

xvi. 32

θεοῦ] So א* B; א^c A C D 81 byz and the versions have *κυρίου*.

xvi. 33

ἐν ἐκείνῃ τῇ ὥρᾳ] Cf. *αὐτῇ τῇ ὥρᾳ*, *ver.* 18.

ἔλουσεν ἀπὸ τῶν πληγῶν] For this use of *ἀπό* cf. Heb. x. 22, *ῥεραντισμένοι . . . ἀπὸ συνειδήσεως πονηρᾶς*. Deissmann (*BS*, p. 227) illustrates *λούειν ἀπό* from inscriptions about ceremonial ablutions. For *ἔλουσεν* D has *ἔλυσεν*, which does not make sense here (cf. the variants *λύσαντι* and *λούσαντι* in Rev. i. 5, followed by *ἐκ τῶν ἁμαρτιῶν ἡμῶν*).

[1] Theodotion's Gk. version of Daniel has it in *Susanna* 26.

ἐβαπτίσθη αὐτὸς καὶ οἱ αὐτοῦ ἅπαντες] For *οἱ αὐτοῦ ἅπαντες* P[45] has *ὁ οἶκος αὐτοῦ ὅλος*. Cf. *ver.* 15, *ἐβαπτίσθη καὶ ὁ οἶκος αὐτῆς*. The washing and the baptism took place after he brought them out of the prison (*ver.* 30) and before he took them into his house (*ver.* 34), probably at a well in the courtyard. The two acts are compared by Chrysostom (*Hom.* xxxvi. 2), *ἔλουσεν αὐτοὺς καὶ ἐλούθη. ἐκείνους μὲν ἀπὸ τῶν πληγῶν ἔλουσεν, αὐτὸς δὲ ἀπὸ τῶν ἁμαρτιῶν ἐλούθη.*

xvi. 34

ἀναγαγών τε αὐτοὺς εἰς τὸν οἶκον] He did not act illegally in doing this; his responsibility was to produce his prisoners when called upon to do so.

παρέθηκεν τράπεζαν] An old and idiomatic expression (similar phrases occur in Homer, e.g. *Iliad* xxiv. 476; *Odyssey* v. 196; vii. 174 f.; xvii. 333 ff.; and the phrase itself occurs in Herodotus vi. 139). An individual table was placed beside each guest.

πανοικεὶ] Here only in NT; it 'is common in the closing greetings of private letters' (MM). Grammatically it may be taken either with *ἠγαλλιάσατο* or *πεπιστευκώς*, in sense it no doubt goes with both.

πεπιστευκὼς τῷ θεῷ] For *πιστεύω* with dat. cf. xviii. 8 and perhaps v. 14. Here D changes *τῷ θεῷ* to *ἐπὶ τὸν θεόν* (similarly in xviii. 8 it changes the dat. to *εἰς* with the acc.).

(g) Paul and Silas asked to leave Philippi, xvi. 35-40

Ἡμέρας δὲ γενομένης ἀπέστειλαν οἱ στρατηγοὶ τοὺς ῥαβδούχους 35
λέγοντες Ἀπόλυσον τοὺς ἀνθρώπους ἐκείνους. ἀπήγγειλεν δὲ ὁ 36
δεσμοφύλαξ τοὺς λόγους πρὸς τὸν Παῦλον, ὅτι Ἀπέσταλκαν οἱ στρα-
τηγοὶ ἵνα ἀπολυθῆτε· νῦν οὖν ἐξελθόντες πορεύεσθε ἐν εἰρήνῃ. ὁ δὲ 37
Παῦλος ἔφη πρὸς αὐτούς Δείραντες ἡμᾶς δημοσίᾳ ἀκατακρίτους,
ἀνθρώπους Ῥωμαίους ὑπάρχοντας, ἔβαλαν εἰς φυλακήν· καὶ νῦν λάθρᾳ
ἡμᾶς ἐκβάλλουσιν; οὐ γάρ, ἀλλὰ ἐλθόντες αὐτοὶ ἡμᾶς ἐξαγαγέτωσαν.
ἀπήγγειλαν δὲ τοῖς στρατηγοῖς οἱ ῥαβδοῦχοι τὰ ῥήματα ταῦτα· ἐφο- 38
βήθησαν δὲ ἀκούσαντες ὅτι Ῥωμαῖοί εἰσιν, καὶ ἐλθόντες παρεκάλεσαν 39
αὐτούς, καὶ ἐξαγαγόντες ἠρώτων ἀπελθεῖν ἀπὸ τῆς πόλεως. ἐξελ- 40
θόντες δὲ ἀπὸ τῆς φυλακῆς εἰσῆλθον πρὸς τὴν Λυδίαν, καὶ ἰδόντες
παρεκάλεσαν τοὺς ἀδελφοὺς καὶ ἐξῆλθαν.

xvi. 35

Ἡμέρας δὲ γενομένης] δ adds *συνῆλθον οἱ στρατηγοὶ ἐπὶ τὸ αὐτὸ εἰς τὴν ἀγορὰν καὶ ἀναμνησθέντες τὸν σεισμὸν τὸν γεγονότα ἐφοβήθησαν καὶ ἀπέστειλαν τοὺς ῥαβδούχους κ.τ.λ.* The addition may be due to a desire to explain the praetors' apparent change of attitude.

After the excitement died down, they probably considered that Paul and Silas had been taught a sufficient lesson by the stripes and the night in prison. They had exercised the police-right of *coercitio*.

ῥαβδούχους] 'lictors', lit., 'rod-bearers'. They carried the *fasces et secures*, the bundles of rods with axes attached (whence 'fascist'), and attended the higher Roman magistrates, in this case the colonial duumvirs.

xvi. 36

ἀπέσταλκαν] The ending -αν instead of classical -ασιν in the 3rd plural perf. indic. act. appears in papyri from 164 B.C. onwards, and secured a firm hold in the vernacular. Cf. Lk. ix. 36; Jn. xvii. 6 f.; Rom. xvi. 7; Col. ii. 1; Jas. v. 4; Rev. xviii. 3; xix. 3; xxi. 6.

ἐν εἰρήνῃ] εἰς εἰρήνην ℵ; om D g. Ropes regarded it as a 'non-western interpolation'.

xvi. 37

ἀκατακρίτους] Only here and xxii. 25. Ramsay regarded it as the equivalent of Lat. *re incognita*, 'without investigating our case'. It is even possible that in a Roman colony Paul, the Roman citizen, used the Latin phrase. The δ text has ἀναιτίους, 'not guilty'.

ἀνθρώπους Ῥωμαίους ὑπάρχοντας] ὑπάρχοντας Ῥωμαίους ἀνθρώπους P45. Cf. Ἰουδαῖοι ὑπάρχοντες, *ver.* 20; Ῥωμαίοις οὖσιν, *ver.* 21. If Paul had heard these expressions, he must have enjoyed his present opportunity to deflate their self-importance. Why did he not appeal to his Roman citizenship the previous day? In the general excitement it might have been useless. (It has been suggested that he did not wish to avail himself of a means of escape that was not open to Silas, but it seems clear from this verse that Silas was a Roman citizen also.) But Paul was careful to claim his citizen rights when arrested in Jerusalem (xxii. 25), as the flogging on that occasion was to be inflicted not with rods but with the murderous scourge (μάστιξ, Lat. *flagrum*). Even if condemned, a Roman citizen was exempt from flogging. By the Valerian and Porcian Laws (passed at various times between 509 and 195 B.C.), Roman citizens were exempted from all degrading forms of punishment (e.g., beating with rods, scourging, crucifixion), though this exemption was not always observed in practice (cf. Cic. *Verr.* ii. 5. 161 f., where it is related how, in spite of his protest *ciuis Romanus sum*, a Roman citizen was publicly beaten in the market-place of Messina).

ἐκβάλλουσιν] The verb suggests the discourtesy of the act. Contrast ἐξαγαγέτωσαν, ' let them conduct us out '.

xvi. 38

τὰ ῥήματα ταῦτα] D adds τὰ ῥηθέντα πρὸς τοὺς στρατηγούς. This was probably the reading of δ in place of τοῖς στρατηγοῖς τὰ ῥήματα ταῦτα, added to D by conflation with the β text.

xvi. 39

καὶ ἐλθόντες κ.τ.λ.] δ has καὶ παραγενόμενοι μετὰ φίλων πολλῶν εἰς τὴν φυλακὴν παρεκάλεσαν αὐτοὺς ἐξελθεῖν εἰπόντες Ἠγνοήσαμεν τὰ καθ' ὑμᾶς ὅτι ἐστὲ ἄνδρες δίκαιοι. καὶ ἐξαγαγόντες παρεκάλεσαν αὐτοὺς λέγοντες Ἐκ τῆς πόλεως ταύτης ἐξέλθατε μήποτε πάλιν συστραφῶσιν ἡμῖν ἐπικράζοντες καθ' ὑμῶν. This addition may well represent the actual situation. The weakness of municipal governments in the Eastern Empire was always a danger to good order. The responsibility of protecting two unpopular Roman citizens was more than the duumvirs were willing to undertake. But Paul's insistence on an official apology may have helped to protect the converts from persecution.

xvi. 40

ἰδόντες] δ adds τοὺς ἀδελφούς, διηγήσαντο ὅσα ἐποίησεν Κύριος αὐτοῖς παρακαλέσαντες αὐτούς, καὶ ἐξῆλθαν.

Paul refers to his Philippi experiences in 1 Th. ii. 2; 2 Cor. xi. 25. The subsequent history of the Philippian church makes pleasant reading; the same kindness as provided the missionaries with hospitality in the house of Lydia was shown in their twice contributing to Paul's needs when he went on to Thessalonica, and later during his imprisonment (Phil. iv. 10 ff.). Luke was apparently left behind to continue the work in Philippi, where he reappears in xx. 5. His stay in Philippi may sufficiently account for his interest in the place.

2. Thessalonica to Athens, xvii. 1-34

(a) Thessalonica, xvii. 1-4

Διοδεύσαντες δὲ τὴν Ἀμφίπολιν καὶ τὴν Ἀπολλωνίαν ἦλθον εἰς 1
Θεσσαλονίκην, ὅπου ἦν συναγωγὴ τῶν Ἰουδαίων. κατὰ δὲ τὸ 2
εἰωθὸς τῷ Παύλῳ εἰσῆλθεν πρὸς αὐτοὺς καὶ ἐπὶ σάββατα τρία διελέξατο αὐτοῖς ἀπὸ τῶν γραφῶν, διανοίγων καὶ παρατιθέμενος ὅτι τὸν 3
χριστὸν ἔδει παθεῖν καὶ ἀναστῆναι ἐκ νεκρῶν, καὶ ὅτι οὗτός ἐστιν ὁ
χριστός, ὁ Ἰησοῦς ὃν ἐγὼ καταγγέλλω ὑμῖν. καί τινες ἐξ αὐτῶν 4
ἐπείσθησαν καὶ προσεκληρώθησαν τῷ Παύλῳ καὶ τῷ Σίλᾳ, τῶν τε
σεβομένων Ἑλλήνων πλῆθος πολὺ γυναικῶν τε τῶν πρώτων οὐκ
ὀλίγαι.

xvii. 1

Διοδεύσαντες] 'taking the road through'; the road was the Via Egnatia, which ran from Neapolis to Dyrrhachium through Philippi and the three towns mentioned in this verse. Perhaps *διοδεύω* is used here instead of *διέρχομαι* in order to emphasize the *ὁδός*. The highways of Empire became for Paul the highways of the Kingdom of Heaven.

Ἀμφίπολιν] Amphipolis on the Strymon (Struma), about 3 miles from the sea, was an important strategic point between Macedonia and Thrace; in earlier times it figured prominently in the Peloponnesian War and the campaigns of Philip. The power in occupation of Amphipolis controlled the bridgehead on the road to the Dardanelles and Black Sea. Under the Romans it was a free town and capital of the first district of Macedonia (see on xvi. 12). It was about 30 miles W.S.W. of Philippi.

Ἀπολλωνίαν] Apollonia lay between the rivers Strymon and Axios (Vardar), on the Egnatian Way, about 27 miles W.S.W. of Amphipolis and 35 miles east of Thessalonica. The reading of D, *κατῆλθον εἰς Ἀπολλωνίδα κἀκεῖθεν εἰς Θεσσαλονίκην*, implies that they halted at Apollonia.

Θεσσαλονίκην] Thessalonica (Saloniki) was originally called Therme, but was refounded by Cassander about 315 B.C. and called Thessalonica after his wife, a step-sister of Alexander the Great. In Macedonian and Roman times alike it was an important city, and after 146 B.C. was the capital of the province of Macedonia. It was made a free city in 42 B.C. If Amphipolis and Apollonia were the only stages on the way from Philippi to Thessalonica, part of the journey must have been done on horseback (see also on xxi. 15).

xvii. 2

κατὰ δὲ τὸ εἰωθὸς] Cf. xiii. 5, 14; xiv. 1 (*κατὰ τὸ αὐτό*).

ἐπὶ σάββατα τρία] 'for three Sabbaths', or for the space of time covered by three Sabbaths (fifteen days at least). For this use of *ἐπί* cf. xiii. 31; xvi. 18. This is the only certain NT example of the use of *σάββατα* as plural in meaning as well as in form (see on xiii. 14; xx. 7). We are not told what space of time elapsed between his leaving the synagogue and leaving the city.

xvii. 3

διανοίγων] Sc. *τὰς γραφάς* (cf. Lk. xxiv. 32).

παρατιθέμενος] Again sc. *τὰς γραφάς*, 'bringing forward as evidence': cf. Plato, *Politicus*, 275B, *τὸν μῦθον παρεθέμεθα, ἵνα ἐνδείξαιτο κ.τ.λ.*

ὅτι . . . καὶ ὅτι] The first *ὅτι* may be, and the second certainly is, *recitantis*.

τὸν χριστὸν ἔδει παθεῖν καὶ ἀναστῆναι ἐκ νεκρῶν] 'the Messiah had to suffer and rise from the dead'; for the insistence on these two facts as the foundation of the Gospel cf. iii. 18; xxiii. 6 ff.; xxvi. 23; Lk. xxiv. 26, 46; 1 Cor. xv. 3 ff.; 1 Pet. i. 11. The necessity (*ἔδει*) lay in their being the subject of OT prophecy, which must be fulfilled, since it expressed 'the determinate counsel and foreknowledge of God' (ii. 23).

οὗτός ἐστιν ὁ χριστός, ὁ Ἰησοῦς κ.τ.λ.] This conclusion depended on the previous one. Once it is accepted that according to OT prophecy the Messiah must die and rise again, the next stage in the argument is that since Jesus is the only one in whom these things came to pass, He must therefore be the Messiah. To prove that they did come to pass in His case, first-hand evidence is cited, as in 1 Cor. xv. 5 ff. For *ὁ χριστός, ὁ Ἰησοῦς* (the reading of B), A D 81 have *Χριστὸς Ἰησοῦς* (cf. WH mg.), ℵ has *Ἰησοῦς Χριστός*, byz has *ὁ χριστός, Ἰησοῦς*. In any case the meaning is, 'This is the Messiah, this Jesus whom I am proclaiming to you'.

xvii. 4

τινες ἐξ αὐτῶν ἐπείσθησαν] i.e., of the Jews, presumably including Jason (*ver.* 5) and Aristarchus and Secundus (xx. 4).

προσεκληρώθησαν] 'joined', lit., 'were allotted to'.

τῶν τε σεβομένων Ἑλλήνων πλῆθος πολύ] The God-fearing Gentiles who addicted themselves to the synagogue-worship (see on x. 2; cf. xiii. 16, 26, etc.).

γυναικῶν τε τῶν πρώτων οὐκ ὀλίγαι] Either 'many of the chief women' (cf. *ver.* 12) or 'many of the wives of the chief men' (for *οἱ πρῶτοι* thus, cf. xiii. 50). Note the characteristic litotes *οὐκ ὀλίγαι* (cf. *ver.* 12). δ inserts *καί* between *σεβομένων* and *Ἑλλήνων*, thus giving four classes of believers instead of three, including pagan Greeks as well as God-fearers. The whole δ text of the verse is *καί τινες ἐξ αὐτῶν ἐπείσθησαν, καὶ προσεκληρώθησαν τῇ διδαχῇ πολλοὶ τῶν σεβομένων, καὶ Ἑλλήνων πλῆθος πολύ, καὶ γυναῖκες τῶν πρώτων οὐκ ὀλίγαι.*

(b) Trouble in Thessalonica, xvii. 5-9

Ζηλώσαντες δὲ οἱ Ἰουδαῖοι καὶ προσλαβόμενοι τῶν ἀγοραίων 5
ἄνδρας τινὰς πονηροὺς καὶ ὀχλοποιήσαντες ἐθορύβουν τὴν πόλιν, καὶ
ἐπιστάντες τῇ οἰκίᾳ Ἰάσονος ἐζήτουν αὐτοὺς προαγαγεῖν εἰς τὸν δῆμον·
μὴ εὑρόντες δὲ αὐτοὺς ἔσυρον Ἰάσονα καί τινας ἀδελφοὺς ἐπὶ τοὺς 6
πολιτάρχας, βοῶντες ὅτι Οἱ τὴν οἰκουμένην ἀναστατώσαντες οὗτοι
καὶ ἐνθάδε πάρεισιν, οὓς ὑποδέδεκται Ἰάσων· καὶ οὗτοι πάντες 7

ἀπέναντι τῶν δογμάτων Καίσαρος πράσσουσι, βασιλέα ἕτερον λέγοντες
εἶναι Ἰησοῦν. ἐτάραξαν δὲ τὸν ὄχλον καὶ τοὺς πολιτάρχας ἀκούοντας 8
ταῦτα, καὶ λαβόντες τὸ ἱκανὸν παρὰ τοῦ Ἰάσονος καὶ τῶν λοιπῶν 9
ἀπέλυσαν αὐτούς.

xvii. 5

Ζηλώσαντες δὲ οἱ Ἰουδαῖοι] The envy of the Jews was aroused, as elsewhere (cf. xiii. 45), at the offer of salvation to the Gentiles. Besides, they probably regarded the God-fearers as half-Jews already, so that in preaching to them Paul was poaching on their preserves. For the hostility of the Thessalonian Jews cf. 1 Th. ii. 14 ff.

ἀγοραίων] 'loafers', 'gangsters', lit., frequenters of the Agora or market-place. For this sense we may compare Plato, *Protagoras* 347C (τῶν φαύλων καὶ ἀγοραίων ἀνθρώπων); Xenophon, *Hellenica* vi. 2. 23 (τὸν ἀγοραῖον . . . ὄχλον); Plutarch, *Aemilius Paullus* 38 (ἀνθρώπους ἀγεννεῖς καὶ δεδουλευκότας, ἀγοραίους δὲ καὶ δυναμένους ὄχλον συναγαγεῖν). In view of the last passage Lake understands the word here of 'agitators', not of 'loafers' (*EEP*, p. 69 *n*.). The two senses are by no means mutually exclusive. See further on σπερμολόγος, *ver*. 18. The sense of ἀγοραῖοι in xix. 38 is quite different.

ὀχλοποιήσαντες] Cf. ὄχλον συναγαγεῖν in the quotation from Plutarch in the previous note. This is the only known example of ὀχλοποιέω. (For compounds in -ποιέω see on ἐμοσχοποίησαν, vii. 41.) ὀχλοποίησις is quoted by Hesychius as equivalent to δημαγωγία.

Ἰάσονα] Jason was a common name in Greece, after the Thessalian hero who led the Argonauts in quest of the Golden Fleece. The Jason of this chapter was probably a Jew. It was customary for Jews to adopt Gentile names with some resemblance to their Hebrew ones; thus Jason corresponds to Joshua, Menelaus to Menahem, and so on. Cf. also i. 23; xii. 12; xiii. 9 for Jewish double names.

εἰς τὸν δῆμον] As Thessalonica was a free city, its citizen-body (δῆμος) discharged legislative and juridical functions. As at Pisidian Antioch, Iconium and Lystra, it is Jews who try to stir up the Gentile authorities against the missionaries. Roman Law depended on voluntary prosecutors (*delatores*) to set it in motion.

xvii. 6

πολιτάρχας] The title πολιτάρχης or πολίταρχος is found in some nineteen inscriptions from the second century B.C. to the third century A.D., being used in the majority of these for magistrates in Macedonian cities. Five of these inscriptions refer to Thessalonica itself, which had five or six politarchs (five under Augustus, six under the Antonines). Cf. E. D. Burton in *AJT* ii (1898), pp. 598 ff.

ὅτι] *recitantis.*

ἀναστατώσαντες] For this verb, meaning 'to stir up sedition', 'upset', cf. xxi. 38; Gal. v. 12. It is not a literary word, but is found in papyri, especially in the famous letter from the bad boy Theon to his father (*P. Oxy.* i. 119. 10, second-third century A.D.), where he quotes his harassed mother as saying ἀναστατοῖ με· ἆρρον αὐτόν ('he upsets me; away with him!').

xvii. 7

ὑποδέδεκται] Classical in this sense, of receiving into one's house.

καὶ οὗτοι πάντες κ.τ.λ.] For a summary of Paul's teaching at Thessalonica cf. 1 Th. i. 9 f. It is clear from 1 and 2 Th. that it contained a prominent eschatological emphasis, which may have lent colour to the accusation.

ἀπέναντι] 'against'. In iii. 16; Mt. xxvii. 24; Rom. iii. 18 it means 'in the presence of', 'before'; in Mt. xxvii. 61; Mk. xii. 41 it means 'over against'.

δογμάτων] 'decrees': see on xvi. 4.

βασιλέα ἕτερον] The Roman Emperor was styled βασιλεύς in the east; when this word is used of him in NT it should be rendered 'emperor'. So here, 'another emperor'. The charge was very subtle; even an unfounded suspicion of this nature was enough to ruin many a man. In this case there was just enough truth in the charge to make it plausible. Cf. the charge brought against our Lord before Pilate, Lk. xxiii. 2; Jn. xix. 12.

xvii. 9

λαβόντες τὸ ἱκανὸν] 'taking security'; λαμβάνειν τὸ ἱκανόν is a Latinism, the equivalent of the legal phrase *satis accipere*, which vet. lat. and vg. have here. (The correlative was *satis dare*, 'to go bail'.) Cf. Mk. xv. 15, τὸ ἱκανὸν ποιῆσαι (*satis facere*), which occurs as early as Polybius. The nature of the security may be inferred from references in 1 and 2 Th. Ramsay (*SPT*, p. 231) suggests that Jason and the others were bound over to send Paul, the alleged cause of the disturbance, away from the city and prevent his return, and that this policy, while it lasted (it probably lapsed when these politarchs demitted office), is the hindrance referred to in 1 Th. ii. 18 (ἐνέκοψεν ἡμᾶς ὁ Σατανᾶς). Paul might well discern Satanic opposition behind the politarchs' decision, though they would no doubt regard it as mild, yet effective. We gather from 1 Th. ii. 13 f., iii. 3, that the Jews continued to organize persecution against the Thessalonian believers; perhaps those who 'fell asleep' so soon (1 Th. iv. 13) were victims of this persecution. The church in Thessalonica became a centre of evangelization (1 Th. i. 8). It included not only Jewish believers and 'God-fearers', but former idolaters (1 Th. i. 9). While in Thessalonica, Paul and his companions had supported themselves by their own work (1 Th. ii. 9; cf. xviii. 3; xx. 34).

(c) Beroea, xvii. 10-15

Οἱ δὲ ἀδελφοὶ εὐθέως διὰ νυκτὸς ἐξέπεμψαν τόν τε Παῦλον καὶ 10
τὸν Σίλαν εἰς Βέροιαν, οἵτινες παραγενόμενοι εἰς τὴν συναγωγὴν τῶν
Ἰουδαίων ἀπῄεσαν· οὗτοι δὲ ἦσαν εὐγενέστεροι τῶν ἐν Θεσσαλονίκῃ, 11
οἵτινες ἐδέξαντο τὸν λόγον μετὰ πάσης προθυμίας, τὸ καθ᾽ ἡμέραν
ἀνακρίνοντες τὰς γραφὰς εἰ ἔχοι ταῦτα οὕτως. πολλοὶ μὲν οὖν ἐξ 12
αὐτῶν ἐπίστευσαν, καὶ τῶν Ἑλληνίδων γυναικῶν τῶν εὐσχημόνων καὶ
ἀνδρῶν οὐκ ὀλίγοι. Ὡς δὲ ἔγνωσαν οἱ ἀπὸ τῆς Θεσσαλονίκης Ἰουδαῖοι 13
ὅτι καὶ ἐν τῇ Βεροίᾳ κατηγγέλη ὑπὸ τοῦ Παύλου ὁ λόγος τοῦ θεοῦ,
ἦλθον κἀκεῖ σαλεύοντες καὶ ταράσσοντες τοὺς ὄχλους. εὐθέως δὲ 14
τότε τὸν Παῦλον ἐξαπέστειλαν οἱ ἀδελφοὶ πορεύεσθαι ἕως ἐπὶ τὴν
θάλασσαν· ὑπέμεινάν τε ὅ τε Σίλας καὶ ὁ Τιμόθεος ἐκεῖ. οἱ δὲ καθισ- 15
τάνοντες τὸν Παῦλον ἤγαγον ἕως Ἀθηνῶν, καὶ λαβόντες ἐντολὴν
πρὸς τὸν Σίλαν καὶ τὸν Τιμόθεον ἵνα ὡς τάχιστα ἔλθωσιν πρὸς αὐτὸν
ἐξῄεσαν.

xvii. 10

τόν τε Παῦλον καὶ τὸν Σίλαν] Probably Timothy too, as he appears at Beroea in *ver.* 14, unless he left Philippi later and rejoined them at Beroea.

Βέροιαν] Beroea (mod. Verria) is about 60 miles west of Thessalonica, south of the Egnatian Way (whence Cicero, *In Pisonem*, xxxvi. 89, calls it *oppidum deuium*, 'an out-of-the-way town'). It was the first city to surrender to the Romans after the battle of Pydna, 168 B.C.

ἀπῄεσαν] om P^{45}. The prefix *ἀπό* is practically otiose here; LC render 'went their way'.

xvii. 11

εὐγενέστεροι] Although *εὐγενής* originally refers to nobility of birth, it came to denote those qualities which were expected in people so born, in the same way as Eng. 'noble'. Moffatt renders 'more amenable'; LC (better) 'more generous', and quote Cicero's '*εὐγενέστερος est etiam quam pater*' (*Att.* xiii. 21a. 4). It is the equivalent of Lat. *generosus*, 'noble', 'liberal', 'free from prejudice'.

οἵτινες] 'for they'.

τὸ καθ' ἡμέραν] B byz; καθ' ἡμέραν ℵ A D P^{45} al.

ἔχοι] The classical use of the optative replacing the indic. in an indirect question in historic sequence: see on xxi. 33.

οὕτως] δ (represented by 383 614 g vg.codd. hcl* Eph Priscill) adds καθὼς Παῦλος ἀπαγγέλλει. The example of these Beroean Jews has been admired and profitably followed by many, and perhaps the majority of people who know the name of Beroea to-day know it only because it was the place where these 'more noble' Jews lived.

xvii. 12

πολλοὶ] Including Sopater son of Pyrrhus (cf. xx. 4). δ has τινες.

ἐπίστευσαν] δ adds τινὲς δὲ ἠπίστησαν (cf. xxviii. 24).

γυναικῶν τῶν εὐσχημόνων] 'of the well-to-do women' (cf. xiii. 50). Cf. *ver.* 4, γυναικῶν . . . τῶν πρώτων. P^{45} has καὶ before τῶν.

οὐκ ὀλίγοι] Cf. *ver.* 4, οὐκ ὀλίγαι. For τῶν Ἑλληνίδων . . . οὐκ ὀλίγοι the δ text has τῶν Ἑλλήνων καὶ τῶν εὐσχημόνων ἄνδρες καὶ γυναῖκες ἱκανοὶ ἐπίστευσαν. For this text's reversal of the order of men and women or toning down of any prominence given to women, cf. *ver.* 34; xviii. 26. It is not clear whether these Greeks were 'God-fearers' or pagans.

xvii. 13

οἱ ἀπὸ τῆς Θεσσαλονικης Ἰουδαῖοι] 'The Jews of Thessalonica'; for this use of ἀπό cf. τῶν ἀπὸ Ἰόππης, x. 23; οἱ ἀπὸ τῆς Ἰταλίας, Heb. xiii. 24.

καὶ ταράσσοντες τοὺς ὄχλους] δ adds οὐ διελίμπανον (this verb occurs also in the δ text of viii. 24, *q.v.*). P^{45} omits καὶ ταράσσοντες. The Thessalonian Jews play in Beroea the same part as the Jews of Pisidian Antioch and Iconium played in Lystra (xiv. 19); they come from the place last visited by Paul to foment opposition to him in the place he visits next.

xvii. 14

ἕως ἐπὶ τὴν θάλασσαν] The use of ἕως with another preposition occurs elsewhere in Luke: cf. xxi. 5; xxvi. 11; Lk. xxiv. 50. D omits ἕως, byz replaces it by ὡς (see below).

ὑπέμεινάν τε ὅ τε Σίλας καὶ ὁ Τιμόθεος ἐκεῖ] With the movements of Paul and his companions from this point onwards we must compare the information in 1 Th. iii. 1 ff. The following reconstruction of the sequence of events is taken chiefly from Lake, *EEP*, p. 74.

1. Paul leaves Silas and Timothy in Beroea, and goes to Athens, whence he sends them a message to rejoin him at once (xvii. 14 f.).
2. They rejoin him in Athens (cf. 1 Th. iii. 1).
3. He sends Timothy to Thessalonica (1 Th. iii. 1 f.) and Silas elsewhere in Macedonia (cf. xviii. 5), probably to Philippi, Ramsay suggests (*SPT*, p. 240).
4. He goes on to Corinth (xviii. 1).
5. Silas and Timothy return from Macedonia to Corinth (xviii. 5 ; cf. 1 Th. iii. 6).
6. From Corinth he writes the two epistles to the Thessalonians.

xvii. 14f.

These two verses are recast in the δ text as follows : *τὸν μὲν οὖν Παῦλον οἱ ἀδελφοὶ ἐξαπέστειλαν ἀπελθεῖν ἐπὶ τὴν θάλασσαν· ὑπέμεινεν δὲ ὁ Σίλας καὶ ὁ Τιμόθεος ἐκεῖ. οἱ δὲ καταστάνοντες τὸν Παῦλον ἤγαγον ἕως Ἀθηνῶν, παρῆλθεν δὲ τὴν Θεσσαλίαν, ἐκωλύθη γὰρ εἰς αὐτοὺς κηρύξαι τὸν λόγον, λαβόντες δὲ ἐντολὴν παρὰ Παύλου πρὸς τὸν Σίλαν καὶ Τιμόθεον ὅπως ἐν τάχει ἔλθωσιν πρὸς αὐτὸν ἐξῄεσαν.* The β text might mean that Paul went to Athens by sea, sailing from Methone or Dium. But Luke usually mentions the port of embarkation, and if we prefer the reading of byz (*ὡς ἐπὶ τὴν θάλασσαν*), we may conclude that the brethren made as if to conduct Paul to the sea, but actually took him overland by Thessaly and did not leave him until they arrived at Athens. This seems to have been the inference of the δ editor,[1] who, as usual, makes his inference explicit (but the omission in D S g sah of either *ἕως* or *ὡς* before *ἐπί* in *ver.* 14 might suggest that he regarded the sea as the sea at Athens, in which case *ver.* 15 would simply recapitulate *ver.* 14). The addition *παρῆλθεν . . . λόγον* is modelled on xvi. 6 ff., even to the peculiar use of the verb *παρέρχομαι* (see on xvi. 8).

xvii. 15

καθιστάνοντες] A B ; *καταστάνοντες* D P^{45} ; *καθιστῶντες* byz. For the classical use of *καθίστημι* meaning ' conduct ' cf. Thuc. iv. 78.6, *οἱ δὲ Περαιβοὶ αὐτὸν . . . κατέστησαν ἐς Δῖον.*

ὡς τάχιστα] Literary ; contrast *ἐν τάχει* of D. This is the only NT occurrence of *τάχιστα*.

(d) Paul waits for his Companions in Athens, xvii. 16-21

Ἐν δὲ ταῖς Ἀθήναις ἐκδεχομένου αὐτοὺς τοῦ Παύλου, παρωξύνετο 16
τὸ πνεῦμα αὐτοῦ ἐν αὐτῷ θεωροῦντος κατείδωλον οὖσαν τὴν πόλιν.

[1] Unless Ropes is right in supposing the δ-text to be based on a corrupt reading *Θεσσαλίαν* for *θάλασσαν* in *ver.* 14 (Ephrem has ' Thessalonica ').

διελέγετο μὲν οὖν ἐν τῇ συναγωγῇ τοῖς Ἰουδαίοις καὶ τοῖς σεβομένοις 17
καὶ ἐν τῇ ἀγορᾷ κατὰ πᾶσαν ἡμέραν πρὸς τοὺς παρατυγχάνοντας.
τινὲς δὲ καὶ τῶν Ἐπικουρίων καὶ Στωικῶν φιλοσόφων συνέβαλλον 18
αὐτῷ, καί τινες ἔλεγον Τί ἂν θέλοι ὁ σπερμολόγος οὗτος λέγειν; οἱ
δέ Ξένων δαιμονίων δοκεῖ καταγγελεὺς εἶναι· ὅτι τὸν Ἰησοῦν καὶ
τὴν ἀνάστασιν εὐηγγελίζετο. ἐπιλαβόμενοι δὲ αὐτοῦ ἐπὶ τὸν Ἄρειον 19
Πάγον ἤγαγον, λέγοντες Δυνάμεθα γνῶναι τίς ἡ καινὴ αὕτη ἡ ὑπὸ
σοῦ λαλουμένη διδαχή; ξενίζοντα γάρ τινα εἰσφέρεις εἰς τὰς ἀκοὰς 20
ἡμῶν· βουλόμεθα οὖν γνῶναι τίνα θέλει ταῦτα εἶναι. Ἀθηναῖοι 21
δὲ πάντες καὶ οἱ ἐπιδημοῦντες ξένοι εἰς οὐδὲν ἕτερον ηὐκαίρουν ἢ
λέγειν τι ἢ ἀκούειν τι καινότερον.

xvii. 16

Ἀθήναις] 'Athens, the eye of Greece, Mother of Arts
And Eloquence, native to famous wits
Or hospitable, in her sweet recess,
City or Suburban, studious walks and shades'—

Athens, the cradle of democracy, attained the foremost place among the Greek city-states early in the fifth century B.C. by reason of the lead she took in resisting the Persian invasions. She was at the height of her power between 478 and 431 B.C., and after her defeat by Sparta in the Peloponnesian War (431-404 B.C.), was not long in regaining much of her earlier influence. In the fourth century she again took the lead in resistance to Philip's aggression, and after his victory at Chaeronea (338 B.C.) was generously treated by him and allowed to retain much of her ancient freedom, which she enjoyed until the Roman conquest of Greece in 146 B.C. The Romans, too, in consideration of her glorious past, left her to carry on her own institutions as a free and allied city within the Empire (*ciuitas libera et foederata*). The sculpture, literature and oratory of Athens in the fifth and fourth centuries B.C. have never been surpassed; in philosophy, too, she took the leading place, being the native city of Socrates and Plato, and the adopted home of Aristotle, Epicurus and Zeno. Her cultural influence in the Greek world is also seen in the fact that it was the Attic dialect of Gk., spoken at first over a very restricted area as compared with Ionic and Doric, which formed the base of the later Koiné. At this time the city was the seat of a famous university (see end of note on Tarsus, ix. 30).

παρωξύνετο] A strong word; cf. the cognate noun in xv. 39. Moffatt renders it 'irritated'; LC 'enraged'. The beauty of the sculpture of Pheidias apparently made no appeal to one brought up in the spirit of the Second Commandment, and could not move him from his fundamental attitude to idolatry, for which cf. Rom.

i. 23 ff.; 1 Cor. x. 20 (ἃ θύουσιν τὰ ἔθνη δαιμονίοις καὶ οὐ θεῷ θύουσιν). Cf. Wisd. xiii. 2-6.

κατείδωλον] 'full of images'; the word is not found elsewhere, but is regularly formed: cf. κατάδενδρος, 'full of trees' (Diod. xvii. 68.5, etc.).

xvii. 17

ἐν τῇ συναγωγῇ] According to his custom (cf. *ver.* 2).

ἐν τῇ ἀγορᾷ] We should observe how subtly and accurately the *ethos* of each city is suggested. Here Paul adapts himself to the Athenian atmosphere. 'In Ephesus Paul taught "in the school of Tyrannus"; in the city of Socrates he discussed moral questions in the market-place. How incongruous it would seem if the methods were transposed!' (Ramsay, *SPT*, p. 238). The Agora lay west of the Acropolis, and S.W. of the Areopagus.

xvii. 18

'Επικουρίων] The Epicureans took their name from Epicurus (341-270 B.C.), whose ethical system, founded on the atomic theory of Democritus, presented pleasure (ἡδονή) as the chief end of life, the pleasure most worth having being a life of tranquillity (ἀταραξία), free from pain, disturbing passions, and superstitious fears. It conceived of the gods as material in essence, existing in eternal calm in intermundane spaces, and having nothing to do with the life of men. The best known exposition of Epicureanism is the *De Rerum Natura* of Lucretius. In Athens the Epicureans frequented the garden of Epicurus.

Στωικῶν] The Stoics regarded Zeno (340-265 B.C.) as their founder, and took their name from the *Stoa Poikile* in Athens, where he taught. Their system aimed at living consistently (ὁμολογουμένως) or according to nature (κατὰ φύσιν). The highest expression of nature was reason or design (λόγος), the principle which combined the elements in various ways so as to produce the universe. God was to the world as the individual soul to the body. The Stoic conception of God as the World-soul was thus thoroughly pantheistic, and their philosophy was no less materialist than the Epicureans', for the World-soul and the individual soul were thought to consist of refined matter. In practice the Stoics laid great emphasis on the supremacy of the rational over the emotional faculty in man, and on individual self-sufficiency. They regarded it as proper to commit suicide when life could no longer be supported with dignity. While Stoicism was at its best marked by great moral earnestness and a high sense of duty, it was coupled with a spiritual pride quite foreign to the spirit of Christianity. Notable Stoics in Roman times were Seneca, Epictetus, and Marcus Aurelius.

σπερμολόγος] This 'word of characteristically Athenian slang' (Ramsay) literally means 'seed-picker', and as such might be used of a gutter-sparrow; then it was used of one who picked up scraps in the market, a worthless character (with a meaning not unlike that of ἀγοραῖος in *ver.* 5; Demosthenes, *De Corona*, 127, calls Aeschines σπερμολόγος, περίτριμμα ἀγορᾶς); and then of one who picked up scraps of learning here and there, which is its meaning here.

ξένων δαιμονίων] 'strange divinities' (in the Greek sense): cf. the accusations brought against Protagoras, Anaxagoras, and Socrates (φησὶ γάρ με ποιητὴν εἶναι θεῶν, καὶ ὡς καινοὺς ποιοῦντα θεούς, τοὺς δ' ἀρχαίους οὐ νομίζοντα, Plato, *Euthyphro* 3B; Σωκράτη φησὶν ἀδικεῖν . . . θεοὺς οὓς ἡ πόλις νομίζει οὐ νομίζοντα, ἕτερα δὲ δαιμόνια καινά, Plato, *Apology* 24B-C).

καταγγελεὺς] 'herald'; found in *OGIS* 456. 10 (καταγγελεῖς τῶν πρώτων ἀ(χ)θησο[μένων ἀγώνων]), in a Mytilenean decree in honour of Augustus.

ἀνάστασιν] Chase (*Credibility*, pp. 205 f.) suggests that if they connected Ἰησοῦς with ἴασις ('healing': cf. the play on words in ix. 34), or with Ἰησώ ('the Healer'), ἀνάστασις might remind them of ἀναστατήρια, a word quoted by Hesychius as meaning sacrifices offered on recovery from sickness. Another suggestion is that they thought Anastasis was a goddess. With this personification of an abstract noun Salomon Reinach (*Orpheus*, p. 420) compares the Virgin's announcement to Bernadette Soubirous at Lourdes, 'I am the Immaculate Conception'.

xvii. 19

ἐπὶ τὸν Ἄρειον πάγον] Short for ἐπὶ τὴν ἐν Ἀρείῳ πάγῳ βουλήν. (Cf. Seneca *De Tranquillitate* 5, '*in qua ciuitate erat Areos pagos, religiosissimum iudicium*'.) The Council of the Areopagus, so called because it met in early times on the Areopagus or Hill of Ares, west of the Acropolis, was the most venerable Athenian court, dating from legendary times. Its traditional power was curtailed as Athens became more democratic, but it retained jurisdiction over homicide and moral questions generally, and commanded great respect because of its antiquity. Under the Romans it increased its prestige. It had supreme authority in religious matters and seems also to have had the power at this time to appoint public lecturers and exercise some control over them in the interest of public order. Cf. Ramsay, *SPT*, pp. 245 ff.; *BRD*, pp. 102 ff.

δυνάμεθα] 'may we?' Attic would prefer ἔξεστιν;

xvii. 20

τίνα θέλει ταῦτα εἶναι] Cf. ii. 12, τί θέλει τοῦτο εἶναι;

xvii. 21

Ἀθηναῖοι δὲ πάντες κ.τ.λ.] This description of the Athenian populace is amply corroborated in ancient literature. Cf. Cleon's description in Thuc. iii. 38.5 (*καὶ μετὰ καινότητος μὲν λόγου ἀπατᾶσθαι ἄριστοι*) and that of Demosthenes in *Phil.* i. 10 (*ἢ βούλεσθε, εἰπέ μοι, περιϊόντες αὐτῶν πυνθάνεσθαι, λέγεταί τι καινόν;*).

Ἀθηναῖοι . . . πάντες] The absence of the article is classical; cf. xxvi. 4, *πάντες Ἰουδαῖοι.*

καινότερον] The comparative in classical Gk. can often be rendered by the positive degree in Eng. We have papyrus parallels for *τι καινότερον.* Ed. Norden describes this characterization of the Athenians as the most Attic thing in NT (*Agnostos Theos*, p. 333).

(e) Paul before the Areopagus, xvii. 22-34

σταθεὶς δὲ Παῦλος ἐν μέσῳ τοῦ Ἀρείου Πάγου ἔφη Ἄνδρες Ἀθη- 22
ναῖοι, κατὰ πάντα ὡς δεισιδαιμονεστέρους ὑμᾶς θεωρῶ· διερχόμενος 23
γὰρ καὶ ἀναθεωρῶν τὰ σεβάσματα ὑμῶν εὗρον καὶ βωμὸν ἐν ᾧ ἐπεγέ-
γραπτο ΑΓΝΩΣΤΩ ΘΕΩ. ὃ οὖν ἀγνοοῦντες εὐσεβεῖτε, τοῦτο ἐγὼ
καταγγέλλω ὑμῖν. ὁ θεὸς ὁ ποιήσας τὸν κόσμον καὶ πάντα τὰ ἐν 24
αὐτῷ, οὗτος οὐρανοῦ καὶ γῆς ὑπάρχων κύριος οὐκ ἐν χειροποιήτοις
ναοῖς κατοικεῖ οὐδὲ ὑπὸ χειρῶν ἀνθρωπίνων θεραπεύεται προσδεόμενός 25
τινος, αὐτὸς διδοὺς πᾶσι ζωὴν καὶ πνοὴν καὶ τὰ πάντα· ἐποίησέν τε 26
ἐξ ἑνὸς πᾶν ἔθνος ἀνθρώπων κατοικεῖν ἐπὶ παντὸς προσώπου τῆς γῆς,
ὁρίσας προστεταγμένους καιροὺς καὶ τὰς ὁροθεσίας τῆς κατοικίας
αὐτῶν, ζητεῖν τὸν θεὸν εἰ ἄρα γε ψηλαφήσειαν αὐτὸν καὶ εὕροιεν, καί 27
γε οὐ μακρὰν ἀπὸ ἑνὸς ἑκάστου ἡμῶν ὑπάρχοντα. ἐν αὐτῷ γὰρ ζῶμεν 28
καὶ κινούμεθα καὶ ἐσμέν, ὡς καί τινες τῶν καθ' ὑμᾶς ποιητῶν
εἰρήκασιν

Τοῦ γὰρ καὶ γένος ἐσμέν.

γένος οὖν ὑπάρχοντες τοῦ θεοῦ οὐκ ὀφείλομεν νομίζειν χρυσῷ ἢ 29
ἀργύρῳ ἢ λίθῳ, χαράγματι τέχνης καὶ ἐνθυμήσεως ἀνθρώπου, τὸ
θεῖον εἶναι ὅμοιον. τοὺς μὲν οὖν χρόνους τῆς ἀγνοίας ὑπεριδὼν ὁ 30
θεὸς τὰ νῦν ἀπαγγέλλει τοῖς ἀνθρώποις πάντας πανταχοῦ μετανοεῖν,
καθότι ἔστησεν ἡμέραν ἐν ᾗ μέλλει κρίνειν τὴν οἰκουμένην ἐν δικαιο- 31
σύνῃ ἐν ἀνδρὶ ᾧ ὥρισεν, πίστιν παρασχὼν πᾶσιν ἀναστήσας αὐτὸν
ἐκ νεκρῶν. ἀκούσαντες δὲ ἀνάστασιν νεκρῶν οἱ μὲν ἐχλεύαζον οἱ 32
δὲ εἶπαν Ἀκουσόμεθά σου περὶ τούτου καὶ πάλιν. οὕτως ὁ Παῦλος 33
ἐξῆλθεν ἐκ μέσου αὐτῶν· τινὲς δὲ ἄνδρες κολληθέντες αὐτῷ ἐπίστευσαν, 34
ἐν οἷς καὶ Διονύσιος ὁ Ἀρεοπαγίτης καὶ γυνὴ ὀνόματι Δάμαρις καὶ
ἕτεροι σὺν αὐτοῖς.

Paul's speech before the Areopagus is just such a speech as we might expect from so versatile a preacher in attempting to influence his philosophic Athenian audience. With his appeal to God's natural revelation we may compare the protest at Lystra (xiv. 15 ff.) and also the argument of Rom. ii. 14-16. As a background to the speech Eduard Norden's *Agnostos Theos* (1913) ought by all means to be studied; and it should be known that the historian, Ed. Meyer, converted him to an admission of the possible genuineness of the speech from the negative view of its authenticity taken in *Agnostos Theos* (*Ursprung und Anfänge des Christentums*, iii, p. 92).[1]

xvii. 22

ἐν μέσῳ τοῦ Ἀρείου Πάγου] 'in the midst of the Council of the Areopagus': see on *ver.* 19, and cf. *ver.* 33, *ἐξῆλθεν ἐκ μέσου αὐτῶν*. In the first century A.D. the Council met in the Agora, before the *Stoa Basileios*.

δεισιδαιμονεστέρους] The context must decide whether this word is used in its better or worse sense. It was, in fact, as vague as 'religious' in Eng., and here we may best translate 'very religious'. But AV 'superstitious' is not entirely wrong; to Paul their religion was mostly superstition, as it also was, though on other grounds, to the Epicureans. We should not lay too much stress on the likelihood of Paul's commencing his talk with a compliment; according to Lucian (*de gymn.* 19) complimentary exordia to secure the goodwill of the Areopagus were forbidden. See on *δεισιδαιμονίας*, xxv. 19. The religious nature of the Athenians is mentioned by several writers, e.g., Sophocles *O.C.* 260 (*τάς γ' Ἀθήνας φασὶ θεοσεβεστάτας εἶναι*); Pausanias i. 17. 1 (*Ἀθηναῖοι . . . θεοὺς εὐσεβοῦσιν ἄλλων πλέον*); Jos. *Ap.* ii. 11 (*τοὺς δὲ εὐσεβεστάτους τῶν Ἑλλήνων*); cf. also Strabo ix. 1. 16; Livy xlv. 27.

xvii. 23

σεβάσματα] 'objects of worship', here of images, as in Wisd. xiv. 20; xv. 17. In 2 Th. ii. 4 *σέβασμα* is used in a wider sense.

ἀγνώστῳ θεῷ] Pausanias (i. 1. 4) says that in Athens there are *βωμοὶ θεῶν ὀνομαζομένων ἀγνώστων*. According to Diogenes Laertius (*Lives of Philosophers*, i. 110) the Athenians during a pestilence sent for Epimenides the Cretan (see on *ver.* 28), who advised them

[1] An important monograph on the speech is M. Dibelius's *Paulus auf dem Areopag* (Heidelberg, 1939). He concludes that the speech was composed by Luke as a suitable discourse for the occasion on the true knowledge of God; the speaker could not have been the Paul whom we know from the Epistles, but rather the forerunner of the Apologists. Meyer's arguments against Norden would be valid also against Dibelius: 'How anyone could have explained this scene as an invention', says Meyer (p. 105), 'is one of the things that have always remained incomprehensible to me'. See also the monograph by N. B. Stonehouse, *The Areopagus Address* (London, 1949).

to sacrifice sheep at various spots τῷ προσήκοντι θεῷ, and to commemorate the occasion altars to unnamed gods (βωμοὶ ἀνώνυμοι) were set up.[1] Philostratus says (*Vit. Apoll. Tyan.* vi. 3. 5) that such altars were common at Athens (καὶ ταῦτα Ἀθήνῃσιν, οὗ καὶ ἀγνώστων δαιμόνων βωμοὶ ἵδρυνται).[2] Jerome (Comm. on Tit. i. 12) and Didymus of Alexandria (on 2 Cor. x. 5) no doubt had such testimonies in mind when they said that Paul changed 'Gods' into 'God'. But there is no reason why there should not have been an altar dedicated exactly as Paul describes.

ὃ . . . τοῦτο] Note the neuter (cf. τὸ θεῖον, *ver.* 29); Paul starts with his hearers' belief in an impersonal divine essence, pantheistically conceived, and leads them to the Living God revealed as Creator and Judge.

ἀγνοοῦντες] Catching up ἀγνώστῳ.

καταγγέλλω] Cf. καταγγελεύς, *ver.* 18.

xvii. 24

ὁ θεὸς ὁ ποιήσας τὸν κόσμον κ.τ.λ.] As at Lystra, Paul begins with the revelation of God in creation (cf. Rom. i. 19 ff.). Cf. Plato, *Timaeus* 28 C, τὸν μὲν οὖν ποιητὴν καὶ πατέρα τοῦδε τοῦ παντὸς εὑρεῖν τε ἔργον καὶ εὑρόντα εἰς πάντας ἀδύνατον λέγειν. See on xiv. 15 ff., and, for the phraseology, iv. 24, with OT parallels mentioned *ad loc.*

χειροποιήτοις] Cf. vii. 48 both for the word and for the thought. Cf. also Euripides, *frag.* 968,

ποῖος δ' ἂν οἶκος τεκτόνων πλασθεὶς ὕπο
δέμας τὸ θεῖον περιβάλοι τοίχων πτυχαῖς;

xvii. 25

οὐδὲ ὑπὸ χειρῶν ἀνθρωπίνων θεραπεύεται κ.τ.λ.] Here are combined the Epicurean doctrine that God needs nothing from men and cannot be served by them, and the Stoic belief that He is the source of all life (see on *ver.* 28). Paul consistently endeavours to have as much common ground as possible with his audience.

ζωὴν καὶ πνοήν] Intentional assonance. The attention paid to style in this speech is marked, as one might expect under the circumstances. For διδοὺς . . . πνοήν cf. Isa. xlii. 5.

xvii. 26

ἐξ ἑνὸς] 'from one man' (i.e., Adam). The Athenians prided themselves on being αὐτόχθονες, sprung from the soil of their native Attica (a claim which simply means that they belonged to the earliest

[1] Cf. Plato, *Laws,* i. 642d; Aristotle, *Ath. Pol.* init.; Plutarch, *Solon,* 12.

[2] Deissmann (*Paul,* pp. 287 ff.) quotes a votive inscription of the second century A.D. from an altar at Pergamum, θεοῖς ἀγν[ώστοις] Καπίτω[ν] δᾳδοῦχο[ς].

wave of Greek immigration into the land, so early that, unlike the later arrivals, the Achaeans and Dorians, they had lost all memory of their immigration). So the Greeks in general considered themselves superior to non-Greeks, whom they called barbarians. Against such claims to racial superiority Paul asserts the unity of all men. The unity of the human race as descended from Adam is fundamental in Paul's theology (cf. Rom. v. 12 ff.). This primal unity, impaired by sin, is restored by redemption (Gal. iii. 28; Col. iii. 11). δ byz add *αἵματος* after *ἑνός*.

ἐπὶ παντὸς προσώπου] This speech is notable for alliteration, especially with *π*, and for the accumulated occurrences of *πᾶς*, often in connection with alliteration. Cf. Lk. xxi. 35 (*ἐπὶ πρόσωπον πάσης τῆς γῆς*); Gen. ii. 6; xi. 8; Jer. xxv. 26 (LXX xxxii. 12), *ἐπὶ προσώπου τῆς γῆς*.

ὁρίσας] Aorist, because earlier than *ἐποίησεν*: 'the determination of man's home *preceded* his creation, in the Divine plan' (J. H. Moulton, *Proleg.*, p. 133).

προστεταγμένους καιροὺς] Cf. *καιροὺς καρποφόρους* (xiv. 17); but here the reference is rather to divinely ordained periods, 'times and seasons': cf. i. 7; Lk. xxi. 24 (*καιροὶ ἐθνῶν*, with which cf. Rom. xi. 25, *τὸ πλήρωμα τῶν ἐθνῶν*); 1 Th. v. 1; Gal. iv. 4; Eph. i. 9 f.; iii. 9; 1 Tim. ii. 6; vi. 15; Tit. i. 3, and perhaps Heb. i. 2 (*ἐποίησεν τοὺς αἰῶνας*).

τὰς ὁροθεσίας τῆς κατοικίας αὐτῶν] The *locus classicus* in OT for the divine fixing of the boundaries of the nations is Dt. xxxii. 8, *ὅτε διεμέριζεν ὁ ὕψιστος ἔθνη, ὡς διέσπειρεν υἱοὺς Ἀδάμ, ἔστησεν ὅρια ἐθνῶν κατὰ ἀριθμὸν ἀγγέλων θεοῦ* (observe that LXX *ἀγγέλων θεοῦ* presupposes Heb. *bĕnē 'Ēl*, 'sons of God', for MT *bĕnē Yisrā'ēl*, 'children of Israel'). The fem. sing. *ὁροθεσία*, as here, is found in an inscription and a papyrus. Galen and Hesychius give the neut. plur. form *ὁροθέσια*.

xvii. 27

ζητεῖν] Epexegetic infin., like *κατοικεῖν* in *ver.* 26. D prefixes *μάλιστα*.

τὸν θεόν] δ has *τὸ θεῖον* (cf. *ver.* 29); so also Clem. *Strom.* i. 19. 91.4, in a quotation of this passage, *ζητεῖν τὸ θεῖον*.

εἰ ἄρα γε ψηλαφήσειαν αὐτὸν καὶ εὕροιεν] A telescoped conditional and final construction. Cf. viii. 22; xxvii. 12, 39. In *ψηλαφάω* we may see the idea of groping after God in the darkness, when the light of His full revelation is not available.

καί γε] A concessive expression; A has *καίτοι*, ℵ *καίτοιγε*. Cf. xiv. 17.

ὑπάρχοντα] The prevalence of *ὑπάρχω* in this speech (cf. *vv.* 24, 29) is in keeping with its elevated style. 'The exordium of an address to Athenian philosophers survives to show us that he could use the language of the higher culture when occasion required' (MH ii, p. 8).

xvii. 28

ἐν αὐτῷ γὰρ ζῶμεν καὶ κινούμεθα καὶ ἐσμέν] Cf. Col. i. 17, *τὰ πάντα ἐν αὐτῷ συνέστηκεν.* The language here is quoted from an address to Zeus by his son Minos: 'They fashioned a tomb for thee, O holy and high—the Cretans, always liars, evil beasts, slow bellies! But thou art not dead; thou art risen and alive for ever, for in thee we live and move and have our being'. The whole of this extract is quoted (in Syriac) by the Syriac father Isho'dad in his commentary on this passage (probably based on Theodore of Mopsuestia). He ascribes the words to a panegyric of Minos over his father Zeus; we learn, however, from Clement of Alexandria (*Strom.* i. 14. 59. 1 f.) that the second line (*Κρῆτες ἀεὶ ψεῦσται, κακὰ θηρία, γαστέρες ἀργαί*), quoted in Tit. i. 12, comes from a work of Epimenides the Cretan (see on *ver.* 23). Rendel Harris (*Exp.* VII. ii [1906], pp. 305 ff.) suggested that the panegyric in question might be the poem by Epimenides on Minos and Rhadamanthys referred to by Diogenes Laertius, i. 112. Or it might come from his *Theogonia* (Diog. Laert., i. 111). The four lines have been turned back into Gk. by Rendel Harris (*Exp.* VII. iii [1907], p. 336) and by A. B. Cook (*Zeus*, i [1914], p. 664). Chrysostom on Tit. i. 12 quotes from Callimachus, *Hymn to Zeus*, 7 f.,

Κρῆτες ἀεὶ ψεῦσται· καὶ γὰρ τάφον, ὦ ἄνα, σεῖο
Κρῆτες ἐτεκτήναντο· σὺ δ' οὐ θάνες· ἐσσὶ γὰρ αἰεί.

These words were probably imitated from Epimenides. In Tit. i. 12 Epimenides is called a *προφήτης* (cf. Plato, *Laws*, i. 642D, where he is called *ἀνὴρ θεῖος*, and Plutarch, *Solon*, 12, where he is called *θεοφιλὴς καὶ σοφὸς περὶ τὰ θεῖα τὴν ἐνθουσιαστικὴν καὶ τελεστικὴν σοφίαν*). Epimenides argues from living men to a living god; our Lord in Lk. xx. 37 f., etc., applies the converse argument from the Living God to living men in a life beyond this. After *ἐσμέν* D adds *τὸ καθ' ἡμέραν.*

ὑμᾶς] B 33 614 have *ἡμᾶς*, which may be right, as Aratus (see below) was a Cilician.

ποιητῶν] om δ. Pesh has *ḥakīme*, 'wise men'.

τοῦ γὰρ καὶ γένος ἐσμέν] From Aratus, *Phainomena* 5. The poem commences *ἐκ Διὸς ἀρχώμεσθα.* Cf. Cleanthes, *Hymn to Zeus*, 4, *ἐκ σοῦ γὰρ γένος ἐσμέν.* The Zeus of these Stoic poets is of course the *λόγος* or world-principle which animates all things. Their language, however, is largely adaptable to the God of revelation. By presenting God as Creator and Judge, Paul emphasizes

His Personality in contrast to the materialistic pantheism of the Stoics.

'Of course Luke is usually credited with Paul's *Areopagitica*, and it may be difficult to prove completely that he wrote his report from full notes, given him not long after by his master. But when we find the Lukan Paul quoting Epimenides (Ac. xvii. 28*a*), and the Paul of the Pastorals citing the very same context (Tit. i. 12), with the Aratus-Cleanthes quotation (*ib.* 28*b*) to match the Menander (1 Co. xv. 33), we may at least remark that the speech is very subtly concocted. Paul was, moreover, much more likely than Luke to know the tenets of Stoics and Epicureans so as to make such delicately suited allusions to them. Luke's knowledge of Greek literature does not seem to have gone far beyond the medical writers who so profoundly influenced his diction' (MH ii. p. 8, *n.* 3).

xvii. 29

γένος οὖν ὑπάρχοντες τοῦ θεοῦ] In OT man is not only the creature of God, but made in His image and after His likeness (κατ' εἰκόνα ἡμετέραν καὶ καθ' ὁμοίωσιν, Gen. i. 26).

οὐκ ὀφείλομεν νομίζειν . . . τὸ θεῖον εἶναι ὅμοιον] Cf. Ps. cxv. 4 (LXX cxiii. 12) and cxxxv. 15 (LXX cxxxiv), τὰ εἴδωλα τῶν ἐθνῶν ἀργύριον καὶ χρυσίον, ἔργα χειρῶν ἀνθρώπων. Cf. also Isa. xl. 18, τίνι ὡμοιώσατε Κύριον, καὶ τίνι ὁμοιώματι ὡμοιώσατε αὐτόν; The argument is also developed in Wisd. xiii. 5, 10; xv. 4, 15 ff.

τὸ θεῖον] 'the divine' (essence or nature), an idiomatic Gk. touch. For the neuter cf. *ver.* 23; cf. also the δ reading in *ver.* 27.

xvii. 30

τοὺς . . . χρόνους τῆς ἀγνοίας] Cf. Rom. i. 21 (γνόντες τὸν θεόν, i.e., knowing of His existence), 28 (οὐκ ἐδοκίμασαν τὸν θεὸν ἔχειν ἐν ἐπιγνώσει); xvi. 25; 1 Cor. i. 21; Gal. iv. 8; Eph. iv. 18; 1 Th. iv. 5; Wisd. xiv. 22; xv. 11. Cf. also xiv. 16, ἐν ταῖς παρῳχημέναις γενεαῖς.

ὑπεριδὼν] 'having overlooked': cf. xiv. 16 with notes and references *ad loc.*; also Rom. iii. 25 f., διὰ τὴν πάρεσιν τῶν προγεγονότων ἁμαρτημάτων ἐν τῇ ἀνοχῇ τοῦ θεοῦ (i.e., judgment was suspended until God's righteousness was demonstrated and vindicated in the Cross); Wisd. xi. 23, παρορᾷς ἁμαρτήματα ἀνθρώπων εἰς μετάνοιαν.

τὰ νῦν] Now that the fulness of God's revelation has been given; cf. Rom. iii. 26 (ἐν τῷ νῦν καιρῷ); xvi. 26 (φανερωθέντος δὲ νῦν); Gal. iv. 9: Eph. iii. 5; v. 8; Col. i. 26.

πάντας πανταχοῦ] For the alliteration and paronomasia on πᾶς see on *ver.* 26. For the turn of phrase cf. xxiv. 3; 1 Cor. iv. 17; 2 Cor. ix. 8; Eph. v. 20; Phil. i. 3.

μετανοεῖν] For the command to repent cf. ii. 38, etc.; Mk. i. 4, 15, etc.

xvii. 31

καθότι] In Hellenistic Gk. *καθότι* passes over to the meaning of *διότι* (' because '), which is the reading of byz here.

ἔστησεν ἡμέραν] For the appointed day of judgment cf. Rom. ii. 5, 16; 1 Cor. i. 8; Phil. i. 6, 10; 1 Th. v. 2, 4; 2 Th. i. 10; ii. 2; Amos v. 18; Isa. ii. 12.

ἐν ᾗ μέλλει] om δ; *κρίνειν* (*κρῖναι* D) will then be epexegetic infin.

κρίνειν τὴν οἰκουμένην ἐν δικαιοσύνῃ] Quoted from Ps. ix. 8 (LXX 9); xcvi. 13 (LXX xcv); xcviii. 9 (LXX xcvii), *κρινεῖ τὴν οἰκουμένην ἐν δικαιοσύνῃ*. The words in their OT context refer to the Messianic reign, but Paul applies them to the judgment with which that reign is to be inaugurated.

ἐν ἀνδρὶ] '*Sic appellat Jesum, pro captu auditorum. Plura erat dicturus audire cupientibus*' (Bengel). That the judgment of the world is entrusted to a Man is taught from Dan. vii. 13 onwards. Cf. Mt. xxiv. 27 ff.; xxv. 31, etc.; Jn. v. 27 (*καὶ ἐξουσίαν ἔδωκεν αὐτῷ κρίσιν ποιεῖν, ὅτι υἱὸς ἀνθρώπου ἐστίν*). For the Semitism *υἱὸς ἀνθρώπου* or *ὁ υἱὸς τοῦ ἀνθρώπου* used in these passages (see on vii. 56) Paul, addressing a Gentile audience to whom such an expression would be unintelligible, substitutes the ordinary word *ἀνήρ*. The use of *ἐν* here may be illustrated from 1 Cor. vi. 2 (*εἰ ἐν ὑμῖν κρίνεται ὁ κόσμος*); cf. also an Athenian inscription of the fourth century B.C., *κρινέσθω ἐν Ἀθηναίοις καὶ τοῖς συμμάχοις* (Dittenberger, *Syll.* 147. 57).

ὥρισεν] For Christ's appointment as Judge cf. x. 42 (*οὗτός ἐστιν ὁ ὡρισμένος ὑπὸ τοῦ θεοῦ κριτὴς ζώντων καὶ νεκρῶν*) and references *ad loc.*; cf. also Rom. i. 4, where the verb is used, as here, in connection with the Resurrection.

πίστιν παρασχὼν] 'having provided proof'. Vettius Valens 277. 29 f. provides an example of *πίστιν παρέχω* in the same sense. Note again alliteration on *π*.

ἀναστήσας αὐτὸν ἐκ νεκρῶν] For the connection between resurrection and judgment cf. x. 41 f.; Jn. v. 25 ff.; 1 Th. i. 10.

xvii. 32

ἀνάστασιν νεκρών] 'a resurrection of dead men': generalizing plural (see on xxvi. 23). Cf. *ver.* 18. The idea of the immortality of the soul was perfectly familiar to the Greek mind, but their philosophies had no room for the idea of the resuscitation of dead bodies. Indeed, one of their own poets had represented the god Apollo as saying, on the occasion when the court of the Areopagus was inaugurated by the city's patron goddess Athene,

> *ἀνδρὸς δ' ἐπειδὰν αἷμ' ἀνασπάσῃ κόνις*
> *ἅπαξ θανόντος, οὔτις ἐστ' ἀνάστασις.*

(Aeschylus, *Eumenides* 647f.)

xvii. 33

ἐκ μέσου αὐτῶν] i.e., from the Areopagites: see on ἐν μέσῳ, *ver.* 22.

xvii. 34

κολληθέντες] Cf. v. 13, κολλᾶσθαι.

ἐπίστευσαν] These are not, however, reckoned as 'the firstfruits of Achaia', a term applied to the household of Stephanas at Corinth (1 Cor. xvi. 15). Perhaps there Achaia is intended in a narrower sense. Zahn and others have held, however, that Stephanas must have been converted in Athens. But cf. Ramsay, *BRD*, ch. xxvi, 'The Firstfruits of Achaia' (pp. 385 ff.).

ἐν οἷς καὶ κ.τ.λ.] 'including in particular Dionysius the Areopagite; and (in addition to the men) a woman named Damaris', etc. There is no need to suppose that καὶ γυνή is included in τινες ἄνδρες . . . ἐν οἷς.

Διονύσιος ὁ Ἀρεοπαγίτης] The Areopagus was a closed body and membership in it was a high distinction. Eusebius (*HE* iii. 4. 11; iv. 23. 3) says that according to Dionysius, bishop of Corinth about A.D. 171, Dionysius the Areopagite was the first bishop of Athens. A considerable body of Neoplatonic literature, dating from the fifth or sixth century A.D., which circulated under his name, profoundly influenced the development of medieval scholasticism. B omits ὁ, D replaces it by τις and adds εὐσχήμων after Ἀρεοπαγίτης.

γυνὴ ὀνόματι Δάμαρις] Her name is a variant of δάμαλις, 'heifer'. Damalis is the reading of h; it was a common female name (for animal names cf. Dorcas, ix. 36, 39). Ramsay thinks she was 'a foreign woman, perhaps one of the class of educated Hetairai', in view of the unlikelihood of an ordinary Athenian woman being present. But e has *mulier honesta* (translated γυνὴ τιμία in E), which probably represents Gk. εὐσχήμων. D omits all mention of Damaris (for the δ text's attitude to women cf. *ver.* 12; xviii. 26), but attaches the gloss εὐσχήμων to Dionysius. (Cf. Ramsay, *CRE*, pp. 161 f.; *SPT*, p. 252.) Chrysostom (*De sacerd.* iv. 7) makes her the wife of Dionysius.

3. Corinth, xviii. 1–17

(a) Paul arrives at Corinth, xviii. 1-4

Μετὰ ταῦτα χωρισθεὶς ἐκ τῶν Ἀθηνῶν ἦλθεν εἰς Κόρινθον. καὶ 1
εὑρών τινα Ἰουδαῖον ὀνόματι Ἀκύλαν, Ποντικὸν τῷ γένει, προσφάτως 2
ἐληλυθότα ἀπὸ τῆς Ἰταλίας καὶ Πρίσκιλλαν γυναῖκα αὐτοῦ διὰ τὸ
διατεταχέναι Κλαύδιον χωρίζεσθαι πάντας τοὺς Ἰουδαίους ἀπὸ τῆς
Ῥώμης, προσῆλθεν αὐτοῖς, καὶ διὰ τὸ ὁμότεχνον εἶναι ἔμενεν παρ' 3
αὐτοῖς καὶ ἠργάζοντο, ἦσαν γὰρ σκηνοποιοὶ τῇ τέχνῃ. διελέγετο 4
δὲ ἐν τῇ συναγωγῇ κατὰ πᾶν σάββατον, ἔπειθέν τε Ἰουδαίους καὶ
Ἕλληνας.

xviii. 1

εἰς Κόρινθον] Corinth, on the Isthmus of Corinth, occupied a most favourable position for commercial enterprise, at the junction of the Saronic and Corinthian Gulfs on the east and west respectively, and of the land-routes north and south. For long it was a commercial and naval rival of Athens. At the time of the Roman conquest of Greece (146 B.C.) Corinth was destroyed by L. Mummius, and lay waste for exactly a century, until it was restored by Julius Caesar as a Roman colony with the name Laus Iulia Corinthus. In 27 B.C. it became the capital of the province Achaia (see on *ver.* 12). The new Corinth was, like the old, a great commercial centre, and—also like the old—noted for sexual immorality, a fact which helps to explain Paul's insistent warnings against such vice in the Epistles to the Corinthians. In the Temple of Aphrodite at Corinth a Hellenized form of the worship of Astarte was cultivated (cf. the similar cults at Antioch and Paphos mentioned in notes on xi. 19; xiii. 6). The city had two ports, Lechaeum on the Corinthian Gulf and Cenchreae on the Saronic Gulf (cf. *ver.* 18).

xviii. 2

Ἀκύλαν] *Ἀκύλας* is a Hellenized form of Lat. Aquila ('eagle').

Ποντικὸν] 'of Pontus'—either the Roman province of that name, which formed an administrative unit with Bithynia (see on xvi. 7), or the kingdom of Pontus farther east; the former is more likely.

καὶ Πρίσκιλλαν γυναῖκα αὐτοῦ] Paul calls her Prisca (Rom. xvi. 3; 1 Cor. xvi. 19; 2 Tim. iv. 19). 'Luke regularly uses the language of conversation, in which the diminutive forms were usual; and so he speaks of Priscilla, Sopatros and Silas always, though Paul speaks of Prisca, Sosipatros and Silvanus' (Ramsay, *SPT*, p. 268). Both Luke and Paul usually put her name before her husband's, from which some have inferred that her rank was superior to his. She may have belonged by birth or manumission to the *gens Prisca*, a noble Roman family. Harnack suggested in *ZNTW*, i. (1900), pp. 32 ff., that she and Aquila were joint-authors of the Epistle to the Hebrews.

διὰ τὸ διατεταχέναι Κλαύδιον χωρίζεσθαι πάντας τοὺς Ἰουδαίους ἀπὸ τῆς Ῥώμης] It is usual to connect this edict with that referred to by Suetonius, *Claud.* xxv. 4, '*Iudaeos impulsore Chresto adsidue tumultuantes Roma expulit*'. Cf. Dio Cassius lx. 6, *τούς τε Ἰουδαίους πλεονάσαντας αὖθις, ὥστε χαλεπῶς ἂν ἄνευ ταραχῆς ὑπὸ τοῦ ὄχλου σφῶν τῆς πόλεως εἰρχθῆναι, οὐκ ἐξήλασε μέν, τῷ δὲ δὴ πατρίῳ βίῳ χρωμένους ἐκέλευσε μὴ συναθροίζεσθαι,* which would in practice amount to their expulsion. Dio places this at the outset of

Claudius's reign, which conflicts with the account of pro-Jewish edicts of that time given in Jos. *Ant.* xix. 5. 2 f.; Orosius (vii. 6.15 f.), more probably, dates it in his ninth year, i.e., A.D. 49-50. There is good evidence for several such anti-Jewish moves, none of which had more than partial and temporary effect. For Claudius see on xi. 28.

The original δ text of *vv.* 2 f. is reconstructed as follows by Ropes, chiefly on the basis of h and hcl. mg: *καὶ εὗρεν Ἀκύλαν, Ποντικὸν τῷ γένει, Ἰουδαῖον, προσφάτως ἐληλυθότα ἀπὸ τῆς Ἰταλίας σὺν Πρισκίλλῃ γυναικὶ αὐτοῦ, καὶ προσῆλθεν αὐτοῖς· οὗτοι δὲ ἐξῆλθον ἀπὸ τῆς Ῥώμης διὰ τὸ τεταχέναι Κλαύδιον Καίσαρα χωρίζεσθαι πάντας Ἰουδαίους ἀπὸ τῆς Ῥώμης· οἳ καὶ κατῴκησαν εἰς τὴν Ἀχαίαν. ὁ δὲ Παῦλος ἐγνωρίσθη τῷ Ἀκύλᾳ διὰ τὸ ὁμόφυλον καὶ ὁμότεχνον εἶναι, καὶ ἔμενεν πρὸς αὐτοὺς καὶ ἠργάζετο· ἦσαν γὰρ σκηνοποιοὶ τῇ τέχνῃ.*

xviii. 3

ἠργάζοντο] ℵ B; *ἠργάζετο* A D; *εἰργάζετο* ℵ^c byz.

σκηνοποιοὶ] Paul's calling was closely connected with the chief manufacture of his native province, *cilicium*, a cloth of goat's hair, used for cloaks, curtains, etc. While the etymological sense of *σκηνοποιός* is 'tent-maker', its actual meaning at that time was 'leather-worker' (cf. how Eng. 'saddler' has a wider meaning than 'maker of saddles'). As all the teaching of scribes and Rabbis had to be gratuitous [1] (in theory at any rate), they had to make their living otherwise, and many practised a trade in addition to the study and teaching of the law, a course recommended by Rabban Gamaliel III (*Pirqe Aboth.* ii. 2). Cf. xx. 34; 1 Th. ii. 9; 2 Th. iii. 8; 1 Cor. ix. 1 ff.

xviii. 4

διελέγετο δὲ κ.τ.λ.] The δ text has this verse in the following form: *εἰσπορευόμενος δὲ εἰς τὴν συναγωγὴν κατὰ πᾶν σάββατον διελέγετο, καὶ ἐντιθεὶς τὸ ὄνομα τοῦ κυρίου Ἰησοῦ, καὶ ἔπειθεν δὲ οὐ μόνον Ἰουδαίους ἀλλὰ καὶ Ἕλληνας.* The addition implies that as the OT scriptures were read Paul explained them by 'inserting the name of the Lord Jesus' where appropriate: cf. the Targumic insertion of 'Messiah' after 'my Servant' in Isa. xlii. 1; lii. 13 (see on iii. 13). 'It is undoubtedly a correct estimate of what Paul did' (LC).

[1] 'R. Zadok said, . . . Make not of the Torah a crown wherewith to aggrandize thyself, nor a spade wherewith to dig. So also used Hillel to say, He who makes a worldly use of the crown of the Torah shall waste away. Hence thou mayest infer, that whosoever derives a profit for himself from the words of the Torah is helping on his own destruction' (*Pirqe Aboth*, iv. 7).

ἐν τῇ συναγωγῇ] The remains of an insertion over a door, found at Corinth, and dated between 100 B.C. and A.D. 200, are deciphered [*συνα*]*γωγὴ Ἑβρ*[*αίων*] (Deissmann, *LAE*, p. 16).

(b) He spends Eighteen Months in Corinth, xviii. 5-11

Ὡς δὲ κατῆλθον ἀπὸ τῆς Μακεδονίας ὅ τε Σίλας καὶ ὁ Τιμόθεος, 5
συνείχετο τῷ λόγῳ ὁ Παῦλος, διαμαρτυρόμενος τοῖς Ἰουδαίοις εἶναι
τὸν χριστὸν Ἰησοῦν. ἀντιτασσομένων δὲ αὐτῶν καὶ βλασφημούντων 6
ἐκτιναξάμενος τὰ ἱμάτια εἶπεν πρὸς αὐτούς Τὸ αἷμα ὑμῶν ἐπὶ τὴν
κεφαλὴν ὑμῶν· καθαρὸς ἐγώ· ἀπὸ τοῦ νῦν εἰς τὰ ἔθνη πορεύσομαι.
καὶ μεταβὰς ἐκεῖθεν ἦλθεν εἰς οἰκίαν τινὸς ὀνόματι Τιτίου Ἰούστου 7
σεβομένου τὸν θεόν, οὗ ἡ οἰκία ἦν συνομοροῦσα τῇ συναγωγῇ. Κρίσπος 8
δὲ ὁ ἀρχισυνάγωγος ἐπίστευσεν τῷ κυρίῳ σὺν ὅλῳ τῷ οἴκῳ αὐτοῦ,
καὶ πολλοὶ τῶν Κορινθίων ἀκούοντες ἐπίστευον καὶ ἐβαπτίζοντο.
Εἶπεν δὲ ὁ κύριος ἐν νυκτὶ δι' ὁράματος τῷ Παύλῳ Μὴ φοβοῦ, ἀλλὰ 9
λάλει καὶ μὴ σιωπήσῃς, διότι ἐγώ εἰμι μετὰ σοῦ καὶ οὐδεὶς ἐπιθήσεταί 10
σοι τοῦ κακῶσαί σε, διότι λαός ἐστί μοι πολὺς ἐν τῇ πόλει ταύτῃ.
Ἐκάθισεν δὲ ἐνιαυτὸν καὶ μῆνας ἓξ διδάσκων ἐν αὐτοῖς τὸν λόγον 11
τοῦ θεοῦ.

xviii. 5

ὅ τε Σίλας καὶ ὁ Τιμόθεος] For the probable movements of Silas and Timothy see on xvii. 14.

συνείχετο τῷ λόγῳ] 'proceeded to devote himself entirely to the preaching'; perhaps supplies brought by Timothy and Silas from Thessalonica and Philippi (cf. 2 Cor. xi. 8; Phil. iv. 15) released him from the necessity of manual labour.

εἶναι τὸν χριστὸν Ἰησοῦν] Note the article; the meaning is, 'that the Messiah (of whom they read in OT) was Jesus (whom Paul now introduced to them)'. For *Ἰησοῦν* the δ text characteristically has *κύριον Ἰησοῦν*, and adds *πολλοῦ δὲ λόγου γινομένου καὶ γραφῶν διερμηνευομένων*.

xviii. 6

ἐκτιναξάμενος τὰ ἱμάτια] In token of abhorrence at the blasphemy (see on xiii. 51).

τὸ αἷμα ὑμῶν ἐπὶ τὴν κεφαλὴν ὑμῶν] Sc. *ἐλθέτω* (cf. Mt. xxiii. 35); for the ellipsis cf. Mt. xxvii. 25; 2 Sam. (LXX 2 K.) i. 16.

εἰς τὰ ἔθνη πορεύσομαι] Cf. xiii. 46; xxviii. 28.

xviii. 7

ἐκεῖθεν] i.e., from the synagogue; *ἀπὸ Ἀκύλα*, the δ reading found in D d h (614 has the conflate *ἐκεῖθεν ἀπὸ τοῦ Ἀκύλα*), 'is probably a misinterpretation; the divergence is wholly inconsistent with the idea of a common authorship for the two forms of the text' (Ropes).

Τιτίου Ἰούστου] So B* D² hcl. The name Titius Iustus suggests that he was a Roman citizen and therefore probably one of the *coloni* (cf. the Latin names of Corinthian Christians in Rom. xvi. 23; 1 Cor. i. 14; xvi. 17). Ramsay identifies him with 'Gaius, mine host' of Rom. xvi. 23; his full name will then have been C. Titius Iustus (cf. 1 Cor. i. 14). For *Τιτίου* ℵ E minn pesh sah boh arm have *Τίτου*, while A B³ D* byz p eth omit. It is possible, as Ropes suggests, that the single name *Ἰούστου* is original, *Τιτίου* having risen from dittography of the final *τι* of *ὀνόματι*.

σεβομένου τὸν θεόν] See on x. 2.

ἦν συνομοροῦσα] For the periphrasis see on i. 10; the construction is much rarer in the second half of Ac. (cf. xxii. 19, translated from an Aramaic speech); but here *συνομοροῦσα* is practically an adjective. No doubt Paul chose a residence near the synagogue in order to keep in touch with the 'God-fearers'.

xviii. 8

Κρίσπος] His baptism by Paul is mentioned in 1 Cor. i. 14; the Gaius similarly mentioned there may be the same as Justus (see on *ver.* 7).

ἀρχισυνάγωγος] See on xiii. 15.

ἐπίστευσεν τῷ κυρίῳ] 'trusted the Lord'; here, as in xvi. 34, where *πιστεύω* is followed by the plain dative, '*accepting the truth of* God's word satisfies the connexion' (*Proleg.* p. 67). Cf. v. 14; Jn. v. 24, 38; viii. 31. For *τῷ κυρίῳ* D substitutes *εἰς τὸν κύριον* (cf. xvi. 34).

σὺν ὅλῳ τῷ οἴκῳ αὐτοῦ] Cf. xi. 14; xvi. 15, 31 ff.

xviii. 9

δι' ὁράματος] Cf. ix. 10, 12; x. 3 ff.; xii. 9; xvi. 9 f.

μὴ φοβοῦ . . . διότι ἐγώ εἰμι μετὰ σοῦ] Cf. Isa. xliii. 5 (*μὴ φοβοῦ, ὅτι μετὰ σοῦ εἰμί*) and Jer. i. 8 (*μὴ φοβηθῇς . . . ὅτι μετὰ σοῦ ἐγώ εἰμι*). *μή* with pres. imperative means 'Stop being afraid'; so *λάλει καὶ μὴ σιωπήσῃς* means 'go on speaking; don't stop'. Paul describes his coming to Corinth as being *ἐν ἀσθενείᾳ καὶ ἐν φόβῳ καὶ ἐν τρόμῳ πολλῷ* (1 Cor. ii. 3).

xviii. 10

οὐδεὶς ἐπιθήσεταί σοι τοῦ κακῶσαί σε] There is emphasis on *κακῶσαι*: he *was* attacked (*ver.* 12), but suffered no harm.

λαός] The word regularly used of the Jewish people as distinct from the Gentiles is here used of the new 'chosen people': cf. xv. 14 (*ἐξ ἐθνῶν λαόν*); Tit. ii. 14; 1 Pet. ii. 9 f.

xviii. 11

ἐκάθισεν] 'he remained'; for *καθίζω* in this sense cf. Lk. xxiv. 49.

ἐνιαυτὸν καὶ μῆνας ἕξ] Probably from late summer of 50 to early spring of 52. During this period he wrote 1 and 2 Th.

(c) Paul before Gallio, xviii. 12-17

Γαλλίωνος δὲ ἀνθυπάτου ὄντος τῆς Ἀχαίας κατεπέστησαν οἱ 12
Ἰουδαῖοι ὁμοθυμαδὸν τῷ Παύλῳ καὶ ἤγαγον αὐτὸν ἐπὶ τὸ βῆμα,
λέγοντες ὅτι Παρὰ τὸν νόμον ἀναπείθει οὗτος τοὺς ἀνθρώπους σέβεσθαι 13
τὸν θεόν. μέλλοντος δὲ τοῦ Παύλου ἀνοίγειν τὸ στόμα εἶπεν ὁ Γαλλίων 14
πρὸς τοὺς Ἰουδαίους Εἰ μὲν ἦν ἀδίκημά τι ἢ ῥᾳδιούργημα πονηρόν,
ὦ Ἰουδαῖοι, κατὰ λόγον ἂν ἀνεσχόμην ὑμῶν· εἰ δὲ ζητήματά ἐστιν 15
περὶ λόγου καὶ ὀνομάτων καὶ νόμου τοῦ καθ' ὑμᾶς, ὄψεσθε αὐτοί·
κριτὴς ἐγὼ τούτων οὐ βούλομαι εἶναι. καὶ ἀπήλασεν αὐτοὺς ἀπὸ 16
τοῦ βήματος. ἐπιλαβόμενοι δέ πάντες Σωσθένην τὸν ἀρχισυνάγωγον 17
ἔτυπτον ἔμπροσθεν τοῦ βήματος· καὶ οὐδὲν τούτων τῷ Γαλλίωνι ἔμελεν.

xviii. 12

Γαλλίωνος] M. Annaeus Novatus, as he originally was, was a son of the elder Seneca, and brother of Seneca the philosopher and of Mela, the father of the poet Lucan. He was born in Cordova, and came with his father to Rome in the reign of Tiberius. He was there adopted by the rhetorician L. Junius Gallio, whose name he thereafter bore. Under Claudius he became proconsul of Achaia. From a Delphian inscription containing a proclamation made by Claudius between the end of 51 and Aug. 52, it seems probable that he was appointed to this proconsulship in July 51. He left his province owing to a fever and went on a cruise for his health (Seneca, *Ep. Mor.* civ. 1). At a later date we find him taking another voyage from Rome to Egypt after his consulship, because of threatened phthisis (Pliny, *NH*, xxxi. 33). On the death of Seneca in 65, Gallio begged successfully for his life (Tac. *Ann.* xv. 73), but later fell a victim to Nero's suspicion, along with his other brother Mela (Dio Cass. lxii. 25). Seneca (*NQ* iv *a*, praef. 11) praises his virtues and lovable character ('*nemo enim mortalium uni tam dulcis est quam hic omnibus*'); Dio (lxi. 35) speaks of his wit.

ἀνθυπάτου ὄντος τῆς Ἀχαίας] 'Achaia was governed by a proconsul from B.C. 27 to A.D. 15, and *from* A.D. 44 *onwards*. It was a province of the second rank, and was administered by Roman officials, after holding the praetorship, and generally before the consulship. Corinth had now become the chief city of Achaia, and the residence of its governors' (Ramsay, *SPT*, p. 258).

For ἀνθυπάτου ὄντος byz has ἀνθυπατεύοντος.

οἱ Ἰουδαῖοι ὁμοθυμαδὸν] B sah boh; ὁμοθυμαδὸν οἱ Ἰουδαῖοι ℵ A D byz (so WH mg., Soden, Ropes). The δ text continues, συνλαλήσαντες μεθ' ἑαυτῶν ἐπὶ τὸν Παῦλον, καὶ ἐπιθέντες τὰς χεῖρας ἤγαγον αὐτὸν πρὸς τὸν ἀνθύπατον (D has ἐπὶ τὸ βῆμα, by contamination with the β text; the true δ text is preserved by h and hcl*). The Jews in the various cities of the Empire were allowed to exercise a considerable degree of jurisdiction over members of their own community, subject to the approval of the Roman authorities.

xviii. 13

λέγοντες] δ has καταβοῶντες καὶ λέγοντες.

παρὰ τὸν νόμον] The Jews probably meant that the apostles were preaching a *religio illicita*. Cf. the charges at Philippi (xvi. 21) and Thessalonica (xvii. 6 f.). There seems to be a studied ambiguity in the words 'contrary to the law'; did they mean Roman or Jewish law? Blass suggests that the 'law' in question is Julius Caesar's decree in favour of Hyrcanus (cf. Jos. *Ant.* xiv. 10. 2), confirming the existing privileges of the Jews. This is doubtful. Gallio replies that he is not interested in Jewish law, and that Paul has committed no offence against Roman law.

ἀναπείθει] The only NT occurrence. MM quote papyrus evidence for this word in the sense of evil persuasion and refer to Jer. xxix. 8 (LXX xxxvi.) and 1 Macc. i. 11. LS[9] refer to Hdt. iii. 148; v. 66, etc. for its use in the sense 'seduce, mislead'.

xviii. 14

ῥᾳδιούργημα] Cf. ῥᾳδιουργία (xiii. 10), which also seems to imply fraud or deception ('false pretences', MM). Both words occur only once in NT.

ὦ Ἰουδαῖοι] δ has ὦ ἄνδρες Ἰουδαῖοι.

κατὰ λόγον] 'reasonably', 'as is reason'.

ἀνεσχόμην] Here, as in 2 Cor. xi. 1, ἀνέχομαι is used of listening patiently while others are allowed to speak.

xviii. 15

περὶ λόγου καὶ ὀνομάτων καὶ νόμου τοῦ καθ' ὑμᾶς] 'about language and names and the law observed by you', as opposed to actual deeds. With the κατά construction cf. xvi. 39 D; xvii. 28; xxvi. 3.

ὄψεσθε αὐτοί] Cf. Mt. xxvii. 4, 24; this use of the fut. indic. is colloquial (cf. Lat. *uideritis*, of which, in this legal context, ὄψεσθε may be an imitation). He directs the Jews to carry their complaint before their own authorities, as it was a matter affecting Jewish law only. Ramsay supposes that it was this refusal of Gallio to interfere with Christian preaching that encouraged Paul a few years later to appeal 'to the supreme tribunal of the Empire' (*SPT*, p. 260).

xviii. 17

Σωσθένην τὸν ἀρχισυνάγωγον] Presumably the successor or colleague of Crispus (*ver.* 8). If he is the Sosthenes of 1 Cor. i. 1, then he too became a Christian. The acc. *Σωσθένην* (common in Attic Gk. from fourth century B.C. for earlier *Σωσθένη*, by analogy with 1st decl.) is governed by *ἔτυπτον*, not *ἐπιλαβόμενοι* (which would take the gen.).

ἔτυπτον] Who beat Sosthenes? Probably the Greeks, taking advantage of the snub Gallio had administered to the Jews to express their own anti-Jewish sentiments. So δ byz, adding *οἱ Ἕλληνες* after *πάντες*.

καὶ οὐδὲν τούτων τῷ Γαλλίωνι ἔμελεν]. 'These things' about which Gallio did not care were the easily roused quarrels between Greeks and Jews, and the Jews' complaints about matters affecting their own law; he is commended for his impartiality, not blamed for his indifference to spiritual matters. Here the δ text (d and h; D is wanting) has 'Gallio pretended not to see', which Clark reconstructs *τότε ὁ Γαλλίων προσεποιεῖτο μὴ ἰδεῖν*.

4. EPHESUS, xviii. 18-xix. 20

(a) Hasty Visit to Palestine, xviii. 18-23

Ὁ δὲ Παῦλος ἔτι προσμείνας ἡμέρας ἱκανὰς τοῖς ἀδελφοῖς 18
ἀποταξάμενος ἐξέπλει εἰς τὴν Συρίαν, καὶ σὺν αὐτῷ Πρίσκιλλα καὶ
Ἀκύλας, κειράμενος ἐν Κενχρεαῖς τὴν κεφαλήν, εἶχεν γὰρ εὐχήν.
κατήντησαν δὲ εἰς Ἔφεσον, κἀκείνους κατέλιπεν αὐτοῦ, αὐτὸς δὲ 19
εἰσελθὼν εἰς τὴν συναγωγὴν διελέξατο τοῖς Ἰουδαίοις. ἐρωτώντων 20
δὲ αὐτῶν ἐπὶ πλείονα χρόνον μεῖναι οὐκ ἐπένευσεν, ἀλλὰ ἀποταξάμενος 21
καὶ εἰπών Πάλιν ἀνακάμψω πρὸς ὑμᾶς τοῦ θεοῦ θέλοντος ἀνήχθη
ἀπὸ τῆς Ἐφέσου, καὶ κατελθὼν εἰς Καισαρίαν, ἀναβὰς καὶ ἀσπασά- 22
μενος τὴν ἐκκλησίαν, κατέβη εἰς Ἀντιόχειαν, καὶ ποιήσας χρόνον τινὰ 23
ἐξῆλθεν, διερχόμενος καθεξῆς τὴν Γαλατικὴν χώραν καὶ Φρυγίαν,
στηρίζων πάντας τοὺς μαθητάς.

xviii. 18

ἡμέρας ἱκανὰς] Cf. ix. 23. He was not likely to hurry away immediately after Gallio's favourable verdict.

κειράμενος . . . τὴν κεφαλήν] It is grammatically possible that it was Aquila whose head was shorn (so h, . . . *Aquila, qui uotum cum fecisset* . . .), but 'the natural emphasis marks Paul as the subject here' (*SPT*, p. 263). Vg has *qui sibi totonderant in Cencris caput, habebant enim uotum,* making the words refer to both. See on xxi. 24, where the verb is *ξυρέω*, 'to shave', whereas *κείρω* means to cut with scissors.

Κενχρεαῖς] Cenchreae was the eastern port of Corinth (see on *ver.* 1). It appears from Rom. xvi. 1 that there was a separate church there.

εἶχεν γὰρ εὐχήν] Cf. xxi. 23, *εὐχὴν ἔχοντες*, i.e., a temporary Nazirite vow. The minimum duration of such a vow was 30 days. The shearing of the hair marked the termination of the vow. Cf. Num. vi. 1-21, and the Mishna tractate *Nazir*.

xviii. 19

κἀκείνους] i.e., Priscilla and Aquila. Between *καὶ* and *ἐκείνους* the δ text inserts *τῷ ἐπιόντι σαββάτῳ*. 'Aquila and Priscilla remained in Ephesus until the end of 55 (1 Cor. xvi. 19); but in 56 they returned to Rome, where they were in the early part of A.D. 57 (Rom. xvi. 3). We may fairly suppose that Timothy came with Paul to Ephesus, and went up on a mission from thence to his native city and the other Churches of Galatia' (Ramsay, *SPT*, p. 263).

Ἔφεσον] Ephesus was situated near the mouth of the Cayster, on the main route from Rome to the east, and was the capital of the province of Asia. At this time it was the greatest commercial city of Asia Minor (*ἐμπόριον οὖσα μέγιστον τῶν κατὰ τὴν Ἀσίαν τὴν ἐντὸς τοῦ Ταύρου*, Strabo xiv. 1. 24), although its harbour required constant dredging because of the Cayster alluvium. Ephesus was a free city, with its own Senate and Assembly (see on xix. 39), an assize town (see on xix. 38), and proud of its title of Warden of the Temple of Artemis (see on xix. 35). Jews lived at Ephesus in great numbers, and the privileges granted them by Dolabella in 44 B.C. were confirmed by the town itself and by Augustus (Jos. *Ant.* xiv. 10. 12, 25; xvi. 6. 2, 4, 7).

διελέξατο] Cf. *ver.* 4, *διελέγετο*, 'conversed', 'discussed', 'debated'.

xviii. 21

εἰπών] δ byz add *δεῖ με πάντως τὴν ἑορτὴν τὴν ἐρχομένην ποιῆσαι εἰς Ἱεροσόλυμα*, which may well give the true reason for Paul's hasty departure, the feast probably being Passover.[1]

[1] If the feast was Passover, there may have been a good reason for his haste; Vegetius (*de re mil.* iv. 39) tells us that the seas were closed until March 10, and in A.D. 52 Passover fell at the beginning of April.

τοῦ θεοῦ θέλοντος] Cf. xxi. 14 (*τοῦ κυρίου τὸ θέλημα γινέσθω*); Jas. iv. 15 (*ἐὰν ὁ κύριος θέλῃ*).

xviii. 22

κατελθὼν εἰς Καισαρίαν] 'landing at Caesarea' (cf. xiii. 4; xiv. 25; xvi. 8 for compounds of *κατά*). When the wind is east of north it is easier to land at Caesarea than at Seleucia.

ἀναβὰς καὶ ἀσπασάμενος τὴν ἐκκλησίαν] Which church? At Caesarea or Jerusalem? The phrase by itself is ambiguous (Moffatt reproduces the ambiguity in his rendering 'went up to the capital'); but the following words *κατέβη εἰς Ἀντιόχειαν* make it plain that Jerusalem is intended; the verb *καταβαίνω* would not be used of going from Caesarea, a seaport, to Antioch, an inland town. (B. H. Streeter, in *JTS*, xxxiv [1933], p. 237, maintains that Caesarea is intended, not Jerusalem, and suggests the insertion here of the δ text of xix. 1, *q.v.*, as explaining why Paul did not carry out the intention expressed in xviii. 21 δ.)

So the second journey ends and the third begins. The succession of participles in *vv.* 22 f. gives the impression of haste. In these two verses and xix. 1 is compressed a journey of 1500 miles. Note how quickly Luke can cover the ground when describing a journey on which he did not accompany Paul.

xviii. 23

τὴν Γαλατικὴν χώραν καὶ Φρυγίαν] This, according to Ramsay, is to be distinguished from *τὴν Φρυγίαν καὶ Γαλατικὴν χώραν* of xvi. 6, 'the Galatian region' here being Lycaonia Galatica, that part of Lycaonia which lay within the province of Galatia, as distinct from Antiochian Lycaonia farther east (see on xiv. 6). But it is perhaps better to understand both Galatia and Phrygia here in the ethnic sense (see also on xvi. 6); the route taken by Paul is summarized in the words *τὰ ἀνωτερικὰ μέρη*, xix. 1 (*q.v.*). See K. Lake in *BC*, v, pp. 239 f.

Now that Paul is on his way back to Ephesus, the record of events there is brought up to date (*vv.* 24 ff.) before we are told of Paul's arrival there (xix. 1).

(b) Apollos, xviii. 24-28

Ἰουδαῖος δέ τις Ἀπολλῶς ὀνόματι, Ἀλεξανδρεὺς τῷ γένει, ἀνὴρ 24
λόγιος, κατήντησεν εἰς Ἔφεσον, δυνατὸς ὢν ἐν ταῖς γραφαῖς. οὗτος 25
ἦν κατηχημένος τὴν ὁδὸν τοῦ κυρίου, καὶ ζέων τῷ πνεύματι ἐλάλει
καὶ ἐδίδασκεν ἀκριβῶς τὰ περὶ τοῦ Ἰησοῦ, ἐπιστάμενος μόνον τὸ

βάπτισμα Ἰωάνου. οὗτός τε ἤρξατο παρρησιάζεσθαι ἐν τῇ συναγωγῇ· 26
ἀκούσαντες δὲ αὐτοῦ Πρίσκιλλα καὶ Ἀκύλας προσελάβοντο αὐτὸν
καὶ ἀκριβέστερον αὐτῷ ἐξέθεντο τὴν ὁδὸν τοῦ θεοῦ. βουλομένου δὲ 27
αὐτοῦ διελθεῖν εἰς τὴν Ἀχαίαν προτρεψάμενοι οἱ ἀδελφοὶ ἔγραψαν
τοῖς μαθηταῖς ἀποδέξασθαι αὐτόν· ὃς παραγενόμενος συνεβάλετο
πολὺ τοῖς πεπιστευκόσιν διὰ τῆς χάριτος· εὐτόνως γὰρ τοῖς Ἰουδαίοις 28
διακατηλέγχετο δημοσίᾳ ἐπιδεικνὺς διὰ τῶν γραφῶν εἶναι τὸν χριστὸν
Ἰησοῦν.

xviii. 24

Ἀπολλῶς] D gives his full name Ἀπολλώνιος. ℵ has Ἀπελλῆς (cf. Horace, *Sat.* i. 5. 100, '*credat Iudaeus Apella*'). The fact that he was accurately acquainted with the story of Jesus, but was ignorant of Christian baptism, and probably of the Pentecostal coming of the Holy Spirit (cf. xix. 2), suggests that his knowledge was not derived along the line of transmission traced in Ac., but perhaps from a Galilean source. He may have been acquainted with a written 'Sayings' Gospel (cf. Blass, *PG*, pp. 29 ff.), although κατηχημένος (*ver.* 25) may rather suggest oral instruction.

Ἀλεξανδρεὺς τῷ γένει] Cf. Ποντικὸν τῷ γένει, *ver.* 2. Alexandria, founded by Alexander the Great in 332 B.C., afforded from its earliest days a home for Jews, who inhabited two out of its five wards, and had their own constitution, independent of the civic government. It was the literary centre of the Hellenistic world, both Gentile and Jewish; here the LXX and the works of Philo saw the light.

ἀνὴρ λόγιος] 'a learned man'; λόγιος has this sense in Mod. Gk. (cf. Jos. *Ant.* xvii. 6. 2). The meaning 'eloquent' (so Lat., Syr., AV), which is deprecated by Phrynichus, was a secondary one; the earliest example of this meaning given in LS⁹ is from Demetrius *de elocutione* 38 (*c.* A.D. 50-100). 'Perhaps some such general sense as "a man of culture" best gives the sense' in this verse (MM).

xviii. 25

κατηχημένος] Usually of oral information; not, as later, of formal catechizing (cf. Lk. i. 4). δ adds ἐν τῇ πατρίδι, implying that Christianity had reached Alexandria by about A.D. 50, which is extremely likely.

ζέων τῷ πνεύματι] Cf. Rom. xii. 11, τῷ πνεύματι ζέοντες. Lit., 'boiling over in his spirit', i.e., full of enthusiasm. But LC take it to mean 'boiling over with the Holy Spirit'.

τὰ περὶ τοῦ Ἰησοῦ] 'the story of Jesus'. Cf. xxviii. 31, Lk. xxiv. 19, 27.

xviii. 26

Πρισκίλλα καὶ Ἀκύλας] Notice the order, as in *ver.* 18; Rom. xvi. 3; 2 Tim. iv. 19. See on *ver.* 2. The δ reviser reverses the order here (not, however, in *ver.* 18, probably because it interpreted *κειράμενος* of Aquila). This is not the only place where δ modifies the prominence of women in Ac.: see on xvii. 4, 12, 34.

ἀκριβέστερον] The comparative force is probably retained here, with reference to *ἀκριβῶς* in *ver.* 25. But for the elative force of the comparative cf. iv. 16 D; xvii. 21; xxiii. 15, 20; xxiv. 22, 26.

xviii. 27

βουλομένου δὲ αὐτοῦ κ.τ.λ.] δ recasts the verse thus: *ἐν δὲ τῇ Ἐφέσῳ ἐπιδημοῦντές τινες Κορίνθιοι καὶ ἀκούσαντες αὐτοῦ παρεκάλουν διελθεῖν σὺν αὐτοῖς εἰς τὴν πατρίδα αὐτῶν. συνκατανεύσαντος δὲ αὐτοῦ οἱ Ἐφέσιοι ἔγραψαν τοῖς ἐν Κορίνθῳ μαθηταῖς ὅπως ἀποδέξωνται τὸν ἄνδρα· ὃς ἐπιδημήσας εἰς τὴν Ἀχαίαν πολὺ συνεβάλλετο ἐν ταῖς ἐκκλησίαις.* This account 'has all the marks of truth, and yet is clearly not original, but a text remodelled according to a good tradition' (Ramsay, *SPT*, p. 267).

προτρεψάμενοι] 'encouraging (him to do so)'.

ἔγραψαν κ.τ.λ.] With this 'letter of commendation' cf. Paul's ironical question in 2 Cor. iii. 1, *ἢ μὴ χρῄζομεν ὥς τινες συστατικῶν ἐπιστολῶν πρὸς ὑμᾶς ἢ ἐξ ὑμῶν;*

συνεβάλετο] 'was helpful' (LC); this translation accords well with the following *γάρ*.

xviii. 28

διακατηλέγχετο] This *hapax legomenon* may be a combination of *διελέγχω* ('confute') and *κατελέγχω* ('convict').

δημοσίᾳ] Cf. xvi. 37; xx. 20.

ἐπιδεικνὺς] δ has *διαλεγόμενος καὶ ἐπιδεικνύς*.

εἶναι τὸν χριστὸν Ἰησοῦν] As in *ver.* 5 (*q.v.*); D has *τὸν Ἰησοῦν εἶναι χριστόν* ('that Jesus was the Messiah'), P^{38} *χριστὸν εἶναι Ἰησοῦν*. The extent of Apollos's influence in the church at Corinth may be gauged from references to him in 1 Cor. Some of the Corinthians declared themselves his special followers (i. 12 ff.), but this partisanship was no doubt as far from his approval as was the existence of the 'I of Paul' party from Paul's. Paul considers that Apollos continued at Corinth the work which he himself had begun (iii. 6), seems to regard him as an apostle (iv. 9), and tells how he pressed him to pay a second visit to Corinth (xvi. 12).

(c) Paul and the Twelve Disciples at Ephesus, xix. 1-7

Ἐγένετο δὲ ἐν τῷ τὸν Ἀπολλῶ εἶναι ἐν Κορίνθῳ Παῦλον διελθόντα 1
τὰ ἀνωτερικὰ μέρη ἐλθεῖν εἰς Ἔφεσον καὶ εὑρεῖν τινὰς μαθητάς, εἶπέν 2
τε πρὸς αὐτούς Εἰ πνεῦμα ἅγιον ἐλάβετε πιστεύσαντες; οἱ δὲ πρὸς
αὐτόν Ἀλλ' οὐδ' εἰ πνεῦμα ἅγιον ἔστιν ἠκούσαμεν. εἶπέν τε Εἰς 3
τί οὖν ἐβαπτίσθητε; οἱ δὲ εἶπαν Εἰς τὸ Ἰωάνου βάπτισμα. εἶπεν 4
δὲ Παῦλος Ἰωάνης ἐβάπτισεν βάπτισμα μετανοίας, τῷ λαῷ λέγων
εἰς τὸν ἐρχόμενον μετ' αὐτὸν ἵνα πιστεύσωσιν, τοῦτ' ἔστιν εἰς τὸν
Ἰησοῦν. ἀκούσαντες δὲ ἐβαπτίσθησαν εἰς τὸ ὄνομα τοῦ κυρίου 5
Ἰησοῦ· καὶ ἐπιθέντος αὐτοῖς τοῦ Παύλου χεῖρας ἦλθε τὸ πνεῦμα 6
τὸ ἅγιον ἐπ' αὐτούς, ἐλάλουν τε γλώσσαις καὶ ἐπροφήτευον. ἦσαν 7
δὲ οἱ πάντες ἄνδρες ὡσεὶ δώδεκα.

xix. 1

Ἐγένετο δὲ κ.τ.λ.] For this beginning δ substitutes *θέλοντος δὲ τοῦ Παύλου κατὰ τὴν ἰδίαν βουλὴν πορεύεσθαι εἰς Ἱεροσόλυμα, εἶπεν αὐτῷ τὸ πνεῦμα ὑποστρέφειν εἰς τὴν Ἀσίαν, διελθὼν δὲ κ.τ.λ.* The δ reviser apparently considered that the church in xviii. 22 (*q.v.*) was the Caesarean one, and inserted this interpolation to explain why Paul did not carry out his intention (expressed in xviii. 21 δ) of going to Jerusalem. Taking his cue from xvi. 6 ff., he attributed the supposed change in plan to the Holy Spirit's prohibition.

τὰ ἀνωτερικὰ μέρη] Recapitulating the geographical note of xviii. 23 (*q.v.*). Instead of taking the main road by the Lycus and Maeander valleys, Paul probably travelled by a higher road farther north, approaching Ephesus from the north side of Mt. Messogis. We gather from Col. ii. 1 that he was a stranger to the Lycus valley.

μαθητάς] Presumably disciples of Christ, in accordance with the meaning elsewhere of *μαθητής* thus used absolutely; had they been disciples of John, we should have expected this to be explicitly stated. They may have received their knowledge of Jesus in some such way as Apollos received his (see on xviii. 24), or even from Apollos himself (cf. xviii. 25).

xix. 2

Εἰ] For *εἰ* introducing direct question cf. vii. 1.

πιστεύσαντες] 'on believing'. Cf. *πιστεύσασιν*, xi. 17; also Eph. i. 13, *ἐν ᾧ καὶ πιστεύσαντες ἐσφραγίσθητε τῷ πνεύματι τῆς ἐπαγγελίας τῷ ἁγίῳ.* 'The coincident aor. ptc. is doctrinally important: cf. RV' (*Proleg.*, p. 131 *n.*).

Ἀλλ' οὐδ' εἰ πνεῦμα ἅγιόν ἐστιν ἠκούσαμεν] The expression 'Holy Spirit', though occurring in OT (cf. Ps. li. 11; Isa. lxiii. 10 f.), was apparently unknown to these 'disciples', who may, of course, have been Gentiles. But the δ reviser felt a difficulty here, and altered the words to ἀλλ' οὐδ' εἰ πνεῦμα ἅγιον λαμβάνουσίν τινες ἠκούσαμεν. Possibly πνεῦμα ἅγιον is to be understood here in a special sense, of the Holy Spirit as sent at Pentecost with outward manifestation: cf. Jn. vii. 39 οὔπω γὰρ ἦν πνεῦμα (where δ byz have similarly tried to smooth a difficulty by adding δεδομένον).

xix. 3

Εἰς τί οὖν ἐβαπτίσθητε;] A connection is suggested between the receiving of the Spirit and baptism (see on ii. 38). As they knew John's baptism, they might have been expected to know John's teaching, that his baptism of repentance prepared the way for the coming of One who should baptize ἐν πνεύματι ἁγίῳ, but this, apparently, they did not know.

Εἰς τὸ Ἰωάνου βάπτισμα] As in Paul's preceding question, εἰς is here equivalent to instrumental ἐν: '(we were baptized) with John's baptism'. For John's baptism cf. i. 5; xi. 16; xiii. 24 f.; xviii. 25; Jn. iii. 22 ff., etc.

xix. 4

βάπτισμα] Internal acc. after ἐβάπτισεν.

εἰς τὸν ἐρχόμενον μετ' αὐτὸν ἵνα πιστεύσωσιν] Note how ἵνα, instead of being at the beginning of the clause, is joined immediately to the verb; this construction throws τὸν ἐρχόμενον μετ' αὐτόν into prominence, thus stressing the preparatory nature of John's ministry. That John directed his hearers to *believe* in the Coming One is not explicitly stated by the Synoptists (according to whom he called for repentance in view of the Coming One's judgment), but it is in thorough accord with his testimony to Jesus in Jn. i. 26 ff.; iii. 25 ff.

τοῦτ' ἔστιν εἰς τὸν Ἰησοῦν] In the Synoptic account John does not explicitly identify the Coming One with Jesus (but cf. Lk. vii. 19). He makes this identification, however, in Jn. i. 29 ff. Some striking agreements between Jn. and Ac. in their presentation of John's ministry and of the Holy Spirit deserve careful study (see also on xiii. 25). Cf. W. F. Lofthouse, 'The Holy Spirit in the Acts and the Fourth Gospel', in *ET*, lii (1940-1), pp. 334 ff.

xix. 5

ἐβαπτίσθησαν εἰς τὸ ὄνομα τοῦ κυρίου Ἰησοῦ] See on viii. 16 for this expression. This is the only case of re-baptism in NT. δ adds *Χριστόν* after *Ἰησοῦν*, and continues ineptly, *εἰς ἄφεσιν ἁμαρτιῶν* (cf. ii. 38), but these disciples had previously been baptized for this.

xix. 6

ἐπιθέντος αὐτοῖς τοῦ Παύλου χεῖρας κ.τ.λ.] Here, as in viii. 15 ff., the Spirit is bestowed after baptism and imposition of apostolic hands. The coming of the Spirit is accompanied, as in ii. 4; x. 44 ff., by glossolalia and prophecy (with *ἐπροφήτευον* here cf. the magnifying of God in ii. 11; x. 46). In Paul's teaching the Spirit is the bestower of supernatural gifts (1 Cor. xii. 8 ff.; Gal. v. 22).

xix. 7

ὡσεὶ δώδεκα] Characteristic Lukan modifying of exact numbers by *ὡσεί* or *ὡς* (see on i. 15).

(d) Paul leaves the Synagogue for the School of Tyrannus, xix. 8-10

Εἰσελθὼν δὲ εἰς τὴν συναγωγὴν ἐπαρρησιάζετο ἐπὶ μῆνας τρεῖς δια- 8
λεγόμενος καὶ πείθων περὶ τῆς βασιλείας τοῦ θεοῦ. ὡς δέ τινες ἐσκλη- 9
ρύνοντο καὶ ἠπείθουν κακολογοῦντες τὴν ὁδὸν ἐνώπιον τοῦ πλήθους,
ἀποστὰς ἀπ᾽ αὐτῶν ἀφώρισεν τοὺς μαθητάς, καθ᾽ ἡμέραν διαλεγόμενος
ἐν τῇ σχολῇ Τυράννου. τοῦτο δὲ ἐγένετο ἐπὶ ἔτη δύο, ὥστε πάντας 10
τοὺς κατοικοῦντας τὴν Ἀσίαν ἀκοῦσαι τὸν λόγον τοῦ κυρίου, Ἰουδαίους
τε καὶ Ἕλληνας.

xix. 8

Εἰσελθὼν δὲ εἰς τὴν συναγωγὴν] He had paid it an earlier visit (xviii. 19). δ adds *ἐν δυνάμει μεγάλῃ* before *ἐπαρρησιάζετο*.

περὶ τῆς βασιλείας τοῦ θεοῦ] See on i. 3; viii. 12; xx. 25.

xix. 9

ἐσκληρύνοντο] 'were obstinate'; lit., 'made themselves difficult'. Cf. *ἀντιτασσομένων*, xviii. 6; *κακολογοῦντες* here corresponds to *βλασφημούντων* there.

ἠπείθουν] 'were disobedient': cf. xiv. 2.

τὴν ὁδὸν] See on ix. 2.

τοῦ πλήθους] 'the congregation': see on iv. 32; xv. 12.

ἀποστὰς ἀπ᾽ αὐτῶν] Cf. xviii. 7, *μεταβὰς ἐκεῖθεν*.

ἐν τῇ σχολῇ Τυράννου] The lecture-hall of Tyrannus (called *σχολή* because it was a place for spending one's *leisure:* cf. Lat. *ludus*) served the purpose in Ephesus that the house of Justus did in Corinth. D changes *Τυράννου* to *Τυραννίου*. δ adds *ἀπὸ ὥρας πέμπτης ἕως δεκάτης*, 'from 11 A.M. to 4 P.M.', a very reasonable guess, if guess it be. Tyrannus no doubt gave his lectures before 11 A.M., at which hour public life in the Ionian cities, as elsewhere, regularly ended. Cf. Martial, iv. 8, '*in quintam uarios extendit Roma labores*'. So we must picture Paul spending the hours from daybreak to 11 A.M. at his manual labour (cf. xx. 34; 1 Cor. iv. 12), and then devoting the next five hours to the still more exhausting business of Christian dialectic. His hearers must have been infected with his keenness and energy, as LC point out that normally more people would be asleep in Ephesus at 1 P.M. than at 1 A.M.

xix. 10

ἐπὶ ἔτη δύο] Now he had ample time to 'preach the word in Asia', which had been his aim previously when he was guided towards Europe (xvi. 6). The period was probably two years and a few months, which with the 3 months of *ver.* 8 make up the 3 years of xx. 31, i.e., 3 years less a few months; probably from autumn of 52 to summer of 55. Many of the events of these years which are not mentioned by Luke can be inferred from Paul's epistles, especially those to Corinth. From these it is evident that, apart from the troubles in the Corinthian church, he had critical experiences in Ephesus of which we learn nothing in Ac.; cf. 1 Cor. xv. 30-32; 2 Cor. i. 8-10. Prof. G. S. Duncan, in *SPEM*, argues that of Paul's frequent imprisonments (cf. 2 Cor. xi. 23) three occurred during this period, and that the 'Captivity Epistles' were written at this time.[1]

ὥστε πάντας τοὺς κατοικοῦντας τὴν Ἀσίαν ἀκοῦσαι κ.τ.λ.] Asia here is probably the district round Ephesus, as in xvi. 6 (*q.v.*). The foundation of the churches of the Lycus valley, at Colossae, Hierapolis and Laodicea (cf. Col. iv. 13) must be dated in this period, although some of these places seem to have been evangelized not by Paul personally, but by his fellow-workers (cf. Col. ii. 1; Colossae was probably evangelized by Epaphras). The province became one of the chief centres of Christianity; possibly all the Seven Churches of Asia addressed in the Apocalypse were founded during these years.

[1] Cf. also Deissmann, 'Zur Ephesinischen Gefangenschaft des Apostels Paulus' in *Anatolian Studies presented to Sir W. M. Ramsay* (Manchester, 1923), pp. 121 ff. The case for an Ephesian provenance seems stronger for Phil. than for Eph., Col. and Philm. See on *ver.* 22.

(e) Signs and Wonders at Ephesus, xix. 11-19

Δυνάμεις τε οὐ τὰς τυχούσας ὁ θεὸς ἐποίει διὰ τῶν χειρῶν Παύλου, 11
ὥστε καὶ ἐπὶ τοὺς ἀσθενοῦντας ἀποφέρεσθαι ἀπὸ τοῦ χρωτὸς αὐτοῦ 12
σουδάρια ἢ σιμικίνθια καὶ ἀπαλλάσσεσθαι ἀπ' αὐτῶν τὰς νόσους, τά
τε πνεύματα τά πονηρὰ ἐκπορεύεσθαι. Ἐπεχείρησαν δέ τινες καὶ 13
τῶν περιερχομένων Ἰουδαίων ἐξορκιστῶν ὀνομάζειν ἐπὶ τοὺς ἔχοντας
τὰ πνεύματα τὰ πονηρὰ τὸ ὄνομα τοῦ κυρίου Ἰησοῦ λέγοντες Ὁρκίζω
ὑμᾶς τὸν Ἰησοῦν ὃν Παῦλος κηρύσσει. ἦσαν δέ τινος Σκευᾶ Ἰουδαίου 14
ἀρχιερέως ἑπτὰ υἱοὶ τοῦτο ποιοῦντες. ἀποκριθὲν δὲ τὸ πνεῦμα τὸ 15
πονηρὸν εἶπεν αὐτοῖς Τὸν μὲν Ἰησοῦν γινώσκω καὶ τὸν Παῦλον
ἐπίσταμαι, ὑμεῖς δὲ τίνες ἐστέ; καὶ ἐφαλόμενος ὁ ἄνθρωπος ἐπ' αὐτοὺς 16
ἐν ᾧ ἦν τὸ πνεῦμα τὸ πονηρὸν κατακυριεύσας ἀμφοτέρων ἴσχυσεν κατ'
αὐτῶν, ὥστε γυμνοὺς καὶ τετραυματισμένους ἐκφυγεῖν ἐκ τοῦ οἴκου
ἐκείνου. τοῦτο δὲ ἐγένετο γνωστὸν πᾶσιν Ἰουδαίοις τε καὶ Ἕλλησιν 17
τοῖς κατοικοῦσιν τὴν Ἔφεσον, καὶ ἐπέπεσεν φόβος ἐπὶ πάντας αὐτούς,
καὶ ἐμεγαλύνετο τὸ ὄνομα τοῦ κυρίου Ἰησοῦ. πολλοί τε τῶν πεπισ- 18
τευκότων ἤρχοντο ἐξομολογούμενοι καὶ ἀναγγέλλοντες τὰς πράξεις
αὐτῶν. ἱκανοὶ δὲ τῶν τὰ περίεργα πραξάντων συνενέγκαντες τὰς βίβ- 19
λους κατέκαιον ἐνώπιον πάντων· καὶ συνεψήφισαν τὰς τιμὰς αὐτῶν
καὶ εὗρον ἀργυρίου μυριάδας πέντε.

xix. 11

δυνάμεις τε οὐ τὰς τυχούσας κ.τ.λ.] With *vv.* 11 f. cf. v. 15 f.

οὐ τὰς τυχούσας] 'unusual', 'extraordinary': cf. xxviii. 2, οὐ τὴν τυχοῦσαν φιλανθρωπίαν. This litotes is characteristic of Luke, as in the frequent οὐκ ὀλίγος (e.g., in *ver.* 23). οὐχ ὁ τυχών is frequent in Vettius Valens (43. 29, 32; 60. 20; 143. 3; 195. 17; 197. 18; 258. 7; 337. 29; 343. 13; 352. 6).

διὰ τῶν χειρῶν] Here there is more emphasis on χείρ than in the Semitism διὰ χειρός (cf. xi. 30, etc.); not merely the agency of Paul is indicated but his personal activity and their contact with him.

xix. 12

χρωτὸς] lit., 'skin'; but it is used in LXX to render Heb. *bāsār*, 'flesh'.

σουδάρια ἢ σιμικίνθια] Both words are of Lat. origin, *sudaria*, 'sweat-rags', kerchiefs worn on the head (cf. Lk. xix. 20; Jn. xi. 44; xx. 7), and *semicinctia*, 'aprons'. Both would be used by Paul at his work. With their effect cf. that of the tassel (κράσπεδον) of Jesus' garment (Lk. viii. 44) and of Peter's shadow (v. 15).

ἀπαλλάσσεσθαι] Cf. Lk. xii. 58; Heb. ii. 15; but this is the only place in NT where it is used of sickness. 'In this use it is one of the words most frequently occurring in the medical writers' (Hobart, p. 47)—as one might expect!

xix. 13

τῶν περιερχομένων Ἰουδαίων ἐξορκιστῶν] 'of the itinerant Jewish exorcists'. This is the only NT example of ἐξορκιστής, and the oldest known example; it occurs also in Lucian, Ptolemy, and the Greek Fathers. In later times exorcists formed an order in the Church. Jews and things Jewish played a prominent part in ancient magic; papyri reveal the use in magic of such Jewish names as Abraham, Sabaoth, Iao or Iabe [1] (Yahweh), etc.

ὁρκίζω ὑμᾶς τὸν Ἰησοῦν] For the use of the name of Jesus by those who were not His disciples cf. Mk. ix. 38 ff.=Lk. ix. 49 f.; cf. also Justin, *Tryph.* 85. The Paris magical papyrus 574 contains the adjuration ὁρκίζω σε κατὰ τοῦ θεοῦ τῶν Ἑβραίων Ἰησοῦ (lines 3018 ff.). Such use of the name of Jesus was censured by the Rabbis (cf. Tosefta, *Ḥullin*, ii. 22 f.; TJ *Shabbath* xiv. 4. 14*d*; TJ *Abodah Zarah* ii. 2. 40*d*-41*a*; TB *Abodah Zarah* 27*b*). The double acc. after ὁρκίζω (cf. Mk. v. 7) is paralleled in inscriptions and in Vettius Valens 172. 31; 263. 19 f.; 293. 26.

xix. 14

ἦσαν δέ τινος κ.τ.λ.] This verse is expanded in the δ text, ἐν οἷς καὶ υἱοὶ Σκευᾶ τινος ἱερέως ἠθέλησαν τὸ αὐτὸ ποιῆσαι (ἔθος εἶχαν τοὺς τοιούτους ἐξορκίζειν), καὶ εἰσελθόντες πρὸς τὸν δαιμονιζόμενον ἤρξαντο ἐπικαλεῖσθαι τὸ ὄνομα λέγοντες, Παραγγέλλομέν σοι ἐν Ἰησοῦ ὃν Παῦλος κηρύσσει ἐξελθεῖν.

Σκευᾶ] Perhaps connected with Heb. Sheba, less probably with Lat. Scaeva.

ἀρχιερέως] It is conceivable that Sceva was related to one of the Jewish high-priestly families; more probably, however, ἀρχιερέως is to be regarded as an advertisement. Luke did not have at his disposal the devices of quotation-marks or the use of '*sic*' to show that he was merely giving Sceva's own account of himself. As a Jewish High Priest had the power to enter the Holy of Holies on the Day of Atonement and pronounce the Ineffable Name, a claim to be such a person would be very impressive. The δ text modifies the difficulty by reading ἱερέως.

ἑπτὰ] See on ἀμφοτέρων, *ver.* 16.

xix. 15

τὸν μὲν Ἰησοῦν γινώσκω καὶ τὸν Παῦλον ἐπίσταμαι] Two different words for 'know' are perhaps used because the two kinds

[1] On the magical use of the Tetragrammaton see Deissmann, *BS*, pp. 322 ff.

of knowledge were different; the demoniac knew of Jesus by hearsay, but knew Paul by sight. But such a conclusion cannot be drawn simply from the respective meanings of γινώσκω and ἐπίσταμαι. For the spirit's recognition of Jesus cf. Mk. i. 24 and elsewhere in the Gospels.

xix. 16

ἀμφοτέρων] The apparent discrepancy between this and ἑπτά in *ver.* 14 was removed in δ(D r)[1] by the omission of ἑπτά (g emends it to *duo*). J. H. Moulton quotes a suggestion by J. B. Shipley that ἑπτά arose from a gloss explaining Σκευᾶ as the equivalent of Heb. *sheba'*, 'seven' (*Proleg.*, p. 246). There is good evidence, however, for ἀμφότεροι in the sense of 'all' in later Koiné and Byzantine Gk. MM refer to a papyrus of A.D. 167 where ἀμφότεροι refers to five men (*P. Lond.* 336[13]), and to two others of A.D. 382 and 386 respectively where the word is used of four men. On the first they quote Kenyon's observation: 'ἀμφότεροι = πάντες in late Byzantine Greek . . . and it is possible that colloquially the use existed earlier.' In hcl and some later versions ἀμφοτέρων is rendered 'all'. If, however, this usage seems insufficiently literary for Luke, we may conclude that we have here the vivid description of an eye-witness, implying that while seven sons attempted the exorcism, only two were attacked by the demoniac.

ἐκ τοῦ οἴκου ἐκείνου] The house has not hitherto been mentioned; this belated mention is 'quite in the manner of Luke' (LC).

xix. 17

ἐγένετο γνωστὸν κ.τ.λ.] Cf. i. 19; ix. 42.

ἐπέπεσεν φόβος ἐπὶ πάντας αὐτούς] Cf. ii. 43; v. 11.

xix. 18

πεπιστευκότων] 'believers'; note the force of the perfect.

ἐξομολογούμενοι καὶ ἀναγγέλλοντες τὰς πράξεις αὐτῶν] 'making confession and revealing their spells'; πρᾶξις is used technically in this sense. As the potency of spells resides largely in their secrecy, their disclosure would be regarded as rendering them powerless.

xix. 19

περίεργα] lit., 'superfluous works', used like Lat. *curiosa* in a magical sense. Deissmann (*BS*, p. 323 *n.*) calls περίεργα 'a *terminus technicus* for *magic*', remarking also on the magical connotation of πράξεις (see on *ver.* 18). For the more general sense of περίεργος, περιεργάζομαι, cf. 2 Th. iii. 11; 1 Tim. v. 13.

[1] P^{38} (a further witness for δ) also omits ἑπτά, but hcl.mg retains it.

βίβλους] Scrolls containing magical spells, like the famous magical papyri in the London, Paris and Leyden collections ; they fetched a high price. The special connection of magical practices with Ephesus is reflected in the term *Ἐφέσια γράμματα* for such scrolls (Anaxilas *ap.* Athen. xii. 548 c ; Plut., *Quaest. Conviv.* 706 e ; Clem. Alex., *Strom.* v. 8. 45. 2). This passage is thus a good touch of local colour.

κατέκαιον ἐνώπιον πάντων] For such public burning of literature as an open repudiation of its contents cf. Livy xl. 29 (of Numa's writings) ; Suet. *Aug.* xxxi. 1 (of prophetic books) ; Diog. Laert. *Lives of Philosophers*, ix. 52 (of the works of Protagoras) ; Lucian, *Alexander*, 47 (of the works of Epicurus). Twentieth century examples will also occur to the reader's mind. Cf. also the burning of objects of luxury in fifteenth century Florence as a result of Savonarola's preaching.

ἀργυρίου μυριάδας πέντε] i.e., drachmae. For the omission of the monetary unit cf. Plut. *Galba*, 17 ; Jos. *Ant.* xvii. 8. 1.

(f) Progress Reported, xix. 20

Οὕτως κατὰ κράτος τοῦ κυρίου ὁ λόγος ηὔξανεν καὶ ἴσχυεν. 20

xix. 20

τοῦ κυρίου] Grammatically the genitive might belong either to *κράτος* or to *λόγος*, more probably to the latter. This sentence is the fifth of six brief reports of progress throughout Ac. : see on vi. 7.

VI. PAUL PLANS TO VISIT ROME VIA JERUSALEM AND ACHIEVES HIS AIM IN AN UNEXPECTED WAY, xix. 21-xxviii. 31

1. He Leaves Ephesus for Macedonia and Greece, xix. 21-xx. 6

(a) Paul makes Plans for the Future, xix. 21-22

Ὡς δὲ ἐπληρώθη ταῦτα, ἔθετο ὁ Παῦλος ἐν τῷ πνεύματι διελθὼν 21
τὴν Μακεδονίαν καὶ Ἀχαίαν πορεύεσθαι εἰς Ἱεροσόλυμα, εἰπὼν
ὅτι Μετὰ τὸ γενέσθαι με ἐκεῖ δεῖ με καὶ Ῥώμην ἰδεῖν. ἀποστείλας 22
δὲ εἰς τὴν Μακεδονίαν δύο τῶν διακονούντων αὐτῷ, Τιμόθεον καὶ Ἔραστον, αὐτὸς ἐπέσχεν χρόνον εἰς τὴν Ἀσίαν.

xix. 21

ὡς δὲ ἐπληρώθη κ.τ.λ.] This verse summarizes the remainder of Ac., referring as it does to the visit to Jerusalem and the journey to Rome, although neither of these turned out exactly as Paul expected. This is Paul's first recorded mention of Rome. For his intention to visit the Imperial City cf. Rom. i. 11 ff.; xv. 23 ff. In the light of these passages this verse reveals what Ramsay calls 'the clear conception of a far-reaching plan' to proceed *via* the Imperial City to evangelize 'the chief seat of Roman civilisation in the West' (i.e. Spain). This decision thus marks a crisis in Paul's career. Cf. *SPT*, pp. 254 f., 274; J. H. Kennedy, *Second and Third Epistles to the Corinthians*, pp. 20 ff.

ἔθετο . . . ἐν τῷ πνεύματι] Either 'purposed in the Spirit' or '. . . in his spirit'; if the latter, cf. v. 4 (*ἔθου ἐν τῇ καρδίᾳ σου*); similarly Lk. i. 66; xxi. 14. For similar ambiguity in the meaning of *πνεῦμα*, cf. xviii. 25; xx. 22. But a reference to the Holy Spirit is the more likely.

διελθὼν κ.τ.λ.] We should take the ptc. with *πορεύεσθαι*, not with *ἔθετο*. This projected visit, then, will be that recorded in xx. 1 ff.; its purpose was to collect the European churches' contribution for the poor members of the Jerusalem church (see on xx. 4). But Paul must have visited Corinth at some time between xviii. 18 and xx. 2*b*, for the visit of xx. 2*b*, 3 was his third (2 Cor. xii. 14; xiii. 1).

ὅτι] *recitantis*.

xix. 22

δύο] For other deputations of two cf. ix. 38; xi. 30; xv. 27, 39 f.

Τιμόθεον] We have not heard of Timothy since his arrival in Corinth from Macedonia (xviii. 5). He may have accompanied Paul to Ephesus or joined him there later. From 1 Cor. iv. 17; xvi. 10, we learn that at some point during Paul's stay in Ephesus Timothy was sent to Corinth; Paul expected him to return to Ephesus (1 Cor. xvi. 11). That was probably not the occasion referred to here, but an earlier one. The visit referred to here may be that mentioned in Phil. ii. 19 (in which case Phil. ii. 24 refers to Paul's Macedonian visit of xx. 1); this identification, however, is possible only if we believe that Phil. was written from Ephesus (see on *ver.* 10).[1]

[1] If so, Phil. i. 13 refers to an Ephesian imprisonment, and the 'Praetorium' there mentioned is the proconsular headquarters at Ephesus (cf. Mk. xv. 16 and parallels); 'they of Caesar's household' (Phil. iv. 22) are members of the imperial civil service, who were mostly the Emperor's freedmen, and the 'true yokefellow' of Phil. iv. 3 is perhaps Luke (see on xvi. 40; xx. 5). But quite apart from the questions of the Captivity Epistles and possible Ephesian imprisonments, the chronology of Paul's movements during his Ephesian ministry and of his relations with the Corinthian church during these years is a complicated study, which would take us outside the scope of this commentary. See literature referred to on p. 39, *n.* 3; p. 40, *n.* 1.

Ἔραστον] He may have been the same as the Erastus of Rom. xvi. 23, the *οἰκονόμος* of Corinth[1] (cf. 2 Tim. iv. 20), but this is not very likely, and the name was quite common.

(b) The Riot at Ephesus, xix. 23-41

Ἐγένετο δὲ κατὰ τὸν καιρὸν ἐκεῖνον τάραχος οὐκ ὀλίγος περὶ 23
τῆς ὁδοῦ. Δημήτριος γάρ τις ὀνόματι, ἀργυροκόπος, ποιῶν ναοὺς 24
ἀργυροῦς Ἀρτέμιδος παρείχετο τοῖς τεχνίταις οὐκ ὀλίγην ἐργασίαν,
οὓς συναθροίσας καὶ τοὺς περὶ τὰ τοιαῦτα ἐργάτας εἶπεν Ἄνδρες, 25
ἐπίστασθε ὅτι ἐκ ταύτης τῆς ἐργασίας ἡ εὐπορία ἡμῖν ἐστίν, καὶ 25
θεωρεῖτε καὶ ἀκούετε ὅτι οὐ μόνον Ἐφέσου ἀλλὰ σχεδὸν πάσης τῆς
Ἀσίας ὁ Παῦλος οὗτος πείσας μετέστησεν ἱκανὸν ὄχλον, λέγων ὅτι
οὐκ εἰσὶν θεοὶ οἱ διὰ χειρῶν γινόμενοι. οὐ μόνον δὲ τοῦτο κινδυνεύει 27
ἡμῖν τὸ μέρος εἰς ἀπελεγμὸν ἐλθεῖν, ἀλλὰ καὶ τὸ τῆς μεγάλης θεᾶς
Ἀρτέμιδος ἱερὸν εἰς οὐθὲν λογισθῆναι, μέλλειν τε καὶ καθαιρεῖσθαι
τῆς μεγαλειότητος αὐτῆς, ἣν ὅλη ἡ Ἀσία καὶ ἡ οἰκουμένη σέβεται.
ἀκούσαντες δὲ καὶ γενόμενοι πλήρεις θυμοῦ ἔκραζον λέγοντες Μεγάλη 28
ἡ Ἄρτεμις Ἐφεσίων. καὶ ἐπλήσθη ἡ πόλις τῆς συγχύσεως, 29
ὥρμησάν τε ὁμοθυμαδὸν εἰς τὸ θέατρον συναρπάσαντες Γαῖον καὶ Ἀρίσ-
ταρχον Μακεδόνας, συνεκδήμους Παύλου. Παύλου δὲ βουλομένου 30
εἰσελθεῖν εἰς τὸν δῆμον οὐκ εἴων αὐτὸν οἱ μαθηταί· τινὲς δὲ καὶ τῶν 31
Ἀσιαρχῶν, ὄντες αὐτῷ φίλοι, πέμψαντες πρὸς αὐτὸν παρεκάλουν
μὴ δοῦναι ἑαυτὸν εἰς τὸ θέατρον. ἄλλοι μὲν οὖν ἄλλο τι ἔκραζον, 32
ἦν γὰρ ἡ ἐκκλησία συνκεχυμένη, καὶ οἱ πλείους οὐκ ᾔδεισαν τίνος
ἕνεκα συνεληλύθεισαν. ἐκ δὲ τοῦ ὄχλου συνεβίβασαν Ἀλέξανδρον 33
προβαλόντων αὐτὸν τῶν Ἰουδαίων, ὁ δὲ Ἀλέξανδρος κατασείσας
τὴν χεῖρα ἤθελεν ἀπολογεῖσθαι τῷ δήμῳ. ἐπιγνόντες δὲ ὅτι Ἰουδαῖός 34
ἐστιν φωνὴ ἐγένετο μία ἐκ πάντων ὡσεὶ ἐπὶ ὥρας δύο κραζόντων
Μεγάλη ἡ Ἄρτεμις Ἐφεσίων. καταστείλας δὲ τὸν ὄχλον ὁ γραμ- 35
ματεύς φησιν Ἄνδρες Ἐφέσιοι, τίς γάρ ἐστιν ἀνθρώπων ὃς οὐ
γινώσκει τὴν Ἐφεσίων πόλιν νεωκόρον οὖσαν τῆς μεγάλης Ἀρτέμιδος
καὶ τοῦ διοπετοῦς; ἀναντιρήτων οὖν ὄντων τούτων δέον ἐστὶν ὑμᾶς 36
κατεσταλμένους ὑπάρχειν καὶ μηδὲν προπετὲς πράσσειν. ἠγάγετε 37
γὰρ τοὺς ἄνδρας τούτους οὔτε ἱεροσύλους οὔτε βλασφημοῦντας τὴν
θεὸν ἡμῶν. εἰ μὲν οὖν Δημήτριος καὶ οἱ σὺν αὐτῷ τεχνῖται ἔχουσιν 38
πρός τινα λόγον, ἀγοραῖοι ἄγονται καὶ ἀνθύπατοί εἰσιν, ἐγκαλείτωσαν
ἀλλήλοις. εἰ δέ τι περαιτέρω ἐπιζητεῖτε, ἐν τῇ ἐννόμῳ ἐκκλησίᾳ 39
ἐπιλυθήσεται. καὶ γὰρ κινδυνεύομεν ἐγκαλεῖσθαι στάσεως περὶ 40
τῆς σήμερον μηδενὸς αἰτίου ὑπάρχοντος, περὶ οὗ οὐ δυνησόμεθα ἀπο-
δοῦναι λόγον περὶ τῆς συστροφῆς ταύτης. καὶ ταῦτα εἰπὼν ἀπέλυσεν 41
τὴν ἐκκλησίαν.

[1] An inscription found in Corinth by T. L. Shear in 1929 mentions an Erastus as being procurator and aedile in the city: ERASTVS PRO. AED. S. P. STRAVIT, 'Erastus, procurator and aedile, made this pavement at his own expense'. (Cf. *JHS*, xlix [1929], p. 221.)

xix. 23

κατὰ τὸν καιρὸν ἐκεῖνον] i.e., about the time of the events of *ver.* 22; xx. 1 implies that the riot happened shortly before Paul's departure from Ephesus. 'It is tempting to believe that the outburst may have been connected with the celebration of the great Ephesian festival of the Artemisia, which took place in March or April' (G. S. Duncan, *SPEM*, p. 140).

τάραχος οὐκ ὀλίγος] Litotes as in xii. 18, etc.

τῆς ὁδοῦ] See on ix. 2; cf. *ver.* 9.

xix. 24

ποιῶν ναοὺς ἀργυροῦς Ἀρτέμιδος] B omits *ἀργυροῦς*. The *ναοί*, according to Ramsay (*SPT*, p. 278), were small shrines for votaries to dedicate in the temple, representing the goddess in a niche or *naiskos*, with her lions beside her. We know of such miniature temples in terra-cotta; this passage is our only evidence for silver ones, which naturally were not allowed to survive. Less probable is the suggestion that *ποιῶν ναούς* reflects *νεωποιός*, 'temple-maker', the official title of members of the Board of Wardens of the temple of Artemis (see E. L. Hicks in *Expositor*, IV, i [1890], pp. 401 ff.). Deissmann quotes a bilingual inscription found in the theatre at Ephesus where C. Vibius Salutaris presents a silver image of Artemis and other statues to be set up in the theatre (see on *ver.* 32).

Ἀρτέμιδος] Artemis of Ephesus was quite distinct in character from the Greek virgin-goddess of the same name. The Ephesian deity was really the great Mother-goddess of Asia Minor, whose worship dates back to the earliest times, and who appears under various names. She was usually portrayed as many-breasted (*πολύμαστος*, *multimammia*). Her priests were eunuchs, called *μεγάβυζοι* (Strabo xiv. 1. 23).

τοῖς τεχνίταις] 'his fellow-craftsmen'.

παρείχετο οὐκ ὀλίγην ἐργασίαν] 'brought no little business': see on xvi. 16, *ἐργασίαν πολλὴν παρεῖχεν*. Here, as there, the Gospel was a danger to vested interests. Cf. Plin., *Ep*. x. 96, where the business of supplying fodder for sacrificial victims is said to have declined through the spread of Christianity.

xix. 25

τοὺς περὶ τὰ τοιαῦτα ἐργάτας] All the workmen engaged in this trade, as well as the *τεχνῖται*, the skilled craftsmen. He was organizing the whole trade in a protest.

Ἄνδρες] δ has *ἄνδρες συντεχνῖται*. For the expansion cf. xviii. 14.

xix. 26

οὐ μόνον Ἐφέσου ἀλλὰ σχεδὸν πάσης τῆς Ἀσίας] The genitive may be either (1) dependent on ὄχλον, or (2) 'genitive of sphere within which'. The former is more probable, in spite of the unusual order. D inserts ἕως before Ἐφέσου.

ὁ Παῦλος οὗτος] δ adds τίς ποτε (D mistakenly has τις τότε), with which Blass (*Gram.*) compares *Clem. Hom.* v. 27, τίς ποτε Ἰουδαῖος ('some Jew or other'). The Lat. equivalent is *nescio quis* (so g has *hic Paulus nescio quem* here, as in xvii. 7 it has *nescio quem Iesum*).

οὐκ εἰσὶν θεοὶ οἱ διὰ χειρῶν γινόμενοι] See on vii. 48; xvii. 24, 29.

xix. 27

οὐ μόνον δὲ . . . ἀλλὰ καὶ . . .] To the threat to their trade he adds a religious sanction. Translate: 'and not only is there this risk for us, that our line of business should come into disrepute, but also that the temple of the great goddess Artemis should become of no account, and that She whom all Asia and the world worships should shortly be cast down from her majesty'. The accumulation of infinitives is difficult but not impossible: ἐλθεῖν, λογισθῆναι and μέλλειν are dependent on κινδυνεύει, καθαιρεῖσθαι on μέλλειν. The δ text makes the construction easier by changing λογισθῆναι and μέλλειν to λογισθήσεται and μέλλει, and τῆς μεγαλειότητος to ἡ μεγαλειότης.

μέρος] MM quote papyrus evidence to show that μέρος can mean 'line of business'.

ἀπελεγμὸν] *Hapax legomenon;* its primary meaning would be 'refutation', from ἀπελέγχω, 'repudiate'. Cf. MM.

τῆς μεγάλης θεᾶς Ἀρτέμιδος] Blass compares an Ephesian inscription τῇ μεγίστῃ θεᾷ Ἐφεσίᾳ Ἀρτέμιδι. She was usually called ἡ θεός (see on *ver.* 37).

ἱερὸν] The temple, successor to that destroyed in 356 B.C., was one of the Seven Wonders of the World. It was situated about 1½ miles N.E. of the city.

εἰς οὐθὲν λογισθῆναι] For the form οὐθέν see on xv. 9. For the predicative use of εἰς see on v. 36; vii. 21; cf. xiii. 22, 47; Rom. ii. 26; iv. 3 (from LXX); ix. 8.

Ἀσία] Here perhaps the whole of Asia Minor; as in *ver.* 26, Demetrius would be more likely to magnify than minimize the extent of her worship.

ἡ οἰκουμένη] In Pauly-Wissowa's *Realencyclopädie*, ii, cols. 1385-6, 33 places are mentioned where she was worshipped. Brit. Mus. Inscr. iii. 482B (*c.* A.D. 161) records her fame [οὐ μόνον] ἐν τῇ ἑαυτῆς πατρίδι . . . [ἀ]λλὰ καὶ παρὰ Ἕλλησίν τε κ[αὶ β]αρβάροις. Cf. W. M. Ramsay in *CR*, vii (1893), pp. 78 f.

xix. 28

πλήρεις] A E L 33 have *πλήρης*, the indecl. form: see on vi. 3, 5.

θυμοῦ] δ adds *δραμόντες εἰς τὸ ἄμφοδον*, 'running into the square', possibly quite true. For *ἄμφοδον* cf. Mk. xi. 4; it occurs in Aristophanes and Hyperides, and is common in papyri of the Roman age.

μεγάλη ἡ Ἄρτεμις Ἐφεσίων] For the exclamation cf. *μέγας ὁ Ἀσκλήπιος* (Aristides i. 467, 471); *μέγας ἐστὶν ὁ Βήλ* (Bel and the Dragon, 18); *μέγας ἐστὶ Κύριος ὁ θεός* (*ib.* 41). Ramsay here and at *ver.* 34 prefers the δ text *μεγάλη Ἄρτεμις Ἐφεσίων* ('Great Artemis of the Ephesians!'), an invocation rather than a declaration, and a common formula in prayer, as attested by inscriptions (*CRE*, pp. 139 ff.).

xix. 29

συγχύσεως] Only here in NT. Cf. *ver.* 32; ii. 6; ix. 22; xxi. 31, for the corresponding verb. LC quote a striking parallel, *ὁ μὲν δᾶμος ἐν οὐ μετρίᾳ συγχύσει γενόμενος . . . μετὰ πάσας προθυμίας συνελθὼν εἰς τὸ θέατρον* (*Brit. Mus. Inscr.* iv. 792, 4 ff.; from Cnidus).

θέατρον] The theatre at Ephesus, the ruins of which have recently been excavated, is estimated to have contained 25,000 people. As in many other Greek towns, the theatre was the most convenient place for a meeting of the citizen-body.

Γαῖον] See on xx. 4.

Ἀρίσταρχον] Cf. xx. 4 (where we learn that he was a Thessalonian); xxvii. 2; Col. iv. 10; Philm. 24. Aristarchus was a well-attested Macedonian name. B. Weiss and others have conjectured that Gaius and Aristarchus were Luke's authorities for this section of the narrative; though one might wonder from the vivid description if Luke himself was not paying a visit to Paul at Ephesus when this happened.

συνεκδήμους] 'fellow-travellers'.

Μακεδόνας] The minuscules 307 431 have *Μακεδόνα*, referring to Aristarchus alone, in conformity with the β text of xx. 4 (*q.v.*), according to which Gaius belonged to Derbe.

xix. 30

δῆμον] The regular term for the citizen-body of a Greek city-state: cf. xvii. 5.

xix. 31

Ἀσιαρχῶν] The foremost men of the cities of Asia, from whose ranks were drawn the annually elected high priests of the cult of Rome and the Emperor. (Cf. Strabo, xiv. i. 42, where they are called *οἱ πρωτεύοντες κατὰ τὴν ἐπαρχίαν*.) Their friendly relations with Paul show that the imperial policy at this time was not hostile to the spread of Christianity, and that the more educated classes did not share the antipathy to Paul felt by the more superstitious populace. See *BC*, v, pp. 256 ff.

xix. 32

ἡ ἐκκλησία] Luke is perhaps being ironical; the town-clerk at any rate did not regard this as a regular meeting of the 'assembly' —the Demos gathered in its legislative capacity. That the Ephesian Ecclesia met in the theatre is shown in a bilingual inscription quoted by Deissmann (*LAE*, pp. 112 f.), in which a Roman official, C. Vibius Salutaris, presents statues *ἵνα τίθηνται κατ' ἐκκλησίαν ἐν τῷ θεάτρῳ ἐπὶ τῶν βάσεων*—Lat., *ita ut* [*om*]*n*[*i e*]*cclesia supra bases ponerentur*. (Observe that Lat. simply transliterates *ecclesia*.) For the statues cf. *ver*. 24. For *κατ' ἐκκλησίαν* cf. xiv. 23.

οἱ πλείους οὐκ ᾔδεισαν τίνος ἕνεκα συνεληλύθεισαν] Whether *ἡ ἐκκλησία* is ironical or not, the humour of this remark is unmistakable. The result of the general ignorance of the purpose of the meeting was that the agitation was as much anti-Jewish as anti-Christian, especially when they saw Alexander.

xix. 33

ἐκ . . . τοῦ ὄχλου] This equivalent of a partitive genitive is to be taken as subject (see on ii. 30).

συνεβίβασαν] A difficult word here, though the meaning 'instructed' (as in LXX) is just possible (see on ix. 22; xvi. 10). More probably it means that they 'conjectured' Alexander to be the cause of the trouble when the Jews put him forward. The δ text has *κατεβίβασαν* (*detraxerunt* g vg); i.e., the crowd pulled him down when the Jews put him up.

κατασείσας τὴν χεῖρα] Inviting silence and attention: cf. xii. 17; xiii. 16; xxi. 40, where the dat. *τῇ χειρί* is used, not the acc. *τὴν χεῖρα* as here.

xix. 34

ἐπιγνόντες . . . φωνὴ ἐγένετο μία ἐκ πάντων . . . κραζόντων] Sense construction, as if the reading were *πάντες μιᾷ φωνῇ ἔκραζον*.

ὡσεὶ] B; *ὡς* ℵ A D byz. See on i. 15.

μεγάλη ἡ Ἄρτεμις Ἐφεσίων] See on *ver*. 28 for the δ reading (here as there). B repeats this phrase, 'picturesquely', say LC, who introduce the double form in their translation, adding, 'It may be a dittography; if so, it is a happy one'.

xix. 35

καταστείλας] 'quieting'; so in 2 Macc. iv. 31; Jos. *BJ*, ii. 21. 5; iv. 4. 4; *Ant.* xx. 8. 8.

γραμματεύς] The 'town-clerk' or executive officer who published the decrees of the Demos was an Ephesian, not a Roman official, but as the most important native official of the provincial capital, he was in close touch with the Roman authorities, who would hold him responsible for the riotous assembly. His speech is a rebuttal of vulgar charges against Christians, and a fine example of the idiomatic spoken Koiné.

γάρ] '(Be quiet), for'.

νεωκόρον] lit., 'temple-sweeper'; then applied as a title of honour first to individuals and later to cities. In *CIG* 2972 there is a reference to Ephesus as *νεωκόρος τῆς Ἀρτέμιδος*, 'Warden of the Temple of Artemis'.

διοπετοῦς] lit., 'fallen from the sky'; probably a meteorite, like the Palladium of Troy, the image of the *Magna Mater* brought from Pessinus to Rome, that of the Tauric Artemis (Eurip., *Iph. in Taur.* 87 f., 1384 f.), of Ceres in Enna (Cicero, *Verr.* ii. 5. 187), and of the god El Gabal of Emesa (Herodian v. 3, 5).

xix. 36

ἀναντιρρήτων] Here the sense is passive, 'not to be disputed'; the adv. is used actively in x. 29.

δέον ἐστὶν] Periphrasis for δεῖ.

xix. 37

ἱεροσύλους] lit., 'temple-robbers', and hence committers of sacrilege. Cf. Rom. ii. 22; Jos. *Ant.* iv. 8. 10; *Ap.* i. 26, 34 f. It has been suggested that their collection for the Jerusalem church had led to an accusation of stealing the statutory Temple-tax, which was authorized and protected by the Emperor; but there is no indication that the town-clerk had such a charge in mind.

οὔτε βλασφημοῦντας] Chrysostom assumes that this was said merely to calm the mob; to a fourth-century Christian it seemed impossible that Paul should not have made a direct assault on the goddess. Paul knew, however, that the best way to defeat error is to present the truth in a convincing fashion. Besides, Jewish Law interpreted Ex. xxii. 28*a* as prohibiting scurrilous abuse of heathen deities (cf. Jos. *Ant.* iv. 8. 10; *Ap.* ii. 33).

τὴν θεὸν] Magnesian inscriptions show that ἡ θεός was the regular term for the great goddess of the city, while other goddesses were *θεαί*. The town-clerk therefore uses the technical term; contrast *ver.* 27. Cf. *Proleg.* p. 244 *n.*

xix. 38

ἀγοραῖοι] Sc. ἡμέραι, lit., 'market-days'; then 'assizes', as these were convenient days for the *conuentus* of citizens to meet under the presidency of the provincial governor. The assizes were held in about nine cities of the province in turn, including Ephesus, Smyrna, Pergamum, Tralles (Pliny, *NH*, v. 105 ff.).

ἄγονται] 'are being held': cf. Tob. xi. 19 (ἤχθη ὁ γάμος); Jos. *Ant.* xiv. 10. 21 (προσελθών μοι ἐν Τράλλεσιν ἄγοντι τὴν ἀγοραῖον). Its use here is possibly a Latinism (*conuentus aguntur*).

ἀνθύπατοι] The proconsul presided at the assizes. This is probably a generalizing plural. The proconsul M. Junius Silanus had recently been poisoned at Agrippina's instigation, shortly after Nero's accession in Oct., A.D. 54 (Tac. *Ann.* xiii. 1; cf. Dio Cassius lxi. 6). G. S. Duncan (*SPEM*, pp. 102 ff.) suggests that the reference may be to Helius and Celer, the officials in charge of the Emperor's affairs in Asia (*rei familiari principis in Asia impositi*), whom Agrippina had employed to murder Silanus, and who may have performed the proconsular functions until the successor of Silanus arrived.[1]

xix. 39

ἐν τῇ ἐννόμῳ ἐκκλησίᾳ] 'in the regular assembly'; such assemblies, according to Chrysostom (*Hom.* xlii. 2), met three times a month. An irregular or unlawful assembly like the present one would not be tolerated by Rome; it might seriously endanger the city's favourable status. The phrase ἐκκλησίας ἐννόμου occurs in Lucian, *Deorum Consil.* 14.

xix. 40

καὶ γὰρ κινδυνεύομεν κ.τ.λ.] 'For indeed we are in danger of being charged with riot on account of to-day's assembly, there being no reason for it; for which cause (or charge, as in Lk. xxiii. 4) we shall not be able to render an account of this uproar.' So β, which is difficult; δ emends by omitting περὶ τῆς and οὐ, the meaning then being, 'For indeed we are in danger of being charged with riot to-day, having no reason for which we shall be able to render an account', etc. β 'may contain some very ancient error' (Ropes). Hort suggests the reading αἴτιοι ὑπάρχοντες for αἰτίου ὑπάρχοντος with the construction μηδένος αἴτιοι ὑπάρχοντες περὶ οὗ οὐ δυνησόμεθα κ.τ.λ. ('although we are guilty of nothing concerning which we cannot', etc.).

περὶ τῆς σήμερον] Sc. ἐκκλησίας.

[1] The same suggestion about Helius and Celer was made by H. M. Luckock, *Footprints of the Apostles as traced by St. Luke in the Acts* (1897), ii. p. 189: see W. M. Ramsay's critical comments in *Exp.* VI. ii. (1900), pp. 334 f.

(c) Paul's Visit to Macedonia and Greece, xx. 1-6

Μετὰ δὲ τὸ παύσασθαι τὸν θόρυβον μεταπεμψάμενος ὁ Παῦλος 1
τοὺς μαθητὰς καὶ παρακαλέσας ἀσπασάμενος ἐξῆλθεν πορεύεσθαι
εἰς Μακεδονίαν. διελθὼν δὲ τὰ μέρη ἐκεῖνα καὶ παρακαλέσας 2
αὐτοὺς λόγῳ πολλῷ ἦλθεν εἰς τὴν Ἑλλάδα, ποιήσας τε μῆνας τρεῖς 3
γενομένης ἐπιβουλῆς αὐτῷ ὑπὸ τῶν Ἰουδαίων μέλλοντι ἀνάγεσθαι εἰς
τὴν Συρίαν ἐγένετο γνώμης τοῦ ὑποστρέφειν διὰ Μακεδονίας. συνεί- 4
πετο δὲ αὐτῷ Σώπατρος Πύρρου Βεροιαῖος, Θεσσαλονικέων δὲ
Ἀρίσταρχος καὶ Σέκουνδος καὶ Γαῖος Δερβαῖος καὶ Τιμόθεος,
Ἀσιανοὶ δὲ Τύχικος καὶ Τρόφιμος· οὗτοι δὲ προσελθόντες ἔμενον 5
ἡμᾶς ἐν Τρῳάδι· ἡμεῖς δὲ ἐξεπλεύσαμεν μετὰ τὰς ἡμέρας τῶν ἀζύμων 6
ἀπὸ Φιλίππων, καὶ ἤλθομεν πρὸς αὐτοὺς εἰς τὴν Τρῳάδα ἄχρι
ἡμερῶν πέντε, οὗ διετρίψαμεν ἡμέρας ἑπτά.

xx. 1

ἐξῆλθεν πορεύεσθαι εἰς Μακεδονίαν] Probably some time in the summer of A.D. 55, shortly after the riot. The purpose of this visit was to collect the contributions of the churches of Macedonia and Achaia for the relief of the needy members of the Jerusalem church (cf. 1 Cor. xvi. 1 ff.; 2 Cor. viii. 1-ix. 15; Rom. xv. 25 ff.). Ramsay suggests (*SPT*, p. 283) that Paul took a coasting vessel from Ephesus, and had to trans-ship in Troas (cf. 2 Cor. ii. 12). At Troas Paul expected to meet Titus, whom he had sent to report on conditions in the Corinthian church; he did not meet him, however, until after his arrival in Macedonia (2 Cor. ii. 13; vii. 6 ff.).[1]

xx. 2

διελθὼν δὲ τὰ μέρη ἐκεῖνα] It was probably at this time that he went as far as Illyricum (Rom. xv. 19). If so, the first ten words of this verse possibly cover the lapse of as much as a year.

Ἑλλάδα] 'Greece', the more popular term, used as a synonym for Achaia, the name of the Roman province, which Luke uses in xviii. 12 (accurately, because 'proconsul of Achaia' was Gallio's title). Luke prefers the popular territorial names; Paul, the Roman citizen, prefers the Roman provincial names (cf. 1 Cor.

[1] W. L. Knox (*St. Paul and the Church of the Gentiles*, p. 144 *n.*) suggests that 2 Cor. ii. 12 f. 'means that Titus was too late to reach Troas by sea, and would necessarily travel overland, and that Paul on the other hand could not risk sailing to Athens to meet him. Paul must have left Troas, in spite of the "open door", when he realized that Titus had missed the last boat [before navigation ceased for the winter: see on xxvii. 9] and would have to come through Macedonia.'

xvi. 15; 2 Cor. i. 1; ix. 2; Rom. xv. 26; see also on xvi. 6). Here the Epistle to the Romans was written (from Corinth: cf. Rom. xvi. 1, 23).

xx. 3

ποιήσας τε μῆνας τρεῖς] For this sense of *ποιέω* cf. xv. 33; Mt. xx. 12; 2 Cor. xi. 25. The three months probably covered the winter 56-57. He did not usually travel in winter (cf. xxvii. 12; xxviii. 11; Tit. iii. 12).

γενομένης ἐπιβουλῆς] Ramsay supposes that Paul intended to take a pilgrim-ship, as he perhaps had done four years previously (cf. xviii. 21 f.), which picked up at the chief ports those who wished to celebrate Passover or Pentecost at Jerusalem. On such a ship it would have been easy to find an opportunity of murdering Paul; having got wind of the plot, therefore, he chose to make his journey by a more circuitous route. Paul's original plan may have been to celebrate *Passover* at Jerusalem (cf. xviii. 21 δ); the delay caused by the plot may have made this impossible, but he determined that he would be in time for *Pentecost* at any rate (*ver.* 16).

μέλλοντι ἀνάγεσθαι εἰς τὴν Συρίαν] Indicating that he intended to go there anyway. The inferior δ reading, *ἠθέλησεν ἀναχθῆναι εἰς Συρίαν* suggests that it was because of the plot that he decided to go to Syria.

ἐγένετο γνώμης] 'he decided'. For the following construction of *τοῦ* with infin., cf. ix. 15; xv. 20; xxvii. 1. δ has *εἶπεν δὲ τὸ πνεῦμα αὐτῷ ὑποστρέφειν διὰ τῆς Μακεδονίας* (observe the characteristic introduction of the Spirit: cf. xix. 1 δ).

xx. 4

συνείπετο δὲ αὐτῷ κ.τ.λ.] Most of these travelling companions were probably delegates from the various churches, bearing their churches' contributions for Jerusalem (cf. 1 Cor. xvi. 3).

Σώπατρος Πύρρου Βεροιαῖος] The delegate from Beroea (cf. xvii. 10), probably the Sosipater of Rom. xvi. 21. As usual, Luke prefers the colloquial form of the name (see on xviii. 2). *Πύρρου* is omitted by byz pesh hcl.

Ἀρίσταρχος] See on xix. 29.

Σέκουνδος] Not mentioned elsewhere.

Γαῖος Δερβαῖος] If he is to be identified with the Macedonian Gaius of xix. 29 (*q.v.*), then *Δουβ[ή]ριος*, the reading of D (*Doberius* g), is probably the right reading here, on the principle *praestat ardua lectio*. Doberus was a Macedonian town, 26 miles from Philippi (cf. Thuc. ii. 98, 99, 100). In later times it sent a bishop to the

Council of Chalcedon (A.D. 451). Blass accepts L. C. Valckenaer's alteration of καί to δέ after Δερβαῖος, making Gaius a Thessalonian along with Aristarchus and Secundus, and Timothy a man of Derbe (though it would be more natural to infer from xvi. 1 f. that Timothy was a Lystran).

Τιμόθεος] We last met him in xix. 22 (*q.v.*), when he and Erastus were sent by Paul to Macedonia. Though not a delegate of any European church, he had perhaps collected some of the contributions.

Ἀσιανοὶ δὲ Τυχικὸς καὶ Τρόφιμος] The δ text, more explicitly, calls them Ἐφέσιοι. For Tychicus cf. Eph. vi. 21 f. ; Col. iv. 7 f. ; Tit. iii. 12 ; 2 Tim. iv. 12. (D has *Εὔτυχος*, by confusion with the man in *ver.* 9.) Trophimus reappears in xxi. 29 ; cf. also 2 Tim. iv. 20.

xx. 5

οὗτοι δὲ προσελθόντες ἔμενον ἡμᾶς ἐν Τρῳάδι] Here a new 'we' section commences. Luke, who had been left at Philippi in ch. xvi, now reappears, perhaps as delegate of the generous Philippian church. He accompanied Paul from Macedonia to Troas, where the other delegates had already arrived. The δ reading *προελθόντες* (D minn vg pesh hcl sah ; so also B²) seems more natural, and may be right (cf. WH mg.). Cf. the variants in *ver.* 13.

xx. 6

μετὰ τὰς ἡμέρας τῶν ἀζύμων] The days of unleavened bread began with the Passover and lasted for a week (see on xii. 3). The time indications in this and the following verses imply that they set sail on a Friday ; Ramsay infers that the days of unleavened bread must have ended on a Thursday, and that the year must therefore have been 57, in which Passover fell on Thursday, 7th April. But whether the year was 57 or not, it is reading too much into the text to suppose that they left Philippi the morning after the days of unleavened bread ended ; however eager Paul was to get off so as to be in Jerusalem by Pentecost, he would have to wait till a boat was due to sail. Nor can the date of Passover in the first century always be fixed to the exact day. But 57 may very likely have been the year (see the argument in the note on xxvii. 9 that the year in which Paul sailed to Rome two years later was 59).

The description of this critical journey to Jerusalem is given in great detail ; cf. in the Third Gospel the detailed narrative of our Lord's last journey to Jerusalem. But much of the detail here is due to the fact that Luke was again with Paul ; contrast the summary nature of *vv.* 1-3.

ἀπὸ Φιλίππων] Actually, no doubt, from Neapolis, the port of Philippi (cf. xvi. 11).

ἄχρι ἡμερῶν πέντε] πεμπταῖοι D.

2. The Journey to Jerusalem, xx. 7-xxi. 17

(a) Paul at Troas ; Fall and Recovery of Eutychus, xx. 7-12

'Εν δὲ τῇ μιᾷ τῶν σαββάτων συνηγμένων ἡμῶν κλάσαι ἄρτον ὁ 7
Παῦλος διελέγετο αὐτοῖς, μέλλων ἐξιέναι τῇ ἐπαύριον, παρέτεινέν
τε τὸν λόγον μέχρι μεσονυκτίου. ἦσαν δὲ λαμπάδες ἱκαναὶ ἐν τῷ 8
ὑπερῴῳ οὗ ἦμεν συνηγμένοι· καθεζόμενος δέ τις νεανίας ὀνόματι 9
Εὔτυχος ἐπὶ τῆς θυρίδος, καταφερόμενος ὕπνῳ βαθεῖ διαλεγομένου
τοῦ Παύλου ἐπὶ πλεῖον, κατενεχθεὶς ἀπὸ τοῦ ὕπνου ἔπεσεν ἀπὸ τοῦ
τριστέγου κάτω καὶ ἤρθη νεκρός. καταβὰς δὲ ὁ Παῦλος ἐπέπεσεν 10
αὐτῷ καὶ συνπεριλαβὼν εἶπεν Μὴ θορυβεῖσθε, ἡ γὰρ ψυχὴ αὐτοῦ
ἐν αὐτῷ ἐστίν. ἀναβὰς δὲ καὶ κλάσας τὸν ἄρτον καὶ γευσάμενος ἐφ' 11
ἱκανόν τε ὁμιλήσας ἄχρι αὐγῆς οὕτως ἐξῆλθεν. ἤγαγον δὲ τὸν παῖδα 12
ζῶντα, καὶ παρεκλήθησαν οὐ μετρίως.

xx. 7

τῇ μιᾷ τῶν σαββάτων] Originally 'the first day after the sabbath'; then 'the first day of the week'. Cf. Lk. xxiv. 1; 1 Cor. xvi. 2. From the primary meaning 'sabbath-day' (see on xiii. 14), σάββατα and σάββατον acquired the extended sense of the interval between two sabbath days, i.e., a week (so δὶς τοῦ σαββάτου, 'twice in the week', Lk. xviii. 12). The cardinal numeral μιᾷ is used in the sense of the ordinal (cf. Tit. iii. 10; title of Ps. xxiii in LXX; see *Proleg.*, p. 96; A. Thumb, *Handbook of the Mod. Gk. Vernacular*, p. 82).

κλάσαι ἄρτον] See on ii. 42, τῇ κλάσει τοῦ ἄρτου. We are probably to understand a meal, in the course of which the Eucharist was celebrated. See on *ver.* 11.

διελέγετο] A conversation rather than an address is indicated, a 'sermon' in the original sense of the word (Lat. *sermo*, 'conversation'). Cf. ὁμιλήσας, *ver.* 11.

τῇ ἐπαύριον] If we compare this with ἄχρι αὐγῆς, *ver.* 11, we infer that for Luke the day did not begin, in the Jewish way, at sunset, but in the Greek way, at dawn; it was therefore not on Saturday evening, but on Sunday evening, that they came together.

παρέτεινέν τε τὸν λόγον] For Paul's lengthy discourses cf. xxviii. 23, ἀπὸ πρωῒ ἕως ἑσπέρας.

xx. 8

λαμπάδες] 'torches'. D has ὑπολαμπάδες, 'windows' (see MM), but d has *faculae*, 'little torches'. We should not attach any ritual significance to the lamps; at that time of day they were required for light.

ὑπερῴῳ] Cf. i. 13; ix. 37, 39.

xx. 9

Εὔτυχος] The δ text of *ver.* 4 (*q.v.*) makes him one of the Ephesian delegates, a confusion due to similarity of name.

θυρίδος] 'window'. Cf. 2 Kings i. 2 (LXX 4 K.), καὶ ἔπεσεν Ὀχοζείας διὰ τοῦ δικτυωτοῦ τοῦ ἐν τῷ ὑπερῴῳ αὐτοῦ.

καταφερόμενος ὕπνῳ βαθεῖ . . . κατενεχθεὶς ἀπὸ τοῦ ὕπνου] The hot, oily atmosphere caused by the crowd and the torches made it difficult for one who had probably put in a hard day's work to keep awake, despite the priceless opportunity of learning truth from apostolic lips. Note the change of tense: καταφερόμενος, 'dropping off to sleep'; κατενεχθείς, 'being sound asleep'. 'The expressing of the different degrees of sleep would be quite natural to a medical writer', says Hobart (p. 48), who quotes parallels from Hippocrates, Galen and Dioscorides.

τριστέγου] For three-storey houses cf. Martial i. 118, '*et scalis habito tribus, sed altis*'.

νεκρός] Luke no doubt means that he was really dead, 'implying apparently that, as a physician, he had satisfied himself on the point. In xiv. 19 he had no authority for asserting that Paul *was* dead, but only that his enemies considered him dead' (*SPT*, pp. 290 f.). In spite of Paul's words in the next verse, we need not doubt that for a short time Eutychus was really dead in the strict medical sense of the word.

xx. 10

ἐπέπεσεν αὐτῷ καὶ συνπεριλαβὼν] Cf. the raising of the widow's son by Elijah (1 K. xvii. 17 ff.), and of the Shunammite's son by Elisha (2 K. iv. 34 f.).

μὴ θορυβεῖσθε] ℵ A byz. 'Stop making a fuss'; present imperative, because they were doing it. B C D have the spelling variant θορυβεῖσθαι.

ἡ γὰρ ψυχὴ αὐτοῦ ἐν αὐτῷ ἐστίν] This has been taken as implying that he was not really dead. (A similar doubt has been felt about Jairus's daughter, Mk. v. 39, in view of the words οὐκ ἀπέθανεν ἀλλὰ καθεύδει.) But Paul's words are not at variance with the statement 'he was taken up dead'; Luke intends us to understand that his life returned to him when Paul embraced him.

xx. 11

κλάσας τὸν ἄρτον] The article points back to *ver.* 7, κλάσαι ἄρτον: it was after midnight (and therefore Monday morning) when they carried out the purpose for which they had met.

γευσάμενος] lit., 'having tasted'; probably 'taken food', in addition to the eucharistic breaking of the bread. For γεύομαι see on x. 10.

ὁμιλήσας] 'having conversed' (Mod. Gk. μιλῶ); as Lat. *sermo* developed into 'sermon' (see on *ver.* 7), so ὁμιλία into 'homily'.

ἄχρι αὐγῆς] See on τῇ ἐπαύριον, *ver.* 7.

xx. 12

ἤγαγον] δ has ἀσπαζομένων δὲ αὐτῶν ἤγαγεν, making Paul himself bring the young man to them. Since this is stated here and not immediately after *ver.* 10, we may conclude that Eutychus recovered consciousness just before Paul's departure. See on next verse.

(b) From Troas to Miletus, xx. 13-16

Ἡμεῖς δὲ προελθόντες ἐπὶ τὸ πλοῖον ἀνήχθημεν ἐπὶ τὴν Ἄσσον, 13
ἐκεῖθεν μέλλοντες ἀναλαμβάνειν τὸν Παῦλον, οὕτως γὰρ διατεταγμένος
ἦν μέλλων αὐτὸς πεζεύειν. ὡς δὲ συνέβαλλεν ἡμῖν εἰς τὴν Ἄσσον, 14
ἀναλαβόντες αὐτὸν ἤλθομεν εἰς Μιτυλήνην, κἀκεῖθεν ἀποπλεύσαντες 15
τῇ ἐπιούσῃ κατηντήσαμεν ἄντικρυς Χίου, τῇ δὲ ἑτέρᾳ παρεβάλομεν
εἰς Σάμον, τῇ δὲ ἐχομένῃ ἤλθομεν εἰς Μίλητον· κεκρίκει γὰρ ὁ 16
Παῦλος παραπλεῦσαι τὴν Ἔφεσον, ὅπως μὴ γένηται αὐτῷ χρονοτρι-
βῆσαι ἐν τῇ Ἀσίᾳ, ἔσπευδεν γὰρ εἰ δυνατὸν εἴη αὐτῷ τὴν ἡμέραν τῆς
πεντηκοστῆς γενέσθαι εἰς Ἰεροσόλυμα.

xx. 13

Ἡμεῖς δὲ] The O. Syr. (perhaps representing the original δ text) seems to have read ἐγὼ δὲ Λουκᾶς καὶ οἱ μετ' ἐμοῦ. Cf. p. 5, and see F. C. Conybeare in *BC* iii, pp. 442 ff.

προελθόντες] ℵ C L 33 (and TR); προσελθόντες A B E H P (cf. the variants in *ver.* 5); κατελθόντες D.

ἐπὶ τὴν Ἄσσον] For Ἄσσον some byz authorities with P^{41} pesh hcl and possibly sah have Θάσον. (Cf. xxvii. 8, vg *Thalassa* for Ἄλασσα, and xxvii. 13, where *celerius* in h may represent a reading θᾶσσον for ἆσσον.) To get to Assos from Troas, the ship had to round Cape Lectum, thus requiring longer time than the land journey, especially as the prevailing wind was the stormy north-easter. 'Paul stayed on to the last moment, perhaps to be assured of Eutychus's recovery, while the other delegates went on ahead in the ship. Thus the fact that Eutychus recovered is in a sense the final incident of the stay at Troas' (Ramsay, *SPT*, p. 291).

πεζεύειν] Here to go by land as opposed to sailing; literally to go on foot as opposed to riding.

xx. 14

συνέβαλλεν] *συνέβαλεν* C D byz. At first sight the aor. is the more natural tense, but the imperf. may imply that Paul was seen and taken in by boat as he was nearing Assos.

Μιτυλήνην] This is the more freq. spelling after 100 B.C. Before that we find *Μυτιλήνη*. Mytilene was the chief town of the island of Lesbos, an early Aeolian settlement, and the cradle of Gk. lyric poetry, being the home of Alcaeus and Sappho.

xx. 15

ἄντικρυς Χίου] Probably near Cape Argennum. Chios is one of the larger Aegean isles, off the middle of the west coast of Asia Minor. It was an early Ionian settlement. Under the Roman Empire it was a free state until the time of Vespasian.

ἑτέρᾳ] *ἑσπέρᾳ* B minn (probably a scribal error).

παρεβάλομεν] It is difficult to decide which meaning of *παραβάλλω* to choose here; it may mean 'pass by', 'cross over to', or even 'stop at'. Perhaps 'cross over to' is most suitable.

Σάμον] Another of the larger Aegean islands, slightly south of the latitude of Ephesus. Like Chios, it was an Ionian settlement, and at this time a free state, a privilege granted it by Augustus in 17 B.C. After *Σάμον*, δ byz have *καὶ μείναντες ἐν Τρωγυλλίᾳ* (-ίῳ), an addition probable in itself, and not likely to have been interpolated. It may have fallen out of the β text at an early stage. Trogyllia (-ium) is a promontory jutting out from the mainland to the S.E. of Samos so as to form a strait less than a mile wide. 'On Wednesday morning they ran straight across to the west point of Samos, and thence kept in towards Miletus; but when the wind fell, they had not got beyond the promontory Trogyllia at the entrance to the gulf, and there, as the Bezan text mentions, they spent the evening' (Ramsay, *SPT*, pp. 293 f.).

Μίλητον] Miletus was the southernmost of the Ionian settlements in Asia Minor; it played a prominent part in the Ionian revolt, and was recaptured by the Persians in 494 B.C. It lay on the south coast of the Latonian Gulf (even then largely silted up by the river Maeander). The presence of Jews in Miletus is attested by an inscription on the seats of the theatre, *τόπος Εἰουδέων τῶν καὶ θεοσεβίον* (i.e., *τόπος Ἰουδαίων τῶν καὶ θεοσεβέων*).

xx. 16

κεκρίκει] For the augmentless pluperf. cf. iv. 22; xiv. 23; xxvi. 32 (AL). This decision had been made probably at Troas; Paul deliberately chose a quick ship which took the straight course from Chios to Samos, across the mouth of the Ephesian gulf, in order to get to Palestine in time.

ὅπως μὴ γένηται αὐτῷ χρονοτριβῆσαι] We may take *χρονοτριβῆσαι* as practically a noun, the subject of *γένηται*, or else regard the construction as analogous to the frequent *ἐγένετο* with the infin. (see on iv. 5). The former is better.

ἐν τῇ Ἀσίᾳ] In the popular sense of the region round Ephesus (see on xvi. 6).

τὴν ἡμέραν τῆς πεντηκοστῆς] See on ii. 1.

(c) Paul's Address to the Elders of Ephesus, xx. 17-38

Ἀπὸ δὲ τῆς Μιλήτου πέμψας εἰς Ἔφεσον μετεκαλέσατο τοὺς πρεσ- 17
βυτέρους τῆς ἐκκλησίας. ὡς δὲ παρεγένοντο πρὸς αὐτὸν εἶπεν αὐτοῖς 18
Ὑμεῖς ἐπίστασθε ἀπὸ πρώτης ἡμέρας ἀφʼ ἧς ἐπέβην εἰς τὴν Ἀσίαν
πῶς μεθʼ ὑμῶν τὸν πάντα χρόνον ἐγενόμην, δουλεύων τῷ κυρίῳ μετὰ 19
πάσης ταπεινοφροσύνης καὶ δακρύων καὶ πειρασμῶν τῶν συμβάντων
μοι ἐν ταῖς ἐπιβουλαῖς τῶν Ἰουδαίων· ὡς οὐδὲν ὑπεστειλάμην τῶν 20
συμφερόντων τοῦ μὴ ἀναγγεῖλαι ὑμῖν καὶ διδάξαι ὑμᾶς δημοσίᾳ καὶ
κατʼ οἴκους, διαμαρτυρόμενος Ἰουδαίοις τε καὶ Ἕλλησιν τὴν εἰς θεὸν 21
μετάνοιαν καὶ πίστιν εἰς τὸν κύριον ἡμῶν Ἰησοῦν. καὶ νῦν ἰδοὺ δεδε- 22
μένος ἐγὼ τῷ πνεύματι πορεύομαι εἰς Ἰερουσαλήμ, τὰ ἐν αὐτῇ συναντήσοντα ἐμοὶ μὴ εἰδώς, πλὴν ὅτι τὸ πνεῦμα τὸ ἅγιον κατὰ πόλιν 23
διαμαρτύρεταί μοι λέγον ὅτι δεσμὰ καὶ θλίψεις με μένουσιν· ἀλλʼ 24
οὐδενὸς λόγου ποιοῦμαι τὴν ψυχὴν τιμίαν ἐμαυτῷ ὡς τελειώσω τὸν
δρόμον μου καὶ τὴν διακονίαν ἣν ἔλαβον παρὰ τοῦ κυρίου Ἰησοῦ,
διαμαρτύρασθαι τὸ εὐαγγέλιον τῆς χάριτος τοῦ θεοῦ. καὶ νῦν ἰδοὺ 25
ἐγὼ οἶδα ὅτι οὐκέτι ὄψεσθε τὸ πρόσωπόν μου ὑμεῖς πάντες ἐν οἷς
διῆλθον κηρύσσων τὴν βασιλείαν· διότι μαρτύρομαι ὑμῖν ἐν τῇ σήμερον 26
ἡμέρᾳ ὅτι καθαρός εἰμι ἀπὸ τοῦ αἵματος πάντων, οὐ γὰρ ὑπεστειλάμην 27
τοῦ μὴ ἀναγγεῖλαι πᾶσαν τὴν βουλὴν τοῦ θεοῦ ὑμῖν. προσέχετε 28
ἑαυτοῖς καὶ παντὶ τῷ ποιμνίῳ, ἐν ᾧ ὑμᾶς τὸ πνεῦμα τὸ ἅγιον ἔθετο
ἐπισκόπους, ποιμαίνειν τὴν ἐκκλησίαν τοῦ θεοῦ, ἣν περιεποιήσατο
διὰ τοῦ αἵματος τοῦ ἰδίου. ἐγὼ οἶδα ὅτι εἰσελεύσονται μετὰ τὴν 29
ἄφιξίν μου λύκοι βαρεῖς εἰς ὑμᾶς μὴ φειδόμενοι τοῦ ποιμνίου, καὶ 30
ἐξ ὑμῶν αὐτῶν ἀναστήσονται ἄνδρες λαλοῦντες διεστραμμένα τοῦ
ἀποσπᾶν τοὺς μαθητὰς ὀπίσω ἑαυτῶν· διὸ γρηγορεῖτε, μνημονεύοντες 31
ὅτι τριετίαν νύκτα καὶ ἡμέραν οὐκ ἐπαυσάμην μετὰ δακρύων νουθετῶν
ἕνα ἕκαστον. καὶ τὰ νῦν παρατίθεμαι ὑμᾶς τῷ κυρίῳ καὶ τῷ λόγῳ τῆς 32
χάριτος αὐτοῦ τῷ δυναμένῳ οἰκοδομῆσαι καὶ δοῦναι τὴν κληρονομίαν
ἐν τοῖς ἡγιασμένοις πᾶσιν. ἀργυρίου ἢ χρυσίου ἢ ἱματισμοῦ οὐδενὸς 33

ἐπεθύμησα· αὐτοὶ γινώσκετε ὅτι ταῖς χρείαις μου καὶ τοῖς οὖσι μετ' 34
ἐμοῦ ὑπηρέτησαν αἱ χεῖρες αὗται. πάντα ὑπέδειξα ὑμῖν ὅτι οὕτως 35
κοπιῶντας δεῖ ἀντιλαμβάνεσθαι τῶν ἀσθενούντων, μνημονεύειν τε
τῶν λόγων τοῦ κυρίου Ἰησοῦ ὅτι αὐτὸς εἶπεν Μακάριόν ἐστιν μᾶλλον
διδόναι ἢ λαμβάνειν. καὶ ταῦτα εἰπὼν θεὶς τὰ γόνατα αὐτοῦ σὺν 36
πᾶσιν αὐτοῖς προσηύξατο. ἱκανὸς δὲ κλαυθμὸς ἐγένετο πάντων, 37
καὶ ἐπιπεσόντες ἐπὶ τὸν τράχηλον τοῦ Παύλου κατεφίλουν αὐτόν,
ὀδυνώμενοι μάλιστα ἐπὶ τῷ λόγῳ ᾧ εἰρήκει ὅτι οὐκέτι μέλλουσιν τὸ 38
πρόσωπον αὐτοῦ θεωρεῖν. προέπεμπον δὲ αὐτὸν εἰς τὸ πλοῖον.

xx. 17

πέμψας εἰς Ἔφεσον] The distance was about 30 miles. Ramsay thinks the elders arrived on the third day of Paul's stay at Miletus.

τοὺς πρεσβυτέρους τῆς ἐκκλησίας] See on xiv. 23. They are called ἐπίσκοποι in *ver*. 28.

xx. 18

εἶπεν αὐτοῖς] The address to the Ephesian elders is different in style and content from all the other speeches in Ac. It is the only example in Ac. of an address to an audience of Christians (apart from Peter's speech in i. 16 ff. and the speeches in ch. xv.). Almost certainly Luke heard it himself (cf. xxi. 1), and may even have taken shorthand notes. It is rich in parallels to the Pauline epistles, many of which are noted below. But that it is not a mere cento of extracts from these is fairly clear from the fact that the author of Ac. shows no sign of acquaintance with Paul's epistles. While hortatory in character, this speech, like the speeches in the remaining part of Ac., is also apologetic. We gather that Paul's opponents had been attacking him in his absence; he defends his teaching and general behaviour by appealing to the Ephesians' own knowledge of him. We may divide the address into three parts; (1) *vv*. 18-21, introduction (the apologetic note is introduced at once); (2) *vv*. 22-32, exhortation; (3) *vv*. 33-35, apologetic and appeal.

ὑμεῖς ἐπίστασθε] For the appeal to their knowledge and remembrance cf. *vv*. 31, 34; 1 Th. ii. 1 f., 5, 10 f.; iii. 3f.; iv. 2; 2 Th. ii. 5; iii. 7; Gal. iv. 13; 1 Cor. iii. 16, etc.; Phil. iv. 15; Eph. ii. 11.

ἀπὸ πρώτης ἡμέρας] Cf. Phil. i. 5, ἀπὸ τῆς πρώτης ἡμέρας.

πῶς μεθ' ὑμῶν τὸν πάντα χρόνον ἐγενόμην] D has ὡς τριετιαν ἢ καὶ πλεῖον ποταπῶς μεθ' ὑμῶν ἦν παντὸς χρόνου (cf. *ver*. 31). The form ἦν for 1st sing. is not otherwise found in NT, but ἤμην.

xx. 19

δουλεύων τῷ κυρίῳ] Cf. Rom. i. 1; xii. 11; Gal. vi. 17; Eph. vi. 7; Phil. ii. 22.

μετὰ πάσης ταπεινοφροσύνης] Cf. Eph. iv. 2; also 1 Th. ii. 6 ff.; 2 Cor. iv. 5; vii. 6.

δακρύων] Cf. *ver.* 31; 1 Cor. ii. 3; 2 Cor. i. 8; ii. 4; Rom. ix. 2; Phil. iii. 18.

πειρασμῶν] A hint of his hard experiences at Ephesus, not described by Luke, but referred to in 1 Cor. xv. 32; xvi. 9; 2 Cor. i. 8-10; xi. 23 (see on xix. 10).

ταῖς ἐπιβουλαῖς τῶν Ἰουδαίων] Cf. *ver.* 3; also xix. 9. These plots brought him face to face with the problem of Israel's unbelief in all its acuteness, with which he had recently dealt in Rom. ix-xi.

xx. 20

οὐδὲν ὑπεστειλάμην . . . τοῦ μὴ ἀναγγεῖλαι] Cf. *ver.* 27. The phrase is equivalent to *ἐπαρρησιασάμην*.

τοῦ μὴ ἀναγγεῖλαι] Epexegetic of *τῶν συμφερόντων* (cf. *ver.* 27; xiv. 18); by failing to announce the truth to them he would have kept back what was to their advantage. For Paul's refusal to water down the truth cf. *ver.* 27; 1 Th. ii. 5; Gal. iv. 16; 2 Cor. ii. 17; iv. 2 ff.

δημοσίᾳ] Cf. xvi. 37; xviii. 28. His discourses in the synagogue and in the lecture-hall of Tyrannus constituted his public teaching.

κατ' οἴκους] 'in your homes', privately as well as publicly. Cf. ii. 46.

xx. 21

Ἰουδαίοις τε καὶ Ἕλλησιν] Cf. 1 Cor. i. 22 ff.; xii. 13; Rom. i. 14 ff.; iii. 9; x. 12.

τὴν εἰς θεὸν μετάνοιαν καὶ πίστιν εἰς τὸν κύριον ἡμῶν Ἰησοῦν] A summary of his message; cf. xxvi. 20; 2 Cor. v. 20 ff.; Rom. x. 9 ff. ℵ A C add *Χριστόν*, D has *διὰ τοῦ κυρίου ἡμῶν Ἰησοῦ Χριστοῦ*.

xx. 22

δεδεμένος . . . τῷ πνεύματι] 'under the constraint of the Spirit': cf. xvi. 6 f.; xix. 21.

πορεύομαι εἰς Ἰερουσαλήμ] Cf. xix. 21; 1 Cor. xvi. 4; Rom. xv. 25.

συναντήσοντα] The fut. ptc. is rare in the Koiné: cf. viii. 27; xxii. 5; xxiv. 11, 17. A D E H minn have the meaningless variant *συναντήσαντα*.

xx. 23

τὸ πνεῦμα τὸ ἅγιον κατὰ πόλιν διαμαρτύρεταί] Speaking through the prophets in the various churches: cf. the disciples at Tyre (xxi. 4) and Agabus (xxi. 11). Already in Ephesus and in Greece he had been the object of Jewish plots (*vv.* 3, 19); these would likely be more numerous and convenient in Jerusalem. Similar apprehensions are implied in Rom. xv. 31*a*.

δεσμὰ] See on xvi. 26. The neut. plur. form here gains in vividness if the distinction there quoted between *δεσμά* and *δεσμοί* be upheld.

xx. 24

ἀλλ' οὐδένος λόγου ποιοῦμαι τὴν ψυχὴν τιμίαν ἐμαυτῷ] For this ready surrender of himself for the sake of Christ and His service cf. 2 Cor. iv. 7 ff.; vi. 4 ff.; xii. 9 f.; Phil. i. 20; ii. 17; iii. 8; Col. i. 24. Translate: 'I reckon my life of no account, as precious to myself' (cf. RV). The expression (א B C sah) is idiomatic enough, if a little awkward. δ expands to *ἀλλ' οὐδένος λόγον ἔχω μοι οὐδὲ ποιοῦμαι τὴν ψυχήν μοι τιμίαν ἐμαυτοῦ* (perhaps for *ἐμαυτῷ*); byz has *ἀλλ' οὐδένος λόγον ποιοῦμαι οὐδὲ ἔχω τὴν ψυχήν μου τιμίαν ἐμαυτῷ* (cf. AV).

ὡς τελειώσω τὸν δρόμον μου] Cf. 2 Tim. iv. 7, *τὸν δρόμον τετέλεκα*. The clause is final, and variants are many. For *ὡς τελειώσω* (א B), A byz have *ὡς τελειῶσαι* (consecutive *ὡς* with infin. is freq. in Josephus; cf. Lk. ix. 52 א B), C has *ὡς τὸ τελειῶσαι*, D has *τοῦ τελειῶσαι*, E 33 minn have *ὥστε τελειῶσαι* (according to Blass the *-τε* of original *ὥστε* fell out before the *τε-* of *τελειῶσαι* and produced the reading of A byz). C byz e add *μετὰ χαρᾶς*.

τὴν διακονίαν] Cf. 2 Cor. iii. 6; iv. 1; v. 18; Col. i. 25; iv. 17; 2 Tim. iv. 5. D adds *τοῦ λόγου* (cf. vi. 4).

ἣν ἔλαβον παρὰ τοῦ κυρίου Ἰησοῦ] Cf. Gal. i. 1, 12; 1 Tim. i. 12.

τὸ εὐαγγέλιον τῆς χάριτος τοῦ θεοῦ] Cf. *ver.* 32; xiv. 3; 2 Cor. vi. 1; Rom. v. 15 ff.; Eph. i. 7f.; ii. 7; iii. 2; Col. i. 6. The grace of God revealed in Christ is the subject of the Good News. It is evident from a comparison of this verse with the next that the preaching of this Gospel is identical with the proclamation of the Kingdom. Before *τὸ εὐαγγέλιον* D adds *Ἰουδαίοις καὶ Ἕλλησιν* (cf. *ver.* 21).

xx. 25

οὐκέτι ὄψεσθε τὸ πρόσωπόν μου ὑμεῖς πάντες] Does this mean that not all, but only some, would see him again; or that none of them would do so? Evidently the latter: cf. *ver.* 38. He did not know what awaited him at Jerusalem, but was prepared for the worst (cf. xxi. 13). If he survived, his intention was to evangelize the western part of the Empire (cf. xix. 21; Rom. i. 15; xv. 23 f.; 28 f.). The Pastoral epistles[1] imply, though they do not explicitly assert, a later visit to Ephesus (cf. 1 Tim. i. 3; 2 Tim. i. 15 ff.). For the bearing of this verse on the question of the date of Ac., see pp. 11 f.; 14, *n*. 2.

κηρύσσων τὴν βασιλείαν] D adds *τοῦ Ἰησοῦ*, byz adds *τοῦ θεοῦ*. Cf. i. 3, 6; viii. 12; xix. 8; xxviii. 23, 31. The proclaiming of the Kingdom is the same as testifying to the good news of God's grace (*ver*. 24).

xx. 27

οὐ γὰρ ὑπεστειλάμην τοῦ μὴ ἀναγγεῖλαι] Cf. *ver*. 20.

πᾶσαν τὴν βουλὴν τοῦ θεοῦ] Cf. Eph. i. 11. 'All the will of God' here corresponds to and explains 'the things that are expedient' in *ver*. 20; the earlier phrase is to be understood in the light of the later. Expediency to Paul meant something much higher than to the majority of men.

xx. 28

προσέχετε ἑαυτοῖς] Cf. 1 Tim. iv. 16, *ἔπεχε σεαυτῷ*.

τῷ ποιμνίῳ] Cf. Jn. x. 16, *μία ποίμνη*.

ἐν ᾧ ὑμᾶς τὸ πνεῦμα τὸ ἅγιον ἔθετο ἐπισκόπους] For the divine appointment cf. i. 24; xiii. 2, 4; 1 Cor. xii. 18, 28; Eph. iv. 11; Col. iv. 17; 1 Tim. i. 12; ii. 7; 2 Tim. i. 6, 7, 11. The church recognized as overseers those whom the Holy Spirit had qualified for the work by bestowing the appropriate *χάρισμα* upon them. They are called *πρεσβύτεροι* in *ver*. 17, and in this verse by implication *ποιμένες* (cf. Eph. iv. 11). For *ἐπίσκοποι* cf. Phil. i. 1; 1 Tim. iii. 1 ff.; Tit. i. 7. Such men are also called *προϊστάμενοι* (1 Th. v. 12; Rom. xii. 8); *προεστῶτες* (1 Tim. v. 17); *ἡγούμενοι* (Heb. xiii. 17).

ποιμαίνειν] Either infin. for imper., or infin. of purpose after *ἔθετο*. The shepherd-ruler idea is constant in OT (cf. also Rev. ii. 27; xii. 5 from Ps. ii. 9); for other NT examples of the shepherd in the church cf. Jn. xxi. 16; Eph. iv. 11; 1 Pet. v. 2 ff.

τὴν ἐκκλησίαν τοῦ θεοῦ ἣν περιεποιήσατο] Cf. Ps. lxxiv. 2 (LXX lxxiii), *μνήσθητι τῆς συναγωγῆς* [Heb. *'ēdāh*] *σου ἧς ἐκτήσω ἀπ' ἀρχῆς*, and Isa. xliii. 21, *λαόν μου ὃν περιεποιησάμην τὰς ἀρετάς μου διηγεῖσθαι*.

[1] On the question of their authenticity, see, in addition to the standard literature, 'The Authenticity and Authorship of the Pastoral Epistles', by E. K. Simpson, in *EQ*, xii. (1940), pp. 299 ff. It is understood that the same writer has in preparation a commentary on these Epistles.

See on v. 11; vii. 38, for *ἐκκλησία*. The words *περιποιέομαι* and *περιποίησις* in OT have a recognized meaning in connection with Israel; for other NT examples of the transference of the idea to the Church cf. 1 Cor. vi. 20; vii. 23; Rom. vi. 22; Eph. i. 14 (see J. A. Robinson *ad loc.*); Tit. ii. 14; 1 Pet. ii. 9. For *θεοῦ* A C δ have *κυρίου*, owing to the difficulty if the following words are taken to mean 'with His own blood' (see below). In byz we find the conflate *κυρίου καὶ θεοῦ*.

διὰ τοῦ αἵματος τοῦ ἰδίου] 'by means of the blood of His own One'. In this sense *ἴδιος* is the equivalent of Heb. *yāḥīd*, 'only', 'well-beloved', elsewhere rendered *ἀγαπητός, ἐκλεκτός, μονογενής*. For the absolute use of *ὁ ἴδιος* cf. iv. 23; xxi. 6; xxiv. 23; Jn. i. 11; xiii. 1; xix. 27. 'In the papyri we find the singular used thus as a term of endearment to near relations, e.g., *ὁ δεῖνα τῷ ἰδίῳ χαίρειν* ["So-and-so to his own (friend), greeting"]' (*Proleg.*, p. 90). It is unnecessary to suppose, with Hort, that *υἱοῦ* may have dropped out after *ἰδίου*. Byz, taking the meaning as 'with His own blood', alters to *διὰ τοῦ ἰδίου αἵματος*.

xx. 29

μετὰ τὴν ἄφιξίν μου] As a derivative from *ἀφικνέομαι, ἄφιξις* ought, of course, to mean 'arrival', 'home-coming'; so Chase, 'after my long journey is over and I have reached my true home' (*Credibility*, pp. 263 f.). This meaning, says J. H. Moulton, 'is hardly likely' (*Proleg.*, p. 26), and there is evidence that the word was sometimes used in the sense 'departure': cf. Jos. *Ant.* ii. 2. 4 (*μὴ προσδηλώσαντες τῷ πατρὶ τὴν ἐκεῖσε ἄφιξιν*); iv. 8. 47 (*θεὸς τήνδε μοι τὴν ἡμέραν τῆς πρὸς ἐκείνους ἀφίξεως ὥρισε*). The word also means 'departure' in Pionius's *Vita Polycarpi* 3, *μετὰ δὲ τὴν τοῦ ἀποστόλου ἄφιξιν*, which is perhaps dependent on the present passage. Such a change of meaning might have been suggested by the prefix *ἀπό* if once the connection with *ἀφικνέομαι* were forgotten.

λύκοι βαρεῖς] For this description of heretical teachers cf. Mt. vii. 15; 4 Ezra v. 18; 1 Enoch lxxxix. 13 ff. They are called wolves by contrast with the true shepherds (cf. Jn. x. 12).

xx. 30

ἐξ ὑμῶν αὐτῶν] The 'wolves' come from without, but dangers from within the flock are also to be apprehended. Cf. 1 Tim. iv. 1 ff. B omits *αὐτῶν*.

τοῦ ἀποσπᾶν τοὺς μαθητὰς ὀπίσω ἑαυτῶν] Cf. Gal. iv. 17; Rom. xvi. 17 f.; Col. ii. 8; 2 Tim. iii. 6; Tit. i. 11.

xx. 31

γρηγορεῖτε] '*Verbum pastorale*' (Bengel). Cf. 1 Th. v. 6, 10; 1 Cor. xvi. 13; Col. iv. 2; also the synonymous *ἀγρυπνέω* in Heb. xiii. 17, *αὐτοὶ γὰρ ἀγρυπνοῦσιν ὑπὲρ τῶν ψυχῶν ὑμῶν.*

τριετίαν] A round figure: see on xix. 10.

μετὰ δακρύων] Cf. *ver.* 19.

νουθετῶν] Cf. 1 Cor. iv. 14; Col. i. 28.

xx. 32

παρατίθεμαι] Cf. 2 Tim. i. 12; for God's guarding cf. 1 Th. iii. 13; v. 23; 2 Th. iii. 3; 1 Cor. i. 8; Rom. xvi. 25; Phil. iv. 19.

κυρίῳ] B 33 257 326 441 g sah boh. The other authorities have *θεῷ*.

τῷ λόγῳ τῆς χάριτος αὐτοῦ] Cf. *ver.* 24; xiv. 3. 'This message of the free bounty of God is the word which has the greatest effect on the heart of man, and so it is *able to build up* the church' (Rackham).

τῷ δυναμένῳ] Cf. 2 Cor. ix. 8; Rom. xiv. 4; xvi. 25; Eph. iii. 20; also Jude 24.

οἰκοδομῆσαι] Cf. 1 Cor. iii. 9 ff.; Eph. ii. 20 ff.; iv. 12 ff.

κληρονομίαν ἐν τοῖς ἡγιασμένοις πᾶσιν] Cf. xxvi. 18; Eph. i. 14; Col. iii. 24; Heb. i. 14; vi. 12. The words recall Dt. xxxiii. 3 f., *καὶ πάντες οἱ ἡγιασμένοι ὑπὸ τὰς χεῖράς σου . . . κληρονομίαν συναγωγαῖς Ἰακώβ.* After *πᾶσιν* the δ text seems to have added *αὐτῷ ἡ δόξα εἰς τοὺς αἰῶνας τῶν αἰώνων. ἀμήν* (so, with variations, 614 minn hcl*; D is corrupt).

xx. 33

ἀργυρίου καὶ χρυσοῦ κ.τ.λ.] For similar swift change of theme cf. 2 Cor. vi. 14; x. 1 (which may be otherwise explained); Phil. iii. 1 f. For the apologia cf. *ver.* 26; 1 Th. ii. 3 ff.; 2 Th. iii. 7 ff.; 1 Cor. ix. 3-18; 2 Cor. iv. 5; x. 1 ff.; xi. 7 ff.; xii. 13. An OT parallel is that of Samuel, 1 S. (LXX 1 K) xii. 3.

ἱματισμοῦ] Part of ancient wealth: cf. Jas. v. 2; Jos. vii. 21 ff.; 2 K. v. 22 ff.; vii. 8 (LXX 4 K.).

οὐδένος] Gen. governed by *ἀργυρίου*, etc. ('no man's silver . . .') rather than in agreement with them ('no silver . . .').

xx. 34

τοῖς οὖσι μετ' ἐμοῦ] lit., 'to those who were with me', but probably compendious construction for *ταῖς τῶν ὄντων μετ' ἐμοῦ.*

αἱ χεῖρες αὗται] These words occupy an emphatic position at the end of the sentence; they were no doubt accompanied by an appropriate gesture.

xx. 35

πάντα] Probably 'always' (adverbial neut. plur.); cf. 1 Cor. ix. 25; x. 33; xi. 2; xiii. 7.

κοπιῶντας] The emphasis on the Christian duty of working was perhaps necessitated by exaggerated eschatological expectations, such as Paul corrects in 2 Th. ii. 1 ff. Cf. 1 Th. iv. 11; v. 12 ff.; 2 Th. iii. 7-12; 1 Cor. iv. 12; Eph. iv. 28.

τῶν ἀσθενούντων] In particular, those who were sick and thus unable to earn their own living: cf. 1 Th. v. 14; Gal. vi. 2; Rom. xv. 1; Eph. iv. 28.

μνημονεύειν τε τῶν λόγων τοῦ κυρίου Ἰησοῦ] They already knew this and presumably other Sayings of our Lord. Collections of His Sayings must have been in circulation by this time. Other references to knowledge of His teaching are in 1 Cor. vii. 10, 12, 25; 1 Tim. v. 18 (cf. Lk. x. 7); vi. 3.

αὐτὸς εἶπεν] Note the reverential *αὐτός*, 'the Master'. Cf. the Pythagorean *αὐτὸς ἔφα*, *ipse dixit*. (Sayings of Christ are introduced with *ipse dixit* by Marius Victorinus, *Adu. Arrium* iii. 17; *Comm. on Eph.* vi. 13.)

μακάριόν ἐστιν μᾶλλον διδόναι ἢ λαμβάνειν] Although this Saying is not found in the Gospels, its spirit is seen in Lk. vi. 38; xi. 9; Jn. xiii. 34, etc. Cf. also Sir. iv. 31 (*μὴ ἔστω ἡ χείρ σου ἐκτεταμένη εἰς τὸ λαβεῖν, καὶ ἐν τῷ ἀποδιδόναι συνεσταλμένη*); *Didaché*, i. 5 (*μακάριος ὁ διδοὺς κατὰ τὴν ἐντολήν*); 1 Clem. ii. 1 (*ἥδιον διδόντες ἢ λαμβάνοντες*); Seneca, *Ep.* lxxxi. 17 ('*errat enim si quis beneficium accipit libentius quam reddit*'). Other parallels are given in LC.

xx. 36

θεὶς τὰ γόνατα] See on vii. 60.

xx. 37

ἐπιπεσόντες ἐπὶ τὸν τράχηλον . . . κατεφίλουν αὐτόν] Cf. for the expression Lk. xv. 20; Gen. xxxiii. 4; xlv. 14; xlvi. 29; Tob. vii. 6 f.; xi. 9, 13.

xx. 38

οὐκέτι μέλλουσιν τὸ πρόσωπον αὐτοῦ θεωρεῖν] See on *ver.* 25.

(d) Arrival at Tyre, xxi. 1-6

Ὡς δὲ ἐγένετο ἀναχθῆναι ἡμᾶς ἀποσπασθέντας ἀπ' αὐτῶν, εὐθυδρο- 1
μήσαντες ἤλθομεν εἰς τὴν Κῶ, τῇ δὲ ἑξῆς εἰς τὴν Ῥόδον, κἀκεῖθεν εἰς
Πάταρα· καὶ εὑρόντες πλοῖον διαπερῶν εἰς Φοινίκην ἐπιβάντες 2
ἀνήχθημεν. ἀναφάναντες δὲ τὴν Κύπρον καὶ καταλιπόντες αὐτὴν εὐώ- 3
νυμον ἐπλέομεν εἰς Συρίαν, καὶ κατήλθομεν εἰς Τύρον, ἐκεῖσε γὰρ

τὸ πλοῖον ἦν ἀποφορτιζόμενον τὸν γόμον. ἀνευρόντες δὲ τοὺς 4
μαθητὰς ἐπεμείναμεν αὐτοῦ ἡμέρας ἑπτά, οἵτινες τῷ Παύλῳ ἔλεγον
διὰ τοῦ πνεύματος μὴ ἐπιβαίνειν εἰς Ἰεροσόλυμα. ὅτε δὲ ἐγένετο 5
ἐξαρτίσαι ἡμᾶς τὰς ἡμέρας, ἐξελθόντες ἐπορευόμεθα προπεμπόντων
ἡμᾶς πάντων σὺν γυναιξὶ καὶ τέκνοις ἕως ἔξω τῆς πόλεως, καὶ θέντες
τὰ γόνατα ἐπὶ τὸν αἰγιαλὸν προσευξάμενοι ἀπησπασάμεθα ἀλλήλους, 6
καὶ ἐνέβημεν εἰς τὸ πλοῖον, ἐκεῖνοι δὲ ὑπέστρεψαν εἰς τὰ ἴδια.

xxi. 1

ἀποσπασθέντας] One is disposed to continue the atmosphere of clinging affection in the previous verses by giving this word its literal force, 'tore ourselves away'; cf. Lk. xxii. 41, *ἀπεσπάσθη ἀπ' αὐτῶν*, which similarly may mean more than 'He was parted from them'.

εὐθυδρομήσαντες] The prevailing wind was N.E.

εἰς τὴν Κῶ] Cos is an island of the Dodecanese, and was at that time included in the province of Asia. It was, like the rest of that group, a Dorian settlement.

Ῥόδον] Rhodes is the name both of the island (then inhabited by Dorian Greeks) and of its chief town, at the island's N.E. extremity, founded in 408 B.C. by the amalgamation of three earlier towns, a great trading port, and a free city under the Roman Empire. It is the city that is meant here.

Πάταρα] A seaport on the south coast of Lycia, which, according to the β text, was the port of trans-shipment on this occasion. The δ text adds *καὶ Μύρα*. Myra also lay on the south coast of Lycia, farther east than Patara. The words may have fallen out of the β text by homoeoteleuton, though it is possible that they were interpolated in the δ text under the influence of xxvii. 5 (*q.v.*).

xxi. 2

εὑρόντες πλοῖον διαπερῶν εἰς Φοινίκην ἐπιβάντες] According to δ, this trans-shipment took place at Myra, which was the great port for cross-sea traffic to Syria and Egypt (see on xxvii. 5). A cross-sea voyage from Myra to Tyre would shorten the journey (see on xx. 16).

xxi. 3

ἀναφάναντες] ℵ B^{vid} minn; *ἀναφανέντες* A B^2 C byz (a grammatically impossible reading here). *ἀναφάναντες* is a Hellenistic form regularly found in verbs in *-αίνω* (Attic *ἀναφήναντες*); the verb is apparently a nautical term for sighting land, lit., 'having made (Cyprus) visible', i.e., making it rise out of the sea on the horizon.

κατήλθομεν εἰς Τύρον] According to Chrysostom the passage from Patara to Tyre took 5 days.

ἦν ἀποφορτιζόμενον] For the construction see on i. 10; here the periphrasis differs in force from the simple imperf.; in Attic the fut. ptc. (rarely found in the Koiné) would probably have been used rather than the pres. The ship was apparently a large merchant vessel, as small vessels hugged the coast. The voyage having been considerably shortened by taking this boat, Paul could afford to wait till the unloading was finished, as the boat was going on to Ptolemais.

xxi. 4

ἀνευρόντες] 'seeking out'; perhaps none of the party knew Tyre.

τοὺς μαθητὰς] The Tyrian church was no doubt the fruit of the Phoenician mission of xi. 19.

διὰ τοῦ πνεύματος] See on xx. 23. Their inspired vision foresaw the difficulties and dangers that lay ahead of Paul (cf. *ver.* 11); they drew the conclusion that he should not go up to Jerusalem (cf. *ver.* 12). We must not infer that his continuing the journey was contrary to God's will; it was 'under the constraint of the Spirit' (xx. 22) that he was going to Jerusalem.

μὴ ἐπιβαίνειν] Pres. infin.; 'to stop going on'.

xxi. 5

ἐξαρτίσαι] 'fulfil', 'complete', a sense apparently not found elsewhere; probably a nautical metaphor.[1]

ἕως ἔξω] For ἕως followed by another prep., cf. xvii. 14.

θέντες τὰ γόνατα] Cf. xx. 36.

αἰγιαλὸν] A smooth beach, as there is at the present day.

xxi. 6

ἀπησπασάμεθα] A rare verb (found also in Tob. x. 12 א). For the kindly farewell cf. xx. 36-38. At Tyre there could not be the longing and sorrow such as arose from long personal friendship at Ephesus. Yet the picture of all the Christian families of Tyre accompanying the little group to the ship at the end of the week is an affecting one, illustrating what a close bond of friendship primitive Christianity was.

εἰς τὰ ἴδια] 'to their own homes'. Cf. Jn. i. 11; xix. 27.

τὸ πλοῖον] The article marks it out as the boat of *vv.* 2 f.

[1] LS[9] quote ἐξαρτίζω in a similar, though not identical, sense of finishing (*a*) a building (*IG* xii. 2. 538), (*b*) documents (*P. Oxy.* 296. 7), (*c*) the legs of a table (Jos. *Ant.* iii. 6. 6).

ἐνέβημεν] ℵ^c B minn; ἐπέβημεν byz. Both these readings may be corrections of the less usual ἀνέβημεν (ℵ A C).

(e) Arrival at Caesarea, xxi. 7-9

Ἡμεῖς δὲ τὸν πλοῦν διανύσαντες ἀπὸ Τύρου κατηντήσαμεν εἰς 7
Πτολεμαΐδα, καὶ ἀσπασάμενοι τοὺς ἀδελφοὺς ἐμείναμεν ἡμέραν
μίαν παρ' αὐτοῖς. τῇ δὲ ἐπαύριον ἐξελθόντες ἤλθαμεν εἰς Καισαρίαν, 8
καὶ εἰσελθόντες εἰς τὸν οἶκον Φιλίππου τοῦ εὐαγγελιστοῦ ὄντος ἐκ
τῶν ἑπτὰ ἐμείναμεν παρ' αὐτῷ. τούτῳ δὲ ἦσαν θυγατέρες τέσσαρες 9
παρθένοι προφητεύουσαι.

xxi. 7

τὸν πλοῦν διανύσαντες] In Bib. Gk. *διανύω* occurs only here and in 2 Macc. xii. 17. The meaning would at first sight be 'having completed the voyage'; but Field points out that in Xenophon Ephesius (second century A.D.) *διανύειν πλοῦν* occurs several times in the sense 'to *continue* a voyage'.

Πτολεμαΐδα] Ptolemais (the Acco of Judg. i. 31; mod. 'Akka or Acre) was so called in honour, apparently, of Ptolemy II (285-246). It has always been a strong fortress, as its history testifies; for that reason it was made a colony by the Romans. The Gospel probably found its way there at the same time as it came to Tyre (cf. xi. 19).

xxi. 8

ἐξελθόντες] This may mean, as in *ver.* 5, that they went out of the city to the ship; it can also mean that they went by road to Caesarea.

εἰς τὸν οἶκον Φιλίππου] We left Philip at Caesarea in viii. 40. We now find him there in a 'we' section. This is one of several indications in this part of Ac. that the 'we' sections are an integral part of the book. See on *ver.* 10.

τοῦ εὐαγγελιστοῦ] The verb *εὐαγγελίζομαι* is used of Philip in viii. 12, 35, 40. Perhaps *τοῦ εὐαγγελιστοῦ* is added to his name here to distinguish him from Philip the apostle, but this did not prevent their being later confused (cf. Euseb., *HE*, iii. 31[1]). Cf. Eph. iv. 11; 2 Tim. iv. 5 for the noun *εὐαγγελιστής*.

[1] Polycrates speaks of Philip, 'one of the Twelve Apostles', as having died in the province of Asia, with two or three of his daughters. But Eusebius, immediately after quoting him, quotes Proclus to the effect that 'Philip's four prophetess-daughters' lived in Hierapolis, and then quotes Ac. xxi. 8. The probability is that it was Philip the Evangelist who later lived in Asia with his daughters: so Zahn, *Forschungen* vi. (1900), pp. 158 ff.; Harnack, *LP*, p. 153. For the contrary view, that it was Philip the Apostle and not the Evangelist who went to Asia with his daughters, see Lightfoot, *Colossians*, pp. 45 ff.; J. Chapman, *John the Presbyter* (1911), pp. 64 ff.

ἐκ τῶν ἑπτά] See on vi. 3. This is another link between a 'we' section and the rest of Ac. The Seven were originally the leaders of the Hellenists in the Jerusalem church, and after the death of Stephen the survivors probably took a leading part among the Hellenists of the dispersion.

xxi. 9

τούτῳ δὲ ἦσαν θυγατέρες τέσσαρες παρθένοι προφητεύουσαι] The introduction of Philip's daughters is significant; there is good evidence that from them Luke received much of the information which he gives in the earlier part of Ac., as well as much of the material peculiar to the Third Gospel. (Cf. Harnack, *LP*, pp. 155 ff.) He certainly had ample opportunity to learn all he could from them, not only during the 'many days' spent in Caesarea on this occasion, but also during the two years of Paul's imprisonment there (xxiv. 27). Eusebius (*HE*, iii. 39) relates on the testimony of Papias, how Philip's daughters were known in later days as informants on the early history of the Church (see on i. 23). Eusebius also quotes references to them by Polycrates and Proclus (*HE*, iii. 31; v. 24).

προφητεύουσαι], i.e., having the gift of prophecy. A romancer would have improved the occasion by relating some of their prophecies.

(f) Agabus Reappears, xxi. 10-14

Ἐπιμενόντων δὲ ἡμέρας πλείους κατῆλθέν τις ἀπὸ τῆς Ἰουδαίας 10
προφήτης ὀνόματι Ἅγαβος, καὶ ἐλθὼν πρὸς ἡμᾶς καὶ ἄρας τὴν ζώνην 11
τοῦ Παύλου δήσας ἑαυτοῦ τοὺς πόδας καὶ τὰς χεῖρας εἶπεν Τάδε
λέγει τὸ πνεῦμα τὸ ἅγιον Τὸν ἄνδρα οὗ ἐστὶν ἡ ζώνη αὕτη οὕτως
δήσουσιν ἐν Ἰερουσαλὴμ οἱ Ἰουδαῖοι καὶ παραδώσουσιν εἰς χεῖρας
ἐθνῶν. ὡς δὲ ἠκούσαμεν ταῦτα, παρεκαλοῦμεν ἡμεῖς τε καὶ οἱ ἐντό- 12
πιοι τοῦ μὴ ἀναβαίνειν αὐτὸν εἰς Ἰερουσαλήμ. τότε ἀπεκρίθη ὁ 13
Παῦλος Τί ποιεῖτε κλαίοντες καὶ συνθρύπτοντές μου τὴν καρδίαν;
ἐγὼ γὰρ οὐ μόνον δεθῆναι ἀλλὰ καὶ ἀποθανεῖν εἰς Ἰερουσαλὴμ ἑτοίμως
ἔχω ὑπὲρ τοῦ ὀνόματος τοῦ κυρίου Ἰησοῦ. μὴ πειθομένου δὲ αὐτοῦ 14
ἡσυχάσαμεν εἰπόντες Τοῦ κυρίου τὸ θέλημα γινέσθω.

xxi. 10

Ἐπιμενόντων] 'Rarely in NT, but frequently in papyri, we find a participle standing by itself in gen. abs. without a noun or pronoun in agreement' (*Proleg.*, p. 74). Cf. *ζητούντων*, *ver.* 31; also Mt. xvii. 14. We find the same thing in classical Gk., where the noun or pronoun can be supplied from the sense, as here.

ἡμέρας πλείους] 'several days'.

ἀπὸ τῆς Ἰουδαίας] Caesarea was officially in Judaea, being its political capital; but it was a Gentile city, and thus not part of Judaea in the ethnic sense.

Ἄγαβος] Cf. xi. 28. Here is another link between this 'we' section and the rest of Ac.; cf. also the similar language with which he is introduced (κατῆλθον ἀπὸ Ἰεροσολύμων προφῆται, xi. 27). The sudden appearances and disappearances of Agabus are 'not fiction, but real life' (LC).

xxi. 11

ἄρας τὴν ζώνην κ.τ.λ.] Acted prophecy of this kind was common in OT times; cf. 1 K. xi. 29 ff. (LXX 3 K.); Isa. xx. 2 ff.; Ezek. iv. 1 ff. For the terms of the prophecy cf. Jn. xxi. 18.

τάδε λέγει τὸ πνεῦμα τὸ ἅγιον] Cf. *ver.* 4; xx. 23. Agabus foresees Paul's imprisonment at Jerusalem, but does not himself deduce that Paul should therefore not go there (contrast the Tyrian Christians, *ver.* 4). The prophecy is couched in words similar to those used by our Lord of Himself (Mk. x. 33, παραδώσουσιν αὐτὸν τοῖς ἔθνεσιν); see on *ver.* 14. In the event, Paul was delivered *by* the Gentiles *from* the Jews, who were forced against their will to hand him over (*vv.* 31 ff.).

xxi. 12

τοῦ μὴ ἀναβαίνειν αὐτὸν] Final construction; here equivalent to μὴ ἀναβαίνειν. Note the pres. infin., 'to stop going up' (cf. *ver.* 4, μὴ ἐπιβαίνειν).

xxi. 13

συνθρύπτοντές μου τὴν καρδίαν] 'bleaching my heart by pounding it like a washerwoman' (J. A. Findlay). Zahn infers from the metaphor that Paul meant 'Why do you try to make me soft?'

ὑπὲρ τοῦ ὀνόματος] Cf. v. 41; ix. 16.

xxi. 14

μὴ πειθομένου δὲ αὐτοῦ] 'As he would not be persuaded'.

ἡσυχάσαμεν, εἰπόντες] 'we ceased speaking, with the words . . .'.

Τοῦ κυρίου τὸ θέλημα γινέσθω] Cf. xviii. 21; Mt. vi. 10. In particular, we are reminded of our Lord's words in Gethsemane, πλὴν μὴ τὸ θέλημά μου ἀλλὰ τὸ σὸν γινέσθω (Lk. xxii. 42). The parallel between the Master's journey to Jerusalem and the servant's is closely drawn by Luke (see on *ver.* 11; xx. 6). Like his Lord, Paul refused to be diverted from the path of duty and suffering by the pleas of well-meaning friends, but 'steadfastly set his face to go to Jerusalem' (cf. Lk. ix. 51). Cf. also Polycarp's answer under similar circumstances, τὸ θέλημα τοῦ θεοῦ γενέσθω (*Mart. Polyc.* vii. 1).

(g) Arrival at Jerusalem, xxi. 15-16

Μετὰ δὲ τὰς ἡμέρας ταύτας ἐπισκευασάμενοι ἀνεβαίνομεν εἰς 15
Ἱεροσόλυμα· συνῆλθον δὲ καὶ τῶν μαθητῶν ἀπὸ Καισαρίας σὺν ἡμῖν, 16
ἄγοντες παρ' ᾧ ξενισθῶμεν Μνάσωνί τινι Κυπρίῳ, ἀρχαίῳ μαθητῇ.

xxi. 15

Μετὰ δὲ τὰς ἡμέρας ταύτας] The 'several days' of *ver.* 10.

ἐπισκευασάμενοι] lit., 'having prepared'; the nature of the preparation is not quite clear. It may mean 'packed our luggage' (cf. RV), or 'hired horses'. Chrysostom (*λαβόντες τὰ πρὸς τὴν ὁδοιπορίαν*) apparently took it in the latter sense, according to Ramsay (*SPT*, p. 302).[1] In classical Gk. the word is used of saddling or equipping a horse (cf. Xen., *Hell.* v. 3. 1, *τούς θ' ἵππους ἐπεσκευασμένους . . . ἔχων*). In any case, that the party used horses to cover the distance from Caesarea to Jerusalem (64 miles) is a very reasonable supposition (cf. xxiii. 23 ff.). D has *ἀποταξάμενοι*, 33 al.pauc *ἀποσκευασάμενοι* (so TR).

xxi. 16

τῶν μαθητῶν] Partitive genitive in place of nominative; 'some of the disciples'.

ἄγοντες παρ' ᾧ ξενισθῶμεν Μνάσωνί τινι Κυπρίῳ, ἀρχαίῳ μαθητῇ] 'bringing (us) to Mnason of Cyprus, one of the early disciples, with whom we were to lodge', presumably in Jerusalem (so Chrysostom). The δ text alters these words to *οὗτοι δὲ ἤγαγον ἡμᾶς πρὸς οὓς ξενισθῶμεν. καὶ παραγενόμενοι εἴς τινα κώμην ἐγενόμεθα παρὰ Μνάσωνί τινι Κυπρίῳ, μαθητῇ ἀρχαίῳ.* This text Ropes calls 'highly improbable'; but others have found in the introduction of an early disciple at a village halfway between Caesarea and Jerusalem the result of the evangelistic activity ascribed to Peter in those parts by the δ text of xi. 2 (*q.v.*). The argument for the δ reading here is put thus by Blass:

> 'It must "seem very strange to us that Paul should have been dependent on a stranger for entertainment at Jerusalem, a place where we should have supposed he could have relied on the hospitality of private friends" (Salmon), and that in order to introduce Paul to Mnason, whose house he might find himself, the disciples of Caesarea should have accompanied him on that long journey. The accompanying, on the other hand, was quite natural, if Mnason lived in a village known to these disciples, but not known to Paul' (*PG*, p. 130).

[1] Ramsay understands *ὑποζύγια* with the phrase quoted from Chrysostom (*Hom.* 45). But it might simply mean 'the supplies for the journey'.

It might be replied that Paul's private friends (whoever they were) might be unable to accommodate his large company ; it was, besides, fitting that arrangement should be made in advance for these Gentile Christians to stay with a Hellenist (and therefore probably liberal) believer. From the description ἀρχαίῳ μαθητῇ we should understand that Mnason had been a disciple since the beginning (ἀρχή) of the Church. For Cypriote Christians cf. iv. 36 ; xi. 20. It is very likely that, like Philip's daughters, he receives explicit mention because, as an early disciple, he could give information about the early days of the Church. Ramsay suggests that Luke was indebted to him for the stories of Aeneas and Dorcas (*BRD*, p. 309 *n*.). Cf. also Luke's interest elsewhere in hosts (cf. ix. 11, 43 ; xvii. 5 ; xviii. 7).

3. Paul at Jerusalem, xxi. 17-xxiii. 30

(a) Meeting with James and the Elders, xxi. 17-26

Γενομένων δὲ ἡμῶν εἰς Ἱεροσόλυμα ἀσμένως ἀπεδέξαντο ἡμᾶς 17
οἱ ἀδελφοί. τῇ δὲ ἐπιούσῃ εἰσῄει ὁ Παῦλος σὺν ἡμῖν πρὸς Ἰάκωβον, 18
πάντες τε παρεγένοντο οἱ πρεσβύτεροι. καὶ ἀσπασάμενος αὐτοὺς 19
ἐξηγεῖτο καθ' ἓν ἕκαστον ὧν ἐποίησεν ὁ θεὸς ἐν τοῖς ἔθνεσιν διὰ τῆς
διακονίας αὐτοῦ. οἱ δὲ ἀκούσαντες ἐδόξαζον τὸν θεόν, εἶπάν τε αὐτῷ 20
Θεωρεῖς, ἀδελφέ, πόσαι μυριάδες εἰσὶν ἐν τοῖς Ἰουδαίοις τῶν πεπισ-
τευκότων, καὶ πάντες ζηλωταὶ τοῦ νόμου ὑπάρχουσιν· κατηχήθησαν 21
δὲ περὶ σοῦ ὅτι ἀποστασίαν διδάσκεις ἀπὸ Μωυσέως τοὺς κατὰ τὰ
ἔθνη πάντας Ἰουδαίους, λέγων μὴ περιτέμνειν αὐτοὺς τὰ τέκνα μηδὲ
τοῖς ἔθεσιν περιπατεῖν. τί οὖν ἐστίν; πάντως ἀκούσονται ὅτι ἐλήλυθας. 22
τοῦτο οὖν ποίησον ὅ σοι λέγομεν· εἰσὶν ἡμῖν ἄνδρες τέσσαρες εὐχὴν 23
ἔχοντες ἀφ' ἑαυτῶν. τούτους παραλαβὼν ἁγνίσθητι σὺν αὐτοῖς καὶ 24
δαπάνησον ἐπ' αὐτοῖς ἵνα ξυρήσονται τὴν κεφαλήν, καὶ γνώσονται
πάντες ὅτι ὧν κατήχηνται περὶ σοῦ οὐδὲν ἔστιν, ἀλλὰ στοιχεῖς καὶ αὐτὸς
φυλάσσων τὸν νόμον. περὶ δὲ τῶν πεπιστευκότων ἐθνῶν ἡμεῖς ἀπεσ- 25
τείλαμεν κρίναντες φυλάσσεσθαι αὐτοὺς τό τε εἰδωλόθυτον καὶ αἷμα
καὶ πνικτὸν καὶ πορνείαν. τότε ὁ Παῦλος παραλαβὼν τοὺς ἄνδρας 26
τῇ ἐχομένῃ ἡμέρᾳ σὺν αὐτοῖς ἁγνισθεὶς εἰσῄει εἰς τὸ ἱερόν, διαγγέλλων
τὴν ἐκπλήρωσιν τῶν ἡμερῶν τοῦ ἁγνισμοῦ ἕως οὗ προσηνέχθη ὑπὲρ
ἑνὸς ἑκάστου αὐτῶν ἡ προσφορά.

xxi. 17

Γενομένων δὲ ἡμῶν] The δ text, linking up with its paraphrase of *ver.* 16, has *κἀκεῖθεν ἐξιόντες ἤλθομεν.*

We are not told if they arrived in time for Pentecost ; probably they did (see on *ver.* 27). In xxi. 17-xxiv. 23 the events of twelve days are narrated ; two years are passed over in xxiv. 24-27 ; then

xxv. 1-xxviii. 7 cover about five months. The space devoted to Paul's arrest and examinations shows the importance attached to these by Luke, and may be compared with the space allotted in the Gospels to the events of Passion Week.

xxi. 18

εἰσῄει ὁ Παῦλος σὺν ἡμῖν] As in xvi. 17, Paul is distinguished from 'us' at the end of a 'we' section. The 'we' narrative is resumed in xxvii. 1. If Luke spent part of the intervening time in Jerusalem, he had access to valuable sources of information, e.g., in the household of Mary the mother of Mark.

Ἰάκωβον] As in xii. 17; xv. 13, James occupies a leading place in the Jerusalem church. From the absence of all mention of the Twelve, it is safe to infer that none of them was in Jerusalem at this time. Clement of Alexandria (*Strom.* vi. 5. 43. 3) quotes from the *Preaching of Peter* (a work to be dated *c.* A.D. 150) a tradition that the Lord commanded the apostles to stay twelve years in Jerusalem and then go out into all the world, that none might say, 'We did not hear'. The tradition appears also in Euseb., *HE*, v. 18. 14. Cf. B. H. Streeter, *The Primitive Church*, pp. 3 ff., for a review of the possibilities of answering the question, 'What became of the Twelve Apostles?'

πάντες τε παρεγένοντο οἱ πρεσβύτεροι] Cf. xi. 30; xv. 4, 6, 22 f.; but no longer do we read, as in ch. xv, of 'the apostles and elders'.

xxi. 19

ἐξηγεῖτο καθ' ἓν ἕκαστον ὧν ἐποίησεν ὁ θεὸς ἐν τοῖς ἔθνεσιν] Cf. xiv. 27; xv. 3 f., 12.

xxi. 20

ἐδόξαζον τὸν θεόν] They had cause to praise God not only for the conversion of the Gentiles, but also for the practical evidence of their conversion in the contributions sent to the Jerusalem Christians, perhaps also for the relief felt at learning that the report of *ver.* 21 was untrue.

πόσαι μυριάδες] 'how many thousands' is our idiom.

ἐν τοῖς Ἰουδαίοις] om ℵ. δ has *ἐν τῇ Ἰουδαίᾳ*, byz *Ἰουδαίων*.

ζηλωταὶ τοῦ νόμου] 'zealous for the law'; the majority probably belonged to the Pharisaic party (cf. xv. 5). Cf. 1 Macc. ii. 27, *πᾶς ὁ ζηλῶν τῷ νόμῳ . . . ἐξελθέτω ὀπίσω μου.* It is from this passage in 1 Macc., according to R. Eisler, that the Zealots (see on i. 13) derived their name; but we should not, with him, take *ζηλωταί* here as meaning 'Zealots' in the party sense, but in the sense in which Paul uses it in Gal. i. 14, *ζηλωτὴς ὑπάρχων τῶν πατρικῶν μου παραδόσεων.*

xxi. 21

κατηχήθησαν] 'they have been informed'; here of false or hostile information. Cf. its use in Lk. i. 4, of true information.

ὅτι ἀποστασίαν διδάσκεις ἀπὸ Μωυσέως] Neither in Ac. nor in his epistles is it suggested that Paul encouraged *Jewish* believers to give up their ancestral observances; indeed, he himself honoured them. But he did insist that these observances must not be imposed upon Gentile believers, that they were not necessary for salvation, and that a man was no worse a Christian for omitting them (cf. Rom. xiv. 5 f.).

πάντας] om A D E 33 d e vg boh.

μὴ περιτέμνειν] 'to stop circumcising'. There is no ground for thinking that Paul forbade *Jews* to practise circumcision; cf. his own action in xvi. 3. His attitude on this and other questions so far as Jews were concerned may have afforded his opponents a pretext for insinuating that despite his protestations to the contrary Paul still taught circumcision (Gal. v. 11).

τοῖς ἔθεσιν περιπατεῖν] 'to walk according to the customs', i.e., the customs ordained by the Jewish law, 'received by tradition from Moses' (vi. 14). For this ethical sense of *περιπατέω* cf. Mk. vii. 5; Eph. ii. 2; Heb. xiii. 9; it is specially common in the Pauline and Johannine epistles. Cf. *στοιχεῖς*, *ver.* 24; *πεπολίτευμαι*, xxiii. 1.

xxi. 22

τί οὖν ἐστίν;] 'What about it, then?' So vi. 3 D; 1 Cor. xiv. 15, 26.

πάντως] 'of course' (cf. xxviii. 4). ℵ A C² D E byz e g vg follow with *δεῖ πλῆθος συνελθεῖν, ἀκούσονται γὰρ κ.τ.λ.*, or the like. This is an attractive and probable addition. For *πλῆθος* ('congregation'), see on iv. 32.

xxi. 23

εὐχὴν ἔχοντες] The vow seems to have been a temporary Nazirite one, like that in xviii. 18 (*q.v.*). Cf. Num. vi. 2 ff. Such a temporary vow commonly lasted 30 days (cf. Jos. *BJ*, ii. 15. 1, where Bernice is said to have taken a vow for this length of time). 'A Nazirite vow that is vowed without a fixed duration is binding for 30 days' (Mishna, *Nazir*, vi. 3). In Paul's readiness to undertake this charge, we have a further example of his self-confessed willingness to be 'all things to all men' (cf. 1 Cor. ix. 19-23).

ἀφ' ἑαυτῶν] 'on their own initiative' (ℵ B minn. pauc sah boh Orig.). Our other authorities have *ἐφ' ἑαυτῶν*, 'upon themselves'.

xxi. 24

ἁγνίσθητι σὺν αὐτοῖς] 'join in the purificatory rite with them'. The men may have had to purify themselves from some defilement (see on *ver.* 27), but Paul could join in the rite without having himself contracted defilement.

δαπάνησον ἐπ' αὐτοῖς] Herod Agrippa I paid the expenses of many Nazirites[1] (Jos. *Ant.* xix. 6. 1). For other indications that Paul had access to money at this time Ramsay adduces the expense of imprisonment and a long lawsuit, Felix's expectation (xxiv. 26), his hiring a lodging in Rome, and his appeal to Caesar: 'there is little doubt that the citizen's right of appeal to the Emperor was hedged in by fees and pledges' (*SPT*, p. 311). From his epistles we gather that he was supported by many of the Gentile churches.

ἵνα ξυρήσονται τὴν κεφαλήν] See on xviii. 18. There the word is *κείρω*, 'shear'; here *ξυρέω*, 'shave'. For the fut. indic. after *ἵνα* cf. Mt. xiii. 15; Rev. vi. 11; xiv. 13. But by this time there was little or no distinction in most verbs between the fut. indic. and the sigmatic aor. subjve., as regards pronunciation.

κατήχηνται] See on *ver.* 21.

στοιχεῖς] Ethically, like *περιπατεῖν*, *ver.* 21. Paul kept the law himself, though he refused to force it on others. Cf. Introduction, pp. 34 ff.

xxi. 25

περὶ δὲ τῶν πεπιστευκότων ἐθνῶν] The letter was addressed to the Gentile brethren in Antioch and Syro-Cilicia (xv. 23), but the intention of those who sent it was no doubt that its terms should be valid for Gentile churches everywhere. Paul himself had carried it beyond the bounds of Syro-Cilicia, to the Galatian churches founded during his first missionary journey (xvi. 4).

ἀπεστείλαμεν] B D minn boh hcl arm (this use without an object is common in LXX); ℵ A C byz have *ἐπεστείλαμεν* (cf. xv. 20). D has *ἀπεστείλαμεν κρίνοντες μηδὲν τοιοῦτον τηρεῖν αὐτοὺς εἰ μὴ φυλάσσεσθαι αὐτοὺς τὸ εἰδωλόθυτον καὶ αἷμα καὶ πορνείαν* (omitting the negative Golden Rule found in the δ text of xv. 20, 29). There is no good reason to infer from this verse, as many do, that Paul had not previously been told of the apostolic decree. Its introduction here is perfectly natural in the context. James and the elders say in effect, 'We are glad to know that you do not teach *Jewish* believers to forsake the law, and we should like you to make this clear to all the Jewish believers here. As for the *Gentile*

[1] This is certainly implied in the statement of Josephus that he directe very many of the Nazirites to have their heads shaved (*διὸ καὶ Ναζιραίων ξυρᾶσθαι διέταξε μάλα συχνούς*).

believers, of course, we have already agreed that nothing is to be required of them except that they refrain from meat sacrificed to idols, etc.' For the various readings in the text of the decree, see on xv. 20, 29.

xxi. 26

εἰσῄει] For this use of *εἰσῄει* without an appreciably imperfect sense, cf. *ver.* 18.

ἐκπλήρωσιν] The time fixed for fulfilment. Cf. I Macc. iii. 49, *τοὺς Ναζιραίους οἳ ἐπλήρωσαν τὰς ἡμέρας.*

τῶν ἡμερῶν τοῦ ἁγνισμοῦ] Cf. Num. vi. 5, *πάσας τὰς ἡμέρας τῆς εὐχῆς τοῦ ἁγνισμοῦ ξυρὸν οὐκ ἐπελεύσεται ἐπὶ τὴν κεφαλὴν αὐτοῦ.*

προσφορά] The offering consisted of one he-lamb, one ewe-lamb, one ram, and accompanying meal and drink-offerings, according to Num. vi. 14 f. Cf. Mishna, *Nazir* vi. 6 ff.

(b) Riot in the Temple ; Paul rescued by the Romans, xxi. 27-36

Ὡς δὲ ἔμελλον αἱ ἑπτὰ ἡμέραι συντελεῖσθαι, οἱ ἀπὸ τῆς Ἀσίας 27
Ἰουδαῖοι θεασάμενοι αὐτὸν ἐν τῷ ἱερῷ συνέχεον πάντα τὸν ὄχλον καὶ
ἐπέβαλαν ἐπ' αὐτὸν τὰς χεῖρας, κράζοντες Ἄνδρες Ἰσραηλεῖται, 28
βοηθεῖτε· οὗτός ἐστιν ὁ ἄνθρωπος ὁ κατὰ τοῦ λαοῦ καὶ τοῦ νόμου
καὶ τοῦ τόπου τούτου πάντας πανταχῇ διδάσκων, ἔτι τε καὶ Ἕλληνας
εἰσήγαγεν εἰς τὸ ἱερὸν καὶ κεκοίνωκεν τὸν ἅγιον τόπον τοῦτον. ἦσαν 29
γὰρ προεωρακότες Τρόφιμον τὸν Ἐφέσιον ἐν τῇ πόλει σὺν αὐτῷ, ὃν
ἐνόμιζον ὅτι εἰς τὸ ἱερὸν εἰσήγαγεν ὁ Παῦλος. ἐκινήθη τε ἡ πόλις 30
ὅλη καὶ ἐγένετο συνδρομὴ τοῦ λαοῦ, καὶ ἐπιλαβόμενοι τοῦ Παύλου
εἷλκον αὐτὸν ἔξω τοῦ ἱεροῦ, καὶ εὐθέως ἐκλείσθησαν αἱ θύραι. Ζητούν- 31
των τε αὐτὸν ἀποκτεῖναι ἀνέβη φάσις τῷ χιλιάρχῳ τῆς σπείρης ὅτι
ὅλη συγχύννεται Ἰερουσαλήμ, ὃς ἐξαυτῆς παραλαβὼν στρατιώτας καὶ 32
ἑκατοντάρχας κατέδραμεν ἐπ' αὐτούς, οἱ δὲ ἰδόντες τὸν χιλίαρχον καὶ
τοὺς στρατιώτας ἐπαύσαντο τύπτοντες τὸν Παῦλον. τότε ἐγγίσας ὁ 33
χιλίαρχος ἐπελάβετο αὐτοῦ καὶ ἐκέλευσε δεθῆναι ἁλύσεσι δυσί, καὶ
ἐπυνθάνετο τίς εἴη καὶ τί ἐστιν πεποιηκώς· ἄλλοι δὲ ἄλλο τι ἐπεφώνουν 34
ἐν τῷ ὄχλῳ· μὴ δυναμένου δὲ αὐτοῦ γνῶναι τὸ ἀσφαλὲς διὰ τὸν
θόρυβον ἐκέλευσεν ἄγεσθαι αὐτὸν εἰς τὴν παρεμβολήν. ὅτε δὲ ἐγένετο 35
ἐπὶ τοὺς ἀναβαθμούς, συνέβη βαστάζεσθαι αὐτὸν ὑπὸ τῶν στρατιωτῶν
διὰ τὴν βίαν τοῦ ὄχλου, ἠκολούθει γὰρ τὸ πλῆθος τοῦ λαοῦ κράζοντες 36
Αἶρε αὐτόν.

xxi. 27

ὡς δὲ ἔμελλον αἱ ἑπτὰ ἡμέραι συντελεῖσθαι] 'When the seven days were going to be fulfilled'; the following events took place at the beginning, not at the end, of the seven days. See on xxiv. 11.

Seven days had to elapse before a Nazirite who had contracted defilement could be purified. Such a man shaved his head on the seventh day and brought his offering on the eighth day (Num. vi. 9 f.; Mishna, *Nazir*, vi. 6).

οἱ ἀπὸ τῆς Ἀσίας Ἰουδαῖοι] Asian Jews would be most likely to recognize Trophimus. The Jews of Asia had already troubled Paul (cf. xx. 19); for the veneration of Jews of the Diaspora for the Temple cf. vi. 9. Jews would be present from all parts now for the Feast of Pentecost.

συνέχεον] For this word used of a riot cf. xix. 32; cf. σύγχυσις, xix. 29.

xxi. 28

ὁ κατὰ τοῦ λαοῦ καὶ τοῦ νόμου καὶ τοῦ τόπου τούτου . . . διδάσκων] Cf. the report of *ver.* 21, and the accusation against Stephen, vi. 13. Nothing was so likely to infuriate Jews of Jerusalem and the Dispersion alike as a suspected disparagement of the Temple; this was the gravamen of the accusation brought against Jesus before the Sanhedrin (cf. Mk. xiv. 57 f.). Yet it was difficult to procure official sanction for a sentence imposed merely for *speaking* against the Jewish religion. A more definite and serious charge was now brought.

πάντας πανταχῇ] Alliteration; cf. *ver.* 39; xvii. 26, 30; xxiv. 3; Mt. xxi. 41; Mk. v. 26; 1 Cor. iv. 17; 2 Cor. viii. 22; ix. 8.

Ἕλληνας εἰσήγαγεν εἰς τὸ ἱερὸν] i.e., beyond the Outer Court. Gentiles might enter the Outer Court, which was therefore known as the Court of the Gentiles; but their progress into the Inner Court was barred. Notices in Greek and Latin were attached to the railing at the foot of the stairs leading to the Inner Court warning Gentiles not to proceed farther (cf. Jos. *BJ*, v. 5. 2; vi. 2. 4; *Ant.* xv. 11. 5; *Ap.* ii. 8; Philo, *Leg. ad Gai.* 212). One of these inscriptions discovered at Jerusalem in 1871, now in Istanbul, reads as follows: μηθένα ἀλλογενῆ εἰσπορεύεσθαι ἐντὸς τοῦ περὶ τὸ ἱερὸν τρυφάκτου καὶ περιβόλου· ὃς δ' ἂν ληφθῇ ἑαυτῷ αἴτιος ἔσται διὰ τὸ ἐξακολουθεῖν θάνατον.[1] J. A. Robinson, on Eph. ii. 14, sees in the μεσότοιχον τοῦ φραγμοῦ there mentioned an allusion to this barrier. The Jews had the right to sentence even Romans to death for a breach of this law, according to the speech of Titus recorded in *BJ*, vi. 2. 4. See on iv. 3.

κεκοίνωκεν] Perfect tense; if the allegation were true, the Temple was now in a state of defilement (κοινόν) as a result.

τὸν ἅγιον τόπον τοῦτον] Cf. vi. 13.

[1] For this inscription, discovered by C. S. Clermont-Ganneau, cf. *PEFQ* 1871, p. 132; τρυφάκτου is, of course, an aberrant spelling of δρυφάκτου. Part of another of these inscriptions was discovered about twelve years ago: cf. *Quarterly of Dept. of Antiquities in Palestine* vi (1938), pp. 1 ff.

xxi. 29

Τρόφιμον] Cf. xx. 4.

ὃν ἐνόμιζον ὅτι εἰς τὸ ἱερὸν εἰσήγαγεν ὁ Παῦλος] Even so, by the letter of the law Trophimus was the guilty party, though Paul would have been guilty of aiding and abetting him.[1]

xxi. 30

ἐκινήθη τε ἡ πόλις ὅλη] News of this kind travels fast.

συνδρομὴ] Elsewhere in Gk. Bible only at Judith x. 18; 3 Macc. iii. 8.

εἷλκον] Imperf.; with the jostling crowd, dragging Paul out was a slow process; they occupied the time in beating him (*ver.* 32).

εὐθέως] As soon as the crowd had got Paul outside.

ἐκλείσθησαν αἱ θύραι] The captain of the Temple (see on iv. 1) probably shut them to prevent further trouble. Some have detected a symbolic significance in the shutting of the doors. Thus T. D. Bernard: '"Believing all things which are written in the Law and in the Prophets", and having "committed nothing against the people or customs of [his] fathers", he and his creed are forced from their proper home. On it as well as him the Temple doors are shut' (*The Progress of Doctrine* [5], p. 121).

xxi. 31

Ζητούντων] See on *ἐπιμενόντων*, *ver.* 10.

φάσις] 'report'; it was probably sent up by the soldiers who patrolled the top of the colonnades to watch for riots.

τῷ χιλιάρχῳ τῆς σπείρης] 'the military tribune in command of the cohort', Claudius Lysias by name (xxiii. 26). Josephus says a *τάγμα* was stationed regularly in the fortress of Antonia, north of the Temple (*BJ*, v. 5. 8). Two flights of steps led down from the fort to the Outer Court (cf. *vv.* 35, 40). The *χιλίαρχος* is perhaps identical with the *φρούραρχος* of Jos. *Ant.* xv. 11. 4; xviii. 4. 3. The court of the Temple had to be under constant military supervision, especially when one of the great feasts was in progress, as at present. The *σπεῖρα* ('cohort': see on x. 1) was a *cohors auxiliaris* of the paper strength of 760 infantry and 240 cavalry.

συνχύννεται] Cf. *ver.* 27. Riots were always more easily stirred up during the feasts, when the city was full of visitors.

[1] J. Klausner (*From Jesus to Paul*, p. 400) thinks 'it is possible that Paul may actually have brought Trophimus into the Temple, since Paul would not have seen any harm in an act like this, after he had put aside the differences between Jew and Greek in all matters pertaining to religion'. However that may be, the idea that Paul, who was taking such pains to conciliate Jewish susceptibilities on this occasion, should have gone out of his way to do anything so outrageously offensive, is absurd.

xxi. 32

ἑκατοντάρχας] As more than one centurion was present, we may infer that at least 200 men were called out.

xxi. 33

ἁλύσεσι δυσί] Perhaps to a soldier on either side; *ἁλύσεις* (cf. xii. 7) were hand-chains, as opposed to *πέδαι* (fetters for the legs). Both are mentioned together in Mk. v. 4; Lk. viii. 29. Cf. Agrippa's chain (*ἅλυσις*) in Jos. *Ant.* xviii. 6. 10.

τίς εἴη] Optative in historic sequence (cf. Lk. i. 29; viii. 9; xviii. 36; xxii. 23). Luke is the only NT writer to use this classical construction.

τί ἐστιν πεποιηκώς] The optative in *τίς εἴη* was appropriate as the prisoner was quite unknown; here the indicative is retained, as the tribune was quite sure that he had done something or other.

xxi. 34

ἄλλοι δὲ ἄλλο τι ἐπεφώνουν] As would naturally happen in an excited crowd (cf. xix. 32).

γνῶναι τὸ ἀσφαλὲς] 'learn the truth'.

εἰς τὴν παρεμβολήν] i.e., the fort or tower of Antonia (see on *ver.* 31).

xxi. 35

ἐγένετο ἐπὶ τοὺς ἀναβαθμούς] 'arrived at the steps': cf. Lk. xxiv. 22, *γενόμεναι ὀρθριναὶ ἐπὶ τὸ μνημεῖον* ('having arrived early at the sepulchre'). The steps connected the outer court of the Temple with the fort (see on *ver.* 31).

συνέβη] Replacing *ἐγένετο*, which has already been used in the sentence.

xxi. 36

Αἶρε αὐτόν] 'Away with him!' Cf. xxii. 22; Lk. xxiii. 18; Jn. xix. 15. A good papyrus parallel is that in the letter of the boy Theon (see on xvii. 6), *ἆρρον αὐτόν* (for *ἆρον αὐτόν*). Cf. also *αἶρε τοὺς ἀθέους*, *Martyrium Polycarpi*, iii. 1; ix. 2.

(c) Paul obtains Leave to address the Crowd, xxi. 37-40

Μέλλων τε εἰσάγεσθαι εἰς τὴν παρεμβολὴν ὁ Παῦλος λέγει τῷ 37
χιλιάρχῳ Εἰ ἔξεστίν μοι εἰπεῖν τι πρὸς σέ; ὁ δὲ ἔφη Ἑλληνιστὶ γινώ-
σκεις; οὐκ ἄρα σὺ εἶ ὁ Αἰγύπτιος ὁ πρὸ τούτων τῶν ἡμερῶν ἀναστα- 38
τώσας καὶ ἐξαγαγὼν εἰς τὴν ἔρημον τοὺς τετρακισχιλίους ἄνδρας τῶν

σικαρίων; εἶπεν δὲ ὁ Παῦλος Ἐγὼ ἄνθρωπος μέν εἰμι Ἰουδαῖος, 39
Ταρσεὺς τῆς Κιλικίας, οὐκ ἀσήμου πόλεως πολίτης· δέομαι δέ σου,
ἐπίτρεψόν μοι λαλῆσαι πρὸς τὸν λαόν. ἐπιτρέψαντος δὲ αὐτοῦ ὁ Παῦλος 40
ἑστὼς ἐπὶ τῶν ἀναβαθμῶν κατέσεισε τῇ χειρὶ τῷ λαῷ, πολλῆς δὲ
σιγῆς γενομένης προσεφώνησεν τῇ Ἑβραΐδι διαλέκτῳ λέγων

xxi. 37

Εἰ] Introducing a direct question (see on i. 6).

Ἑλληνιστὶ γινώσκεις;] Sc. *λαλεῖν*. 'Can you (speak) Greek?'

xxi. 38

οὐκ ἄρα σὺ εἶ] 'Then you are not . . .', in a tone of surprise.

ὁ Αἰγύπτιος] According to Jos. *BJ*, ii. 13. 4 f.; *Ant.* xx. 8. 6, this Egyptian came to Jerusalem about A.D. 54, claiming to be a prophet, and led a multitude of 30,000 to the Mount of Olives, promising that the city walls would fall down at his command, that they might march in. Felix sent soldiers against them, who killed 400 and captured 200. The Egyptian himself escaped and disappeared. No doubt some, impressed by his apparently miraculous deliverance, looked for his triumphant return. Luke's report seems quite independent of Josephus's. The more moderate figure (4000) given here is more likely; in Gk. the signs for 4000 (,Δ) and for 30,000 (,Λ) could easily be confused. This Egyptian is possibly to be identified with the false prophet called Ben Stada in the Talmud (cf. J. Klausner, *Jesus of Nazareth* [1929], pp. 20 ff.).

ἀναστατώσας] See on xvii. 6.

ἐξαγαγὼν εἰς τὴν ἔρημον] As Moses had done. Josephus tells us that many impostors at this time led people into the wilderness, promising to perform miracles (cf. Mt. xxiv. 26).

τῶν σικαρίων] 'of the Assassins' (Lat. *sicarius*, from *sica*, 'dagger'). They began to be active in the time of Felix, and after murdering the former High Priest Jonathan (see on iv. 6), appeared as bitter enemies of the Romans and of pro-Roman Jews. They mingled with the crowds at festivals and stabbed their opponents unobserved. Their activities added to the horrors of Jerusalem's last days. Cf. Jos. *BJ*, ii. 13. 3; *Ant.* xx. 8. 5, 10.

xxi. 39

Ἐγὼ ἄνθρωπος μέν εἰμι . . . δέομαι δὲ σοῦ] Observe the balance of *μέν* and *δέ*. 'I, as regards your question to me, am a man . . ., but, as regards my question to you, I ask . . .' (Page).

οὐκ ἀσήμου πόλεως πολίτης] Cf. Euripides, *Ion*, 8, *ἔστιν γὰρ οὐκ ἄσημος Ἑλλήνων πόλις* (i.e., Athens). Note the litotes, and also the alliteration *πόλεως πολίτης* (cf. *ver.* 28). He was not merely a native, but a citizen of Tarsus, and, though he does not mention it at this point, his Roman citizenship placed him among the élite of the citizens of Tarsus. But his Tarsian citizenship made no such impression on the tribune as his Roman citizenship did when later revealed (xxii. 28 f.).

xxi. 40

κατέσεισε τῇ χειρὶ] A characteristic action: cf. xiii. 16. (Cf. also xii. 17; xix. 33.)

τῇ Ἑβραΐδι διαλέκτῳ] 'in the Aramaic tongue', for so we should understand this expression or the adverb *Ἑβραϊστί* in NT except in Rev. ix. 11; xvi. 16. The use of Aram. was perhaps calculated *ad captandam beniuolentiam*. Besides being the Palestine vernacular, Aram. was the *lingua franca* of non-Greek speakers in the eastern Roman world and of the Parthian Empire. The first draft of *BJ* was written by Josephus in Aram. for the Jews of Babylonia.

(d) Paul addresses the Crowd; he relates his Conversion, xxii. 1-16

Ἄνδρες ἀδελφοὶ καὶ πατέρες, ἀκούσατέ μου τῆς πρὸς ὑμᾶς νυνὶ 1
ἀπολογίας.—ἀκούσαντες δὲ ὅτι τῇ Ἑβραΐδι διαλέκτῳ προσεφώνει 2
αὐτοῖς μᾶλλον παρέσχον ἡσυχίαν. καί φησιν— Ἐγώ εἰμι ἀνὴρ 3
Ἰουδαῖος, γεγεννημένος ἐν Ταρσῷ τῆς Κιλικίας, ἀνατεθραμμένος δὲ
ἐν τῇ πόλει ταύτῃ παρὰ τοὺς πόδας Γαμαλιήλ, πεπαιδευμένος κατὰ
ἀκρίβειαν τοῦ πατρῴου νόμου, ζηλωτὴς ὑπάρχων τοῦ θεοῦ καθὼς
πάντες ὑμεῖς ἐστὲ σήμερον, ὃς ταύτην τὴν ὁδὸν ἐδίωξα ἄχρι θανάτου, 4
δεσμεύων καὶ παραδιδοὺς εἰς φυλακὰς ἄνδρας τε καὶ γυναῖκας, ὡς 5
καὶ ὁ ἀρχιερεὺς μαρτυρεῖ μοι καὶ πᾶν τὸ πρεσβυτέριον· παρ' ὧν καὶ
ἐπιστολὰς δεξάμενος πρὸς τοὺς ἀδελφοὺς εἰς Δαμασκὸν ἐπορευόμην
ἄξων καὶ τοὺς ἐκεῖσε ὄντας δεδεμένους εἰς Ἰερουσαλὴμ ἵνα τιμωρηθῶσιν. Ἐγένετο δέ μοι πορευομένῳ καὶ ἐγγίζοντι τῇ Δαμασκῷ 6
περὶ μεσημβρίαν ἐξαίφνης ἐκ τοῦ οὐρανοῦ περιαστράψαι φῶς ἱκανὸν
περὶ ἐμέ, ἔπεσά τε εἰς τὸ ἔδαφος καὶ ἤκουσα φωνῆς λεγούσης μοι Σαοὺλ 7
Σαούλ, τί με διώκεις; ἐγὼ δὲ ἀπεκρίθην Τίς εἶ, κύριε; εἶπέν τε 8
πρὸς ἐμέ Ἐγώ εἰμι Ἰησοῦς ὁ Ναζωραῖος ὃν σὺ διώκεις. οἱ δὲ σὺν 9
ἐμοὶ ὄντες τὸ μὲν φῶς ἐθεάσαντο τὴν δὲ φωνὴν οὐκ ἤκουσαν τοῦ λαλοῦντός μοι. εἶπον δέ Τί ποιήσω, κύριε; ὁ δὲ κύριος εἶπεν πρός με 10
Ἀναστὰς πορεύου εἰς Δαμασκόν, κἀκεῖ σοι λαληθήσεται περὶ πάντων
ὧν τέτακταί σοι ποιῆσαι. ὡς δὲ οὐκ ἐνέβλεπον ἀπὸ τῆς δόξης τοῦ 11
φωτὸς ἐκείνου, χειραγωγούμενος ὑπὸ τῶν συνόντων μοι ἦλθον εἰς
Δαμασκόν. Ἁνανίας δέ τις ἀνὴρ εὐλαβὴς κατὰ τὸν νόμον, μαρτυ- 12
ρούμενος ὑπὸ πάντων τῶν κατοικούντων Ἰουδαίων, ἐλθὼν πρὸς ἐμὲ 13
καὶ ἐπιστὰς εἶπέν μοι Σαοὺλ ἀδελφέ, ἀνάβλεψον· κἀγὼ αὐτῇ τῇ

ὥρᾳ ἀνέβλεψα εἰς αὐτόν. ὁ δὲ εἶπεν Ὁ θεὸς τῶν πατέρων ἡμῶν 14
προεχειρίσατό σε γνῶναι τὸ θέλημα αὐτοῦ καὶ ἰδεῖν τὸν δίκαιον καὶ
ἀκοῦσαι φωνὴν ἐκ τοῦ στόματος αὐτοῦ, ὅτι ἔσῃ μάρτυς αὐτῷ πρὸς 15
πάντας ἀνθρώπους ὧν ἑώρακας καὶ ἤκουσας. καὶ νῦν τί μέλλεις; 16
ἀναστὰς βάπτισαι καὶ ἀπόλουσαι τὰς ἁμαρτίας σου ἐπικαλεσάμενος
τὸ ὄνομα αὐτοῦ.

xxii. 1

Ἄνδρες ἀδελφοὶ καὶ πατέρες, ἀκούσατε] The opening words of Stephen's defence, vii. 2.

ἀκούσατέ μου τῆς . . . ἀπολογίας] 'Hear my defence'; take *μου* with *ἀπολογίας* rather than with *ἀκούσατε*, though the latter is possible.

xxii. 2

τῇ Ἑβραΐδι διαλέκτῳ] See on xxi. 40.

μᾶλλον παρέσχον ἡσυχίαν] As though a bilingual Irish or Welsh audience, expecting a speech in English, suddenly became aware that they were being addressed in Irish or Welsh.

xxii. 3

ἐγώ εἰμι ἀνὴρ Ἰουδαῖος, γεγεννημένος ἐν Ταρσῷ τῆς Κιλικίας] Cf. xxi. 39. Yet there is a difference between the two verses; to the tribune he emphasizes his Tarsian citizenship; to the Jerusalem crowd, his Jewish birth and Rabbinical upbringing.

παρὰ τοὺς πόδας Γαμαλιήλ] 'The pupils sat on the ground during the instruction of the teacher, who was on an elevated place' (Schürer II. i. 326).[1] Cf. Lk. ii. 46; viii. 35; x. 39. For Gamaliel see on v. 34. His tolerant attitude there contrasts with the persecuting zeal of his pupil; it is by no means unusual for the pupil to be more extreme than his master. B Ψ 614 minn inflect *Γαμαλιήλου* (cf. Mt. xxiv. 15 D, *Δανιήλου*). It is possible that we should punctuate after *ταύτῃ*, and construe *παρὰ τοὺς πόδας Γαμαλιήλ* with *πεπαιδευμένος*.

κατὰ ἀκρίβειαν τοῦ πατρῴου νόμου] 'according to the strict letter of our ancestral law'. Cf. xxiv. 14; Mk. vii. 3; 1 Pet. i. 18; Jos. *Ant.* xiii. 10. 6 (*ἐκ πατέρων διαδοχῆς*); 16. 2 (*κατὰ τὴν πατρῴαν παράδοσιν*); cf. also Gorgias, *Epitaphius*, for the phrase *νόμου ἀκριβείας*.

ζηλωτὴς ὑπάρχων τοῦ θεοῦ] Cf. xxi. 20; Rom. x. 2; Gal. i. 14 (*ζηλωτὴς ὑπάρχων τῶν πατρικῶν μου παραδόσεων*). His zeal was

[1] The Mishnaic idiom for sitting at the feet of teachers is *hith'abbaq ba'ăphar raglēhem*, lit. 'to cover oneself with the dust of their feet' (cf. *Pirqe Aboth*, i. 4).

shown by his persecuting the church: cf. Phil. iii. 6 (the whole context in Phil. iii. 4 ff. should be compared with the present passage). For τοῦ θεοῦ vg has *legis;* hcl* has 'of my ancestral traditions' (representing τῶν πατρικῶν μου παραδόσεων, from Gal. i. 14).

xxii. 4

ταύτην τὴν ὁδὸν] See on ix. 2.

ἄχρι θανάτου] In *ver.* 20 below he mentions his complicity in the death of Stephen; and cf. ix. 1, ἐνπνέων ἀπειλῆς καὶ φόνου. For ἄχρι θανάτου cf. Rev. ii. 10, xii. 11; cf. μέχρι θανάτου Phil. ii. 8, 30; ἕως θανάτου, Mk. xiv. 34.

xxii. 5

ἀρχιερεὺς] 614 minn hcl* add Ἁνανίας (cf. xxiii. 2).

μαρτυρεῖ] ἐμαρτύρει B.

τὸ πρεσβυτέριον] 'the elderhood', i.e., the Sanhedrin (see on iv. 5, 15). The word is used in this sense in Lk. xxii. 66, and of the elders of a Christian church in 1 Tim. iv. 14.

παρ' ὧν καὶ ἐπιστολὰς δεξάμενος] Cf. ix. 2 ff. This is the second account in Ac. of Paul's conversion. In ch. ix. we have Luke's narrative; in chs. xxii and xxvi we have the story told by Paul himself to two very different audiences. Here the story is told in such a way as would naturally appeal to a Jerusalem audience; the contrasts with the two other accounts are significant.

πρὸς τοὺς ἀδελφοὺς] The 'brethren' here are Jews (cf. xxviii. 21); Paul speaks as a Jew to Jews.

ἄξων] Fut. ptc. expressing purpose: cf. viii. 27; (xx. 22;) xxiv. 11, 17.

ἐκεῖσε] Used in the sense of ἐκεῖ (cf. xxi. 3), which is the D reading here. If we press the original force of ἐκεῖσε ('thither'), the reference will be to those Christians who had gone to Damascus to escape the persecution in Jerusalem (viii. 1*b*).

εἰς 'Ιερουσαλὴμ] D has ἐν 'Ιερουσαλήμ, which must be taken with ἵνα τιμωρηθῶσιν.

xxii. 6

ἐγένετο δέ μοι πορευομένῳ καὶ ἐγγίζοντι . . . περιαστράψαι φῶς] For the construction cf. *ver.* 17; see on iv. 5.

περὶ μεσημβρίαν] Cf. ἡμέρας μέσης, xxvi. 13. Contrast κατὰ μεσημβρίαν, viii. 26.)

περιαστράψαι] Cf. περιήστραψεν, ix. 3.

xxii. 7

ἤκουσα φωνῆς λεγούσης μοι] See on ix. 4, *ἤκουσεν φωνὴν λέγουσαν αὐτῷ*, for the difference in construction. In g hcl.mg *τῇ Ἑβραΐδι διαλέκτῳ* is added (from xxvi. 14).

τί με διώκεις;] Followed in E 255 e g vg.codd hcl.mg Athan by *σκληρόν σοι πρὸς κέντρα λακτίζειν* (from xxvi. 14).

xxii. 8

Ἐγώ εἰμι Ἰησοῦς ὁ Ναζωραῖος ὃν σὺ διώκεις] Dalman (*Jesus-Jeshua*, p. 18) suggests *'anā Yēshūa' Nāṣĕrāyā dĕ-'att rādĕphinnēh* as the original Aramaic. The words *ὁ Ναζωραῖος* are not found in the accounts in ix. 5 or xxvi. 15. See on ii. 22.

xxii. 9

τὴν δὲ φωνὴν οὐκ ἤκουσαν τοῦ λαλοῦντός μοι] For the apparent contradiction with ix. 7 (*ἀκούοντες μὲν τῆς φωνῆς*) see note *ad loc.*

xxii. 10

Ἀναστὰς] More than a Semitic redundant ptc. here (see on v. 6, 17), as he had fallen to the ground.

περὶ πάντων ὧν τέτακταί σοι ποιῆσαι] HS 1765 minn Chr have *τί σε δεῖ ποιῆσαι* (*or ποιεῖν*), under the influence of ix. 6.

xxii. 11

ὡς δὲ] δ (1611 d g hcl.mg) prefixes *ἀναστὰς δὲ οὐκ ἐνέβλεπον.*

οὐκ ἐνέβλεπον] *οὐδὲν ἔβλεπον* B (so WH mg.).

ἀπὸ τῆς δόξης] The causal use of *ἀπὸ* (cf. xi. 19 ; xii. 14 ; xx. 9 ; Lk. xix. 3) has parallels both in classical and vernacular Gk.

χειραγωγούμενος] Cf. ix. 8, *χειραγωγοῦντες*.

xxii. 12

Ἁνανίας δέ τις ἀνὴρ εὐλαβὴς κατὰ τὸν νόμον] Ananias is here referred to as a pious Jew, in terms calculated to appeal to pious Jews, and the part played by him in Paul's conversion is emphasized. There is no real discrepancy between this account and Gal. i. 1, 12 ; the difference arises from the point of view. In Gal. Paul is concerned to show that he received his Gospel and his commission to preach it from God, not from the Twelve. A private Christian like Ananias could not in any case have commissioned him ; he simply communicated to Paul the message which God had given him to deliver.

xxii. 13

Σαοὺλ ἀδελφέ, ἀνάβλεψον] A summary of the words of Ananias in ix. 17.

αὐτῇ τῇ ὥρᾳ] See on xvi. 18.

ἀνέβλεψα εἰς αὐτόν] Here *ἀναβλέπω* has the double meaning 'recover sight' (*ἀνά*, 'again') and 'look up' (*ἀνά*, 'up').

xxii. 14

ὁ θεὸς τῶν πατέρων ἡμῶν κ.τ.λ.] The words of Ananias are such as a pious Jew might use. They are not given in the other accounts of the conversion, but cf. the words spoken by the Lord to Ananias in ix. 15 f. Ananias communicated to Paul the revelation he had received from the Lord concerning him.

προεχειρίσατο] Cf. *προκεχειρισμένον*, iii. 20; *προχειρίσασθαι*, xxvi. 16.

γνῶναι τὸ θέλημα αὐτοῦ] Cf. Rom. ii. 18; xii. 2; Col. i. 9. From Rom. ii. 18 we may infer that the phrase was current in Jewish circles.

τὸν δίκαιον] For 'the Righteous One' as a title of Messiah see on iii. 14.

xxii. 15

ὅτι ἔσῃ μάρτυς] 'For you shall be a witness'; cf. *μάρτυρα*, xxvi. 16.

πρὸς πάντας ἀνθρώπους] Cf. ix. 15, *ἐνώπιον τῶν ἐθνῶν τε καὶ βασιλέων υἱῶν τε Ἰσραήλ*.

ὧν ἑώρακας καὶ ἤκουσας] Cf. xxvi. 16, *ὧν τε εἶδές με ὧν τε ὀφθήσομαί σοι*. He had seen the risen Christ; he had heard His voice. In xxvi. 16 ff. Paul represents the communication he received from Ananias as part of the heavenly vision. Cf. ix. 12, where Paul in a vision foresees the visit of Ananias.

xxii. 16

τί μέλλεις;] 'Why do you delay?'

ἀναστὰς βάπτισαι καὶ ἀπόλουσαι τὰς ἁμαρτίας σου] Here *ἀναστάς* may be the Semitic redundant ptc. (see on *ver.* 10). The imperatives are in the middle voice: 'get yourself baptized and get your sins washed away'. Cf. *ἀπελούσασθε*, 1 Cor. vi. 11; *ἐβαπτίσαντο*, 1 Cor. x. 2. His baptism was the 'outward and visible sign' of his inward and spiritual cleansing. For Paul's own developed teaching on the significance of baptism, cf. Rom. vi. 3 ff.

ἐπικαλεσάμενος τὸ ὄνομα αὐτοῦ] 'invoking His name'; and thus being baptized in (*or* with) that Name: see on ii. 38.

(e) Paul Relates his Vision in the Temple, xxii. 17-21

Ἐγένετο δέ μοι ὑποστρέψαντι εἰς Ἰερουσαλὴμ καὶ προσευχομένου 17
μου ἐν τῷ ἱερῷ γενέσθαι με ἐν ἐκστάσει καὶ ἰδεῖν αὐτὸν λέγοντά μοι 18
Σπεῦσον καὶ ἔξελθε ἐν τάχει ἐξ Ἰερουσαλήμ, διότι οὐ παραδέξονταί
σου μαρτυρίαν περὶ ἐμοῦ. κἀγὼ εἶπον Κύριε, αὐτοὶ ἐπίστανται 19
ὅτι ἐγὼ ἤμην φυλακίζων καὶ δέρων κατὰ τὰς συναγωγὰς τοὺς πιστεύοντας
ἐπὶ σέ· καὶ ὅτε ἐξεχύννετο τὸ αἷμα Στεφάνου τοῦ μάρτυρός σου, καὶ 20
αὐτὸς ἤμην ἐφεστὼς καὶ συνευδοκῶν καὶ φυλάσσων τὰ ἱμάτια τῶν
ἀναιρούντων αὐτόν. καὶ εἶπεν πρός με Πορεύου, ὅτι ἐγὼ εἰς ἔθνη 21
μακρὰν ἐξαποστελῶ σε.

xxii. 17

ἐγένετο δέ μοι ὑποστρέψαντι . . . καὶ προσευχομένου μου . . . γενέσθαι με] An awkward sentence in more ways than one, e.g., in the double sense of *γίνομαι*, avoided in xxi. 35; in the lack of concord in the pronouns *μοι . . . μου . . . με* (cf. xv. 22); in the gen. abs. *προσευχομένου μου* referring to a noun or pronoun already in the sentence, with no attempt to assimilate the cases (cf. Mt. i. 18; viii. 1; ix. 18; Mk. xiii. 1; Lk. xii. 36).

ὑποστρέψαντι εἰς Ἰερουσαλὴμ] Cf. ix. 26. Ramsay, on inadequate and unconvincing grounds, places the vision of *vv.* 17-21 during Paul's second visit to Jerusalem, soon after the vision of 2 Cor. xii. 2 ff. (*SPT*, pp. 60 ff.) Paul certainly preached to Gentiles, in Tarsus and Antioch, before his second Jerusalem visit (cf. also Gal. ii. 7, *πεπίστευμαι τὸ εὐαγγέλιον τῆς ἀκροβυστίας*).

ἐν ἐκστάσει] Cf. x. 10; xi. 5. For *ἐν ἐκστάσει γενέσθαι* we may also cf. Vettius Valens 201. 16 f., *ἐν ἐκστάσει φρενῶν γίνονται.*

xxii. 18

Σπεῦσον καὶ ἔξελθε κ.τ.λ.] Cf. ix. 29 f., where the Jerusalem brethren, getting wind of the plot against Paul, convoy him to Caesarea. This is not the only place where action is taken in response both to divine revelation and coincident human advice. Cf. Gal. ii. 2.

xxii. 19

Κύριε, αὐτοὶ ἐπίστανται κ.τ.λ.] In *vv.* 19 f. Paul argues that he is just the very man to convince the Jews. We may paraphrase his argument: 'They know how whole-heartedly I opposed the Christians; they remember the part I played at Stephen's martyrdom; they must realize therefore that there must be overwhelmingly cogent reasons for my change of attitude'.

ἤμην φυλακίζων καὶ δέρων] Cf. viii. 3; ix. 1 f. For the construction see on i. 10; in a speech translated from Aram. we may reasonably regard the periphrasis as an Aramaism.

xxii. 20

μάρτυρος] 'witness'; this use of the word is a step in the direction of the later meaning 'martyr' (cf. Rev. ii. 13).

ἤμην ἐφεστὼς καὶ συνευδοκῶν καὶ φυλάσσων κ.τ.λ.] Cf. vii. 58; viii. 1*a*. Periphrastic construction as in *ver.* 19.

τῶν ἀναιρούντων αὐτόν] In vii. 58 (*q.v.*) they are called the witnesses. In an execution for blasphemy the witnesses took the chief part. With ἀναιρούντων cf. ἀναιρέσει, viii. 1; ἀναιρουμένων, xxvi. 10.

xxii. 21

εἰς ἔθνη μακρὰν ἐξαποστελῶ σε] And so, when the Jerusalem brethren had convoyed him to Caesarea, they sent him off to Tarsus, where he had every opportunity of preaching to Gentiles (cf. Gal. i. 21 with ii. 2, 7 ff.). For ἐξαποστελῶ (א A C byz), B Chr have ἀποστελῶ (so WH mg.), D ἐξαποστέλλω.

(f) The Tumult renewed; Paul Reveals his Roman Citizenship, xxii. 22-29

Ἤκουον δὲ αὐτοῦ ἄχρι τούτου τοῦ λόγου καὶ ἐπῆραν τὴν φωνὴν 22
αὐτῶν λέγοντες Αἶρε ἀπὸ τῆς γῆς τὸν τοιοῦτον, οὐ γὰρ καθῆκεν αὐτὸν
ζῆν. κραυγαζόντων τε αὐτῶν καὶ ῥιπτούντων τὰ ἱμάτια καὶ κονιορτὸν 23
βαλλόντων εἰς τὸν ἀέρα ἐκέλευσεν ὁ χιλίαρχος εἰσάγεσθαι αὐτὸν εἰς 24
τὴν παρεμβολήν, εἴπας μάστιξιν ἀνετάζεσθαι αὐτὸν ἵνα ἐπιγνῷ δι' ἣν
αἰτίαν οὕτως ἐπεφώνουν αὐτῷ. ὡς δὲ προέτειναν αὐτὸν τοῖς ἱμᾶσιν 25
εἶπεν πρὸς τὸν ἑστῶτα ἑκατόνταρχον ὁ Παῦλος Εἰ ἄνθρωπον Ῥωμαῖον
καὶ ἀκατάκριτον ἔξεστιν ὑμῖν μαστίζειν; ἀκούσας δὲ ὁ ἑκατοντάρχης 26
προσελθὼν τῷ χιλιάρχῳ ἀπήγγειλεν λέγων Τί μέλλεις ποιεῖν; ὁ
γὰρ ἄνθρωπος οὗτος Ῥωμαῖός ἐστιν. προσελθὼν δὲ ὁ χιλίαρχος 27
εἶπεν αὐτῷ Λέγε μοι, σὺ Ῥωμαῖος εἶ; ὁ δὲ ἔφη Ναί. ἀπεκρίθη 28
δὲ ὁ χιλίαρχος Ἐγὼ πολλοῦ κεφαλαίου τὴν πολιτείαν ταύτην ἐκτησάμην.
ὁ δὲ Παῦλος ἔφη Ἐγὼ δὲ καὶ γεγέννημαι. εὐθέως οὖν ἀπέστησαν 29
ἀπ' αὐτοῦ οἱ μέλλοντες αὐτὸν ἀνετάζειν· καὶ ὁ χιλίαρχος δὲ ἐφοβήθη
ἐπιγνοὺς ὅτι Ῥωμαῖός ἐστιν καὶ ὅτι αὐτὸν ἦν δεδεκώς.

xxii. 22

Ἤκουον δὲ αὐτοῦ ἄχρι τούτου τοῦ λόγου] The mention of the Gentiles was the last straw so far as the audience was concerned; it reminded them of their main grievance against Paul. It was not that they did not believe in proselytizing Gentiles, but Paul was offering Gentiles equal privileges with Jews, without requiring them to submit to the obligations of the Law.

Αἶρε ἀπὸ τῆς γῆς τὸν τοιοῦτον] See on xxi. 36.

καθῆκεν] The imperf. indic. in classical Gk. may indicate necessity or possibility when the opposite is taking place; but the usage is extended in the Koiné to cover what in classical Gk. would be expressed by the present. For *καθῆκεν* here classical usage would require *προσήκει*. Cf. Eph. v. 4; Col. iii. 18.

xxii. 23

ῥιπτούντων] From *ῥιπτέω*, a variant of *ῥίπτω*. Field suggests that it means 'shaking' or 'waving' (Lat. *iactatio togarum*) rather than 'throwing off', though both are probably implied. See on xiv. 14 for the *rending* of clothes as a gesture of horror at blasphemy.

κονιορτὸν] 'dust'. 'In England mud is more frequently available' (LC). See also on xiii. 51.

xxii. 24

ἐκέλευσεν . . . εἴπας] Coincident aor. ptc.; cf. iv. 19; xi. 30; xv. 8 f.

μάστιξιν] The scourge (Lat. *flagrum, flagellum*) was a murderous instrument of torture, quite different from the lictors' rods at Philippi. Here Paul at once protests his Roman citizenship, which, by the Valerian and Porcian Laws (see on xvi. 37), exempted him from such treatment. A slave or alien might be scourged in order to make him confess the truth.

ἀνετάζεσθαι] MM refer to a papyrus of A.D. 127 (*P. Oxy*. 34. i. 13) in which a prefect uses this word in directing Government clerks whose business was to 'examine' documents before filing them.

ἵνα ἐπιγνῷ δι' ἣν αἰτίαν οὕτως ἐπεφώνουν αὐτῷ] 'that he might ascertain for what reason they were shouting against him so'. The tribune of course did not understand Paul's speech in Aramaic. For *ἐπιφωνέω* cf. xii. 22; xxi. 34; Lk. xxiii. 21.

xxii. 25

προέτειναν αὐτὸν τοῖς ἱμᾶσιν] Pesh renders *mathūy bĕ-'arqe*, 'they were stretching him with thongs' (Lat. *loris*). Syr. *mĕtaḥ*, 'stretch', is used technically of tying up a person for whipping, and this may be the meaning here. Cf. R. H. Connolly, 'Syriacisms in St. Luke', *JTS*, xxxvii (1936), p. 383. Otherwise *τοῖς ἱμᾶσιν* may mean 'for the lash'.

Εἰ] Introducing direct question as in xxi. 37.

Ῥωμαῖον καὶ ἀκατάκριτον] We find large numbers of Jews with Roman citizenship, especially in Asia Minor. For the privileges of Roman citizenship see on xvi. 37, as also for the force of *ἀκατάκριτος*. The two passages, xvi. 37 ff. and xxii. 25 ff., should be compared.

xxii. 26

Τί μέλλεις ποιεῖν;] 'What are you about to do?' The sense of *μέλλεις* here is to be distinguished from that in *ver.* 16.

xxii. 27

ἔφη Ναί] D has *εἶπεν Εἰμί*, the sort of variant which lends colour to Torrey's theory that δ is a re-translation of a translation (see p. 45).

xxii. 28

Ἐγὼ πολλοῦ κεφαλαίου τὴν πολιτείαν ταύτην ἐκτησάμην] The δ text has *ἐγὼ οἶδα πόσου κεφαλαίου τὴν πολιτείαν ταύτην ἐκτησάμην*, which may be sarcastic: 'It cost *me* a huge sum; it seems to have become cheap nowadays'.[1] Probably Paul's appearance after his deliverance from the mob was not such as one usually associated with a Roman citizen.

πολλοῦ κεφαλαίου] The monetary sense of *κεφάλαιον* is found in Demosthenes, *Aphobus* i. 10, where it means 'capital', and in Plato *Laws* 742 C and LXX Lev. vi. 5; Num. v. 7, where it denotes the 'principal' of a debt. The tribune's *nomen*, Claudius, implies that he acquired the citizenship under Claudius. Under Claudius the citizenship was commonly bought for money (cf. Dio Cassius, lx. 17. 5 f.).

δὲ καὶ] Emphasizing the adversative force of *δέ*.

γεγέννημαι] How Paul's father or earlier ancestor acquired Roman citizenship we cannot tell. According to Ramsay, a large number of Jews became citizens of Tarsus as early as 171 B.C. (cf. xxi. 39), and some citizens of Tarsus probably received Roman citizenship under Pompey (*The Cities of St. Paul*, pp. 169 ff.).

xxii. 29

ἀπέστησαν] lit., 'stood away from'.

ἀνετάζειν] See on *ver.* 24.

ἐφοβήθη ἐπιγνοὺς ὅτι Ῥωμαῖός ἐστιν] Cf. xvi. 38.

ἦν δεδεκώς] Periphrastic form of pluperfect.

[1] Cf. Bede *ad loc.*: 'Alia editio manifestius quid dixerit insinuat: *dixit tribunus, tam facile te dicis ciuem Romanum esse? ego enim scio quanto pretio ciuitatem istam possedi*'.

(g) Paul before the Sanhedrin, xxii. 30-xxiii. 10

Τῇ δὲ ἐπαύριον βουλόμενος γνῶναι τὸ ἀσφαλὲς τὸ τί κατηγορεῖται 30
ὑπὸ τῶν Ἰουδαίων, ἔλυσεν αὐτόν, καὶ ἐκέλευσεν συνελθεῖν τοὺς
ἀρχιερεῖς καὶ πᾶν τὸ συνέδριον, καὶ καταγαγὼν τὸν Παῦλον ἔστησεν
εἰς αὐτούς. ἀτενίσας δὲ Παῦλος τῷ συνεδρίῳ εἶπεν Ἄνδρες ἀδελφοί, 1
ἐγὼ πάσῃ συνειδήσει ἀγαθῇ πεπολίτευμαι τῷ θεῷ ἄχρι ταύτης τῆς
ἡμέρας. ὁ δὲ ἀρχιερεὺς Ἁνανίας ἐπέταξεν τοῖς παρεστῶσιν αὐτῷ 2
τύπτειν αὐτοῦ τὸ στόμα. τότε ὁ Παῦλος πρὸς αὐτὸν εἶπεν Τύπτειν 3
σε μέλλει ὁ θεός, τοῖχε κεκονιαμένε· καὶ σὺ κάθῃ κρίνων με κατὰ τὸν
νόμον, καὶ παρανομῶν κελεύεις με τύπτεσθαι; οἱ δὲ παρεστῶτες 4
εἶπαν Τὸν ἀρχιερέα τοῦ θεοῦ λοιδορεῖς; ἔφη τε ὁ Παῦλος Οὐκ 5
ᾔδειν, ἀδελφοί, ὅτι ἐστὶν ἀρχιερεύς· γέγραπται γὰρ ὅτι Ἄρχοντα τοῦ
λαοῦ σου οὐκ ἐρεῖς κακῶς. Γνοὺς δὲ ὁ Παῦλος ὅτι τὸ ἓν μέρος ἐστὶν 6
Σαδδουκαίων τὸ δὲ ἕτερον Φαρισαίων ἔκραζεν ἐν τῷ συνεδρίῳ Ἄνδρες
ἀδελφοί, ἐγὼ Φαρισαῖός εἰμι, υἱὸς Φαρισαίων· περὶ ἐλπίδος καὶ ἀνασ-
τάσεως νεκρῶν κρίνομαι. τοῦτο δὲ αὐτοῦ λαλοῦντος ἐγένετο στάσις 7
τῶν Φαρισαίων καὶ Σαδδουκαίων, καὶ ἐσχίσθη τὸ πλῆθος. Σαδ- 8
δουκαῖοι γὰρ λέγουσιν μὴ εἶναι ἀνάστασιν μήτε ἄγγελον μήτε πνεῦμα,
Φαρισαῖοι δὲ ὁμολογοῦσιν τὰ ἀμφότερα. ἐγένετο δὲ κραυγὴ μεγάλη, 9
καὶ ἀναστάντες τινὲς τῶν γραμματέων τοῦ μέρους τῶν Φαρισαίων
διεμάχοντο λέγοντες Οὐδὲν κακὸν εὑρίσκομεν ἐν τῷ ἀνθρώπῳ τούτῳ·
εἰ δὲ πνεῦμα ἐλάλησεν αὐτῷ ἢ ἄγγελος—. Πολλῆς δὲ γινομένης 10
στάσεως φοβηθεὶς ὁ χιλίαρχος μὴ διασπασθῇ ὁ Παῦλος ὑπ' αὐτῶν
ἐκέλευσεν τὸ στράτευμα καταβὰν ἁρπάσαι αὐτὸν ἐκ μέσου αὐτῶν,
ἄγειν εἰς τὴν παρεμβολήν.

xxii. 30

γνῶναι τὸ ἀσφαλὲς] As in xxi. 34.

τὸ τί κατηγορεῖται] The def. art. controls the noun clause, just as it would an ordinary noun.

ἔλυσεν αὐτόν] i.e., from prison. Then if Paul had satisfied the Sanhedrin he would presumably have gone free.

τοὺς ἀρχιερεῖς καὶ πᾶν τὸ συνέδριον] 'the chief priests and all the Sanhedrin' (see on iv. 5, 15). They constituted the chief Jewish court, and if Paul had broken the Jewish law in a matter of which Rome took cognizance, it was their business to try and sentence him, and the Roman governor's to ratify a capital sentence.

xxiii. 1

ἀτενίσας] See on i. 10.

πεπολίτευμαι] This ethical sense of *πολιτεύομαι* (cf. *περιπατέω*, xxi. 21 ; *στοιχέω*, xxi. 24) is found not only in Bib. Gk. (e.g. Phil. i. 27; 2 Macc. vi. 1 ; xi. 25 ; 3 Macc. iii. 4 ; 4 Macc. ii. 8, 23 ; iv. 23 ;

v. 16), but also in Philo (e.g., *de uirtutibus* 161), Josephus (*vit.* 2), 1 Clem. vi. 1, later Christian writers, and the papyri.

συνειδήσει ἀγαθῇ] Cf. 1 Pet. iii. 16, 21; 1 Tim. i. 5, 19; 1 Clem. xli. 1; cf. also *ἀπρόσκοπον συνείδησιν*, xxiv. 16; *ἐν καθαρᾷ συνειδήσει*, 1 Tim. iii. 9; 2 Tim. i. 3; *καλὴν συνείδησιν*, Heb. xiii. 18; *συνείδησιν θεοῦ*, 1 Pet. ii. 19. The word *συνείδησις* is not current in classical Gk. It belonged to the vernacular tongue and did not attain literary status long before the Christian era; though it became current in non-philosophic writers, it was not generally adopted by philosophers (though LS[9] quotes it from Bias and Periander *apud Stobaeum* in the sense 'consciousness of right or wrong doing', and from Democritus and Chrysippus in the sense 'awareness'). Cf. H. Osborne in *JTS*, xxxii (1931), pp. 167 ff. It occurs twice or thrice in LXX (Eccles. x. 20; Wisd. xvii. 11; Sir. xlii. 18 ℵ). 'The word would seem, therefore, to have been "baptized" by Paul into a new and deeper connotation, and to have been used by him as equivalent to *τὸ συνειδός*' (MM). In this sense it means 'consciousness with (oneself)', i.e., consciousness of one's own good or bad behaviour, and is spoken of as a sort of independent witness (cf. Rom. ii. 15; ix. 1).[1] For Paul's good conscience even in his persecuting days cf. xxvi. 9; Phil. iii. 6.

τῷ θεῷ] 'in the sight of God' or 'in a godly manner': cf. xxiv. 16; Rom. vi. 10 f.; xiv. 8 (with which cf. Lk. xx. 38); Gal. ii. 19; 1 Pet. ii. 19.

xxiii. 2

Ἀνανίας] Ananias, the son of Nedebaeus, a notoriously unscrupulous and rapacious politician, had been appointed High Priest by Herod of Chalcis about A.D. 47. He was, like most of the High Priests, a Sadducee. About 52 he was sent to Rome by Quadratus, legate of Syria, as responsible for risings in Judaea, but was acquitted and was now at the height of his power. Even after his supersession in 58-59 he wielded great authority. He was assassinated in 66 in revenge for his pro-Roman policy. The Talmud (TB *Pesaḥim* 57*a*) refers to him as being a great glutton. See *BJ*, ii. 12. 6; 17. 6, 9; *Ant.* xx. 5. 2; 6. 2; 9. 2, 4.

xxiii. 3

Τύπτειν σε μέλλει ὁ θεός] Some have seen the fulfilment of this 'predictive curse' in his death nine years later at the hands of 'brigands' (*λῃσταί*, as Josephus calls them: perhaps Zealots).

[1] Cf. Philo's use of *τὸ συνειδός*, as examining and passing judgment on conduct, e.g., *de opificio mundi* 128, *τὸν τοῦ συνειδότος ἔλεγχον, ὃς ἐνιδρυμένος τῇ ψυχῇ καθάπερ δικαστὴς ἐπιπλήττων οὐ δυσωπεῖται.*

τοιχὲ κεκονιαμένε] 'whitewashed wall'. Cf. Mt. xxiii. 27, *παρομοιάζετε τάφοις κεκονιαμένοις*, contrasting the decent exterior with the unclean contents. But we need not suppose that Paul alluded to those words of Christ; if he alludes to anything, it may be to the wall of Ezek. xiii. 10 ff., which looked stable enough, but collapsed before the stormy wind.

καὶ σὺ κάθῃ] *καὶ indignantis:* 'do you actually sit?' N.B. thematic *κάθῃ* for classical *κάθησαι*, as in Hyperides, *frag.* 115; *P. Oxy.* 33. iii. 13 (2nd cent. A.D.); cf. imperative *κάθου* for *καθῆσο* in ii. 34.

παρανομῶν] Emphatic; the Jewish law presumed innocence until guilt was proved.

xxiii. 4

Τὸν ἀρχιερέα τοῦ θεοῦ λοιδορεῖς;] Cf. the bystander's words to Christ before the Sanhedrin in Jn. xviii. 22, *οὕτως ἀποκρίνῃ τῷ ἀρχιερεῖ;*—words which were actually accompanied by a slap on the face. As in the journey to Jerusalem, so now before the Sanhedrin, Luke seems to draw parallels between the experiences of the Master and the servant.

xxiii. 5

Οὐκ ᾔδειν, ἀδελφοί, ὅτι ἐστὶν ἀρχιερεύς] Various reasons have been suggested for Paul's failure to recognize him; e.g., his alleged weak eyesight, a change of High Priests since Paul's last visit, or irony ('I did not think that a man who spoke like that could possibly be the High Priest'). Before A.D. 70 the High Priest was normally president of the Sanhedrin.[1] This was an extraordinary meeting of the Sanhedrin, summoned by the tribune. Ramsay insists that the tribune must have presided, having the Sanhedrin on one hand and Paul on the other, with Luke and others in the audience (*corona adstantium*). After *ver.* 6, he supposes, the Pharisaic members of the council crossed the floor and took their place by Paul (*BRD*, pp. 90 ff.). This reconstruction seems rather unlikely; however, it may have been so.

[1] That this was so is clear from Josephus (e.g. *Ant.* xiv. 9. 3 ff.; xx. 9. 1) and the NT (cf. Mt. xxvi. 57 ff.= Mk. xiv. 53 ff.; Jn. xviii. 19 ff.; Ac. v. 17; vii. 1; see also on iv. 6, 15). When the Supreme Court was reconstituted by Yohanan ben Zakkai at Jabneh after A.D. 70, its president was no longer a priest, but a rabbi, the *nāsī* or *rōsh bēth dīn*. The Mishna carries this later state of affairs back to the time of the Second Commonwealth, anachronistically representing scholars like Hillel and Gamaliel I as presidents of the Sanhedrin (*Ḥagīgāh* ii. 2). That Gamaliel occupied no such office is clear from v. 34. See Schürer, II, i. 180 ff.

ἄρχοντα τοῦ λαοῦ σου οὐκ ἐρεῖς κακῶς] From Ex. xxii. 28 (LXX 27), *ἄρχοντας τοῦ λαοῦ σου οὐ κακῶς ἐρεῖς*. (See on xix. 37 for Jewish exegesis of the earlier part of this verse.) Cf. Jude 8 f.; 2 Pet. ii. 10 f.

xxiii. 6

Σαδδουκαίων . . . Φαρισαίων] For Sadducees see on iv. 1; for Pharisees see on v. 34. Though the priestly party was mainly Sadducaean, the Pharisees were also strongly represented in the Sanhedrin.

ἐγὼ Φαρισαῖός εἰμι, υἱὸς Φαρισαίων] Cf. xxvi. 5; Phil. iii. 5. True to his policy of being all things to all men, Paul, who had appealed to Claudius Lysias as a Roman, now appeals to the Jews as a Pharisee.

ἐλπίδος καὶ ἀναστάσεως νεκρῶν] Hendiadys: 'the hope of the resurrection of the dead'. The hope of Israel, as Paul saw it, was bound up with the resurrection of Christ, and thus with the general principle (held by the Pharisees) of the resurrection of the dead; 'for if the dead are not raised, neither hath Christ been raised' (1 Cor. xv. 16). Therefore Paul's message could be fitted into the Pharisaic framework, but not into the Sadducaean; that his argument was not frivolous is shown by the presence of Pharisees in the Jerusalem church (xv. 5; xxi. 20). We cannot imagine a Sadducee becoming a Christian, unless he ceased to be a Sadducee. Cf. xxiv. 15; xxv. 19; xxvi. 6 ff., 22 ff.; xxviii. 20. It is unduly squeamish to blame Paul for this outburst, as if his only purpose were by a disingenuous claim to set his accusers by the ears; xxiv. 21 is not a confession of fault.

κρίνομαι] Read *ἐγὼ κρίνομαι* (B g omit *ἐγώ*).

xxiii. 7

λαλοῦντος] B; *λαλήσαντος* C byz; *εἴπαντος* ℵ*; *εἰπόντος* ℵ^c A.
ἐγένετο] ℵ A C byz; *ἐπέπεσε* B.
τὸ πλῆθος] 'the company': see on iv. 32.

xxiii. 8

Σαδδουκαῖοι γὰρ λέγουσιν κ.τ.λ.] After *Σαδδουκαῖοι* add *μέν* with ℵ A C byz (B omits). For the Sadducaean denial of resurrection cf. Mt. xxii. 23 = Mk. xii. 18 = Lk. xx. 27; Jos. *BJ*, ii. 8. 14; *Ant.* xviii. 1. 4. By this denial they renounced the Messianic hope in the form which it had taken in post-exilic times. The doctrine of resurrection and retribution (cf. Dan. xii. 2) was regarded by now as belonging to genuine Judaism; from this point of view the Sadducees represented a sectarian opinion. The statement of their disbelief in angels and spirits, though not explicitly confirmed elsewhere, is in keeping with their general attitude; the developed angelology and demonology of the time, like the belief in resurrection, they would reject as a late accretion to the original Jewish faith.[1] For *μή* with infin. see on xxv. 25.

Φαρισαῖοι δὲ ὁμολογοῦσιν τὰ ἀμφότερα] The two beliefs referred to by *τὰ ἀμφότερα* are (1) in resurrection, (2) in angels and spirits. (But it is just possible that *τὰ ἀμφότερα* means 'all three': see on xix. 16.) For the Pharisaic doctrine cf. *BJ*, ii. 8. 14; *Ant.* xviii. 1. 3. This doctrine is perpetuated in the Mishna: 'He who says that the resurrection of the dead is not to be inferred from the law has no part in the Age to come' (*Sanh.* x. 1). According to Josephus, the Pharisees and Sadducees also differed in their views about divine providence and freewill.

xxiii. 9

τινὲς τῶν γραμματέων] The scribes were mostly Pharisees: see on iv. 5; cf. Mk. ii. 16; Lk. v. 30. With their reaction to Paul's words, cf. the scribe's admiration of Christ's reply to the Sadducees on the question of resurrection, Mk. xii. 28; Lk. xx. 39.

εἰ δὲ πνεῦμα ἐλάλησεν αὐτῷ ἢ ἄγγελος] Referring to his experience near Damascus (xxii. 6 ff.) or, less probably, in the Temple (xxii. 17 ff.). The apodosis is suppressed; byz supplied it with *μὴ θεομαχῶμεν* (cf. v. 39).

xxiii. 10

τὸ στράτευμα] i.e., the detachment of soldiers on duty at the time: cf. Lk. xxiii. 11.

καταβὰν] From the Fortress of Antonia (the *παρεμβολή*); the Sanhedrin apparently met in the outer Temple precincts.

ἄγειν] Add *τε* (omitted, probably by accident, in B 69).

(h) The Lord Appears to Paul by Night, xxiii. 11

Τῇ δὲ ἐπιούσῃ νυκτὶ ἐπιστὰς αὐτῷ ὁ κύριος εἶπεν Θάρσει, ὡς 11
γὰρ διεμαρτύρω τὰ περὶ ἐμοῦ εἰς Ἰερουσαλὴμ οὕτω σε δεῖ καὶ εἰς
Ῥώμην μαρτυρῆσαι.

[1] 'What they rejected was the developed doctrine of the two kingdoms with their hierarchies of good and evil spirits' (T. W. Manson, *BJRL*, xxii. [1938], p. 154 *n.*).

xxiii. 11

ἐπιστὰς] ' standing over '.

ὁ κύριος] Jesus. For other visions received by Paul cf. ix. 4; xvi. 9; xviii. 9; xxii. 17; xxvii. 23 f.

θάρσει] δ byz add *Παῦλε* (cf. xxvii. 24).

εἰς Ῥώμην] Thus confirming Paul's own purpose (xix. 21).

(i) The Plot against Paul, xxiii. 12-15

Γενομένης δὲ ἡμέρας ποιήσαντες συστροφὴν οἱ Ἰουδαῖοι ἀνεθεμά- 12
τισαν ἑαυτοὺς λέγοντες μήτε φαγεῖν μήτε πεῖν ἕως οὗ ἀποκτείνωσιν
τὸν Παῦλον. ἦσαν δὲ πλείους τεσσεράκοντα οἱ ταύτην τὴν συνωμοσίαν 13
ποιησάμενοι· οἵτινες προσελθόντες τοῖς ἀρχιερεῦσιν καὶ τοῖς πρεσ- 14
βυτέροις εἶπαν Ἀναθέματι ἀνεθεματίσαμεν ἑαυτοὺς μηδενὸς γεύσασθαι
ἕως οὗ ἀποκτείνωμεν τὸν Παῦλον. νῦν οὖν ὑμεῖς ἐμφανίσατε τῷ χιλι- 15
άρχῳ σὺν τῷ συνεδρίῳ ὅπως καταγάγῃ αὐτὸν εἰς ὑμᾶς ὡς μέλλοντας
διαγινώσκειν ἀκριβέστερον τὰ περὶ αὐτοῦ· ἡμεῖς δὲ πρὸ τοῦ ἐγγίσαι
αὐτὸν ἕτοιμοί ἐσμεν τοῦ ἀνελεῖν αὐτόν.

xxiii. 12

συστροφὴν] In LXX this sometimes means conspiracy', 'plot'. We should regard it here as synonymous with *συνωμοσίαν* (*ver.* 13) and *ἐνέδραν* (*ver.* 16).

οἱ Ἰουδαῖοι] δ byz have *τινὲς τῶν Ἰουδαίων*, which accords better with *ver.* 13; but if this had been the original text, it is not easy to see why it should have been changed to *οἱ Ἰουδαῖοι*.

ἀνεθεμάτισαν ἑαυτοὺς] 'laid themselves under a curse'; i.e., 'May God curse me if I fail to perform this'. Cf. the OT formula, 'So may God do to me, and more also, if . . .'. The Rabbis held that relief could be given from such vows as could not be fulfilled ' by reason of constraint ' (cf. Mishna, *Nedarim*, iii. 1, 3).

μήτε φαγεῖν μήτε πεῖν] Cf. Jerome's account of James the Just, taken from the 'Gospel according to the Hebrews': '*iurauerat enim Iacobus se non comesurum panem ab illa hora, qua biberat calicem Domini, donec uideret eum resurgentem a dormientibus*' (*De Vir. Ill.* 2). Deissmann (*LAE*, p. 203) compares *οὐ μὴ φάγω, οὐ μὴ πείνω* from the boy Theon's letter (see on xvii. 6).

πεῖν] This, the Koiné form, is found in B here and in *ver.* 21; other MSS. have the classical form *πιεῖν*.

xxiii. 14

τοῖς ἀρχιερεῦσιν καὶ τοῖς πρεσβυτέροις] i.e., to the Sanhedrin (cf. iv. 23; xxv. 15; Lk. xxii. 52), or rather to a section of it, as we may gather from *σὺν τῷ συνεδρίῳ*, *ver.* 15. The would-be assassins would naturally approach that section which had shown itself most hostile to Paul.

ἀναθέματι ἀνεθεματίσαμεν] For the Semitic construction see on ii. 17, 30; iv. 17; v. 28.

xxiii. 15

νῦν οὖν κ.τ.λ.] δ (represented by g h Lucifer hcl.mg sah and reconstructed by Ropes after Zahn) expands thus: νῦν οὖν ἐρωτῶμεν ὑμᾶς τοῦτο ἡμῖν παρέχειν· συναγαγόντες τὸ συνέδριον ἐμφανίσατε τῷ χιλιάρχῳ ὅπως καταγάγῃ αὐτὸν εἰς ὑμᾶς.

ἐμφανίσατε] 'lay information before': cf. *ver.* 22; xxiv. 1; xxv. 2, 15; Esth. ii. 22; 2 Macc. iii. 7. The word is also found in papyri.

σὺν τῷ συνεδρίῳ] i.e., with the rest of the Sanhedrin: see on *ver.* 14.

διαγινώσκειν] Including the ideas of inquiry and decision: cf. xxiv. 22; xxv. 21.

ἀκριβέστερον] MM suggest on papyrus evidence that the use of this comparative with verbs denoting inquiry was evidently a formula (cf. *ver.* 20). Here it plainly retains its comparative force: cf. xviii. 26.

ἕτοιμοί ἐσμεν τοῦ ἀνελεῖν αὐτόν] The sense would equally well be expressed without τοῦ. But Luke is fond of τοῦ with infin.; for various ways in which he uses it cf. iii. 2, 12; vii. 19; x. 25; xiv. 9; xv. 20; xx. 3; xxi. 12; xxvi. 18. With the men's statement cf. the activities of the *Sicarii* (see on xxi. 38), described in Jos. *Ant.* xx. 8. 5. δ (represented by 614 2147 h hcl.mg) adds ἐάν δέῃ καὶ ἀποθανεῖν, 'even if we must die for it'.

(j) Paul's Nephew reveals the Plot to the Tribune, xxiii. 16-22

Ἀκούσας δὲ ὁ υἱὸς τῆς ἀδελφῆς Παύλου τὴν ἐνέδραν παραγενό- 16
μενος καὶ εἰσελθὼν εἰς τὴν παρεμβολὴν ἀπήγγειλεν τῷ Παύλῳ.
προσκαλεσάμενος δὲ ὁ Παῦλος ἕνα τῶν ἑκατονταρχῶν ἔφη Τὸν νεανίαν 17
τοῦτον ἄπαγε πρὸς τὸν χιλίαρχον, ἔχει γὰρ ἀπαγγεῖλαί τι αὐτῷ.
ὁ μὲν οὖν παραλαβὼν αὐτὸν ἤγαγεν πρὸς τὸν χιλίαρχον καί φησιν 18
Ὁ δέσμιος Παῦλος προσκαλεσάμενός με ἠρώτησεν τοῦτον τὸν
νεανίαν ἀγαγεῖν πρὸς σέ, ἔχοντά τι λαλῆσαί σοι. ἐπιλαβόμενος δὲ 19
τῆς χειρὸς αὐτοῦ ὁ χιλίαρχος καὶ ἀναχωρήσας κατ' ἰδίαν ἐπυνθάνετο
Τί ἐστιν ὃ ἔχεις ἀπαγγεῖλαί μοι; εἶπεν δὲ ὅτι Οἱ Ἰουδαῖοι συνέθεντο 20
τοῦ ἐρωτῆσαί σε ὅπως αὔριον τὸν Παῦλον καταγάγῃς εἰς τὸ συνέδριον
ὡς μέλλων τι ἀκριβέστερον πυνθάνεσθαι περὶ αὐτοῦ· σὺ οὖν μὴ 21
πεισθῇς αὐτοῖς, ἐνεδρεύουσιν γὰρ αὐτὸν ἐξ αὐτῶν ἄνδρες πλείους
τεσσεράκοντα, οἵτινες ἀνεθεμάτισαν ἑαυτοὺς μήτε φαγεῖν μήτε πεῖν

ἕως οὗ ἀνέλωσιν αὐτόν, καὶ νῦν εἰσὶν ἕτοιμοι προσδεχόμενοι τὴν ἀπὸ
σοῦ ἐπαγγελίαν. ὁ μὲν οὖν χιλίαρχος ἀπέλυσε τὸν νεανίσκον παραγ- 22
γείλας μηδενὶ ἐκλαλῆσαι ὅτι ταῦτα ἐνεφάνισας πρὸς ἐμέ.

xxiii. 16

ὁ υἱὸς τῆς ἀδελφῆς Παύλου] The sudden introduction of Paul's nephew is interesting; we wish we knew more about Paul's relations with his family, which might provide a background to this incident.

ἐνέδραν] lit., 'ambush'; here practically synonymous with *συστροφήν* (*ver.* 12) and *συνωμοσίαν* (*ver.* 13).

παραγενόμενος] 'having been present'; probably to be taken with *ἀκούσας*. If he was present at the conspiracy, either his relation to Paul was unknown, or Paul's bitterest enemies may have been those of his own household, in which case the presence of one of Paul's relatives would have occasioned no misgivings. Possibly, however, *παραγενόμενος* means 'having arrived (at the barracks)'; cf. vg *uenit et intrauit in castra*.

ἀπήγγειλεν τῷ Παύλῳ] Paul was kept in honourable captivity, was allowed to receive visitors, and (as we see from *ver.* 17) could give orders to a centurion.

xxiii. 18

ὁ δέσμιος Παῦλος] Paul is fond of giving himself the title *δέσμιος* (cf. Eph. iii. 1; iv. 1).

νεανίαν] B byz; *νεανίσκον* ℵ A E 33 81 (so WH mg., Soden): cf. *vv.* 17, 22.

xxiii. 20

ὅτι] *recitantis.*

μέλλων] A B 81 boh eth; *μέλλον* ℵ 33 (so Ropes); *μελλόντων* ℵ[c] 431 614 Chr; *μέλλοντα* byz (HLPS 383); *μέλλοντες* minn.pler g h vg pesh hcl arm sah (so TR).

ἀκριβέστερον] See on *ver.* 15.

xxiii. 21

ἐνεδρεύουσιν] lit., 'are lying in wait for': cf. *ἐνέδραν*, *ver.* 16.

πεῖν] See on *ver.* 12.

ἐπαγγελίαν] 'consent'.

xxiii. 22

παραγγείλας μηδένι ἐκλαλῆσαι ὅτι ταῦτα ἐνεφάνισας πρὸς ἐμέ] For the mixture of indirect and direct speech cf. *vv.* 23 f.; i. 4; xxv. 4 f.; Lk. v. 14.

(k) Lysias prepares to send Paul away, xxiii. 23-25

Καὶ προσκαλεσάμενός τινας δύο τῶν ἑκατονταρχῶν εἶπεν Ἑτοιμά- 23
σατε στρατιώτας διακοσίους ὅπως πορευθῶσιν ἕως Καισαρίας, καὶ
ἱππεῖς ἑβδομήκοντα καὶ δεξιολάβους διακοσίους, ἀπὸ τρίτης ὥρας τῆς
νυκτός, κτήνη τε παραστῆσαι ἵνα ἐπιβιβάσαντες τὸν Παῦλον διασώσωσι 24
πρὸς Φήλικα τὸν ἡγεμόνα, γράψας ἐπιστολὴν ἔχουσαν τὸν τύπον 25
τοῦτον.

xxiii. 23

στρατιώτας . . . ἱππεῖς . . . δεξιολάβους] The escort was composed of heavy infantry, cavalry, and light-armed troops (*leuis armatura*), the three constituents of the Roman army. The unusual word *δεξιολάβος* (this is its first appearance, and it does not occur again until the sixth century) seems to mean 'spearman' (cf. LS[9]), lit., 'taking (a spear) in the right hand' (cf. vg *lancearios*). A has *δεξιοβόλους*, 'slingers' or 'javelin-throwers', lit., 'throwing with the right hand' (so pesh *shādyay bĕ-yamīnā*). See MH ii, pp. 272 f.

xxiii. 24

κτήνη τε παραστῆσαι κ.τ.λ.] The direct speech gives place to indirect; contrast the opposite change in *ver.* 22.

κτήνη] Horses or mules (LC).

διασώσωσι] 'bring safely through'.

Φήλικα τὸν ἡγεμόνα] *ἡγεμών* is a general word for a governor; here it refers to a procurator (Gk. *ἐπίτροπος*). In Lk. ii. 2 *ἡγεμονεύω* is used of the imperial legate (*legatus pro praetore*, Gk. *ἀντιστράτηγος*) of Syria. Antonius Felix was a brother of Pallas, the favourite freedman of Claudius. His gentile name Antonius suggests that, like Pallas, he was a freedman of Claudius's mother Antonia. According to Josephus (*BJ*, ii. 12. 8; *Ant.* xx. 7. 1), he succeeded Ventidius Cumanus as procurator in 52; but even before that he held office in Palestine, as Tacitus (*Ann.* xii. 54) makes him governor of Samaria while Cumanus ruled Galilee (48-52). We may infer, by comparing the two accounts, that Cumanus was procurator of Judaea from 48 to 52, while Felix occupied a subordinate post in Samaria, and that when Cumanus was disgraced in 52, Felix was promoted to procuratorship of the whole province, an unprecedented honour for a freedman. His term of office was marked by fierce attacks on insurgents, which disaffected a great part of the nation. His recall (see on xxiv. 27) was due to his violent but unsuccessful intervention in riots between the Jewish and Gentile populations of Caesarea. Tacitus sums up his character in the well-known epigram: '*per omnem saeuitiam ac libidinem ius regium seruili ingenio exercuit*' (*Hist.* v. 9). Of his three wives, all princesses according to Suet. *Claud.* 28, the first was a granddaughter of Antony and Cleopatra, the third was Drusilla, the daughter of Herod Agrippa I (see on xxiv. 24). Cf. Jos. *BJ*, ii. 12. 8-13. 7; *Ant.* xx. 7. 1-8. 9.

xxiii. 25

ἔχουσαν τὸν τύπον τοῦτον] For this use of *τύπος* cf. 3 Macc. iii. 30, *καὶ ὁ μὲν τῆς ἐπιστολῆς τύπος οὕτως ἐγέγραπτο.* Cf. also the commoner expressions *ἔχειν τὸν τρόπον τοῦτον* (1 Macc. xi. 29; 2 Macc. i. 24; Jos. *Ant.* xi. 6. 12) and *περιέχειν τὸν τρόπον τοῦτον* (1 Macc. xv. 2; 2 Macc. xi. 16; Jos. *Ant.* xi. 6. 6; xii. 4. 11). The δ text of *vv.* 23-25 may be tentatively reconstructed from the evidence of P^{48} 88 614 915 1611 2147 g h p hcl.mg hcl*: *καὶ προσκαλεσάμενος δύο τῶν ἑκατονταρχῶν εἶπεν Ἑτοιμάσατε στρατιώτας ἐνόπλους ὅπως πορευθῶσιν ἕως Καισαρείας, ἱππεῖς ἑκατὸν καὶ δεξιολάβους διακοσίους· οἱ δὲ εἶπαν ὅτι Ἕτοιμοί εἰσι πορεύεσθαι. ὁ δὲ ἐκέλευσε τοὺς ἑκατοντάρχας καὶ κτήνη παραστῆσαι ἵνα ἐπιβιβάσαντες τὸν Παῦλον νυκτὸς διασώσωσιν εἰς Καισαρείαν πρὸς Φήλικα τὸν ἡγεμόνα. ἐφοβήθη γὰρ μήποτε ἁρπάσαντες αὐτὸν οἱ Ἰουδαῖοι ἀποκτείνωσι, καὶ αὐτὸς μεταξὺ ἔγκλησιν ἔχῃ ὡς ἀργύριον εἰληφώς· ἔγραψε δὲ ἐπιστολὴν περιέχουσαν τάδε.*

(1) Letter from Lysias to Felix, xxiii. 26-30

Κλαύδιος Λυσίας τῷ κρατίστῳ ἡγεμόνι Φήλικι χαίρειν. Τὸν ἄνδρα 26 27
τοῦτον συλλημφθέντα ὑπὸ τῶν Ἰουδαίων καὶ μέλλοντα ἀναιρεῖσθαι
ὑπ' αὐτῶν ἐπιστὰς σὺν τῷ στρατεύματι ἐξειλάμην, μαθὼν ὅτι Ῥωμαῖός
ἐστιν, βουλόμενός τε ἐπιγνῶναι τὴν αἰτίαν δι' ἣν ἐνεκάλουν αὐτῷ 28
κατήγαγον εἰς τὸ συνέδριον αὐτῶν· ὃν εὗρον ἐγκαλούμενον περὶ ζητη- 29
μάτων τοῦ νόμου αὐτῶν, μηδὲν δὲ ἄξιον θανάτου ἢ δεσμῶν ἔχοντα
ἔγκλημα. μηνυθείσης δέ μοι ἐπιβουλῆς εἰς τὸν ἄνδρα ἔσεσθαι ἐξαυτῆς 30
ἔπεμψα πρὸς σέ, παραγγείλας καὶ τοῖς κατηγόροις λέγειν πρὸς αὐτὸν
ἐπὶ σοῦ.

Whether Luke had access at Caesarea to the actual letter or not, this reproduction of it is very true to life, especially in the exaggerated place which Lysias gives to his own part in the events, and in the slight twisting of the truth at the end of *ver.* 27.

xxiii. 26

Κλαύδιος] He acquired this gentile name when he purchased his citizenship (see on xxii. 28), probably because it was the gentile name of the Emperor.

κρατίστῳ] Cf. xxiv. 3; xxvi. 25; Lk. i. 3. The title is given to Felix in virtue of his office; it belonged properly to members of the equestrian order, from which such procurators were usually drawn. See on i. 1.

χαίρειν] See on xv. 23.

xxiii. 27

τὸν ἄνδρα τοῦτον κ.τ.λ.] Lysias skilfully presents the facts in a manner calculated to reflect credit on his own action. It is amusing to contrast his account with that of Tertullus (xxiv. 6 f.), which is equally calculated to reflect *dis*credit on him.

τῷ στρατεύματι] See on *ver.* 10.

μαθὼν ὅτι Ῥωμαῖός ἐστιν] Actually, it was later, when he had ordered Paul to be scourged, that he learned he was a Roman. Lysias passes over his *faux pas* in such a way as to make his behaviour seem the more praiseworthy.

xxiii. 28

αἰτίαν] The meaning may be 'reason', 'charge', or 'crime'. Cf. xiii. 28; xxv. 18, 27; xxviii. 18; αἴτιον in xix. 40; Lk. xxiii. 4, 14, 22; αἰτίωμα in xxv. 7.

κατήγαγον εἰς τὸ συνέδριον αὐτῶν] Omitted by B 81, but it is added in the margin of B, with αὐτόν after κατήγαγον.

xxiii. 29

περὶ ζητημάτων τοῦ νόμου αὐτῶν] Cf. xviii. 15. After αὐτῶν the δ text (614 2147 hcl.mg) adds Μωυσέως καὶ Ἰησοῦ τινος (cf. xxv. 19).

μηδὲν δὲ ἄξιον θανάτου ἢ δεσμῶν ἔχοντα ἔγκλημα] Only here and in xxviii. 6 is the ptc. negatived by μή in indirect speech. As in the Gospel Luke is at pains to emphasize Pilate's finding no fault with Jesus (Lk. xxiii. 4, 14 f., 22), so now in the mouth of many official witnesses he emphasizes Paul's innocence of the charge brought against him (cf. xxv. 18; xxvi. 31 f.). After ἔγκλημα the δ text (614 2147 g hcl*) adds ἐξήγαγον αὐτὸν μόλις τῇ βίᾳ (cf. xxiv. 7).

xxiii. 30

μηνυθείσης δέ μοι ἐπιβουλῆς εἰς τὸν ἄνδρα ἔσεσθαι] Blass points out that in a construction of this kind classical Gk. would require the acc. (or gen.) abs. of the neut. sing. ptc. followed by the acc. and infin., thus: μηνυθὲν (or μηνυθέντος) δέ μοι ἐπιβουλὴν εἰς τὸν ἄνδρα ἔσεσθαι. What we have here is a mixed construction, the gen. abs. passing into an indirect statement.

ἔσεσθαι] The fut. infin. hardly existed in the Koiné; *ἔσεσθαι* is the one real exception, and rare at that: here it occurs in an official letter (cf. xi. 28; xxiv. 15; xxvii. 10, there because *μέλλειν ἔσεσθαι* is a set phrase). Cf. also *καταντήσειν*, xxvi. 7 (WH mg.); *χωρήσειν*, Jn. xxi. 25; *εἰσελεύσεσθαι*, Heb. iii. 18. See MH ii, p. 219.

ἐξαυτῆς] 'immediately': so B byz; ℵ A E 33 81 have *ἐξ αὐτῶν*.

ἔπεμψα] 'I am sending'; epistolary aorist.

παραγγείλας κ.τ.λ.] Cf. xxiv. 8 δ. It is characteristic of Luke to introduce in a speech or letter matter not mentioned in the accompanying narrative: cf. xi. 12; xv. 26; xxii. 6; Lk. iv. 23; xxiv. 34.

πρὸς αὐτὸν] 'against him'; read with 81 byz sah *τὰ πρὸς αὐτόν*, 'the things concerning him' (so Soden, Ropes); ℵ A have *αὐτούς*.

ἐπὶ σοῦ] ℵ 81 byz add *ἔρρωσο* (cf. *ἔρρωσθε*, xv. 29).

4. Paul at Caesarea; He appears before Felix and Festus, xxiii. 31-xxv. 12

(a) Paul taken to Caesarea, xxiii. 31-35

Οἱ μὲν οὖν στρατιῶται κατὰ τὸ διατεταγμένον αὐτοῖς ἀναλαβόντες 31
τὸν Παῦλον ἤγαγον διὰ νυκτὸς εἰς τὴν Ἀντιπατρίδα· τῇ δὲ ἐπαύριον 32
ἐάσαντες τοὺς ἱππεῖς ἀπέρχεσθαι σὺν αὐτῷ ὑπέστρεψαν εἰς τὴν
παρεμβολήν· οἵτινες εἰσελθόντες εἰς τὴν Καισαρίαν καὶ ἀναδόντες 33
τὴν ἐπιστολὴν τῷ ἡγεμόνι παρέστησαν καὶ τὸν Παῦλον αὐτῷ.
ἀναγνοὺς δὲ καὶ ἐπερωτήσας ἐκ ποίας ἐπαρχείας ἐστὶν καὶ πυθόμενος 34
ὅτι ἀπὸ Κιλικίας Διακούσομαί σου, ἔφη, ὅταν καὶ οἱ κατήγοροί σου 35
παραγένωνται· κελεύσας ἐν τῷ πραιτωρίῳ τοῦ Ἡρῴδου φυλάσσεσθαι
αὐτόν.

xxiii. 31

Ἀντιπατρίδα] Antipatris, mod. Ras el 'Ain, about 10 miles north of Lydda and 25 miles south of Caesarea, was built by Herod the Great on the site of the earlier Kaphar-Saba, and called after his father Antipater. It lay in a well-watered and well-wooded plain. The main road to it ran through Lydda, but possibly on this occasion the party kept to the hill road by Bethel. Cf. Jos. *BJ*, i. 4. 7; 21. 9; *Ant.* xiii. 15. 1; xvi. 5. 2.

xxiii. 32

ἐάσαντες τοὺς ἱππεῖς ἀπέρχεσθαι σὺν αὐτῷ ὑπέστρεψαν] From Antipatris onward the country was open, and mainly inhabited by Gentiles. As the conspirators had now been left far behind, the large escort was no longer necessary.

xxiii. 33

οἵτινες] i.e., the horsemen.

Καισαρίαν] About 60 miles from Jerusalem.

ἀναδόντες] MM quotes several papyrus examples of *ἀναδίδωμι* in the sense of 'presenting' a document to an official.

xxiii. 34

ἀναγνοὺς κ.τ.λ.] δ (614 2147 hcl.mg) gives this verse in the more vivid direct speech: *ἀναγνοὺς δὲ τὴν ἐπιστολὴν ἐπηρώτησε τὸν Παῦλον, Ἐκ ποίας ἐπαρχίας εἶ; ἔφη, Κίλιξ. καὶ πυθόμενος ἔφη . . . .*

ποίας] Equivalent in Koiné to *τίνος*. It is pedantic to suppose with Wendt that Felix meant 'From what kind of province—imperial or senatorial?' Cf. Pilate's question in Lk. xxiii. 6 f.

xxiii. 35

διακούσομαι] A legal term for 'holding a hearing' (cf. Job ix. 33); it is used thus in Hellenistic writers, inscriptions and papyri. δ (614 2147) has *ἀκούσομαι*.

κελεύσας] Not necessarily a simultaneous or futuristic aor. ptc.; it 'may perfectly well mean that Felix first told his soldiers where they were to take Paul, and then assured the prisoner of an early hearing, just before the guards led him away' (*Proleg.*, p. 133).

πραιτωρίῳ] The praetorium (originally the headquarters of the praetor or military commander) was the official residence of the Roman governor of a province; the word is used here of a palace in Caesarea, built by Herod the Great, which served as a residence for the procurator. Cf. Mk. xv. 16 and Jn. xviii. 28 (of the procurator's Jerusalem headquarters); Phil. i. 13 (either of the headquarters of the Praetorian Guard in Rome, or the residence in Ephesus of the proconsul of Asia; see footnote on xix. 22).

(b) Paul Accused before Felix, xxiv. 1-9

Μετὰ δὲ πέντε ἡμέρας κατέβη ὁ ἀρχιερεὺς Ἁνανίας μετὰ πρεσ- 1
βυτέρων τινῶν καὶ ῥήτορος Τερτύλλου τινός, οἵτινες ἐνεφάνισαν τῷ
ἡγεμόνι κατὰ τοῦ Παύλου. κληθέντος δὲ αὐτοῦ ἤρξατο κατηγορεῖν 2
ὁ Τέρτυλλος λέγων Πολλῆς εἰρήνης τυγχάνοντες διὰ σοῦ καὶ διορ-
θωμάτων γινομένων τῷ ἔθνει τούτῳ διὰ τῆς σῆς προνοίας πάντῃ τε 3
καὶ πανταχοῦ ἀποδεχόμεθα, κράτιστε Φῆλιξ, μετὰ πάσης εὐχαριστίας.
ἵνα δὲ μὴ ἐπὶ πλεῖόν σε ἐνκόπτω, παρακαλῶ ἀκοῦσαί σε ἡμῶν συν- 4
τόμως τῇ σῇ ἐπιεικίᾳ. εὑρόντες γὰρ τὸν ἄνδρα τοῦτον λοιμὸν καὶ 5
κινοῦντα στάσεις πᾶσι τοῖς Ἰουδαίοις τοῖς κατὰ τὴν οἰκουμένην
πρωτοστάτην τε τῆς τῶν Ναζωραίων αἱρέσεως, ὃς καὶ τὸ ἱερὸν 6

ἐπείρασεν βεβηλῶσαι, ὃν καὶ ἐκρατήσαμεν, παρ' οὗ δυνήσῃ αὐτὸς 8
ἀνακρίνας περὶ πάντων τούτων ἐπιγνῶναι ὧν ἡμεῖς κατηγοροῦμεν
αὐτοῦ. συνεπέθεντο δὲ καὶ οἱ Ἰουδαῖοι φάσκοντες ταῦτα οὕτως 9
ἔχειν.

xxiv. 1

ῥήτορος Τερτύλλου τινος] Tertullus is a common name. This advocate seems to have been a Jew (cf. *ἐκρατήσαμεν*, *ver.* 6, etc.), probably a Hellenist.

ἐνεφάνισαν] 'laid information': cf. xxiii. 15.

xxiv. 2

Πολλῆς εἰρήνης κ.τ.λ.] Tertullus begins his speech with a great flourish, after the rhetorical fashion of the times; the rest of the speech, unfortunately, does not fulfil the promise of the exordium, and it tails away in a lame conclusion. The flattering mention of the 'great peace' enjoyed under Felix's rule is in glaring contrast to the facts related by Josephus and Tacitus. The Jews of Jerusalem had co-operated with Felix in putting down the Egyptian mentioned in xxi. 38. The language here is reminiscent of 2 Macc. iv. 6, *ἄνευ βασιλικῆς προνοίας ἀδύνατον εἶναι τυχεῖν εἰρήνης*.

τῷ ἔθνει τούτῳ] See on *ver.* 10.

xxiv. 3

πάντῃ τε καὶ πανταχοῦ] Rhetorical alliteration: cf. xvii. 30; xxi. 28.

κράτιστε Φῆλιξ] See on xxiii. 26.

xxiv. 4

ἐνκόπτω] 'hinder' (as in 1 Th. ii. 18). It might, however, mean 'weary' (so pesh.), in the sense of *κόπτω* (the apparent reading of A*): cf. *ἔγκοπον ποιέω*, Job xix. 2; Isa. xliii. 23.

συντόμως] Ancient speakers, like those of later days, considered it advisable to promise to be brief at the outset of their speeches; Tertullus at any rate seems to have kept his promise.

ἐπιεικίᾳ] 'moderation', 'clemency'; the word is found in papyri in exactly such complimentary addresses to officials.

xxiv. 5

εὑρόντες κ.τ.λ.] He 'arrives at the goal by way of anacoluthon —Luke cruelly reports the orator *verbatim*' (*Proleg.*, pp. 224 f.). With *εὑρόντες* cf. *εὕραμεν* in Lk. xxiii. 2, where also the word introduces a threefold indictment; here the accusation is that Paul is (1) a troublesome pest, (2) a ringleader of the Nazarenes, (3) a desecrator of the Temple. The first charge put him in the same category as many who stirred up strife about that time; the second associated him with a Messianic movement, and was calculated to arouse suspicion in a Roman official who knew how much trouble had lately been caused by political Messianism, and could not distinguish the political from the purely religious variety; the third marked him as an opponent of the established order, and thus repugnant to the ruling priestly class, whose privileges were protected by the Romans.

λοιμὸν] lit., 'plague', 'pest', a common term of abuse.

πρωτοστάτης] 'ringleader'; nowhere else in NT; used from Thuc. onward in the sense 'a man of the front rank'.

αἱρέσεως] 'party': cf. v. 17; xv. 5. The word is not used by Christians of their own community. Its use here (cf. xxviii. 22) implies that by the Jews the Christians were still regarded as a heretical Jewish sect.

Ναζωραίων] So called from their Founder, Jesus the Nazarene (see on ii. 22). In Hebrew, Christians are called *Noṣrīm* to this day. The name *Ναζωραῖοι* was later appropriated by a Judaeo-Christian sect (Epiphanius, *Pan.* xxix. 7) and (in the Syriac form *Nāṣĕrāye*) by the Mandaeans. Some take it to mean 'observants', from *nāṣar*, 'observe'. Cf. *BC*, v, pp. 356 f., 386 f.

xxiv. 6-8

βεβηλῶσαι] Cf. xxi. 28, where the word used is *κοινόω*, appropriate in a Jewish setting; here the Gentile word *βεβηλόω* is used in addressing Felix.

ἐκρατήσαμεν] 'we arrested'; an excessively refined description of an attempt at lynching! Lysias was not the only one who manipulated the details of this incident in his own interests. The δ text (EΨ 614 minn [and TR] e g vg.codd pesh hcl eth) adds *καὶ κατὰ τὸν ἡμέτερον νόμον ἠθελήσαμεν κρίνειν. παρελθὼν δὲ Λυσίας ὁ χιλίαρχος μετὰ πολλῆς βίας ἐκ τῶν χειρῶν ἡμῶν ἀπήγαγε, κελεύσας τοὺς κατηγόρους αὐτοῦ ἔρχεσθαι ἐπὶ σοῦ.* This addition bears marks of genuineness, and the misleading and reproachful reference to the tribune's 'violence' in rescuing Paul is an amusing travesty of the real facts (though *μετὰ πολλῆς βίας* may be compared with *μόλις τῇ βίᾳ*, xxiii. 29 δ). No mention is here made of the 'great violence' of the Jewish attack on Paul. But by presenting this attack as an orderly arrest, Tertullus tries to score a point against Lysias, who had no right to interfere with the High Priest's prerogative of maintaining the temple law. Observe the antithesis of *τὸν ἡμέτερον νόμον* and *ἐπὶ σοῦ*.

xxiv. 8

παρ' οὗ] According to the β text, the antecedent is Paul; according to the δ text, it seems to be Lysias.

ἐπιγνῶναι κ.τ.λ.] 'get at the facts': cf. xxii. 24; Lk. i. 4.

xxiv. 9

συνεπέθεντο] 'joined in the attack'.

(c) Paul's Defence before Felix, xxiv. 10-21

Ἀπεκρίθη τε ὁ Παῦλος νεύσαντος αὐτῷ τοῦ ἡγεμόνος λέγειν 10
Ἐκ πολλῶν ἐτῶν ὄντα σε κριτὴν τῷ ἔθνει τούτῳ ἐπιστάμενος εὐθύμως
τὰ περὶ ἐμαυτοῦ ἀπολογοῦμαι, δυναμένου σου ἐπιγνῶναι, ὅτι οὐ 11
πλείους εἰσίν μοι ἡμέραι δώδεκα ἀφ' ἧς ἀνέβην προσκυνήσων εἰς Ἰερουσαλήμ, καὶ οὔτε ἐν τῷ ἱερῷ εὗρόν με πρός τινα διαλεγόμενον ἢ ἐπί- 12
στασιν ποιοῦντα ὄχλου οὔτε ἐν ταῖς συναγωγαῖς οὔτε κατὰ τὴν πόλιν,
οὐδὲ παραστῆσαι δύνανταί σοι περὶ ὧν νυνὶ κατηγοροῦσίν μου. 13
ὁμολογῶ δὲ τοῦτό σοι ὅτι κατὰ τὴν ὁδὸν ἣν λέγουσιν αἵρεσιν οὕτως 14
λατρεύω τῷ πατρῴῳ θεῷ, πιστεύων πᾶσι τοῖς κατὰ τὸν νόμον καὶ
τοῖς ἐν τοῖς προφήταις γεγραμμένοις, ἐλπίδα ἔχων εἰς τὸν θεόν, ἣν 15
καὶ αὐτοὶ οὗτοι προσδέχονται, ἀνάστασιν μέλλειν ἔσεσθαι δικαίων
τε καὶ ἀδίκων· ἐν τούτῳ καὶ αὐτὸς ἀσκῶ ἀπρόσκοπον συνείδησιν 16
ἔχειν πρὸς τὸν θεὸν καὶ τοὺς ἀνθρώπους διὰ παντός. δι' ἐτῶν δὲ 17
πλειόνων ἐλεημοσύνας ποιήσων εἰς τὸ ἔθνος μου παρεγενόμην καὶ
προσφοράς, ἐν αἷς εὗρόν με ἡγνισμένον ἐν τῷ ἱερῷ, οὐ μετὰ ὄχλου 18
οὐδὲ μετὰ θορύβου, τινὲς δὲ ἀπὸ τῆς Ἀσίας Ἰουδαῖοι, οὓς ἔδει ἐπὶ 19
σοῦ παρεῖναι καὶ κατηγορεῖν εἴ τι ἔχοιεν πρὸς ἐμέ,—ἢ αὐτοὶ οὗτοι 20
εἰπάτωσαν τί εὗρον ἀδίκημα στάντος μου ἐπὶ τοῦ συνεδρίου ἢ περὶ 21
μιᾶς ταύτης φωνῆς ἧς ἐκέκραξα ἐν αὐτοῖς ἑστὼς ὅτι Περὶ ἀναστάσεως
νεκρῶν ἐγὼ κρίνομαι σήμερον ἐφ' ὑμῶν.

xxiv. 10

λέγειν] In hcl.mg there is a curious expansion, 'to make his defence, and taking up a godlike attitude, he said'.

Ἐκ πολλῶν ἐτῶν κ.τ.λ.] Paul also has a complimentary exordium, but shorter and less involved than that of Tertullus. Felix had been governor of the whole province for about 5 years, but if we add his term of office in Samaria during the procuratorship of Cumanus (see on xxiii. 24), the total will be 8 or 9 years. Note the fondness for introducing a part of πολύς at the beginning of a speech (cf. *ver.* 2).

τῷ ἔθνει τούτῳ] As in *ver.* 2. For ἔθνος used by Jews of their own nation cf. also xxvi. 4; xxviii. 19 (where Paul is again the speaker); Lk. vii. 5; xxiii. 2. It is used of the Jewish nation by Gentiles in x. 22. The word in the sing. was used of an organized political community, e.g., of the Jews at Alexandria, with the ἐθνάρχης at their head.

εὐθύμως . . . ἀπολογοῦμαι] Cf. xxvi. 2.

xxiv. 11

οὐ πλείους εἰσίν μοι ἡμέραι δώδεκα] lit., 'there are not more days than twelve'; for the omission of ἤ before a numeral cf. the corresponding Lat. omission of *quam*. The notes of time in this section of Ac. are fairly full: cf. xxi. 15, 18, 26, 27; xxii. 30; xxiii. 11 f., 23, 32; xxiv. 1. Comparing these with the note here, we have to conclude that the seven days of xxi. 27 (*q.v.*) were only beginning when Paul was arrested.

προσκυνήσων] 'on pilgrimage' (see on viii. 27). With the classical use of the fut. ptc. to express purpose cf. ποιήσων, *ver*. 17.

xxiv. 12

καὶ οὔτε ἐν τῷ ἱερῷ κ.τ.λ.] Paul's lawyer-like speech is more than a match for the ineffective rhetoric of Tertullus.

ἐπίστασιν ποιοῦντα ὄχλου] Cf. ὀχλοποιέω, xvii. 5. For ἐπίστασιν, byz has ἐπισύστασιν, as in 2 Cor. xi. 28.

ἐν ταῖς συναγωγαῖς] See on vi. 9.

xxiv. 13

παραστῆσαι] 'provide proof'; lit., 'to set (the evidence) alongside (the charge)'. The word is so used in the Attic orators and philosophers: cf. Plato, *Repub*. 600 D, τοῖς ἐφ' ἑαυτῶν παριστάναι κ.τ.λ.

xxiv. 14

τὴν ὁδὸν ἣν λέγουσιν αἵρεσιν] For 'the Way', see on ix. 2. For αἵρεσις cf. *ver*. 5. δ seems to have omitted τὴν ὁδόν (*secundum sectam quam dicunt isti* g; *dĕ-beh bĕ-hānā yūlpānā d'āmrīn* pesh). 'The Way' was evidently the name favoured by the Christians themselves; it was non-Christians who called them a αἵρεσις.

τῷ πατρῴῳ θεῷ] Cf. xxii. 3; xxviii. 17. The adj. 'ancestral' is important; Judaism was a *religio licita*, and Paul ever insisted that he had not forsaken the faith of his fathers.

xxiv. 15

ἐλπίδα] See on xxiii. 6; cf. also xxvi. 6 ff.; xxviii. 20.

ἣν καὶ αὐτοὶ οὗτοι προσδέχονται] Presumably some of the elders of *ver*. 1 were Pharisees.

ἀνάστασιν μέλλειν ἔσεσθαι δικαίων τε καὶ ἀδίκων] Again, as in xxiii. 6, Paul insists that his teaching, with which Israel's national hope is bound up, hinges on the doctrine of the resurrection of the dead. This is the only recorded place where Paul explicitly mentions the resurrection of the unjust. For the resurrection of the just cf. 1 Cor. xv. 12 ff.; Lk. xiv. 14; xx. 35 f.; for the resurrection of unjust as well as just cf. Dan. xii. 2; Jn. v. 28 f.; Rev. xx. 12 ff.

μέλλειν ἔσεσθαι] Cf. xi. 28; xxvii. 10; see also on xxiii. 30.

xxiv. 16

ἐν τούτῳ] 'Therefore'; for causal *ἐν*, cf. vii. 29 (from LXX).

ἀσκῶ] 'exercise myself'; the only NT occurrence of the word, which has a note of moral strictness about it, without the later sense of asceticism.

ἀπρόσκοπον συνείδησιν ἔχειν κ.τ.λ.] For *συνείδησις* see on xxiii. 1. For *ἀπρόσκοπος* cf. 1 Cor. x. 32; Phil. i. 10. In the papyri it often means 'unharmed'. The word is also quoted from Sextus Empiricus i. 195, in the sense 'giving no offence'.

xxiv. 17

δι' ἐτῶν δὲ πλειόνων] 'And after an interval of several years'; it must have been four or five years since the hasty visit to Palestine of xviii. 22; but he may be thinking of the last occasion when he spent any length of time in Jerusalem, viz. at the Apostolic Council. For this use of *διά* cf. i. 3; Gal. ii. 1.

ἐλεημοσύνας ποιήσων εἰς τὸ ἔθνος μου . . . καὶ προσφοράς] These were the sums contributed by the Gentile churches for the poor believers at Jerusalem, who were still regarded as an integral part of the Jewish nation. The collection is referred to in 1 Cor. xvi. 1 ff.; 2 Cor. viii. 1 ff.; Rom. xv. 25 ff.; see also on xx. 4. Paul took it very seriously; not only was it in his eyes a requital in some measure of the spiritual debt owed by the Gentile churches to those from whom the Gospel first proceeded, but a means of conciliating the Judaistic extremists in the Jerusalem church, and of thus welding Jews and Gentiles in the Church into one body, by making each section feel dependent on, and grateful to, the other. For *ἔθνος* see on *ver.* 10.

xxiv. 19

τινὲς δὲ ἀπὸ τῆς Ἀσίας Ἰουδαῖοι] Cf. xxi. 27. The previous part of the sentence is left unfinished—a not unnatural anacoluthon.

οὓς ἔδει ἐπὶ σοῦ παρεῖναι καὶ κατηγορεῖν] A good point in Paul's argument; the alleged eyewitnesses made no appearance.

κατηγορεῖν εἴ τι ἔχοιεν πρὸς ἐμέ] 'bring whatever accusation they had against me'; for the optative after *εἰ* in Ac. cf. xx. 16; xxvii. 39. Here Paul breaks off with another anacoluthon.

xxiv. 20

αὐτοὶ οὗτοι] Cf. *ver.* 15.

xxiv. 21

ἢ περὶ μιᾶς ταύτης φωνῆς κ.τ.λ.] Cf. xxiii. 6 He does not blame himself (he has just repeated the same argument about the centrality of the resurrection in his teaching, *ver.* 15); he simply insists that the only valid charge that can be brought against him is a theological one, and one in which all who believe in the resurrection should share.

ἧς ἐκέκραξα] *ἧς*, by Attic attraction for *ἥν*. The reduplicated aor. *ἐκέκραξα* is the regular form in LXX.

(d) Felix Adjourns the Proceedings, xxiv. 22-23

Ἀνεβάλετο δὲ αὐτοὺς ὁ Φῆλιξ, ἀκριβέστερον εἰδὼς τὰ περὶ τῆς 22
ὁδοῦ, εἴπας Ὅταν Λυσίας ὁ χιλίαρχος καταβῇ διαγνώσομαι τὰ καθ'
ὑμᾶς· διαταξάμενος τῷ ἑκατοντάρχῃ τηρεῖσθαι αὐτὸν ἔχειν τε ἄνεσιν 23
καὶ μηδένα κωλύειν τῶν ἰδίων αὐτοῦ ὑπηρετεῖν αὐτῷ.

xxiv. 22

ἀνεβάλετο] 'put off'; Blass compares Lat. *pronuntiauit 'amplius'* (cf. Cic. *Verr.* ii. 1. 74).

ἀκριβέστερον] Cf. xxiii. 15, 20. The sense is here elative, 'pretty accurately' (cf. *κάλλιον*, xxv. 10). Felix may have been indebted for his knowledge to his wife Drusilla.

τὰ περὶ τῆς ὁδοῦ] See on *ver.* 14.

διαγνώσομαι] 'I shall examine': cf. xxiii. 15.

xxiv. 23

διαταξάμενος] This aor. ptc., like *εἴπας* in the previous verse, denotes one of the items in the action described by *ἀνεβάλετο*.

ἔχειν τε ἄνεσιν] This is the only non-Pauline example of *ἄνεσις* in NT, where it always occurs with the contrast to *θλῖψις* at least implied. MM suggest that it refers here to a kind of *libera custodia*. So Moffatt, 'allow him some freedom'. Cf. Jos. *Ant.* xviii. 6. 10, *φυλακὴ μὲν γὰρ καὶ τήρησις ἦν, μετὰ μέντοι ἀνέσεως τῆς εἰς τὴν δίαιταν.*

τῶν ἰδίων αὐτοῦ] 'of his own (friends)': see on iv. 23; xx. 28.

(e) Paul's Interviews with Felix, xxiv. 24-26

Μετὰ δὲ ἡμέρας τινὰς παραγενόμενος ὁ Φῆλιξ σὺν Δρουσίλλῃ τῇ 24
ἰδίᾳ γυναικὶ οὔσῃ Ἰουδαίᾳ μετεπέμψατο τὸν Παῦλον καὶ ἤκουσεν
αὐτοῦ περὶ τῆς εἰς Χριστὸν Ἰησοῦν πίστεως. διαλεγομένου δὲ 25
αὐτοῦ περὶ δικαιοσύνης καὶ ἐγκρατείας καὶ τοῦ κρίματος τοῦ μέλλοντος

ἔμφοβος γενόμενος ὁ Φῆλιξ ἀπεκρίθη Τὸ νῦν ἔχον πορεύου, καιρὸν
δὲ μεταλαβὼν μετακαλέσομαί σε· ἅμα καὶ ἐλπίζων ὅτι χρήματα 26
δοθήσεται αὐτῷ ὑπὸ τοῦ Παύλου· διὸ καὶ πυκνότερον αὐτὸν μετα-
πεμπόμενος ὡμίλει αὐτῷ.

xxiv. 24

σὺν Δρουσίλλῃ τῇ ἰδίᾳ γυναικὶ οὔσῃ Ἰουδαίᾳ] Drusilla was the youngest daughter of Herod Agrippa I (see on xii. 1), being born in A.D. 38 (Jos. *Ant.* xix. 9. 1). She was betrothed by her father to Epiphanes, son of the king of Commagene, but did not marry him, as he refused to be circumcised. Her brother Agrippa II (see on xxv. 13) gave her in marriage to Azizus, king of Emesa; but Felix, by the mediation of a Cypriote magician named Atomos,[1] persuaded her to leave her husband and join himself as his third wife (A.D. 54). Their son Agrippa perished in the eruption of Vesuvius in 79. (Cf. *Ant.* xx. 7. 1 f.) After *Ἰουδαίᾳ*, hcl.mg (representing δ) adds 'who asked to see Paul and hear him speak; so wishing to satisfy her he summoned Paul'. We are to regard *ἰδίᾳ* as an example of the 'exhausted' *ἴδιος* (according to Deissmann), merely serving as a possessive; 'Luke is not ironically suggesting the poverty of Felix's title' (*Proleg.*, p. 88).

xxiv. 25

περὶ δικαιοσύνης καὶ ἐγκρατείας καὶ τοῦ κρίματος τοῦ μέλλοντος] 'about righteousness, self-control, and the coming judgment'—the very subjects that Felix and Drusilla most needed to hear about.

ἔμφοβος γενόμενος] Cf. x. 4; Lk. xxiv. 5, 37; Rev. xi. 13.

τὸ νῦν ἔχον] A good Hellenistic idiom: cf. Tob. vii. 11, *ἀλλὰ τὸ νῦν ἔχον ἡδέως γίνου.*

καιρὸν δὲ μεταλαβὼν] 'and when I have spare time'. Luke paints Roman officials in a favourable light, so far as their attitude to the Gospel is concerned; and Felix is more interested than Gallio, his 'fairly accurate knowledge of the Way' being perhaps due to his Jewish wife. The material consideration mentioned in the next verse was a subsidiary motive for his frequent intervals with Paul; we need not doubt his real interest in theological discussion kept, of course, within purely academic limits.

xxiv. 26

ἅμα καὶ ἐλπίζων] 'hoping at the same time also', i.e., in addition to the interest he felt. Cf. xxvii. 40, *ἅμα ἀνέντες*. For the question

[1] Jos. *Ant.* xx. 7. 2, Ambrosian MS. and Epitome; some MSS. call him Simon. There may be some connection between his name and Etymas, the name given in δ to the Cypriote magician in xiii. 8 (*q.v.*).

of Paul's financial resources at this time see on xxi. 24. The taking of bribes was forbidden by the *Lex Iulia de repetundis*, which was, however, more often than not violated by governors. The procurator Albinus was an outstanding example of venality (cf. Jos. *BJ*, ii. 14. 1; *Ant.* xx. 9. 5). Cf. the δ addition between xxiii. 24 and 25.

πυκνότερον] Either 'very often' (elative; cf. *ver.* 22), or 'the more often' (because of his financial expectations).

ὡμίλει αὐτῷ] 'he conversed with him'; see on xx. 11.

(f) Festus Succeeds Felix; Paul Left in Custody, xxiv. 27

Διετίας δὲ πληρωθείσης ἔλαβεν διάδοχον ὁ Φῆλιξ Πόρκιον Φῆστον· 27
θέλων τε χάριτα καταθέσθαι τοῖς Ἰουδαίοις ὁ Φῆλιξ κατέλιπε τὸν
Παῦλον δεδεμένον.

xxiv. 27

Διετίας δὲ πληρωθείσης] This is most usually and easily understood as meaning that Paul had been in custody for two years when the change of governors took place. But Petavius, Wellhausen, E. Schwartz and K. Lake take it to mean that Felix was removed after two years in office (cf. *BC*, v, pp. 465 f., 471 *n.*). The difficulty in taking it in the more natural way is that Felix, when accused in Rome after his recall from Palestine, escaped punishment through the influence of his brother Pallas (Jos. *Ant.* xx. 8. 9). Pallas, however, according to Tacitus (*Ann.* xiii. 14) was deposed from office by Nero in 55. This date agrees with that given by Eusebius (followed by Jerome) for the accession of Festus, viz., the second year of Nero (55-56). It is, however, difficult to bring Paul to Jerusalem so early as this, and it is best to take the 'two years' of Paul's imprisonment,[1] and suppose that if Josephus is right, Pallas must have exerted some influence even after his deposition from office. See C. H. Turner in *HDB*, i, p. 419.

ἔλαβεν διάδοχον] 'received as successor'; διάδοχος survives in Mod. Gk. as the title of the heir to the throne.

Πόρκιον Φῆστον] We have no information about Festus outside the writings of Luke and Josephus. The *gens Porcia* was a well-known one. Eusebius brings him to Judaea in 55-56, as we have seen, to be succeeded by Albinus 4 or 5 years later. But the impression we get from Josephus is that the rule of Festus was short

[1] For Luke these two years 'were doubtless the opportunity of collecting material for his Gospel and the earlier parts of *Acts*. Did he trouble to acquire Aramaic for the purpose?' (MH ii. p. 19). If a native of Antioch, he may have known some already. Cf. R. H. Connolly in *JTS*, xxxvii. (1936), op. 374 ff.

as compared with Felix's, and 58 or 59 is a more likely year for the change of procurators. The administration of Festus was not marked by the excesses of his predecessor and successors. Cf. *BJ*, ii. 14. 1 ; *Ant.* xx. 8. 9 ff.

θέλων τε χάριτα καταθέσθαι τοῖς Ἰουδαίοις] 'and wishing to ingratiate himself with the Jews'. Cf. xxv. 9, where the same phrase is used of Festus. Felix desperately needed to do something to court the favour of the Jews, who lodged an indictment against him for his behaviour when he intervened in the riots between the Jewish and Gentile citizens of Caesarea. The unusual acc. χάριτα (contrast χάριν, xxv. 9) is well supported in the vernacular of the imperial age.

(g) Festus Visits Jerusalem, xxv. 1-5

Φῆστος οὖν ἐπιβὰς τῇ ἐπαρχείᾳ μετὰ τρεῖς ἡμέρας ἀνέβη εἰς 1
Ἱεροσόλυμα ἀπὸ Καισαρίας, ἐνεφάνισάν τε αὐτῷ οἱ ἀρχιερεῖς καὶ 2
οἱ πρῶτοι τῶν Ἰουδαίων κατὰ τοῦ Παύλου, καὶ παρεκάλουν αὐτὸν 3
αἰτούμενοι χάριν κατ' αὐτοῦ ὅπως μεταπέμψηται αὐτὸν εἰς Ἰερουσαλήμ, ἐνέδραν ποιοῦντες ἀνελεῖν αὐτὸν κατὰ τὴν ὁδόν. ὁ μὲν οὖν 4
Φῆστος ἀπεκρίθη τηρεῖσθαι τὸν Παῦλον εἰς Καισαρίαν, ἑαυτὸν δὲ
μέλλειν ἐν τάχει ἐκπορεύεσθαι· Οἱ οὖν ἐν ὑμῖν, φησίν, δυνατοὶ 5
συνκαταβάντες εἴ τί ἐστιν ἐν τῷ ἀνδρὶ ἄτοπον κατηγορείτωσαν αὐτοῦ.

xxv. 1

ἐπιβὰς τῇ ἐπαρχείᾳ] 'having entered upon his province'. For ἐπαρχείᾳ ℵ A have ἐπαρχείῳ. The word is an adj. used as a substantive (sc. either ἐξουσίᾳ or χώρᾳ). Cf. Jos. *Ant.* xiv. 12. 4, ἐπιβῆναι τῆς ἐπαρχείας ἡμῶν. The substantive proper is ἐπαρχία, which naturally is confused in MSS. with ἐπαρχεία.

xxv. 2

ἐνεφάνισαν] Cf. xxiii. 15 ; xxiv. 1.

οἱ ἀρχιερεῖς καὶ οἱ πρῶτοι τῶν Ἰουδαίων] Probably yet another way of referring to the Sanhedrin ; with οἱ πρῶτοι τῶν Ἰουδαίων cf. xiii. 50, τοὺς πρώτους τῆς πόλεως.

xxv. 3

χάριν] 'a favour' : cf. *vv.* 11, 16 ; xxiv. 27. LC compare the Cambridge expression, 'a Grace of the Senate', i.e., a decision (*placitum*).

κατ' αὐτοῦ] 'against him'.

ἐνέδραν] Cf. xxiii. 16 ; hcl.mg has an addition to the effect that this plot was made by the same people as bound themselves by a vow in xxiii. 12.

xxv. 4

ὁ μὲν οὖν Φῆστος] 'Festus, however'.

τηρεῖσθαι τὸν Παῦλον] 'that Paul was being kept'.

ἑαυτὸν δὲ μέλλειν κ.τ.λ.] We might have expected αὐτός for ἑαυτόν, but where there is a contrasted clause (as here, τηρεῖσθαι τὸν Παῦλον), the acc. of the reflexive may be kept even in classical Gk. See on *ver.* 21.

xxv. 5

δυνατοὶ] 'men of power *or* influence'; a term freq. in Josephus (e.g., *BJ*, i. 12. 4; *Ant.* xiv. 13. 1). These δυνατοί would be more or less identical with the πρῶτοι of *ver.* 2.

ἄτοπον] 'amiss', lit., 'out of place': cf. xxviii. 6 (litotes, as here); Lk. xxiii. 41; 2 Th. iii. 2.

(h) Paul Appeals to Caesar, xxv. 6-12

Διατρίψας δὲ ἐν αὐτοῖς ἡμέρας οὐ πλείους ὀκτὼ ἢ δέκα, καταβὰς 6
εἰς Καισαρίαν, τῇ ἐπαύριον καθίσας ἐπὶ τοῦ βήματος ἐκέλευσεν τὸν
Παῦλον ἀχθῆναι. παραγενομένου δὲ αὐτοῦ περιέστησαν αὐτὸν οἱ 7
ἀπὸ Ἱεροσολύμων καταβεβηκότες Ἰουδαῖοι, πολλὰ καὶ βαρέα αἰτιώματα καταφέροντες ἃ οὐκ ἴσχυον ἀποδεῖξαι, τοῦ Παύλου ἀπολογου- 8
μένου ὅτι Οὔτε εἰς τὸν νόμον τῶν Ἰουδαίων οὔτε εἰς τὸ ἱερὸν οὔτε
εἰς Καίσαρά τι ἥμαρτον. ὁ Φῆστος δὲ θέλων τοῖς Ἰουδαίοις χάριν 9
καταθέσθαι ἀποκριθεὶς τῷ Παύλῳ εἶπεν Θέλεις εἰς Ἱεροσόλυμα
ἀναβὰς ἐκεῖ περὶ τούτων κριθῆναι ἐπ' ἐμοῦ; εἶπεν δὲ ὁ Παῦλος Ἑστὼς 10
ἐπὶ τοῦ βήματος Καίσαρός εἰμι, οὗ με δεῖ κρίνεσθαι. Ἰουδαίους
οὐδὲν ἠδίκηκα, ὡς καὶ σὺ κάλλιον ἐπιγινώσκεις. εἰ μὲν οὖν ἀδικῶ 11
καὶ ἄξιον θανάτου πέπραχά τι, οὐ παραιτοῦμαι τὸ ἀποθανεῖν· εἰ δὲ
οὐδέν ἐστιν ὧν οὗτοι κατηγοροῦσίν μου, οὐδείς με δύναται αὐτοῖς
χαρίσασθαι· Καίσαρα ἐπικαλοῦμαι. τότε ὁ Φῆστος συνλαλήσας μετὰ 12
τοῦ συμβουλίου ἀπεκρίθη Καίσαρα ἐπικέκλησαι, ἐπὶ Καίσαρα πορεύσῃ.

xxv. 6

ἡμέρας οὐ πλείους ὀκτὼ ἢ δέκα] The same construction as in xxiv. 11, οὐ πλείους . . . ἡμέραι δώδεκα (see *ad loc.*).

καθίσας ἐπὶ τοῦ βήματος] 'having sat down on the judgment-seat'; this was a necessary formality in order that his decision might have legal effect. Cf. Mt. xxvii. 19; Jn. xix. 13; Jos. *BJ*, ii. 9. 3; 14. 8; iii. 10. 10. See Schürer, I, ii. 15.

xxv. 7

παραγενομένου δὲ αὐτοῦ περιέστησαν αὐτὸν] Note the change of case; cf. xix. 30; xxi. 17; xxviii. 17.

αἰτιώματα] 'charges'. Less classical than *αἰτιάματα*; MM quote it from an illiterate Fayum papyrus of A.D. 95-6 in the sense of 'blame'.

ἃ οὐκ ἴσχυον ἀποδεῖξαι] 'which they were not able to prove'.

xxv. 8

οὔτε . . . οὔτε . . . οὔτε . . .] Cf. the form of his reply before Felix, xxiv. 12. In *οὔτε εἰς τὸν νόμον τῶν Ἰουδαίων οὔτε εἰς τὸ ἱερόν* he answers the old charges; in *οὔτε εἰς Καίσαρα* he replies to a new one of activity contrary to the Emperor's interests. Probably his opponents raked up something on the lines of the old charges at Thessalonica (xvii. 6 f.) Cf. again the accusation against Jesus (Lk. xxiii. 2; Jn. xix. 12).

xxv. 9

θέλων τοῖς Ἰουδαίοις χάριν καταθέσθαι] The same words as are used of Felix, xxiv. 27, except that the commoner form, *χάριν*, is used here (but A has *χάριτα*).

ἀποκριθεὶς . . . εἶπεν] See on iv. 19. Only here and at xix. 15 is this idiom used in a non-Semitic part of Ac.

θέλεις εἰς Ἰεροσόλυμα κ.τ.λ.] The suggestion was plausible enough; as the alleged crime was committed at Jerusalem, that might be the most convenient place for the trial, and Festus himself proposed to act as judge (*κριθῆναι ἐπ' ἐμοῦ*). But, having begun to conciliate the Jews in this much, he might be tempted to conciliate them in more. No doubt they wished Paul to be handed over to their own jurisdiction, but if so, they overreached themselves by accusing him of offences against Caesar.

xxv. 10

ἑστὼς . . . εἰμι] For the construction see on i. 10; here the periphrasis produces a more solemn and rhetorical expression. B repeats *ἑστώς* after *Καίσαρος* ('standing at Caesar's tribunal, I am standing where I ought to be judged'), an attractive reading, approved by LC, though WH and Ropes (following ℵ) omit the second and Soden (following the other authorities) the first *ἑστώς*.

κάλλιον] Here the comparative is definitely elative, 'very well'. Cf. xxiv. 22.

xxv. 11

εἰ μὲν οὖν . . . εἰ δὲ . . .] Antithetic *μέν* and *δέ*, in the classical manner; cf. xxi. 39.

ἀδικῶ] 'I am guilty', an Attic use.

οὐ παραιτοῦμαι τὸ ἀποθανεῖν] 'I do not beg myself off from death' (cf. Lat. *deprecor*).[1] Cf. Jos. *Vita*, 29, *θανεῖν μὲν εἰ δίκαιόν ἐστιν οὐ παραιτοῦμαι.*

εἰ δὲ οὐδέν ἐστιν] Even after *εἰ*, the negative *οὐδέν* is here preferred to *μηδέν*, as denoting greater absoluteness, 'nothing at all'.

χαρίσασθαι] 'give up by way of ingratiation': cf. *ver.* 16; iii. 14; xxvii. 24.

Καίσαρα ἐπικαλοῦμαι] The right of appeal to the Emperor (*prouocatio ad Caesarem*) arose out of the earlier appeal to the people (*ad populum*), one of the most ancient rights of a Roman citizen, traditionally dating from 509 B.C. The right was usually exercised by appealing against a magistrate's verdict, but might be exercised at any earlier stage of the proceedings, 'claiming that the investigation be carried on at Rome and the judgment pronounced by the emperor himself' (Schürer, I, ii. 59). The right of *appellatio*, the appeal to a magistrate to veto the action of his colleague, and in particular to a tribune to exercise his power of absolute veto, was now also directed to the Emperor, in whom the powers of the tribune (*tribunicia potestas*) were vested. Thus under the Empire these two citizen-rights, formerly distinct, were practically coincident. See *BC*, v, pp. 312 ff.

The procurator could judge a Roman citizen and Paul was quite willing to submit his case to the Emperor's representative (he had previous favourable experiences of the justice of imperial officials), but when he saw that Festus was prepared to make concessions to the Jews, he feared that the trial would no longer be impartial.

Ordinary provincials, unlike Roman citizens, had no such right of appeal, as they had no rights under the Valerian and Porcian laws (see on xvi. 37; xxii. 25). In Pliny's letter to Trajan about the Christians in Bithynia (*Ep.* x. 96), he says: '*fuerunt alii similis amentiae, quos quia ciues Romani erant adnotaui in urbem remittendos*'.

The Emperor at this time was Nero, who succeeded his stepfather, Claudius, in 54 and ruled till 68. The first five years of his reign, while he was under the influence of Seneca and Burrus, were regarded as a miniature Golden Age, the *quinquennium Neronis*.

xxv. 12

μετὰ τοῦ συμβουλίου] 'with his council'; these were the governor's assessors (*σύνεδροι, comites*), of whose advice he might avail himself, though the decision lay in his hands alone. They included both the higher officials of his court and the younger men who accompanied him to gain experience in provincial administration.

[1] Mr. H. H. Huxley points out to me a good example of this use of *deprecor* in Virgil, *Aeneid* xii. 931: '*equidem merui, nec deprecor*'.

ἐπὶ Καίσαρα πορεύσῃ] So said Festus, glad, no doubt, at being thus happily relieved of an awkward responsibility. It is possible that Paul simply appealed to Caesar in the person of his representative, who sat on Caesar's judgment-seat, insisting on his right to be tried there, and not handed over to the Jews; whether this is so or not, Festus seized a way out of a difficult situation and took his plea as an appeal direct to the Emperor in person at Rome (so H. J. Cadbury in *BC*, v, p. 319).

If we understand Paul's appeal in the usual way, as an appeal to the Emperor in person, we may conclude that it was made not so much for the sake of his personal safety, as from a desire to win recognition for the churches in the Empire as practising a *religio licita* distinct from Judaism. Gallio's decision (xviii. 15) may have encouraged him to hope for this.

5. PAUL AND AGRIPPA, XXV. 13-XXVI. 32

(a) Agrippa II and Bernice visit Festus, xxv. 13-22

Ἡμερῶν δὲ διαγενομένων τινῶν Ἀγρίππας ὁ βασιλεὺς καὶ Βερνίκη 13
κατήντησαν εἰς Καισαρίαν ἀσπασάμενοι τὸν Φῆστον. ὡς δὲ πλείους 14
ἡμέρας διέτριβον ἐκεῖ, ὁ Φῆστος τῷ βασιλεῖ ἀνέθετο τὰ κατὰ τὸν
Παῦλον λέγων Ἀνήρ τίς ἐστιν καταλελιμμένος ὑπὸ Φήλικος δέσμιος,
περὶ οὗ γενομένου μου εἰς Ἰεροσόλυμα ἐνεφάνισαν οἱ ἀρχιερεῖς καὶ 15
οἱ πρεσβύτεροι τῶν Ἰουδαίων, αἰτούμενοι κατ᾽ αὐτοῦ καταδίκην· πρὸς 16
οὓς ἀπεκρίθην ὅτι οὐκ ἔστιν ἔθος Ῥωμαίοις χαρίζεσθαί τινα ἄνθρωπον
πρὶν ἢ ὁ κατηγορούμενος κατὰ πρόσωπον ἔχοι τοὺς κατηγόρους τόπον
τε ἀπολογίας λάβοι περὶ τοῦ ἐγκλήματος. συνελθόντων οὖν ἐνθάδε 17
ἀναβολὴν μηδεμίαν ποιησάμενος τῇ ἑξῆς καθίσας ἐπὶ τοῦ βήματος
ἐκέλευσα ἀχθῆναι τὸν ἄνδρα· περὶ οὗ σταθέντες οἱ κατήγοροι οὐδεμίαν 18
αἰτίαν ἔφερον ὧν ἐγὼ ὑπενόουν πονηρῶν, ζητήματα δέ τινα περὶ τῆς 19
ἰδίας δεισιδαιμονίας εἶχον πρὸς αὐτὸν καὶ περί τινος Ἰησοῦ τεθνηκότος,
ὃν ἔφασκεν ὁ Παῦλος ζῆν. ἀπορούμενος δὲ ἐγὼ τὴν περὶ τούτων ζήτησιν 20
ἔλεγον εἰ βούλοιτο πορεύεσθαι εἰς Ἰεροσόλυμα κἀκεῖ κρίνεσθαι
περὶ τούτων. τοῦ δὲ Παύλου ἐπικαλεσαμένου τηρηθῆναι αὐτὸν εἰς 21
τὴν τοῦ Σεβαστοῦ διάγνωσιν, ἐκέλευσα τηρεῖσθαι αὐτὸν ἕως οὗ
ἀναπέμψω αὐτὸν πρὸς Καίσαρα. Ἀγρίππας δὲ πρὸς τὸν Φῆστον 22
Ἐβουλόμην καὶ αὐτὸς τοῦ ἀνθρώπου ἀκοῦσαι. Αὔριον, φησίν,
ἀκούσῃ αὐτοῦ.

xxv. 13

ἡμερῶν δὲ διαγενομένων τινῶν] 'And after an interval of some days'; for διά in διαγενομένων cf. xxiv. 17.

Ἀγρίππας ὁ βασιλεὺς] Herod Agrippa II, described on his coins as Marcus Julius Agrippa, was the son of Herod Agrippa I (see on xii. 1), born in A.D. 27. He was in Rome when his father died in 44, and Claudius was disposed to give him the kingdom, but was dissuaded, and Judaea again became a Roman province under a procurator. In 50, however, Claudius gave Agrippa the kingdom of Chalcis (N.E. of Palestine) in succession to his uncle Herod, together with the right of appointing the Jewish High Priest. In 53 he exchanged Chalcis for Batanea, Gaulonitis, Trachonitis and Abila, which had formed part of his father's kingdom; and three years later Nero gave him in addition the regions of Tiberias and Tarichaea, and Julias in Peraea, with 14 neighbouring villages. As a compliment to this Emperor he changed the name of his capital from Caesarea Philippi to Neronias. Like his father he called himself βασιλεὺς μέγας φιλόκαισαρ εὐσεβὴς καὶ φιλορώμαιος. He did his best to avert the Jewish War (see his speech in *BJ*, ii. 16. 4); when his efforts failed, he remained loyal to the Empire throughout the war, and was rewarded with a further increase of territory. He was promoted to praetorian rank in 75 at Rome. Later he corresponded with Josephus about the latter's *Jewish War*. He died childless about the end of the century. Cf. Jos. *BJ*, ii. 12. 1, 7 f.; 15. 1; 16. 4; vii. 2. 1; *Ant*. xix. 9. 2; xx. 5. 2; 6. 3; 7. 1; 8. 4; 9. 6; *Vita* 65.

Βερνίκη] This form replaced the earlier Βερενίκη by the operation of 'Kretschmer's Law' (which states that in the Koiné an unstressed vowel after μ, ν, ρ or λ dropped out when the same vowel stood in the preceding syllable). Berenice was a common name in the Macedonian royal families. It was Latinized as Veronica. The corresponding Attic form was Φερενίκη.

This Bernice was the elder daughter of Herod Agrippa I, born in A.D. 28, and given in marriage by her father to his brother Herod, king of Chalcis. When her husband died in 48, she lived in the house of her brother Agrippa. Later she married Polemon, king of Cilicia, but soon left him and returned to her brother. (Cf. Juvenal, *Sat*. vi. 156 ff., for the current gossip about her relations with Agrippa.) In Jerusalem, in the spring of 66, she performed a Nazirite vow and attempted in vain, not without personal risk, to prevent the massacre of the Jews by the procurator Gessius Florus; later, however, when her house had been burned by Jews, she became an ardent pro-Flavian, like her brother. She attracted the attention of Titus during the war, and later lived with him as his wife in the Palatine, when she came to Rome with Agrippa in 75. Popular disapproval made Titus sever his connection with her. Cf. Jos. *BJ*, ii. 11. 6; 15. 1; 17. 6; *Ant*. xix. 5. 1; 9. 1; xx. 7. 3; Tacitus, *Hist*. ii. 2; Suetonius, *Titus*, 7; Dio Cass. lxv. 15, lxvi. 18.

κατήντησαν . . . ἀσπασάμενοι τὸν Φῆστον] i.e., to pay him a

complimentary visit on his assumption of the procuratorship. The aor. ptc. was early felt to be a difficulty, and altered in some MSS. (Ψ 81 minn—whence TR) to ἀσπασόμενοι, the fut. ptc. expressing intention ; ' but the aorist participle is probably defensible. It describes the condition of the visit, not any time relation between coming to Caesarea and welcoming Festus ' (LC). We may regard κατήντησαν . . ἀσπασάμενοι as equivalent to κατήντησαν καὶ ἠσπάσαντο, taking the aor. ptc. as roughly coincident in force (cf. i. 24 ; xi. 30 ; xv. 8 f. ; xvii. 26 ; xxii. 24 ; xxiii. 35 ; xxiv. 22 ; Lk. xix. 6). Cf. Pindar, *Pyth.* iv. 189, λέξατο ἐπαινήσαις (' mustered and praised them '), where, so far as time relation goes, ἐπαινήσαις is subsequent to λέξατο.

xxv. 14

πλείους ἡμέρας] Cf. xxi. 10.

ἀνέθετο] ' communicated ', with a view to consultation ; cf. Gal. ii. 2 ; 2 Macc. iii. 9. MM illustrate this late sense of ἀνατίθεμαι from a papyrus of A.D. 233.

xxv. 15

ἐνεφάνισαν] Cf. *ver.* 2 ; xxiii. 15 ; xxiv. 1.

xxv. 16

οὐκ ἔστιν ἔθος Ῥωμαίοις κ.τ.λ.] A vindication of the justice of Roman law. Field quotes Appian, *Bell. ciu.* iii. 54, ὁ μὲν νόμος, ὦ βουλή, δικαιοῖ τὸν εὐθυνόμενον αὐτὸν ἀκοῦσαί τε τῆς κατηγορίας καὶ ἀπολογησάμενον ὑπὲρ αὐτοῦ κρίνεσθαι.

πρὶν ἢ . . . ἔχοι] Optative in historic sequence after ἀπεκρίθην. Cf. Lk. ii. 26, πρὶν ἢ ἂν ἴδῃ (where the subjunctive is retained in vivid construction even in historic sequence).

κατὰ πρόσωπον] For the adverbial use of this phrase (Lat. *coram*), cf. 2 Cor. x. 1 ; Gal. ii. 11 ; it is a recognized Gk. usage. See also on iii. 13.

τόπον] ' opportunity ' ; Lat. *locus* is similarly used. Cf. Heb. xii. 17 ; Jos. *Ant.* xvi. 8. 5, μήτ' ἀπολογίας μήτ' ἐλέγχου τόπον ἕως ἀληθείας ἐχόντων.

xxv. 17

ἀναβολὴν] Cf. ἀνεβάλετο, xxiv. 22.

τῇ ἑξῆς] Sc. ἡμέρᾳ.

xxv. 18

πονηρῶν] א^c B 81 minn ; πονηράν A C 33 ; πονηρά א C^2 ; om byz.

xxv. 19

ζητήματα] Cf. xv. 2; xviii. 15; xxiii. 29; xxvi. 3, and ζήτησις, *ver.* 20; xv. 2, 7.

τῆς ἰδίας δεισιδαιμονίας] 'their own religion' or 'their own superstition'; the more complimentary sense is required here, as Festus was addressing the 'secular head of the Jewish church'. LC, however, suggest '*his* own superstition', i.e. Paul's. See on δεισιδαιμονεστέρους, xvii. 22.

περί τινος Ἰησοῦ τεθνηκότος, ὃν ἔφασκεν ὁ Παῦλος ζῆν] The puzzled allusion of the pagan Festus contains the crux of the dispute; Paul's insistence (ἔφασκεν) on the resurrection (of men in general, and of Christ in particular) had impressed itself on his mind.

xxv. 20

ζήτησιν] Cf. ζητήματα in previous verse; Jos. *Ant.* xiv. 10. 2, ἂν δὲ μεταξὺ γένηταί τις ζήτησις περὶ τῆς Ἰουδαίων ἀγωγῆς, ἀρέσκει μοι κρίσιν γίνεσθαι παρ' αὐτοῖς. For the acc. after ἀπορέω or ἀπορέομαι cf. Plato, *Cratylus*, 409 D, τὸ πῦρ ἀπορῶ.

xxv. 21

τηρηθῆναι αὐτὸν . . . τηρεῖσθαι αὐτόν] The aor. does not include his custody to date; the pres. does: 'to continue being kept', 'to remain in custody'.

τηρηθῆναι αὐτόν] We might have expected the reflexive ἑαυτόν (cf. *ver.* 4).

εἰς τὴν τοῦ Σεβαστοῦ διάγνωσιν] 'for His Majesty's examination and decision'. Σεβαστός is the equivalent of the Lat. title Augustus (transliterated, not translated, in Lk. ii. 1, Αὐγοῦστος, because Augustus in the case of the *first* Emperor was considered a personal name as much as a title). With διάγνωσις (Lat. *cognitio*) cf. διαγινώσκω in xxiii. 15; xxiv. 22. In *IG*, xiv. 1072 the office *a cognitionibus Augusti* is rendered ἐπὶ . . . διαγνώσεων τοῦ Σεβαστοῦ (end of second century A.D.). Cf. *P. Hib.* i. 93^{10} (*c.* 250 B.C.), ἡ διάγ[νωσις περὶ αὐτοῦ ἔσ]τω πρὸς βασ[ιλικά (MM).

ἀναπέμψω] Used, like Lat. *remitto*, of 'remanding' to a higher tribunal.

xxv. 22

Φῆστον] C E 81 byz add ἔφη (cf. ix. 5, 11).

ἐβουλόμην] 'I should like': cf. the similar use of the imperf. in Rom. ix. 3; Gal. iv. 20; Philm. 13. The corresponding classical construction εὐξαίμην ἄν occurs in xxvi. 29. Less probably Agrippa may mean that he has already heard of Paul and wished to see him: 'I was wishing' (cf. the desire of Antipas to see Jesus, Lk. ix. 9; xxiii. 8).

(b) Paul brought before Agrippa, xxv. 23-27

Τῇ οὖν ἐπαύριον ἐλθόντος τοῦ Ἀγρίππα καὶ τῆς Βερνίκης μετὰ 23
πολλῆς φαντασίας καὶ εἰσελθόντων εἰς τὸ ἀκροατήριον σύν τε χιλιάρχοις
καὶ ἀνδράσιν τοῖς κατ' ἐξοχὴν τῆς πόλεως καὶ κελεύσαντος τοῦ
Φήστου ἤχθη ὁ Παῦλος. καί φησιν ὁ Φῆστος Ἀγρίππα βασιλεῦ 24
καὶ πάντες οἱ συνπαρόντες ἡμῖν ἄνδρες, θεωρεῖτε τοῦτον περὶ οὗ
ἅπαν τὸ πλῆθος τῶν Ἰουδαίων ἐνέτυχέν μοι ἔν τε Ἱεροσολύμοις καὶ
ἐνθάδε, βοῶντες μὴ δεῖν αὐτὸν ζῆν μηκέτι. ἐγὼ δὲ κατελαβόμην 25
μηδὲν ἄξιον αὐτὸν θανάτου πεπραχέναι, αὐτοῦ δὲ τούτου ἐπικαλεσαμένου τὸν Σεβαστὸν ἔκρινα πέμπειν. περὶ οὗ ἀσφαλές τι γράψαι τῷ 26
κυρίῳ οὐκ ἔχω· διὸ προήγαγον αὐτὸν ἐφ' ὑμῶν καὶ μάλιστα ἐπὶ σοῦ,
βασιλεῦ Ἀγρίππα, ὅπως τῆς ἀνακρίσεως γενομένης σχῶ τί γράψω·
ἄλογον γάρ μοι δοκεῖ πέμποντα δέσμιον μὴ καὶ τὰς κατ' αὐτοῦ αἰτίας 27
σημᾶναι.

xxv. 23

ἐλθόντος τοῦ Ἀγρίππα καὶ τῆς Βερνίκης] Bernice also sat by Agrippa when he made his appeal to the Jews to avert the war (*BJ*, ii. 16. 3 ff.).

μετὰ πολλῆς φαντασίας] *Fantasia* is still used in Palestinian Arabic for a procession (cf. 'pomp' from Gk. πομπή, the reverse process). Cf. Polyb. xvi. 21. 1 (μετὰ φαντασίας); Vettius Valens 38. 26 *et saepe* (cf. MM).

ἀκροατήριον] 'audience-chamber'; doubtless in Herod's praetorium. Cf. *auditorium* in *Digest*, iv. 4. 18. 1 of a room used by the Emperor for hearing trials.

χιλιάρχοις] There were at Caesarea five cohorts, each of which would be commanded by a military tribune (Jos. *Ant.* xix. 9. 2).

τοῖς κατ' ἐξοχὴν τῆς πόλεως] 'the leading men of the city', i.e., of Caesarea. These would be chiefly, if not entirely, Gentiles. Cf. τοὺς πρώτους τῆς πόλεως, xiii. 50. Hcl.mg (representing δ) has 'who had come down from the province', which may be reconstructed with Ropes, τοῖς κατελθοῦσιν [καταβεβηκόσιν Zahn, Clark] ἀπὸ τῆς ἐπαρχείας.

xxv. 24

συνπαρόντες ἡμῖν ἄνδρες] Called in xxvi. 30 οἱ συνκαθήμενο αὐτοῖς. Cf. the συμβούλιον in *ver.* 12.

πλῆθος] 'community', 'people'; so Deissmann (*BS*, p. 232), who compares τὸ πλῆθος τῶν Ἰουδαίων in 1 Macc. viii. 20; 2 Macc. xi. 16 (= ὁ δῆμος τῶν Ἰουδαίων, 2 Macc. xi. 34); Aristeas 308.

ἐνέτυχεν] B ; read *ἐνέτυχον* (WH mg.) with ℵ A C 81 byz.

καὶ ἐνθάδε] δ (represented chiefly by hcl.mg and partly by vg. cod. ardmach and the Old Bohemian version) continues : 'that I should hand him over to them for punishment without any defence. But I could not hand him over, on account of the commands which we have from Augustus. But if anyone was going to accuse him, I said he should follow me to Caesarea, where he was in custody ; and when they came, they clamoured that he should be put to death'.

xxv. 25

ἐγὼ δὲ κατελαβόμην κ.τ.λ.] Hcl. mg (representing δ) has : 'But when I heard one side and the other, I found that he was in no respect guilty of death. But when I said, "Are you willing to be judged before them in Jerusalem?" he appealed to Caesar.'[1]

ἐγὼ δὲ κατελαβόμην μηδὲν ἄξιον αὐτὸν θανάτου πεπραχέναι] For *μή* with the infin. instead of *οὐ* after *κατελαβόμην*, cf. xxiii. 8 and the similar construction after *λογίζομαι* in 2 Cor. xi. 5.

ἔκρινα] Festus has already decided to send Paul to Rome ; he wants Agrippa's help in preparing a report on a puzzling case.

xxv. 26

ἀσφαλές] 'certain', 'definite'.

γράψαι] *Digest*, xlix. 6. 1 refers to such a report as *litterae dimissoriae siue apostoli*.

τῷ κυρίῳ] In Egypt and the East the Emperor was called *Κύριος* as the Ptolemies and other potentates had been ; and in the time of Nero and his successors there is a remarkable rise in the frequency of such ascriptions (Deissmann, *LAE*, pp. 353 ff.). According to Dio Cassius (lxii. 5. 2), Tiridates of Armenia paid homage to Nero as his 'master' (*δεσπότης*) and 'god'.

ἀνακρίσεως] 'preliminary investigation' is the proper meaning ; perhaps it is used here in the looser sense of 'inquiry'.

xxv. 27

τὰς κατ' αὐτοῦ αἰτίας] 'the charges against him'.

(c) Paul's 'Apologia Pro Vita Sua,' xxvi. 1-23

Ἀγρίππας δὲ πρὸς τὸν Παῦλον ἔφη Ἐπιτρέπεταί σοι ὑπὲρ σεαυ- 1
τοῦ λέγειν. τότε ὁ Παῦλος ἐκτείνας τὴν χεῖρα ἀπελογεῖτο Περὶ πάν- 2
των ὧν ἐγκαλοῦμαι ὑπὸ Ἰουδαίων, βασιλεῦ Ἀγρίππα, ἥγημαι ἐμαυτὸν
μακάριον ἐπὶ σοῦ μέλλων σήμερον ἀπολογεῖσθαι, μάλιστα γνώστην 3

[1] The δ text of *vv.* 24*b*, 25 is restored as follows by Clark : *ὅπως παραδῶ αὐτὸν εἰς βάσανον ἀναπολόγητον· οὐκ ἠδυνήθην δὲ παραδοῦναι αὐτόν, διὰ τὰς ἐντολὰς ἃς ἔχομεν παρὰ τοῦ Σεβαστοῦ. ἐὰν δέ τις αὐτοῦ κατηγορεῖν θέλῃ, ἔλεγον ἀκολουθεῖν μοι εἰς Καισάρειαν οὗ ἐφυλάσσετο· οἵτινες ἐλθόντες ἐβόων ἵνα ἀρθῇ ἐκ τῆς ζωῆς. ἀκούσας δὲ ἀμφοτέρων κατελαβόμην ἐν μηδένι αὐτὸν ἔνοχον εἶναι θανάτου· εἰπόντος δέ μου· Θέλεις κρίνεσθαι μετ' αὐτῶν ἐν Ἱεροσολύμοις ; Καίσαρα ἐπεκαλέσατο.*

ὄντα σε πάντων τῶν κατὰ Ἰουδαίους ἐθῶν τε καὶ ζητημάτων· διὸ
δέομαι μακροθύμως ἀκοῦσαί μου. Τὴν μὲν οὖν βίωσίν μου ἐκ νεό- 4
τητος τὴν ἀπ' ἀρχῆς γενομένην ἐν τῷ ἔθνει μου ἔν τε Ἰεροσολύμοις
ἴσασι πάντες Ἰουδαῖοι, προγινώκοντές με ἄνωθεν, ἐὰν θέλωσι μαρτυρεῖν, 5
ὅτι κατὰ τὴν ἀκριβεστάτην αἵρεσιν τῆς ἡμετέρας θρησκείας ἔζησα
Φαρισαῖος. καὶ νῦν ἐπ' ἐλπίδι τῆς εἰς τοὺς πατέρας ἡμῶν ἐπαγγελίας 6
γενομένης ὑπὸ τοῦ θεοῦ ἕστηκα κρινόμενος, εἰς ἣν τὸ δωδεκάφυλον 7
ἡμῶν ἐν ἐκτενείᾳ νύκτα καὶ ἡμέραν λατρεῦον ἐλπίζει καταντῆσαι· περὶ
ἧς ἐλπίδος ἐγκαλοῦμαι ὑπὸ Ἰουδαίων, βασιλεῦ· τί ἄπιστον κρίνεται 8
παρ' ὑμῖν εἰ ὁ θεὸς νεκροὺς ἐγείρει; Ἐγὼ μὲν οὖν ἔδοξα ἐμαυτῷ πρὸς 9
τὸ ὄνομα Ἰησοῦ τοῦ Ναζωραίου δεῖν πολλὰ ἐναντία πρᾶξαι· ὃ καὶ 10
ἐποίησα ἐν Ἰεροσολύμοις, καὶ πολλούς τε τῶν ἁγίων ἐγὼ ἐν φυλακαῖς
κατέκλεισα τὴν παρὰ τῶν ἀρχιερέων ἐξουσίαν λαβών, ἀναιρουμένων
τε αὐτῶν κατήνεγκα ψῆφον, καὶ κατὰ πάσας τὰς συναγωγὰς πολλάκις 11
τιμωρῶν αὐτοὺς ἠνάγκαζον βλασφημεῖν, περισσῶς τε ἐμμαινόμενος
αὐτοῖς ἐδίωκον ἕως καὶ εἰς τὰς ἔξω πόλεις. Ἐν οἷς πορευόμενος εἰς 12
τὴν Δαμασκὸν μετ' ἐξουσίας καὶ ἐπιτροπῆς τῆς τῶν ἀρχιερέων ἡμέρας 13
μέσης κατὰ τὴν ὁδὸν εἶδον, βασιλεῦ, οὐρανόθεν ὑπὲρ τὴν λαμπρότητα
τοῦ ἡλίου περιλάμψαν με φῶς καὶ τοὺς σὺν ἐμοὶ πορευομένους· πάντων 14
τε καταπεσόντων ἡμῶν εἰς τὴν γῆν ἤκουσα φωνὴν λέγουσαν πρός
με τῇ Ἑβραΐδι διαλέκτῳ Σαοὺλ Σαούλ, τί με διώκεις; σκληρόν
σοι πρὸς κέντρα λακτίζειν. ἐγὼ δὲ εἶπα Τίς εἶ, κύριε; ὁ δὲ κύριος 15
εἶπεν Ἐγώ εἰμι Ἰησοῦς ὃν σὺ διώκεις· ἀλλὰ ἀνάστηθι καὶ στῆθι 16
ἐπὶ τοὺς πόδας σου· εἰς τοῦτο γὰρ ὤφθην σοι, προχειρίσασθαί σε
ὑπηρέτην καὶ μάρτυρα ὧν τε εἶδές με ὧν τε ὀφθήσομαί σοι, ἐξαιρού- 17
μενός σε ἐκ τοῦ λαοῦ καὶ ἐκ τῶν ἐθνῶν, εἰς οὓς ἐγὼ ἀποστέλλω σε
ἀνοῖξαι ὀφθαλμοὺς αὐτῶν, τοῦ ἐπιστρέψαι ἀπὸ σκότους εἰς φῶς καὶ 18
τῆς ἐξουσίας τοῦ Σατανᾶ ἐπὶ τὸν θεόν, τοῦ λαβεῖν αὐτοὺς ἄφεσιν ἁμαρτιῶν καὶ κλῆρον ἐν τοῖς ἡγιασμένοις πίστει τῇ εἰς ἐμέ. Ὅθεν, 19
βασιλεῦ Ἀγρίππα, οὐκ ἐγενόμην ἀπειθὴς τῇ οὐρανίῳ ὀπτασίᾳ, ἀλλὰ 20
τοῖς ἐν Δαμασκῷ πρῶτόν τε καὶ Ἰεροσολύμοις, πᾶσάν τε τὴν χώραν
τῆς Ἰουδαίας, καὶ τοῖς ἔθνεσιν ἀπήγγελλον μετανοεῖν καὶ ἐπιστρέφειν
ἐπὶ τὸν θεόν, ἄξια τῆς μετανοίας ἔργα πράσσοντας. ἕνεκα τούτων με 21
Ἰουδαῖοι συλλαβόμενοι ἐν τῷ ἱερῷ ἐπειρῶντο διαχειρίσασθαι. ἐπι- 22
κουρίας οὖν τυχὼν τῆς ἀπὸ τοῦ θεοῦ ἄχρι τῆς ἡμέρας ταύτης ἕστηκα
μαρτυρόμενος μικρῷ τε καὶ μεγάλῳ, οὐδὲν ἐκτὸς λέγων ὧν τε οἱ προφῆται ἐλάλησαν μελλόντων γίνεσθαι καὶ Μωυσῆς, εἰ παθητὸς ὁ 23
χριστός, εἰ πρῶτος ἐξ ἀναστάσεως νεκρῶν φῶς μέλλει καταγγέλλειν
τῷ τε λαῷ καὶ τοῖς ἔθνεσιν.

xxvi. 1

ὑπὲρ] B byz; *περί* ℵ A C E H 33 81 minn.

Παῦλος] Hcl.mg (representing δ) adds, ‘confident, and encouraged in the Holy Spirit’, which Clark reconstructs, **θαρρῶν καὶ ἐν πνεύματι ἁγίῳ παράκλησιν λαβών.**

ἐκτείνας τὴν χεῖρα] For the gesture cf. xiii. 16; xxi. 40, though this is somewhat different, perhaps a salute of respect.

ἀπελογεῖτο] 'made his defence'. Of all Paul's speeches recorded in Ac., this may best claim to be regarded as his *Apologia pro Vita Sua*. The speech (*vv.* 2-23) may be divided thus:—

(1) Exordium (*vv.* 2 f.);
(2) As a Pharisee, he stands for the hope of Israel, which includes a belief in resurrection (*vv.* 4-8);
(3) He recalls his persecuting zeal (*vv.* 9-11);
(4) The heavenly vision (*vv.* 12-18);
(5) His preaching activity in obedience thereto (*vv.* 19 f.);
(6) His arrest (*ver.* 21);
(7) The substance of his preaching (*vv.* 22 f.).

(1) Exordium

xxvi. 2

Περὶ πάντων κ.τ.λ.] For the elaborate structure and complimentary style of the prooemium cf. xxiv. 10.

ὑπὸ Ἰουδαίων] For the anarthrous Ἰουδαίων cf. *vv.* 3, 4, 7, 21; xxv. 10. Blass points out that in Attic forensic speeches names of opponents are anarthrous. In xxv. 8 (τῶν Ἰουδαίων) the article is due to the preceding τὸν νόμον (*Gr.* § 46, 12).

βασιλεῦ Ἀγρίππα] The position of the vocative is unusual (cf. *vv.* 7, 13, 27), for stylistic effect. The style and language of this speech are mostly of a high literary quality.

ἥγημαι ἐμαυτὸν μακάριον] Cf. εὐθύμως (xxiv. 10) for the *captatio beniuolentiae*, but Paul meant what he said. The perf. ἥγημαι with present meaning 'is one of the literary touches characteristic of the speech before Agrippa' (*Proleg.*, p. 148).

xxvi. 3

μάλιστα] This may go with the whole following phrase, as giving a special reason for Paul's pleasure (so EV), or with γνώστην (' because you are specially expert ').

γνώστην ὄντα σε] The accusatives are left hanging in air, though in *sense* they agree with σοῦ. ℵc A C 33 614 al pesh improve the construction by adding ἐπιστάμενος (cf. xxiv. 10) after ζητημάτων. When Paul got into his stride he was apt to lapse from the studied purity of his Attic diction, which was not his natural mode of expression.

ἐθῶν τε καὶ ζητημάτων] 'customs and disputes'; for ζήτημα cf. xxv. 19.

μακροθύμως] He does not promise to speak concisely (συντόμως) as Tertullus had done (xxiv. 4); probably he expected that

Agrippa would be sufficiently interested to listen to a fairly long statement; but he asks for a patient hearing.

(2) His Pharisaic Position

xxvi. 4

μὲν οὖν] 'Well, then'.

βίωσιν] The two other earliest known occurrences of this word are also Jewish; they appear in the preface to Sir. (τῆς ἐννόμου βιώσεως) and in an inscription dated A.D. 60-80 recording how Jews of Phrygia were honoured by their synagogue διά τε τὴν ἐνάρετον αὐτῶν [βί]ωσιν κ.τ.λ. (Ramsay, *Cities and Bishoprics of Phrygia*, ii, p. 650). Its first known use in papyri is in the sixth century A.D.

ἐν τῷ ἔθνει μου] For this use of ἔθνος see on xxiv. 10. Here the phrase may refer particularly to his fellow-Jews in Cilicia, as it seems to be contrasted with the following ἔν τε Ἱεροσολύμοις.

ἴσασι] The classical form, instead of Koiné οἴδασι.[1]

'St. Paul, too, when he was called to speak before King Agrippa, and Queen Berenice, and the Praeses (or Procurator) Festus, and the most distinguished society of Caesarea and of the whole province, took care (if we trust, as we ought to do, Luke's account in Acts xxvi.) not to employ vulgar inflections of the verbs, but to say ἴσασιν πάντες Ἰουδαῖοι, not οἴδασιν. In his epistles, he constantly has οἴδαμεν, —ατε, —ασι; but his schoolmaster at Tarsus had warned him against such vulgarisms: "ἴσμεν, ἴστε, ἴσασιν," he must have said, "are the true forms which you must employ if you care to be considered a cultivated speaker or writer"' (Blass, *PG*, p. 9).

xxvi. 5

ἄνωθεν] 'for a long time', but not necessarily going as far back as ἀπ' ἀρχῆς (*ver.* 4). Cf. the parallelism between these two phrases in Lk. i. 2 f. (the prologue to Lk., like this speech, is very classical).

ἐὰν θέλωσι μαρτυρεῖν] Cf. xxii. 5.

ἀκριβεστάτην] True superlative force ('strictest'); 'this speech is much affected by literary style' (*Proleg.*, p. 78 *n.*). This is the only superlative in -τατος in NT, except the elative ἁγιώτατος in Jude 20, and ἁπλούστατοι (a gloss for ἀκέραιοι) in Mt. x. 16 D.

αἵρεσιν] Cf. v. 17; xv. 5; xxiv. 5, 14; xxviii. 22.

θρησκείας] 'cultus', 'ritual': cf. Col. ii. 18; Jas. i. 26 f.

ἔζησα Φαρισαῖος] Cf. xxiii. 6; Phil. iii. 5; also Gal. i. 14.

xxvi. 6

ἐλπίδι] Cf. xxiii. 6; xxiv. 15; xxviii. 20.

ἐπαγγελίας] Cf. Lk. i. 55, 72; Rom. ix. 4 f.; the promise was made in particular to the patriarchs Abraham, Isaac and Jacob.

[1] Cf. ἴστε in Eph. v. 5.

xxvi. 7

δωδεκάφυλον] Properly an adj. (sc. ἔθνος). This is the first known occurrence of the word; later it appears in 1 Clem. lv. 6; Protevang. Jac. i. 1; Sib. Or. iii. 248; Josephus, *Hypomnesticum* (cf. MM *s.v.*). Cf. Jas. i. 1, ταῖς δώδεκα φυλαῖς, with Hort's note *ad loc.* Observe that Paul knows nothing of the fiction of the ten 'lost' tribes.

ἐν ἐκτενείᾳ] Cf. ἐκτενῶς, xii. 5; ἐκτενέστερον, Lk. xxii. 44; in both these places the word is associated with prayer.

λατρεῦον ἐλπίζει καταντῆσαι] The δ text is perhaps represented by the fragmentary P^{29}, λατρεύει ἐν] ἐλπίδι κ̣[αταντῆσαι . . . (Grenfell's reconstruction): cf. g *deseruiunt in spe.*

καταντῆσαι] καταντήσειν B. See on xxiii. 30 for the fut. infin. in NT. If καταντήσειν were better attested here, it might be allowed, as being in keeping with the classical style of the speech.

ὑπὸ Ἰουδαίων] Perhaps emphatic; they least of all ought to prosecute a man for asserting the hope of Israel. See on *ver.* 2.

xxvi. 8

τί ἄπιστον κρίνεται κ.τ.λ.] Nestle, followed by Moffatt, suggests that this verse should be inserted between *vv.* 22 and 23, leading on to the εἰ clauses of *ver.* 23. It is difficult to see how the dislocation could have come about. The verse is very much in place here, owing to the close connection in Paul's mind between the hope and the resurrection (see on xxiii. 6). P^{29} seems to omit τί ἄπιστον κρίνεται παρ' ὑμῖν.

παρ' ὑμῖν] Emphatic; 'among you Jews'.

εἰ ὁ θεὸς νεκροὺς ἐγείρει] 'that God raises dead people'. The resurrection of Christ is bound up with the resurrection of men in general: cf. *ver.* 23.

(3) His Persecuting Zeal

xxvi. 9

Ἐγὼ μὲν οὖν] Emphatic: 'Pharisee though I was, and thus in theory a believer in the resurrection of the dead, I yet judged it incredible in this particular case, and thought it my duty to oppose such a heresy'.

With this section of the speech cf. viii. 1*a*, ix. 1 f.; xxii. 4 f. This forms the introduction to the story of his conversion, which is now to be told for the third time in Ac., and for the second time by Paul himself.

ἔδοξα ἐμαυτῷ] In later years Paul thought himself unfit to form any judgment by himself (2 Cor. iii. 5).

πρὸς τὸ ὄνομα Ἰησοῦ τοῦ Ναζωραίου] For the emphasis on the Name cf. ii. 38; iii. 6; v. 41, etc.

xxvi. 10

ὃ καὶ] *καί* simply emphasizes ὅ (cf., e.g., xi. 30).

πολλούς τε] B omits τε.

τῶν ἁγίων] Cf. ix. 13 for this name for Christians.

ἐν φυλακαῖς κατέκλεισα] Cf. viii. 3 ; xxii. 4, 19. For ἐν φυλακαῖς cf. 2 Cor. vi. 5 ; xi. 23 ; also Vettius Valens 65. 9 f.

τὴν παρὰ τῶν ἀρχιερέων ἐξουσίαν λαβών] Cf. ix. 2, 14.

ἀναιρουμένων] Cf. xxii. 20 (and the noun ἀναιρέσει in viii. 1*a*), where the word is used of Stephen's martyrdom.

κατήνεγκα ψῆφον] 'gave my vote against'. The phrase may be used officially or unofficially, like συνευδοκέω in viii. 1*a* ; xxii. 20, and cannot be said to *prove* that Paul was a member of the Sanhedrin. F. C. Conybeare (*Exp.* VIII. vi [1913], pp. 466 ff.) argues that he acted as herald at the martyrdom of Stephen, proclaiming the name of the accused and the crime which he was expiating.

xxvi. 11

κατὰ πάσας τὰς συναγωγάς] Cf. ix. 2 ; xxii. 19.

ἠνάγκαζον] 'I tried to compel them'; imperf. tense (cf. the force of συνήλλασσεν, vii. 26). He does not say that he succeeded in making them blaspheme, as AV implies.

βλασφημεῖν] To say ἀνάθεμα Ἰησοῦς (cf. 1 Cor. xii. 3), or something similar. Cf. Pliny, *Ep.* x. 96, '. . . *male dicerent Christo, quorum nihil cogi posse dicuntur, qui sunt re uera Christiani*'. Cf. xiii. 45.

ἐμμαινόμενος] This verb occurs in Jos. *Ant.* xvii. 6. 5 ; after that it is not found until Epiphanius *Pan.* xxvi. 10 (fourth century).

ἕως καὶ εἰς] For ἕως with a following preposition cf. xvii. 14 ; xxi. 5 ; Lk. xxiv. 50.

τὰς ἔξω πόλεις] Cities outside Palestine ; probably he is thinking of Damascus in particular.

(4) The Heavenly Vision

xxvi. 12

ἐν οἷς] 'under these circumstances': cf. xxiv. 18 byz.

πορευόμενος εἰς τὴν Δαμασκὸν κ.τ.λ.] Cf. ix. 2 f. ; xxii. 5.

xxvi. 13

ἡμέρας μέσης] Cf. περὶ μεσημβρίαν, xxii. 6.

οὐρανόθεν] Literary (cf. xiv. 17) ; ix. 3 and xxii. 6 have ἐκ τοῦ οὐρανοῦ. Cf. 4 Macc. iv. 10, quoted in note on ix. 3.

ὑπὲρ τὴν λαμπρότητα τοῦ ἡλίου] This picturesque phrase is the equivalent of ἱκανόν in xxii. 6.

περιλάμψαν] The verb in ix. 3 and xxii. 6 is περιαστράπτειν.

xxvi. 14

πάντων τε καταπεσόντων] In the other versions of the story Paul only is said to have fallen; this is one of several additions in this account; it does not necessarily contradict ix. 7 (*ἱστήκεισαν*); if his companions fell with him, they probably rose before he did. After *γῆν* the δ text (614 1611 2147 hcl.mg) adds *διὰ τὸν φόβον*.

ἤκουσα φωνὴν] Cf. *ἤκουσεν φωνήν*, ix. 4 (xxii. 7 has *ἤκουσα φωνῆς*). Before *ἤκουσα* the δ text (614 1611 2147 hcl.mg) has *ἐγὼ μόνος*.

τῇ Ἑβραΐδι διαλέκτῳ] i.e., in Aramaic (cf. xxi. 40). We have already gathered that this was the language employed from the choice of the form *Σαούλ* (see on ix. 4).

σκληρόν σοι πρὸς κέντρα λακτίζειν] The Aram. may have been something like *qĕshē lākh li-mĕba'āṭā bĕ-ziqtayyā*. The proverb has not been found in an Aram. source, but it is the sort of saying that might be current in any agricultural community. It is frequent in classical literature: cf. Pindar, *Pyth.* ii. 94 f. (*ποτὶ κέντρον δέ τοι λακτιζέμεν τελέθει ὀλισθηρὸς οἶμος*); Aeschylus, *Agam.* 1624 (*πρὸς κέντρα μὴ λάκτιζε*); *P.V.* 323 (*πρὸς κέντρα κῶλον ἐκτενεῖς*); Euripides, *Bacch.* 795 (*πρὸς κέντρα λακτίζοιμι*); Terence, *Phormio* i. 2. 27, '*aduorsum stimulum calces*'. (Cf. *ver.* 26 for another proverbial tag.) Paul evidently had been uneasy in mind about his persecution of the Christians, especially since the death of Stephen, whose arguments had been convincing him against his will.

xxvi. 15

Ἰησοῦς] δ (181 614 g vg.codd pesh hcl*) adds *ὁ Ναζωραῖος* (from xxii. 8).

xxvi. 16

ἀλλὰ ἀνάστηθι κ.τ.λ.] *Verses* 16 and 17 summarize the commissions given by the Lord to Paul both in the way (ix. 6; xxii. 10), through Ananias (ix. 15; xxii. 14 ff.), and in the Temple (xxii. 17 ff.), The passage is full of OT language; for the accumulation of infinitives with or without *τοῦ* cf. the *Benedictus*, Lk. i. 72 ff. Ananias is not mentioned in this account; Agrippa would not be so interested as a Jerusalem audience in the important part played by this 'devout man according to the law'.

στῆθι ἐπὶ τοὺς πόδας σου] From Ezek. ii. 1, where the words are spoken to Ezekiel, who had fallen to the ground when first he saw 'visions of God'; their repetition to Paul under similar circumstances suggested that he, too, was now called to prophetic service. (B omits *καὶ στῆθι*, by homoeoteleuton.)

ὤφθην σοι] Cf. 1 Cor. xv. 8, *ὤφθη κἀμοί.*

προχειρίσασθαι] Cf. xxii. 14 (where the appointment here made by the risen Lord is ascribed to 'the God of our fathers'); also iii. 20.

ὑπηρέτην καὶ μάρτυρα] Cf. Lk. i. 2, *αὐτόπται καὶ ὑπηρέται.*

ὧν τε εἶδές με ὧν τε ὀφθήσομαί σοι] 'of the visions which you both have had and will have of me': cf. xxii. 15, *ὧν ἑώρακας καὶ ἤκουσας.* For other visions cf. xviii. 9; xxii. 17; xxiii. 11; xxvii. 23; 2 Cor. xii. 1 ff.; 2 Tim. iv. 17.

xxvi. 17

ἐξαιρούμενός σε ἐκ τοῦ λαοῦ καὶ ἐκ τῶν ἐθνῶν] Cf. Jer. i. 8. *μετὰ σοῦ εἰμι τοῦ ἐξαιρεῖσθαί σε* (also at the beginning of a prophetic commission); 1 Chr. xvi. 35, *καὶ ἐξελοῦ ἡμᾶς ἐκ τῶν ἐθνῶν.* But Paul needed deliverance from his own people (*λαός*) much more than from the Gentiles (*ἔθνη*). The sense of *ἐξαιρέομαι* here is certainly 'deliver', though its classical sense is 'choose'.

εἰς οὓς ἐγὼ ἀποστέλλω σε] Cf., from prophetic commissions cited above, *πρὸς πάντας, οὓς ἐὰν ἐξαποστείλω σε, πορεύσῃ*, Jer. i. 7; *ἐξαποστέλλω ἐγώ σε πρὸς τὸν οἶκον τοῦ Ἰσραήλ*, Ezek. ii. 3.

xxvi. 18

ἀνοῖξαι ὀφθαλμοὺς] Cf. Isa. xlii. 7, *ἀνοῖξαι ὀφθαλμοὺς τυφλῶν*, in the first 'Servant' section of the prophecy.

τοῦ ἐπιστρέψαι ἀπὸ σκότους εἰς φῶς καὶ τῆς ἐξουσίας Σατανᾶ ἐπὶ τὸν θεόν] Cf. Isa. xlii. 16, *ποιήσω αὐτοῖς τὸ σκότος εἰς φῶς*, also Col. i. 13, *ὃς ἐρύσατο ἡμᾶς ἐκ τῆς ἐξουσίας τοῦ σκότους καὶ μετέστησεν εἰς τὴν βασιλείαν τοῦ υἱοῦ τῆς ἀγάπης αὐτοῦ.*

ἄφεσιν ἁμαρτιῶν] Cf. Col. i. 14, *ἐν ᾧ ἔχομεν τὴν ἀπολύτρωσιν, τὴν ἄφεσιν τῶν ἁμαρτιῶν.*

κλῆρον ἐν τοῖς ἡγιασμένοις] Cf. Col. i. 12, *τῷ ἱκανώσαντι ὑμᾶς εἰς τὴν μερίδα τοῦ κλήρου τῶν ἁγίων ἐν τῷ φωτί.* The inheritance is associated with sanctification rather than with forgiveness; cf. xx. 32; 1 Th. ii. 12; 1 Pet. v. 10. Cf. the connection between *ἡγιασμένοι* and *κληρονομία* in Dt. xxxiii. 3 f.

πίστει τῇ εἰς ἐμέ] 'by faith which (is placed) in me'. Cf. the use of *εἰς* after *πιστεύω* (see on x. 43).

(5) His Preaching Activity in Obedience to the Vision

xxvi. 19

οὐκ ἐγενόμην ἀπειθὴς] Litotes.

τῇ οὐρανίῳ ὀπτασίᾳ] *οὐράνιος* is here used as an adj. of two terminations: cf. *στρατιᾶς οὐρανίου*, Lk. ii. 13 (it has three terminations in Attic). For ὀπτασία (from ὀπτάνω, cf. i. 3), cf. Lk. i. 22 ; xxiv. 23 (it occurs 9 times in LXX).

xxvi. 20.

πᾶσάν τε τὴν χώραν τῆς Ἰουδαίας] As it stands, the β text is corrupt or solecistic ; byz mends it by adding εἰς before πᾶσαν.

'As Greek, the text without εἰς is hardly tolerable. The omission may be a very ancient accidental error (-OICEIC), but with so firmly attested a text the theory of a Semitism suggests itself, in view of the strikingly Semitic cast, and grammatical difficulties of *vv.* 16-18. Cf. Deut. i. 19, ἐπορεύθημεν πᾶσαν τὴν ἔρημον τὴν μεγάλην καὶ τὴν φοβεράν' (Ropes).

Blass's emendation εἰς πᾶσάν τε χώραν Ἰουδαίοις καὶ τοῖς ἔθνεσιν (approved by Ramsay, *SPT*, p. 382) removes both the trouble here and the discrepancy with Gal. i. 22, and may well be nearer the original text than any of the extant MSS. traditions. P^{29} (representing δ?) seems to have had simply κα[ὶ τῇ Ἰουδαίᾳ] (Grenfell's reconstruction).

ἀπήγγελλον] ἐκήρυξα P^{29} ; ἀπαγγέλλων byz, perhaps going with ἐγενόμην.

μετανοεῖν καὶ ἐπιστρέφειν ἐπὶ τὸν θεόν] These and the following words give an epitome of apostolic exhortation : cf. xx. 21 ; also ix. 35 ; xiv. 15 ; xv. 19. For μετανοεῖν καὶ ἐπιστρέφειν see on iii. 19.

ἄξια τῆς μετανοίας ἔργα πράσσοντας] 'doing works worthy of their repentance' : cf. Mt. iii. 8 ; Eph. ii. 10 ; Tit. ii. 14 ; iii. 8.

'None more firmly than Paul rejected works, before or after conversion, as a ground of salvation ; none more firmly demanded good works as a consequence of salvation (G. H. Lang, *The Gospel of the Kingdom*, p. 23).

(6) His Arrest

xxvi. 21

ἕνεκα τούτων] Blass regards this Attic ἕνεκα as suitable to a speech in the presence of royalty.

ἐπειρῶντο] Attic ; elsewhere the Hellenistic verb πειράζω is used (cf. xxiv. 6).

διαχειρίσασθαι] Cf. v. 30.

(7) The Substance of His Preaching

xxvi. 22

ἐπικουρίας οὖν τυχὼν] This is the one NT occurrence of the good classical word ἐπικουρία (it also occurs once in LXX, Wisd. xiii. 18). It is used with τυγχάνω in Polybius, Diodorus, Josephus, and the papyri.

μικρῷ τε καὶ μεγάλῳ] i.e., to all. Cf. *ver.* 29, καὶ ἐν ὀλίγῳ καὶ ἐν μεγάλῳ.

οὐδὲν ἐκτὸς λέγων] For *οὐ* with ptc. cf. vii. 5; xxviii. 17, 19; parallels are also quoted from papyri. 'In many of these examples we can distinctly recognise, it seems, the lingering consciousness, that the proper negative for a statement of a downright fact is *οὐ*' (*Proleg.*, pp. 231 f.).

ὧν τε οἱ προφῆται] For *ὧν οἵ τε προφῆται*, a not uncommon backward attraction of *τε*.

οἱ προφῆται . . . καὶ Μωυσῆς] i.e., the OT scriptures: cf., in a similar context, Lk. xxiv. 27, 44. Paul insists throughout that his Gospel was but the logical and necessary fulfilment of the OT revelation: cf. Rom. i. 2; xvi. 26; 1 Cor. xv. 3 f.

μελλόντων γίνεσθαι] Note the attraction of *μελλόντων* (for *μέλλειν*) to *ὧν*, itself an example of Attic attraction.

καὶ Μωυσῆς] *scriptum est enim in Moyse* e h (probably to help the difficult *εἰ* construction in the next verse).

xxvi. 23

εἰ παθητὸς ὁ χριστός] 'whether the Messiah is to suffer'. This and the following *εἰ* clause may be regarded as headings from a collection of Messianic proof-texts or Testimonies (see on i. 20). 'Must the Messiah suffer?'; 'Must He rise from the dead?', and so on. See J. R. Harris, *Testimonies*, i, pp. 19 f. Cf. Justin (*Dial.* 89), *παθητὸν μὲν τὸν χριστὸν ὅτι αἱ γραφαὶ κηρύσσουσι, φανερόν ἐστιν.* By these headings Luke summarizes the arguments from OT used by Paul to Agrippa. For insistence elsewhere on the Passion and Resurrection as the subject of prophecy cf. iii. 18; xvii. 3; Lk. xxiv. 25 ff., 44 ff. Nestle and Moffatt, without adequate warrant, transfer *ver.* 8 between *vv.* 22 and 23, to introduce the *εἰ* clauses. The reading of h is *si passibilis Christus ex resurrexione mo[rtuorum] lux annuntiabit plebi et gentibus.*

πρῶτος ἐξ ἀναστάσεως νεκρῶν] 'first out of the resurrection of the dead', i.e., 'the first that should rise from the dead' (AV): cf. 1 Cor. xv. 20, *ἀπαρχὴ τῶν κεκοιμημένων.* As pointed out already, for Paul the resurrection of the dead in general cannot be separated from the resurrection of Christ in particular (see on xxiii. 6). For the use of the plur. *νεκρῶν* where the resurrection of Christ Himself is in view cf. xvii. 32; Rom. i. 4, *ἐξ ἀναστάσεως νεκρῶν.*

φῶς μέλλει καταγγέλλειν τῷ τε λαῷ καὶ τοῖς ἔθνεσιν] Cf. xiii. 47 (with OT references in note *ad loc.*); Lk. ii. 32.

(d) Interchange between Festus, Paul and Agrippa, xxvi. 24-29

Ταῦτα δὲ αὐτοῦ ἀπολογουμένου ὁ Φῆστος μεγάλῃ τῇ φωνῇ φησίν 24
Μαίνῃ, Παῦλε· τὰ πολλά σε γράμματα εἰς μανίαν περιτρέπει. ὁ δὲ 25
Παῦλος Οὐ μαίνομαι, φησίν, κράτιστε Φῆστε, ἀλλὰ ἀληθείας καὶ

σωφροσύνης ῥήματα ἀποφθέγγομαι. ἐπίσταται γὰρ περὶ τούτων ὁ 26
βασιλεύς, πρὸς ὃν παρρησιαζόμενος λαλῶ· λανθάνειν γὰρ αὐτὸν τούτων
οὐ πείθομαι οὐθέν, οὐ γάρ ἐστιν ἐν γωνίᾳ πεπραγμένον τοῦτο. πισ- 27
τεύεις, βασιλεῦ Ἀγρίππα, τοῖς προφήταις; οἶδα ὅτι πιστεύεις. ὁ 28
δὲ Ἀγρίππας πρὸς τὸν Παῦλον Ἐν ὀλίγῳ με πείθεις Χριστιανὸν
ποιῆσαι. ὁ δὲ Παῦλος Εὐξαίμην ἂν τῷ θεῷ καὶ ἐν ὀλίγῳ καὶ ἐν 29
μεγάλῳ οὐ μόνον σὲ ἀλλὰ καὶ πάντας τοὺς ἀκούοντάς μου σήμερον
γενέσθαι τοιούτους ὁποῖος καὶ ἐγώ εἰμι παρεκτὸς τῶν δεσμῶν τούτων.

xxvi. 24

μεγάλῃ τῇ φωνῇ] Note the predicative position of the adj.: cf. Mk. viii. 17; Jn. v. 36; 1 Cor. xi. 5; Heb. vii. 24.

μαίνῃ, Παῦλε] h has *insanisti, Paule, insanisti*, whence we may infer that δ had μαίνῃ, Παῦλε, μαίνῃ or μέμηνας, Παῦλε, μέμηνας.

τὰ πολλά σε γράμματα] For the position of the pronoun cf. Lk. xviii. 18; Jn. xiii. 6; Rom. i. 11; 1 Cor. v. 1; Heb. iv. 11. The effect is an added emphasis both on σε and τὰ πολλὰ γράμματα. For γράμματα, 'learning', cf. Jn. vii. 15.

εἰς μανίαν περιτρέπει] Cf. Lucian, *The Disowned* 30, εἰς μανίαν περιέτρεψεν. The remark was not offensive; both μαίνομαι and μανία are cognate with μάντις, 'seer', 'inspired person'; Plato, for example, declares that without μανία no one can be a true poet (*Phaedrus*, 245 A). See the comments on these words by Ramsay (*SPT*, p. 313) and LC (*ad loc.*).

xxvi. 25

Παῦλος] om δ (g h) and byz.

κράτιστε Φῆστε] Cf. xxiii. 26; xxiv. 3.

σωφροσύνης] In Mk. v. 15 = Lk. viii. 35, σωφροσύνη is the antithesis of demon-possession (cf. 2 Cor. v. 13); here Paul uses it as the antithesis of μανία. Cf. Plato, *Protag.* 323 B, ὃ ἐκεῖ σωφροσύνην ἡγοῦντο εἶναι τἀληθῆ λέγειν, ἐνταῦθα μανίαν. According to Xenophon, *Mem.* i. 1. 16; iii. 9. 6-7, σωφροσύνη or σοφία is the opposite of μανία.

ἀποφθέγγομαι] Of solemn utterance: cf. ii. 4, 14.

xxvi. 26

παρρησιαζόμενος] א A 33 81 byz prefix καί (WH mg., Soden, Ropes); B omits.

αὐτόν] א A 33 81 byz add τι (WH mg., Soden); B omits.

οὐθέν] For the form see on xv. 9.

οὐ γάρ ἐστιν ἐν γωνίᾳ πεπραγμένον τοῦτο] Another classical tag (cf. *ver.* 14 for a previous one): cf. Plato, *Gorgias* 485 D (ἐν γωνίᾳ . . . ψιθυρίζοντα); Epictetus, *diss.* ii. 12. 17 (τὸν γὰρ ποιοῦντα αὐτὸ οὐκ ἐν γωνίᾳ δηλονότι δεήσει ποιεῖν) ; Terence, *Adelphoe*, v. 2. 10, '*in angulum aliquo abeam*'. This proverb contains the element of litotes so dear to Luke and Paul ; the evangelic events had taken place and the Gospel had been preached openly.

xxvi. 27

πιστεύεις, βασιλεῦ Ἀγρίππα, τοῖς προφήταις;] Not content with assuring Festus that Agrippa can vouch for the truth and sanity of his report, Paul now turns to the king himself with a direct appeal for his corroborating testimony. If Agrippa believed the prophets, as Paul was persuaded he did, then he must agree with Paul, whose message contained ' nothing beyond what the prophets and Moses said should happen '.

xxvi. 28

ὁ δὲ Ἀγρίππας πρὸς τὸν Παῦλον] Sc. *ἔφη* (for the omission cf. xxv. 22), supplied in byz and probably in δ (*ait* h). If Agrippa says ' No ', his reputation for orthodoxy is gone ; if he says ' Yes ', he suddenly realizes that he is being manoeuvred into a position of public agreement with Paul ; academic interest is one thing, but confession of Christianity quite another.

ἐν ὀλίγῳ με πείθεις Χριστιανὸν ποιῆσαι] ' In short, you are trying to persuade me to act the Christian '. For *ἐν ὀλίγῳ* cf. *ver.* 29 (where it does not necessarily have the same sense ; Paul could easily play on words and phrases) ; Eph. iii. 3 (' in few words '). For the idiom *Χριστιανὸν ποιῆσαι* A. Nairne in *JTS*, xxi (1920), pp. 171 f., refers aptly to 1 K. xxi. 7 (LXX 3 K. xx), *σὺ νῦν οὕτως ποιεῖς βασιλέα ἐπὶ Ἰσραήλ;* ' Is it thus that you now play the king over Israel? ' See further E. A. Sophocles, *Lexicon*, s.v. *ποιέω*, No. 3. The overlooking of this idiom has led to several variants ; A has *πείθῃ* for *πείθεις* (similarly Hort suggested *πέποιθας* for *με πείθεις*) ; while for *ποιῆσαι*, byz has *γενέσθαι*, from *ver.* 29 (similarly vg and pesh).

xxvi. 29

ὁ δὲ Παῦλος] byz adds *εἶπεν*, δ (Ψ minn) *ἔφη*.

εὐξαίμην ἂν] ' I could pray ' ; this is the classical use of the optative with *ἄν* to express a softened assertion, the ' potential optative '. (Cf. *ἐβουλόμην*, xxv. 22.) The whole sentence is very elegantly expressed.

καὶ ἐν ὀλίγῳ καὶ ἐν μεγάλῳ] ' with few words or with many ', ' with ease or with difficulty '—playing on Agrippa's *ἐν ὀλίγῳ*.

παρεκτὸς τῶν δεσμῶν τούτων] Indicating his chain (*ἅλυσις*, cf. xxi. 33) with a gesture (cf. xx. 34).

(e) Agreement on Paul's Innocence, xxvi. 30-32

Ἀνέστη τε ὁ βασιλεὺς καὶ ὁ ἡγεμὼν ἥ τε Βερνίκη καὶ οἱ συνκαθή- 30
μενοι αὐτοῖς, καὶ ἀναχωρήσαντες ἐλάλουν πρὸς ἀλλήλους λέγοντες ὅτι 31
Οὐδὲν θανάτου ἢ δεσμῶν ἄξιον πράσσει ὁ ἄνθρωπος οὗτος. Ἀγρίππας 32
δὲ τῷ Φήστῳ ἔφη Ἀπολελύσθαι ἐδύνατο ὁ ἄνθρωπος οὗτος εἰ μὴ
ἐπεκέκλητο Καίσαρα.

xxvi. 30

ἀνέστη τε] δ (h hcl*) byz have *καὶ ταῦτα εἰπόντος αὐτοῦ ἀνέστη*.

τε . . . καὶ . . . τε . . . καὶ] For the distribution of *τε . . . καὶ* cf. i. 13; ii. 10 f.; xiii. 1: this gathering in pairs is purely stylistic.

xxvi. 31

ἐλάλουν πρὸς ἀλλήλους] Cf. *συνλαλήσας μετὰ τοῦ συμβουλίου*, xxv. 12.

ἐλάλουν . . . λέγοντες] Redundant ptc.: cf. viii. 26.

ὅτι] *recitantis.*

οὐδὲν θανάτου ἢ δεσμῶν ἄξιον πράσσει κ.τ.λ.] Here and in the next verse Luke emphasizes the official agreement on Paul's innocence: cf. Herod and Pilate's agreement on Christ's innocence in Lk. xxiii. 14 f.

πράσσει] ℵ A 33 81 prefix *τι*. Note the present continuous tense, referring to Paul's whole manner of life and his Christian activity in particular.

xxvi. 32

ἐπεκέκλητο] The plupf. expresses more than the aorist would have done; Paul's appeal to Caesar was not a mere act in the past, but had put him into a definite position in the eyes of the law. (A L omit the augment: cf. iv. 22; xiv. 23.)

6. The Voyage and Shipwreck of Paul, xxvii. 1-44

This chapter is one of the most vivid pieces of descriptive narrative in the whole of Ac., or indeed in the whole NT. H. J. Holtzmann (*Handcommentar zum NT*, p. 421) called it 'one of the most instructive documents for the knowledge of ancient seamanship'. In ancient times the narrative of a Mediterranean voyage almost invariably contained the account of a storm or a shipwreck, from the *Odyssey* of Homer onwards. Indeed, Homer really set the fashion in which narratives of storms and shipwrecks at sea continued to be told long after his day (see on *vv.* 29, 41 for Homeric reminiscences in this chapter). In Heb. literature we have the storm-narrative of Jonah i. 4 ff., to the diction of which this chapter is also indebted. At a later date we have the shipwrecks described by Josephus (*Vita* 3), and by Lucian in *The Ship*, 7 ff. The last-named ought especially to be compared with the Lukan narrative.

The leading Eng. work on this chapter is *The Voyage and Shipwreck of St. Paul*, by James Smith of Jordanhill (4th ed., 1880), to which the following notes are greatly indebted. Among German works, much valuable information may be found in A. Breusing, *Die Nautik der Alten* (1886).

Human life has been very often compared to a stormy voyage. It is not surprising, therefore, that many readers have found in this chapter an allegory of the soul's experience, or even of the history of the Church. Those who wish to pursue such methods of exegesis can work the correspondences out for themselves; here we confine ourselves to an exposition *ad litteram*.

(a) The Voyage to Myra, xxvii. 1-5

Ὡς δὲ ἐκρίθη τοῦ ἀποπλεῖν ἡμᾶς εἰς τὴν Ἰταλίαν, παρεδίδουν τόν 1
τε Παῦλον καί τινας ἑτέρους δεσμώτας ἑκατοντάρχῃ ὀνόματι Ἰουλίῳ
σπείρης Σεβαστῆς. ἐπιβάντες δὲ πλοίῳ Ἀδραμυντηνῷ μέλλοντι 2
πλεῖν εἰς τοὺς κατὰ τὴν Ἀσίαν τόπους ἀνήχθημεν, ὄντος σὺν ἡμῖν
Ἀριστάρχου Μακεδόνος Θεσσαλονικέως· τῇ τε ἑτέρᾳ κατήχθημεν 3
εἰς Σιδῶνα, φιλανθρώπως τε ὁ Ἰούλιος τῷ Παύλῳ χρησάμενος
ἐπέτρεψεν πρὸς τοὺς φίλους πορευθέντι ἐπιμελείας τυχεῖν. κἀκεῖθεν 4
ἀναχθέντες ὑπεπλεύσαμεν τὴν Κύπρον διὰ τὸ τοὺς ἀνέμους εἶναι
ἐναντίους, τό τε πέλαγος τὸ κατὰ τὴν Κιλικίαν καὶ Παμφυλίαν 5
διαπλεύσαντες κατήλθαμεν εἰς Μύρρα τῆς Λυκίας.

xxvii. 1

ὡς δὲ ἐκρίθη κ.τ.λ.] δ (represented in part by 97 421 pesh, and fairly completely by h hcl.mg) paraphrases thus: 'So then the governor decided to send him to Caesar; and next day he called a certain centurion named Julius, of the Augustan cohort, and delivered to him Paul along with other prisoners as well' (Clark: *οὕτως οὖν ἔκρινεν ὁ ἡγεμὼν ἀναπέμπεσθαι αὐτὸν Καίσαρι. καὶ τῇ ἐπαύριον προσκαλεσάμενος ἑκατοντάρχην τινὰ ὀνόματι Ἰούλιον, σπείρης Σεβαστῆς, παρεδίδου αὐτῷ τὸν Παῦλον σὺν καὶ ἑτέροις δεσμώταις*).

ἐκρίθη τοῦ ἀποπλεῖν ἡμᾶς] With this construction cf. especially xv. 20; xx. 3.

ἡμᾶς] Marking the resumption of the 'we' narrative. Where Luke had spent the time since the end of the last 'we' section (xxi. 18), we are not told; probably he was never very far away from Paul.

παρεδίδουν] The subject is not specified; 'they', i.e., the Roman authorities. The form in *-ουν* is borrowed from the contracted verbs (classical *-οσαν*). It is difficult to say why the imperf. is used here and not the aor.

τόν τε Παῦλον καί τινας ἑτέρους δεσμώτας] A Roman citizen who had appealed to Caesar would occupy a very different position from ordinary prisoners.

ἑκατοντάρχῃ ὀνόματι Ἰουλίῳ σπείρης Σεβαστῆς] Cf. x. 1. Ramsay, following Mommsen, supposes that 'the troop of the Emperor' was a popular name for the corps of officer-couriers (*frumentarii*) detailed for communication-service between the Emperor and his armies (*SPT*, p. 315). Julius, a legionary centurion, would be one of these couriers. (See on xxviii. 16.) This cohort may not have been one of the five cohorts of *Σεβαστηνοί* (Jos. *BJ*, ii. 3. 4, etc.); '*Σεβαστή* is rather an exact translation of *Augusta*, a title of honour very frequently bestowed upon auxiliary troops' (Schürer, I. ii. 53).[1] This cohort is perhaps the same as the *Cohors Augusta I* which was in Syria in the time of Augustus (Dessau, *ILS*, 2683), which may reappear as *σπείρης Αὐ[γούστης]* in the time of Agrippa II at Batanea (*OGIS*, 421). (Cf. the similarly named *Cohors III Augusta* in *CIL*, vi. 3508.) See *BC*, v, pp. 443 f.

xxvii. 2

Ἀδραμυντηνῷ] Of Adramyttium, in Mysia, opposite Lesbos. The ship was a coasting vessel, and Julius no doubt expected to find a ship bound for Rome at one of the ports in Asia at which the Adramyttian ship touched. The spelling varies; A B 33 boh arm have it, as here, with infixed nasal.

τοὺς κατὰ τὴν Ἀσίαν τόπους] 'the places along the coast of Asia'. For *κατά* used thus cf. *ver.* 5; ii. 10; xvii. 28.

ὄντος σὺν ἡμῖν Ἀριστάρχου Μακεδόνος Θεσσαλονικέως] It has been generally supposed, with reason, that Aristarchus accompanied Paul to Rome (cf. Col. iv. 10; Philm. 24); it is possible, however, that he was at this time on his way home to Thessalonica. δ (614 1518 hcl) adds the name of Secundus, from xx. 4.

xxvii. 3

πρὸς τοὺς φίλους] 'to his friends'; but Harnack (*Mission and Expansion of Christianity*, i, pp. 419 ff.) suggests 'to the Friends', regarding *οἱ φίλοι* as perhaps another name by which Christians knew each other, and comparing 3 Jn. 15 (see on xi. 26).

[1] Schürer believed that it was one of the cohorts of *Sebasteni* [men of Sebaste], called perhaps *Cohors Augusta Sebastenorum*.

κατήχθημεν εἰς Σιδῶνα] 'we put in at Sidon', about 69 miles north of Caesarea. Achilles Tatius (i. 1) calls it the mother-city of the Phoenicians (*μήτηρ Φοινίκων ἡ πόλις*) and says it had a double harbour.

ἐπιμελείας τυχεῖν] Like *φιλανθρώπως . . . χρησάμενος*, an idiomatic expression. This is the only NT occurrence of *ἐπιμέλεια*. Cf. *ἐπιμελέομαι*, Lk. x. 34 f., of medical attention.

xxvii. 4

ὑπεπλεύσαμεν τὴν Κύπρον] 'we sailed under the lee of Cyprus', i.e., east and north of the island, the prevailing wind in the Levant through the summer months being W. or N.W. Thus a ship going from Syria to Myra coasted, helped probably by the land breeze which blows, especially at night, about 90° to the shore; while a ship doing the reverse journey fared directly over the sea, passing west of Cyprus (cf. xxi 1-3).

xxvii. 5

τό τε πέλαγος . . . διαπλεύσαντες] 'and sailing across . . . the open sea'. δ (614 1518 2147 h vg.cod.ardmach hcl*) adds *δι' ἡμερῶν δεκάπεντε*, a very probable estimate, if they had to hug the coast for the greater part of the voyage. Lucian (*Ship*, 7) gives 9 days for a voyage from Sidon to the Lycian coast.

Μύρρα] Myra, where they now trans-shipped, was the place where Paul trans-shipped on his voyage to Jerusalem, according to the δ text of xxi. 1 f. The form *Μύρρα* (B) is not found elsewhere; byz *Μύρα* is preferable. Myra was one of the chief ports of the Egyptian service. According to Strabo (xiv. 3. 7), the city was 20 stades inland. The ruins of the theatre and tombs remain.

(b) They Trans-ship at Myra and Sail to Crete, xxvii. 6-8

Κἀκεῖ εὑρὼν ὁ ἑκατοντάρχης πλοῖον Ἀλεξανδρινὸν πλέον εἰς τὴν 6
Ἰταλίαν ἐνεβίβασεν ἡμᾶς εἰς αὐτό. ἐν ἱκαναῖς δὲ ἡμέραις βραδυπλο- 7
οῦντες καὶ μόλις γενόμενοι κατὰ τὴν Κνίδον, μὴ προσεῶντος ἡμᾶς τοῦ
ἀνέμου, ὑπεπλεύσαμεν τὴν Κρήτην κατὰ Σαλμώνην, μόλις τε παρα- 8
λεγόμενοι αὐτὴν ἤλθομεν εἰς τόπον τινὰ καλούμενον Καλοὺς Λιμένας,
ᾧ ἐγγὺς ἦν πόλις Λασέα.

xxvii. 6

πλοῖον Ἀλεξανδρινὸν πλέον εἰς τὴν Ἰταλίαν] This ship of Alexandria appears from *ver.* 38 to have been a corn-ship. Egypt was the chief granary of Rome, and the corn-trade between Rome and Egypt was of the greatest importance. The service of ships devoted to this Alexandrian trade was a department of state, 'the oldest and best organized corn fleet of Rome . . . organized for the service of the state as early as the Ptolemaic period', says M. Rostovtzeff in *The Social and Economic History of the Roman Empire* (1926), p. 595. See on *ver.* 11. With a steady wind from the west, the best route from Alexandria to Rome was by Myra. From Myra a northerly wind would take the ship to Sicily; thence a change to the west would bring it to Ostia or Puteoli. Lucian's ship, attempting the straight run from Alexandria to Myra, was driven to Sidon.

xxvii. 7

βραδυπλοοῦντες καὶ μόλις γενόμενοι κατὰ τὴν Κνίδον] 'sailing slowly and arriving with difficulty off Cnidus'. The difficulty was due to the strong N.W. wind. Smith (p. 75) compares Cicero, *Fam.* xiv. 5. 1, '*cum sane aduersis uentis usi essemus, tardeque et incommode nauigassemus*'. Cnidus, according to Thuc. viii. 35, was frequented by merchant-ships from Egypt. It was a Peloponnesian colony on the Carian promontory of Triopium, and had two harbours, that on the east being particularly large.

ὑπεπλεύσαμεν τὴν Κρήτην κατὰ Σαλμώνην] 'We sailed under the lee of Crete off Salmone', i.e., east and south of Crete, being thus sheltered from the N.W. wind. According to Smith (pp. 75 f.), the ship would not have been prevented from pursuing the normal course north of Crete had not the wind been W. of N.N.W.; she could not have fetched Cape Salmone had not the wind been N. of W.N.W.; the wind was therefore N.W., 'precisely the wind which might have been expected in those seas towards the end of summer'. Cf. Aristotle, *de mundo*, iv. 15, *οἱ δὲ θέρους, ὡς οἱ ἐτησίαι λεγόμενοι, μίξιν ἔχοντες τῶν τε ἀπὸ τῆς ἄρκτου φερομένων καὶ ζεφύρων.* Salmone is the promontory at the east end of Crete.

xxvii. 8

παραλεγόμενοι αὐτὴν] 'coasting along it'—either Salmone or Crete; if the former, the difficulty might be due to the rocks round the cape.

Καλοὺς Λιμένας] A small bay 2 leagues east of Cape Matala, mod. Limeônas Kaloús. It is protected by small islands, but was not a very good winter harbour, as it stands open to nearly half the compass. After Fair Havens the coast tends northwards, and would therefore no longer afford such good protection from a N.W. wind.

Λασέα] The Lasos or Alos of Pliny, *NH* iv. 59. It has been identified with ruins a little to the east of Fair Havens. h has

Anchis, perhaps through a misreading of ἄγχι, which may have replaced ἐγγύς of the β text. A 181 460 hcl.mg have Ἄλασσα (whence vg *Thalassa:* cf. *ver.* 13, and the variant Θάσον for Ἄσσον in xx. 13).

(c) Paul's Advice Neglected, xxvii. 9-12

Ἱκανοῦ δὲ χρόνου διαγενομένου καὶ ὄντος ἤδη ἐπισφαλοῦς τοῦ 9
πλοὸς διὰ τὸ καὶ τὴν νηστείαν ἤδη παρεληλυθέναι, παρῄνει ὁ Παῦλος
λέγων αὐτοῖς Ἄνδρες, θεωρῶ ὅτι μετὰ ὕβρεως καὶ πολλῆς ζημίας οὐ 10
μόνον τοῦ φορτίου καὶ τοῦ πλοίου ἀλλὰ καὶ τῶν ψυχῶν ἡμῶν μέλλειν
ἔσεσθαι τὸν πλοῦν. ὁ δε ἑκατοντάρχης τῷ κυβερνήτῃ καὶ τῷ ναυκλήρῳ 11
μᾶλλον ἐπείθετο ἢ τοῖς ὑπὸ Παύλου λεγομένοις. ἀνευθέτου δὲ τοῦ 12
λιμένος ὑπάρχοντος πρὸς παραχειμασίαν οἱ πλείονες ἔθεντο βουλὴν
ἀναχθῆναι ἐκεῖθεν, εἴ πως δύναιντο καταντήσαντες εἰς Φοίνικα παρα-
χειμάσαι, λιμένα τῆς Κρήτης βλέποντα κατὰ λίβα καὶ κατὰ χῶρον.

xxvii. 9

ὄντος ἤδη ἐπισφαλοῦς τοῦ πλοός] According to Vegetius, *de re militari*, iv. 39, the dangerous season for navigation lasted from Sept. 14 to Nov. 11; from the latter date all navigation on the open sea ceased for the remainder of the winter. With ἐπισφαλοῦς τοῦ πλοός Smith compares πλοῦς ἀσφαλής (*Julius Pollux*, i. 105).

διὰ τὸ καὶ τὴν νηστείαν ἤδη παρεληλυθέναι] The Fast was the Day of Atonement (*Yōm Kippūrīm*), on the 10th Tishri. Cf. τῇ τῆς νηστείας ἡμέρᾳ, *Ant.* xiv. 4. 3; also xvii. 6. 4; Philo, *Vit. Moys.* ii. 23; *de spec. leg.* i. 186; ii. 193; *leg. ad Gai.* 306; Mishna, *Menaḥoth* xi. 9 ('the Day of Fasting'). For other Jewish time-notes cf. i. 12; xii. 4; xviii. 21 (δ); xx. 6, 16. Paul, we may take it, observed the Fast at Fair Havens; the ship, however, had probably set sail from there before the Feast of Tabernacles began on 15th Tishri, otherwise Luke would have mentioned that date and not the Fast. The καί before τὴν νηστείαν is important; it has point only if the Fast fell rather late that year, and in A.D. 59 it fell about October 5. So Luke's meaning is: 'Not only had the dangerous time for sailing begun; the Fast also (*or* even the Fast) was now past'—so it was more dangerous than ever. A late date for the Fast is demanded, moreover, by the subsequent time-notes of the voyage to Rome. They cannot have sailed more than about 50 or 60 miles to get under the lee of Cauda, and it was on the fourteenth night from Cauda (*ver.* 27) that they drew near land, and the following day they landed at Malta, where they spent three months (xxviii. 11). The seas were closed until the beginning of February at the earliest (see on xxviii. 11); the three months spent in Malta must therefore have been (roughly) November, December and January; they must have left Fair Havens not much earlier than the middle of October, and this reckoning accords with the date of the Fast in A.D. 59 (Oct. 5), but not in any of the neighbouring years from 57 to 62, when it fell earlier. See W. P. Workman in *ET*, xi (1899-1900), pp. 316 ff.

παρῄνει] Imperf., 'offered his advice'. Paul was a traveller of great experience, both by land and sea (cf. 2 Cor. xi. 25 f.). Ramsay supposes that his advice was offered at a council held on board, presided over by the centurion.

xxvii. 10

ὅτι . . . μέλλειν ἔσεσθαι τὸν πλοῦν] Mixture of the *ὅτι* construction with the acc. and infin. construction. Cf. xvi. 19 D (*ὅτι ἀπεστερῆσθαι*); Xenophon, *Hell.* ii 2. 2 (*εἰδὼς ὅτι ὅσῳ ἂν πλείους συλλέγωσιν εἰς τὸ ἄστυ καὶ τὸν Πειραιᾶ θᾶττον τῶν ἐπιτηδείων ἔνδειαν ἔσεσθαι*).

ὕβρεως] 'injury'. LC compares Jos. *Ant.* iii. 6. 4, *τὴν ἀπὸ τῶν ὄμβρων ὕβριν.* Paul's positive advice, as we gather from *ver.* 21, was that they should winter in the port where they were.

'Considering the suddenness, the frequency, and the violence with which gales of northerly wind spring up, and the certainty that, if such a gale sprang up in the passage from Fair Havens to Lutro, the ship must be driven off to sea, the prudence of the advice given by the master and owner was extremely questionable, and . . . the advice given by St. Paul may probably be supported even on nautical grounds' (Smith, p. 85, n. 2).

xxvii. 11

ὁ δὲ ἑκατοντάρχης κ.τ.λ.] 'But the centurion paid more heed to the pilot and the shipowner than to Paul's arguments'. The *ναύκληρος* was a merchant-shipowner, who usually acted as captain of his own ship. As this ship was part of a state-service (see on *ver.* 6), the *ναύκληρος* (Lat. *nauicularius*) was thus a contractor for the state transport of corn. Ramsay (*SPT*, pp. 324 f.) quotes from an inscription *οἱ ναύκληροι τοῦ πορευτικοῦ Ἀλεξανδρεινοῦ στόλου.* On the basis of further inscriptional evidence Rostovtzeff says: 'I am convinced that from the very beginning the corporations of merchants and shipowners who dealt in some of the necessities of life, and especially the latter, were recognized by the state because they were agents of the state—more or less concessionaires of the Roman government' (*op. cit.*, p. 532). The final decision was left to the centurion, who naturally followed expert advice.

Ramsay explains that as it was a state ship, the centurion, as the highest official on board, ranked as commanding officer.

xxvii. 12

ἀνευθέτου] 'unsuitable', because of the reason given in note on *ver.* 8. This is the first known occurrence of *ἀνεύθετος* (for *εὔθετος* cf. Lk. ix. 62; xiv. 35; Heb. vi. 7).

εἴ πως δύναιντο κ.τ.λ.] A telescoped conditional and final construction; 'in order that, if possible, they might . . .'; for the construction cf. *ver.* 39; viii. 22; xvii. 27; Lk. xiv. 28; Rom. i. 10; Phil. iii. 11.

Φοίνικα] One of the many place-names showing the extent of Phoenician influence in ancient times. According to Smith, it is to be identified with Lutro, 'the only secure harbour in all winds on the south coast of Crete'. The difficulty with this identification is that while Lutro is open towards the east, the description of Phoenix, *βλέποντα κατὰ λίβα καὶ κατὰ χῶρον*, suits rather a harbour facing west. Can *βλέποντα κατά* mean 'looking down' the direction *towards* which these winds blow? It is an unnatural way to take the phrase, and Smith's quotations from Herodotus iv. 110, of a ship being driven *κατὰ κῦμα καὶ ἄνεμον*, and Arrian, *Periplus Euxini*, 5, of a cloud which *ἐξερράγη κατ' εὖρον* (Lat. tr., *ab Euro . . . erupit*) are not exactly parallel. Nor is the parallel in Jos. *Ant.* xv. 9. 6 much better, where Joppa and Dora are said not to provide good havens *διὰ τὰς κατὰ λίβα προσβολάς*, even if we take that to mean that they are approached 'down the south-west wind', for, after all, Joppa and Dora face west, not east like Lutro. Smith supports his interpretation by saying that the island of Lutro gives the harbour two entrances, one *κατὰ λίβα* and the other *κατὰ χῶρον*. The name Phoenix has survived in Phineka, which lies a short distance west of Lutro, on the other side of the peninsula of Muros, and which, to judge by the map, seems open to any westerly wind. It has been identified with Phoenix by Wordsworth, Page, and C. H. Prichard (cf. LC). It may have had quite a good harbour in the first century; the two streams shown entering the bay may have silted it up since then. The fact that Phineka retains the name Phoenix is another point in favour of this identification.

βλέποντα κατὰ λίβα καὶ κατὰ χῶρον] 'facing S.W. and N.W.'; *λίψ* is the 'Libyan'[1] wind (Lat. *Africus*); *χῶρος* (found here only) represents Lat. *caurus*. Ioannes Lydus (sixth cent.) has *κῶρος*. RV mg. translates literally, '(looking) down the south-west wind and down the north-west wind', which is interpreted in RV text as 'looking north-east and south-east' (a rendering due probably to the identification with Lutro). But see previous note.

[1] A popular etymology; the real derivation of *λίψ* is uncertain.

(d) They are caught by the Wind Euraquilo, xxvii. 13-20

Ὑποπνεύσαντος δὲ νότου δόξαντες τῆς προθέσεως κεκρατηκέναι 13
ἄραντες ἆσσον παρελέγοντο τὴν Κρήτην. μετʼ οὐ πολὺ δὲ ἔβαλεν κατʼ 14
αὐτῆς ἄνεμος τυφωνικὸς ὁ καλούμενος Εὐρακύλων· συναρπασθέντος 15
δὲ τοῦ πλοίου καὶ μὴ δυναμένου ἀντοφθαλμεῖν τῷ ἀνέμῳ ἐπιδόντες
ἐφερόμεθα. νησίον δέ τι ὑποδραμόντες καλούμενον Καῦδα ἰσχύσαμεν 16
μόλις περικρατεῖς γενέσθαι τῆς σκάφης, ἣν ἄραντες βοηθείαις ἐχρῶντο 17
ὑποζωννύντες τὸ πλοῖον· φοβούμενοί τε μὴ εἰς τὴν Σύρτιν ἐκπέσωσιν,
χαλάσαντες τὸ σκεῦος, οὕτως ἐφέροντο. σφοδρῶς δὲ χειμαζομένων 18
ἡμῶν τῇ ἑξῆς ἐκβολὴν ἐποιοῦντο, καὶ τῇ τρίτῃ αὐτόχειρες τὴν σκευὴν 19
τοῦ πλοίου ἔριψαν. μήτε δὲ ἡλίου μήτε ἄστρων ἐπιφαινόντων ἐπὶ 20
πλείονας ἡμέρας, χειμῶνός τε οὐκ ὀλίγου ἐπικειμένου, λοιπὸν περιῃρεῖτο ἐλπὶς πᾶσα τοῦ σώζεσθαι ἡμᾶς.

xxvii. 13

ὑποπνεύσαντος δὲ νότου] ' a south wind having sprung up ', which would favour the westerly voyage.

ἄραντες] ' having set out ' from Fair Havens.

ἆσσον παρελέγοντο τὴν Κρήτην] ' they coasted along (the shore of) Crete, (keeping) close in (to the land) '. This was necessary until they rounded Cape Matala, about two leagues west of Fair Havens. For the literary *ἆσσον* (the comparative of *ἄγχι*), vg has *de Asson*, sah ' from Alasos ' (see on *ver.* 8), boh ' from Assos '. h *celerius* probably represents a variant *θᾶσσον* (cf. *Θάσον* for *Ἄσσον* in xx. 13, and vg *Thalassa* from *Alassa* in *ver.* 8).

xxvii. 14

ἔβαλεν κατʼ αὐτῆς] ' there rushed down from it ', i.e., from Crete.

ἄνεμος τυφωνικὸς] The adj. refers to the whirling motion of the clouds and sea caused by the meeting of opposite currents of air. Pliny calls the typhoon ' *praecipua nauigantium pestis non antennas modo uerum ipsa nauigia contorta frangens* ' (*NH*, ii. 132).

Εὐρακύλων] The word is not found elsewhere, although the wind is well-known. It is a hybrid compound of *Εὖρος*, the east wind, and Lat. *Aquilo*, the north wind. The wind was actually E.N.E., and blowing down from Mt. Ida, would be very dangerous to a ship with one large sail; if it did not capsize her, it would probably drive her to the Syrtes. For *Εὐρακύλων* (א A B vg sah boh) there is a variant *Εὐροκλύδων* (byz pesh hcl).

xxvii. 15

ἀντοφθαλμεῖν] ' face ', ' head up ' (LC). Cf. vi. 11 D; the word occurs also in Polybius i. 17. 3, etc.; Wisd. xii. 14; 3 Baruch

vii. 4[1] (*οὗ τὴν θέαν οὐκ ἠδυνήθημεν ἀντοφθαλμεῖν καὶ ἰδεῖν*); Ep. Barnab. v. 10 (*οὐκ ἰσχύουσιν εἰς τὰς ἀκτῖνας αὐτοῦ ἀντοφθαλμῆσαι*); 1 Clem. xxxiv. 1 (*ὁ νωθρὸς καὶ παρειμένος οὐκ ἀντοφθαλμεῖ τῷ ἐργοπαρέκτῃ αὐτοῦ*).

τῷ ἀνέμῳ] May go with either *ἀντοφθαλμεῖν* or *ἐπιδόντες* (probably the former; in sense with both). In δ it must go with *ἀντοφθαλμεῖν*, as in it *ἐπιδόντες* is provided with a separate dative (see below).

ἐπιδόντες ἐφερόμεθα] 'we scudded before it'. After *ἐπιδόντες* the δ text (614 1518 hcl*) adds *τῷ πνέοντι* (614 1518 have *τῷ πλέοντι* by error) *καὶ συστείλαντες τὰ ἱστία*, to which hcl* adds 'and as it happened' (*κατὰ τὸ συμβαῖνον*, Blass).

xxvii. 16

ὑποδραμόντες] 'running (before the wind) under the lee of'. Cf. *ὑπεπλεύσαμεν*, *vv.* 4, 7.

Καῦδα] The mod. Gavdho (Ital. Gozzo), in the vicinity of which the Battle of Cape Matapan was fought on March 28, 1941. It lay about 23 miles to leeward of the point which they had reached when the wind struck them. The variant *Κλαῦδα* (א* A 33 81 vg.codd sah boh hcl; cf. byz *Κλαύδην*) is found in ancient authors; Hierocles and Ptolemy have *Κλαῦδος*, Pliny and Mela have Gaudos and Caudos respectively.

ἰσχύσαμεν κ.τ.λ.] Three operations are to be distinguished: (1) hauling in the boat; (2) undergirding the ship with cables, to strengthen it lest it should be disintegrated by the violence of wind and wave; (3) lowering the gear (but see on next verse).

ἰσχύσαμεν μόλις περικρατεῖς γενέσθαι τῆς σκάφης] 'we were able with difficulty to secure the boat'. The dinghy was normally towed at the stern, not kept on deck. The 1st pers. *ἰσχύσαμεν* suggests that Luke himself helped (any landlubber could haul on a rope), and *μόλις* has been thought to hint at the painful memory of his blisters.

xxvii. 17

ἄραντες] 'taking up'. LC suggest that the foremast, which sloped forward, was used as a derrick.

βοηθείαις ἐχρῶντο ὑποζώννυντες τὸ πλοῖον] For *βοηθεῖαι* cf. Aristotle, *Rhet.* ii. 5. 18 (*ὥσπερ ἐν τοῖς κατὰ θάλατταν κινδύνοις οἵ τε ἄπειροι χειμῶνος θαρροῦσι τὰ μέλλοντα καὶ οἱ βοηθείας ἔχοντες διὰ τὴν ἐμπειρίαν*); Philo, *de Iosepho*, 33 (*ὥσπερ γὰρ κυβερνήτης ταῖς τῶν πνευμάτων μεταβολαῖς συμμεταβάλλει τὰς πρὸς εὔπλοιαν βοηθείας*).

[1] I.e. the *Greek* Apocalypse of Baruch: Charles's *Apocrypha and Pseudepigrapha*, ii. pp. 527 ff.

S. A. Naber, in *Mnemosyne*, xxiii (1895), pp. 267 ff., conjectured *βοείαις*, 'ropes of ox-hide', which would give excellent sense, but is unnecessary in view of the cited occurrences of *βοηθεῖαι* in a nautical context. The 'helps' in this case might more technically be called *ὑποζώματα*, used thus in Plato, *Republic*, x. 616 C; *Laws*, xii. 945 C; in Callixenus, Herodotus medicus, and many inscriptions. The verb *ὑποζώννυμι* is found in this sense of 'bracing' a ship in Polybius xxvii. 3. 3 and in inscriptions. See *BC* v, pp. 345 ff.

Σύρτιν] The Syrtes are quicksands off the Libyan coast. They were still far distant, but the wind might blow for many days, and it was driving them right in the direction of the Greater Syrtis, west of Cyrene.

χαλάσαντες τὸ σκεῦος] 'lowering the gear'. The phrase is ambiguous, and may be understood in various ways, e.g., (1) 'setting sail' (so pesh and some minn which have *τὰ ἱστία* instead of *τὸ σκεῦος*);[1] (2) 'dropping a sea-anchor', the dragging of which would act as a brake (cf. g *uas quoddam dimiserunt quod traheret*, rendering *χαλάσαντες τὸ σκεῦος οὕτως ἐφέροντο*); (3) according to Smith, *σκεῦος*, 'when applied to a ship, means appurtenances of every kind, such as spars, sails, rigging, anchors and cables, etc. Now, every ship situated as this one was, when preparing for a storm, sends down upon deck the "top-hamper", or gear connected with the fair-weather sails, such as the *suppara*, or top-sails' (p. 111): cf. s *depositis uelis*.

οὕτως ἐφέροντο] 'away they drifted'; according to Smith, on the starboard tack (i.e., with the right side to the wind), with storm sails set. Cf. Homer, *Odyssey*, ix. 70, *αἱ μὲν ἔπειτ' ἐφέροντ' ἐπικάρσιαι.* The use of *οὕτως* to resume a series of participles is idiomatic.

xxvii. 18

χειμαζομένων] 'making heavy weather'.

ἐκβολὴν ἐποιοῦντο] 'they began to jettison the cargo': cf. Jonah i. 5, *ἐκβολὴν ἐποιήσαντο τῶν σκευῶν τῶν ἐν τῷ πλοίῳ εἰς τὴν θάλασσαν τοῦ κουφισθῆναι ἀπ' αὐτῶν.* See on *ver.* 38.

xxvii. 19

ἔριψαν] *ἐρρίψαμεν* byz (which Ramsay favours). δ adds *εἰς τὴν θάλασσαν* (614 minn g vg.codd sah hcl*).

τὴν σκευὴν] 'the spare gear'. 'As with *σκεῦος* in verse 17 we are uncertain whether *σκευή* here has not a technical meaning which is now lost' (LC). Cf. Jonah i. 5, quoted above. Smith supposes that the main-yard is meant, 'an immense spar, probably as long

[1] This may reflect the original δ text, for *χαλάζειν τὰ ἱστία* is the reverse action to *συστέλλειν τὰ ἱστία* ('shorten sail') of *ver.* 15 δ.

as the ship, which would require the united efforts of passengers and crew to launch overboard' (p. 116).

αὐτόχειρες] The use of this emphatic word marks a climax of precautionary operations, with an implication of increasing danger.

xxvii. 20

μήτε δὲ ἡλίου μήτε ἄστρων ἐπιφαινόντων] Thus they were left in ignorance of their course.

οὐκ ὀλίγου] Lukan litotes : see on xii. 18.

λοιπὸν] om B (probably accidentally).

περιῃρεῖτο ἐλπὶς] An idiomatic expression. The imperf. implies that the situation was continually getting worse.

(e) Paul's Encouragement, xxvii. 21-26

Πολλῆς τε ἀσιτίας ὑπαρχούσης τότε σταθεὶς ὁ Παῦλος ἐν μέσῳ 21
αὐτῶν εἶπεν Ἔδει μέν, ὦ ἄνδρες, πειθαρχήσαντάς μοι μὴ ἀνάγεσθαι
ἀπὸ τῆς Κρήτης κερδῆσαί τε τὴν ὕβριν ταύτην καὶ τὴν ζημίαν. καὶ 22
τὰ νῦν παραινῶ ὑμᾶς εὐθυμεῖν, ἀποβολὴ γὰρ ψυχῆς οὐδεμία ἔσται ἐξ
ὑμῶν πλὴν τοῦ πλοίου· παρέστη γάρ μοι ταύτῃ τῇ νυκτὶ τοῦ θεοῦ 23
οὗ εἰμί, ᾧ καὶ λατρεύω, ἄγγελος λέγων Μὴ φοβοῦ, Παῦλε· Καίσαρί 24
σε δεῖ παραστῆναι, καὶ ἰδοὺ κεχάρισταί σοι ὁ θεὸς πάντας τοὺς
πλέοντας μετὰ σοῦ. διὸ εὐθυμεῖτε, ἄνδρες· πιστεύω γὰρ τῷ θεῷ 25
ὅτι οὕτως ἔσται καθ' ὃν τρόπον λελάληταί μοι. εἰς νῆσον δέ τινα δεῖ 26
ἡμᾶς ἐκπεσεῖν.

xxvii. 21

Πολλῆς τε ἀσιτίας ὑπαρχούσης] Their abstinence from food might be due to various reasons—difficulty of cooking, spoiling of food by sea-water, sea-sickness, etc. Cf. ἄσιτοι διατελεῖτε, *ver*. 33.

ἔδει μέν, ὦ ἄνδρες, κ.τ.λ.] We appreciate this human touch in Paul ; he is a man of like passions with us and not above saying 'I told you so!'

κερδῆσαί τε τὴν ὕβριν ταύτην καὶ τὴν ζημίαν) 'and have gained this damage and loss' : note the oxymoron. Cf. Euripides, *Cycl.* 312, πολλοῖσι γὰρ/κέρδη πονηρὰ ζημίαν ἠμείψατο, and Pliny, *NH*, vii. 129, '*quam quidem iniuriam lucri fecit ille*'.

xxvii. 22

πλὴν] 'but only', by brachylogy ; the lit. meaning is 'except'.

xxvii. 23

παρέστη γὰρ κ.τ.λ.] Cf. the vision of xxiii. 11.

ταύτῃ τῇ νυκτὶ] 'last night' (cf. Fr. *cette nuit*).

xxvii. 24

Μὴ φοβοῦ] Cf. *θάρσει*, xxiii. 11.

Καίσαρί σε δεῖ παραστῆναι] Cf. xxiii. 11, *οὕτω σε δεῖ καὶ εἰς Ῥώμην μαρτυρῆσαι.*

κεχάρισται] 'has given as a present'—for the saving of life, as in iii. 14; not for the destroying of it, as in xxv. 11, 16. Cf. Gen. xviii. 26 for the principle that the presence of good men is a protection to a community.

xxvii. 25

πιστεύω γὰρ τῷ θεῷ] 'For I trust God', i.e., I believe what He says (see on v. 14).

xxvii. 26

ἐκπεσεῖν] 'be cast up', 'cast ashore'.

(f) They Approach Land, xxvii. 27-29

Ὡς δὲ τεσσαρεσκαιδεκάτη νὺξ ἐγένετο διαφερομένων ἡμῶν ἐν 27
τῷ Ἀδρίᾳ, κατὰ μέσον τῆς νυκτὸς ὑπενόουν οἱ ναῦται προσάγειν τινὰ
αὐτοῖς χώραν. καὶ βολίσαντες εὗρον ὀργυιὰς εἴκοσι, βραχὺ δὲ δια- 28
στήσαντες καὶ πάλιν βολίσαντες εὗρον ὀργυιὰς δεκαπέντε· φοβούμενοί 29
τε μή που κατὰ τραχεῖς τόπους ἐκπέσωμεν ἐκ πρύμνης ῥίψαντες
ἀγκύρας τέσσαρας ηὔχοντο ἡμέραν γενέσθαι.

xxvii. 27

τεσσαρεσκαιδεκάτη νὺξ] Thirteen or fourteen days would be almost exactly the time required to reach Malta from Cauda under such conditions, according to Smith's calculations (pp. 124 ff.).

διαφερομένων ἡμῶν] 'while we were drifting across', not 'up and down'. Cf. *ver.* 5, *διαπλεύσαντες*, for this sense of *διά* in composition.

ἐν τῷ Ἀδρίᾳ] i.e., the sea between Italy, Malta, Crete and Greece. Strabo (*c.* A.D. 19) says the Ionian Sea is part of Adria (*ὁ δ' Ἰόνιος κόλπος μέρος ἐστὶ τοῦ νῦν Ἀδρίου λεγομένου*, ii. 5. 20). Pausanias (v. 25. 3) says the straits of Messina unite the Adriatic and Tyrrhenian Seas. Ptolemy (iii. 4. 1; 15. 1) makes the Adriatic Sea (as distinct from the Adriatic Gulf) the whole sea as far south as Sicily and Crete. Cf. Jos. *Vita*, 3, *βαπτισθέντος γὰρ ἡμῶν τοῦ πλοίου κατὰ μέσον τὸν Ἀδρίαν.*

κατὰ μέσον τῆς νυκτὸς] Cf. xvi. 25, *κατὰ τὸ μεσονύκτιον.*

προσάγειν τινὰ αὐτοῖς χώραν] 'that some land was approaching': this is described by Smith as the 'graphic language of seamen'

(p. 120 n.). The reading of B*, προσαχεῖν, is very attractive, and explains the reading of g s, *resonare*. The form προσαχεῖν is Doric (Attic προσηχεῖν); MH suggest that it was a term first used by sailors outside the Ionic-Attic area, and later used more generally as a technical term (*Gr.* ii. p. 71). Ramsay (*SPT*, pp. 334 f.) suggests that they heard the breakers; had it been daylight they would have seen them too. According to Smith (p. 121) no ship can enter St. Paul's Bay from the east without passing within a quarter of a mile of the point of Koura, and when she comes within this distance (and not until then) it is impossible not to observe the breakers, which are particularly violent at Koura in a N.E. wind.

xxvii. 28

καὶ βολίσαντες κ.τ.λ.] The soundings agree with the direction of a ship passing Koura on her way into St. Paul's Bay, the 20 fathoms' depth being close to the spot where they had indications of land, and bearing E. by S. from the 15 fathom depth, at such a distance as would allow preparation for anchoring as they did; Smith estimates half an hour's lapse.

βραχὺ δὲ διαστήσαντες] Cf. v. 34; Lk. xxii. 58. The time was about half an hour: see previous note.

xxvii. 29

ἐκ πρύμνης ῥίψαντες ἀγκύρας τέσσαρας] Smith quotes from the sailing directions that in St. Paul's Bay, 'while the cables hold there is no danger, as the anchors will never start'. Here the anchors were intended to act as a brake. Casting them from the stern was an unusual procedure, but advantageous in the circumstances; for had they anchored by the bow the ship would have swung round from the wind, whereas now the prow kept pointing to the shore. Smith shows from the figure of a ship in the *Antichità di Ercolano* that this was possible, for the ship is depicted with hawse-holes aft, through which anchor-cables could be passed if required; though in ancient as in modern times the rule was *ancora de prora iacitur*. Appian (viii. 18. 123) tells how the Romans won a victory against the Carthaginians through anchoring by the stern, thus obviating the necessity of exposing the ships' weak points to the enemy in turning round. For the same reason Nelson anchored by the stern at the Battle of the Nile.

ηὔχοντο ἡμέραν γενέσθαι] Cf. Homer, *Odyssey*, ix. 151, 306, 436, ἐμείναμεν ἠῶ δῖαν. Much of the language of the *Odyssey* became part of a literary tradition in nautical matters: see on ναῦν, *ver.* 41.

(g) The Sailors' Attempt to Escape Frustrated, xxvii. 30-32

Τῶν δὲ ναυτῶν ζητούντων φυγεῖν ἐκ τοῦ πλοίου καὶ χαλασάντων 30
τὴν σκάφην εἰς τὴν θάλασσαν προφάσει ὡς ἐκ πρῴρης ἀγκύρας μελλόντων ἐκτείνειν, εἶπεν ὁ Παῦλος τῷ ἑκατοντάρχῃ καὶ τοῖς στρατιώταις 31
Ἐὰν μὴ οὗτοι μείνωσιν ἐν τῷ πλοίῳ, ὑμεῖς σωθῆναι οὐ δύνασθε.
τότε ἀπέκοψαν οἱ στρατιῶται τὰ σχοινία τῆς σκάφης καὶ εἴασαν 32
αὐτὴν ἐκπεσεῖν.

xxvii. 30

χαλασάντων τὴν σκάφην] They had taken it up in *ver.* 16. The wind must have fallen greatly to allow them now to lower it.

προφάσει ὡς . . . μελλόντων ἐκτείνειν] 'as if they were going to let out anchors from the bow'. Note *προφάσει* with *ὡς* and ptc., meaning 'as if'; for the same idea expressed by *ὡς* with the ptc. without *προφάσει* cf. xxiii. 15, 20.

xxvii. 31

εἶπεν ὁ Παῦλος κ.τ.λ.] For the third time in this narrative Paul shows outstanding presence of mind. Had the sailors made good their escape, there would not have been enough skilled hands to work the ship. As it was, all they had to do was to wait for the storm to abate, and then row ashore in the dinghy. But the soldiers seem to have misunderstood Paul's advice.

xxvii. 32

ἀπέκοψαν τὰ σχοινία τῆς σκάφης] 'cut away the falls of the dinghy'. In doing this, the soldiers took effective means to prevent the sailors escaping, but also rendered the business of getting ashore more difficult.

(h) Paul again Encourages the Ship's Company, xxvii. 33-38

Ἄχρι δὲ οὗ ἡμέρα ἤμελλεν γίνεσθαι παρεκάλει ὁ Παῦλος 33
ἅπαντας μεταλαβεῖν τροφῆς λέγων Τεσσαρεσκαιδεκάτην σήμερον
ἡμέραν προσδοκῶντες ἄσιτοι διατελεῖτε, μηθὲν προσλαβόμενοι· διὸ 34
παρακαλῶ ὑμᾶς μεταλαβεῖν τροφῆς, τοῦτο γὰρ πρὸς τῆς ὑμετέρας
σωτηρίας ὑπάρχει· οὐδενὸς γὰρ ὑμῶν θρὶξ ἀπὸ τῆς κεφαλῆς ἀπολεῖται.
εἴπας δὲ ταῦτα καὶ λαβὼν ἄρτον εὐχαρίστησεν τῷ θεῷ ἐνώπιον πάντων 35
καὶ κλάσας ἤρξατο ἐσθίειν. εὔθυμοι δὲ γενόμενοι πάντες καὶ αὐτοὶ 36
προσελάβοντο τροφῆς. ἤμεθα δὲ αἱ πᾶσαι ψυχαὶ ἐν τῷ πλοίῳ ὡς 37
ἑβδομήκοντα ἕξ. κορεσθέντες δὲ τροφῆς ἐκούφιζον τὸ πλοῖον ἐκβαλ- 38
λόμενοι τὸν σῖτον εἰς τὴν θάλασσαν.

xxvii. 33

Ἄχρι . . . οὗ] lit., ' until ' ; here probably ' when '.

παρεκάλει] Cf. *παρῄνει*, *ver*. 9.

μεταλαβεῖν τροφῆς] Cf. *ver*. 34 ; also *προσελάβοντο τροφῆς*, *ver*. 36.

Τεσσαρεσκαιδεκάτην σήμερον ἡμέραν κ.τ.λ.] An idiomatic Gk. expression, ' this is the fourteenth day that . . .'. Cf. Demosthenes, *Olynth*. iii. 4, *ἀπηγγέλθη Φίλιππος . . . τρίτον ἢ τέταρτον ἔτος τουτὶ Ἡραῖον τεῖχος πολιορκῶν*.

ἄσιτοι διατελεῖτε] ' you continue without taking food '. For the omission of *ὄντες* cf. W. G. Rutherford, *The New Phrynichus*, pp. 342 f. Like *ἀσιτία* in *ver*. 21, *ἄσιτος* implies not absence of food but abstinence from it. Cf. *εἴποτε ἄσιτος διετέλεσεν*, Galen, *On Phlebotomy* xi. 242.

μηθὲν προσλαβόμενοι] For the spelling of *μηθέν* see on xv. 9. For *προσλαβόμενοι* cf. *ver*. 36.

xxvii. 34

πρὸς τῆς ὑμετέρας σωτηρίας] This use of *πρός* with the gen. is literary, and is the one NT occurrence. Blass compares Thuc. iii. 59. 1, *οὐ πρὸς τῆς ὑμετέρας δόξης, ὦ Λακεδαιμόνιοι, τάδε*. The taking of food was essential to their health, and the physical well-being which it would promote might play its part in saving their lives.

οὐδένος γὰρ ὑμῶν θρὶξ ἀπὸ τῆς κεφαλῆς ἀπολεῖται] A proverbial expression, for which we may compare 1 Sam. xiv. 45 ; 2 Sam. xiv. 11 ; 1 K. i. 52 ; Mt. x. 30 = Lk. xii. 7 ; Lk. xxi. 18. The clause requires only the omission of *γάρ* to be a perfect hexameter.

xxvii. 35

εὐχαρίστησεν] ' he gave thanks ' ; we need not find a sacramental significance in Paul's act, though we are naturally reminded of the occasions when Jesus acted similarly : cf. Mk. vi. 41 ; viii. 6 f. ; xiv. 22 f. ; Lk. xxiv. 30. Giving thanks for one's food was a normal Jewish custom.

ἤρξατο ἐσθίειν] Semitizing use of *ἄρχομαι* (cf. ii. 4, etc.). After *ἐσθίειν* the δ text (614 1611 2147 hcl* sah) adds *ἐπιδιδοὺς καὶ ἡμῖν*. Ramsay supposes that *ἡμῖν* means Luke and Aristarchus, and that they along with Paul celebrated the Lord's Supper.

xxvii. 36

καὶ αὐτοὶ] In addition to Paul (with the δ text of *ver*. 35 it might mean ' in addition to us ').

προσελάβοντο τροφῆς] Cf. *ver*. 33, *μεταλαβεῖν τροφῆς . . . μηθὲν προσλαβόμενοι*.

xxvii. 37

ὡς ἑβδομήκοντα ἕξ] For Luke's *ὡς* with numerals see on i. 15; but *ὡς* seems out of place with so exact a statement of number. This reading (B sah) is probably to be rejected in favour of the much better attested *διακόσιοι ἑβδομήκοντα ἕξ* (*ΠΛΟΙΩΩCΟF* could easily have arisen out of *ΠΛΟΙΩCΟF*). There is no improbability in the larger number; Josephus set sail for Rome in a ship which had 600 on board (*Vita*, 3). Breusing thinks the number is mentioned at this point because the food had to be rationed. We should certainly look for no significance in the fact that 276 is the sum of all whole numbers from 1 to 23 inclusive (for such 'triangular numbers' cf. 120 in i. 15; 153 in Jn. xxi. 11; 666 in Rev. xiii. 18).

xxvii. 38

ἐκβαλλόμενοι τὸν σῖτον] For *σῖτον* S. A. Naber conjectured *ἱστόν*, 'mainmast' (*Mnemosyne* ix. [1881], p. 293; xxiii. p. 269), because the cargo had already been jettisoned (*ver.* 18). But they must have kept some as food and to serve as ballast. Now, however, it was desirable that the ship should draw as little water as possible, and so run aground well up the beach.

(i) The Shipwreck, xxvii. 39-41

Ὅτε δὲ ἡμέρα ἐγένετο, τὴν γῆν οὐκ ἐπεγίνωσκον, κόλπον δέ τινα 39
κατενόουν ἔχοντα αἰγιαλὸν εἰς ὃν ἐβουλεύοντο εἰ δύναιντο ἐκσῶσαι
τὸ πλοῖον. καὶ τὰς ἀγκύρας περιελόντες εἴων εἰς τὴν θάλασσαν, ἅμα 40
ἀνέντες τὰς ζευκτηρίας τῶν πηδαλίων, καὶ ἐπάραντες τὸν ἀρτέμωνα
τῇ πνεούσῃ κατεῖχον εἰς τὸν αἰγιαλόν. περιπεσόντες δὲ εἰς τόπον 41
διθάλασσον ἐπέκειλαν τὴν ναῦν, καὶ ἡ μὲν πρῷρα ἐρείσασα ἔμεινεν
ἀσάλευτος, ἡ δὲ πρύμνα ἐλύετο ὑπὸ τῆς βίας.

xxvii. 39

κόλπον δέ τινα κατενόουν ἔχοντα αἰγιαλὸν] 'but they noticed a creek with a sandy beach'. The combination of this creek with the 'rocky places' of *ver.* 29 and the 'place between two seas' of *ver.* 41 agrees, as Smith demonstrated, with St. Paul's Bay. He points out that the west side of the bay, though rocky, has two creeks, and while the creek which best suits the description here has now no sandy beach, it is very likely that it has been 'worn away by the wasting action of the sea'.

κατενόουν] Imperf.; perhaps one after another of them noticed.

εἰ δύναιντο] Classical use of opt. in historic sequence for *ἐὰν δυνώμεθα* of direct speech.

ἐκσῶσαι] B C minn sah boh arm. The homophone *ἐξῶσαι* (from *ἐξωθέω*), the reading of ℵ A B² 81 byz g vg, is to be preferred as a more natural expression for running a ship ashore (as, e.g., in Thuc. ii. 90. 5).

xxvii. 40

τὰς ἀγκύρας περιελόντες] 'weighing anchor'; take *περί* as intensive (MH ii. p. 321). See on xxviii. 13. If we take the verb here in the same sense as in *ver.* 20, the meaning would be 'slipping anchors'.

ἅμα ἀνέντες τὰς ζευκτηρίας τῶν πηδαλίων] 'while at the same time they unleashed the lashings of the steering-paddles'; in ancient ships steering-paddles served as rudders. In papyri the word *ζευκτηρίαι* is used for yokes and for straps in connection with water-wheels.

ἐπάραντες τὸν ἀρτέμωνα] 'hoisting the foresail'. Juvenal (*Sat.* xii. 68 f.) describes the entry of a disabled ship into harbour thus:

> *uestibus extentis et, quod superauerat unum,*
> *uelo prora suo—*

on which a scholiast says, '*Vestibus: funibus aut uestibus uelis accipe aut quod dicunt artemonem. Velo: id est artemone solo uelificauerunt*'. This is by far the earliest instance of the word in Gk.; it was used in mediaeval Italian for the foresail, in Fr. for the mizzen. It was probably a small sail on the foremast. Cf. S. A. Naber in *Mnemosyne* xxiii. (1895), p. 269: '*ἀρτέμωνα, quo nomine tunc Graeci appellabant uelum minus in anteriore nauis parte, quo uelo non augetur celeritas, sed dirigitur cursus*'.

τῇ πνεούσῃ] Sc. *αὔρᾳ*.

xxvii. 41

περιπεσόντες] 'coming upon', frequently of an unpleasant surprise.

εἰς τόπον διθάλασσον] 'into a place between two seas', identified by Smith with the narrow channel between Malta and the island of Salmonetta, which shelters St. Paul's Bay on the N.W.

ἐπέκειλαν τὴν ναῦν] 'they ran the ship aground'. For *ἐπέκειλαν* (from *ἐπικέλλω*), B² byz have *ἐπώκειλαν* (from *ἐποκέλλω*). Elsewhere in the chapter the ship is called *πλοῖον*; this is the only NT occurrence of *ναῦς*. The use of the classical but obsolete *ναῦς* here is plausibly ascribed to a Homeric reminiscence; cf. *Odyssey*, ix. 148 (*νῆας . . . ἐπικέλσαι*), 546 (*νῆα . . . ἐκέλσαμεν*). The verb *ἐπικέλλω* is also poetical. 'Must we not accept it for a certainty that Luke, the physician of Antioch, had gone through his Homer?'

(Blass, *PG*, p. 186; and cf. his commentary *ad loc.*). See on *ver.* 29 for another parallel to *Odyssey* ix. After ναῦν hcl* adds 'on a place where there was a quicksand'.

ἡ μὲν πρῷρα ἐρείσασα] Cf. Pindar, *Isthm.* i. 36, ἐρειδόμενον ναυαγίαις. Smith explains that a ship driven by a gale into a creek such as those in St. Paul's Bay would strike a bottom of mud graduating into tenacious clay, in which the forepart would stick fast while the stern would be exposed to the force of the waves.

ἐλύετο] 'began to be broken up'.

ὑπὸ τῆς βίας] ℵ^{c} C 33 81 byz boh add τῶν κυμάτων, g vg add *maris;* sah adds 'of the wind'.

(j) They all get safe to Land, xxvii. 42-44

Τῶν δὲ στρατιωτῶν βουλὴ ἐγένετο ἵνα τοὺς δεσμώτας ἀποκτείνωσιν, 42
μή τις ἐκκολυμβήσας διαφύγῃ· ὁ δὲ ἑκατοντάρχης βουλόμενος δια- 43
σῶσαι τὸν Παῦλον ἐκώλυσεν αὐτοὺς τοῦ βουλήματος, ἐκέλευσέν τε
τοὺς δυναμένους κολυμβᾶν ἀπορίψαντας πρώτους ἐπὶ τὴν γῆν ἐξιέναι,
καὶ τοὺς λοιποὺς οὓς μὲν ἐπὶ σανίσιν οὓς δὲ ἐπί τινων τῶν ἀπὸ τοῦ 44
πλοίου· καὶ οὕτως ἐγένετο πάντας διασωθῆναι ἐπὶ τὴν γῆν.

xxvii. 42

Τῶν δὲ στρατιωτῶν βουλὴ ἐγένετο] g *tunc cogitauerunt milites,* which probably implies a δ text with the characteristic τότε.

βουλὴ] 'plan'.

xxvii. 43

ὁ δὲ ἑκατοντάρχης κ.τ.λ.] This verse and the following appear in g thus: *centurio autem prohibuit hoc fieri praecipue propter Paulum ut saluum illum faceret. Et iussit illos qui possent enatare primos exire ad terram et reliquos quosdam in tabulis saluos fieri. Et sic omnes animae saluae ad terram uenerunt.* This probably represents a δ text: ὁ δὲ ἑκατοντάρχης ἐκώλυσε τοῦτο γενέσθαι μάλιστα διὰ τὸν Παῦλον, ἵνα αὐτὸν διασώσῃ. ἐκέλευσέν τε τοὺς δυναμένους κολυμβᾶν πρώτους ἐπὶ τὴν γῆν ἐξιέναι, καὶ τοὺς λοιπούς τινας ἐπὶ σανίσιν διασωθῆναι, καὶ οὕτως πᾶσαι αἱ ψυχαὶ διεσώθησαν ἐπὶ τὴν γῆν.

βουλήματος] 'purpose': cf. βουλή, *ver.* 42.

ἀπορίψαντας] 'leaping off'; intrans., like ῥίπτω in poetry and late writers.

xxvii. 44

σανίσιν] 'planks'; Breusing and Blass think their purpose had been to keep the cargo in place. Blass compares Galen, *Therapeutic*

Method, x. 377: κυβερνήτῃ δι' ἀμέλειαν περιτρέψαντι τὸ πλοῖον εἶτ' ἐγχειρίζοντι σανίδα τῶν πλωτήρων τινί, καὶ συμβουλεύοντι διὰ ταύτης πορίζεσθαι τὴν σωτηρίαν. Cf. Xenophon Ephes. ii. 11 (ἐναντίῳ δὲ πνεύματι κατεχόμενοι καὶ τῆς νεὼς διαρραγείσης μόλις ἐν σανίδι τινὲς σωθέντες ἐπ' αἰγιαλοῦ τινος ἦλθον); *Anth. Pal.* vii. 289,

Ἀνθέα τὸν ναυηγὸν ἐπὶ στόμα Πηνειοῖο
νυκτὸς ὑπὲρ βαιῆς νηξάμενον σανίδος.

ἐπί τινων τῶν ἀπὸ τοῦ πλοίου] 'on some of the (things) from the ship'; or, conceivably, 'on some of the (people) from the ship', i.e., on the backs of the crew. Observe that τινῶν is gen., while σανίσιν is dat. For τινὲς τῶν ἀπό cf. xii. 1; xv. 5.

καὶ οὕτως ἐγένετο πάντας διασωθῆναι ἐπὶ τὴν γῆν] 'and so it turned out that all got safely to land'. For ἐγένετο with acc. and infin. see on iv. 5.

7. In Malta, xxviii. 1-10

(a) Welcome at Malta; Paul and the Viper, xxviii. 1-6

Καὶ διασωθέντες τότε ἐπέγνωμεν ὅτι Μελιτήνη ἡ νῆσος καλεῖται. 1
οἵ τε βάρβαροι παρεῖχαν οὐ τὴν τυχοῦσαν φιλανθρωπίαν ἡμῖν, ἅψαντες 2
γὰρ πυρὰν προσελάβοντο πάντας ἡμᾶς διὰ τὸν ὑετὸν τὸν ἐφεστῶτα καὶ
διὰ τὸ ψύχος. συστρέψαντος δὲ τοῦ Παύλου φρυγάνων τι πλῆθος 3
καὶ ἐπιθέντος ἐπὶ τὴν πυράν, ἔχιδνα ἀπὸ τῆς θέρμης ἐξελθοῦσα καθῆψε
τῆς χειρὸς αὐτοῦ. ὡς δὲ εἶδαν οἱ βάρβαροι κρεμάμενον τὸ θηρίον 4
ἐκ τῆς χειρὸς αὐτοῦ, πρὸς ἀλλήλους ἔλεγον Πάντως φονεύς ἐστιν ὁ
ἄνθρωπος οὗτος ὃν διασωθέντα ἐκ τῆς θαλάσσης ἡ δίκη ζῆν οὐκ εἴασεν.
ὁ μὲν οὖν ἀποτινάξας τὸ θηρίον εἰς τὸ πῦρ ἔπαθεν οὐδὲν κακόν· οἱ 5 6
δὲ προσεδόκων αὐτὸν μέλλειν πίμπρασθαι ἢ καταπίπτειν ἄφνω νεκρόν.
ἐπὶ πολὺ δὲ αὐτῶν προσδοκώντων καὶ θεωρούντων μηδὲν ἄτοπον εἰς
αὐτὸν γινόμενον, μεταβαλόμενοι ἔλεγον αὐτὸν εἶναι θεόν.

xxviii. 1

ἐπέγνωμεν ὅτι Μελιτήνη ἡ νῆσος καλεῖται] Μελιτήνη is the reading of B* g vg hcl.mg.gr boh arm; but Μελίτη, the reading of the other authorities, ℵ A B [2.3] C byz vg.codd pesh hcl sah eth, is probably to be preferred. Μελιτήνη (prob. the adj. from Μελίτη) may have arisen by dittography, *ΜΕΛΙΤΗΝΗΗΝΗCOC* for *ΜΕΛΙΤΗΗΝΗCOC* (the reverse process would be due to haplography). The island is, of course, Malta; the idea that it is Meleda off the Dalmatian coast (called Μελιτήνη by Ptolemy, ii. 16. 9) is due to a misunderstanding of 'Adria' in xxvii. 27. Euraquilo could not have driven them to Dalmatia.

If the sailors did not recognize the island at first, this may have been because they were accustomed to landing at Valetta.

J. R. Harris (*ET*, xxi. [1909-10], p. 18) suggested an allusion to the meaning of the island's Phoenician name *mĕlīṭā* ('refuge', 'escape'): 'we recognized that the island deserved its name'.

xxviii. 2

οἱ βάρβαροι] 'the natives'. The use of *βάρβαρος* is a characteristic mark of Greek authorship. The Maltese were not uncivilized; they had been for many centuries in touch with the Phoenicians and Romans. They were of Phoenician extraction and spoke a Phoenician dialect; hence they were *βάρβαροι* to the Greeks. (Mod. Maltese is an Arabic dialect.)

παρεῖχαν] For the ending *-αν* for 3rd plur. imperf. (ℵ A B), cf. viii. 10 (ℵ); xxviii. 6 (B).

οὐ τὴν τυχοῦσαν] 'no ordinary', i.e., extraordinary. For the same litotes cf. xix. 11.

φιλανθρωπίαν] Cf. *φιλανθρώπως*, xxvii. 3.

πυρὰν] 'a bonfire', of brushwood in the open.

προσελάβοντο πάντας ἡμᾶς] 'brought us all to it'. It is better, with Ropes, to read *προσανελάμβανον* (ℵ Ψ 614 1518 minn; cf. vg *reficiebant*), 'they refreshed us'.

τὸν ἐφεστῶτα] 'impending', or better, 'which had set in'.

xxviii. 3

συστρέψαντος] 'twisting together'. Paul can make himself useful in small matters as in great. The Maltese had got the fire going; he will help to keep it going.

φρυγάνων τι πλῆθος] 'a bundle of brushwood'.

ἔχιδνα κ.τ.λ.] Cf. T. E. Lawrence, *Revolt in the Desert*, p. 107;

> 'When the fire grew hot a long black snake wound slowly out into our group; we must have gathered it, torpid, with the twigs.'

There are now no poisonous snakes in Malta. It has been suggested that this was *coronella austriaca*, which looks like a viper (*ἔχιδνα*), but is not poisonous (cf. Ramsay, *Luke the Physician*, pp. 63 ff.). There may, however, have been vipers there in Paul's time. (So, in Ireland, there were snakes before Patrick, but none, we are told, since his day.)

ἀπὸ τῆς θέρμης] 'from the heat'; the only NT example of *θέρμη*, which was used by Hippocrates, Thucydides, Plato, Aristotle and others both in this sense and in the sense of 'feverish heat'.

καθῆψε] 'fastened'; active used with genitive. This meaning will suit *coronella austriaca*. LC insist on the meaning 'bit' (so Blass, *momordit*), as vipers do not coil. Dioscorides uses *καθάπτομαι* of poisonous matter invading the body; cf. Galen, *Medicus*, 13 (Hobart, pp. 288 f.). Cf. also Harnack, *LP*, p. 177.

xxviii. 4

θηρίον] Common in Mod. Gk. for a snake (lit., 'wild beast', as in Rev. xiii. 2).

'St. Luke used this word here exactly in the same way as the medical writers, who employed it to denote venomous serpents, and of these they applied it in particular to the viper (ἔχιδνα), so much so that an antidote, made chiefly from the flesh of vipers, was termed θηριακή' (Hobart, p. 51). Cf. Harnack, *op. cit.*, p. 178.

πάντως] 'of course': cf. xxi. 22.

φονεύς ἐστιν ὁ ἄνθρωπος οὗτος] *Anth. Pal.* vii. 290 tells of one who, escaping from a storm at sea, was shipwrecked on the Libyan coast and killed by a viper.

δίκη] 'Justice'. The Maltese may have referred to a goddess of their own, whose native name Luke replaces by Dikē, just as the names of the Lycaonian deities in xiv. 12 are replaced by Zeus and Hermes.

xxviii. 6

προσεδόκων] Imperf.; they stood watching him for some time.

πίμπρασθαι] 'to swell'; this word, 'peculiar to St. Luke [in NT], was the usual medical word for inflammation' (Hobart, p. 50). See on πρηνής, i. 18.

μηδὲν ἄτοπον εἰς αὐτὸν γινόμενον] Only here and at xxiii. 29 do we find in NT μή with ptc. in indirect speech. μηδὲν ἄτοπον (or οὐδὲν ἄτοπον, Lk. xxiii. 41) 'must also be noted—a phrase used by St. Luke alone among the evangelists. It is used by physicians not only to describe something unusual, but also to describe something fatal[1] . . . the whole section xxviii. 3-6 is tinged with medical colouring' (Harnack, *LP*, p. 179).

ἔλεγον αὐτὸν εἶναι θεόν] 'they began to say (imperf.) that he was a god'. The sudden reversal of opinion about Paul may be compared and contrasted with the attitude of the Lycaonians in xiv. 11 ff., who first acclaimed him as a god, and later nearly stoned him to death. There may be a reflection of this incident in the long Markan appendix (ὄφεις ἀροῦσιν, Mk. xvi. 18).

(b) Deeds of Healing in Malta, xxviii. 7-10

Ἐν δὲ τοῖς περὶ τὸν τόπον ἐκεῖνον ὑπῆρχεν χωρία τῷ πρώτῳ τῆς 7
νήσου ὀνόματι Ποπλίῳ, ὃς ἀναδεξάμενος ἡμᾶς ἡμέρας τρεῖς φιλοφρόνως
ἐξένισεν. ἐγένετο δὲ τὸν πατέρα τοῦ Ποπλίου πυρετοῖς καὶ δυσεν- 8
τερίῳ συνεχόμενον κατακεῖσθαι, πρὸς ὃν ὁ Παῦλος εἰσελθὼν καὶ προσευξάμενος ἐπιθεὶς τὰς χεῖρας αὐτῷ ἰάσατο αὐτόν. τούτου δὲ 9

[1] It is, of course, the adjective ἄτοπον itself which has the sense 'unusual' or 'fatal'.

γενομένου καὶ οἱ λοιποὶ οἱ ἐν τῇ νήσῳ ἔχοντες ἀσθενείας προσήρχοντο καὶ ἐθεραπεύοντο, οἳ καὶ πολλαῖς τιμαῖς ἐτίμησαν ἡμᾶς καὶ ἀναγομένοις ἐπέθεντο τὰ πρὸς τὰς χρείας.

xxviii. 7

Ἐν δὲ τοῖς περὶ τὸν τόπον κ.τ.λ.] 'In the district round that place there was an estate belonging to the chief man of the island'.

τῷ πρώτῳ τῆς νήσου] The appropriateness of this title in a Maltese context is evidenced by the inscriptions: *Κα[στρί]κιος Κυρ(είνᾳ) Πούδηνς ἱππεὺς Ῥωμ(αίων) πρῶτος Μελιταίων καὶ πάτρων, ἄρξας καὶ ἀμφιπολεύσας θεῷ Αὐγούστῳ*, *IG*, xiv. 601; [*munic*]*ipii Mel*(*itensium*) *primus omni*[*um*], *CIL*, x. 7495.

Ποπλίῳ] The Gk. form of Publius. Luke, a Greek, has little time for the technicalities of Roman nomenclature (so Polybius regularly calls P. Cornelius Scipio simply *Πόπλιος*). Ramsay suggests that the peasantry on the estate called Publius by his *praenomen*, and that Luke uses the name he commonly heard.

xxviii. 8

ἐγένετο δὲ] Followed by acc. and infin. without a temporal clause, as in xxvii. 44.

πυρετοῖς] 'fever', i.e., gastric fever. The plur. may imply 'attacks of intermittent fever' (Hobart, p. 52). 'Malta has always a peculiarly unpleasant fever of its own' (LC).

δυσεντερίῳ] 'dysentery' (having trouble in the *ἔντερα*). The form in *-ιον* is later than that in *-ία* (Moeris, the second century A.D. grammarian, calls the former Hellenistic and the latter Attic), and is perhaps due to the influence of *μεσεντέριον*. In Hippocrates *δυσεντερία* is often joined with *πυρετός* (Hobart, *ib.*).

συνεχόμενον] Cf. Lk. iv. 38, *συνεχομένη πυρετῷ μεγάλῳ*, for the less technical *πυρέσσουσα* of Mk. i. 30 = Mt. viii. 14.

προσευξάμενος ἐπιθεὶς τὰς χεῖρας αὐτῷ] For the imposition of hands in healing cf. ix. 17; Lk. iv. 40; Mk. xvi. 18; see also vi. 6 and xiii. 3 for prayer as an accompaniment to the laying on of hands.

ἰάσατο] 'healed': see on *ἐθεραπεύοντο*, *ver.* 9.

xxviii. 9

ἐθεραπεύοντο] 'were tended', 'were treated'; contrast aor. *ἰάσατο* in *ver.* 8. Harnack (*LP*, p. 16) suggests that they received medical attention from Luke (cf. *ἡμᾶς*, *ver.* 10).

xxviii. 10

τιμαῖς] 'honours' or 'fees'? The latter suits the medical context; cf. the ambiguity in 1 Tim. v. 17; Sir. xxxviii. 1 (*τίμα* ἰατρὸν πρὸς τὰς χρείας τιμαῖς αὐτοῦ, a passage remarkably similar to this) ; Cicero, *Fam.* xvi. 9. 3, '*ut medico honos haberetur*'.

ἡμᾶς] Harnack (*ib.*) suggests that the absence of an expressed agent with ἐθεραπεύοντο in the previous verse prepares the way for ἡμᾶς here. After his remarks on the medical colouring of *vv.* 3-6, he adds, 'and seeing that in verses 7-10 both subject-matter and phraseology are medical, therefore the whole story of the abode of the narrator in Malta is displayed in a medical light' (*LP*, p. 179).

ἐπέθεντο] 'bestowed on us' or 'put on board'; hcl* understands the latter, adding 'in the ship' (perhaps representing δ).

8. ROME ! xxviii. 11-31

(a) The Last Lap ; "And so we came to Rome," xxviii. 11-15

Μετὰ δὲ τρεῖς μῆνας ἀνήχθημεν ἐν πλοίῳ παρακεχειμακότι ἐν τῇ 11
νήσῳ Ἀλεξανδρινῷ, παρασήμῳ Διοσκούροις. καὶ καταχθέντες εἰς 12
Συρακούσας ἐπεμείναμεν ἡμέρας τρεῖς, ὅθεν περιελόντες κατηντή- 13
σαμεν εἰς Ῥήγιον. καὶ μετὰ μίαν ἡμέραν ἐπιγενομένου νότου
δευτεραῖοι ἤλθομεν εἰς Ποτιόλους, οὗ εὑρόντες ἀδελφοὺς παρεκλήθημεν 14
παρ' αὐτοῖς ἐπιμεῖναι ἡμέρας ἑπτά· καὶ οὕτως εἰς τὴν Ῥώμην
ἤλθαμεν. κἀκεῖθεν οἱ ἀδελφοὶ ἀκούσαντες τὰ περὶ ἡμῶν ἦλθαν εἰς 15
ἀπάντησιν ἡμῖν ἄχρι Ἀππίου Φόρου καὶ Τριῶν Ταβερνῶν, οὓς ἰδὼν
ὁ Παῦλος εὐχαριστήσας τῷ θεῷ ἔλαβε θάρσος.

xxviii. 11

μετὰ δὲ τρεῖς μῆνας] i.e., in Feb., A.D. 60. Pliny (*NH*, ii. 122) says that the seas are re-opened to navigation in spring, which commences when the west winds (*fauonii*) begin to blow on February 8; Vegetius (*de re mil.* iv. 39) says the seas are closed till March 10. In actual practice, the state of the weather would determine the date. For the influence of the seasons of navigation on Paul's movements cf. xx. 3; xxvii. 9; 1 Cor. xvi. 6 ff.; Tit. iii. 12; 2 Tim. iv. 21; see also Jos. *BJ*, ii. 10. 5.

ἐν πλοίῳ . . . Ἀλεξανδρινῷ] 'in an Alexandrian ship which had wintered in the island', probably in the harbour of Valetta. It presumably belonged to the same grain-fleet as the ship which they boarded at Myra (xxvii. 6).

παρασήμῳ Διοσκούροις] 'having as its figurehead the Heavenly Twins'. Plutarch (*Symp.* 162 A) seems to distinguish παράσημος from ὄνομα. Blass, however, points out that ships, like inns, took their names from their figureheads. Ramsay suggests that the name was the first thing Luke learned of the ship, when news came across the island that the *Dioskouroi* was in harbour at Valetta. The *Dioskouroi* (' sons of Zeus '), Castor and Pollux, were patrons of navigation, and were commonly worshipped by sailors, receiving invocations and vows in bad weather. Their constellation (Gemini) was a sign of good fortune in a storm (Horace, *Odes*, i. 3. 2; iii. 29. 64).

xxviii. 12

Συρακούσας] Syracuse, the famous port on the east coast of Sicily, with two harbours, was the chief city of the island. It was founded as a Corinthian colony in 734 B.C., and had been Roman since 212 B.C.

ἐπεμείναμεν ἡμέρας τρεῖς] The delay may have been caused by the wind falling. B has *ἡμέραις τρισίν*.

xxviii. 13

περιελόντες] ℵ B g (*et inde tulimus et*). This seems to be a technical nautical term whose meaning we cannot determine; it may be a shorter expression for *τὰς ἀγκύρας περιελόντες* (as in xxvii. 40, *q.v.*), ' weighing anchor ', ' casting loose '. Uncertainty of the meaning of *περιελόντες* seems to have given rise to the variant *περιελθόντες* of ℵ[c] A 066 33 81 byz (' sailing round ' or ' tacking '), as if referring to the sharp angle to be turned in getting through the straits of Messina. The (south ?) wind which had brought them from Malta had fallen, and tacking was now necessary (in a N.W. wind?); good seamanship, however, got them to Rhegium, and after a day there, a south wind rose again, and they crossed to Puteoli.

Ῥήγιον] Rhegium (mod. Reggio di Calabria) was a Greek colony in the toe of Italy, about 6 or 7 miles across the strait from Messana (Messina) in Sicily. Its harbour was important because of its position on the strait.

δευτεραῖοι] ' on the second day ': cf. *πεμπταῖοι*, xx. 6 D.

Ποτιόλους] Puteoli (mod. Pozzuoli), in the Bay of Naples, was the principal port in S. Italy, and an important emporium, especially for eastern trade. It was one of the chief ports of arrival of the Alexandrian grain fleet (the other being Ostia). In such an important seaport it is not surprising that Christians were to be found. The Jewish community of Puteoli was apparently the oldest in Italy after that of Rome; we find Jews there in 4 B.C. (Jos. *BJ*, ii. 7. 1; *Ant*. xvii. 12. 1).

xxviii. 14

παρεκλήθημεν] ' we were invited '.

καὶ οὕτως εἰς τὴν Ῥώμην ἤλθαμεν] Ramsay distinguishes the meaning of Rome here from that in *ver*. 16 by supposing that the reference here is to the wider area of the *ager Romanus* (cf. also D. Plooij in *ET*, xxiv [1912-13], p. 186). This is an unnecessary and untenable distinction (see next note). Luke first states the fact of their arrival in Rome, and then goes back to relate what happened on the way there.

xxviii. 15

κἀκεῖθεν] 'and from there', i.e., from the Rome of *ver.* 14, which must therefore be the city proper, as Appii Forum and Tres Tabernae lay within the *ager Romanus*.

ἦλθαν εἰς ἀπάντησιν ἡμῖν] *ἀπάντησις* appears to have been a sort of technical term for the official welcome of a newly arrived dignitary by a deputation which went out from the city to greet him and to escort him there; there is thus deep significance in the use of this word to describe the welcome received by Paul from the Roman church. Cf. Mt. xxv. 6; 1 Th. iv. 17, and the synonymous *εἰς ὑπάντησιν* in Mt. viii. 34; xxv. 1; Jn. xii. 13. (In LXX *εἰς ἀπάντησιν* is used more widely as a convenient literal rendering of Heb. *liqra'th.*) See MM, and *Proleg.*, pp. 14, 242. Cf. Cicero, *Att.* viii. 16. 2; xvi. 11. 6.

Ἀππίου Φόρου] Appii Forum, a market town about 43 miles from Rome on the Appian Way. Cf. Horace, *Sat.* i. 5. 3,

inde Forum Appi
differtum nautis, cauponibus atque malignis.

Τριῶν Ταβερνῶν] 'The Three Taverns' (*Tres Tabernae*), i.e., shops or huts. This was a station on the Appian Way about 33 miles from Rome, mentioned along with Appii Forum by Cicero (*Att.* ii. 10).

ἔλαβε θάρσος] He might well be encouraged by this assurance that he was by no means friendless in the Eternal City. He had long had a desire to go there (cf. xix. 21); he had communicated to the Roman Christians the exposition of his Gospel about three years previously; now his prayer was granted and, in circumstances unforeseen when he wrote his epistle, he saw them face to face.

(b) Paul handed over to be kept under Guard, xxviii. 16

Ὅτε δὲ εἰσήλθαμεν εἰς Ῥώμην, ἐπετράπη τῷ Παύλῳ μένειν καθ' 16
ἑαυτὸν σὺν τῷ φυλάσσοντι αὐτὸν στρατιώτῃ.

xxviii. 16

Ὅτε δὲ εἰσήλθαμεν εἰς Ῥώμην] See on *ver.* 14. He must have entered the city by the Porta Capena. With this clause the third 'we' section of Ac. comes to an end.

ἐπετράπη τῷ Παύλῳ] δ (reprd. by 614˺ byz g p vg.codd hcl* sah eth) has *ὁ ἑκατόνταρχος παρέδωκε τοὺς δεσμίους τῷ στρατοπεδάρχῳ, τῷ δὲ Παύλῳ ἐπετράπη*. According to Mommsen, followed by Ramsay, the stratopedarch was the *princeps peregrinorum* (so g), the commander of the *castra peregrinorum* on the Caelian hill, where the *frumentarii* (see on xxvii. 1) resided when they were in Rome. The *frumentarii* and all officials of the *castra peregrinorum*, including the *princeps*, were of centurial rank (see *BC*, v. p. 444). Another explanation is that this stratopedarch was the praetorian prefect, to whom prisoners from the provinces were handed over. Cf. Pliny, *Ep*. x. 57, where Trajan directs Pliny to send a prisoner in chains to the prefects of the praetorian guard. The *praefectus praetorii* from 51 to 62 was the honest Afranius Burrus.

καθ' αὑτόν] δ (614 1611 2147 g p vg.codd Ambst hcl*) adds *ἔξω τῆς παρεμβολῆς* (cf. Heb. xiii. 11; Lev. xvi. 27).

σὺν τῷ φυλάσσοντι αὐτὸν στρατιώτῃ] To whom he would be lightly chained by the wrist, with the *ἅλυσις* to which he refers in *ver*. 20. Mommsen (*Römisches Strafrecht*, p. 317) points out that the Digest contrasts *militi tradere* (or *committere*) with *carceri* or *uinculis tradere*. Cf. *ὑπὸ στρατιώτην ὄντα*, *BGU*, 151.

(c) Paul's First Interview with the Roman Jews, xxviii. 17-22

Ἐγένετο δὲ μετὰ ἡμέρας τρεῖς συνκαλέσασθαι αὐτὸν τοὺς ὄντας τῶν 17
Ἰουδαίων πρώτους· συνελθόντων δὲ αὐτῶν ἔλεγεν πρὸς αὐτούς
Ἐγώ, ἄνδρες ἀδελφοί, οὐδὲν ἐναντίον ποιήσας τῷ λαῷ ἢ τοῖς ἔθεσι
τοῖς πατρῴοις δέσμιος ἐξ Ἰεροσολύμων παρεδόθην εἰς τὰς χεῖρας τῶν
Ῥωμαίων, οἵτινες ἀνακρίναντές με ἐβούλοντο ἀπολῦσαι διὰ τὸ μηδε- 18
μίαν αἰτίαν θανάτου ὑπάρχειν ἐν ἐμοί· ἀντιλεγόντων δὲ τῶν Ἰουδαίων 19
ἠναγκάσθην ἐπικαλέσασθαι Καίσαρα, οὐχ ὡς τοῦ ἔθνους μου ἔχων
τι κατηγορεῖν. διὰ ταύτην οὖν τὴν αἰτίαν παρεκάλεσα ὑμᾶς ἰδεῖν 20
καὶ προσλαλῆσαι, εἵνεκεν γὰρ τῆς ἐλπίδος τοῦ Ἰσραὴλ τὴν ἅλυσιν
ταύτην περίκειμαι. οἱ δὲ πρὸς αὐτὸν εἶπαν Ἡμεῖς οὔτε γράμματα 21
περὶ σοῦ ἐδεξάμεθα ἀπὸ τῆς Ἰουδαίας, οὔτε παραγενόμενός τις τῶν
ἀδελφῶν ἀπήγγειλεν ἢ ἐλάλησέν τι περὶ σοῦ πονηρόν. ἀξιοῦμεν δὲ 22
παρὰ σοῦ ἀκοῦσαι ἃ φρονεῖς, περὶ μὲν γὰρ τῆς αἱρέσεως ταύτης γνωστὸν
ἡμῖν ἐστὶν ὅτι πανταχοῦ ἀντιλέγεται.

xxviii. 17

τοὺς ὄντας] See on v. 17; xiii. 1.

τοὺς ὄντας τῶν Ἰουδαίων πρώτους] Cf. xxv. 2, *οἱ πρῶτοι τῶν Ἰουδαίων*.

ἔλεγεν] 'he proceeded to say'.

ἄνδρες ἀδελφοί] For this address to Jews, cf. ii. 29, etc.

οὐδὲν ἐναντίον ποιήσας κ.τ.λ.] Cf. xxiv. 12 ff. ; xxv. 8.

τοῖς ἔθεσι τοῖς πατρῴοις] Cf. xxiv. 14.

παρεδόθην εἰς τὰς χεῖρας τῶν Ῥωμαίων] 'I was handed over into the hands of the Romans' : cf. xxi. 11 ; also the words of Jesus, *ὁ γὰρ υἱὸς τοῦ ἀνθρώπου μέλλει παραδίδοσθαι εἰς χεῖρας ἀνθρώπων*, Lk. ix. 44 ; *παραδοθήσεται γὰρ τοῖς ἔθνεσιν*, Lk. xviii. 32. In Paul's case the handing over was unwilling.

xxviii. 18

οἵτινες ἀνακρίναντές με] After *οἵτινες* the δ text (614 2147 hcl*) adds *πολλά*. With *ἀνακρίναντες* cf. xxiv. 8.

ἐβούλοντο ἀπολῦσαι] Cf. iii. 13.

διὰ τὸ μηδεμίαν αἰτίαν θανάτου ὑπάρχειν ἐν ἐμοί] Cf. xxv. 18 ; also xiii. 28.

xxviii. 19

ἀντιλεγόντων δὲ τῶν Ἰουδαίων] 614 1518 hcl* (probably representing δ) add *καὶ ἐπικραζόντων· Αἶρε τὸν ἐχθρὸν ἡμῶν*.

οὐχ ὡς τοῦ ἔθνους μου ἔχων τι κατηγορεῖν] He insists that he is strictly on his defence ; he has no complaint to make against his people (for *ἔθνος* see on xxiv. 10). The δ text (614 1518 minn g p vg.codd hcl*) adds *ἀλλ' ἵνα λυτρώσωμαι τὴν ψυχήν μου ἐκ θανάτου*.

xxviii. 20

παρεκάλεσα ὑμᾶς ἰδεῖν καὶ προσλαλῆσαι] 'I invited you that I might see you and talk to you' (*ὑμᾶς* is probably the object both of *παρεκάλεσα* and of *ἰδεῖν καὶ προσλαλῆσαι*).

τῆς ἐλπίδος τοῦ Ἰσραήλ] The expectation of the Messiah, and the belief in resurrection which, for Paul, was so closely bound up with it. See on xxiii. 6 ; xxvi. 6 ff.

τὴν ἅλυσιν ταύτην περίκειμαι] See on *ver.* 16 ; xxi. 33.

xxviii. 21

Ἡμεῖς οὔτε γράμματα περὶ σοῦ ἐδεξάμεθα κ.τ.λ.] It may be surprising that the Jerusalem authorities had made no communication to the Roman Jews about Paul, but that is no reason for rejecting the truth of this statement. It is, indeed, doubtful whether they communicated with Rome at all about Paul, probably realizing that if they could not proceed successfully against him before provincial magistrates, there was still less hope of success before the supreme court of the Empire. Roman law was severe on unsuccessful prosecutors ; it is likely, therefore, that they allowed the case to go by default (see on *ver.* 30).

τῶν ἀδελφῶν] 'of our brethren', i.e., the Jerusalem Jews.

ἀπήγγειλεν ἢ ἐλάλησεν] 'reported (officially) or spoke (unofficially)'. The Roman Jews were probably anxious to have as little as possible to do with the prosecution of a Roman citizen who had received favourable verdicts from Festus and Agrippa.

xxviii. 22

περὶ μὲν γὰρ τῆς αἱρέσεως ταύτης γνωστὸν ἡμῖν ἐστιν ὅτι πανταχοῦ ἀντιλέγεται] 'This much we do indeed know about this party, that it is everywhere spoken against'. For αἵρεσις used of the Christians cf. xxiv. 5. No doubt they had had some experience of Christians in Rome itself. There were Christians in Rome from a very early date (the Gospel was perhaps taken back there by some of the 'visitors from Rome' present in Jerusalem on the Day of Pentecost, ii. 10). It has also been inferred from the terms in which Suetonius describes Claudius's decree of banishment against the Roman Jews (see on xviii. 2) that the cause of the trouble was a dispute between Christian and non-Christian Jews. At any rate, the Jewish leaders whom Paul met now were obviously unwilling to commit themselves on the question.

(d) Paul's Second Interview with the Roman Jews, xxviii. 23-29

Ταξάμενοι δὲ αὐτῷ ἡμέραν ἦλθαν πρὸς αὐτὸν εἰς τὴν ξενίαν 23
πλείονες, οἷς ἐξετίθετο διαμαρτυρόμενος τὴν βασιλείαν τοῦ θεοῦ πείθων
τε αὐτοὺς περὶ τοῦ Ἰησοῦ ἀπό τε τοῦ νόμου Μωυσέως καὶ τῶν
προφητῶν ἀπὸ πρωὶ ἕως ἑσπέρας. Καὶ οἱ μὲν ἐπείθοντο τοῖς λεγο- 24
μένοις οἱ δὲ ἠπίστουν, ἀσύμφωνοι δὲ ὄντες πρὸς ἀλλήλους ἀπελύοντο, 25
εἰπόντος τοῦ Παύλου ῥῆμα ἓν ὅτι Καλῶς τὸ πνεῦμα τὸ ἅγιον ἐλάλησεν
διὰ Ἠσαίου τοῦ προφήτου πρὸς τοὺς πατέρας ὑμῶν λέγων Πορεύθητι 26
πρὸς τὸν λαὸν τοῦτον καὶ εἰπόν Ἀκοῇ ἀκούσετε καὶ οὐ μὴ συνῆτε, καὶ
βλέποντες βλέψετε καὶ οὐ μὴ ἴδητε· ἐπαχύνθη γὰρ ἡ καρδία τοῦ 27
λαοῦ τούτου, καὶ τοῖς ὠσὶν βαρέως ἤκουσαν, καὶ τοὺς ὀφθαλμοὺς
αὐτῶν ἐκάμμυσαν· μή ποτε ἴδωσιν τοῖς ὀφθαλμοῖς καὶ τοῖς ὠσὶν ἀκού-
σωσιν καὶ τῇ καρδίᾳ συνῶσιν καὶ ἐπιστρέψωσιν, καὶ ἰάσομαι αὐτούς.
γνωστὸν οὖν ὑμῖν ἔστω ὅτι τοῖς ἔθνεσιν ἀπεστάλη τοῦτο τὸ σωτήριον 28
τοῦ θεοῦ· αὐτοὶ καὶ ἀκούσονται.

xxviii. 23

εἰς τὴν ξενίαν] 'to his lodging', or better, 'to receive his hospitality' (the usual sense of ξενία: cf. Philm. 22).

διαμαρτυρόμενος τὴν βασιλείαν τοῦ θεοῦ πείθων τε αὐτοὺς περὶ τοῦ Ἰησοῦ] 'bearing witness of the kingdom of God and seeking to persuade them about Jesus'. The kingdom of God and the story of Jesus are closely connected in the preaching of the Gospel: see on *ver.* 31; i. 3; viii. 12; xx. 24 f.

ἀπό τε τοῦ νόμου Μωυσέως καὶ τῶν προφητῶν] Cf. xxvi. 22, etc.

xxviii. 24

ἐπείθοντο] 'gave heed'; the imperf. does not necessarily imply that they were actually persuaded.

ἠπίστουν] 'would not believe'. Cf. xiv. 1 f., where the contrasted verbs are *πιστεύω* and *ἀπειθέω.*

xxviii. 25

ἀπελύοντο] 'they began to break up'.

ῥῆμα ἕν] 'Paul always gets the last word—generally with devastating effect' (LC).

Καλῶς κ.τ.λ.] Cf. the language with which another quotation from Isa. (xxix. 13) is applied to the Jews by our Lord in Mk. vii. 6, *καλῶς ἐπροφήτευσεν Ἡσαίας περὶ ὑμῶν τῶν ὑποκριτῶν.* The present quotation (from Isa. vi. 9 f., LXX) is also used of the Jews by our Lord (Mt. xiii. 13 ff. = Mk. iv. 12 = Lk. viii. 10; cf. Jn. xii. 39 f.). Paul had already used it of the unbelieving Jews in Rom. xi. 8. The point of the repeated quotation is to show that the Jewish rejection of Jesus as the Christ was a fulfilment of prophecy. See J. R. Harris, *Testimonies*, ii, pp. 65, 74, 137.

xxviii. 28

γνωστὸν οὖν ὑμῖν ἔστω] For the solemn expression cf. ii. 14; iv. 10; xiii. 38.

τοῖς ἔθνεσιν ἀπεστάλη τοῦτο τὸ σωτήριον τοῦ θεοῦ] Cf. Ps. lxvii. 2 (LXX lxvi. 3), *τοῦ γνῶναι ἐν τῇ γῇ τὴν ὁδόν σου, ἐν πᾶσιν ἔθνεσιν τὸ σωτήριόν σου,* and Ps. xcviii. 3 (LXX xcvii), *εἴδοσαν πάντα τὰ πέρατα τῆς γῆς τὸ σωτήριον τοῦ θεοῦ ἡμῶν.*

τοῦτο τὸ σωτήριον] Cf. xiii. 26, *τῆς σωτηρίας ταύτης.*

αὐτοὶ καὶ ἀκούσονται] As in other cities since the days of his preaching in Pisidian Antioch (cf. xiii. 46), the Jews in Rome, having received the first offer of the Gospel, refuse it, and he turns to the Gentiles. Thus, while Ac. records the expansion of the Gospel among the Gentiles, it also records progressively its rejection by the greater part of the Jewish nation. Cf. Paul's treatment of the problem thus raised in Rom. ix-xi. 'The narrative reaches a solemn climax—rejection on the one side, unchecked success and hope on the other' (Chase, *Credibility*, p. 52).

xxviii. 29 (not in WH)

The δ text (byz g p vg.codd hcl*) adds *ver.* 29, *καὶ ταῦτα αὐτοῦ εἰπόντος ἀπῆλθον οἱ Ἰουδαῖοι, πολλὴν ἔχοντες ἐν ἑαυτοῖς συζήτησιν* (*v.l.* *ζήτησιν*).

(e) The Gospel Advances Unhindered in Rome, xxviii. 30-31

Ἐνέμεινεν δὲ διετίαν ὅλην ἐν ἰδίῳ μισθώματι, καὶ ἀπεδέχετο πάντας 30
τοὺς εἰσπορευομένους πρὸς αὐτόν, κηρύσσων τὴν βασιλείαν τοῦ θεοῦ 31
καὶ διδάσκων τὰ περὶ τοῦ κυρίου Ἰησοῦ Χριστοῦ μετὰ πάσης παρρησίας
ἀκωλύτως.

xxviii. 30

διετίαν ὅλην] After two years the case probably went by default.[1] See *BC*, v. pp. 325 ff. Cf. Philo, *Flacc.* 128f., where Lampon is said to have been kept in prison for two years (*ἐπὶ διετίαν*), which is described as *πρὸς μήκιστον χρόνον* (this, however, may not mean 'for the longest period allowed' but 'for a very long time'); Pliny, *Ep.* x. 56 f., also shows a *biennium* fixed as a term of grace by the Senate, but in a different matter.

ἐν ἰδίῳ μισθώματι] 'on his own earnings' or 'at his own expense' rather than 'in his own hired lodgings', a sense which cannot be proved for *μίσθωμα*. The conditions of Paul's *libera custodia* probably permitted of his carrying on his tent-making.

xxviii. 31

κηρύσσων τὴν βασιλείαν τοῦ θεοῦ καὶ διδάσκων τὰ περὶ τοῦ κυρίου Ἰησοῦ Χριστοῦ] See on *ver.* 23.

'Evidently on purpose are the two expressions combined in this final summary, in order to show that the preaching of the kingdom and the preaching of Christ are one: that the original proclamation has not ceased, but that in Christ Jesus the thing proclaimed is no longer a vague and future hope, but a distinct and present fact. In the conjunction of these words the progress of doctrine appears. All is founded upon the old Jewish expectation of a kingdom of God; but it is now explained how that expectation is fulfilled in the person of Jesus, and the account of its realization consists in the unfolding of the truth concerning him (*τὰ περὶ τοῦ Ἰησοῦ*). The manifestation of Christ being finished, the kingdom is already begun. Those who receive *him*

---

[1] Ramsay (*The Teaching of Paul*, pp. 346 ff.) shows reason to believe that the two years consisted of the statutory eighteen months within which the prosecution might state its case, *plus* such time as was necessary for the formalities attending Paul's release. But for the contrary view see J. V. Bartlet in *Exp.* VIII. v. (1913), pp. 464 ff. He argued that the prosecutors gave notice within the eighteen months' time-limit of their intention to proceed with the case, that they arrived in Rome early in 62 and successfully prosecuted Paul as a disturber of the peace of the provinces (cf. xxiv. 5), that the original readers of Ac. knew from Nero's record what the inevitable result of such a prosecution before him would be (the more so in view of Poppaea's pro-Jewish sentiments) and would therefore not need to be told explicitly of Paul's condemnation and execution, and that there is an ominous note in Agrippa's remark (xxvi. 32): 'This man might have been set free, *if he had not appealed to Caesar*'. Bartlet thus rejected Ramsay's theory of a second imprisonment and trial of Paul at Rome, and dated the Pastoral Epistles during the two years of xxviii. 30 (*Exp.* VIII. v. pp. 325 ff.).

enter into *it*. Having overcome the sharpness of death, he has opened the kingdom of heaven to all believers' (T. D. Bernard, *The Progress of Doctrine*[5], p. 112).

μετὰ πάσης παρρησίας] 'with all freedom of speech'.

ἀκωλύτως] 'without let or hindrance'. 'The word is legal to the last', say MM, who speak of 'the triumphant note on which it brings the Acts of the Apostles to a close'. Cf. Clem. Alex., *Strom.* vi. 18, 167. 5, *μένει δὲ ἀκώλυτος*. Foakes Jackson calls the conclusion 'highly artistic'. Ramsay's dictum is thus a gross exaggeration: 'No one can accept the ending of *Acts* as the conclusion of a rationally conceived history' (*SPT*, pp. 351 f.). Very many can and do so accept it.

The ending is weakened by the δ addition, found with variations in p vg.codd hcl: 'saying that this is the Messiah, Jesus the Son of God, by whom the whole world is to be judged'.

Luke has reached the objective of his history by bringing Paul to Rome, where he proclaims the Gospel without let or hindrance. The programme mapped out in i. 8 has been carried through. '*Victoria Verbi Dei*', says Bengel; '*Paulus Romae, apex evangelii, Actorum finis. . . . Hierosolymis coepit: Romae desinit. Habes, Ecclesia, formam tuam: tuum est, servare eam, et depositum custodire.*'

There is no sufficient ground to suppose, with Ramsay, Zahn and others, that Luke projected a third volume of his work *ad Theophilum*. Certainly no such deduction can be made from the use of *πρῶτον* in i. 1 (see *ad loc.*).

Yet, artistic and powerful as the conclusion is, it is strange that Luke has not told us explicitly what the result of Paul's appeal was. It may be a sufficient answer to say that this formed no part of his project; it would be more satisfactory to suppose that he wrote no more because he knew no more—because he completed his book at the end of the two years of *ver.* 30, probably early in A.D. 62.[1] (See Introduction, pp. 11 ff.)

[1] J. de Zwaan ('Was the book of Acts a posthumous edition?' *HTR* xvii [1924], pp. 95 ff.) and H. Lietzmann (*The Founding of the Church Universal* [1938], p. 100) take the view that the absence of any reference to Paul's death in Ac. is due to Luke's dying before the work was finished. T. W. Manson, who holds that Lk.-Ac. was written *c.* A.D. 70 'as a public defence of the Christian Church against the suspicion of being mixed up with the rebellious Jews, and a public assurance that the Christian Gospel was no seditious propaganda but a message of universal peace and goodwill,' surmises that Luke went to Achaia and did not hear what Paul was doing or where he went (supposing the apostle was released at the end of the two years). But he would certainly hear of Paul's martyrdom, and his failure to mention it, 'supposing that it occurred anywhere near the dates usually given for it, is very difficult to explain; so difficult as to call for a reconsideration of the traditions which are held to testify to it' (*BJRL* xxviii [1944], p. 403).

INDEX